Second Edition

CRIME PREVENTION

Theory and
Practice

Second Edition

CRIME PREVENTION

Theory and Practice

Stephen Schneider
St. Mary's University
Halifax, Nova Scotia, Canada

CRC Press
Taylor & Francis Group
Boca Raton London New York

CRC Press is an imprint of the
Taylor & Francis Group, an **informa** business

CRC Press
Taylor & Francis Group
6000 Broken Sound Parkway NW, Suite 300
Boca Raton, FL 33487-2742

First issued in paperback 2020

ISBN-13: 978-1-4665-7711-4 (hbk)
ISBN-13: 978-0-367-73867-9 (pbk)

Visit the Taylor & Francis Web site at
http://www.taylorandfrancis.com

and the CRC Press Web site at
http://www.crcpress.com

DEDICATION

To Evangeline

CONTENTS

Contents

PART IV
Planning, Implementing, and Evaluating a Crime Prevention Project

PREFACE TO THE SECOND EDITION

As a writer and an academic, it is an immensely humbling experience to be published. Having a second edition of one's book published is perhaps even more rewarding. I am forever grateful to all of those who purchased the first (and second) edition of this book, including practitioners and course instructors (not to mention all those students obliged to purchase the textbook as a required course reading).

The main revisions to this edition are twofold. The first is the addition of a new chapter applying crime prevention through social development principles to adolescents and young adults. This new chapter is a recognition of the disproportionate rate of offending by adolescents and young adults as well as the distinctive risk factors faced by these groups. This chapter also emphasizes the unique nature of applying social problem-solving solutions to adolescents and young adults who have been in formal contact with the criminal justice system. Indeed, this chapter very much focuses on recidivism prevention, an oft-ignored, but critical aspect of crime prevention.

The second major revision to this book is updates on the extant literature on crime prevention, in particular the addition of research that has been published since the first edition of this book. To a lesser extent, new case studies have been added.

As with the first edition, I hope readers find this book informative and educational (and perhaps may even be motivated by the book to undertake a crime prevention project of their own).

A web site has also been created that contains supplemental materials for use by both instructors and students. These materials can be found at http://www.stephenschneider.ca.

Stephen R. Schneider
Halifax, Nova Scotia, Canada

PREFACE TO THE FIRST EDITION

This textbook explores the discipline of crime prevention, which can be broadly defined as any preemptive intervention intended to block or reduce the likelihood of the occurrence of a criminal act at a given location or the onset of criminal behavior within an individual (Ekblom et al., 1996; Tolan, 2002, 109; Lab, 2004, 23; Crawford, 2007, 871). This expansive definition is purposeful, for it reflects the expansiveness of the crime prevention field, both theoretically and in applied terms. This highly inclusive definition is also an acknowledgment of the unfinished debate among scholars as to the conceptual parameters that should be applied to crime prevention to distinguish it from traditional criminal justice approaches to crime.

Despite disagreements as to what should be defined as crime prevention, within a theoretical context this field is distinguished from the criminal justice system by its proactive nature, the central role played by private citizens and communities, the importance of multiagency and multisectoral partnerships, and its *problem-oriented* methodology (which advocates a focus on the causes of crime and criminality, while emphasizing solutions that are tailored to the unique circumstances of each problem).

As an academic discipline within the social and behavioral sciences, crime prevention is characterized by its interdisciplinary and applied nature. It is highly interdisciplinary in that it is influenced by and incorporates concepts, theories, principles, and strategies from such diverse fields as psychology, sociology, criminology, health care, architecture, urban planning and design, education, economics, social work, and community development. The study of crime prevention is also heavily tilted toward developing and evaluating interventions for application in real-world settings, with far less emphasis placed on its theoretical development. (In fact, crime prevention has been criticized for lacking any coherent, unified theoretical framework.)

This textbook reflects the predominantly applied nature of the crime prevention field. While most chapters explore basic concepts and theories that inform this discipline, one of the preeminent goals of this book is to impart to the reader the knowledge and skills necessary to plan, implement, evaluate, and sustain effective crime prevention interventions.

With that said, the overriding objective of this textbook is to provide an introduction to and overview of the crime prevention field, which includes examining substantive approaches (situational, social development, community crime prevention, recidivism prevention, and community policing) as well as process-oriented issues essential to its application (planning, implementing, and evaluating a crime prevention project). In short, this book attempts to balance a scholarly analysis of the subject while imparting knowledge and useful skills that can be applied by practitioners working in the field or by postsecondary students working on a term paper or some other school project).

The specific objectives of this textbook are as follows:

- Provide an introduction to and overview of the theory and practice of crime prevention, which includes exploring, advancing, and critically analyzing definitions, descriptions, theories, research, and dominant crime prevention approaches
- Nurture an understanding of how etiological theories of crime and criminal behavior inform the field of crime prevention
- Encourage the development of knowledge, expertise, and practical skills among crime prevention practitioners that can be applied in *real-world* settings.
- Contribute to the planning, implementation, evaluation, and maintenance of successful crime prevention interventions
- Contribute to the development of critical analytical thinking, communication, and writing skills of the reader

In keeping with its dual theoretical and applied aspirations, this textbook has been written for two audiences. The first is postsecondary students, in particular those taking degrees, diplomas, or certificates in such disciplines as criminology, criminal justice, sociology, social work, policing, or community development. The second group is practitioners—those working in the field who can benefit from a combination of a scholarly examination of crime prevention plus illustrative case studies and practical instructions on how to plan, implement, and assess a crime prevention project.

The pedagogical approach of this book reflects the balance it endeavors to strike between a theoretical and empirical understanding of crime prevention, on the one hand, and its practical application on the other. The first two-thirds of the book explores crime prevention theories, concepts, research findings, and case studies (with each chapter dedicated to a dominant crime prevention approach). The last part of the book imparts practical knowledge and skills essential to planning, implementing, and evaluating a crime prevention project.

Each chapter follows a uniform structure, which in turn incorporates the dual emphasis on theory and practice. The reader will first encounter the learning objectives for the chapter. An introduction to and overview of the chapter contents is then provided. Crime causation theories that inform the respective crime prevention topic of each chapter are then discussed. This is followed by a theoretical and empirical examination of the crime prevention topic covered by the chapter. A conclusion includes a summary of research examining the extent to which strategies pursued under each crime prevention approach have met their objectives in real-world applications. Critiques of theory and practice of the crime prevention topic are also presented. Each chapter ends with a list of key concepts (i.e., important terms) explored in the chapter. Discussion questions and exercises are then provided. Instead of asking questions that merely require the regurgitation of material presented in the chapter, emphasis is placed on questions and exercises that can invoke the reader's critical reflection and practical application of the particular topic presented in the chapter. This includes having the reader research instances of the topic on the Internet or in their own neighborhood or city. Further reading and Internet resources relevant to the subject under examination in the chapter are then listed.

In most chapters, numerous case studies that illustrate a particular crime prevention theory, concept, or strategy are presented. Particular attention has been paid to including case studies that exemplify a specific theory or strategy or those that have proven successful based on evaluations. Another bias of the author has been to include innovative and creative examples of applied crime prevention projects. An effort has also been made to present applied projects that have undergone rigorous evaluations.

Indeed, as this textbook concerns the application of crime prevention theories, concepts, and strategies, it is paramount that the evaluation results of crime prevention projects be included, at the very least to determine what works and what does not work. This entails not only presenting evaluation findings of individual case studies, but also summarizing the research and evaluation data on crime prevention approaches examined in the book.

A number of caveats should be considered when reviewing the results of experiments and project evaluations that test crime prevention theories and strategies. First, many studies are not particularly rigorous as far as their methodology is concerned, and as such their findings may not be accurate. Research into crime prevention also suffers from a lack of longitudinal research; that is, most experiments and project evaluations measure only the immediate, short-term impact of the intervention. As a result, there is a paucity of data indicating whether positive outcomes can be sustained over a long period of time. Many studies also fail to account for whether the outcomes were influenced by events or circumstances other than the intervention being tested. Even if one study indicated that a particular crime prevention strategy worked (or did not work) in a particular time and place, this does not mean these results can necessarily be generalized.

There are significant methodological challenges inherent in evaluating crime prevention projects. Clarke (1997, 34) writes, "Crime prevention measures are not like drugs, i.e., treatments with precisely measurable and controllable chemical constituents. Rather, they consist of a complex interaction of several related social and physical elements. This makes it impossible to be certain about the precise causes of any effect demonstrated by the experiment." These challenges and methodological problems, and the resulting lack of reliable and empirical data that has been generated through studies, are perhaps the most significant weaknesses in crime prevention scholarship (especially given the applied nature of the discipline). With that said, in recent years a growing body of meta-analytical studies have been conducted that aggregate and statistically analyze the results of existing evaluations of and (rigorous) experiments testing crime prevention projects to determine if a particular approach is in fact effective. As MacKenzie (2012, 476) writes, "Like literature reviews, meta-analysis is a method of drawing conclusions about a group of studies. However, in contrast to literature reviews, meta-analysis uses a specific statistical methodology. Quantitative data from a group of studies is used in the analysis to draw conclusions about effectiveness."

A final cautionary note: as an academic subject within a postsecondary school setting, crime prevention should be considered an advanced topic that requires students to already have an understanding of basic criminological concepts and theories. While this book explains the criminological theories that serve as a foundation for scientifically developed crime prevention theories and strategies, it assumes the reader has a grounding in criminology and hence understands basic terms and the conceptual differences between, for example, a crime (a criminal act) and criminality (criminal behavior).

While it is not necessary to take a criminology course before undertaking some form of crime prevention strategy, it should be understood that crime is a complex issue, both theoretically and in applied terms. Crime problems can be highly intransigent, while many offenders are highly adaptive and resilient. The social problems that help create criminal behavior in the first place are also pervasive and omnipresent.

Most crime problems or criminogenic preconditions cannot be solved through spur-of-the-moment, arbitrary actions based on gut feelings or *common sense*. What is most often required is a problem-oriented approach that relies on rigorous information collection and analysis and the application of crime prevention strategies that have been proven to work. This systematic approach includes putting together a plan that entails a basic understanding of crime and criminality in general, researching and understanding crime problems and their causes and aggravating factors within a particular setting, understanding the environment in which the problems are taking place, identifying and mobilizing community members and other key partners, developing a strategy to address the identified problems (and their causes), implementing the strategy, sustaining the strategy, as well as evaluating it to ensure it works.* Anyone interested in reducing crime must be prepared to invest time and energy—both intellectual and physical. This book is one modest effort to assist people and communities in this endeavor.

---

* Preventing crime is a lot like losing weight; for most people it is difficult to shed the superfluous weight and even tougher to keep the pounds off on a permanent basis. The same can be said for preventing crime and criminality; it can be very difficult to reduce or prevent the occurrence of crime problems or the onset of criminal behavior (especially within high-crime, low-income, disadvantaged neighborhoods) and it can be even harder to maintain this momentum over a long-term period.

AUTHOR

Stephen R. Schneider, PhD, is an associate professor in the Department of Sociology and Criminology at Saint Mary's University in Halifax, Nova Scotia, Canada. His main areas of expertise and interest include crime prevention, organized crime, and policing and law enforcement. He has worked in the field of crime prevention for more than 20 years as a scholar, researcher, community-based practitioner, consultant, and government policy analyst. He is the author of three other books: *Refocusing Crime Prevention: Collective Action and the Quest for Community* (University of Toronto Press, Toronto, 2007), *Money Laundering in Canada: Chasing Dirty and Dangerous Dollars* (coauthored with Margaret Beare, University of Toronto Press, Toronto, Ontario, Canada, 2007), and *Iced: The Story of Organized Crime in Canada* (John Wiley & Sons, Toronto, Ontario, Canada, 2009). His first book, *Refocusing Crime Prevention*, was based on his PhD dissertation and explored the obstacles to the effective implementation of community crime prevention initiatives in disadvantaged, high-crime communities.

In 2006, Schneider received a $380,000 grant from the Canadian government for a three-year project to research, implement, and evaluate a comprehensive developmental program for disadvantaged children. This research experiment tested theories and principles of crime prevention through social development, with emphasis on enhancing the resilience of at-risk children and youth through tutoring, mentoring, social and critical thinking skills development, and physical activity. The experiment tested whether such interventions can decrease personal and social environmental factors that place children at risk for future criminal behavior. In addition to his research work, Dr. Schneider has worked as a community crime prevention coordinator in Vancouver, British Columbia, and has assisted numerous community groups in developing and implementing crime prevention plans. He most recently completed a report on how to prevent and control serious and chronic criminal offending by youth and young adults for the Halifax Mayor's Roundtable on Violence. Currently, Prof. Schneider, in conjunction with the Nova Scotia Department of Corrections, is implementing a recidivism prevention project he developed that helps at-risk young people and youth in custody finish high school and enter a post-secondary institution.

PART I

CRIME PREVENTION: AN OVERVIEW

CHAPTER 1

THEORY AND PRACTICE OF CRIME PREVENTION

An Overview

CONTENTS

1.1 LEARNING OBJECTIVES

By the end of this chapter, you should have a better understanding of the unique theoretical and conceptual constructs of crime prevention, including

- Difficulties in establishing conceptual boundaries and definitions of crime prevention
- Different definitions and descriptions of crime prevention
- Fundamental differences between crime prevention and the criminal justice system
- Various ways of categorizing crime prevention strategies
- Basic characteristics of crime prevention
- An overview of the institutions through which crime prevention strategies are delivered

1.2 INTRODUCTION

Since at least the late 1960s, there has been an exponential increase in theories, strategies, activities, and programs that can be classified as *crime prevention*.

It will become apparent as you read this chapter that there is no universally accepted definition of this term, nor is there any consensus as to the scope and boundaries of the crime prevention field. For example, social problem-solving approaches that address the root causes of criminal behavior clearly strive to be preventive in nature. But do we classify positive parenting skills or job training (two other important ways to reduce the risk of delinquency and future offending) as crime prevention? Should policing or prisons be classified as preventive? Crime prevention strategies are generally differentiated from traditional criminal justice approaches, yet both policing and correctional systems can potentially prevent crime; by arresting offenders and putting them in jail, further crimes may very well be prevented. Moreover, in recent years, policing has increasingly integrated proactive, preventive approaches through the adoption of community-based and problem-oriented policing principles.

There are a number of philosophies, strategies, programs, and practices that could potentially be classified as *crime prevention*. Some have suggested that we should determine whether a particular strategy or program is preventive by its results or consequences, and not by its methods or intentions (Sherman et al., 2006, 3–4). That is, if a particular approach addresses crime in a proactive and preventive manner, then it should fall under the broad rubric of crime prevention.

With that said, there are a number of characteristics that help define crime prevention and distinguish it from traditional criminal justice approaches. In particular, crime prevention is inherently proactive, assumes a risk-based (targeted) approach, emphasizes a *problem-oriented* methodology, involves the participation of nonstate actors (neighborhood residents, community groups, the private sector), stresses informal social control, and is highly contingent on partnerships and collaboration.

For this book, crime prevention initiatives are demarcated into the following broad categories: (1) crime prevention through social development (interventions designed to prevent the onset of criminal and violent behavior by addressing their root causes, especially among *at-risk* children and youth), (2) situational crime prevention (SCP) (interventions designed to prevent the opportunities for a crime to occur in a particular time and place through the management, design, or manipulation of the physical and/or human environment), (3) community crime prevention (the mobilization of neighborhood residents to prevent crime through informal social control and/or community development measures), (4) recidivism prevention (initiatives to help offenders desist from criminal and violent behavior), and (5) police and the criminal justice system (CJS) (emphasizing proactive, community-oriented, and problem-oriented policing as well as harm reduction approaches, such as drug courts, which ameliorate the causes of criminal behavior).

Because the field of crime prevention involves such a diverse range of interventions, there is a myriad of individuals, professions, groups, and institutions through which these programs and practices are formulated and delivered. The institutional settings through which crime prevention interventions, programs, and practices are executed can be divided into eight categories: (1) families, (2) schools, (3) labor markets, (4) neighborhoods/communities, (5) places, (6) (mental) health-care systems, (7) police and other criminal justice branches, and (8) other government agencies and institutions.

1.3 DEFINITIONS AND DESCRIPTIONS

Crime prevention remains a vague concept that can mean different things to different people. The challenge in attempting to conceptualize crime prevention is to create a definition that encompasses the diverse array of approaches that can integrate the principles of this crime control philosophy, while avoiding a definition that is so broad and inclusive that it is rendered vague and meaningless. Below are some examples of crime prevention definitions that have emerged over the years. Following each definition is a brief analysis of its strengths and weaknesses as it endeavors to precisely, yet comprehensively, define this concept.

The National Crime Prevention Institute (1978, 1) defines crime prevention as the "anticipation, recognition, and appraisal of a crime risk and the initiative of some action to remove it." The strengths of this definition (beyond its conciseness) are that it highlights the proactive nature of crime prevention (*anticipation* and *crime risk*) as well as its problem-oriented strategy of determining the scope and nature of a crime problem and then formulating an appropriate response (*recognition and appraisal*). The most significant weakness of this definition is that it may be too broad in scope and therefore too vague.

Van Dijk and De Waard (1991, 483) define crime prevention as "the total of all private initiatives and state policies, other than the enforcement of criminal law, aimed at the reduction of damage caused by acts defined as criminal by the state." The strengths of this definition are that it encompasses efforts by governments as well as nongovernmental actors (*private initiatives* undertaken by individual citizens, neighborhoods, community groups, businesses, etc.) and distinguishes crime prevention from traditional criminal justice approaches. By expressly omitting *the enforcement of criminal law*, this definition provides some boundaries that can help with the conceptual clarity of the term *crime prevention*. However, the definition says nothing about the proactive underpinnings of crime prevention (in fact, by emphasizing the *damage caused* by criminal acts, this definition appears to define crime prevention as largely reactive).

Crime prevention is defined by Ekblom (1996, 2) as "an intervention in mechanisms that cause criminal events, in a way which seeks to reduce the probability of an occurrence." The strengths of this definition are that it stresses proactive measures that address the causes of crime while implicitly acknowledging that efforts can never guarantee the prevention of a criminal act or the onset of criminal behavior (i.e., only a reduction in the *probability of occurrence*). One weakness of this definition is that not all crime prevention strategies focus on the *causes* of crime: SCP, for example, attempts to limit the *opportunity* for a crime to occur in a particular time and place.

Lab (2004, 23) defines crime prevention as "any action designed to reduce the actual level of crime and/or perceived fear of crime." Like others, this definition is quite vague and could apply to any effort to address crime or the fear thereof, especially given that it does not appear to emphasize the proactive nature of crime prevention.

For Sherman et al. (2006, 3–4), crime prevention should be defined not by *intentions*, but rather by its *consequences*. That is, the actual approach is not as important as the results; if a strategy or program has served to prevent a criminal act from occurring or criminal behavior from emerging, it should be classified as such. These outcomes can be defined in a number of ways: a reduction in or prevention of specific criminal events; a reduction in the number of criminal offenders, the extent to which harm was prevented or reduced; or a reduction in the number of victims harmed. The strength of this characterization is that it focuses primarily on results: the prevention of crime and criminal behavior. By defining this concept through results, a broad universe of approaches can potentially be included, from working with at-risk children to incarcerating chronic adult offenders. Yet, this inclusiveness can also be viewed as a potential weakness because it ensures that the concept of crime prevention remains vague and ill defined. If you measure crime prevention by the outcome of interventions, you can include almost any crime control tactic under this definition (including the traditional criminal justice approach of cops, courts, and corrections).

Some crime prevention purists call for the application of the dictionary definition of the word *prevent*—to keep something from happening or existing. From this perspective, Tolan (2002, 109) writes, the definition of crime prevention should be "limited to actions intended to prevent the onset of criminal activity in individuals or the occurrence of criminal activities within a given location." Tolan is emphatic that "most legal procedures and punishment-based actions should not be considered prevention."

Think about It!

How would you define crime prevention? Do you believe it should be defined broadly or narrowly? Should it be defined by its methods or its consequences? What parameters would you apply to a definition of crime prevention?

As you read through the remainder of this chapter—and the entire book—you should be thinking about how you would define *crime prevention*. This includes determining what you would and would not include as a crime prevention strategy.

Moreover, think about whether certain traditional criminal justice strategies (policing and law enforcement, the courts, corrections, parole) can be considered preventative in nature. If not, how could these be modified to incorporate the basic principles of crime prevention discussed in this book?

1.4 IDENTIFYING THE TARGETS OF CRIME PREVENTION

Adopting Tolan's definitional parameters makes it a little easier to identify and classify the main *targets* of crime prevention strategies and programs. The theory and practice of crime prevention spends relatively little time addressing offenders (which is the main focus of the CJS). Instead, in keeping with its proactive philosophy, crime prevention theories and applied strategies focus on *potential offenders* (at-risk children and youth), *potential victims* (neighborhood residents and businesses), and *potential crime sites* (places).

Crime prevention through social development (CPSD) primarily targets children and youth who are at risk of developing delinquent and criminal behaviors due to, for example, poor parenting, an impoverished social environment, or behavioral problems. SCP and crime prevention through environmental design (CPTED)—which ignores the root causes of crime and instead focuses on reducing the opportunity for a crime to occur in a particular time and place—are primarily aimed at places that are vulnerable to crime.

CASE STUDY 1.1

COMPREHENSIVE COMMUNITY-BASED EFFORTS TO TACKLE CRIME IN A POOR, INNER-CITY TORONTO NEIGHBORHOOD

Standing near a bright new playground, watching smiling children taking tennis lessons and neighbors chatting as they tend a community garden, Stephanie Payne marvels at how quickly the scene has changed at Toronto's most notorious intersection.

"Two years ago, everyone was scared and cautious. There were a lot of kids hanging out and smoking and swearing. You don't see that anymore," said the Barbados-born Ms. Payne, who helped organize a community effort that cut the rate of major crimes by half in a troubled trio of apartment buildings on the northeast corner of Jane and Finch.

A survey done in 2000 showed that the crime rate in the area of high-rise buildings and malls near York University was well over twice the national average, and much of it was youth related. Assaults, shootings, stabbings, and standoffs with police occurred with alarming frequency.

Breaking the cycle required creative thinking and a lot of detailed work, but the success can serve as a model for other communities, said Kevin Green, principal of Greenwin Property Management, which owns the buildings and manages 50,000 apartment units across Canada. "We had a vision that we could get the community involved and bring down crime, but landlords are not the ones most renters turn to unless the heat is off," Mr. Green said.

He approached Ms. Payne and other prominent tenants to start the San Romanoway Revitalization Association, which includes residents, businesses, and the police.

Ms. Payne, who has lived in Canada since 1967 and works as a nurse, said she knew that giving the residents a sense of community and empowerment was important, but she was skeptical.

"Over the years there's been a lot of negativity attached to the area," she said. "I hemmed and hawed but I finally said I'll give it a try."

Complicating matters were the 76 different languages spoken by tenants of the three buildings on San Romanoway. They are mostly recent immigrants from the Caribbean, Guyana, South and East Asia, and Africa, all of whom are still adapting to life in a new country. Of the 4400 residents, nearly 3000 are under the age of 18.

Because many of the residents come from places where speaking out can invite trouble, the association's early meetings drew as few as half a dozen residents, Ms. Payne said. But as people talked, momentum and membership grew. They found everyone wanted more security but had been waiting for someone else to do something about it. They also wanted more recreational and social activities for children, who played noisily and destructively in the hallways.

The crime figures became the basis of Ms. Payne's proposal to the National Crime Prevention Centre, a federal Justice Department initiative that provides up to $100,000 a year in project support for up to 3 years if a group can get local corporate and private partners.

Meanwhile, Greenwin worked with the Toronto-based private firm Intelligarde International to rethink the security system to keep out people who do not belong. Brighter lighting and security cameras were installed around the complex to eliminate places where people could congregate without being seen, Mr. Green said.

But there were challenges within as well. A few tenants who were perennial problems, such as drug dealers who had set up shop in apartments, were evicted.

Then, the association began to get corporate help to find activities and jobs for the youthful residents.

Rogers Cable donated computers and Internet access for a computer center that is continually busy. Tennis Canada refinished a long-neglected tennis court, and the Ontario Tennis Association agreed to provide free tennis lessons. In the past year, 120 children enrolled in the course.

Human Resources Development Canada (HRDC) is paying the salaries of counselors for a 9-week children's day-camp program this summer. As part of a $300,000 HRDC grant, a youth internship program was also set up with the Jewish Vocational Services of Greater Toronto.

The latest addition is the playground, completed last weekend with the help of 200 volunteers and material provided by Home Depot Canada. The inspiration for that was a tenant who found a website for KaBOOM!, a US-based foundation linking corporations to community groups seeking to build safe play spaces.

Andrea Allen, a single parent of two boys who came to Toronto from Jamaica 3 years ago, says she wonders why people used to be wary of living at Jane and Finch.

"Honestly, I would not want to leave here." (Immen, 2003, A10*)

1.5   CRIME PREVENTION VERSUS THE CRIMINAL JUSTICE SYSTEM

One way to define and characterize crime prevention is to distinguish its principles and strategies from the traditional criminal justice approach to crime control. In fact, the contemporary field of crime prevention began to emerge in the 1960s as a critique of and an alternative to the CJS. In particular, during the time of a precipitous increase in crime rates and social unrest, the traditional *cops, courts, and corrections* approach was seen as insufficient to unilaterally control, prevent, or deter acts that threaten public safety. In this sense, crime prevention is based upon the assumption that the CJS is unable to cope with the actual quantity of crime, fails to identify many criminal offenders and bring them to justice, fails to rehabilitate those offenders who are identified by the CJS, and fails to address the underlying factors associated with crime and criminality (Parliament of Canada, 1993, 1).

Moreover, while dominant crime prevention strategies are predicated on empirically supported criminological theories as to the causes of criminal acts and criminal behavior, an ever-growing body of research has increasingly shown that the theoretical basis for the preventative tenets of CJS is tenuous at best. In particular, deterrence theory—which assumes that crime results from a rational calculation of the costs and benefits of criminal activity and therefore potential offenders can be swayed from such behavior through the threat of punishment—"rests on the false premise that altering criminal

---

* *Printed with permission from CTVglobemedia Publishing Inc.*

penalties will alter behavior" (Spohn and Holleran, 2002, 329–330). In fact, according to these criminologists, "scholarly research generally concludes that increasing the severity of penalties will have little, if any, effect on crime." More specifically, research has shown that the severity of a punishment does not have a significant effect on preventing crime, although increasing the certainty of punishment may have a deterrent effect (Wright, 2010). Research also indicates that criminal justice sanctions and incarceration, in particular, do not have a significant impact on preventing recidivism (Petrosino et al., 2010; Bales and Piquero, 2012). Criticisms of the CJS also include its enormous costs, the high rate of incarceration generally and of nonviolent offenders specifically (especially in the United States), the negative impact that a criminal record and incarceration can have on people, and systemic injustices perpetrated against the innocent, racial minorities, and the poor.

Based explicitly on these critiques, in theory, crime prevention is antithetical to the CJS in many respects:

- It is inherently proactive, not reactive.
- It avoids the *cookie-cutter* approach of the CJS, which generally relies on the same set of strategies in controlling crime (arrest, prosecute, punish); instead, crime prevention places emphasis on an analytical, problem-oriented approach that stresses flexibility in applying solutions that are individualized for specific circumstances and generally avoid the CJS.
- It is based on rigorous theories of crime causation.
- Responsibility for crime prevention is primarily in the hands of citizens, not the state (governments).
- Greater emphasis is placed on *informal social control* (which is carried out by private actors—citizens, community groups, businesses) and not *formal social control* (which is exercised by the state).
- The focus is shifted from the offender (as is the case with the CJS) to the (potential) offender and the (potential) victim.
- It targets not only crime but also fear, disorder, and public incivilities.

Greenwood (2006, 12–13) distinguishes between the ultimate goals of delinquency prevention and the CJS. He asserts that the main role of the CJS in helping to produce a civil and orderly society is the *control of individuals*—in particular offenders, although it can be argued that the state's social control function also targets the broader public through the general deterrence effect of criminal laws, enforcement, and punishment. In contrast, crime prevention through social development (delinquency prevention)—through its emphasis on social problem solving, community cohesion, informal social control, and strong local institutions (e.g., schools, families, communities)—is ultimately geared toward the improved functioning of the individual. Indeed, the crime prevention roles played by nurturing and loving families, socially cohesive communities, well-functioning schools, a strong social welfare system, and accessible quality health care are in fact a by-product of their ultimate mission in society, which is to contribute to the cultivation of well-functioning, well-adjusted, healthy, prosocial, law-abiding, civically engaged people. Table 1.1 summarizes the differences between crime prevention and the CJS (with contributions from Greenwood [2006, 15]).

Table 1.1
Comparison of Crime Prevention and the CJS

	Crime Prevention	CJS
Timing	Proactive	Reactive
Approach	Predict, assess, and intervene	Intervene (no real prediction)
Response	Problem oriented (wide range of appropriate solutions)	Narrow range of solutions
Lead responsibility	Citizenry (community based)	State (police, CJS)
Organizations providing services	Public health, community organizations, social workers, volunteers	Prisons, jails, training schools, institutions
Control	Informal social control	Formal social control
Scope	Criminal act, criminality (causes), disorder, incivilities, fear	Criminal act
Targets	Victim and potential offender	Offender
Setting	Natural: home or community	Artificial: institution
Primary goal	Improved functioning	Control of individuals

1.6 DEFINING CHARACTERISTICS OF CRIME PREVENTION

The earlier section identifies some of the characteristics that distinguish crime prevention from traditional criminal justice approaches. This section elaborates on these characteristics by identifying and describing the following defining traits of crime prevention:

- Crime prevention is inherently proactive.
- Crime prevention assumes a risk-based (targeted) approach.
- Crime prevention emphasizes a *problem-oriented* methodology.
- Crime prevention initiatives are evidence based.
- Responsibility for crime control is partially shifted to private (nonstate) actors.
- (Community) crime prevention stresses informal social control.
- Focus is shifted from the offender to the potential victim and potential offender.
- Central to crime prevention are partnerships and collaboration.
- Crime prevention targets not only the criminal act but also criminality, fear, and disorder.

1.6.1 Crime Prevention Is Inherently Proactive

One critique of the CJS is that it is largely reactive and does not have the capacity (nor was it created) to address the root causes of crime and disorder. In contrast, a fundamental characteristic of crime prevention is that it is proactive in dealing with crime and criminality. It strives to anticipate and prevent crime, either by reducing the opportunity for a crime to occur in a particular time or place or by preventing the onset of criminal behavior by addressing its root causes. Indeed, the proactive nature of crime prevention is epitomized by social problem-solving interventions that target young people who are at risk of future delinquent and criminal behavior.

CASE STUDY 1.2

ADDRESSING THE ROOT CAUSES OF CRIMINALITY THROUGH AN INTENSIVE PRESCHOOL PROGRAM IN MICHIGAN

The Perry Preschool Project, which began in the early 1960s, is the best-known example of a preschool project setup with the objective of reducing the risk of delinquency. The project (which actually began as a research experiment) initially enrolled disadvantaged African-American children ages 4 and 5 years in a preschool curriculum that promoted their intellectual and social development. Nearly half the families in the program were headed by one parent who generally had a low level of education, a poor employment record, and lived in overcrowded dwellings in poor neighborhoods. All children tested for a low IQ and were considered at high risk for school failure.

The program provided the children with 2 years of preschool education and weekly home visits. Teams of teachers were employed on very high student–teacher ratios for 2.5 h/day for 30 weeks in each year. The program emphasized learning through active and direct child-initiated experiences rather than direct teaching. Children were involved in the planning of classroom activities and were encouraged to engage in play activities that involve making choices and problem solving. The curriculum, which was intended to promote a child's intellectual, social, and emotional learning and development, did not include defined subject matter. Instead, teachers were to listen closely to what students plan and then actively work with and question them to extend their activities to developmentally appropriate exercises and experiences. Each mother and child also received a home visit from a teacher once a week for approximately 1.5 h. The home visits were intended to involve the mother in the educational process and to help her provide her child with education support and implement the curriculum within the child's home.

An accompanying study randomly allocated 123 African-American children, and regular analyses of the children's social and intellectual development were undertaken and compared with a control group of children. Over the next 30 years, longitudinal data were collected. The results showed that children who attended the program performed better in school, had more favorable opinions toward school, were more likely to complete high school and obtain employment, and were less likely to have received any form of welfare assistance. Teenage pregnancies were about half the number in the control group. By the age of 19, arrest rates of those in the preschool program were 40% lower compared to those in the control group. By age 27, 1 in 3 of the control group had been arrested five or more times compared with only 1 in 14 of those who had attended the preschool program. At this age, those in the treatment group also had significantly higher earnings, they were more likely to be homeowners, and more of the women were married with fewer children born outside marriage (Berrueta-Clement et al., 1984; Schweinhart et al., 1993). By the age of 40, longitudinal research found that program participants were less likely to be arrested than control group participants (Schweinhart et al., 2005).

1.6.2 Crime Prevention Assumes a Risk-Based (Targeted) Approach

Crime prevention theories and strategies have increasingly assumed a risk-based orientation. Within the context of social problem-solving approaches that address the root causes of criminality, emphasis is placed on targeting communities, families, children, and youth where there is a high crime rate and a high risk of future offending by young people.

Crime and (public) violence also tend to cluster in what are called *hot spots*. As such, place-based approaches to preventing and controlling crime and violence assume a targeted geospatial approach through SCP and policing measures that strive to reduce the opportunity for crime and violence to occur in these hot spots. Finally, a particular emphasis of community crime prevention is mobilizing residents in high-crime neighborhoods.

This targeted, risk-based approach also requires an intimate understanding of the specific risk factors, and the relative importance of each risk factor, in either promoting the root causes of crime and violence or promoting opportunities for crime and violence in a particular time and place (Wyrick and Howell, 2004, 23). This targeted risk-based approach appears to have supplanted a more universal approach to preventing crime, in part due to research suggesting that a small number of chronic offenders commit a disproportionate amount of crime, the results of research indicating that proactive strategies are most fruitful in controlling crime and violence when focused on high-risk individuals and places, and the finite resources available to fund crime prevention initiatives. In short, as McGarrell et al. (2013b, 41) write in their analysis of gun and gang violence prevention programs, "given that a small number of cities, places, gangs, and people drive levels of the most serious violence, then maximum program impact" will come from programs aimed at the "few cities, places, gangs, and people at highest risk for generating serious violence."

1.6.3 *Crime Prevention Emphasizes a* Problem-Oriented *Methodology*

In theory, crime prevention emphasizes a systematic *problem-oriented* approach that, in general, encompasses three components:

1. It involves an *analytical process* whereby the scope and nature of a potential crime problem or criminal behavior are predicted and assessed through the gathering and analysis of relevant information (which includes identifying and separating the causes of the problem from symptoms and aggravating factors).
2. The intervention is *crafted specifically for the (potential) crime problem being addressed.* That is, the scope and nature of the crime prevention strategy are commensurate with the scope and nature of the problem while also being appropriate for the setting in which the problem is occurring or may occur. This includes determining the most appropriate institutions through which interventions can be delivered, as well as determining who should be involved in delivering these interventions.
3. *A wide range of alternative and flexible solutions* is considered in anticipation of or reaction to a crime risk or onset of criminal behavior (recognizing the highly individualized nature of each risk).

The three elements that make up a problem-oriented approach translate into four phases that should be undertaken in any crime prevention intervention:

1. *Anticipating and assessing the potential problem,* whether this involves gauging the level of risk and predicting the type of crime that may occur in a particular setting or identifying children and youth who are at risk of future offending and assessing the factors that put them at risk

by

2. *Gathering and analyzing* relevant information to assess the scope, nature, and impact of the (potential) problem

13

CASE STUDY 1.3

DEVELOPMENTAL PROGRAM FOR CHILDREN AT RISK OF CONDUCT PROBLEMS

Early Risers is an intensive and comprehensive developmental program for elementary school children (ages 6–10 years) who are at heightened risk for early onset of serious conduct problems. This includes children who display such criminogenic risk factors as aggression, defiance, hyperactivity, and impulsivity. The scientifically developed program operates on the empirically established assumption that early, comprehensive, and sustained intervention is necessary for children who exhibit multiple risk factors. "The enhanced competence gained through the program leads to the development of positive self-image, independent decision making, healthy problem solving, assertive communication, and constructive coping. Once acquired, these attributes and skills collectively enable youths to resist personal and social forces that encourage early substance use and potential abuse and dependency" (Office of Juvenile Justice and Delinquency Prevention, n.d.).

The multidimensional program integrates child-, school-, and family-focused interventions to help at-risk children develop prosocial behaviors and achieve academic successes essential to their positive development. This is attained by promoting such social competencies and life skills as self-control, social problem solving, conflict resolution, anger management, and positive peer networking. The program also strives to improve the child's academic ability, which includes developing a positive attitude toward learning and a strong bond to schools. The program also provides support and training to parents that can help them promote the goals of the program with their child through proper discipline, monitoring, and communication.

The child-focused component of the program has three parts: (1) a 6-week long summer day camp, which provides social competency skills training, reading enrichment, and creative arts experiences supported by a strong behavioral management regime; (2) school year friendship groups, which are offered during or after school and work to maintain and advance the skills learned over the summer; and (3) school support, which is provided throughout the school year and is intended to assist the child's schooling while promoting positive behaviors at school. In nurturing these skills among at-risk children, the program uses various instructional techniques (teaching, behavioral modeling, role paying, coaching, positive reinforcement) and mediums (videos, books, puppets, sports, creative arts, in-class demonstrations).

The family-focused component has two parts: (1) family nights with parent education, in which the parents meet in small groups five nights per year for education and skills training, and (2) family support, an individualized plan for each participating family to address risk factors through goal setting, a strategy to reach those goals, skills training for the parent, and referral to organizations that could assist parents in reaching the goals set for themselves and their children.

A professional trained as a *family advocate* is responsible for providing the services to the participating children and parents. For the child-centered component, the advocate conducts assessments of the child and the family, consults with teachers, visits the child's school, mentors the child, teaches the child social competency skills, conducts home visits, develops supportive relationships with parents, assists the family in setting goals and strategic planning, finds supportive community services, and facilitates communication between parents and the school.

Assessments of the program indicate that when compared with a control group, the children enrolled in the program showed greater academic success, lower rates of attention and concentration problems, increased self-control, anger management, and greater rates of improvement in social skills and overall social competence (August et al., 2002, 2003). All of these achievements can be considered protective factors that can help stave off future delinquent and criminal behavior.

and then

3. *Intervening,* by developing and employing individualized strategies that cater to the nature and scope of the identified risks and actual problems (applying solutions that best solve the problem, which frequently involves working outside the CJS)

and finally

4. *Monitoring* and assessing the effectiveness of the interventions (ensuring they address the cause of the problem) and recalibrating the intervention if necessary

In the context of problem-oriented policing, Sampson and Scott (1999, 30) emphasize that "a proactive, problem-solving approach is markedly different from the traditional approach to addressing crime and fear in our communities. It involves tailoring solutions to unique neighborhood problems, based on thoughtful, in-depth analysis. It involves moving away from generic crime-control models or off-the-shelf solutions, because each community's crime problems are unique." As Shaw notes, this problem-oriented approach mimics the methodology used in public health by "defining the problem, its incidence and trends through extensive data collection, identifying the causes and associated risk and protective factors, designing and implementing interventions targeting those causes, evaluating their effectiveness, and disseminating the results of successful practice to educate the public (more on how the field of public health has influenced the field of crime prevention is discussed in Box 1.1). "Thus initiatives target individual, family, community, and social factors, drawing on evidence-based research and practice of well-implemented and evaluated programmes" (Shaw, 2005, 6).

In their adoption of the problem-oriented approach, many police forces follow the *SARA* model, which is an acronym for scan, analyze, respond, and assess. (Eck and Spelman, 1987; see Chapter 7 for more information on the SARA model within the context of problem-oriented policing.) Other mnemonic methodological models that encapsulate this problem-oriented philosophy include Read and Tilley's (2000) *PROCTOR* (problem, cause, tactic/treatment, output, and result), Ekblom's (2005) *5Is* (intelligence, intervention, implementation, involvement, and impact), and the Royal Canadian Mounted Police's (2008) *CAPRA* (clients, acquire/analyze information, partnerships, response, and assessment of action taken) (as cited in Clare et al., 2010, 8).

CASE STUDY 1.4

APPLYING PROBLEM-ORIENTED PRINCIPLES IN GREEN BAY, WISCONSIN

This case study provides one example of how the problem-oriented SARA model has been applied in the context of crime prevention and problem-oriented policing.

Scan: Two Green Bay police officers were assigned full time to address a problem that had long plagued Wisconsin's largest city. Broadway Street had a squalid reputation. Liquor bottles littered the streets. Homeless people and panhandlers were everywhere and slept on park benches outside of neglected, decaying buildings. There was an overabundance of seedy bars, some of which sold drugs. Drunks and drug addicts aimlessly wandered the streets. Broadway Street became known as the *Wild West* of Green Bay; many city residents avoided the area and most area businesses suffered financially. Police simply reacted to the problems by responding to complaints, issuing warnings for public drunkenness, and arresting those involved in property, drug, or violent crime.

The two police officers determined that they would try to address the causes underlying the problems in this neighborhood and set out to achieve the following objectives: eliminate illegal activity from the neighborhood, reduce calls for police and rescue services, bring businesses to the area by improving the public's perception of the Broadway business district, and restore faith in the ability of the police department by building a cooperative working relationship with local residents, community groups, and businesses.

Analyze: In their problem-oriented approach to the identified problems, the police officers began by talking with local residents, groups, and businesses, while also analyzing police data. Through their research of the neighborhood, they discovered a crime rate that was much higher than the rest of the city and a disproportionate demand for police and rescue services. They also found that it was the same 20 people who were at the center of the vast majority of complaints. Analysis of police data showed that most victims of serious crimes in the area, such as stabbings, shootings, and assaults, were patrons of a few taverns. Repeat calls were made to the same bars for fights and other alcohol-related problems. Victimization rates were very low for citizens in the area who did not patronize these taverns.

Wisconsin state law provides a judicial process for local governments to regulate liquor licenses. However, the two officers found that the municipal government rarely exercised its authority to revoke or suspend the licenses of problem taverns. In fact, the city's Protection and Welfare Committee, which regulates liquor licenses, often approved and renewed licenses in the area with little scrutiny.

The two officers undertook a safety audit of the Broadway area and found numerous physical design deficiencies that contributed to the crime and disorder problems. Several taverns had dark alcoves and doorways facing alleys, which facilitated quick and discrete access and escape for drug dealers and users, violent patrons, and other offenders. Poorly designed landscaping on Broadway Street also created hiding places for people who were intoxicated and living on the street.

Respond: In response to what they perceived as the causes and facilitators of these problems, the two police officers pursued the following five initiatives:

1. No serve list: The police officers provided liquor store and tavern owners with a list of people who were habitually intoxicated, accompanied by a letter from the police department requesting that service be denied to them.
2. Operation *hot seat*: Police stepped up enforcement of ordinance violations in the neighborhood, by issuing citations and arresting people for behavior and actions that would have resulted in warnings in the past. Several offenders were placed on probation, and the two officers worked closely with probation officers to enforce the probation conditions.
3. Environmental design: A number of design modifications were made to the neighborhood to reduce the opportunities for future problems to occur: overgrown shrubs that concealed illegal activity were trimmed; the Broadway district's park benches were modified to prevent people from lying down; access to an abandoned building that was used by homeless people as well as drug dealers and consumers was boarded up; the Broadway district's park grounds were better maintained, removing the litter and bedding generated by people who lived on the streets; lighting in the dark alcoves behind taverns was improved to increase visibility and surveillance opportunities, while the rear doors of taverns were modified to permit exit only.
4. Increased regulation of liquor licenses: The police department worked with the city attorney's office to enforce new municipal ordinances. The result was that police officers could now cite bar owners even if they were not present when offenses were committed. The city attorney's office developed a system in which points were assessed against the liquor license upon conviction of an alcohol-related offense allowing the municipal court to automatically suspend a license and close a tavern for a designated period of time after 12 points had been accumulated.
5. Community mobilization: Police felt that many citizens were unaware of the licensing regulations governing liquor establishments. Therefore, they educated people about how they could influence the actions of the Protection and Welfare Committee, which had the power to issue and rescind licenses. The two officers provided citizens with dates and times of the committee meetings, the names and telephone numbers of council members who sat on the committee, and the proper procedure for addressing the committee. Meetings once conducted in a small room in city hall had to be moved to city council chambers to accommodate the increased number of people attending. The local community also came together to support the police by donating office space (in a housing complex for the elderly) as well as equipment (computers, a cellular telephone, police bicycles, and office furniture).

Assess: After the problem-solving initiative began in 1995, and along with some economic development support from the city, Broadway Street slowly transformed into a prosperous business district. An assessment of the results of the initiative showed that the area experienced a 65% reduction in total police calls and a 91% decrease in the demand for rescue squad services to handle injuries resulting from assaults. From 1995 to February 2000, the Broadway business district gained more than $8.4 million in new public and private investment, 410 new jobs, and 33 new businesses (United States. Department of Justice, 1999, 7–13).

1.6.4 Crime Prevention Initiatives Are Evidence Based

Another salient characteristic of crime prevention theory and practice is that it is increasingly based on strong empirical evidence as to what is effective (i.e., *best practices*) in controlling crime. Critiques of criminal justice policies, practices, and programs often center on the lack of a strong theoretical basis as well as the absence of techniques, strategies, or programs that research has shown to be effective. Stated differently, one constant in ineffective crime control measures—whether they are proactive or reactive—is that they use techniques and strategies that rigorous research and program evaluations have shown to be ineffective or counterproductive. Because criminal justice policies and programs are ultimately in the hands of politicians, they can be shaped by politics and ideology, which may run counter to what the research may say is effective. As Homel and Homel (2012, 424) write, "politics has trumped science, with evidence based crime prevention being largely abandoned for projects proposed by community group set up often are not built in sound scientific foundations." Bergin (2013), for example, explains that the proliferation of boot camps in the United States during the 1980s and 1990s—despite the mounting evidence that these approaches were ineffective in reducing recidivism rates—was due to a conservative political climate in a racially charged environment that also included such influences as the popularity of *tough-on-crime* approaches among the electorate and the high number of military veterans as policy makers and voters.

Given the finite resources available to combat crime, it is imperative that policy makers and program developers emphasize policies and techniques that have shown to work based on rigorous experimental research or program evaluations (or at the very least have a strong theoretical foundation). This is what is commonly referred to as an *evidence-based* or *knowledge-based* approach to crime prevention and control. As Welsh (2007, 1) writes, "evidence-based crime prevention ensures that the best available evidence is considered in the decision to implement a program designed to prevent crime." According to Welsh and Farrington (2001, 166), "In an evidence-based society, government crime prevention policy and local practice would be based on interventions with demonstrated effectiveness in preventing crime and offending. Equally important, governments would put an end to those interventions that do not work and, more important, to those that are harmful or iatrogenic. The key here, of course, is fostering high quality research—using experimental and quasi-experimental evaluation designs—on the effects of interventions." For Petrosino (2000, 635), "an evidence-based approach requires that the results of rigorous evaluation be rationally integrated into decisions about interventions by policy-makers and practitioners alike." The International Centre for the Prevention of Crime (2008) states, "Knowledge-based prevention includes approaches that use good evidence as the basis for action, ranging from diagnosis to evaluation. Such approaches are also used to reinforce, and where necessary, challenge public policies" (155). Rigorous experimental research and especially program evaluations of "crime prevention practices helps to establish a rational and scientific basis" and "has made it possible to identify 'what works', what is less effective, and why this is so" (15–16).

According to Welsh (2007), the contemporary impetus for an evidence-based approach to crime prevention began with a 1997 report to the US Congress, led by criminologist Lawrence Sherman, entitled *Preventing Crime: What Works, What Doesn't, What's Promising* (Sherman et al., 1997). The meta-analysis of federally sponsored programs used scientifically derived scales to rate different evaluations of crime prevention programs, and, based upon this analysis, the authors drew evidence-based conclusions on what appeared to be effective and ineffective programs and approaches. Another important development in the evolution of evidence-based crime prevention movement was the creation of the Center for the Study of Violence Prevention and at the University of Colorado Boulder, the mandate of which is to "identify evidence-based prevention and intervention programs that are effective in reducing antisocial behavior and promoting a healthy course of youth development" (Center for the Study of Violence Prevention, n.d.). In addition, in 2000, the Campbell Collaboration Crime and Justice Group was created and constitutes "an international network of researchers that prepares and disseminates systematic reviews of high-quality research on methods to reduce crime and delinquency and improve the quality of justice" (Campbell Collaboration Crime and Justice Group, n.d.). According to the International Centre for the Prevention of Crime (2008, 162), "By carefully selecting projects which meet their standards for scientific measurement, and using systematic metaanalysis to compare the results from similar studies obtained in different countries or contexts, the group has been able to demonstrate clear crime reduction outcomes from particular kinds of interventions. They have also been able to demonstrate some clear cost-benefits and cost-savings."

In short, there has been a "marked trend toward knowledge-based" crime prevention; that is, "an increasing use of prevention approaches which have a strong scientific basis." In many countries, "prevention policies are now likely to be based on more reliable data, including that collected and analysed by independent authorities" (International Centre for the Prevention of Crime, 2008, 15–16). The movement toward a more evidence-based approach to crime control is reflective of the trend toward evidence-based public policy making generally. According to the International Centre for the Prevention of Crime (2008, 155), the "development of knowledge-based policies is not limited to the field of crime prevention and community safety. It forms part of a larger trend encouraging decision-makers to base their decisions on more scientific information, making better use of recent knowledge in their respective fields of action, and taking into consideration lessons learned from past initiatives."

1.6.5 Responsibility for Crime Control Is Partially Shifted to Private (Nonstate) Actors

The CJS is symptomatic of a state-imposed, top-down approach to social problem solving: The government defines the problem (through laws and legislation) and then takes responsibility for addressing the problem (through the enforcement of criminal laws by police, prosecutors, the judiciary, correctional facilities, parole agencies, etc.).

In contrast, crime prevention is theoretically premised on a bottom-up approach, which in turn is based on the assumption that private citizens play a major role in maintaining order in a free society and therefore should accept some responsibility for the prevention of crime, criminality, and incivilities. The significance of this paradigmatic shift is that responsibility for crime control has been partially transferred from the state to the citizenry. Indeed, while governments still have a major role to play in crime prevention (through the CJS, schools, social policies and programs, program funding, etc.), the lead responsibility for the *prevention of crime* should rest with citizens and not the state. The significance of this philosophical shift is quite profound and far reaching: not only should individual citizens and other nonstate actors play a greater role in

CASE STUDY 1.5

MOBILIZING AN INNER-CITY NEIGHBORHOOD IN VANCOUVER, CANADA

The South Vancouver Community Police Centre (CPC) serves the south–central and south-eastern portions of Vancouver, which are historically working-class areas and today are largely made up of middle- and lower–middle-class residents. In addition to its traditional Caucasian population, South Vancouver has long been home to a large Indo-Canadian population (which is now made up of first, second, and third generations) as well as Chinese and Vietnamese Canadians (many of whom are new immigrants). The CPC is located in a strip mall on a major thoroughfare and is highly visible, due in part to its large blue electric sign that simply reads, *Community Policing.* While the office is connected to the Vancouver Police Department, it is governed by a board of directors made up of local residents, run by a civilian coordinator, and staffed mostly by volunteers.

In a 2003 interview, the CPC coordinator stated that the office has approximately 160 volunteers, including a *hard core* group of 60–80 people. The volunteer base is diverse and includes businesspeople, students, homemakers, and retirees, many of which have been *volunteering at the office for a number of years.* The volunteer base also includes *lots of immigrant families.* Commitment and attachment to the local community are key factors in influencing one's decision to volunteer at the CPC, according to the coordinator, although people "also get involved because of a specific crime issue." The coordinator credits the "healthy, positive dynamics in this office" where "we have lots of fun."

Ongoing outreach and communications target existing crime prevention participants, such as Neighborhood Watch Block Captains, *to make them feel important and needed.* As the coordinator put it, "These people are essential, so we must keep in constant contact." Emphasis is also placed on reaching out to visible minority and immigrant residents. To this end, the office is staffed with volunteers who speak the dominant languages of the neighborhood, pamphlets are available in different languages, and workshops have also been held specifically for the local Vietnamese, Hispanic, and Indo-Canadian populations. The outreach and communications stress a positive message (*we get in their face constantly … but in a nice way*) and are *as personalized as possible* (including personal contact by the CPC coordinator or police officers). This personal contact is particularly important because, in the experience of this CPC coordinator, many community members who use the services of or volunteer at the office heard about it through word of mouth.

The volunteer base, including board members, is reflective of the demographic diversity of the neighborhoods served by this CPC, which *helps with promoting the office among different racial and ethnic groups through word-of-mouth.*

The coordinator estimated that in 2002, the CPC organized 132 community events, including many beautification projects, such as an annual garbage cleanup and a graffiti removal project that attracted more than 200 volunteers. A wide variety of SCP and community development programs help to increase the visibility of the office while appealing to different needs, interests, and priorities of community members. The CPC also provides incentives to encourage participation and efforts to help keep the neighborhood clean and attractive; for example, local businesses that keep their area clean are rewarded with cedar planters, plaques, or flower boxes.

The coordinator also stressed that this CPC pays "close attention to our volunteers," making sure "their time spent at the office is meaningful" and assigning tasks and responsibilities that "brings benefits to volunteers," such as improving their work skills. The coordinator cited leadership as a key factor in attracting volunteers and program participants and stressed that CPC coordinators must be prepared to "invest a lot of time" in reaching out to and working with volunteers. Success in attracting volunteers and program participants is also the result of nurturing a strong working relationship with other local community groups, businesses, and the Vancouver Police Department (Schneider, 2007a, 141–142).

preventing crime, but this bottom-up approach emphasizes that government agencies should be subordinate to private citizens and nongovernmental groups in planning and implementing crime prevention interventions. The result of this assumption is a de facto division of labor between private citizens and the government as far as crime control is concerned: The state is responsible for *reacting to crime* (through laws and the CJS), while private citizens and nongovernmental organizations should take the lead in community-based initiatives that *prevent* crime from occurring. (In practice, this theoretical division of labor is not as clear-cut as police often take the lead in initiating crime prevention projects.)

Because responsibility for crime prevention is primarily entrusted to the citizenry, community-based organizations have a far greater role in crime prevention when compared to criminal justice approaches to crime. With that said, as Hastings and Jamieson (2002) point out, "not all crime prevention programs and activities require community involvement. Preventive actions can occur in many different spheres." In particular, governments play a major role in crime prevention, beyond their traditional criminal justice responsibilities. Thus, crime prevention is ultimately a shared responsibility between local communities and government policy makers and agencies. Because the state does have a role to play in crime prevention, government agencies and public services can be integral to a proactive, preventive approach to crime. In addition to police, these government agencies, professionals, and services include schools, social workers, publicly funded health-care facilities and professionals, municipal engineering and urban planning departments, and municipal recreational facilities and community centers, to name just a few.

1.6.6 *(Community) Crime Prevention Stresses Informal Social Control*

The implication of the shift in crime *prevention* responsibilities from the state to local communities is that greater emphasis is placed on *informal forms of social control* exerted by individuals acting collectively, as opposed to the *formal methods of social control*, which are state-imposed sanctions codified in written laws and regulations and enforced by the police and the courts.

Informal social control is a central concept in crime prevention. Community crime prevention in particular is concerned with reinforcing or modifying the individual and collective behaviors of local residents to produce or strengthen a local social environment that can informally regulate itself, including the regulation and prevention of criminal, delinquent, disorderly, and uncivil behavior. Informal social control is based on custom, common agreement, or social norms, and, in the neighborhood context, it refers to the observance and enforcement of implicit local rules for behavior that is consistent with, and supportive of, the values, standards, and tolerance levels of a particular neighborhood.

Informal social control is said to restrict crime and disorder through a vigorous enforcement of norms and standards that the community holds (Greenberg et al., 1983). As a response to undesirable behavior, expressions of informal social control range from the most spontaneous and subtle (e.g., raised eyebrows, gossip, or ridicule), to direct confrontation (e.g., verbal reprimands, warnings, or physical intervention), to structured activities of neighborhood groups (e.g., organizing a neighborhood watch program) (Greenberg et al., 1985, 1; Rosenbaum, 1988, 327).

Community-based initiatives that are premised on informal social control have increasingly been seen as an alternative to the formal approaches to social control carried out by the state. However, within the context of a collaborative approach to preventing crime, the two should not be seen as mutually exclusive: Informal social control by citizens supplements the formal social control mechanisms of government. As detailed in Chapter 5, the effective functioning of informal social control is contingent upon a strong sense of community or local social cohesion.

1.6.7   Focus Is Shifted from the Offender to the Potential Victim and Potential Offender

The CJS is overwhelmingly focused on offenders—catching them, charging them, prosecuting them, sentencing them, punishing them, and, to a lesser extent, rehabilitating them. In contrast, a major criticism of the CJS is that it has traditionally paid little attention to victims. In the field of crime prevention, offenders are still a preoccupation insofar as many proactive interventions—especially situational strategies—are geared toward stopping or deterring them. However, the field of crime prevention also places great emphasis on the potential victim or target; not only are SCP strategies geared toward protecting people and places from victimization, but the planning and implementation of these interventions are often carried out by the very people who are at risk of becoming crime victims. Attention has also shifted from the offender to the potential offender. This is the hallmark of social developmental approaches, which target factors that place children and youth at risk of (future) delinquency and criminality.

1.6.8   Crime Prevention Is Contingent upon Partnerships

Central to many crime prevention strategies and programs is a collaborative, multiagency, multisectoral approach in which all relevant service providers and other stakeholders work as a team in a coordinated, seamless fashion. The literature on prevention, for example, shows that the most successful interventions "are those which combine multiple approaches and emphasize multi-agency involvement (e.g. the police, community, school, family, prisoners, ex-gang members, youth workers, peers and health practitioners)" (Maher, 2010, 318). The diverse range of criminogenic risk factors that produce serious and chronic offenders cuts across the jurisdictions, mandates, expertise, and resources of different governments, government agencies, and other sectors of society. As such, no single government or organization is equipped to deal with crime and violence or the underlying causes thereof in their totality.

> Partnerships are assumed to bring together diverse agencies in individuals, leverage more resources to address the problem, and coordinate the development and application of interventions. In theory, therefore, partnerships are expected to be more inclusive and responsive to community priorities than single agencies; achieve a

greater understanding of risk factors; develop more diverse, creative, and comprehensive strategies; reduce duplication of services and provide better coordination of strategies across agencies; increase agency accountability; strengthen local community organizations; and provide more political clout to garner additional resources.

Rosenbaum and Schuck (2012, 228)

Therefore, according to Wyrick and Howell (2004, 22–23), addressing the multiplicity of criminogenic risk factors among individuals, families, and communities requires "a coordinated partnership" that "must be developed and managed with a broad understanding of local risk factors across domains." Further, a collaborative approach must take place at all levels: policy making, program development, program implementation, and program evaluation. Perhaps most importantly, this collaborative, integrated approach must be implemented at the local (neighborhood) level. The importance of collaboration and coordination permeates other prevention-based approaches to crime, including community policing, the defining characteristic of which is partnerships between the police and the communities they serve. (For more on community policing and its defining characteristics, see Chapter 7.)

According to Berry et al. (2011, 2), a theoretical perspective on multiagency models of crime reduction identifies seven potential benefits of effective partnerships:

1. Crime and drug problems are complex and require complex, innovative, and comprehensive solutions.
2. Partnerships are better than individual agencies at identifying and defining problems of greatest community concern.
3. Partnerships are better able to develop creative and targeted interventions (because they bring together a diverse group of agencies with different approaches).
4. Multiple interventions are generally more effective than single agency interventions with potentially higher levels of the intervention being delivered (e.g., greater number of prevention activities being undertaken).
5. Partnerships bring more resources and new ideas to the problem-solving arena.
6. Multiple interventions are likely to maximize the impact on any particular target audience.
7. Exposure to different interventions may yield new benefits (where the combined interaction of two or more interventions may generate greater effects).

Berry and colleagues (2011, 2) also cite the work of Rosenbaum (2002), who "identified several additional benefits of partnership activity over and above the impact on crime reduction. In particular, he suggests that when partnerships work effectively they can:

• Increase the accountability of organisations;
• Reduce duplication and fragmentation of services;
• Build public-private linkages;
• Increase public awareness of and participation in crime reduction initiatives;
• Serve to strengthen local community organisations; and,
• Be transformational, permanently altering the way agencies do business (better data-driven decision making, emphasis on problem solving and prevention).

Finally, Rosenbaum and Schuck (2012, 240) identify the "common set of conditions" necessary to create and sustain successful community partnerships:

> (1) a supportive start-up environment with adequate funding and a history of collaborative partnerships; (2) a common purpose or mission that unifies all participating stakeholders; (3) a lead agency that is respected by other agencies; (4) leadership they can champion the cause, stimulate problem solving, resolve conflicts and maintain group cohesiveness; (5) a formalized structure, including a steering committee (with appropriate community group representation) that can develop strategies, make decisions, and leverage resources for implementation, and a working group and fully execute action plans and strategies; (6) the commitment to evidence-based practice and prevention science; and (7) access to training and technical assistance to build competency the individual, organizational, programmatic, and relational levels.

1.6.9 Crime Prevention Targets not only the Criminal Act but also Criminality, Fear, and Disorder

As implied earlier, crime prevention through social development focuses on addressing the root causes of crime and delinquency. This of course contrasts with the CJS, which was never really created for such purposes (although corrections-based treatment and rehabilitation, do attempt to prevent recidivism among offenders). Crime prevention interventions do not simply address crime, but in some cases, they also target the fear of crime by providing individuals and communities with the education, tools, power, and collective security that can potentially contribute to alleviating fear.

CASE STUDY 1.6

ADDRESSING THE HOMELESS PROBLEM IN CALIFORNIA THROUGH PARTNERSHIP-BASED PROBLEM-SOLVING METHODS

For a number of years, the City of Fontana, California, had been experiencing problems involving large homeless and transient populations. Businesses identified homelessness as the largest single public safety-related problem in the city. Piecemeal enforcement strategies implemented on a block-by-block basis simply resulted in the displacement of homeless people from one area of the city to another. Police, in cooperation with businesses and community groups, then embarked on a citywide strategy that attempted to lower the number of homeless people on the street. Police partnered with local charities that worked with the homeless, and an agreement was reached to open a referral office. Homeless people identified by business owners, community groups, and police officers would be referred to staff at this volunteer-run agency who then referred them to organizations and programs that would meet their needs and help them get off the streets. Police also became more aggressive in enforcing violations of nuisance laws committed by homeless people, while local business groups agreed to supply jobs and job training programs. Local charitable groups that had been supplying free shelter, meals, and clothing to homeless people (which was identified as a major attractor for the homeless to Fontana) now began encouraging them to work with the referral agency.

As a result of the multipronged partnership-based strategy, the number of homeless people in Fontana decreased by 90% and calls for service related to homelessness decreased by 50% (Center for Problem-Oriented Policing, 1998).

CASE STUDY 1.7

DESIGN MODIFICATIONS TO REDUCE FEAR IN TORONTO'S SUBWAY SYSTEM

Surveys consistently show that women are generally more fearful than men in enclosed public spaces, such as underground parking garages or subways. In 1989, a collaborative effort between the Toronto Transit Commission (TTC), the Metropolitan Toronto Police Service, and the Metro Action Committee on Public Violence against Women (METRAC) produced a number of measures to make the Toronto subway system and the surface transit system safer for women. An ancillary goal was to decrease fear that women may feel while waiting for subway trains (which was also meant to serve to increase ridership by women).

One of the first products to emerge from this joint effort was the *safety audit kit*, a checklist to evaluate the design features of specific public transit settings. In particular, the kit was used to evaluate the design of 65 subway stations in greater Toronto. The audit identified a number of design factors that made women feel unsafe, including poor lighting, isolation, lack of sight lines, no access to help, hiding and entrapment spots, and inadequate security measures. A 1989 audit of Toronto's public transit system resulted in 63 recommendations to reduce the risk of sexual assault. These recommendations were documented in a report entitled *Moving Forward: Making Transit Safer for Women* (Toronto Transit Commission, 1989). A result of this report was a comprehensive review of the design of Toronto subway stations and the adoption of a number of physical design measures to increase the safety and security of those waiting for trains. Some of these key measures are summarized in the following:

1. Public telephones: To facilitate 911 emergency calls, public telephones are located on all subway station platforms, at station entrances, and in many bus and streetcar terminal areas.
2. Security mirrors: Mirrors are located at a number of points on and around the subway platform. Areas where the mirrors are most prevalent include stairwells and any other places where blind corners may exist. These mirrors are intended to eliminate blind spots and help transit riders see around corners or into other passageways.
3. Designated waiting areas (DWAs): DWAs are located on all subway- and surface-level rapid transit platforms to enhance the safety of passengers while they wait for trains. A DWA has brighter lights, an intercom, a closed-circuit television camera, and is situated near public telephones. On the subway platform, the DWA is also located where the subway guard's car stops. For easy recognition by subway users, the guard's car is distinguished from the rest of the train by an orange or white light on the outside. Boarding from the DWA, a passenger can ride in a subway car with a TTC employee for additional safety.
4. Intercoms: Intercoms, which let passengers talk directly to a station collector or other TTC staff, are located in each of the DWAs, outside elevator entrances, and at subway entrances not staffed by a TTC station collector.
5. Visibility: To increase visibility and decrease fear, bright lighting is consistently placed throughout subway platforms. Walls and columns within subway platforms are painted white to maximize light reflectance.

In addition to the subway system, design modifications that take into consideration the safety of women were also made at surface-level transit stations. This included maximizing lighting in and around transit stops, installing public telephones, relocating transit stops to safer locations, and redesigning transit stop shelters to maximize sight lines, surveillance, and easy egress for passengers.

The TTC also has its own force of special constables who have the same powers as police officers whose duties include reviewing and recommending improvements to transit stations to decrease safety concerns. The special constables also provide security awareness training to frontline TTC employees "to help them carry out their role as TTC Safety Partners" (Toronto Transit Commission, 2014b).

According to the Corporate Security Department of the TTC, one indication of the impact of the safety improvements has been a 23% decrease in crime at five subway stations. A 50% decrease in crime occurred at one subway station, the site of a comprehensive safety upgrade (Scarborough Surface Transit, 1991; Toronto Transit Commission, 1989, 2014a,b).

Certain crime prevention theories and strategies also advocate a focus on disorder and incivilities. These are problems that are not illegal as defined by criminal law but, according to some theories and research, can contribute to local instability that may invite more serious crime problems. (Broken windows is the oft-cited theoretical basis for preventative efforts aims at disorder and incivility problems. This theory is described in Chapter 2). For Lab (2004, 15), there are two categories of disorder and incivilities: physical and social. Physical signs include "the physical deterioration of buildings, litter, graffiti, vandalism, and abandoned buildings and cars, among others." Some of the social signs of disorder and incivilities are "public drunkenness, vagrancy, groups of loitering youths, harassment (such as begging and panhandling), and visible drug sales and use." Disorder and incivilities may be addressed by mobilizing and organizing neighborhood residents, which include invigorating a level of informal social control that is strong enough to help prevent such physical or social incivilities. Some SCP and law enforcement strategies emphasize *zero tolerance*, which means preventing, quickly catching, and punishing incivilities and disorder problems. This approach is premised on the belief that the enforcement of disorder problems may help address some of the factors that precipitate or encourage more serious crime problems (Wilson and Kelling, 1982).

1.7 CLASSIFYING CRIME PREVENTION APPROACHES

Another way to explore the conceptual parameters of crime prevention, and its wide range of applied interventions, is to divide its many different strategies into distinguishable categories. Below are some examples of how the field of crime prevention has been demarcated based on the differing types of interventions that can be pursued within the broad parameters of this field.

1.7.1 Five Pillars of Crime Prevention

Crime prevention strategies can be classified into five categories:

1. Crime prevention through social development: Social problem-solving interventions designed to prevent the onset of criminal and violent behavior in individuals by addressing their root causes, especially among *at-risk* children and youth
2. SCP: Interventions designed to prevent the occurrence of criminal and violent acts by reducing opportunities in a particular time and place through the management, design, or manipulation of the immediate physical and/or human environment

CASE STUDY 1.8

PREVENTING CRIME AND INCIVILITIES IN OAKLAND, CALIFORNIA

The Beat Health Program of the Oakland Police Department relies on civil remedies—procedures and sanctions codified in municipal laws and regulations—to prevent and reduce not just crime problems but incivilities that can also negatively impact the livability of a neighborhood. Civil remedies generally aim to persuade third parties, such as landlords, property owners, or the management of licensed establishments, to take responsibility for and action to prevent criminal and uncivil behavior on their property. The Beat Health Program places particular emphasis on using civil remedies to "control drug and disorder problems by focusing on the physical decay and property management conditions of specific commercial establishments, private homes, and rental properties" (Mazerolle and Roehl, 1999, 2).

A group of patrol officers work with personnel from municipal government agencies to inspect problem premises, pressure landowners to clean up and maintain blighted properties, implement proper safety and security measures, enforce municipal regulations and health and safety codes, and initiate court proceedings against property owners who fail to comply with bylaw and regulatory citations. The Beat Health patrol officers often coordinate site visits with the city's Specialized Multi-Agency Response Team, which is made up of city inspectors working in such areas as housing, fire, health, utilities, and sewage. These officials are invited to inspect and enforce city codes and to use their civil powers to close down or force the cleanup of residential and commercial establishments that may be the source of local crime or disorder problems.

Mazerolle and Roehl (1999) describe one successful case involving the Beat Health team that followed up on an anonymous tip to a police-operated hotline concerning drug trafficking, abandoned vehicles, and garbage at a single-family home in a nice neighborhood. "The Beat Health Team contacted the owner, who said the problems were probably due to an illegal tenant staying at the house with the permission of the legal tenant. Police records revealed that the illegal tenant was on probation for drug charges." An inspection was conducted by the Specialized Multi-Agency Response Team and the city inspectors found a number of violations, such as missing stair banisters, broken windows, possible electrical tampering, overgrown weeds, trash, two pit bulls, dog waste, large cracks in the sidewalk, and abandoned cars and engine parts in the yard. "Following the inspection, which resulted in numerous citations for violations, both the legal tenant and the owner contacted the Beat Health officer. Within 3 months, the illegal tenant was evicted, the yard cleared of abandoned vehicles and trash, and code violations fixed. The case was closed 6 months after it was opened: the property was being restored and no new calls or complaints were received" (Mazerolle and Roehl, 1999, 7).

An evaluation of the Beat Health program in a number of sites in Oakland showed a decline in public signs of disorder, decreases in drug trafficking, and increases in signs of civil behavior in public places and on private properties (Mazerolle and Roehl, 1999; Mazerolle et al., 2000).

3. Community crime prevention: The mobilization of neighborhood residents based on two different (yet complementary) approaches: (i) the community defense approach (in which residents work together to prevent crime, primarily through opportunity reduction measures) and (ii) the community development approach (in which the causes and aggravating factors that promote crime and criminality locally are addressed through social, economic, and physical development)

4. Recidivism prevention: Initiatives to help offenders desist from criminal behavior, emphasizing community-based, social problem-solving interventions, emphasizing treatment and the creation of positive, alternative opportunities (such as social reintegration, education, and job training)
5. Police and the CJS: The use of proactive, community-based, and/or problem-oriented policing approaches that have shown to work (e.g., community policing, problem-oriented policing, hot spot policing, CompStat) as well as harm reduction approaches implemented by other criminal justice branches that address the root causes of criminal offending (e.g., drug courts, mental health courts)

1.7.2   *Primary, Secondary, and Tertiary Approaches (Public Health Typology)*

Brantingham and Faust (1976) created one of the first classifications of crime prevention by adapting a public health typology for disease prevention and control that incorporates three levels: primary, secondary, and tertiary. Each level differs primarily by the extent to which treatment is proactive: primary prevention is concerned with stemming the conditions that may give rise to an infectious disease (or criminal behavior). The latter two categories entail responses that are concerned with treating and reducing the consequences of an emergent disease (or criminal act).

Specifically, within the public health model, primary prevention involves measures that attempt to avoid the onset of a particular disease. Examples of such primary prevention interventions include sewage treatment, mosquito extermination, or smallpox vaccinations. Similarly, primary crime prevention strategies address immediate social and physical environmental conditions that may provide opportunities for a crime to occur, such as the poor design of buildings, a lack of physical security, or an absence of informal social control within a neighborhood. Primary crime prevention tends to encompass situational measures that focus on the immediate physical and human environment, such as *hardening the target* (through locks, gates, reinforced windows) or organizing local residents (e.g., neighborhood watch or citizen patrols).

Secondary prevention within the public health field is concerned with interventions directed toward groups or individuals who exhibit the early symptoms of a disease. Examples include screening tests for cancer or regular checkups for people who may be at heightened risk of contracting a disease or illness (e.g., low-birth-weight babies, seniors, coal miners). Secondary crime prevention generally includes social developmental approaches that are directed toward individuals or groups who are at high risk of becoming offenders. Examples of secondary (social developmental) crime prevention approaches include mentoring; social competency programs; remedial education; treatment of psychological, behavioral, and learning disorders; and sports and recreational programs.

Tertiary prevention within the public health model involves medical help for people who have already contracted a disease or have become injured. The goal is to overcome the disease and/or prevent its reoccurrence and may involve surgery, drugs, therapy, or rehabilitation. Tertiary crime prevention focuses on individuals who have already committed offenses and aims to intervene in their lives in a way that will stop them from committing further offenses. Otherwise known as recidivism prevention, this might be achieved through deterrence, treatment, and/or incarceration (Brantingham and Faust, 1976; Graham, 1995, 10; Lab, 2004, 24) (see Box 1.1).

BOX 1.1

APPLYING THE PUBLIC HEALTH MODEL TO CRIME AND VIOLENCE

In recent years, there have been growing calls to augment the traditional criminal justice approach to criminal violence with a public health approach. This is not surprising given the symmetry between the principles, strategies, and methodologies of crime prevention and those of public health. The public health model has been defined as "the science and art of preventing disease, prolonging life and promoting health through the organized efforts and informed choices of society, organizations, public and private, communities and individuals" (Winslow, 1920). It is primarily concerned with ameliorating threats to a population's health and improving health and quality of life through the prevention and treatment of disease and other physical and mental health conditions. As Krug et al. (2002, 3) write, by addressing conditions and problems that can lead to widespread health problems, a public health approach strives to "provide the maximum benefit for the largest number of people."

The problem-oriented methodology of crime prevention has also been greatly influenced by the public health approach to ameliorating social problems. According to the US surgeon general (2001), the basic methodology behind the public health approach to diagnosing problems and developing solutions for entire population groups comprises four basic steps:

1. Define the problem, through rigorous research using "processes designed to gather data that establish the nature of the problem and the trends in its incidence and prevalence."
2. Identify potential causes, "through epidemiological analyses that identify risk and protective factors associated with the problem."
3. Design, develop, and evaluate "the effectiveness and generalizability of interventions."
4. Disseminate "successful models as part of a coordinated effort to educate and reach out to the public."

In its 2001 report, the US surgeon general stressed the need to treat youth violence as a public health crisis and, therefore, apply a public health approach to diagnosing and treating this social problem on a wide scale (a position also taken by the World Health Organization's 2002 report on violence and health). According to the US surgeon general, "The designation of youth violence as a public health concern invites an approach that focuses more on prevention than on rehabilitation, which means identifying behavioral, environmental, and biological risk factors associated with violence" and then taking steps "to educate individuals and communities about, and protect them from, these risks." According to Welsh (2005, 35), a public health approach to youth violence

> ... recognizes the complex causes of violence. It emphasizes preventative interventions in collaboration with other key stakeholders to tackle proximal and distal causes of juvenile violence. It is very much about working to change behavior to prevent juvenile violence, either directly through violence prevention curricula in high schools or community outreach activities, or indirectly through home visitation services for new mothers or by providing families with advice and information on effective child-rearing methods. Public health goes a long way toward improving society's response to preventing and reducing juvenile criminal violence.

The surgeon general (2001) argues that compared to the CJS, the public health approach can be more effective in reducing the number of injuries as well as fatalities stemming from youth crime and violence. In making this argument, the surgeon general cites past public health approaches to traffic facilities or deaths attributed to tobacco, both of which have declined significantly in recent years.

In sum, as Shaw (2005, 3) notes, a "broader consensus has emerged on the long-term benefits of a public health and community safety approach to youth violence," in part because research shows "it is better for policies and programmes to invest in and support young people (and their families) through preventive approaches, than to exclude or incarcerate them." However, a public health approach "is not a panacea to the problem of juvenile criminal violence." While "it emphasizes primary prevention, views violence as a threat to community health rather than community order, and adheres to scientific principles, it should be seen as not so much a challenge to law and order but rather as a complement to it—part of an effort to create a more balanced, comprehensive, and sustainable strategy in preventing and reducing juvenile criminal violence" (Welsh, 2005, 23, 28–29).

1.7.3 *Collective versus Individualistic Crime Prevention*

One way to classify crime prevention strategies is to make a distinction between those that are individualistic and those that are collective in nature. Individualistic crime prevention involves measures undertaken by individuals acting alone to avoid victimization. This includes locking doors, installing alarms, using steering column locks for cars, placing bars on windows, avoiding certain parts of a city at night, carrying pepper spray or a gun, or taking self-defense classes. These measures generally only benefit the individual undertaking them and rarely do they contribute to making public spaces safer. Collective crime prevention entails two or more people getting together to maximize their own safety, the safety of those around them, and that of their surrounding environment (and, as such, includes public spaces, such as a residential street and a local park). Collective crime prevention forms the core of *community defense* strategies, such as neighborhood watch or citizen patrols. (See Chapter 5 for more details on neighborhood watch and other collective crime prevention strategies.) Thus, central to a community-based crime prevention effort is a collective response in which individuals jointly act to undertake measures to prevent or reduce crime problems that they could not accomplish on their own (Barker and Linden, 1985, 15). Collective action may also contribute indirectly to community safety by fostering social interaction and cohesion within a block, an apartment building, or a neighborhood, which in turn bolsters the informal social control that is so central to community crime prevention.

Both individual and collective approaches involve the modification of the behavior of community residents. However, the former is often viewed as negative modification, resulting in increased fear and isolation. On their own, individualized crime prevention measures have been criticized because they do little to promote a collective sense of security; target hardening may make one's home more secure but it does little to make the surrounding public spaces safe.

CASE STUDY 1.9

TERTIARY (RECIDIVISM PREVENTION) PROGRAM FOR YOUTH RELEASED FROM CUSTODY IN INDIANA

Programs that attempt to prevent recidivism among juvenile offenders epitomize the public health tertiary approach to crime prevention.

Early et al. (2013) write that there is growing interest in

> community-based juvenile reentry services that engage parents and caregivers in the treatment process as a way to reduce high rates of recidivism among youth released from correctional custody. These family-focused interventions are based on the theory that the family plays a pivotal role in reducing risk—directly, through social support and the exercise of supervision and guidance, and indirectly, by mitigating the influence of antisocial peers, antisocial thought patterns, and other potential risk factors.

> One of the advantages of community-based treatment for delinquent youth is that it offers the opportunity to intervene not only with the youth, but also to target risk factors associated with parents and the family. Juvenile offenders released from confinement often return to disorganized, chaotic family environments. The youth may have attained skills while in residential commitment, but the family may have remained largely unchanged in the interim. Addressing this issue becomes critical to reducing juvenile recidivism.

> **Early et al. (2013, 2, 3)**

Greenwood (2008, 198) corroborates this argument when he writes, "the most successful community-based programs are those that emphasize family interactions, probably because they focus on providing skills to the adults who are in the best position to supervise and train the child."

The Reentry Model of Parenting with Love and Limits (PLL Reentry) is based on the original PLL program, which was designed for adolescents who have been diagnosed with oppositional defiant or conduct disorder. "PLL integrates group and family therapy into one system of care. Parents and teens learn specific skills in group therapy and then meet in individual family therapy to role-play and practice these new skills. This integration of group and family therapy enables parents to transfer these new skills to real-life situations" (Crimesolutions.gov, n.d.). The approach is grounded in family systems theory, which has support in the literature to be an effective method for reducing adolescent conduct disorders (Early et al., 2013, 6). The effectiveness of PLL is supported by a number of studies and, as a result, has been designated as a model or promising program by the University of Colorado Blueprints for Violence Prevention project, the Substance Abuse and Mental Health Administration's National Registry of Evidence-Based Programs and Practices, the Model Programs Guide from the Office of Juvenile Justice and Delinquency Prevention, and the National Institute of Justice's crimesolutions.gov.

In 2007, PLL introduced its reentry model as part of a pilot project implemented through the St. Joseph County Probate Court in Indiana. As part of this pilot project, PLL Reentry targeted juvenile offenders (ages 14–17) who exhibited serious emotional and behavioral problems, including aggression, criminality, drug or alcohol abuse, sexual offending, conduct disorder, running away, and/or chronic truancy. Like the PLL program, the main treatment interventions of PLL Reentry are parenting groups (to educate parents and help them develop necessary parenting skills) combined with family therapy. In addition, community-based wraparound services are provided to the youth, such as job or educational placement, medication management, and mentoring (Early et al., 2013, 6).

PLL Reentry begins with the youth and family during the period in which the youth is confined. This is unique as traditionally juvenile aftercare services only begin after a young offender has been released from custody. The philosophy underlying this approach is to help the youth prepare for postrelease, which not only smoothes this difficult transition but helps to facilitate earlier release to the community (and hence a reduction in the overall length of incarceration, "thereby moderating the adverse effects associated with incarceration, including those resulting from commingling with negative peers."). Another hallmark of the program is continuity in services by having the same PLL therapist work with the youth and family from the time the youth is incarcerated through postrelease treatment (Early et al., 2013, 6, 15).

PLL Reentry is divided into three implementation stages: (1) intensive, (2) transition, and (3) aftercare. On average, stage one lasts approximately 3 months and consists of parent-only group modules and family therapy. Stage two lasts approximately 1–2 months and also entails family therapy as well as transition services (ensuring the community-based wraparound services are in place for the youth). Stage three involves further family therapy as well as relapse prevention services, refresher sessions, and the provision of the wraparound services to the youth (Early et al., 2013, 6–7).

An evaluation was conducted of the impact of the PLL Reentry pilot project on juvenile recidivism compared with a matched sample of youth who received standard programming through the St. Joseph County Probate Court in Indiana. This study found that 81% of the youth and families admitted to the program completed PLL Reentry services. Youth participating in the PLL Reentry program had a shorter incarceration than the control group, while "the family-focused reentry program also reduced recidivism compared with standard aftercare programming in the study site" (Early et al., 2013, 6–7). In another study examining PLL with juvenile offenders, Sells et al. (2011) found that participants in the PLL treatment group had fewer offenses during the 12 months after program completion than the control group (16% of PLL participants reoffended compared with 55% for the control group). Additionally, youth in the treatment group spent a total of 72 days in detention, while those in the control group spent 543 days in detention.

Think about It!

Should community crime prevention be considered the third dominant crime prevention approach along with the situational and social developmental approaches? While some may view the *neighborhood* as simply the spatial locale in which SCP or CPSD programs are implemented, the sociological concept of *community* in and of itself forms the heart of a distinct crime prevention philosophy and institution. The goal of the community organizing for crime prevention is to ensure the existence of local informal social control, by modifying or reinforcing the collective behavior of local residents to assume a safe, secure, well-maintained, and socially cohesive neighborhood. This crime prevention approach is explored in more detail in Chapter 5.

1.7.4 Program versus Practice

Finally, a distinction should be made between a crime prevention *program* and a crime prevention *practice*. The latter is an ongoing routine or activity that is well established in a particular setting. In the context of crime prevention, a practice is most often an individualized measure that people undertake in their everyday lives, such as automatically locking the doors of homes and cars. An important goal of community crime prevention is to promote more collective community safety practices among neighbors, such as keeping an eye out for anything that may be suspicious. Practices can also be considered commonly accepted standards that help ensure the proper functioning and health of a society, such as strong parenting, good schools, and respect for the law. In contrast, a program is a focused and organized effort to change, restrict, or create a routine practice in a crime prevention setting, such as neighborhood watch.

1.8 INSTITUTIONS THROUGH WHICH CRIME PREVENTION PROGRAMS AND PRACTICES ARE DELIVERED

Because crime prevention involves such a diverse range of interventions, there are a myriad of individuals, professions, groups, and institutions through which these programs and practices are formulated and delivered. The institutional settings through which crime prevention interventions, programs, and practices are delivered can be divided into eight categories: (1) families, (2) schools, (3) labor markets, (4) places, (5) neighborhoods/communities, (6) (mental) health-care systems, (7) police and other criminal justice institutions, and (8) other government agencies and institutions.

1.8.1 Families

The family is society's most crucial institution in promoting or hindering the development of future criminogenic behavior in a child. This is because the family is a child's most immediate and influential environment affecting his/her development and socialization. The development and socialization of young people is highly influenced by various family characteristics and practices, including family structure, parent–child relationships, disciplinary practices, family mental health, nutrition, the occurrence of neglect or abuse, and family history of substance abuse or criminal behavior. Because family risk factors are the single most important determinant of whether child assumes delinquent or criminal behavior later in life, effective and nurturing family practices (especially in child rearing) are key to protecting children from a future life that may include chronic delinquency, criminality, or other antisocial behaviors.

A significant focus of crime prevention through social development interventions is to strengthen families by helping them develop and support good parenting skills while addressing problems experienced by parents that can affect their children (such as poverty, substance abuse, aggression, and poor parenting practices). In addition to focusing on parents, social problem-solving approaches to criminality prevention also entail initiatives that cater directly to at-risk children by increasing their personal resilience (including remedial education, mentoring, psychological counseling, social and life skills development, and recreational activities).

Graham (1995, 2) lists seven forms of intervention that can enhance the capacity of families to reduce or prevent the development of criminal propensities among children and youth: (1) preventing teenage pregnancies, (2) providing support and advisory services for mothers during pregnancy and infancy, (3) providing guidance for improving the quality of parenting, (4) providing preschool education for children living in deprived families or experiencing specific difficulties, (5) offering support to parents at specific times of stress, (6) developing strategies for preventing child abuse and keeping families intact, and (7) preventing youth homelessness.

1.8.2 Schools

The crucial role of schools in educating and helping to positively socialize young people means they are second only to families in their importance as crime and violence prevention institutions. This is especially true given the strong causal relationship between certain school-based risk factors (academic failure, an inability to bond to schools, chronic truancy, expulsion, and dropping out of high school) and future criminal and violent behavior. Education is a crucial protective factor that promotes resilience and offsets criminogenic conditions. As a crime prevention institution, perhaps the most important role that schools can play is to teach kids to read, write, compute, and think. School-based initiatives that cater to students who struggle academically; who are frequently absent from school; who frequently misbehave, act out, and cause disturbances; who are suspended from school; and who are at risk of dropping out also serve as significant criminality and violence prevention initiatives. Like families, schools also provide young people with an environment that is critical to their positive socialization and the development of basic social competencies.

Many innovative approaches to school culture and pedagogy have been introduced in recent years that can also help prevent criminal and violent behavior insofar as such innovations promote learning, attendance, and prosocial behavior among struggling and high-risk students. This includes individualizing academic programs to the needs of each student; tutoring and other forms of remedial support; introducing alternative curriculum (such as vocational skills training); providing material incentives for academic achievement or consistent attendance; high-intensity dropout prevention, and recovery initiatives; nurturing a school culture that is inclusive and condemns bullying and other forms of harassment and violence; and implementing programs that foster important social competencies and life skills that can prevent future delinquency, criminality, or other forms of antisocial or risky behavior. Finally, schools have become a central vehicle through which programs are delivered to reduce nonacademic, criminogenic risk factors, such as aggression, bullying, substance abuse, contempt for the law, gang involvement, and interpersonal violence.

1.8.3 Labor Markets

Unemployment can correlate with criminal behavior, although the relationship is not always so clear-cut at the individual, community, or societal level. It is no coincidence, however, that those communities with the highest crime rates often have the highest unemployment rates as well. Furthermore, a disproportionate amount of crime and violence is committed by adolescent males, which is also a demographic group that tends to have a relatively high unemployment rate. There is a long history of attempting to prevent the onset of criminal behavior by pulling at-risk youth and young adults

CASE STUDY 1.10

MULTILEVEL PARENT TRAINING PROGRAM IN AUSTRALIA

The goal of the Positive Parenting Program, which was implemented in Queensland, Australia, by the Parenting and Family Support Centre at the University of Queensland, is to "prevent severe behavioral, emotional, and developmental problems in children," which in turn can increase their susceptibility to criminal and other antisocial behavior (Gant and Grabosky, 2000, 32).

The program is a "multilevel model of behavioral family intervention that aims to prevent and treat the risk factors associated with severe behavioral and emotional problems in preadolescent children" (Gant and Grabosky, 2000, 32). This is accomplished by providing parents with the knowledge and the skills to promote their children's social, emotional, and behavioral development while dealing with a variety of childhood behavior problems and developmental issues, through safe, nurturing, and nonviolent family environments (Sanders et al., 2004, 266). Specifically, the program aims to "(1) increase parents' competence in managing common behavior problems and developmental issues found among children with disabilities; (2) reduce parents' use of coercive and punitive methods of disciplining children; (3) improve parents' personal coping skills and reduce parenting stress; (4) improve parents' communication about parenting issues and help parents support one another in their parenting roles; and (5) develop parents' independent problem-solving skills" (Sanders et al., 2004, 273).

The flexible program includes five levels of intervention. Each level increases in intensity and corresponds to the scope of the child's behavioral and family functioning problems. That is, each level is designed to offer a parent the intervention type and intensity and modes of delivery that are appropriate to the nature and scope of the child's behavioral problems as well as parent and family functioning issues that may be contributing to these behavioral problems.

The first level is a universal information dissemination strategy that provides parents with access to useful information and tips concerning general parenting issues that can help solve minor developmental and behavioral problems. The mode of delivery is a "coordinated information campaign using print and electronic media and other health promotion strategies to promote awareness of parenting issues and normalize participation in parenting programs…" (Sanders et al., 2004, 269). It may also include contact between a parent and a professional staff (e.g., through a telephone information line).

The second level involves the provision of information and advice for a specific parenting concern that may arise over common behavior problems or developmental transitions, such as toilet training, nutrition, or putting kids to bed. The mode of delivery includes booklets, wall charts, and videos for parents and may involve face-to-face or telephone contact with professionals.

The third level is for parents who have children with *discrete* behavioral problems such as tantrums, fighting with siblings, or who lack appropriate developmental self-care skills (such as oral hygiene and getting dressed in the morning). At this level, parents are trained to acquire skills to deal with such issues. The training lasts about 80 min over four sessions and teaches parents to manage their child's discrete behavioral problem.

The fourth level is for parents of children with multiple and more severe behavioral problems and psychological disorders, such as aggression, oppositional defiance disorder, or conduct disorder. This level entails approximately 10 h of intensive training over 8–10 sessions and is meant to provide parents with skills to address a broad range of problematic behaviors.

Level five is for families experiencing a combination of child behavior and psychological problems, parenting problems, and family dysfunction. Parents participate in an intensive, individually tailored, multicomponent program that includes skills training (up to 11 sessions that last 60–90 min each) and home visits by professionals (Sanders et al., 2007, 266).

A number of studies have demonstrated the effectiveness of the Positive Parenting Program in nurturing parenting skills and overcoming both minor and severe behavioral problems in children (Martin and Sanders, 2003; Ralph and Sanders, 2003; Markie-Dadds and Sanders, 2006). The program was the recipient of the Overall National Winner of the Australian Violence Prevention Awards in 1997.

into the labor market, while job training and placement have also been promoted as positive alternative opportunities for offenders and gang members. Employment-based approaches to crime and violence prevention typically target youth and adults that are at a high risk of criminality, are involved in gangs, are convicted (and paroled) offenders, and/or are chronically unemployed. Some examples of employment-based crime prevention programs include summer job or subsidized work programs, job training, pretrial diversions for offenders that make employment training a condition of case dismissal, community development-based employment for at-risk youth or convicted offenders, transitional employment assistance for offenders released from jail, *enterprise zones* that provide no- or low-interest loans for budding entrepreneurs in high-crime neighborhoods, and wage and work transportation subsidies.

1.8.4 *Places*

Within the context of crime and violence prevention, the concept of *place* refers to any physical or spatial structure or small environment—such as houses, apartment buildings, schools, office buildings, businesses, retail stores, parks, streets, parking lots, and hospitals—where criminal offending and victimization take place. While *place* may appear to be a vague concept, it is critical to opportunity reduction (situational) approaches to crime prevention, which are premised on the assumption that most crimes occur in a particular place. The concept of *place* is of central importance to preventing and controlling crime because research has shown that some locations are so prone to criminal and violent acts that they are labeled *hot spots*. Place is also important in the theory and practice of crime prevention as well as community safety and security, because "place is more than just a location. Places can acquire meaning. People develop their own sense of place. Potential users can see a park as either a place of safety or a risk to be avoided. A potential offender can see the park as an attractive place of criminal opportunity" (Hilborn, 2009, 3). Place-based crime prevention is especially pertinent to public spaces. According to Shehayeb (2008, 107), "The importance of providing a sense of security among people in public spaces cannot be underestimated. Besides being a basic human need, failing to have a sense of security in one's everyday environment can have various negative consequences." Further, when people begin to feel they can no longer safely enjoy certain public spaces, they ultimately abandon them (International Centre for the Prevention of Crime, 2008, 106).

Place-based (or place-focused) crime prevention entails measures that target public or private locations, such as homes, stores, parks, public transport facilities, street corners, schools, and even nonstationary places, for instance, buses and subways (Eck, 2006, 242). The focus of SCP is removing or reducing the opportunities for a criminal act to occur in a particular time and place. The argument behind SCP is if a particular place

CASE STUDY 1.11

COMPREHENSIVE SCHOOL-BASED PROGRAM TO PROMOTE GOOD BEHAVIOR

The Promoting Alternative Thinking Strategies (PATHS) curriculum is a comprehensive school-based program for promoting emotional and social competencies and reducing aggression and behavior problems in elementary school-aged children while enhancing the educational process in the classroom. This curriculum is designed to be used by educators and counselors as part of a multiyear, universal prevention program that can potentially pre-empt a broad range of future antisocial behaviors. Although primarily focused on the school and classroom settings, information and activities are also included for use by parents.

The curriculum, taught three times per week for a minimum of 20–30 min/day, provides teachers with systematic lessons, materials, and instructions for teaching students self-control, positive peer relationships, interpersonal problem solving, stress reduction, reading and interpreting social cues, empathy, self-awareness and self-confidence, verbal and nonverbal communication, and how to understand, express, and manage emotions. A key objective in promoting these skills is to prevent or reduce behavioral and emotional problems.

In their evaluations, Greenberg et al. (1995), Greenberg (1996), and Kam et al. (2004) found that students who were exposed to the PATHS curriculum achieved gains in such areas as greater self-control; improved understanding and knowledge of one's feelings and the ability to recognize the feelings of others; increased ability to tolerate frustration; increased use of more effective conflict resolution strategies; improved thinking and planning skills; decreased symptoms of sadness, anxiety, and depression; and decreased conduct problems, including aggression.

PATHS has been designated a *Model Program* by the Center for the Study and Prevention of Violence at the University of Colorado at Boulder. In a summary of the evaluations of the program, the center reports that PATHS program participants, relative to a control group, showed

- Lower rate of conduct problems and externalizing behaviors (e.g., aggression)
- Lower internalizing scores and depression
- Improvements in social problem solving, emotional understanding, and self-control
- Better understanding of cues for recognizing feelings in others
- Higher scores on peer sociability and social school functioning
- Better ability to resolve peer conflicts, identify feelings, and identify problems and greater empathy for others
- Less anger and attribution bias
- Reduction in ADHD symptoms
- Better scores on measures of authority acceptance, cognitive concentration, and social competence (University of Colorado at Boulder, 2014)

is properly designed, protected, and managed, the opportunity for a criminal or violent act to occur is reduced or prevented. The theory and practice of CPTED is also heavily predicated on the concept of places. An assumption underlying CPTED is that some types of physical and spatial designs are more likely than others to precipitate certain behaviors that may result in a greater incidence of crime. Conversely, the proper design and effective use of the built environment can lead to a reduction in the opportunity for crimes to occur.

CASE STUDY 1.12

VOCATIONAL TRAINING AND PLACEMENT PROGRAM FOR INCARCERATED YOUTH IN NORTH CAROLINA

The Vocational Delivery System is one example of a corrections-based transitional employment program for incarcerated youth. The program, which was implemented in two North Carolina juvenile detention centers for 18- to 22-year-old males, entails the following components: "(1) working individually with inmates to identify vocational interests and aptitudes, (2) developing individual plans of study for improving vocational skills, (3) providing the identified training as well as other needed services, and (4) helping inmates secure postrelease employment" (Lattimore et al., 1990, 118).

The process begins with the inmate undergoing a battery of tests administered by a trained vocational counselor to determine his employment interests and aptitudes. The results are discussed with the inmate and the two work to identify potential career paths based on the results of the tests. The inmate's correctional case manager will then help him develop a personal plan, which includes steps that must be taken by the inmate to achieve his career goals. The case manager and the inmate will also discuss job opportunities in the chosen career with a job development specialist (who is responsible for prerelease employment assistance) and the Employment Security Commission (which assists the inmate in finding a job once he is released). If employment prospects in the chosen career appear favorable for the inmate, the case manager will arrange for appropriate vocational training, along with other important preparatory and complementary education and counseling, such as completion of a grade 12 equivalent, the mandatory Community Reentry Training program (which teaches job preparation skills, such as conducting oneself at a job interview), and counseling (e.g., substance abuse treatment). The case manager will also work with the inmate to facilitate completion of the correctional plan, which includes such incentives as the designation of a parole date, which is contingent upon the inmate's completion of the plan (a specified parole date is meant to facilitate postrelease employment placement as the employer now has a date as to when the inmate will be available for work). Once released, the inmate either begins the job identified prior to his release or continues to work with job placement specialists until suitable employment is found.

The results of one study that evaluated the Vocational Delivery System showed that those who participated in the program had a significantly lower recidivism rate upon release compared to a control group of inmates who did not participate in the program (Lattimore et al., 1990).

1.8.5 Neighborhoods and Communities

In the lexicon of crime prevention theorists and practitioners, the concept of *community* has traditionally been defined in spatial terms, in particular the residential neighborhood. *Community* can also be defined in sociological terms, as an organic unit of social organization among people characterized by enduring personal ties and networks, a high level of social interaction and cohesion, a sense of belonging and common goals, and a sense of wholeness (Crank, 1994, 336–337; Leighton, 1988, 359). A dominant etiological theory of crime upon which community crime prevention is premised is that the loss of the socially cohesive community within advanced Western societies has contributed to crime and disorder. Accordingly, the efficacy of community-based

CASE STUDY 1.13

SITUATIONAL CRIME PREVENTION IN A GOVERNMENT-SUBSIDIZED HOUSING ESTATE IN ENGLAND

The Hopwood Triangle, a 91-unit, government-subsidized housing complex located in the English city of Preston, had been slipping into a spiral of decline, fed by an increase in burglaries, prostitution, and drug trafficking. In January 2002, the Preston City Council spearheaded a long-term development initiative that included the application of a number of SCP and CPTED strategies. Based on a safety audit of the premises, the following modifications were made: improved lighting (to increase visibility); closure of certain pathways leading into the estate (to control access of people into the housing complex); more fencing and railings (also to reduce access points into the estate); installation of closed-circuit video cameras (to increase surveillance); better maintenance of the grounds, including cleaning up garbage and more aesthetic landscaping (to promote a more livable environment and a greater sense of ownership by residents); pruning of hedges (to improve natural surveillance opportunities by residents and police); and demolition of derelict garages (to remove concealment areas for drug dealers and the homeless). Other crime prevention initiatives undertaken entailed the identification and eviction of problem tenants, targeted enforcement of offenders by police, formation of the Hopwood Residents Association and Neighborhood Forum, implementation of a neighborhood watch program, and formation of Operation Curb/Safer Sex Works, which targets prostitution in and around the area.

An assessment of these place-focused prevention initiatives revealed that after 2 years, the overall crime rate declined by 52%, burglary decreased by 28%, vehicle crime declined by 80%, calls to police decreased by 38%, and property damage decreased by 73%. Occupancy also increased, as did the sense of community among residents. "In particular, through participation in the Residents Association and Neighborhood Forums, citizens are now empowered to preserve the cohesive and increasingly safe neighborhood in which they live" (Center for Problem-Oriented Policing, 2004).

crime prevention programs is often contingent on the existence of local social cohesion or a sense of *community*. As such, while some may view the neighborhood as simply the spatial locale in which situational or social developmental crime prevention programs are implemented, the sociological concept of community in and of itself forms the heart of a distinct crime prevention philosophy and institution. Community crime prevention is concerned with reinforcing or modifying the individual and collective behaviors of community residents to produce or strengthen a local social environment that can informally regulate itself, including the regulation and prevention of (public) criminal, violent, and disorderly behavior. The existence of this *informal social control* is contingent upon the existence of a strong sense of local social cohesion. This means that in neighborhoods where it does not presently exist, social cohesion must be fostered as a fundamental prerequisite for informal social control and community crime prevention. In short, imbued with the essential crime prevention prerequisites of social cohesion, collective action, and informal social control, the community is viewed as a crime prevention institution, like the family, the school, or the labor market. Thus, an

CASE STUDY 1.14

NURTURING COMMUNITY COHESION AS A CRIME PREVENTION STRATEGY IN AUSTRALIA

In Newcastle, Australia, one of the major issues documented in a crime prevention plan for the city was the "perceived decline in community cohesion." Arising from a number of community safety forums was the belief that "if there were a stronger sense of community spirit, if people felt more a part of their community and community bonds were strengthened, they would more likely be safer communities and to experience less crime." In particular, "stronger community bonds may offer the opportunity for greater security of homes and community resources" as a result of increased vigilance of community members.

Accordingly, one of the first goals of the 2001 crime prevention plan for Newcastle was to "promote stronger communities and community cohesion between and among communities" and to "promote community cohesiveness as a positive crime prevention measure" (City of Newcastle, 2001, 2–3).

underlying goal (or prerequisite) of community crime prevention is to transform the neighborhood as a spatial entity into an enduring institution: a community.

1.8.6 Police and the Criminal Justice System

No branch of the CJS plays a greater role in crime prevention than police. In addition to traditional reactive law enforcement, community policing and problem-oriented policing are seen as the two most important proactive, crime prevention philosophies carried out by police. The former is concerned with improving the relationship between police and the communities they serve, while the latter is focused on more effective and lasting methods to preventing and controlling crime by focusing more on causes. In addition, there have been a number of innovations in evidence-based, proactive policing techniques in recent years that have shown positive results, including intelligence-led policing, CompStat, and predictive policing. (The role of police in crime prevention is detailed in Chapter 7.)

As discussed, the CJS has been criticized as an institution that relies on a limited number of reactive and inflexible responses to crime and violence, through its main emphasis on suppression, deterrence, punishment, and incapacitation of offenders. It is true that the CJS is largely reactive when it comes to crime. However, three points should be made that may lessen the critiques of the CJS as a crime prevention institution. First, informal social control must be coupled with and supported by formal social control for a comprehensive approach to managing crime in any society. Second, although controversial, one must consider the preventive role that the CJS plays in deterring and preventing crime, whether it is through the patrol and rapid response function of police, criminal penalties, or the incarceration of offenders. Third, even the most ardent critics should acknowledge that in some countries, the CJS and its component parts have at least partially internalized some of the precepts of crime prevention. Police services throughout the Western world have pursued community-based and problem-oriented policing, juvenile justice systems rely more heavily on community-based sanctions, specialty courts divert offenders to treatment instead of incarceration, and offenders released from prison are increasingly enrolled in reentry programs that include treatment, job training, and other social programming.

1.8.7 *Other Government Agencies, Services, and Policies*

In addition to the CJS, governments, at the national, state/provincial, regional/county, and municipal levels, can play a critical role in preventing crime and violence through numerous other public policies, agencies, services, and programs. In addition to the public education system, other branches of government that play a role in crime prevention include public schools, the health-care system, housing and urban development, employment assistance, family and child welfare programs, and community centers, to name just a few. Government social assistance agencies can play an important role in helping families create a nurturing environment for children by assisting parents, especially during times of crisis. The state also has the legal responsibility to determine when an at-risk child should be removed from a household and placed in custodial care. Governments at the federal, state, and municipal levels are key players in funding and carrying out community development in poor, high-crime neighborhoods and providing affordable housing, both of which are important community-based approaches to crime prevention.

1.8.8 *(Mental) Health-Care Systems*

Psychological and mental health problems can increase the risk of offending and other antisocial and risky behaviors that are tied to offending, such as substance abuse and homelessness. Research has demonstrated that childhood psychological disorders, such as attention deficit disorder or oppositional defiance disorder, are risk factors for future offending. (See Chapters 3 and 4 for more details on mental health and psychological factors that put individuals at risk of criminal behavior.) Studies have also shown that more than half of all adult inmates in US prisons had a mental health problem (James and Glaze, 2006) and that the US adult prison population has rates of mental illness that are up to four times greater than rates for the general population (Human Rights Watch, 2003). One study suggested that at least two-thirds of the population of youth correctional facilities in the United States have one or more mental disorders (Rapp-Palicchi and Roberts, 2004).

Given these findings, the timely diagnosis and treatment of psychological and mental health disorders may reduce the risk of offending. Moreover, social problem-solving programs have been developed that can help prevent the onslaught of mental health problems by instilling in children and youth strong problem-solving and coping skills that can potentially carry into adulthood. Early interventions to prevent and/or identify, diagnose, and treat mental health and substance abuse disorders within children and adolescents are particularly important, according to Kinscherff (2012, 1), given that the CJS "was not designed to identify and respond as a clinical service system to meet the needs of these youth."

> Juvenile justice programs and facilities often lack established policies and practices, sufficient clinical and staff resources, and/or adequate training to effectively meet the needs of these youth. Youth with significant mental health needs who do not

pose heightened public safety risks may be nonetheless incarcerated. Youth may be detained because mental health services are not available. When detained or incarcerated in juvenile justice facilities, many youth will have poor or no mental health care.

Kinscherff (2012, 1)

Consistent and easy access to health-care services (and not just mental health care) for children and youth is a highly important part of effective preventive care (and not just crime and violence prevention). According to Graham (1995, 16), government policies to promote better health, nutrition, and psychological well-being need to be integrated and coordinated with broader prevention programs and easily accessible to those most in need, through local hospitals, clinics, schools, and in-home visits. Kinscherff (2012, i, 2) concurs, arguing that interventions that deter youth with mental health disorders from offending and coming into contact with the CJS must include a combination of both prevention and treatment, must be delivered through "comprehensive community-based services and supports" that are "tailored to local needs and conditions," and must emphasize "planned and thoughtful programs, strong interagency collaboration, and sustained funding."

1.9 CONCLUSION

Crime prevention interventions encompass and are often delivered through society's most basic institutions by a wide range of governmental and nongovernmental groups and services, including those whose mandate is tangential to crime control. These include day-care and preschool facilities, schools, social welfare agencies, faith-based groups, community centers, substance abuse clinics, neighborhood associations, youth drop-in centers, employment training agencies, and health-care facilities, to name just a few. As Sherman (1997a, 1) writes, "most crime prevention results from the web of institutional settings of human development and daily life." All of the aforementioned institutions and organizations can contribute to the prevention of crime and criminality, yet we don't usually view them in such a narrow vein.

At the same time, programs and groups have arisen over the years specifically to prevent crime and criminality. Some have expressly capitalized on the important role that the aforementioned institutions and organizations can play in criminality prevention, such as introducing programs in schools that reduce criminogenic risk factors. Others attempt to organize or reinvigorate the basic tenets of civil society as a means to prevent crime, like the mobilization of local communities through Neighborhood Watch or citizen patrols.

While the crime prevention institutions and strategies described in this chapter have been listed separately, the impact and success of each are maximized when they work in a coordinated and complementary fashion. In other words, "the necessary condition for successful crime prevention practices in one setting is adequate support for the practice in related settings. Schools cannot succeed without supportive families, labor markets cannot succeed without well-policed safe streets, and police cannot succeed without community participation in the labor market" (Sherman, 1997a, 5).

This observation underscores the importance of a comprehensive approach to crime prevention, especially in disadvantaged neighborhoods where residents are often confronted with a myriad of different problems that can give rise to and facilitate crime and criminal behavior. A comprehensive approach to crime prevention, according to the National Crime Council in Ireland, must aim to reduce crime by "reducing the opportunities to commit crime; promoting social inclusion and reducing the socio-economic, educational, societal and environmental factors that can leave children and young people 'at risk' of engaging in criminal activities; reducing recidivism through the re-integration of young and adult offenders into the community in a planned and supportive way, involving training and education, skills development and personal support; and providing appropriate interventions through an interagency/partnership approach where knowledge, expertise and best practice are shared to the maximum" (National Crime Council of Ireland, 2003, 20). In a similar vein, the 2002 United Nations Guidelines for the Prevention of Crime contend that crime prevention in any country should be based on the following eight basic principles:

1. Government leadership: All levels of government should play a leadership role.
2. Socioeconomic development and inclusion: Crime prevention considerations should be integrated into all relevant social, health, and economic policies and programs.
3. Cooperation/partnerships: Cooperation/partnerships should be an integral part of effective crime prevention.
4. Sustainability/accountability: Crime prevention requires adequate and sustained resourcing with clear accountability for funding and achievement of results.
5. Knowledge base: Crime prevention strategies, policies, programs, and actions should be based on a broad, multidisciplinary foundation of knowledge.
6. Human rights/rule of law/culture of lawfulness: The rule of law and those human rights recognized in international instruments must be respected.
7. Interdependency: National crime prevention diagnoses and strategies should take account of links between local criminal problems and international organized crime.
8. Differentiation: Prevention strategies should recognize the different needs of men and women and consider the special needs of vulnerable members of society (as cited in Husain, 2007, 6–7).

1.10   DISCUSSION QUESTIONS AND EXERCISES

1. Discuss and debate the various definitions of crime prevention. Which one do you think is precise yet comprehensive?
2. How would you define crime prevention? What parameters (if any) would you place around the concept of crime prevention?
3. Should the CJS be included within the field of crime prevention? Regardless of your answer, research some innovative crime control strategies that have been adopted by criminal justice agencies and institutions that satisfy your definition of crime prevention.
4. Apply the problem-oriented methodology to a crime or disorder issue in your neighborhood or city (focusing on a thorough analysis that distinguishes causes from symptoms and aggravating factors).
5. Identify and discuss different forms of crime control approaches in your city. Demarcate these approaches based on whether they are a *formal* or *informal* means to promote social control.

6. Provide examples of crime prevention approaches that fall into the primary, secondary, and tertiary conceptual categories.
7. Identify various institutions, organizations, and agencies within your city or neighborhood that can potentially play a role in preventing crime, and describe the role they could play.

1.11   IMPORTANT TERMS

Community
Crime
Crime prevention
Crime prevention through social development
Criminal Justice System
Criminality
Criminality prevention
Disorder
Families
Formal social control
Labor markets
Incivilities
Informal social control
Neighborhoods
Opportunity reduction
Place
Primary prevention
Problem oriented
Schools
Secondary prevention
Situational crime prevention
Tertiary prevention

FURTHER READING

Fisher, B. and Lab, S.P., *Encyclopedia of Victimology and Crime Prevention*, SAGE Publications, Thousand Oaks, CA, 2010.

International Centre for the Prevention of Crime, *The 2012 International Report on Crime Prevention and Community Safety*, ICPC, Montreal, Quebec, Canada, 2012.

Lab, S.P., *Crime Prevention Approaches, Practices, and Evaluations*, 6th edn., Anderson Publishing (Lexis Nexis), New York, 2007.

Sherman, L.W. et al. *Preventing Crime: What Works, What Doesn't, What's Promising*, Research in Brief, National Institute of Justice, Washington, DC, July 1998, http://www.ncjrs.org/pdffiles/171676.pdf.

Sherman, L.W., Farrington, D.P., Welsh, B.C., and MacKenzie, D.L., Eds., *Evidence-Based Crime Prevention*, revised edn., Routledge, London, U.K., 2006.

Tilley, N., Ed., *Handbook of Crime Prevention and Community Safety*, Willan Publishing, Devon, U.K., 2005.

Welsh, B.C. and Farrington, D.P., Eds., *The Oxford Handbook of Crime Prevention*, Oxford University Press, New York, 2012.

INTERNET RESOURCES

Crime Prevention Organizations

Center for Crime Prevention and Control, John Jay School of Criminal Justice, http://johnjayresearch. org/ccpc/.

Crimereduction.gov.uk (United Kingdom), http://www.crimereduction.gov.uk/.

International Centre for the Prevention of Crime, http://www.crime-prevention-intl.org/.

Institute for the Prevention of Crime (University of Ottawa), http://www.sciencessociales.uottawa. ca/ipc/eng/.

National Crime Prevention Centre (Canada), http://www.publicsafety.gc.ca/cnt/cntrng-crm/ crm-prvntn/ntnl-crm-prvntn-cntr-eng.aspx.

National Crime Prevention Council (United States), http://www.ncpc.org/.

National Crime Prevention Program (Australia), http://www.crimeprevention.gov.au/.

United Nations Office on Drugs and Crime, http://www.unodc.org/unodc/index.html.

Evidence-Based Crime Prevention Programs

Campbell Collaboration Library of Systematic Review, Crime and Justice, http://www. campbellcollaboration.org/reviews_crime_justice/.

Center for Problem-Oriented Policing, http://www.popcenter.org/.

Center for the Study and Prevention of Violence, University of Colorado Boulder, http://www. blueprintsprograms.com/.

National Institute of Justice, http://www.crimesolutions.gov/.

Office of Juvenile Justice and Delinquency Prevention Model Programs, http://www.ojjdp.gov/ mpg/Program.

U.S. Interagency Working Group on Youth Programs, http://www.findyouthinfo.gov/ evidence-innovation.

PART II

DOMINANT CRIME PREVENTION APPROACHES

CHAPTER 2

SITUATIONAL CRIME PREVENTION AND CRIME PREVENTION THROUGH ENVIRONMENTAL DESIGN

CONTENTS

2.1 LEARNING OBJECTIVES

By the end of this chapter, you should have a better understanding of the following:

- Definitions and parameters of Situational Crime Prevention (SCP) and Crime Prevention through Environmental Design (CPTED)
- Theories and assumptions of crime that inform SCP and CPTED
- Theoretical and conceptual constructs of SCP and CPTED (how they work to prevent crime)
- Specific SCP and CPTED principles and strategies
- Critiques of SCP and CPTED

2.2 INTRODUCTION

Situational crime prevention (SCP) is distinguished from traditional criminal justice system approaches to crime in that it is focused on the immediate environmental setting for criminal acts, rather than focusing on those committing the criminal acts (Clarke, 1997, 2). And while SCP is also distinguished from the criminal justice system in its proactive, preventive philosophy, unlike social problem-solving approaches to crime (see Chapter 3), it does not attempt to address the root causes of criminal behavior. Instead, the goal is to make a criminal act less attractive to and less likely for the motivated, rationally thinking offender. As Clarke puts it (1992, 3), SCP is "... a preventive approach that relies, not upon improving society or its institutions, but simply upon reducing opportunities for crime."

SCP operates on the fact that the vast majority of crimes occur in a specific time and place and, as such, it focuses on removing or reducing the opportunity for a criminal act to occur in a particular time and place. As Clarke and Eck (2005, 16) write, "for environmental criminologists, 'opportunity makes the thief' is more than just a popular saying; it is the cornerstone of their approach. They believe that if opportunity increases so will crime...In fact, crime levels are as much determined by the opportunities afforded by the physical and social arrangements of society as by the attitudes and dispositions of the population."

Broadly speaking, opportunity-reduction approaches to crime prevention can assume one of two (complementary) forms. First, criminal opportunities can be reduced through the management, design, or manipulation of the *immediate physical environment* to enhance its safety and security. The most common measure that directly reduces the opportunity for crime is *target hardening*, which includes the use of deadbolt locks, window bars, locking gates, and safes. Crime Prevention through Environmental Design (CPTED) is another opportunity-reduction approach that advocates certain designs and uses of the built and physical environment (houses, buildings, landscapes, streets, parks, and entire neighborhoods) to reduce the opportunity for crime to occur. Second, criminal opportunities can be reduced through the *immediate human environment*, that is, measures that influence or mobilize people to work toward deterring crime in a particular locale. At the core of these people-based SCP measures is surveillance by the legitimate users of an environment, which is epitomized by Neighborhood Watch (NW) program citizen patrols.

The most common critiques of SCP and CPTED are that they do little to address the root causes of crime and they may not really prevent crime but simply deflect it to another place or time.

2.3 THEORETICAL ASSUMPTIONS UNDERLYING SITUATIONAL CRIME PREVENTION

This section outlines some of the theoretical assumptions about crime upon which situational approaches are based. In particular, SCP operates on three hypotheses concerning crime:

1. Most criminal acts require convergence of motivated offenders and potential victims at a particular time and place.
2. Many types of crime—and property crime in particular—are opportunistic; that is, offenders take advantage of certain opportunities they perceive can be exploited within a particular physical (and human) environment.
3. Criminal behavior is purposive in the sense that it is intended to meet an immediate or long-term need and may also be characterized as a rational decision-making process whereby the offender calculates the advantages and disadvantages of a specific criminal act (although SCP theory recognizes that not all offenders act rationally).

Each of these hypotheses draws attention to one of the most important theoretical and empirical assumptions underlying SCP: that human behavior can be affected by the immediate physical environment. According to Felson and Clarke (1998, 1–2), within the context of crime and its prevention, this precept asserts that specific settings can create opportunities for an illegal act to occur by transforming thoughts or inclinations into a criminal act. "The theory of crime settings rests on a single principle: that easy or tempting opportunities entice people into criminal action." This theoretical tenet is expressed in the *opportunity theories of crime* that inform SCP, including routine activity theory, rational choice theory, crime pattern theory, offender search theory, broken windows theory, and crime hot spots.

2.3.1 Routine Activity Theory

Cohen and Felson (1979) were the first to articulate *routine activity theory*, which seeks to explain the circumstances required for criminal acts to occur. A later version of this theory argues that most criminal acts require the convergence of three factors: (1) an offender, (2) a suitable target (a potential victim), and (3) the absence of a *controller.*

An offender is anyone who for any reason might commit a crime, while a suitable target may be an object worth stealing, a physical structure that can be vandalized, or a person who can be victimized. Based on this theory of criminal offending, there are three types of *controllers*, each of which corresponds to the three routine elements (offender, target, and place) that make up a criminal event:

> For the target/victim, this is the capable guardian of the original formulation of routine activity theory – usually people protecting themselves, their own belongings or those of family members, friends, and co-workers. Guardians also include public police and private security. For the offender, this is the handler, someone who knows the offender well and who is in a position to exert some control over his or her actions. Handlers include parents, siblings, teachers, friends and spouses. Probation and parole authorities often augment or substitute for normal handlers. For the place, the controller is the manager, the owner or designee who has some responsibility for controlling behavior in the specific location such as a bus driver or teacher in a school, bar owners in drinking establishments, landlords in rental housing, or flight attendants on commercial airliners.
>
> **Clarke and Eck (2005, 14)**

In short, routine activity theory contends that most criminal acts are undertaken by motivated offenders against a target or potential victim, at a particular time and place. Furthermore, "crime problems arise when offenders and targets come together in a context where such key 'controllers' (handlers, guardians, managers) fail to prevent crime due to a limited sphere of influence resulting from either a lack of awareness, low capacity or sheer unwillingness to assert control" (Cherney, 2008, 635). This theoretical proposition lays the foundation for prescriptions as to how to reduce the opportunity for a criminal act to occur. Based on routine activity theory, "a crime is discouraged when the likely offender is supervised by the intimate handler, the suitable target is protected by the capable guardian and the time and space where the converge occurs is monitored by the place manager" (Fisher and Lab, 2010, 797). The theoretical relationship between the three crime occurrence variables (target/victim, offender, place) and their respective corresponding crime prevention agents (guardian, handler, manager) is depicted in Figure 2.1.

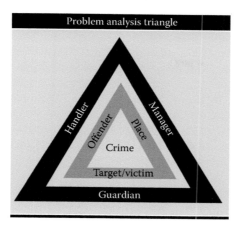

Figure 2.1
The SCP problem analysis triangle. (From Clarke, R. and Eck, J., Crime Analysis for Problem Solvers in 60 Small Steps, Office of Community Oriented Policing, Washington, DC, 2005, p. 14.)

2.3.2 Rational Choice Theory

SCP is also premised on the rational choice theory of offender decision making, which argues that criminals make (opportunistic) choices and decisions in the course of planning and carrying out a criminal act and thus can be deterred (Clarke and Cornish, 1985). SCP theory recognizes that not all offenders are rational, self-maximizing decision makers who carefully and deliberatively calculate the advantages and disadvantages of committing a specific criminal act (this is especially true of those committing crimes of passion, offenders with a mental illness or under the influence of alcohol or drugs, and drug addicts who commit property crimes to finance their next fix).

Nonetheless, SCP is implicitly premised on the assumption that many offenders do exercise some form of rational thinking; they will weigh the potential costs (the chance of getting caught) against the potential benefits (the rewards that can be gained from committing a criminal act). At the very least, most crimes are carried out through what Clarke (1997, 10) calls *purposive behavior*, which is designed to satisfy the offender's need for money, status, sex, or excitement. In their quest to meet these needs, the offender will make decisions and choices (no matter how rudimentary, impulsive, or careless the decision-making process may be).

In sum, a premise underlying SCP is that offenders engage in some form of decision-making process and purposive behavior (no matter how irrational) in the course of committing a criminal act. This assumption is paramount to SCP theories and strategies because this crime prevention approach is fundamentally about influencing the decision-making process of the offender, largely by increasing the perceived risks of getting caught or increasing the effort required to commit an offense. In other words, an underlying assumption of SCP is that the decision-making process of criminal offenders can be influenced by preventative measures.

2.3.3 Crime Pattern Theory (Environmental Criminology)

Environmental criminology is concerned with how environmental or contextual factors (in particular, time, space, and physical properties) can influence the decision-making process of the criminal offender. As a means to determine patterns in where, when, and how crimes occur, this theoretical framework focuses on the spatial–temporal aspect of criminal acts and in doing so analyzes the "location of crimes, characteristics of those locations, the movement paths that bring offenders and victims together at those locations, and people's perception of crime locations" (Brantingham and Brantingham, 1981, 8). Environmental criminology contends that criminal acts do not occur randomly in time or space but are influenced by the routine movements of offenders and victims. Furthermore, the theory argues that "the level and the type of criminal activity can be predicted through an analysis of a city's geographic environment, such as land use patterns, street networks, and transportation systems" (Lersch, 2007, 91). The theory's crime pattern aspect is based on three main concepts: nodes, paths, and edges. Nodes are the areas where people travel to and from in the course of their daily activities, such as work, home, school, or the shopping center, while paths are the travel routes that run between the nodes. Both are important in the context of victimization because crimes are frequently committed in the areas near an offender's personal nodes or along their usual travel paths (or *movement corridors*). Edges refer to a "sharp visual break between different types of land-use, between different socioeconomic and demographic residential and commercial areas" (Brantingham and Brantingham, 1998, 33). Edges are "premier locations for criminal offending," according to Paynich and Hill (2010, 111–112). "This is because the level of diversity encountered here (in people from both sides of the edge and their activities) limits the surveillance capabilities of potential guardians."

In short, "crimes are patterned, decisions to commit crimes are patterned; and the process of committing a crime is patterned" (Brantingham and Brantingham, 2008, 79). By fostering a greater understanding of crime patterns along a time, space, and offender decision-making continuum, environmental criminology has "proven useful in explaining crime probabilities at vulnerable points and along movement corridors" (Schneider, 2005, 275). As such, it provides a strong theoretical foundation for interventions to reduce the opportunity for criminal acts to occur at these locations.

2.3.4 Offender Search Theory

Underlying many of the theories discussed in this chapter is the idea that the opportunistic behavior of offenders is provoked by cues given out by the physical and built environment. Social and physical environments provide cues that can set the occasion for certain criminal acts by communicating to an individual that such acts can be executed without detection or apprehension. For example, a motivated, rationally thinking, criminal offender will target a home that presents certain cues (e.g., signs that no one is home, a lack of security alarms). The physical environment provides cues as to one's appropriate behavior in a given context; to this end, they are known as *releaser cues* because they may stimulate the opportunistic release of otherwise inhibited behavior. Some studies suggest that deviant behavior may be encouraged if people are exposed to opportunities where the risk of being caught is perceived as being low. In one of the earliest field experiments testing this theory (Zimbardo, 1973), a car was left abandoned on a New York street, and as researchers watched surreptitiously, the car was stripped little by little until all that remained was a hunk of metal. Researchers were surprised when they found that some of those involved in vandalizing the vehicle appeared to be *ordinary* people as opposed to hard-core offenders or delinquent youth. "Thus, it seems that the opportunity itself motivated the offence" (Gabor, 1990, 54).

In their application of environmental cues to residential burglary, Brantingham and Brantingham (1984) suggest that one of the criterion that offenders look for as part of their decision-making process is ease of entry into and exit from a locale. The attractiveness of targets is also influenced by locational characteristics. In particular, targets of property crime tend to become more attractive the closer they are to major transportation paths (automobile, public transit, and pedestrian). Environmental psychologists Brown and Altman (1981) found that burglarized homes were more likely to be on streets with cues that create the perception that they are busy public thoroughfares where strangers might commonly be found. Nonburglarized blocks had a more private look and feel to them and appeared better protected by the owners. Through interviews with young offenders in a housing project, Merry (1981) found they were conscious of an area's architectural features. Several of her interviewees mentioned that they looked for places where they had less chance of being spotted, such as narrow, enclosed pathways, poorly lit roads or alleys, or yards where they could hide behind trees or shrubs.

2.3.5   Broken Windows Theory

Wilson and Kelling (1982) have implicitly pursued the study of releaser cues in their attempt to explain vandalism. In an influential, yet controversial article, they argue that if a window in a building is broken and left unrepaired, there is a greater chance that the remaining windows will also soon be broken. Their conclusion is that if the broken windows are not repaired, a message is conveyed that nobody cares about or is around to maintain or defend the building. As such, the untended broken window sends out releaser cues to people that this building is not sufficiently guarded, thereby increasing the opportunity for vandalism or theft. The authors also use the broken windows example as a metaphor for deviant behavior and minor incivilities that go unaddressed. The *broken windows* theory contends that if the police and society at large do not crack down on disorderly behavior and minor incivilities—such as public drunkenness, public drug use, public urination, and jumping over subway turnstiles, graffiti walls, and dilapidated buildings—this can lead to the perception among potential offenders that their transgressions will be tolerated, unnoticed, and/or unpunished. In turn, this will lead to more serious crimes and can help send certain places and perhaps entire neighborhoods into a cycle of decline and lawlessness. This theory has been particularly influential in crime prevention and policing strategies that target minor incivilities and antisocial behavior, including opportunity-reduction measures undertaken by community residents and police.

2.3.6   Crime Hot Spots

As discussed in Chapter 1, the concept of *place* is of central importance to preventing and controlling criminal opportunities because research has shown that some locations are so prone to criminal and violent acts that they are labeled *hot spots* (Braga, 2012). Eck et al. (2005, 2) define a crime hot spot as "an area that has a greater than average number of criminal or disorder events, or an area where people have a higher than average risk of victimization." As Eck (2002, 242) writes,

"The scientific basis of place-focused crime prevention comes from epidemiological studies showing that a small percentage of persons, places, times, and situations account for a disproportionately large share of serious crime. For example, it is estimated that across the United States 10% of the places are sites for around 60% of the crimes." At an even more finite level are the so-called *hot spots* (also called *risky facilities*), which are specific addresses that are engaged in illegal activities (such as a crack house or automobile *chop shop*) or legitimate businesses that are considered *crime prone* because they "tend to attract persistent criminal and police attention for a variety of reasons" (Exum et al., 2010, 271) and may cause or contribute to crime, violence, and disorder problems in local surrounding areas (e.g., bars). Braga (2012, 320) summarizes the research indicating that facilities such as bars, churches, convenience stores, abandoned buildings, and apartment buildings "have been found to affect crime rates in their immediate environment depending on the type of persons they attract and the way the space is managed, or the possible crime controllers present such as owners, security, or police." Because of this spatial concentration of crime, place-based approaches to community safety assume a targeted geospatial approach through SCP, CPTED, community crime prevention, and policing measures that strive to reduce the opportunity for crime and violence to occur in these hot spots. In short, the theory and practice of SCP has increasingly been influenced by research demonstrating that crime and disorder problems are concentrated geospatially.

2.4 SITUATIONAL CRIME PREVENTION: DEFINITIONS AND DESCRIPTIONS

Clarke (1997, 4) defines SCP as "opportunity-reducing measures that (1) are directed at highly specific forms of crime; (2) involve the management, design, or manipulation of the immediate environment in as systematic and permanent a way as possible; (3) make crime more difficult and risky, or less rewarding and excusable as judged by a wide range of offenders." Also included in SCP are efforts by people to deter crime in a particular locale, primarily through *watch-and-report* strategies, such as NW or citizen patrols. In sum, SCP entails measures that involve managing, designing, or manipulating the physical environment or influencing legitimate users of a space, to reduce the opportunities for crimes to occur.

The first third of Clarke's definition is necessary because situational preventative measures should be tailored to the unique characteristics of specific types of crimes or disorder problems as well as the unique circumstances of each occurrence (the time, the place, the victim, security measures, etc.). In other words, to be successful, the development and implementation of SCP measures should follow the problem-oriented approach described in Chapter 1. The second part of Clarke's definition is an explicit recognition that SCP is concerned with manipulating the *immediate* physical and human environment to reduce the opportunity for a crime to occur and does not entail long-term solutions that ameliorate the root causes of criminal behavior. The last third of his definition represents the ultimate goal of SCP: to stop or deter an offender from committing a crime, either by making the criminal act more difficult to commit or by influencing the thought process of the offender to dissuade him from committing an offense in a particular time and place.

The most distinguishable characteristic of SCP is that it focuses on reducing the *opportunity* for a criminal act to occur in a particular time and place. As such, SCP is also referred to as an *opportunity-reduction* approach to crime prevention. Because SCP strategies intervene directly in the opportunistic portion of the criminal process, its solutions are restricted to variables that can be manipulated in the context of the relationship between people and their physical environment. With this in mind, opportunity-reduction approaches to crime prevention have been grouped into five categories:

1. Increasing the effort of the offender by making the targets of crime harder to get at or otherwise hindering the commission of crime
2. Increasing the risks to the offender, whether real or perceived, of detection and apprehension
3. Reducing the rewards to the offender, which in some cases may involve removing the targets of crime altogether
4. Removing people's excuses to commit crimes
5. Reducing the provocations that may contribute to a criminal act or criminal behavior (Clark, 1997; Cornish and Clarke, 2003)

Based on the above, SCP theory contends that motivated criminal offenders "may nonetheless be deterred from committing crime if they perceive a potential target to (1) involve too much risk, (2) require too much effort, (3) yield too meager a profit, (4) induce too much guilt or shame to make the venture worthwhile, or (5) reduce provocations that create criminal opportunities" (La Vigne and Lowry, 2011, 11). These categories are summarized in Table 2.1.

2.4.1 Increase the Effort Necessary to Commit a Crime

One obvious way to reduce the opportunity for a crime to occur is to increase the effort the offender must expend to commit the crime. The dominant opportunity-reduction strategies that increase the effort required to commit a crime are target hardening, access control, deflection of offenders, and controlling the facilitators of crime.

The most frequently used strategy to increase the effort of offenders is referred to as *target hardening*, which entails the use of such physical barriers and security devices as locks, window bars, fences, and reinforced materials to make it more difficult for an offender to physically enter a particular place. Clarke (1983) argues that the effectiveness of target hardening in reducing specific types of residential crime has been clearly demonstrated through research. Crime and victimization statistics have shown that residences with the most basic type of target hardening (i.e., locked doors) are less likely to be burglarized than those with no such type of device (Bureau of Justice Statistics, 1987). According to Poyner (1983), studies have shown that target hardening has enjoyed a greater amount of success relative to other crime prevention initiatives. In their review of target hardening studies, Bell and Bell (1987) also found that it can reduce the fear of crime. Mayhew (1984), who is critical of the efficacy of target hardening measures, nonetheless notes that the best argument for its effectiveness is implied by the large number of forced entries through insecure points that are recorded in burglary reports.

Table 2.1
25 SCP Techniques

Increase the effort	*Harden target* (deadbolt locks, fences, window bars)
	Access control (entry phones, prickly shrubs, psychological barriers)
	Deflect offenders (bus stop placement, tavern location, road closures)
	Control crime facilitators (gun control, plastic cups, caller ID, credit card photo)
Increase the risk	*Natural surveillance* (CPTED, NW, street lighting)
	Surveillance by employees (undercover security, raised kiosks)
	Intentional surveillance (security mirrors, CCTV, security guards, citizen patrols)
	Entry/exit screening (airport metal detectors, retail theft exit controls)
	Guardianship (being at home, carrying a cell phone, police, security guards)
	Place managers (apartment manager, bus driver, teacher, flight attendant)
	Reduce anonymity (school uniforms, taxi ID badges, *how's my driving truck* decals)
Reduce the rewards	*Property marking* (engraving valuable electronics, automobile VIN, cattle branding)
	Remove/conceal targets (removable car stereo, move items to car trunk)
	Deny benefits (ink merchandise tags, security codes for electronics, graffiti removal)
	Disrupt markets for stolen goods (regulate/crack down on pawn shops, street vendors)
Reduce provocations	*Reduce frustration and stress* (providing needed information to agitated people)
	Avoid disputes (standardized taxi fares from airport to city center)
	Reduce arousal and temptation (gender-neutral listings, restricting jobs for pedophiles)
	Neutralize peer pressure (*friends don't let friends drink and drive* ad campaign)
	Discourage imitation (regulate violence in movies, remove graffiti and vandalism)
Remove excuses	*Set rules* (government laws, code of conduct regulations in taverns and public places)
	Stimulate conscience (roadside speedometers, *shoplifting is stealing* signs)
	Facilitate compliance (easy library checkout, public lavatories, public trash bins)
	Control disinhibitors (no liquor after a certain time, V-chip, ignition lock)
	Post instructions (road signs, code of conduct signs)

Sources: Adapted from Clarke, R., Introduction, in Situational Crime Prevention: Successful Case Studies, Clarke, R.V., Ed., 2nd edn., Harrow and Heston, Albany, New York, 1997, pp. 2–43; Clarke, R. and Eck, J., Crime Analysis for Problem Solvers in 60 Small Steps, Office of Community Oriented Policing, Washington, DC, 2005; Smith, M. and Clarke, R., Situational crime prevention: Classifying techniques using 'good enough' theory, in The Oxford Handbook of Crime Prevention, Welsh, B.C. and Farrington, D.P., Eds., Oxford University Press, Oxford, U.K., 2012, pp. 291–315.

CASE STUDY 2.1

RESIDENTIAL BURGLARY REDUCTION PROJECT IN CHULA VISTA, CALIFORNIA

In 1997, police in Chula Vista, a city in San Diego County, California, applied a problem-oriented approach to residential burglaries following an increase in the number of reports, growing concern among residents, and in anticipation of the 300,000 new housing units to be built in and around the city over the next 20 years. Police began by conducting a study of factors that attracted burglars to homes as well as those protective devices that were most effective at preventing burglaries. As part of this study, more than 300 victims and suspects were interviewed, dozens of safety audits were undertaken, and more than 1000 police reports on residential break and enters were analyzed.

The study found that doors without deadbolt locks and windows with single panes were easily broken into, while doors with deadbolt locks and double-paned windows were far less frequently used as access points. The study also found that basic factory window latches could be pried open with a screwdriver or crowbar, sliding glass doors without specialized pin locks were easily rocked off their tracks, and many targeted properties had numerous hidden points of entry concealed by high shrubbery or solid fencing.

As a result of their analysis, police made the following target hardening recommendations to representatives from the real estate development and home construction industries for integration into new single-family homes: upgrading window locks, installing only double-paned glass, using some form of automatic locking mechanism that engages windows as they close, installing deadbolt locks on all side and rear home doors (including garage doors), and affixing keyed channel locks or slide bolts on sliding glass doors.

While not all developers followed the recommendations, enough did so that some decrease in burglaries of new homes was realized. Evaluations indicated that homes built with the recommended security enhancements had less than half the burglary rate of homes in neighborhoods that did not have such enhancements (Center for Problem-Oriented Policing, 2001).

Access control refers to any crime prevention measure that somehow regulates who can enter a certain area, allowing entry only to those who have a legitimate reason to be there (Lab, 2004, 38). Access control is most commonly employed in spaces that may have a variety of users. In this sense, an access control system regulates who is allowed to enter, where they are allowed to enter, and when they are allowed to enter. Access control approaches include apartment building entry phones, pass card readers for automatically locking doors or parking garages, card-operated subway turnstiles (Figure 2.2), office building reception areas or security check points, and biotechnology security that reads palm prints. Access control also includes the use of personal identification numbers (for ATM machines), passwords (for computer accounts), and engine immobilization security (for automobiles).

Poyner and Webb (1987) found that a combination of access controls implemented in a social housing complex in London, England—including fencing, entry phones that allow residents to screen visitors, pass card-restricted access to the enclosed parking garage, and a new reception desk on the ground floor of a high rise—resulted in a significant reduction in vandalism, theft, and graffiti. Poyner (1997)

Figure 2.2
The card-operated turnstiles at a New York City subway terminal is one example of access control.

describes how the demolition of enclosed walkways linking buildings in another social housing complex in London eliminated robberies and purse snatching that occurred on the walkways but did not result in a broader reduction in burglaries for the entire housing complex as hoped. The installation of locked gates at entrances to alleys that run behind terraced residential properties in a part of Liverpool, England, resulted in a 37% decline in burglaries. The effectiveness of the locked gates was evidenced by an increase in the proportion of burglaries in which entrance to the property by offenders was gained through other, more vulnerable entry points (Bowers et al., 2004).

Deflecting offenders involves measures that attempt to steer would-be criminals away from a particular location or, more generally, to deter people from the temptation to engage in criminal or disorderly behavior at a particular time or place. Scheduling the last bus to leave immediately after a bar closes is also intended to avoid late-night, alcohol-induced problems. Crowds of drunken young people on the streets at closing time may also be reduced by avoiding the concentration of licensed bars and pubs in one part of a city. Alternatively, the closing times of several bars in close proximity to one another can be staggered to avoid a large number of drunks in one area at the same time. Road closures have been used to deflect cruising by customers of street prostitutes or even drive-by shootings by gang members. In Santa Ana, California, street closures, traffic calming signs, written warnings, and controlling the movement of cars by police helped dramatically reduce cruising-related criminal acts associated with drug and alcohol use as well as violent conflicts along a major thoroughfare (Center for Problem-Oriented Policing, 1997). To reduce brawls at football matches in the United Kingdom, rival groups of fans are often segregated in the stadium's stands, while their arrival and departure times are scheduled to avoid waiting periods and loitering that may cause trouble (Clarke, 1983).

CASE STUDY 2.2

DEFLECTING BURGLARS FROM A FLORIDA CONVENIENCE STORE

A Florida convenience store was the victim of frequent robberies following its 1973 founding. The store had a robbery prevention program in place when it opened for business and implemented further security in 1979; however, the robberies continued to be a frequent occurrence. A safety audit conducted in 1981 revealed a gap in the store's security: A large parking lot located behind the store had exits in two directions, which provided easy access to and a quick getaway from the store.

Following the audit, a 6 ft high chain link fence was installed between the store and the parking lot, making it more difficult for robbers to escape into the parking lot and then drive away. Six months following the installation of the fence, there was one robbery, but in the following 3 years, there was none (Chambers, 1988). The addition of the fence can be considered an example of *access control* (regulating the entry and exit of cars accessing the store), *deflecting offenders* (deflecting them from the parking lot), and even *controlling facilitators* (in this case, the crime facilitator being controlled was the parking lot).

Controlling facilitators entails regulating certain items that can be used to aid in the commission of a crime. Gun control measures are perhaps the most salient example that falls within this category. (Gun control measures are described in more detail in violence prevention strategies in Section 2.7 of this chapter.) Another example of a strategy that can help control facilitators of crime and violence is serving beer in plastic cups to prevent bottles or glasses from being used as weapons or thrown as projectiles in bars or sports stadiums. The category of controlling facilitators is not simply limited to the use of potential weapons. To deter drug dealing in high-risk areas, public telephones are often modified to prohibit incoming calls, are disabled during certain periods (e.g., at night when demand for drugs is higher), or are completely removed from high-risk locations. Caller ID, which has proven to be an effective way to reduce obscene and unwanted telephone calls, can also be considered a way to control the use of the telephone as a facilitator for harassment and other incivilities.

2.4.2 Increase the Risks of Detection

SCP also seeks to increase the risks of an offender being detected, primarily through the use of surveillance and entry and exit screening. Some research supports the correlation between crime prevention and the offender's perception of increased risks; interviews with residential burglars suggest that they pay more attention to the immediate chances of getting caught than to the severity of the punishment they may receive at a later date (Clarke, 1997, 14).

Surveillance is the most effective human-based method of increasing the chance that an offender may be detected. Surveillance simply means introducing or increasing opportunities for the legitimate users of a space—such as neighborhood residents, retail storeowners, passersby, security guards, or police—to monitor that space. The fundamental assumptions underlying surveillance are that (1) legitimate users of a space

CASE STUDY 2.3

CONTROLLING FACILITATORS AND INCREASING THE RISK OF DETECTION FOR CREDIT CARD FRAUD AT A NEW JERSEY RETAILER

In the early 1990s, Tops Alliance City, Inc., a New Jersey electronics and appliance retailer, implemented a security program called *CardWatch*, which was intended to cut down on the use of fraudulent credit cards. Anyone wishing to apply for a store credit card had to have their pictures taken by a store clerk. These pictures were stored on the computer, and when someone made a purchase on the credit card, a store clerk was able to compare the picture in the computer to the customer.

The new system cut down on the use of credit cards as a crime facilitator; people were dissuaded from applying for credit cards under someone else's name, in part because their pictures would be maintained by the store, which could then be provided to police as evidence if a crime was committed. The new security system also resulted in a 45% reduction in claims by customers that someone else had made a purchase with their card. Overall, the annual losses from credit card fraud at the retailer dropped 93% following implementation of the new measures (Masuda, 1996).

will be more likely to notice intruders and (2) potential offenders will be deterred from these sites due to the risk of being caught. Studies involving interviews with burglars have demonstrated that they can be deterred by surveillance (Brown, 1985). Strategies that maximize surveillance opportunities for residents and other legitimate users of public spaces are essential to situational and community crime prevention as well as CPTED. According to Poyner (1994, 139), even very heavy use of hardware and security technology may prove inadequate without good surveillance measures in place.

Surveillance can be carried out naturally; as part of their routine activities, neighborhood residents are asked to keep an eye out for suspicious activity or people. *Natural surveillance* (also called *passive* or *informal* modes of surveillance) can be encouraged through the design of the physical environment so that legitimate users of that space can see and be seen. This includes situating windows in frequently used rooms of homes and apartment buildings to facilitate casual surveillance of entrances and nearby spaces, ensuring each dwelling entry is visible from as many other dwellings as possible, and erecting fences that enable people to see out but limit views into dwellings and private open spaces (Geason and Wilson, 1989, 26–28; Crowe, 1991, 106–107). Figure 2.3 provides a photo of the façade of a ground-level suite at Collingwood Village in Burnaby, British Columbia. This planned community was the first large-scale urban development in Canada to comprehensively integrate situational and CPTED principles into its design. Note the large windows that are meant to facilitate natural surveillance over both the immediate private and public spaces. The ground-level windows and doors have also been fortified (*target hardened*) for extra security.

NW programs can also fall under the natural surveillance category because residents are asked to look out for suspicious people and behavior in the course of the routine activities. (Neighborhood Watch is discussed in more detail in Chapter 4, which deals with community crime prevention.)

Figure 2.3
The façade of a ground-level suite at Collingwood Village in Burnaby, British Columbia, Canada.

Retail businesses have also implemented design measures to boost surveillance opportunities for staff, especially in convenience stores that are highly vulnerable to shoplifting and burglaries. In such stores, surveillance is facilitated by elevating cashier kiosks a foot or two above the floor, positioning store shelves laterally toward the kiosk, and affixing convex mirrors in the corners. Many convenience stores have also stopped placing large promotional posters on their windows to facilitate the store employee's view of the parking lot and to make it possible for passersby to view the inside of the store (which can help deter or catch robbers). To allow clear sight lines from the store onto the street (and vice versa), cashier kiosks are often moved to the front of the store. Bright floodlights are frequently used on the exterior of stores to increase the surveillance opportunities of staff.

Intentional surveillance refers to technology or activities in which the sole or primary function is to watch out for criminal or disorderly acts as a means to deter such acts or to apprehend those carrying them out (Hough et al., 1980, 7). Citizen patrols, security guards, and surveillance cameras are all examples of intentional forms of surveillance. Evaluations of the impact of security guards have been mixed. Barclay et al. (1996) found that bike-riding security guards in large suburban parking lots in Vancouver, Canada, reduced thefts. Poyner (1994) concluded that the use of security attendants to control vehicle access onto a London (England) housing estate helped reduce certain crime problems. In an evaluation of security guards in Rotterdam, Holland, Hesseling (1995) uncovered no impact on thefts from vehicles, but this might have been the result of how the guards were deployed. Employing technology to facilitate surveillance, such as security cameras, is often referred to as artificial surveillance. The goals of a closed-circuit television (CCTV) system are to both deter and detect offenders. While CCTV cameras are primarily located on commercial premises, they are increasingly being used in high-density multiresidential housing and parking lots and even on public streets. Welsh and Farrington (2009) conducted a meta-analysis of 44 studies that assessed the crime prevention effect of CCTV systems in three settings: (1) city centers and public housing, (2) public transportation, and (3) parking facilities. "The results suggest that CCTV caused a modest (16%) but significant decrease in crime in experimental areas compared with control areas.

CASE STUDY 2.4

THE CITY GUARD PROGRAM IN THE NETHERLANDS

The *Stadswacht* (City Guard) program began in 1989 in the city of Dordrecht in the Netherlands. Recruits are drawn from the chronically unemployed and receive 8 weeks of training in law, first aid, and security. City Guards are primarily responsible for patrolling public areas as uniformed civilians (with no police powers) but also take reports on crime, disorder vandalism, and physical security problems. The City Guard program has expanded to more than 150 other cities and towns in Holland.

One evaluation showed a reduction of 17% in reported crime in inner-city neighborhoods of Dordrecht patrolled by City Guards. In the year following the 1992 introduction of City Guards in the city of Nieuwegein, there was a 36% decrease in bicycle thefts (from 250 to 160), a 16% reduction in car thefts (from 229 to 193), and a 62% drop in pickpocketing (from 81 to 31) (Hauber et al., 1994; Koopman, 1996 as cited in International Centre for the Prevention of Crime, n.d., 14).

This overall result was largely driven by the effectiveness of CCTV schemes in car parks, which caused a 51% decrease in crime. Schemes in most other public settings had small and nonsignificant effects on crime: a 7% decrease in city and town centers and in public housing communities. Public transport schemes had greater effects (a 23% decrease overall), but these were still nonsignificant" (Welsh and Farrington, 2009, 716).

Exterior lighting is another widely touted SCP technique. By increasing visibility in dark or secluded areas, it is argued that criminal acts can be better detected, which creates a deterrent effect. In this respect, lighting reinforces surveillance as a means to prevent crime through detection and deterrence. The use of lighting for safety and security can be demarcated into two general categories: exterior lighting around residential or commercial buildings and public street lighting. Fennelly (1982, 35–36) provides the following checklist to ensure optimal exterior lighting for residences:

- Is the lighting adequate to illuminate vulnerable areas?
- Is there an even distribution of light? Is there sufficient lighting over entrances?
- Are the perimeter areas sufficiently illuminated to assist police surveillance?
- Is there an auxiliary electrical system in place if the primary power source goes out?
- Are the fixtures secure from tampering or vandalism?

The contribution of streetlights in reducing crime has been supported by research. According to Lavrakas and Kushmuk (1986), a significant reduction in crime was noted after the installation of high-intensity lighting along a commercial strip in Portland, Oregon (although it should be noted that improved lighting was only one of several physical and social interventions in the target area). Following improvements to street lighting in a Glasgow (Scotland) neighborhood, Ditton et al. (1992) describe how a survey of residents in the area reported 50% less victimization. Automobile-related crimes dropped to 4% of the total recorded before the lighting improvement campaign. Pedestrians, however, reported the same number of victimizations before and after relighting.

In 2002, an evaluation of three enhanced lighting programs in Bristol, Stoke-on-Trent, and Birmingham, England, found that each was effective in reducing criminal activity in crime *hot spots* (Farrington and Welsh, 2002, 31). For a public housing estate in Stoke-on-Trent, a victimization survey indicated a 42.9% decrease in overall crime, including a reduction in burglaries, thefts from autos, and violent crimes. Based on police reports, enhanced lighting in a city market in Birmingham resulted in a 79% reduction in personal thefts. In two residential neighborhoods in Bristol, enhanced lighting resulted in a reduction of the overall crime rate as well as theft from autos. In his review of the literature on the crime prevention effects of street lighting, Pease (1999, 47) concludes that "precisely targeted increases in street lighting generally have crime reduction effects" and "more general increases in street lighting seem to have crime prevention effects, but this outcome is not universal." In their meta-analysis of 13 studies on the effects of street lighting on crime, Welsh and Farrington (2004) found improved street lighting to be effective in reducing crime in public space, with an overall crime reduction of 22% in experimental areas compared with control areas.

Entry screening differs from access control in that it is not about excluding or deterring potential offenders from entering a particular area but increasing the likelihood of detecting those not conforming to entry requirements. These requirements may relate to prohibited goods and objects or to ensure people are in possession of valid tickets (e.g., at a concert, in a sporting event, or in a public transit) or valid documents (such as passports to enter a country). Airport metal detectors attempt to screen out (i.e., detect) individuals carrying firearms or other weapons. Searches by custom officials at ports of entry are another example of entry screening. In contrast, *exit screening* is meant to deter property theft by detecting objects that should not be removed from the protected area, such as items being shoplifted from a retail store. Many retail stores now have electronic exit screening devices located at the front entrance that are meant to detect any merchandise that has not been paid for and scanned at the checkout. To reduce the theft of books, most libraries now have exit screening systems in place.

As emphasized in routine activity theory, *guardians* refer to people protecting themselves, their own belongings, or those of family members, friends, and coworkers (and can include police and security guards). A place manager is someone who is given responsibility, as an ancillary part of their job, for controlling behavior in a specific location, such as an apartment building manager, a bus driver, a teacher in a school, or a flight attendant on a commercial airline (Clarke and Eck, 2005, 14, 78).

Reducing anonymity refers to efforts to help identify an individual who may be vulnerable to victimization or someone who may have committed a crime or bylaw infraction. As Clarke and Eck (2005, 78) explain,

> ... people spend increasing periods of time among anonymous strangers. The building of large schools has contributed to this trend because pupils are less well known to staff and other pupils. Reducing anonymity is a promising but rarely used situational technique. Some schools are now requiring uniforms, partly to reduce the anonymity of pupils on their way to and from school. Cab driver ID badges and "How's my driving?" decals with 1-800 numbers on trucks are two further ways of reducing anonymity.

2.4.3   Reduce the Rewards

As the heading implies, this category entails efforts to minimize the rewards that an offender may enjoy as a result of his/her criminal activities. One example is *property marking*, whereby one's assets are electronically engraved with some form of identification. Property marking is often used in relation to high-value electronic equipment (such as televisions, stereo equipment, or laptop computers) that is highly sought after by thieves due to the relative ease with which it can be pawned or resold. Property marking is also used with motor vehicles, through the use of vehicle identification numbers (which are mandatory in most jurisdictions). As a reward–reduction strategy, the goals of marking property are twofold. First, it is intended to deter offenders by lowering the economic gain of a theft (the potential likelihood of a stolen item being traced or the reluctance of someone buying marked property will reduce its resale value) and increasing the risk of apprehension (by linking recovered property to a specific crime). The second goal is to increase the probability of recovering and returning stolen property to the victim. In a study of property marking in two isolated communities in Wales, Laycock (1985) concluded that such measures can be successful. After police conducted a property marking program among homes in one neighborhood, a survey determined that burglaries decreased by 40% in the following year. The author also claims that there was no displacement of burglaries from participants to nonparticipants. In their review of burglary prevention strategies, Millie and Hough (2004, 6) conclude that a property marking scheme implemented as part of broader crime prevention initiatives in multiple neighborhoods in Southern England and Wales resulted in a drop in burglary in "the specific streets and blocks targeted for property marking." According to the researchers,

> The property marking plausibly contributed to this fall. Potential burglars may have been deterred by intervention publicity and by window stickers used that labelled a house as "postcode protected." The fact that it was the police who visited each household to do the marking may have been just as important, effectively making the intervention one of high visibility policing. Other police operations in the area at this time may also have been an influence.
>
> **Millie and Hough (2004, 6)**

In contrast, an assessment of a property marking program in a Canadian neighborhood found there was a 75% increase in seasonally adjusted burglaries per dwelling following its implementation (Gabor, 1981).

In some cases, reducing rewards may involve removing and/or concealing a target of crime. For example, signs in the parking lots of shopping malls remind customers to move any items from their car into the trunk. Car stereo manufactures facilitate this technique by designs that allow the stereo to be easily removed from the dashboard. Some parking lot companies are switching to machines where customers pay for parking through credit and debit cards only. This trend is the result of thefts of change from coin-operated machines. Some municipal governments are moving away from coin-operated parking meters for the same reason. Many medical clinics carry only a very small supply of drugs (and post visible signs as such) in order to avoid theft. In Charlotte, North Carolina, the removal of kitchen appliances from homes still under construction until the new owners had taken up residence resulted in a decrease in thefts, with no evidence of a displacement of thefts to surrounding areas (Clarke and Goldstein, 2002).

Another form of reducing rewards is to deny the criminal offender the benefits after something has been stolen. For example, retail stores attach *ink tags* to clothes that, if tampered by shoplifters, will leave an indelible stain on the garments (only the store staff have the technology to safely remove the tag). Many high-value electronic devices, such as car stereos, tablets, laptop computers, and cell phones, can only be operated if a secret security code is enabled. Ekblom (2012, 386) describes the Puma folding bike, which has "a down-tube (the diagonal part of the frame) made of tension steel cable that unfastens and doubles as a locking device that can wrap around a bike stand - cut the cable and the release bike is now useless. This reduces the reward."

Smith (2003) writes that the "repair of damage and removal of defacement" has been used as an effective benefit denial technique for over 30 years and has been employed in British public housing revitalization schemes and as part of citywide campaigns against graffiti in the United States. In 1984, the transit authority in New York City implemented the Clean Car Program, which had as its goal the removal of graffiti from subway cars within 2 h of the cars being vandalized. Teams of cleaners were employed at the end of train lines to immediately remove graffiti or to pull tagged cars from service. The policy was that no vandalized car would be put back into service until the graffiti had been removed. The goal behind the Clean Car Program was to deny offenders the gratification of seeing their work on public display. The program was deemed a great success, in part because it was held responsible for dramatically reducing future incidents of graffiti on subway cars (showing that this strategy can have a deterrent effect). To maximize the deterrent effect of this benefit denial strategy, the repair of vandalism or the removal of graffiti must be done as quickly and comprehensively as possible (Sloan-Hewitt and Kelling, 1992).

Reducing the rewards to offenders also includes strategies that disrupt markets that sell contraband goods (i.e., those that are stolen, counterfeited, and strictly regulated, such as cigarettes and alcohol). According to Clarke and Eck (2005, 80) "if there were no market for stolen goods there would be few persistent burglars and few thefts of trucks carrying large loads of tobacco and alcohol." Disrupting markets as a crime prevention strategy includes regulating and/or cracking down on pawn shops and street vendors.

2.4.4   *Reduce Provocations*

While SCP focuses mostly on risk factors that create the opportunity for crimes to occur in a particular time and place, this category recognizes that there are features of a particular situation that may precipitate or induce criminal behavior. Thus, SCP includes measures that reduce or remove such provocations or inducements. Reducing frustration and stress that may lead to violent altercations can be accomplished by providing agitated people with the information or services they need or desire especially in the context of a crisis situation. Disputes can also lead to violent altercations and can be prevented through situational measures. For example, in many cities, taxi fares from an airport to a certain part of a city are fixed at a standard amount to avoid possible accusations of cheating by the customer. Given the opportunistic nature of many crimes, strategies that reduce temptation may also be effective in deterring crime. *Temptation-reduction* measures include phone directories or resident entry-phone listings on apartment buildings that are gender neutral (i.e., includes only the first initial of a first name), which are meant to inhibit obscene phone calls or even the targeting of women for sexual assault. A mural on an exterior wall of a building may reduce the temptation to graffiti the wall. Reducing arousal and temptation is also pertinent to preventing sexual offenses and can include ensuring that convicted pedophiles are not given jobs around children or that convicted sex offenders are provided with medication to avoid arousal. Peer pressure is a significant risk factor for binge drinking by young men (which is a risk factor for violence as well drinking and driving) and can be prevented by ad campaigns, such as the ubiquitous *Friends don't let friends drink and drive*. Criminal offenders are also known to copy criminal acts or behavior that they may have seen through entertainment (TVs, the movies, video games) or in the news media.

As such, one provocation reduction strategy is to discourage *copycat* crimes, which can include regulating violence in the entertainment industry, minimizing the publicity of certain criminal techniques in the media, and removing graffiti and fixing vandalized property quickly (Clarke and Eck, 2005, 82–83).

2.4.5 Remove Excuses

This category includes any measure that removes an individual's excuse to commit a crime or a disorderly act. Of all the SCP strategies, this one is the most overt in directly trying to change behaviors, primarily by making a moral appeal to people to behave appropriately. The first way to remove excuses is to establish and communicate rules, procedures, or limits that ensure there is no ambiguity as to what behavior is expected in a certain place or at a certain time. Government laws are, in effect, rules that people are expected to follow; criminal laws or municipal bylaws are implemented to establish certain rules and are backed up by the threat of punishment as an extra incentive to deter people from breaking such rules. Taverns, parks, and sports stadiums are just a few examples where rules for appropriate behavior are posted. Another example of *rule setting* is refund policies at retail stores, where cash refunds are only provided if the customer produces a legitimate receipt. This policy has been implemented to reduce refund fraud. Another technique to remove excuses is to stimulate people's conscience, which involves reminding people that a certain act or behavior is wrong or even illegal. The posting of electronic road signs connected to radar guns, which tell drivers their speed (in an attempt to shame speeders into slowing down), is one example.

In addition to, or instead of, setting and conveying rules, excuses can be removed by encouraging people to do the right thing. *Facilitating compliance* is a crime and

---

CASE STUDY 2.5

SETTING STANDARDS FOR BEHAVIOR IN SURREY, ENGLAND

While crimes such as burglary and auto theft were falling in the Guildford Town Centre in Surrey, England, violent crime and disorderly behavior were increasing, especially among young males. This contributed to an increase in fear by others who used this space, which in turn led to avoidance of this part of the city by many. After consulting with NW coordinators, police identified five types of behavior by young people that caused people the greatest distress: obscene language, throwing objects, obstructing roads, public drunkenness, and urinating in the street. In 2002, police began targeting incivilities by enforcing a standard of behavior that involved issuing a yellow/red card warning system similar to that used in football (an ingenious tactic given the passion that many British youth have for the sport, combined with their familiarity of the penalty card system). Youth who commit one of the aforementioned incivilities are warned and issued a yellow card. If they reoffend the same evening, they are shown a red card and handed a summons.

An evaluation showed that the strategy reduced crime and disorder problems in the targeted area by 30%, while the number of arrests decreased by 38%. During the test period, 214 people were warned for antisocial behavior and issued yellow cards. Only five subsequently came to the notice of Surrey Police (Center for Problem-Oriented Policing, 2003).

---

disorder prevention technique that incorporates measures that make it easy and convenient for people to follow rules and standards for appropriate behavior. For example, garbage cans that are easily accessible to the public can help limit littering. Free rides on public transit after midnight can also dissuade people from drinking and driving. Some universities and public libraries now have technology whereby borrowers can check out books themselves, an attempt to promote the legal removal of books from a library.

Controlling disinhibitors involves limiting people's access to things that reduce their ability to think and behave inappropriately. The most common example is limiting access to alcohol, a strategy that is relevant to reducing drinking and driving as well as vandalism and violence in and around licensed establishments. Sporting events often stop serving liquor an hour or more before a game is expected to end. Another way to minimize alcohol-related problems in licensed premises is to implement responsible beverage service policies, such as those that require staff to refuse to serve inebriated customers. Research suggests that such policies can have positive effects on alcohol-related problems in bars and surrounding areas (see Homel et al., 1997).

A final way to remove excuses for criminal behavior is to post instructions either to prevent people claiming ignorance of the rules or to show precisely where these apply. The most obvious example of instruction posting is road signs that govern driving or parking. "Studies have found that warning signs significantly reduce illegal parking in spaces reserved for disabled drivers. Many other facilities—parks, colleges, transit lines and housing projects—also post signs to govern a wide range of behaviors" (Clarke and Eck, 2005, 84).

2.5 CPTED

CPTED is a strategy intended to reduce the opportunity for crime through the proper design and use of the physical environment (including the built and natural environments). The underlying theory of CPTED is that the physical environment plays a role in promoting and deterring criminal behavior and, as such, its proper design and effective use can lead to a reduction in the incidence of crime and fear of crime as well as promote greater responsibility and vigilance over private and public spaces by the legitimate users of these spaces.

Sociologists, psychologists, architects, and urban planners have long studied how the immediate physical environment can influence people's behavior. Theories and strategies that attempt to draw a cause–effect relationship between the physical environment and crime contend that some types of physical and spatial designs are more likely than others to precipitate certain behaviors that result in a greater incidence of crime. To this end, crime causation theories underlying CPTED are in line with those of SCP, which is that the immediate physical environment can be a factor in an offender's decision to commit a crime.

Specifically, it is hypothesized that the design of the physical environment (houses, buildings, landscapes, streets, parks, other public spaces, and entire neighborhoods) can influence the behavior of the legitimate users of that space, which may inhibit or promote crime opportunities. Some contemporary theories that advocate a relationship between crime and the physical environment suggest that the use of modern architectural and spatial designs minimizes social interaction, breaks down community cohesiveness, and destabilizes informal social control. This, in turn, contributes to increases in crime. In her influential 1961 book, *The Death and Life of Great American*

Cities, Jane Jacobs observed that certain neighborhoods experience relatively less crime despite being found in urban settings where the surrounding areas have high crime rates. She attributed this lower crime rate to a neighborhood design that provided increased (natural) surveillance opportunities to legitimate residents and pedestrians. One of her major criticisms of urban planning and architecture of the day was the way modern design—such as high-rise buildings, narrow sidewalks, and wide streets that encourage cars—undermines the proclivity of people to use and observe public spaces, to socially interact, and to feel a sense of attachment to their neighborhood. She hypothesized that this leads to a breakdown in informal social control, which translates into greater opportunities for crime. According to Mair and Mair (2003, 212),

> Jacobs identified three main qualities that safe streets in thriving city neighborhoods possessed by promoting surveillance and mutual policing. First, there must be a clear separation between public and private space so that the area needing surveillance is unequivocally defined. Second, safety requires "eyes upon the street," which Jacobs refers to as "the natural proprietors of the street." Buildings therefore should be oriented to allow an easy view of the street. Finally, sidewalks should be used fairly continuously to add to the number of eyes on the street and to induce people inside adjacent buildings to watch the sidewalks. Jacobs also argued that streets must accommodate mixed uses (e.g., residential housing, restaurants, stores) attracting people to the area and promoting 24-hour surveillance.

In short, she advocated that neighborhoods be designed to create opportunities for people to use public spaces and to see and be seen. This, in turn, would foster informal social control through interpersonal social interaction and mutual surveillance.

Following up on this early environmental design hypothesis, Oscar Newman (1972) introduced his theory of *Defensible Space*, which would become one of the most prominent (and controversial) crime prevention theories dealing with the relationship between the physical environment and human behavior. As a basis for this theory, Newman asserted a significant relationship between building design, the loss of social cohesion, and crime. In particular, he found a correlation between the height of residential apartment buildings and the rate of crime in and around such buildings. His research suggests that crime and vandalism rates in multi-storey public housing projects were relatively high because tall buildings foster a disassociation between dwellings and street activities and promote a sense of alienation from the surrounding neighborhood and from other residents living in the housing complex (larger buildings are used by more people, so residents are less able to differentiate neighbors from intruders and, as such, criminals are less likely to be deterred due to their perception of a low probability of detection).

Newman (1996) later revised his theories on the relationship between environmental design and safety by making them less environmentally deterministic, in part through a increased recognition of the role social and managerial factors play in influencing crime. In particular, he suggested that the human environment was equally important in predicting crime especially with respect to the nature and scope of residents' use of the surrounding public spaces and the level of their social interaction and cohesion. In turn, these factors influence the extent to which they are vigilant in protecting their neighborhood from crime. The International Centre for the Prevention of Crime (2008, 110) summarized his conclusions as such: "the impact of physical, social and managerial predictor variables on crime, fear and insecurity is through mediating variables which are use of space, social interaction and control of space."

Finally, research has confirmed the relationship between the fear of crime and the physical environment; that is, environmental features can signal to legitimate users that a particular locale is either safe or threatening. Research by Fisher and Nasar (1992) that looked at the relationship between exterior site characteristics and fear of crime suggests that places offering offenders refuge and victims limited prospects for escape will be seen as unsafe to legitimate users of that space. Fear of crime was highest in areas that are dimly lit, are secluded, and have plenty of overgrown bushes.

In theory, CPTED operates in two basic ways: like SCP in general, design strategies are meant to prevent crime both directly (by managing the physical environment to influence the behavior and actions of potential offenders) and indirectly (by influencing the behavior of the legitimate users of a space). First, it is hypothesized that CPTED can work directly to prevent crime by restricting access to property and removing criminal opportunities through the design and management of the physical environment that satisfy the basic principles of SCP (increase the effort, increase the risk, reduce the rewards, reduce provocations, remove excuses). In addition, CPTED relies on design principles that may not create real impediments to committing a crime but try to create the perception in the minds of potential offenders that they are at a higher risk of being detected.

Second, safe environmental designs can work indirectly to reduce crime, fear, and related problems by influencing the social behavior of legitimate users of a particular space. Newman's defensible space theory contends that the physical environment can be designed to spur residents to assume a proprietary interest in their neighborhood (Newman, 1972). In his own words, the goal of a design that creates defensible space is "to release the latent sense of territoriality and community among inhabitants so as to allow these traits to be translated into inhabitants' assumption of responsibility for preserving a safe and well-maintained living environment" (Newman, 1976, 4). Newman suggested that the physical layout of multiresidential complexes, and public housing in particular, can influence residents to help contribute to a safe environment through four mechanisms:

> (a) by creating "perceived zones of territorial influences" or objectively recognizable areas that residents control and defend (territoriality); (b) by providing opportunities for residents to survey nonprivate areas of their housing environment (natural surveillance); (c) by designing buildings, grounds, and streets that do not stigmatize or isolate the residents (image); and (d) by locating the housing site adjacent to areas with safe activities (milieu).

Mair and Mair (2003, 212)

Thus, CPTED theories are not restricted simply to changes in the physical environment exclusively, but rather how these changes can influence human behavior, including that of legitimate users (through designs that ultimately promote vigilance) and potential offenders (through designs that send the message that certain areas are well protected). CPTED principles can be applied to new and existing developments, including single-family houses and multiresidential complexes (apartment buildings, townhouses, hotels), neighborhoods and subdivisions and public spaces (streets, parks, pathways), semiprivate spaces (hospitals, college campuses, parking lots, malls), and industrial sites. Some of the key strategies pursued within the CPTED field are summarized in the following.

2.5.1 Territoriality/Informal Social Control/Defensible Space

Some have argued that residential neighborhoods can be designed to help foster residents' proprietary interest and vigilance over their home and their neighborhood as a whole.

CASE STUDY 2.6

ENVIRONMENTAL DESIGN MODIFICATIONS IN CLASON POINT, NEW YORK CITY

One row house development located in Clason Point, a collection of neighborhoods located in the south–central Bronx, was an original test site for Newman's defensible space hypotheses. In an effort to reduce crime during the 1970s, four environmental design measures were pursued: (1) the installation of attractive 6 ft iron fences to enclose the areas immediately behind each row house block, (2) the use of paths and low curbs to delineate individual front yards for each unit in what formerly was public space in front of each block, (3) resurfacing amorphous building facades in varying colors and textures so that each unit became visually distinct from the one next door, and (4) fostering greater use of streets and other public spaces by people through the creation of sidewalks, ample street lighting, benches for sitting, and other appropriate street furniture.

These changes converted 80% of the previously public grounds into spaces that were designed and designated for private use (controlled or *defensible* space). Within a year, researchers found that most residents also began to personalize their own private spaces. The crime rate reportedly decreased in the area by more than 50%, a decline attributed to the design modifications. Researchers concluded that the design changes prompted a greater vigilance by residents, which was reflected in the increase in the number of tenants who believed they had a right to question strangers in the housing complex following the modifications (Newman and Franck, 1980, as cited in Cisneros, 1995, 10). While this research has been quite influential, it has also been subjected to numerous critiques, based largely on accusations of a weak methodology.

Public and semipublic areas can be made more defensible by providing a clear definition of *controlled space*, creating signs of ownership and vigilance over public spaces, designing clearly marked transitional zones for people moving from public to private spaces, attracting local residents to use public spaces, promoting surveillance opportunities among the legitimate users of public and private spaces, and maintaining the aesthetics of the local environment (e.g., by fixing dilapidated buildings, removing graffiti, or erecting public art) to show that people care about their community. Through such measures, it is hypothesized that the physical environment can be designed to release the latent sense of *territoriality* (informal social control) among inhabitants, which turns local public and private property into *defensible space* (i.e., where the perception is created that residents are ready and willing to defend their space against unwanted intruders).

2.5.2 Spatial Hierarchy

In the context of CPTED, a spatial hierarchy refers to design principles that clearly delineate private from public spaces. The purpose of this spatial hierarchy is to signal to potential offenders that they are entering private space, which is intended to increase perceptions of heightened risks (because it is argued that the offender's chance of being spotted, confronted, and/or reported to police is heightened as residents are generally more vigilant in private spaces compared to public spaces). In other words, the ultimate goal of a spatial hierarchy is to create the perception of increased risks for the would-be offender. Defensible space theory is also premised on the belief that private areas are less susceptible to crime and vandalism than public areas. This delineation between private and public spaces relies on the use of physical markers that create a sense of ownership, control, and vigilance (Perkins et al., 1993, 31). A spatial hierarchy can be created to delineate controlled space by marking out private territory through a series of transitional zones for people moving from public to private spaces. This can be accomplished by increasing lighting at the entrance or just prior to the entrance of a home, changing the texture or patterns of a walkway as one gets closer to a private entrance (e.g., a public sidewalk is concrete and a private path is brick), changing the level of a private walkway (e.g., private footpaths may be one or two steps higher than a public sidewalk or gradually slope upward to the doorway), or using real or symbolic barriers such as fences, shrubbery, or even signs to define borders (Geason and Wilson, 1989, 15–16). In short, residential environments should be designed to help identify ownership by clearly delineating public space such as streets, sidewalks, or community spaces (e.g., playground, communal laundries) from private space (such as the actual dwelling or private open spaces such as yards).

2.5.3 Natural Surveillance

The safe design of any environment should maximize the ability of legitimate users to spot suspicious people and activities. Natural surveillance opportunities can be enhanced by orienting windows to entry ways, vulnerable points, or public spaces; designing landscapes that allow unobstructed views of surrounding areas; improving visibility with lighting, transparent building materials, or white paint; and avoiding the creation of entrapment areas. As mentioned earlier, maximizing natural surveillance opportunities for legitimate users of a space is said to contribute to fostering territoriality and defensible space.

2.5.4 Activity Support

The design of public spaces should encourage the intended use of this space by legitimate users. This can be achieved by designing public or semipublic spaces to include parks, playgrounds, benches, lighting, or promenade-style sidewalks. In the early 1990s, police in Stockholm, Sweden, complemented a crackdown of drug trafficking in a park by locating a *dog toilet* on a hill where many of the illegal drug deals were occurring. This initiative attracted many dog owners to the spot, thereby encouraging natural surveillance opportunities and *ownership* of the area by legitimate users (key goals of activity support). Providing communal areas for residents in public spaces is also meant to stimulate social interaction, which in theory can lead to greater levels of social cohesion and informal social control (territoriality). Activity support in public and semipublic spaces is central to the defensible space theory. Newman emphasizes the importance of creating the perception of a *controlled space*, which is a powerful environmental cue affecting the behavior and predispositions of both legitimate and illegitimate users of that space (Crowe, 1991, 106). Legitimate users of public and semipublic spaces must *mark* this territory by creating the perception that it is *controlled space*. As such, designs that promote the use of public space by legitimate users help satisfy an important objective of defensible space, which is to *privatize* public and semipublic areas so that territorial motivation is aroused, strangers are more easily recognizable, and residents develop a sense of personal responsibility for maintaining a secure environment.

CASE STUDY 2.7

APPLYING CPTED PRINCIPLES TO THE BEACH NEIGHBORHOOD IN VANCOUVER

Beach Neighborhood is located along the northern shore of False Creek in the densely populated West End of downtown Vancouver, Canada. The neighborhood is characterized by high-rise apartment buildings, low-rise townhouses, retail offices, commercial sites, a waterfront parkette, and a walkway along the shore of False Creek. A high-density redevelopment of Beach Neighborhood took place during the early to mid-1990s, and in its development guidelines, city planners required that safe design principles be incorporated into the construction and layout of the buildings and surrounding areas. Specific crimes and disorder problems that were to be taken into consideration include auto and bicycle theft in the underground parking areas, residential burglaries, graffiti, and sleeping alcoves by homeless people. Easing fear should also be of paramount concern, especially in the design of places with minimal natural surveillance opportunities or *controlled space* such as the underground parking garages.

The CPTED principles that were emphasized in the redesign include access control, hierarchy of space, activity support, and surveillance.

The ground-level townhouses were designed to address the high number of break-ins in the neighborhood by reducing areas of concealment outside the units and maximizing surveillance opportunities by residents and passersby. The sidewalks are wide and running parallel to them are grass boulevards with small palm trees, creating a promenade effect that is meant to invite pedestrians (leading to what Jacobs calls more *eyes on the street*). A spatial hierarchy is created between the private front entrance of individual residences and the public sidewalks by setting the entrances 3 ft above grade, differing surface styles between the sidewalk and the front *porch*, and creating a small semiprivate area before one enters the elevated front door through rows of small shrubbery and a small fence. Target hardening measures for the ground-level units include the use of small-paned windows and fully secured swing doors rather than sliding doors (which are more vulnerable to break-ins). An alcove on the side of the townhouses that houses the water meters is enclosed by a locked gate to remove hiding spots for offenders or sheltered sleeping prospects for homeless people.

Visitor and public parking in the high-rise apartment buildings are separated from resident parking and secured with an overhead gate and electronic communication to residential units. Elevator access into the garage from the lobby can only be operated through a card access system. To minimize easy access into the garage by offenders, entry into the underground parking from the sidewalk is only available through a gated, locked door. An open exit stairwell on the outside of the building is located in a semiprivate space where it can be watched by residents from their units.

A small park was created to act as an activity generator for residents and was designed with clear sight lines. Apartment buildings with ground-level retail shops and cafes surround and overlook the public space and the small marina located just off the park, thereby maximizing surveillance opportunities. Interconnected paving stones are used as the pavement within the public space to deter skateboarding (City of Vancouver, 1996).

Figure 2.4 provides a photo of the front of a Beach Neighborhood condominium development that has incorporated CPTED principles into its design.

Figure 2.4
Ground-level townhouses along Beach Avenue.

2.5.5   Access Control

A safe design should control access to a site, limiting unnecessary traffic and most importantly deterring offenders from entering residential complexes, houses, buildings, parking lots, schools, neighborhoods, etc. Access control can be achieved by ensuring that entrances are clearly defined, well lit, and overlooked by windows; installing security hardware; or designing streets to prevent quick and easy entry and exit.

2.5.6   Location/Surrounding Environment

A safe design or location decision should take into consideration the surrounding environment and user groups. The potential negative impact on a site by the surrounding environment should be considered, primarily by avoiding the use of the site by incompatible groups (such as building a high school next to a senior citizens' residence or a tavern).

2.5.7   Second-Generation CPTED

As detailed in Section 2.8 of this chapter, CPTED has been leveled with criticisms that its theories about the relationship between design and crime are too deterministic and simplistic. Critics charge that CPTED proponents give too much weight to the role of the environment in influencing crime and criminal behavior and that social and demographic variables are more important in predicting crime rates (see Section 2.8). Moreover, environmental design only has the potential for invoking social control, informal social control, or releasing defensive behavior under certain social conditions (e.g., stable, homogenous neighborhoods).

CASE STUDY 2.8

DEFENSIBLE SPACE THROUGH MODULE LOTTING IN MISSISSAUGA, CANADA

Trelawny is a single-family home development located in Mississauga, Ontario, a suburb of Toronto. The neighborhood is characterized by the use of modular lots, where each home is placed on an angle relative to the street. By angling the homes, *module lotting* is said to foster territoriality and defensible space because a group of houses visually shares the same outdoor space, including the street, the cul-de-sac, and the spaces between the houses. The rear yards are also visually shared and can be overseen by two adjacent dwellings (indicated by the arrows in Figure 2.5). The elimination of dark areas along the sides of homes removes potential hiding spots for offenders. Not only is this design meant to foster greater surveillance opportunities, but the shared space is also meant to create *controlled space* and hence greater territoriality (defensible space). Territoriality and defensible space are also said to be fostered by a combination of modular lotting and street design, which together are meant to create the perception of a private street.

The design of Trelawny is meant to promote social interaction and cohesion, which theoretically is supposed to increase territoriality, defensible space, and informal social control.

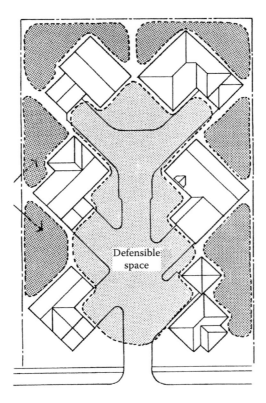

Figure 2.5
Modular lotting.

The street upon which the houses are located is narrower than the main street to which it is connected (providing a spatial hierarchy). The homes at the mouth of the larger *feeder* street create an almost gatelike effect, which contributes to the private feel of the residential street. The other end of the street is designed as a cul-de-sac, which not only is an access and exit control technique but is also meant to foster controlled (defensible) space and territoriality. There are a limited number of homes on the street (which can foster controlled space). Homes are designed with front porches, which are meant to encourage *eyes and ears* on the street while promoting social interaction and cohesion among neighbors. The angling of the houses maximizes residents' opportunities to see those entering their street (from the single entry point). It can also create the perception among those entering this street that they are being watched by the houses (First City Development Corp. Ltd., n.d.). Many of these CPTED features can be seen in the photo of one street in the Trelawny development (Figure 2.6).

These critiques have given rise to the development of *second-generation CPTED* that seeks to address these critiques and the limitations of first-generation CPTED theories and strategies. It does so through a particular focus "on improving social cohesion and social capital in neighborhoods and encouraging connectivity between residents in neighborhoods" (Raynald, 2011, 77). Saville and Cleveland (1998) initially developed second-generation CPTED to move beyond its strict focus on environmental design and to reintegrate some of the original community-building and social programming intentions of CPTED's pioneers, in particular Jane Jacobs. Second-generation CPTED "recognizes the most valuable aspects of safe community lie not in structures of the brick and mortar type, but rather in structures of family, of thought and, most importantly of behavior. We may benefit from starting with an examination of the physical aspects of place, but we must end up looking at the social aspects of home and neighborhood—the affective environment" (Saville and Cleveland, 1998, 1–2).

Figure 2.6
Trelawny neighborhood.

This revised approach recognizes that modifying the physical and built environment is only the first step in promoting community safety; vigilance and territoriality among local residents requires a foundation of social cohesion and collective efficacy that may require some form of community building through localized social programming (especially in high-crime, disadvantaged neighborhoods). Thus, this addition to CPTED "is a new form of ecological, sustainable development" that moves beyond the "rational offender model, which is too narrow and offender-centered" (Saville and Cleveland, 1998, 8), and "the design-affects-crime debate," which is too environmentally deterministic (Saville and Cleveland, 2013, 94). Instead, it incorporates a wide range of community-building and "social crime prevention strategies in a holistic way but it does so in specific situations in local places." This specificity is a hallmark of new CPTED strategies, according to the progenitors of this revised approach: second-generation CPTED addresses "the cultural, social, and emotional needs of people at the specific locales where crime is most acute" (Saville and Cleveland, 2010, 81).

For Saville and Cleveland (2010, 2013), the community-building aspect of this new approach to CPTED and community safety involves four main components:

1. Social cohesion: Building social cohesion is to second-generation CPTED what *territoriality* was to the first generation. Social cohesion is a critical foundation for effective crime prevention strategies and safe communities. (See Chapter 5 for more details on the role of social cohesion in crime prevention.) Social cohesion is built on "social glue" strategies "that bring members of the community together to take responsibility for their street, block, organization, or town" and "positive esteem," which is "characteristics that individuals within the neighborhood need for cohesion to occur" (Saville and Cleveland, 2013, 96).

2. Connectivity: This is about promoting a neighborhood's positive relations and influences with outside agencies (such as city planners or government funding sources) by providing residents with "access to grant-writing expertise" or fostering "neighborhood empowerment teams for participatory planning." These connections can serve to empower local residents by giving them greater influence over their community (Saville and Cleveland, 2013, 97).

3. Community culture: This includes strategies meant to bring people together to develop a unique, inclusive, and common local culture ("this is how local residents begin to share a sense of place and why they bother to exert territorial control in the first place") (Saville and Cleveland, 2013, 98).

4. Threshold capacity: This concept is about establishing balanced, or more diverse, land uses and social activities through "social stabilizers" that attempt to instill in residents a strong sense of belonging and shared bonds with others. "Stabilizers include safe congregation areas of events for young people while minimizing destabilizing activities that tip and area into crime, such as illegal pawn shops and abandoned buildings." Stabilizing strategies also attempt to address factors that contribute to "community imbalances," which refer to the "capacity of any given activity or space to properly support the intended use." For example, stabilizing strategies would attempt to address an overabundance of abandoned homes or taverns, both of which can contribute to local crime problems (Saville and Cleveland, 2010, 84).

In sum, some common CPTED guidelines from both the first and second generations include the following:

- Maximize residents' opportunities for surveillance of dwellings and public spaces in residential neighborhoods.
- Clearly define the boundaries between public and private spaces.
- Limit the number of access and exit points and routes into and out of a neighborhood.
- Maximize interior and exterior lighting, stressing bright white lights.
- Avoid any building design or ground-level planting that may provide concealment or entrapment areas.
- Keep the surrounding area clean, well-maintained, graffiti-free, and attractive to prevent a perception of neglect and insecurity by potential offenders.
- Promote legitimate use of public spaces by designing for or building attractors, such as playgrounds, wide sidewalks, and community gardens.
- Consider the safety and security implications of a site when deciding how that site will be used (i.e., ensure that the use of the site is compatible with the surrounding area and consider how certain land uses, for example bars or roadways, may create a crime *tipping point* for the local community).
- Design spaces to promote social interaction, social cohesion, collective efficacy, and territoriality among residents.
- Build local social capital, collective efficacy, and social cohesion through social programming as a foundation for the essential elements of local crime prevention initiatives and practices (territoriality, natural surveillance, vigilance).
- Empower local residents to become involved in planning and designing CPTED and broader community safety strategies while also forging strong relationships with relevant external agencies and professionals.

2.6 REDUCING CRIME OPPORTUNITIES BY MODIFYING THE BEHAVIOR OF POTENTIAL VICTIMS

The strategies described earlier involve the management, design, or manipulation of the physical environment as a means to prevent and deter crime. Opportunity-reduction strategies also include efforts to influence and organize people to prevent or reduce criminal opportunities.

According to Eck and Rosenbaum (1994, 14–15), there are five SCP roles people can play:

1. They can watch out for and report suspicious people or behavior to police.
2. They can actively patrol areas, confront suspicious individuals, and ask them to leave or change their behavior.
3. They can change their own behavior so that they do not become victims of a crime.
4. They can pressure others to act (such as demanding more police resources, lobbying government for services or resources, launching civil suits against slum landlords who turn a blind eye to crime and disorder problems on their property).
5. They can authorize police to act on their behalf.

CASE STUDY 2.9

FIRST- AND SECOND-GENERATION CPTED APPLIED TO THE SAN ROMANOWAY LOW-INCOME APARTMENT BUILDING

Saville and Cleveland (2010, 84–86) describe how second-generation CPTED concepts and strategies were applied to a low-income apartment complex in Toronto (which was initially presented as a case study in Chapter 1).

The preliminary recommendations included improving the lighting, installing boarder fencing to reinforce access control, and improving the on-site maintenance to enhance image. Additional recommendations also included second-generation strategies such as conducting a series of meetings with residents. These meetings ended up in the creation of a permanent local association to coordinate preventive actions and help encourage local cohesion.

Survey results suggested major implications for building social cohesion. Data indicated over 20% relied on welfare or government disability payments to survive, and one in four was unemployed. Over 30% indicated they immigrated to Canada within the past 5 years. Since different cultures have various methods of socializing and different groups tended to cluster in different buildings on-site, community building needed strategies tailored to the site and common to everyone (and not one-size-fits-all social programs).

The foundation document confirmed that access control or natural surveillance strategies, in and of themselves, will have little effect on an environment where residents may not know who is trespassing and may be too fearful to take action. Territoriality must include community building and involvement of residents in order to be effective.

The project team was convinced there were security, physical, and social strategies to bring people together that might have lasting impacts. This required a much stronger sense of social cohesion and community culture, especially if residents were to begin to feel a stronger sense of territoriality and ownership over their own affairs in the neighborhood.

The property owners were reluctant to spend their own resources to implement some of the security or first-generation CPTED changes. Boundary access control fencing and modifications to landscaping were very expensive. However, the tennis court and nearby area fencing was improved. No further extension of the fencing took place, and lighting was also not initially improved due to reluctance to spend funds. However, funds from an outside agency were obtained to build a community garden and also construct a safe playground area for children. This reinforced the importance of connectivity during project work. It also led new project managers to focus exclusively onto second-generation CPTED.

Second-generation CPTED made an impact. For example, since connectivity infers a neighborhood should encourage connections with external agencies, outreach efforts targeted outside funding agencies. Local politicians were brought into the project and appeared during media photo opportunities. Eventually over $500,000 grant funds were directed to San Romanoway, mostly for second-generation CPTED initiatives.

These initiatives include programs such as anger management training, youth mentoring, and computer classes in a new computer room. Additionally they funded a full-time teacher and social worker to help students expelled from school. Community cultural programs include a cultural dance group, tennis clubs, and a homework club. Today, residents themselves work together and participate in the nonprofit association formed by residents called the San Romanoway Revitalization Association to coordinate activities on site.

This section describes an amalgam of the different, but complementary, SCP functions that can be realized through the education and mobilization of people. Promoting a greater vigilance and territoriality of neighborhood residents, exercised primarily through their surveillance of private and public spaces, is at the core of these people-based SCP approaches. Keeping an eye out for suspicious people or activities while going for a walk around the block is just one example of an informal surveillance-based approach to SCP that emphasizes the human touch. The most formal, active, and organized approach to people-centered SCP is NW, where local residents make a commitment to be more vigilant in watching each other's homes and public spaces and reporting suspicious people or activity to police and one another. Thus, at the opportunity-reduction core of NW is surveillance; residents are encouraged to act as the eyes and ears of police by watching out for and reporting suspicious individuals and incidents in their neighborhood. (See Chapter 5 for more details on Neighborhood Watch.)

Another example of situational measures that entails the direct participation of people is citizen patrols, which are generally comprised of community members who walk, bike, or drive around their neighborhood intentionally keeping an eye out for suspicious individuals or activities, checking on property and buildings, and reporting security problems (e.g., open windows, unlocked car doors) to owners and suspicious incidents to the police (Graham, 1995, 65). Citizen patrols can take on different forms: they can be initiated and organized by neighborhood residents, local community groups, and even police; they can be on foot, on bicycles, or in cars; and they can be either formal (whereby residents are organized, trained, and patrol on a set schedule) or informal (residents can be loosely organized into patrols that take advantage of their daily routines). Assessing more than 100 citizen patrols in 15 American cities, Yin et al. (1977) concluded that they resulted in less crime and fear of crime. Latessa and Allen (1980) found that paid citizen patrols in Columbus, Ohio, led to a significant drop in crime in the patrol areas. A review of the literature by Titus (1984) also shows that citizen patrols can reduce burglary rates in patrol areas by 20%–50%. Those conducting patrols are discouraged from intervening in specific criminal acts, which speaks to the predominant danger of citizen patrols that participants might actually confront offenders, which could put them in harm's way. Police also worry about the potential for vigilante action that may stem from citizen patrols.

The most formal of these human-based, opportunity-reduction approaches to crime and disorder is carried out by paid employees: security guards, store employees, concierges, and police. In fact, even under the rubric of community or problem-oriented policing, most preventive and proactive work by police is mostly confined to opportunity-reduction measures. The broken windows theory of Wilson and

---

CASE STUDY 2.10

FORMAL CITIZEN PATROLS IN THE UNITED STATES

The Guardian Angels differ from ordinary citizen patrol groups insofar as they are specially trained, wear a uniform, may physically intervene in criminal acts, and may make citizen arrests. Unlike most citizen patrols, which are generally ad hoc and informally organized, the Guardian Angels are an organized group with branches in a number of cities in and outside the United States. The Guardian Angels are also distinguished from traditional citizen patrols in that the latter are usually made up of residents who walk the beat in their own neighborhood. In contrast, the Guardian Angels recruit individuals for *safety patrols* of high-crime areas that may be outside their own neighborhood (Graham, 1995, 66).

Kenney (1986) found that there was no discernable impact of the Guardian Angels' patrol of New York subway stations compared to other stations that did not have a patrol presence. Kenney argues that this may be because crime was generally too low in these stations for any effect to be detected. An evaluation of the Guardian Angels in San Diego, California, shows they had little impact on crime in the areas they patrolled. Violent crime dropped by 22% in their patrol areas, but there was also a 42% drop in crime in areas where there were no patrols (Pennell et al., 1986). While their impact on crime may be minimal, Pennell et al. (1986) did find that people in the areas patrolled by the Guardian Angels reported greater feelings of safety when the Angels were on duty.

Kelling (1982), described in Section 2.3.5 of this chapter, has influenced certain municipal police forces in North America in their efforts to reduce and prevent crime. Those who subscribe to this theory advocate an approach that targets low-level, highly visible, and/or destabilizing crime problems, rule breaking, bylaw infractions, incivilities, and disorderly acts as a means to restore order and ameliorate an environment that fosters crime. (See Chapter 8 for more details on *broken windows* [order maintenance] policing.)

2.7 OPPORTUNITY-REDUCTION APPROACHES TO VIOLENCE PREVENTION

A limited number of SCP measures have been applied to reducing violent crimes. As mentioned in Section 2.4.1 of this chapter, efforts to control the facilitators of crime and violence have focused overwhelming on guns. One example is gun buyback programs, whereby illegal and legal guns are turned over to police in exchange for money or some other type of material incentive. According to Sherman (1997c, 30), gun buyback programs are based on two hypotheses: "One is that the more guns in a community, the more gun violence there is. There is substantial evidence to support that claim (Reiss and Roth, 1993). The second hypothesis, however, is not supported by the evidence. That hypothesis is that offering cash for guns in a city will reduce the number of incidents in which guns are used in crime in that city." Sherman reviewed four evaluations of gun buyback programs in the United States and concluded that they showed no impact on local gun violence and gun-related crimes. He cites the following reasons why buyback programs may fail to reduce gun violence: "they often attract guns from areas far from the program city; they may attract guns that are kept locked up at home, rather than being carried on the street; potential gun offenders may use the cash from the buyback program to buy a new and potentially more lethal firearm; and the buyback cash value for their old gun may exceed market value substantially" (Sherman, 1997c, 30–31). In addition to gun buyback programs, other initiatives undertaken to control firearms include improving gun safety (such as trigger locks), reducing the availability of guns (such as local or state laws banning gun ownership or carrying concealed weapons), and restricting the ownership, sales, and transfers of guns (Sherman, 2000).

Some countries have pursued more far-reaching measures to control gun violence and gun-related crime, including the implementation of strict gun control laws that operate at the national level and which limit the distribution, ownership, possession, and use of firearms. Canada enacted its first gun control legislation in 1977, which was amended and strengthened in 1991 and 1995. The 1977 Firearms Control Initiative was implemented with the aim of preventing firearm accidents and gun-related crime and violence. Under the initiative, the *Criminal Law Amendment Act of 1977* was introduced, which established regulatory controls on access to and the use of guns. It also increased the power of police to search for and seize firearms where reasonable grounds exist to believe that possession of the firearm poses a safety threat. In addition, the Firearms Acquisition Certificate was introduced, which is required for everyone who owns a firearm. New regulations also required gun owners to receive mandatory training on the safe handling and use of guns as well as federal firearm laws. The Canadian Department of Justice evaluated the effects of the legislation, which included reviewing homicide rates in which guns were and were not involved. The assessment concluded that the gun control initiative contributed to a 55% reduction in homicides between 1977 and 1993 (Department of Justice Canada, 1996, as cited in International Centre for the Prevention of Crime, n.d., 31). In 1995, the Canadian federal government enacted the *Firearms Act*, which some consider the strictest gun control legislation ever brought into force in that country. The legislation required all gun owners to be registered and licensed (which must be renewed every 5 years), set mandatory requirements for the proper storage of all firearms, increased penalties for crimes involving the use of guns, and created the Canadian Firearms Registry, a nationwide database of all legal gun owners. All of these provisions are still in effect today. The one exception is the firearms registry; in 2012, the Conservative Government passed legislation that repealed the requirement to register nonrestricted firearms (long guns).

Gang violence interventions can also include opportunity-reduction approaches, according to Braga and Weisburd (2007, 11–12). "Based loosely on theories and principles of situational (opportunity reduction) crime prevention, one central tenet of gang and gun violence interventions is to address immediate proximate conditions that may create or facilitate opportunities for gang/youth/gun violence to occur. The assumption underlying situational approaches to gang and gun violence is that the latter is partially the result of a rational decision-making process by the offenders."

Lasley (1998, 2) agrees, suggesting that "gangs may choose a particular street to commit a crime because they rationally determine that the way the street is situated provides them with ready access and exit, thereby creating an opportunity to more easily elude arrest." This supposition challenges "the popular notion that gang rivalries are so deep seated, emotionally charged, and irrational that they cannot be mitigated or stopped by specific deterrence measures" (Lasley, 1998, 1–2). Using a problem-oriented approach, effective interventions are contingent on a complete analysis and understanding of the proximate factors that give rise to a particular gang violence problem and then developing a solution that addresses these immediate factors in a particular time and place. For example, an analysis of a gang violence problem may well reveal that much of it is retaliatory in nature or that it is concentrated in certain areas. "As such, police interventions to reduce gang violence may well address relevant features of places, offenders, and victims" (Braga and Weisburd, 2007, 11–12).

One notable situational gang violence prevention strategy is manipulating and managing the design of the physical and built environment to deflect potential offenders. This involves measures that attempt to steer would-be offenders away from a particular location and, more generally, to deter people from the temptation to engage in criminal or disorderly behavior at a particular time or place. The deflection of offenders is an appropriate situational strategy for violence prevention given the public nature of gun violence related to the drug trade and/or gangs. A predominant opportunity-reduction, offender-deflection approach to gang-related gun violence, and drive-by shootings in particular, is street closures. (Other crime prevention measures targeting gangs and gang violence are described in Chapter 4.)

Situational measures have also been introduced to address violence against women. This includes safety audits for women, which "allows participants to identify safe and unsafe spaces and recommend how the unsafe spaces can be improved" (Whitzman et al., 2009, 205), modifications to public transportation systems to make them safer for female passengers for women (Metro Action Committee on Public Violence Against Women and Children, 1989), and the introduction of quick response alarms in households to address domestic violence (Lloyd et al., 1994).

Finally, Mair and Mair (2003, 216–217) summarize the principles underlying the relationship between environmental design, violence, and violence prevention:

- Physical design and immediate situational factors of a place may encourage or inhibit violence.
- Physical design and immediate situational factors can create a sense of territoriality in the legitimate users of a space and induce them to act on that attachment in order to protect against violence and other illegitimate use.
- Modifications can be made to the environment to reduce opportunities for violence by making the commission of the violent event appear more risky, more difficult, less rewarding, and less excusable to the potential offender.
- The effectiveness of specific environmental modifications to reduce violence depends on the type of violence and the particular setting (place, context) in which it occurs.
- Though environmental modifications alone will not prevent all violence in all settings, they offer a promising prevention and control strategy.

CASE STUDY 2.11

DEFLECTING VIOLENT OFFENDERS
THROUGH STREET CLOSURES

In an attempt to prevent a cycle of drive-by shootings by rival gangs in Los Angeles, in 1990, the L.A. Police Department embarked on an experiment to *design out* violence by reducing the opportunities for drive-by shootings to be committed. As part of the Operation Cul-de-Sac (OCDS), traffic barriers were erected at the mouth of streets to block access by automobiles in neighborhoods where drive-by shootings and other gang-related violence were common. Specifically, the intervention site was a 10-block area that had the highest average number of drive-by shootings, gang homicides, and street assaults for L.A. in 1989.

According to Lasley (1998, 2), "OCDS focused on a proximate cause rather than a 'root cause,' with the goal of using traffic barriers to decrease the mobility of rival neighborhood gangs traveling to and from gang crime 'hot spots.' In this way the barriers change the situations in which gangs perceive opportunities to carry out 'hit-and-run' crimes such as drive-by shootings."

As part of the strategy, the LAPD employed a problem-oriented approach that involved collecting and analyzing information on the opportunistic nature of drive-by shootings in order to more strategically and effectively use traffic barriers to prevent violence. "Initial data showed that the majority of violence occurred in hot spots connected to major roadways on the periphery of the neighborhoods. Researchers believed that gangs committed crimes on streets that afforded easy automobile access to crime opportunities and escape from arrest" (Mair and Mair, 2003, 215). As Lasely (1998, 3) explains,

> When police and researchers examined hot spots in the OCDS program area, they found a systematic pattern of opportunity. The majority of drive-by shootings and violent gang encounters occurred in clusters linked to major thoroughfares. To stem the violence, the police closed all major roads leading to and from the identified hot spots by placing standard cement K-rails (freeway dividers) at the end of the streets that led directly to these roads. This reconfiguration, which essentially created cul-de-sacs, was completed within the relatively short period of a week. Later, the K-rails were replaced with fixed iron fences which featured a locked gate that could be opened to permit access by emergency vehicles. Most of the traffic barrier configurations generally allowed one unrestricted roadway entrance/exit point.

An evaluation of the initiative after it had been in effect for 2 years found that "the number of homicides and assaults in the OCDS area fell significantly during the 2 years the program was operating, and rose after it ceased operations, while in the comparison area the level of these crimes remained constant" (Lasely, 1998, 2). Assaults also decreased during the 2-year test period, while they rose after the barriers were removed. The research also indicated that drive-by shootings and other targeted violence were not displaced to other neighborhoods. Moreover, "there is no reason to believe that criminals adapted to the OCDS traffic closures; that is, adjusted their modus operandi to the closures and used the barriers to their criminal advantage" (Lasely, 1998, 4).

2.8 CRITIQUES OF SITUATIONAL CRIME PREVENTION AND CPTED

Despite its widespread popularity and empirically tested effectiveness, the substance of many individual SCP and CPTED assumptions, concepts, and strategies have come under scrutiny. Some question the original suppositions of Jacobs (1961) that crime is deterred with an increase in the number of *eyes on the street*. Studies suggest that increases in public activity are counterbalanced by a lessened sense (diffusion) of responsibility and a diminished ability to judge what is suspicious behavior. As Linden (1990, 34) notes, the "presence of more people does not necessarily increase feelings of community." Maxfield (1987) argues that more people lead to crowding, greater incivilities, and increased cover for many types of crime.

More sophisticated criminals can often circumvent SCP measures. By way of illustration, the security that has been added to credit cards, such as the hologram, was meant to prevent the counterfeiting of cards, yet police cases have turned up fake cards that are the exact replicas, including sophisticated holograms (Calgary Herald, 2002; Canadian Press, 2002). SCP measures, especially target hardening, can provoke an aggressive escalation of offenders, such as the gasoline-fuelled attacks on bullet-proof token booths on the New York subway (Dwyer, 1991). Alternatively, at least one study has shown that environmental design modifications have actually been used by criminals to their own advantage. In a study of 21 crime sites, Atlas (1991) found that offenders use safe design features that maximize surveillance opportunities to spot the police or others approaching the area, report problems to those in command, provide a communications network to warn of approaching police, and erect barriers to slow down police. Atlas argues that as criminals feel more proprietary and responsible for space, they maintain and defend it more. Criminal groups, such as gangs, drug users, and drug dealers, are more likely to exert territorial control over nearby spaces than legitimate users.

SCP's focus on the opportunity portion of the criminal process has come under considerable attack by critics who charge that crime will simply be displaced to another location or to some other time, especially if SCP measures are not practiced widely. "Displacement occurs when offenders change their behavior to thwart preventive actions." A related concept is "adaptation," which "refers to a longer term process whereby the offender population as a whole discovers new crime vulnerabilities after preventive measures have been in place for a while" (Clarke and Eck, 2005, 20). As Clarke (1983, 246) observes, "within easy reach of every house with a burglar alarm or car with an antitheft device are many others without such protection." Waples et al. (2009, 208–209) summarize the different types of displacement that may result from opportunity-reduction measures:

- Spatial/geographical displacement: The same crime is moved from one location to another.
- Temporal displacement: The same crime in the same area but committed at a different time.
- Tactical displacement: The offender uses new means (modus operandi) to commit the same offense.
- Target displacement: Offenders choose a different type of victim within the same area.
- Functional displacement: Offenders change from one type of crime to another, for example, from burglary to robbery.

- Perpetrator displacement: It occurs where a crime opportunity is so compelling that even if one person passes it by, others are available to take their place.

Some of the leading SCP researchers, however, are adamant that opportunity-reduction approaches do not displace crime. One of the "10 principles of crime opportunity theory" put forth by Felson and Clarke (1998, vi) is the following:

> Reducing opportunities does not usually displace crime. Evaluations have usually found little displacement following the implementation of situational prevention. No studies have found displacement to be complete. This means that each person or organization reducing crime can accomplish some real gain. Even crime which is displaced can be directed away from the worst targets, times or places.

In his analysis of evaluations of place-based crime prevention strategies, Eck (2006, 282) concludes, "Reviews of empirical studies find no evidence to suggest that these interventions increase crime by displacing, that there is often no displacement, but when displacement does occur it does not overwhelm other gains from blocking crime opportunities." While Eck adds that "perhaps more displacement would be found if evaluators were more diligent in searching for it," he follows this caveat by stating that "recent studies designed explicitly to detect displacement find little of it." The accumulated evidence on the displacement of crime as a result of opportunity-reducing strategies is more complicated; many situational prevention studies have found evidence of some *partial* displacement (see Clarke, 1997, 28; Brantingham and Brantingham, 2003, 120–121). Finally, based on their review of the literature, Johnson et al. (2012, 348) conclude that the "results are clear: geographic displacement is not an inevitable consequence" of SCP. "In fact, across the studies examined, rarely was it the case that crime increased in the catchment areas following intervention. Rather, in line with previous reviews, crime appears just as likely (or perhaps slightly more so) to decrease in the areas that surround the treatment area following intervention."

Theories about the relationship between design and crime have been criticized at length for their environmental determinism. Critics charge that CPTED proponents give too much weight to the role of the environment in influencing crime and criminal behavior and that social and demographic variables are more important in predicting crime rates. The defensible space theory has been particularly weakened by what many view as an overly optimistic and naive view of the foundation of territoriality and surveillance: neighbor or bystander intervention. No matter how much territoriality is exerted in a particular area, there is no guarantee that people will intervene if they see a criminal event in progress. Latanne and Daley (1970) have suggested that in order to intervene, the public must go through a series of deliberations that may minimize their motivation to intercede. Even when aware of an incident, people frequently decide not to intervene because of the fear of personal injury, the fear of embarrassment of mistakenly intervening in a private quarrel, and the inconvenience of becoming involved (Mayhew, 1981).

Studies have demonstrated that housing units that exhibit defensible space and other CPTED principles have experienced high crime rates, suggesting that personal safety and the security of the home are "affected more dramatically by the predisposition of one's neighbors than by the physical design and layout of the neighborhood" (Moughtin and Gardiner, 1990, 11). For example, in a study of 66 neighborhoods in Baltimore, Maryland, Taylor et al. (1984) found that the apparent strong link between design and crime disappeared after they controlled for the social status variable. On the prevention side, Hope (1984, 54–55) argues that Newman's defensible space theory is inadequate because it oversimplifies the complex relationship between local social interaction and cohesion on the one hand and the built environment on the other:

> The built environment actually influences crimes such as burglary only in conjunction with social and perceptual processes. These include: offender's residential proximity to their targets; offenders' perceptions of risk and reward; the social patterns and preferences which the built environment reflects; and the patterns of activity which building design facilitates or inhibits. All these create a complex web of relationships which suggest that it is both difficult and unrealistic to seek a simple, relatively independent relationship between building design and burglary.

Although the link between design features and the actual act of intervention is still not completely understood, proponents of defensible space are also vague about the process by which residents come to define spaces as their territory and act to defend it. There is still a lack of hard evidence that environmental design promotes the essential requisites of the social behavior required to maximize territoriality, sense of community, a desire to intervene in criminal situations, or other behavioral expressions of informal social control. Newman's theory of the *latent territoriality* of people, derived from popularized versions of animal psychology, is said to grossly misinterpret the process that leads to residents' exercising control over their environment. This must be seen as a *social* process, which can vary according to different factors and circumstances, rather than a universal human quality influenced by physical design (Hope, 1984, 46). SCP may, in fact, undermine the collective underpinnings of community crime prevention because there is a tendency for people to rely on individualistic, target hardening approaches (the fortress mentality) at the expense of collective measures.

For Merry (1981), environmental design only has the potential for invoking informal social control or releasing defensive behavior under certain social conditions. These conclusions are based on that author's efforts to try to understand the conditions under which residents of an American inner-city housing project act and fail to act to defend both architecturally defensible and indefensible spaces. Merry studied a four-story building that reflected several of the design factors recommended by Newman, yet it had the highest per-capita robbery and assault rates in the city. She substantiated this finding by highlighting the heterogeneous ethnic composition of the residents, which helped create "a neighborhood of strangers" (the subtitle of her 1981 book). Few friendships stretched across racial or cultural lines, and each of the groups harbored strong and often negative stereotypes of the others. Thus, for Merry, what accounted for the undefended defensible space was the lack of social cohesion of its residents, attributed primarily to ethnic fragmentation. She asserts that while design can provide preconditions for effective control, it cannot create such control if the social fabric of the community is fragmented. Merry made a critical distinction between space that is *defensible* and space that is actually *defended* and in doing so corroborated earlier conclusions in this field: physical design may establish the preconditions for citizens to exercise social control (defensible space), but it cannot guarantee such behaviors (defended space). As Merry (1981, 398) notes, while poor design may facilitate crime, good design will not necessarily prevent it; thus, "defensible space design appears to be a necessary, but not a sufficient condition for crime prevention" (Merry, 1981, 420). To his credit, Newman's later theories acknowledged the mediating role that social variables play in the relationship between environmental design and crime. Second-generation CPTED explicitly recognizes the importance of building social cohesion and collective efficacy before environmental design can truly contribute to community safety.

Another critique of SCP and CPTED is that they are not always congruent with other design and planning priorities. For example, while tall high-rise buildings can be considered a poor design concept as far as promoting defensible space is concerned, they are viewed favorably by environmentalists because the high-density design counters urban sprawl. Limiting access and exit control within buildings can also go against fire emergency design principles. Surveillance, especially surveillance cameras in public places, can be highly intrusive and may infringe upon people's privacy.

Finally, critics of SCP charge that opportunity-reduction measures fall seriously short of the more fundamental need to address the social causes of criminal behavior. For SCP and CPTED ignore the problems and inequalities within society that give rise to crime and criminal behavior, which concentrates such problems within disadvantaged neighborhoods or certain demographic groups. Moreover, the redesign of a built environment can be expensive and, as such, can only be afforded by the middle class and the rich, which may contribute even further to the concentration of crime in poor communities. Civil rights advocates have also argued that police approaches that are based on the broken windows theory target and infringe upon the civil rights of the most vulnerable (e.g., the homeless, the mentally ill) or the most harassed (racial minority groups, youth) groups in society.

2.9 CONCLUSION

SCP is intended to "make specific locations unattractive for offenders to commit crimes. These interventions do not necessarily result in the arrest or incarceration of offenders, nor do they usually assist in the rehabilitation of offenders. They may not even keep offenders away. They just make offenders less willing to choose to commit crimes at the location where these interventions are deployed" (Eck and Guerette, 2012, 355).

Fuelled in part by the positive evaluations of SCP measures, SCP theories, research, and strategies have been applied to a wide range of other criminal problems, including child sexual abuse (Wortley and Smallbone, 2006; Terry and Ackerman, 2008), riots (Verma, 2007), terrorism and political extremism (Shaftoe et al., 2007; Ekici et al., 2008), corporate and economic crime (Alvesalo et al., 2006), organized crime (Van de Bunt and Van der Schoot, 2003), Internet-based crimes (Newman and Clarke, 2003; Morris, 2004; Taylor and Quayle, 2006), and illegal drug markets (Natarajan and Hough, 2000).

In his analysis of findings from the National Crime Survey, Lab (1990) identifies the most popular crime prevention measures undertaken by survey participants in the United States as surveillance (informally and through programs like NW), avoiding certain parts of a city at certain times, locks, property marking, alarms, peepholes on doors, and personal security (e.g., mace). Using information from the 1994 British Crime Survey, Lab and Hope (1998) found that the most popular security measures in that country were taking precautions in the evening, NW, technological security measures, target hardening, and self-defense (as cited in Lab, 2004, 80).

In a comprehensive analysis of studies concerned with "preventing crime at places" (which only includes the management of the physical environment, and not the human environment), John Eck concludes that "blocking crime opportunities at places reduces crime in many circumstances. Over 90 percent of the interventions reported evidence of crime reduction following the installation of an opportunity-blocking tactic." These findings are consistent across a number of evaluations, and in some cases, the reductions were large (Eck, 2006, 281). In one comprehensive meta-analysis of crime prevention measures published in the late 1990s, Eck and Sherman et al. (1998, 9) contend that "there are as yet no place-focused crime prevention programs proved to be ineffective" (although they concede that more rigorous studies are needed). One community-based situational measure that Sherman and colleagues did suggest was ineffective was that of gun buyback programs. This conclusion was based on a review of such programs implemented and evaluated in St. Louis and Seattle, which failed to reduce gun violence in those cities (Sherman et al., 1998, 8). According to one review of the empirical research (Sherman et al., 1998), among those SCP measures that have been proven to work are the following:

- Target hardening
- Improved street lighting
- CCTV systems
- Civil remedies (or the threat of civil actions) against landlords for not address-ing drug problems on the premises (which reduces drug trafficking in privately owned rental housing)
- Street closures, barricades, and rerouting, which have reduced several types of crime, including burglary, homicides, and violent crime
- Addition of a second clerk at convenience stores, which may reduce robberies in stores that have already been robbed (but probably does not prevent rob-beries in convenience stores that have never been robbed)
- Redesigning the layout of retail stores to reduce shoplifting
- Proper training and management of bar and tavern staff to reduce violence at licensed premises
- Metal detectors to reduce the number of weapons being brought into schools (although they do not necessarily reduce assaults within or outside schools)
- Airport metal detectors or sky marshals, which reduce airplane hijackings

Based on his review of the research, Welsh (2007, 28) identifies only three types of place-focused programs that have been found to be effective in preventing crime: (1) nuisance abatement, (2) CCTV surveillance cameras, and (3) improved street lighting.

Contrary to critics who contend SCP and CPTED simply displaces crime, according to Clarke and Eck (2005) "researchers looking for displacement have sometimes found precisely its reverse."

> Rather than finding that crime has been pushed to some other place or time, they have found that crime has been reduced more widely than expected, beyond the intended focus of the measures ... These are all examples of the "diffusion of benefits" resulting from crime prevention measures. It seems that potential offenders may be aware that new prevention measures have been introduced, but they are often unsure of their precise scope. They may believe the measures have been implemented more widely than they really have, and that the effort needed to commit crime, or the risks incurred, have been increased for a wider range of places, times, or targets than really is the case. This means that diffusion can take several forms, paralleling the different kinds of displacement ... Diffusion of ben-efits is a windfall that greatly increases the practical appeal of situational crime prevention, but we do not yet know how to deliberately enhance it. One important

method may be through publicity. A publicity campaign helped to spread the benefits of video surveillance cameras across an entire fleet of 80 buses in the North of England, although these were installed on just a few of the buses.

Clarke and Eck (2005, 24)

Partially as a result of criticisms that SCP does not address the root causes of crime in society, advocates of SCP and CPTED measures contend that, ideally, they should be implemented as part of, and work best in the context of, a comprehensive approach to crime and disorder problems (Royal Canadian Mounted Police, 1985; Crowe, 1991). At the very least, crime prevention interventions should employ a wide range of situational measures. For example, in his study of CCTV in parking garages, Tilley (1993) suggests that its effect appears to be enhanced when complemented by other strategies, such as lighting, fencing, the deployment of visible security personnel, access control, and signs alerting people to the presence of a CCTV system. Gardiner (1982, 44–45) sums up this need for a comprehensive approach to (situational) crime prevention:

> If solutions are to be found, it is necessary to first understand the basic environmental organization of neighborhoods and the complex series of causes and effects that allow the occurrence of opportunity crimes. To respond to these complex problems requires a range of reinforcing solutions, both physical and social—in other words, a comprehensive environmental approach. This concept of multiple reinforcements is contrary to the unfortunate tendency to look for single, simple answers to complex problems. The neighborhood environment is dynamic and ever-changing. Overdependence on any one tool, whether law enforcement, social, or physical, will not only fail but will ultimately diminish the effectiveness of the tool being used.

2.10   DISCUSSION QUESTIONS AND EXERCISES

1. Review the crime causation theories upon which SCP theories and approaches are based. Do they provide a plausible foundation for SCP theories and strategies? What are the strengths and weaknesses of these crime causation theories as a foundation for the theory and practice of SCP?
2. Walk around your neighborhood and describe physical characteristics that you believe increase the opportunity for a crime to occur. Walk around your neighborhood and take pictures of examples of design principles that adhere to CPTED.
3. Critics charge that SCP simply deflects crime to another time and place and that it does not address the root causes of the problem. How would you defend SCP in the face of such criticism? Do you believe that the design of the physical environment can actually affect people's behavior in those spaces? Do you believe that design can help motivate people to assume more interest in the safety of their neighborhood?
4. SCP is not without controversy. Research and discuss some of the more controversial claims in recent years, such as (1) gun control laws (consider whether they prevent gun-related violence and infringe upon the individual's right to bear arms in America and whether such infringement should be considered for the sake of collective safety and security) and (2) the use of CCTV cameras, especially on public streets.

2.11   IMPORTANT TERMS

Access and exit control
Administrative criminology
Broken windows
Citizen patrols
Closed-circuit television
Crime Prevention through Environmental Design
Defensible space
Environmental criminology
Exit/entrance screening
Hierarchy of space
Informal social control
Neighborhood watch
Offender search theory
Opportunity reduction
Physical environment
Private space/public space/semiprivate space
Rational choice theory
Routine activity theory
Situational crime prevention
Surveillance
Target hardening
Target removal
Territoriality

FURTHER READING

Atlas, R.E., Ed., *21st Century Security and CPTED: Designing Critical Infrastructure Protection and Crime Prevention*, CRC Press, Boca Raton, FL, 2013.

Braga, A.A., High crime places, times, and offenders, in *The Oxford Handbook of Crime Prevention*, Welsh, B.C. and Farrington, D.P., Eds., Oxford University Press, New York, 2012, Chap. 16, pp. 316–336.

Colquhoun, I., *Design out Crime: Creating Safe and Sustainable Communities*, Architectural Press, Oxford, U.K., 2004.

Crowe, T., *Crime Prevention through Environmental Design*, 2nd edn., Butterworth-Heinemann, Oxford, U.K., 2000.

Eck, J.E. and Guerette, R.T., Place-based crime prevention: Theory, evidence, and policy, in *The Oxford Handbook of Crime Prevention*, Welsh, B.C. and Farrington, D.P., Eds., Oxford University Press, New York, 2012, Chap. 18, pp. 354–383.

Johnson, S.D., Guerette, R.T., and Bowers, K.J., Crime displacement and diffusion of benefits, in *The Oxford Handbook of Crime Prevention*, Welsh, B.C. and Farrington, D.P., Eds., Oxford University Press, New York, 2012, Chap. 17, pp. 337–353.

Knutsson, J. and Clarke, R., Eds., *Putting Theory to Work: Implementing Situational Prevention and Problem-Oriented Policing* (Crime Prevention Studies, Vol. 20), Criminal Justice Press, Monsey, NY, 2006.

Smith, M.J. and Clarke, R.V., Situational crime prevention: Classifying techniques using 'good enough' theory, in *The Oxford Handbook of Crime Prevention*, Welsh, B.C. and Farrington, D.P., Eds., Oxford University Press, New York, 2012, Chap. 15, pp. 291–316.

Smith, M.J. and Cornish, D.B., *Theory for Practice in Situational Crime Prevention* (Crime Prevention Studies, Vol. 16), Criminal Justice Press, Monsey, NY, 2003.

Von Hirsch, A., Garland, D., and Wakefield, A., *Ethical and Social Perspectives on Situational Crime Prevention* (Studies in Penal Theory and Penal Ethics), Hart Publishing, Oxford, U.K., 2004.

Wilson, J. and Kelling, G., Broken windows, *Atlantic Monthly*, pp. 29–38, March 31, 1982.

INTERNET RESOURCES

Clarke, R., Ed., *Situational Crime Prevention: Successful Case Studies*, 2nd edn., Harrow and Heston, Albany, NY, 1997, http://www.popcenter.org/library/reading/PDFs/scp2_intro.pdf.

CPTED Ontario, http://www.cptedontario.ca/.

Design Centre for CPTED Vancouver, http://www.designcentreforcpted.org/.

International CPTED Association, http://www.cpted.net/.

Newman, O., *Creating Defensible Space*, U.S. Department of Housing and Urban Development, Office of Policy Development and Research, Washington, DC, 1996, http://www.defensiblespace.com/book.htm.

Rutgers University, School of Criminal Justice, Crime Prevention Services for Business, http://crimeprevention.rutgers.edu/index.htm.

Rutgers University, School of Criminal Justice, Crime Prevention Service, Strategies and Case Studies, http://crimeprevention.rutgers.edu/topics.htm.

Taylor, R.B. and Harrell, A.V., *Physical Environment and Crime*, National Institute of Justice, Washington, DC, 1996, http://www.ncjrs.gov/txtfiles/physenv.txt.

CHAPTER 3

CRIME PREVENTION THROUGH SOCIAL DEVELOPMENT

CONTENTS

3.1   LEARNING OBJECTIVES

By the end of this chapter, you should have a better understanding of the following:

- Theories regarding the root causes of criminal behavior and how they relate to crime prevention through social development (CPSD)
- Factors that put children and youth at risk of future criminal behavior
- Differences between personal risk factors and social environmental risk factors
- Underlying philosophy and theory of CPSD
- Concept of *resilience* and its importance to CPSD
- Dominant CPSD approaches and their essential elements
- Differences between CPSD interventions that *directly* or *indirectly* target an at-risk child or youth
- Key players (institutions) in delivering CPSD services and programs
- CPSD program design and implementation principles
- Critiques of and challenges facing CPSD

3.2   INTRODUCTION

This chapter focuses on social developmental approaches to crime prevention, that is, theories and strategies that attempt to address the root causes of criminal and delinquent behavior.

Research shows that many chronic offenders come from some type of disadvantaged background. Crime prevention through social development (CPSD) interventions operate on the premise that the root causes of criminality are often a combination of social environmental risk factors (e.g., parental neglect or abuse, poverty, negative role models, inadequate schools) and personal risk factors (e.g., behavioral, neurological, cognitive, psychological, and mental health problems). As such, CPSD relies on targeted, problem-solving strategies (ideally during childhood) to reduce, eliminate, or offset these *criminogenic risk factors*. Given the aforementioned root causes, CPSD interventions are directed toward one of two (complementary) targets: an at-risk child's deleterious social environment (e.g., by promoting more positive and effective parenting) or the young person's personal risk factors (e.g., through tutoring, mentoring, life skills training, mentoring, cognitive–behavioral therapy [CBT]). In other words, the protective factors delivered through CPSD interventions can either benefit the child indirectly (by nurturing a positive social environment) or directly (by nurturing the child's personal resilience). Despite these conceptual differences, an ideal social problem-solving strategy for at-risk children and youth is one that addresses both social environmental and personal risk factors while being sufficiently individualized to each child's unique set of circumstances.

CPSD interventions also target older youth and young adults. One goal of criminality prevention programs for youth is to foster their personal development through a positive socialization process and integration into their local communities. On a practical level, this means providing meaningful educational, recreational, and employment opportunities. It also means ensuring that young people are made to feel useful, appreciated, and of value while making certain there are clear, fair, consistent, and meaningful consequences for their actions (good and bad). Education and employment-based programs, including high school completion and job training and placement, are the most common CPSD approaches for older youth and adults. For chronic teenage and adult offenders, therapy delivered in the community has proven to reduce recidivism. (CPSD interventions for youth and young adults, including recidivism prevention, are described in Chapter 4.)

In general, developmental approaches that contribute to, or directly focus on, criminality prevention can be divided into four categories:

1. *Basic, commonly accepted practices and social institutions*: The most important tools that societies have to stem delinquency, criminality, and other forms of antisocial behavior are well-functioning and stable social institutions, in particular: families, schools, communities, the health-care system, the labor market, and the local economy. Loving and nurturing parents, vibrant and peaceful neighborhoods, universal educational opportunities, good schools, a robust economy that provides for gainful employment, an accessible health-care system, civic engagement in social and political affairs, and a tolerant society that respects diversity and guarantees basic human rights are the best measures to prevent the onset of criminal behavior in any society.

2. *Universal social welfare policies and services*: Since at least the end of World War II, many governments have fostered and fortified the aforementioned social institutions and practices through social welfare policies and programs. Many of the welfare programs delivered by governments (e.g., education, health care, unemployment insurance, financial support for families) were never meant to address crime. Yet, these policies and programs can play a key role in the prevention of delinquent, criminal, and other antisocial behaviors by contributing to the long-term positive development, socialization, and prosperity of children, young people, and adults so that they can become stable, prosperous, and contributing members of society.

3. *Programs and services targeting disadvantaged families*: This category includes programs and services for disadvantaged families and communities and includes free or subsidized health care, day care, preschool programs, meals, after-school programs, remedial education, job training, and financial support. As with the universal social welfare practices and services described earlier, these targeted programs are not specifically concerned with criminality prevention but can play an important role as such by promoting the positive development and socialization of disadvantaged (at-risk) children and youth.

4. *Targeted CPSD interventions*: This category includes strategies and programs that have been developed specifically to address children, youth, and adults who are at risk of (future) delinquent and criminal behavior. CPSD interventions overlap with programs and services that target disadvantaged families but also include services and programs that have been developed specifically to address criminogenic risk factors, such as social competency skills training, CBT, and recidivism prevention.

The remainder of this chapter is concerned with exploring the theoretical tenets, strategies, and specific programs that fall under the rubric of CPSD (while also examining relevant programs and services that target disadvantaged children, youth, families, and communities).

3.3 ETIOLOGICAL (CRIME CAUSATION) THEORIES UNDERLYING CPSD

CPSD is informed by certain assumptions and theories regarding what causes the onset of criminal, delinquent, and/or antisocial behaviors. This section discusses some of the criminality causation theories that have been used as a foundation for CPSD theories and strategies. It is important to note that just as there is no one cause of crime, there is no one etiological* theory that can adequately or comprehensively account for the causes of criminal behavior. With that said, one of the common themes linking the theories presented in the following is that the causes and facilitators of criminal behavior are overwhelmingly rooted in the immediate social environment of a child, youth, or adult. In other words, criminality is not the product of an inherently pathological individual; instead, for at-risk children and youth, it is more accurate to say that it is the immediate social environment that is pathological. With that said, there is an emergent body of theories and research indicating that certain personal risk factors (e.g., neurological issues, cognitive deficits, mental health disorders) that can contribute to criminal behavior. The implications of these etiological theories for CPSD are that to prevent the onset of criminal behavior, interventions must target both dysfunctional social environments and personal risk factors.

3.3.1 Anomie and Strain Theory

The French sociologist Emile Durkheim introduced the concept of anomie in his book *The Division of Labor in Society*, which was first published in 1893. He used the term *anomie* to denote the breakdown of certain norms and rules that dictate how people should behave with one another. For Durkheim, anomie refers to a state where social norms are confused, unclear, or rejected by people. Crime and deviance are seen as a product of anomie; a lack of commonly held norms leads to deviant behavior in society. Some people may adapt and internalize values and behaviors that do not conform to the conventional norms. This is most likely to occur in environments characterized by rapid social change, complexity, and relative social disorganization, where familial, communal, and social controls become increasingly ineffective in exerting a positive conforming influence. Like many sociologists, Durkheim's thinking was a reflection of his times; in the late nineteenth century, Europe and North America were undergoing great transformations, due to industrialization, urbanization, and international migration. Durkheim argued that rapid changes and transformations in a society contributed to a destabilization of that society. This leads to a breakdown in commonly accepted

---

* *Aetiology/n./(U.S. etiology): (1) The assignment of cause or reason to help explain a certain phenomenon. (2) The philosophy of causation. (3) Med. The science of the causes of disease.*

norms (*anomie*), which in turn facilitates the rise of deviant and criminal norms. While Durkheim's theories were a product of his times, he was one of the first scholars to suggest that criminal and antisocial behavior may be provoked, in part, by social conditions.

Robert Merton postulated a theory of crime that continued Durkheim's tradition of locating the causes of deviance in the broad social environment. His strain theory suggests that society, through conflicts and contradictions between its goals and the means to attain them, exerts a pressure on some people to behave in deviant and criminal ways. Strain may result when people experience the contradiction between goals that they are expected to achieve (e.g., material wealth) and the opportunities available to them to actually achieve those goals. Some people may experience strain, reject conventional norms, and turn to crime when they are blocked from achieving the goals that society promises them (Merton, 1938). Merton's theories are most apparent when we consider how those social and economic goals that are held in the highest esteem in Western societies are often unequally distributed (due to racism, anti-Semitism, gender bias, regional disparities, lack of local economic opportunities, etc.). This argument is epitomized by the culture-defining *American dream*, which urges all citizens to succeed while distributing the opportunity to succeed unequally (Figure 3.1). When the channels of vertical mobility are closed or narrowed in a society that places a high premium on economic affluence and social advancement, criminal behavior may result. In other words, criminality stems, in part, from a lack of opportunities available to certain members of society who have been implicitly promised such opportunities. This is of central importance in understanding the motives and drives of those situated in the underclass, the poor, ethnic or racial minorities, immigrants, and others who may feel excluded but who have at the same time embraced the omnipresent cultural value of material success. Merton says that people at the bottom of the economic

Figure 3.1
Louisville Flood Victims, the 1937 photo by Margaret Bourke White, graphically symbolizes the historical relevance of anomie/strain theory in America. (Courtesy of Margaret Bourke-White/Life Magazine © TimePix, https://docs.google.com/presentation/d/1-28gQSx-e8YjSXIaWg9B6QOReG Hqptlmyg7C8uUoLi8/edit#slide=id.i56.)

ladder may resort to crime to succeed if that drive is strong enough and if their sense of frustration is acute enough. People turn to crime to realize success because it is the goal that is important, not the means used to reach that goal.

One of the goals of social developmental programs is to alleviate the preconditions for strain in society by providing at-risk children, youth, and adults with the behavioral, emotional, academic, vocational, and social skills necessary to (1) take advantage of the opportunities available in society to succeed and prosper, (2) avoid the deviant behavior that may result from feelings of strain, and (3) resist feelings of frustration that may result from blaming external forces—society, others, fate, chance, and luck—rather than their own actions for any lack of success in their lives.

3.3.2   Differential Association Theory

According to the differential association theory, criminal behavior is not simply a reaction to blocked aspirations or an instinctive response to frustration. For Sutherland (1973), just as individuals will tend to conform if their socialization emphasizes a *respect* for prevailing norms, so they will tend to become deviant if their socialization emphasizes *contempt* for these norms. An underlying assumption of this theory is that many social behaviors are learned (especially during the formative childhood and teenage years), and this is no different for deviant and criminal behavior. For Sutherland, a criminal orientation is not solely based on thwarted opportunities. The tendency to turn to crime can be bolstered if the *frustrated* individual lives in an environment where deviant and criminal behavior can be observed, learned, and emulated—primarily through associations with others, especially those from intimate personal groups such as the family, peer networks, or role models who are involved in deviant and/or criminal activities. The more one is surrounded by individuals who are contemptuous of the prevailing cultural norms and laws (and who *teach* or indoctrinate such violations intentionally or unintentionally to the neophyte), the greater the probability the *student* will follow in similar footsteps. In short, criminal and other forms of deviant behavior are often learned via a sustained social contact and interaction with those already committed to law breaking or other forms of deviant behavior and also because of their relative isolation from those committed to obeying the law (Kelly, 1987, 19; Volk and Schmalleger, 2005, 383).

This is an exceptionally powerful theory in criminology because the more we learn about the causes of criminal behavior, the more we realize that chronic offenders came from negative childhood backgrounds where they were exposed to, learned from, and emulated poor role models (i.e., *monkey see, monkey do*). As discussed in the following, children whose parents are abusive are at a higher risk of being abusive and violent themselves. Young people living in impoverished neighborhoods may want to follow in the footsteps of a high-profile local drug dealer because he appears to be the richest and most successful person on the block. Teenagers who hang around with offenders are at a higher risk of becoming offenders themselves (through peer pressure). Some argue that violent television programs, movies, or video games may also teach children and young people to be more violent. All the aforementioned examples have one thing in common:

deviant and criminal behaviors are observed and learned by children and young people, especially those who grow up in dysfunctional social environments and who are exposed to poor role models.

Informed by the differential association theory, a paramount CPSD strategy is nurturing a positive social environment for at-risk children and youth. Most importantly, this entails promoting a loving and stable family life in which parents model prosocial behavior and employ positive parenting skills (which can be instilled through parental training or family therapy programs). Alternatively, CPSD strategies may involve placing at-risk children and youth in a more positive social environment (such as foster homes, sports leagues, summer camps) to offset a negative family or community environment. Mentoring programs that expose children and youth to positive adult role models, like Big Brothers/Big Sisters, are also meant to offset a child's negative home life and poor familial and community role models. Some CPSD programs attempt to enhance the *resilience* of children and youth to help them withstand a negative family and community environment by fostering their critical thinking, problem-solving, and coping skills.

3.3.3 Social Learning Theory

Within the field of criminology, social learning theory is closely associated with differential association theory as both are premised on the assumption that behavior is learned from one's social environment and that deviance is often brought about by observing the behaviors of others within that environment. As such, social learning theory "explains human behavior in terms of continuous reciprocal interaction between cognitive, behavioral, and environmental influences" (Bandura, 1977, vii).

Bandura (1962, 1975) and Bandura and Walters (1959) adapted existing social learning theories to explain aggressive behavior among children. He argued that aggression and violence are not intrinsic to any individual; instead, this behavior is influenced by (and learned from) family members, the media, and their social environment in general. In particular, he believed that aggression is learned through a process called *behavior modeling* (also called *vicarious learning*) in which children are *trained* to act aggressively and use violence by modeling their behavior upon that of adults who display aggression and act violently. Displays of aggression and violence by parents is considered the most prominent source of such behavior modeling, as these individuals are the most intimate and influential people in the life of a child. Bandura reported that children are more apt to use the same aggressive tactics their parents use when dealing with other individuals or circumstances in their lives. For example, children who have been abused or have witnessed spousal abuse are at higher risk of replicating that behavior later in life. This replication occurs because children will have learned to use aggression and violence as a means to control behavior or to solve conflicts or other problems (i.e., it becomes a natural response or coping mechanism). If the violence witnessed by a child or youth appears to solve a problem, this positively reinforces the efficacy of such behavior in the eyes of an impressionable child. In sum, learning, behavioral modeling, and positive reinforcement are all believed to help form and maintain aggressiveness and violent behavior, especially in the context of certain family dynamics (Brezina, 1998). Bandura (1977) believed that if aggression was diagnosed early in a child's life, that child would be less at risk of future violent behavior.

Similarly, the cycle of violence theory (Widom, 1989a,b) purports that the violent victimization of children, especially physical abuse perpetrated by caregivers, can increase the likelihood of subsequent violent behavior during adolescence. Widom's longitudinal research examining the short- and long-term effects of child physical abuse found that victims were significantly more likely than those without records of childhood abuse to be arrested for violent crimes during adolescence and young adulthood (Widom, 1989b; Maxfield and Widom, 1996). Wright and Fagen (2013) cite other recent studies that have established a correlation between child abuse and subsequent violent behavior.

Most CPSD programs targeting aggression and violent behavior assert that such behavior (or the preconditions thereof) can be prevented and/or treated through targeted interventions. These interventions include inculcating such skills as anger management, conflict resolution, positive problem solving, empathy, impulse control, and the ability to proactively recognize and anticipate the consequences of negative (violent) behavior.

3.3.4 Control Theory/Social Bond Theory

In the late 1960s, sociologist Travis Hirschi developed a theory of criminality that focuses not on why people commit crime but why people do not. Through his social bond theory, Hirschi (1969) contends that crime needs no special motivation. Rather, there is a need to explain why people do *not* commit crime. The answer to this question lies in the concept of social control. Through social bonds, society encourages individuals to forego their selfish motivations and conform to certain rules and norms. Without social bonds, people are at higher risk of pursuing their selfish interests, which may lead to criminal behavior. Gottfredson and Hirschi (1990) suggest that self-control, internalized early in life, determines an individual's ability or inability to resist crime. For some, criminal behavior fulfills short-term gratification. By implication, law-abiding people do not fall victim to the seduction of criminal behavior because of a strong sense of self-control, which allows them to resist such antisocial temptations. As such, low self-control arises from defective socialization; those who exhibit antisocial behavior are more likely not to have received effective socialization early in life.

Hirschi (1969) identifies four social control variables—attachment, commitment, involvement, and belief—each of which represents a significant bond that encourages positive socialization by inculcating certain values in children and youth as they grow up. Ties with and *attachments* to parents, the family, peers, and other important institutions such as the school and the local community are viewed as the most important bond that results from the positive socialization of a child. The quantity and quality of time a child and parent(s) spend together, their feelings toward one another, their level of intimacy, as well as bonding and mutual identification represent some key determinants of the attachment variable. Hirschi also found that an inability to do well in school is indirectly linked with delinquency. Intellectual, cognitive, and academic problems can result in poor school performance, which can lead to a dislike of school and a rejection of teachers and authority. In turn, this can increase the risk of delinquency. In short, weak ties and attachments to parents and schools undermine a positive socialization process, which can inhibit self-control and increase impulsivity, placing an individual at higher risk for deviant or criminal tendencies.

There are at least two implications of control theory for CPSD. The first is the importance of interventions that nurture the bonds between a young person and his or her parents as well as other important social institutions, in particular schools. The second implication centers on the importance of impulse control in criminality prevention initiatives. A theoretical premise of some CPSD programs is that chronic offenders tend to have a low level of self-control, are impulsive, poor problem solvers, and imprudent risk takers and do not think through the consequences of their actions. Regardless of the causes of these social competency deficits, all are said to contribute to delinquent, criminal, and violent behavior. Central to CPSD interventions are those that directly address low self-control by promoting impulse control, critical thinking, problem-solving skills, the assumption of personal responsibility, and the recognition and anticipation of the consequences of one's actions.

3.3.5 Developmental Criminology: Identifying Risk Factors among Children and Youth

CPSD is greatly informed by the field of developmental or *life-course* criminology. David Farrington, a scholar who specializes in longitudinal studies of criminal careers, argues that "offending is part of a larger syndrome of antisocial behavior that arises in childhood and tends to persist into adulthood" (Farrington, 2007, 603). Research shows that chronic offenders differ considerably from nonoffenders in the prevalence of criminogenic risk factors in their childhood, adolescence, and adulthood. Farrington (2007, 604) defines risk factors as "prior factors that increase the risk of occurrence of the onset, frequency, persistence or duration of offending." He cites research from a number of countries showing that "many risk factors for offending are well established and highly replicable." By way of example, he summarizes two longitudinal surveys in London and Pittsburgh (Farrington and Loeber, 1999) that reveal numerous "personal and social environmental predictors of delinquency over time and place, including impulsivity, hyperactivity, attention problems, aggressiveness, a low educational attainment, poor parental supervision, parental conflict, an antisocial parent, a young mother, poverty, and a dysfunctional family" (Farrington, 2007, 604). Similarly, Waller and Sansfaçon (2000, 5) write:

> ... large-scale longitudinal surveys on both sides of the Atlantic have studied how the development of individuals from birth to adulthood affects their propensity to be involved with crime. Studies have shown that a small group of individuals (5 to 10 percent) accounts for most offenses (50 to 70 percent) committed each year. Researchers have concluded that youth exposed to any or all of the following conditions are more likely to commit delinquent acts than those who are not: relative poverty and inadequate housing, inconsistent and insufficient parental or guardian guidance, limited social and cognitive abilities, exclusion from school, family violence, few opportunities for employment and economic exclusion, a culture of violence.

CASE STUDY 3.1

CONTROLLING IMPULSES THROUGH A BOARD GAME

The Franklin Learning Systems Company of Westport, Connecticut, markets the *Impulse Control* board game (Figure 3.2), which is for children in grades 2–8. The game teaches specific skills to help players control their impulses and to make good decisions through deliberative thought (while having fun in the process). According to the facilitator booklet (Franklin Learning Systems, Inc., 2007, 1) that comes with the game, players will learn "(1) to understand the benefits of impulse control; (2) to evaluate alternatives before acting; (3) to use self-talk to build their impulse control; (4) to look at likely consequences of their actions; (5) the benefits of delayed gratification; and (6) to read social cues, so that they will know when to stop and think before acting."

Like many board games, players are given a token (in this case a car) and are instructed to make their way through a maze of roads to get to the finish line. Players roll the dice to determine how many spaces along the road they can move their car. At each intersection of the maze/road they have to make a decision regarding the best route. The game board is designed so that the easy way to the finish line is not always the optimal route. Some routes to the finish line are shorter but contain a number of hazards (represented by road signs). For example, a yield sign means that the player must go back two spaces. Therefore, players must avoid rash decisions, evaluate their options, and select their routes in a way that anticipates the potential consequences of each.

To do well in the game, players are forced to plan ahead, which includes making decisions only after the consequences of their moves have been considered. The game also compels players to apply impulse control and problem-solving skills to their own life. This is accomplished by game cards that are read by each player after landing on a designated space along the road. These game cards require the player to participate in scientifically proven techniques to help with impulse control: (1) stop and think about the consequences of certain actions (e.g., "You are getting into the lunch line at school and have the impulse to cut in front of someone who is not paying attention. STOP and THINK. What might happen?"),

Figure 3.2
The Impulse Control board game. (From Research Press Publishers, https://www.researchpress. com/books/599/impulse-control-game, accessed July 20, 2014. With permission.)

(2) generate multiple solutions to problems (e.g., "You have a classmate who keeps bumping your desk when he walks by. Name two to three solutions to this problem"), (3) practice self-talk out loud (e.g., "Say out loud two times, My impulse control helps me be a better listener. Then tell about a time when you were a good listener"), (4) practice delayed gratification (e.g., "You can take one point right now or you can have two points at the start of the next turn. It's your choice"), (5) practice stopping an activity (e.g., "Hum something until the person on your left tells you: STOP"), and (6) read social cues (e.g., "Ask the player opposite you to make an angry face. MIRROR it back to him, paying special attention to what he does with his mouth and eyes"). By fulfilling the request of the card, a player earns points (which are meant to work as an incentive). Players can win the game in one of two ways: by getting to the finish line first or by accumulating the largest number of points.

More recently, a survey of youth in custody in the United States by Sedlak and McPherson (2010) indicates that most suffer from a range of risk factors, including a learning disability, academic failure, family breakup, foster care placement, and homelessness.

Just because a young person may be suffering from one or more risk factors does not mean that criminal behavior is inevitable. It simply means that these children and youth are at a higher risk of offending compared to others who are more fortunate. The probability of becoming a chronic offender will depend upon the type of risk factors present, when the risk factors emerge during their life, how long they persist without being treated, and how many there are. Regardless, the risk factors that may give rise to future criminality are highly individualized. As Wasserman et al. (2003a, 2) put it, "although some risk factors are common to many child delinquents, the patterns and particular combination of risk factors vary from child to child." In general, the risk factors underlying delinquent and criminal behavior can be demarcated into two broad categories:

1. *Social environment*: Risk factors produced by a deleterious social environment that surrounds an individual or a group. Family risk factors are generally considered the most influential of all social environmental risk factors.
2. *Personal*: Neurological, cognitive, behavioral, psychological, mental health, and physiological factors that may or may not be influenced by an individual's social environment.

Those factors that researchers correlate with a high risk of developing future criminal behavior can be divided into five categories, as depicted in Box 3.1.

Risk factors can also be distinguished based on whether they are *static* or dynamic. Static risk factors are *historical* in the sense that they are rooted in the past and therefore the facts or existence of these risk factors cannot be changed. Examples of static risk factors may include early antisocial behavior, neglect or abuse by parents, episodes of substance abuse, or prior criminal history. Dynamic risk factors are those that continue to be part of an individual's *daily experiences* (Milkman and Wanberg, 2007, xxv) and that are amenable to change through deliberate interventions. This may include anger management issues, impulsivity, negative peer networks, or a mental health disorder, among others.

3.3.5.1 Personal Risk Factors A certain degree of misbehavior, experimentation, or independence seeking is common among children and youth (Kelly et al., 1997). But children who persistently and progressively exhibit problem behaviors, are diagnosed with a psychological or mental health disorder, or significantly underachieve in their

BOX 3.1

CHILDHOOD RISK FACTORS FOR FUTURE JUVENILE AND ADULT OFFENDING

Personal Risk Factors

- Sociobiological factors (neuropsychological or cognitive deficits, prefrontal or frontal deficits, low resting heart rate, alcohol fetal syndrome)
- Early antisocial behavior/conduct problems (aggressive behavior and anger management problems)
- Low self-control, impulsivity
- Poor problem-solving, critical thinking, and abstract reasoning skills; inability to recognize and anticipate the consequences of one's actions; failure to consider positive solutions to problems
- Low levels of empathy
- Psychopathology
- Certain psychological disorders (e.g., oppositional defiance disorder, conduct disorder, ADHD)
- Certain mental health disorders (paranoid schizophrenia)
- Substance abuse
- Academic failure, lack of commitment to schools, truancy, school exclusion, dropping out of school

Family Risk Factors

- Parent characteristics
  - Parental psychopathology
  - Criminality and deviance
  - Substance abuse
  - Family violence (spousal abuse)
  - Parental conflict
- Parenting practices
  - Conflict with children
  - Harsh or erratic parenting skills
  - Poor parental supervision
  - Neglect
  - Coldness/rejection
  - Physical or sexual abuse/child maltreatment
- Family characteristics
  - Large family
  - Family disruption and breakup
  - Low socioeconomic status/poverty

School/Academic Risk Factors

- Unchecked bullying, harassment, and violence within school settings
- High absentee rate, frequent expulsion from school, and dropping out of school
- Overreliance on reactive, punitive disciplinary techniques
- Lack of support and evidence-based measures for struggling students

Community Risk Factors

- Neighborhood disadvantage/*disorganized* neighborhoods
- Poor housing and neighborhood conditions
- Negative role models
- Concentration of delinquent peer groups
- A high rate of localized crime and violence
- Availability of crime facilitators (drugs, guns, liquors stores)
- Lack of local employment opportunities

Peer Risk Factors

- Association with deviant peers
- Spending a large amount of unsupervised time with peers
- Peer rejection
- Involvement with gangs

Situational Risk Factors

- Involvement in drug trafficking
- Access to weapons

Sources: Loeber, R. and Stouthamer-Loeber, M., Family factors as correlates and predictors of juvenile conduct problems and delinquency, in *Crime and Justice*, M. Tonry and N. Morris, Eds., University of Chicago Press, Chicago, IL, 1986, pp. 29–149; Blackburn, R., *The Psychology of Criminal Conduct*, Wiley, Chichester, U.K., 1993; Gottfredson, D.C., School-based crime prevention, in *Preventing Crime: What Works, What Doesn't, What's Promising*, A Report to the United States Congress, L.W. Sherman et al., Eds., National Institute of Justice, Washington, DC, 1997, Chap. 5; Kelly, B.T. et al., *Developmental Pathways in Boys' Disruptive and Delinquent Behavior*, Office of Juvenile Justice and Delinquency Prevention, Washington, DC, 1997; Wasserman, G.A. et al., Risk and protective factors of child delinquency, Child delinquency bulletin series, Office of Juvenile Justice and Delinquency Prevention, Washington, DC, April 2003, http://www.ncjrs.gov/pdf-files1/ojjdp/193409.pdf; National Institute on Drug Abuse, *Preventing Drug Abuse among Children and Adolescents. A Research Based Guide for Parents, Educators and Community Leaders*, U.S. Department of Health and Human Services, Washington, DC, 2003; Bor, W. et al., *Aust. N. Z. J. Psychiatry*, 38, 365, 2004; Farrington, D.P., Childhood risk factors and risk-focused prevention, in *The Oxford Handbook of Criminology*, 4th edn., M. Maguire, R. Morgan, and R. Reiner, Eds., Oxford University Press, Oxford, U.K., 2007, pp. 602–640; International Centre for the Prevention of Crime, *International Report Crime Prevention and Community Safety: Trends and Perspectives*, ICPC, Montreal, Quebec, Canada, 2008; Savignac, J., *Families, Youth and Delinquency: The State of Knowledge, and Family-Based Juvenile Delinquency Prevention Programs*, National Crime Prevention Centre, Ottawa, Ontario, Canada, 2009; Farrington, D.P. et al., Risk and protective factors for offending, in *The Oxford Handbook of Crime Prevention*, B.C. Welsh and D.P. Farrington, Eds., Oxford University Press, Oxford, U.K., 2012, pp. 70–88.

academic studies are at risk of criminal and other antisocial behaviors later in life. The personal risk factors discussed in the following include those that research has shown to correlate strongly with future delinquent and criminal behavior. These risk factors are grouped into the following categories: early antisocial behavior; hyperactivity; low self-control/impulsiveness; poor problem-solving and abstract thinking skills; low levels of empathy; poor academic achievement, underdeveloped cognitive skills, learning disabilities; and mental health disorders.

3.3.5.1.1 Early Antisocial Behavior Antisocial behavior and conduct problems occurring during childhood and adolescence entail "a range of behaviors that are related to such constructs as delinquency, aggression, violence, disruptive behaviors, and externalizing disorders" and have a "far-reaching effects on future life-course outcomes," according to Litschge et al. (2010, 21, 22). For Wasserman and colleagues (2003a, 2), the early onset of antisocial behavior (including various forms of oppositional defiance, rule breaking, aggression, violence, theft, and vandalism) may be the best predictor of later delinquency while early and persistent aggressive behavior may be the single most significant behavioral trait in predicting delinquency before the age of 13. Thornberry et al. (2004, 14–15) cite a body of research suggesting, "youth who start their delinquency careers before age 13 are at higher risk of becoming serious and violent offenders than those who start their delinquency careers later."

The implications of conduct problems are particularly deleterious if they begin during childhood, are persistent, and continue into adolescence. While it is quite normal for adolescents to occasionally engage in antisocial acts, "persistent and serious forms of antisocial behavior place youth at greater risk for imprisonment and political disenfranchisement, family disruption, unemployment, and drug dependence" (Litschge et al., 2010, 21). Lösel and Bender (2012, 102–103) cite research showing "Approximately one-third of the early antisocial children continue their problem behavior into youth, and this group has a particularly high rate of serious and persistent offending… Early conduct problems are also with sound predictor of other psychiatric problems later in life." According to the Promising Practices Network on Children Families and Communities (2002), three principal factors are associated with early onset of antisocial behavior:

> The first factor is neurodevelopmental impairment of the fetus. Children of women who engage in risky behaviors (cigarette, alcohol, and drug use) are more at risk for this kind of impairment. The second factor is dysfunctional care giving, which generally refers to an inadequate parental provision of material and emotional care. The third factor is maternal life-course development. Children of women who are on welfare, are unmarried, are high school dropouts, or who have three or more children are more likely to have reported behavioral problems.

3.3.5.1.2 Hyperactivity Studies suggest that hyperactivity is a strong predictor of future delinquency and offending (Farrington et al., 1990; Brennan et al., 1993; Klinteberg et al., 1993; Lynam, 1997; Bor et al., 2004). Moreover, the risks of future delinquent and criminal behavior can be heightened when hyperactivity is combined with other behavioral disorders, such as attention deficit problems (leading to attention deficit hyperactivity disorder [ADHD]) or impulsivity (hyperactivity impulsivity attention deficit disorder [HIAD]). Studies show that a large number of children with ADHD self-report delinquent behavior by early adolescence and that delinquent youth diagnosed with or displaying symptoms of ADHD and HIAD are at risk of becoming chronic and even violent adult offenders (Satterfield, 1987; Farrington et al., 1990; Moffitt, 1990; Farrington, 1991). Some researchers believe that impulsivity interacts with neighborhood factors to influence juvenile offending. For example, one study showed that impulsive boys were at greatest risk for delinquent and criminal behavior in Pittsburgh's poorest neighborhoods, compounded perhaps by lower levels of parental supervision and informal social controls (Loeber and Hay, 1994; Browning and Loeber, 1999). These psychological disorders can also indirectly lead to future delinquent, criminal, and other antisocial behaviors by destabilizing a child's academic performance and cognitive abilities (through their inability to focus in school and difficulty in understanding abstract concepts), by undermining their ability to interact with others (leading to peer rejection and social exclusion), and by contributing to aggressiveness. Other research suggests that hyperactivity is not a good predictor of future delinquency if resulting conduct problems are controlled for. Lahey et al. (2000) suggest that hyperactivity can lead to delinquency, but only when it occurs along with defiant or aggressive behavior. This suggests that like many other psychological, cognitive, or behavioral risk factors, hyperactivity is not a direct cause of delinquency or criminality but can indirectly lead to such behavior (by contributing to poor performance in school, an inability to make friends, aggressiveness, etc.).

3.3.5.1.3 Low Self-Control/Impulsiveness According to Farrington (2007, 611), "impulsiveness is the most crucial personality dimension that predicts offending." Citing the extant literature, Doran et al. (2012, 751) state, "researchers have suggested that early childhood impulsivity is typically the first step on the developmental pathway toward delinquency, substance use, and criminality." Some researchers believe that impulsivity interacts with neighborhood factors to influence juvenile offending. For example, one study showed that impulsive boys were at greatest risk for delinquent and criminal behavior in Pittsburgh's poorest neighborhoods, compounded perhaps by lower levels of parental supervision and informal social controls (Loeber and Hay, 1994; Browning and Loeber, 1999). As previously discussed, low self-control and impulsiveness are key determinants in criminology's social bond theory (Hirschi, 1969) and associated self-control theories (Gottfredson and Hirschi, 1990).

3.3.5.1.4 Poor Problem-Solving and Abstract Thinking Skills This category includes any deficits that may inhibit an individual's ability to preface his/her actions with a deliberative process of critical or creative thinking, problem solving, consequence recognition, and a search for the most positive option to pursue. In other words, there is an insufficient link between thinking (deliberation) and behavior (action). Many studies suggest that chronic and serious offenders are reactive, impulsive, unnecessary risk takers who do not think through the consequences of their actions. Underlying these cognitive and behavioral deficits are poor problem-solving skills and the inability or unwillingness to reason abstractly, think ahead, envision positive solutions to a particular problem, or learn from experience (Blackburn, 1993, 204–209).

3.3.5.1.5 Low Empathy The argument has been made that low empathy is a personality trait common among offenders, with the assumption being that "people who can appreciate or experience a victim's feelings (or both) are less likely to victimize someone" (Farrington, 2007, 610). Thus, a lack of empathy is seen as a risk factor among children and youth for future delinquency, offending, and violence. Farrington (2007, 612) writes:

> Offenders are often said to be self-centred and callous, with low empathy. They are relatively poor at role-taking and perspective-taking, and may misinterpret other people's intentions. Their lack of empathy, awareness or sensitivity to other people's thoughts and feelings impairs their ability to form relationships and to appreciate the effects of their behaviour on other people. They show poor social skills in interpersonal interactions, fidgeting and avoiding eye contact rather than listening and paying attention.

Farrington makes the distinction "between cognitive empathy (understanding or appreciating other people's feelings) and emotional empathy (actually experiencing other people's feelings)." In one meta-analysis of 35 studies comparing empirical measures of empathy with official recorded measures of delinquent or criminal behavior, Jolliffe and Farrington (2004) found that low cognitive empathy positively correlates with offending, but low *emotional empathy* was only weakly related. "Most importantly, the relationship between low empathy and offending was greatly reduced after controlling for intelligence or socio-economic status, suggesting that they might be more important risk factors or that low empathy might mediate the relationship between these risk factors and offending" (Farrington, 2007, 610).

3.3.5.1.6 Poor Academic Achievement, Underdeveloped Cognitive Skills, and Learning Disabilities Research shows that poor cognitive development, academic performance, educational achievement as well as a lack of attachment to schools are all significant risk factors for future criminal offending (Farrington, 1990; Farrington and West, 1993; Maguin and Loeber, 1996). All of these risk factors can set in motion a chain of negative events and conditions later in life (e.g., academic failure, persistent truancy, dropping out of school, chronic unemployment, association with antisocial peers), which can then potentially lead to criminality, violence, and other antisocial behaviors.

Academic failure has been defined as "the failure to acquire skills sets expected to be learned and the failure to acquire official documentation of achievement by the school system" (Spiebelger, 2004, 2). The most detrimental culmination of academic failure is when a young person drops out of school or has been the subject of multiple expulsions or a permanent expulsion. Research reveals a strong correlation between academic failure, on the one hand, and delinquent, criminal, and violent behavior among adolescents and adults (Mayor's Task Force on Safer Cities, 1992; LeBlanc et al., 1993; Maguin and Loeber, 1996; Hawkins et al., 1998; Lipsey and Derzon, 1998; Office of Surgeon General, 2001; Felson and Staff, 2006; Samaha, 2006, 64; Farrington and Welsh 2007; World Health Organization, 2010). Herrenkohl and colleagues (2001, 223) note that children and youth with "low academic performance, low commitment to school, and low educational aspirations during the elementary and middle school grades are at higher risk for child delinquency…"

Other studies show a correlation between academic failure and violence. In their report reviewing violence prevention research, the World Health Organization (2010, 35) concludes that low academic achievement and truancy are risk factors for violent behavior. The FBI estimates that increasing the high school graduation rate in the United States from 71% to 81% would prevent more than 3,000 murders and nearly 175,000 aggravated assaults each year (Federal Bureau of Investigation, 2006).

Howell (2010, 7) cites studies that establish a relationship between a student's level of academic achievement and gang membership. Poor school performance on math tests, for example, predicts male gang membership (Thornberry et al., 2003). Future gang members perform poorly in elementary school and generally have a low degree of commitment to and involvement in school (Le Blanc and Lanctot, 1998; Hill et al., 1999) as well as a weak attachment to teachers (Thornberry et al., 2003).

In its review of criminogenic risk factors, the John Howard Society of Alberta (1995) writes, a "significant factor associated with risk of criminality is poor school performance or failure to thrive in school, often leading to early school leaving." Indeed, statistics and empirical research have established a strong correlation between dropping out of school or expulsion and formal contact with the criminal justice system (Wald and Losen, 2003; Rocque and Paternoster, 2011). In the United States, one study estimates that high school dropouts are 3.5 times more likely to be arrested than those youth who have graduated from high school (Catterall, 1985), while another estimates they are eight times more likely to be incarcerated (Bridgeland et al., 2006).

Wald and Losen (2003) use the terms "prison track" and "school-to-prison" pipeline to epitomize the relationship between academic failure and incarceration, which is corroborated by the following revealing American statistics:

> Approximately 68 percent of state prison inmates in 1997 had not completed high school. Seventy-five percent of youths under age eighteen who have been sentenced to adult prisons have not passed tenth grade. An estimated 70 percent of the juvenile justice population suffer from learning disabilities, and 33 percent read below the fourth grade level. The single largest predictor of later arrest among adolescent females is having been suspended, expelled, or held back during the middle school years.
>
> **Wald and Losen (2003, 11)**

For Kim et al. (2010, 4), the school-to-prison pipeline is the result of "the confluence of education policies in under resourced public schools and a predominantly punitive juvenile justice system that fails to provide education and mental health services for our most at-risk students and drastically increases the likelihood that these children will end up with a criminal record rather than a high school diploma."

The causal relationship between academic failure and criminal behavior is complex and multifaceted. In the short term, dropping out of school means young people have less adult supervision, while in the long term, adults without a high school diploma often lack the skills necessary to find work in the labor market, thereby increasing the risk of becoming involved in criminal endeavors to make a living. Siegel and Welsh (2011) contend that academic failure leads to emotional and psychological problems, which can contribute to antisocial behavior. Students who fail school often feel frustrated and rejected. As a result, they believe that they cannot achieve success through conventional means, such as school or the legitimate labor market. They are also at a higher risk of associating with others exhibiting similar antisocial behavior. For Zamora (2005, 42), the "school failure hypothesis suggests that the failure experienced in school by juveniles with learning disabilities is the first of many negative experiences that will result in delinquency because of the development of a negative self-image."

3.3.5.1.7 Mental Health and Substance Abuse Disorders Mental health disorders can increase the risk of offending, recidivism, violence (both self-directed and interpersonal), and other antisocial and risky behaviors, such as substance abuse and homelessness. In one large study that employed standardized mental health assessments, Copeland et al. (2009) found that children with behavior disorders were more likely to offend in young adulthood compared to children without such disorders.

According to Kinscherff (2012, 1), in the United States, it has been "well established that a high prevalence of youth who come into contact with the juvenile justice system have significant mental health needs." Of the more than 2 million children, youth, and young adults who come into formal contact with the youth justice system, research shows that a substantial proportion (between 65% and 70%) have at least one diagnosable mental health need, and between 20% and 25% have serious emotional issues (Kinscherff, 2012, i). One influential study conducted by Shufelt and Cocozza (2006) estimated that 55% of the young men and women who had formal contact with the juvenile justice system in the United States had two or more co-occurring mental health diagnoses. Similar estimates were produced by Teplin and colleagues (2006), who found that nearly two-thirds of males and three quarters of females in juvenile detention facilities had a mental health disorder, and Wasserman et al. (2010), whose research showed that close to 65% of incarcerated American youth met the criteria for a mental health disorder.

This means that youth who have been incarcerated in the United States are far more likely to have one or more mental health disorders compared to youth in the general population (Vermeiren et al., 2006; Colins et al., 2010; Wasserman et al., 2003b, 2010). Citing past literatures, Hoeve et al. (2013, 289) estimate that mental health disorders affect about 15% of American adolescents. According to Hoeve et al. (2013, 289), while "prevalence figures for mental health problems differ across types of juvenile justice setting" in the United States, there is a higher rate of mental health disorders among those youth who have more frequent contact with the justice system or are subject to more severe sanctions (i.e., commit more serious offenses). Further, "several studies have found that youth with mental health concerns are more likely to reoffend, but findings with regard to reoffense severity are lacking" (Hoeve et al., 2013, 290). Common diagnoses among youth in the American juvenile justice system include anxiety disorders, mood disorders, schizophrenia, antisocial personality disorder, attention deficit disorders, substance abuse disorders, depression, and trauma disorders (Fazel et al., 2009; Kinscherff, 2012, 7–11).

Substance use disorders (SUDs) in youth are also strongly "associated with aggression, delinquency, and involvement with the juvenile justice and mental health systems," according to Doran et al. (2012, 748). In one large study, Schubert et al. (2011) found that incarcerated young offenders with a SUD were more likely to reoffend compared to incarcerated youth without one, even when controlling for criminogenic factors (in particular, peer influence and antisocial history). "While evidence indicates etiological overlap, SUDs also confer risk for aggression and delinquent behavior. SUDs and aggression are each influenced by executive functions that develop as youth transition toward adult roles. Additionally, the effects of substance use on the adolescent brain impair neurocognitive function and increase the risk for aggression and further substance use" (Doran et al., 2012, 748). In regard to treatment, Doran et al. (2012, 748) argue that youth with SUDs "tend to be underserved, particularly when they are also involved with the juvenile justice system."

3.3.5.2 Family (Parental) Risk Factors As discussed, the family figures prominently in some of the most powerful etiological theories of criminal and violent behavior. The family environment, and parenting practices in particular, can have a significant influence on the future delinquency and criminality prospects of a child. Families that are at higher risk of producing criminal offenders are characterized by parents who are antisocial or criminal; practice poor child-rearing methods (poor supervision, no rule setting, coldness and rejection, a lack of involvement with their children); and impose physical or inconsistent punishment, abuse, maltreat, or neglect their children (Tremblay and Craig, 1995, 158). Savignac (2009, 3) groups family environmental risk factors into three categories: (1) family dynamic and functioning (bad parenting practices, lack of supervision, parental criminality, family violence, child mistreatment, parental substance abuse), (2) family characteristics (single-parent families, large families, broken families), and (3) area of residence (living in socially disadvantaged neighborhoods).

According to Loeber and Stouthamer-Loeber (1986), the four main clusters of family influences that increase the risk of offending are "(1) neglect, where parents spend little time interacting with and supervising their children, (2) conflict, where parents exert inconsistent or inappropriate discipline and one party rejects the other, (3) deviance, where parents are themselves involved in offending and/or condone law-breaking, and (4) disruption, where neglect and conflict arise from marital discord and the breakup of the marriage, with the subsequent absence of one parent (usually the father)" (as cited in Graham, 1995, 17). Farrington (2007, 613) classifies family risk factors into five categories: (1) criminal and antisocial parents, (2) large family size, (3) child-rearing methods (poor supervision, poor discipline, coldness and rejection, low parental involvement with the child), (4) abuse (physical or sexual) or neglect, and (5) disrupted families. Inadequate parenting practices are among the most powerful predictors of early antisocial behavior among children and particular types of negative or inadequate child-rearing methods can place a child at heightened risk of future delinquency, criminality, and other antisocial behavior. Wasserman et al. (2003a, 5) contend that there are three specific parental practices that correlate strongly with early conduct problems: (1) a high level of conflict with a child, (2) poor supervision of a child, and (3) a low level of positive involvement with a child.

3.3.5.3 School Risk Factors This category of risk factors is concerned with the school not only as the main educational institution in the lives of young people but also as a critical socializing institution. Indeed, because schools play such an important role in the socialization of children, they can also contribute to antisocial behavior. Based on their review of the relevant literature, Wasserman and colleagues (2003a, 9) write:

> When schools are poorly organized and operated, children are less likely to value their education and do well on academic tasks and more likely to experience peer influences that promote delinquency and opportunities for antisocial behavior (Gottfredson, 2001). For example, schools with fewer teacher resources and large enrollments of students have higher levels of teacher victimization by pupils. Teacher victimization is also higher in schools with lower cooperation between teachers and administrators and with poor rule enforcement. Furthermore, poor rule enforcement within schools has been associated with higher levels of student victimization. Disciplinary problems are also more common in schools with less satisfied teachers.
>
> **Ostroff (1992)**

Gottfredson et al. (2006, 56) identify several school-related precursors to delinquency that have been identified by research:

> These factors include characteristics of school and classroom environments as well as individual-level school-related experiences and attitudes, peer group experiences, and personal values, attitudes, and beliefs. School environment factors related to delinquency include availability of drugs, alcohol, and other criminogenic commodities such as weapons; characteristics of the classroom and school social organization such as strong academic mission and administrative leadership; and a climate of emotional support. School-related experiences and attitudes that often precede delinquency include poor school performance and attendance, low attachment to school, and low commitment to schooling. Peer-related experiences, many of which are school-centered, include rejection by peers and association with delinquent peers. And individual factors include early problem behavior, impulsiveness

or low levels of self-control, rebellious attitudes, beliefs favoring law violation, and low levels of social competency skills such as identifying likely consequences of actions and alternative solutions to problems, taking the perspective of others, and correctly interpreting social cues.

In sum, schools that are poorly organized and governed when carrying out their basic mandate to educate and graduate students, as well as positively socialize children and youth, can contribute to the onset of delinquency and criminality, especially when failing to adequately cater to struggling students and at-risk children and youth.

3.3.5.4 Neighborhood and Community Risk Factors The neighborhood is another social environmental focal point for situating the causes and facilitators of criminal characteristics; there may very well be something about a neighborhood that shapes and influences both the local crime rate and the root causes of criminality. In other words, some neighborhoods may be breeding grounds for criminal behavior due to ecological conditions. Community-based criminogenic risk factors include concentrated poverty, poor housing, physical deterioration, rapid population turnover, instability, the availability of weapons and drugs, a high concentration of unemployed and undereducated young males, and the absence of strong local institutions, social cohesion, and informal social control.

As part of their highly influential research beginning in the 1930s, sociologists at the University of Chicago found that crime and delinquency in the city occurred in areas characterized by "social disorganization," which includes inadequate housing; physical deterioration; a large percentage of immigrant, non-white, and lower income families; and a rapid turnover of the population. As a result of this social pathology and the absence of strong positive local institutions, children were considered ineffectually socialized and controlled, leading to their rejection of social norms and the acceptance of alternative values (i.e., delinquency and crime). In turn, delinquent traditions became established and passed on within that neighborhood (Shaw and McKay, 1931, 1942).

Within this context, the prevailing idea is that crime results from a breakdown of community life. This school of thought is very much a reflection of the aforementioned theories (anomie, strain, differential association, social learning), all of which are highly relevant to poor, high-crime neighborhoods. As Farrington (2007, 619) writes, "adolescents living in physically deteriorated and socially disorganized neighborhoods disproportionally tend also to come from families with poor parental supervision and erratic parental discipline and tend also to have high impulsivity and low intelligence." In other words, uneven development, social disorganization, strain, and differential association are concentrated and most intense in disadvantaged neighborhoods, where local institutions—the family, schools, faith-based groups, police, and even the community itself—are too weak to exert a positive socializing influence. This, in turn, leads to an environment that nurtures crime and delinquency.

Since the pioneering work of the Chicago School of Sociology, numerous studies have established that children who are raised in poor families and neighborhoods are at greater risk for delinquency and criminality than children raised in relatively affluent families or neighborhoods. Poverty and related negative circumstances at the neighborhood level are also viewed as a contributor to antisocial behaviors among children and youth. Levels of informal social control are often much lower in disadvantaged neighborhoods, allowing for criminal and disorderly actions to go unchecked. Children and youth living in such neighborhoods are more frequently exposed to norms favorable to criminality, which fosters a negative socialization, especially when regularly surrounded by *successful* criminal role models such as drug dealers or gang leaders (Sampson and Lauritsen, 1994; Elliott and Menard 1996; Sampson et al., 1997; Morenoff et al., 2001; Nicholas et al., 2005; Wang, 2010).

3.3.5.5 Peer Group Risk Factors   Young offenders tend to have friends who are also involved in delinquent and criminal activities. The influence of peers on delinquency and criminality usually appears later in an individual's life compared to personal or family risk factors. Two of the most significant criminogenic risk factors related to peer influences are associating with deviant peers and rejection by one's peers. Wasserman et al. (2003a, 6–7) conclude that three interdependent risk factors combine to account for chronic offending during the teenage years: (1) the individual's own antisocial tendencies, (2) the negative consequences of peer rejection that can result from these tendencies, and (3) the resulting deviant peer associations. Wasserman and colleagues believe that peer influence has an impact on delinquency in two ways: (1) it can initiate offending of relatively "late starters" and (2) it can lead to the escalation of serious offending among the "early starters."

3.3.5.6 Biosocial Risk Factors   Given its dominant sociological underpinnings, the discipline of criminology has traditionally focused on the role of one's social environment in promoting the onset of delinquent and criminal behavior. And while empirical research strongly supports theories postulating a causal relationship between social environment risk factors and criminality, there is a growing body of literature suggesting that genetics and biology may also play a role in promoting or hindering antisocial and criminal behavior. However, this literature emphasizes one decisive caveat: "biological influences do not exist in a vacuum and the social context must always be taken into account" (Wilson and Scarpa, 2012, 366). Indeed, Walsh and Beaver (2009, 80) are unequivocal when they write, "Let us make it clear that there is no such thing as a strictly biological theory of criminality; all theories of human behavior that integrate biological insights are biosocial." This biosocial criminology "is a perspective that takes seriously the fact that any meaningful human action is always the result of individual propensities interacting with environmental instigation" (Walsh and Beaver, 2009, 79). For Wilson and Scarpa (2012, 366), the result of theorizing and research that examines "the interaction effect between biological and social influences" is a "more holistic picture of criminal behavior." As such, "criminologists should strive to create an integrative model of criminality that addresses both the more traditional sociological factors, in addition to the biological correlates…" (Wilson and Scarpa, 2012, 377).

Moffitt (1993) was one of the first contemporary criminological theorists to postulate how biological and social environmental risk factors interact to foster criminality. In her prominent theory of life-course persistent offending, she argues that serious and chronic offenders are the product of neuropsychological deficits (e.g., due to genetics or a brain injury), combined with a dysfunctional and adverse family environment (e.g., abuse, neglect, deviant parents).

Walsh and Beaver (2009) contend that other leading sociological theories of criminality causation, such as anomie/strain theory, social learning theory, and differential association theory, could explain more robustly and rigorously the onset of criminal behavior if biological variables are taken into consideration. A study by Wright and Beaver (2005) challenged Gottfredson and Hirschi's (1990) assertion that low self-control arises from defective socialization (i.e., that parents are primarily responsible for their children's self-control). Their study did find a "modest relationship between parental practices and children's self-control," but this relationship "disappeared when genetic information was added" (Walsh and Beaver, 2009, 81). Indeed, according to Rocque et al. (2012, 308), "while criminologists often think of impulsivity and negative emotionality as personality traits, research has indicated that they have biological underpinnings," including genetics or even brain impairment. "For example, impulsive homicides are associated with reduced glucose metabolism in the prefrontal cortex, a part of the brain involved in the control and regulation of behavior." Wright and Beaver (2005, 1190) conclude, "for self-control to be a valid theory of crime it must incorporate a more sophisticated understanding of the origins of self-control." In support of this conclusion, Lilly et al. (2007, 110) state, "research suggests that parents may affect levels of self control less by their parenting styles and more by genetic transmission." While it is still unclear whether low self-control or a high rate of impulsivity is caused by biological factors, social environmental conditions, or a combination of the two, the aforementioned conclusions highlight the dangers of relying solely on a sociological perspective in criminology. Furthermore, it epitomizes the argument made by proponents of a more biologically informed approach to understanding the causes of criminality: "not using genetically informed methods leads researchers to misidentify important causal influences" (Walsh and Beaver, 2009, 81).

The identification of biological risk factors is especially important given the research demonstrating that "the relationship between physiological factors and anti-social behaviors is stronger in individuals who do not have sociological risk factors" (Wilson and Scarpa, 2012, 367). This is what is called the "social push hypothesis," which argues, "if an antisocial individual is not exposed to social risk factors that would 'push' him or her towards antisocial behavior, then physiological influences will likely better account for his/her antisocial tendencies" (Wilson and Scarpa, 2012, 367). The biological determinants of this social push hypothesis may help explain why certain individuals, who come from stable, loving, supportive, privileged backgrounds, engage in delinquent and criminal activity. (See Chapter 4 for a discussion on biosocial theories as to why adolescents are disproportionately involved in crime and violence.)

There are numerous studies demonstrating the salience of a biosocial approach in understanding the causes of criminal behavior, many of which illustrate the correlation between deficits in brain functioning and criminal or antisocial behavior. As Rocque et al. (2012, 307) explain,

> One of the strongest correlates of later criminal behavior (and other life-course problems) is neuropsychological or cognitive deficits in childhood... Individuals with cognitive deficits may have trouble conforming to social expectations and delaying gratification or adjusting to society... Low intelligence is likely (in part) a function of generalized cognitive impairment across a number of neurocognitive domains.... These deficits are associated with behavioral difficulties early in childhood (e.g., conduct disorder) that tend to extend throughout the life course.

The causes of neuropsychological or cognitive deficits have been traced to specific parts of the brain (e.g., the frontal lobe) "and are thought to be caused in part by events early on in fetal or child development (e.g., in utero drug or alcohol use)." Alternatively, "some forms of cognitive deficits appear to be caused later in child development, for example, by trauma events or experiencing abuse" (Rocque et al., 2012, 307). According to Adams (2010, 2), youth who have experienced trauma sometime in their lives

> ... may be more likely to be involved in illegal behavior for a variety of reasons, including the neurological, psychological and social effects of trauma. A growing body of research in developmental neuroscience has begun to uncover the pervasive detrimental effects of traumatic stress on the developing brain. The majority of brain development is completed during the first five years of life, with the most critical development occurring within the first two years. Brain structures responsible for regulating emotion, memory and behavior develop rapidly in the first few years of life and are very sensitive to damage from the effects of emotional or physical stress, including neglect.

Wilson and Scarpa (2012, 374) state, "A considerable amount of research has been dedicated to pinpointing the functional and structural brain differences of individuals who engage in criminal behavior."

> For example, some of the areas that have been identified as impaired in antisocial populations include the dorsal and ventral regions of the prefrontal cortex, amygdala, hippocampus, angular gyrus, and posterior cingulate ... Of note, there is some overlap between the areas that have been identified as impaired in criminal populations and those areas identified as related to moral cognition and emotionality. Specifically, the antisocial, violent, and psychopathic behaviors observed in criminals may in part stem from deficits in the areas of the brain related to moral reasoning and emotions (e.g., dorsal and ventral prefrontal cortex, amygdala).

The use of medical technology, in particular functional magnetic resonance imaging (MRI), has helped to increase an understanding of the relationship between structural abnormalities in the brain and serious and chronic criminal offending. Studies conducted at the King's College Institute of Psychiatry in London that scanned the brains of men convicted of murder, rape, and violent assaults found strong evidence of structural abnormalities in their brains. The study revealed that psychopaths, who are characterized by a profound lack of empathy, had less gray matter in the parts of the brain that are critical to understanding and appreciating the emotions of other people (Kellan, 2012).

Other biological factors have been identified as potential causes of antisocial and criminal behavior. Wilson and Scarpa (2012, 367) summarize studies showing that "antisocial individuals tended to have lower resting heart rates than nonantisocial individuals" and that a "low resting heart rate as a risk factor of antisocial behavior is particularly strong in individuals who do not have sociological risk factors." The authors provide two theories as to why a low resting heart rate may lead to antisocial and even criminal behavior. The first is the *sensation seeking theory*, which argues, "criminals are chronically underaroused, as evidenced by their lower resting heart rates, which leads them to engage in stimulating activities to increase their arousal level to a more optimal level" and these "stimulation seeking tendencies may make these individuals more likely to engage in behaviors, such as violence or crime" (Wilson and Scarpa, 2012, 372). The second explanation is *fearlessness theory*, which contends that people with a lower resting heart rate have a lower level of fear. In turn, individuals with a lower level of fear are more willing to take more danger-inducing risks and are "less likely to be influenced by social constraints, such as punishment" (Wilson and Scarpa, 2012, 373). For Wilson and Scarpa (2012, 373), both the sensation seeking and fearlessness theories represent "the intersection of biological mechanisms, social and personality factors, and criminal behavior."

While the research and theorizing in the field of biosocial criminology has yet to produce a robust biosocial crime prevention body of knowledge, findings show that developmentally-based interventions for at-risk young people "likely have myriad effects on biological risk factors" (Rocque et al., 2012, 310). In particular, programs and services that seek to improve the social environment of the child or youth (e.g., a more positive family environment) and/or nurture personal protective factors (e.g., cognitive and social competency skills), have been held out as effective preventative approaches to biosocial risk factors. In particular, early intervention programs, such as enriched pre-school programs that provide "economically disadvantaged children with cognitively stimulating and enriching experiences" have shown to encourage healthy brain development and offset cognitive deficits (Duncan and Magnuson, 2004, 105). A biosocial perspective also encourages "early screening for neuropsychological or pre-frontal cortical deficits" especially for children from high-risk environments. From a treatment and offender rehabilitation perspective, "stimulation therapy may be beneficial" for those "stimulation seekers" with low resting heat rates while "neurorehabilitation" may be used for those with cognitive impairment.

Rocque et al. (2012, 310)

3.3.6 Summary: Risk Factors among Children and Youth

As this preceding discussion demonstrates, risk factors "exist in every area of life—individual, family, school, peer group, and community" (Office of the Surgeon General, 2001). Farrington et al. (2012, 48) list the criminogenic risk factors that they believe should be prioritized in development-based, early intervention programs: "school achievement, child-rearing methods, young mothers, child abuse, parental conflict, disrupted families, poverty, delinquent peers and deprived neighborhoods." Research also demonstrates how criminogenic risk factors are highly individualized. According to Wasserman et al. (2003a, 2) "although some risk factors are common to many child delinquents, the patterns and particular combination of risk factors vary from child to child."

In its 2001 report on youth violence, the U.S. Surgeon General stressed that to understand why some youth become involved in violence, while others do not, it is important to examine how "personal characteristics interact over time with the social contexts in which they live. This perspective considers a range of risks over the life course, from prenatal factors to factors influencing whether patterns of violent behavior in adolescence will persist into adulthood." In other words, risk factors will vary and change based on the age and/or developmental level of the individual. As children move from infancy to early adulthood, some risk factors will become more important and others less important. With respect to future delinquent and criminal behavior, the most deleterious risks early in a child's life stem from *personal* factors (e.g., birth complications, hyperactivity, and temperamental difficulties) and family factors (e.g., parental antisocial or criminal behavior, substance abuse, poor child-rearing practices). As children grow older, new risk factors related to their social environment, such as their community, their school, their peer network, and the media begin to become more influential (Wasserman et al., 2003a, 2).

The probability of becoming a chronic offender often increases with the number of risk factors present in the life of a child or youth (Farrington, 2002). As the Surgeon General (2001) puts it, "risk factors do not operate in isolation—the more risk factors a child or young person is exposed to, the greater the likelihood that he or she will become violent." Those most at risk of becoming involved in crime are often struggling with several problems. The old adage *when it rains it pours* is quite applicable when considering the range of personal, family, school, and community risk factors that children and youth, especially those living in disadvantaged neighborhoods, must endure. According to Canada's National Crime Prevention Centre (2008, 1), "not only do the effects of risk factors accumulate, but the factors also interact with each other: the effects of one multiply the effects of another and so on. For example, parental alcoholism causes family conflicts, which then increase the risks of substance abuse." As Agnew (2005, 112) succinctly states, "a cause is more likely to increase crime when other causes are present."

As biosocial criminology emphasizes, it is especially important to recognize that personal risk factors and environmental risk factors are not mutually exclusive, but critically interconnected. Bonnie et al. (2012) argue, "adolescent risk-taking and delinquent behavior result from the interaction between the normal developmental attributes" of youth as well as "the environmental influences to which they are exposed before and during this stage of development. Put simply, the brain plays an enormous role in determining behavior, but individual development is affected strongly by the interplay between the brain and an adolescent's environment. In particular, the likelihood and seriousness of offending, as well as the effects of interventions, are strongly affected by the adolescent's interactions with parents, peers, schools, communities and other elements of their social environment" (Bonnie et al., 2012, 2).

When anticipating future criminal behavior, this conclusion underlines the importance of looking at risk factors in combination with each other and recognizing that they may interact and are often linked in a causal relationship (e.g., hyperactivity can lead to poor academic achievement, which can result in dropping out of school, which can lead to negative peer relationships, unemployment, or drug abuse, which can result in criminal behavior). Indeed, the causal relationship between one particular risk factor and criminal behavior is made more complex by how other risk factors may influence this bilateral relationship (and is itself a recognition of how our lives are differentially affected by numerous people, environments, and events). For example, as important as parenting practices are in promoting or hindering the prosocial behavior of children and youth, "parenting does not occur in isolation; rather children and youth are exposed to many contexts beyond the home that may influence the relationship between parenting strategies and youth behavioural outcomes" (Fitzgerald, 2010, 5). When discussing criminogenic risk factors specifically, research has shown that the impact of poor parental supervision is amplified when the unsupervised youth are also exposed to delinquent peers or a negative school environment (Fitzgerald, 2010, 4). Similarly, social bond theory argues that the prospect of criminal behavior among those with weak bonds to society is heightened in neighborhoods rife with criminogenic influences (Hirschi, 1969).

The implication of developmental criminology for the field of crime prevention is that social problem-solving interventions should assume a risk-based, early intervention approach; that is, children and youth who suffer from serious and chronic risk factors (and as such are most at risk of serious and chronic criminal offending) should be the particular targets of CPSD initiatives. As such, a scientifically developed approach to CPSD first identifies and analyzes social environmental and personal risk factors among children and then, based on this evidence, individualized interventions are developed to address these risk factors. Notwithstanding the aforementioned, no single risk factor or combination of risk factors can predict criminal or violent behavior with unerring accuracy. The good news is that many children and youth who suffer from untreated risk factors do not become involved in criminal behavior, let alone develop into serious or chronic criminal offenders (Office of the U.S. Surgeon General, 2001). Furthermore, as detailed throughout this chapter, research indicates that even the most severe and chronic risk factors can be prevented or ameliorated through targeted CPSD interventions.

3.4 CRIME PREVENTION THROUGH SOCIAL DEVELOPMENT

CPSD is comprised of interventions that attempt to ameliorate the root causes of criminal behavior, particularly among at-risk children and youth. Also known as *crime prevention through social problem solving, social crime prevention,* and *criminality prevention,* CPSD is the most proactive of all crime prevention strategies in that it is ultimately geared toward preventing criminal predispositions from developing in the first place. CPSD is defined in the 2002 *United Nations Standards and Norms in Crime Prevention* as approaches that "promote the well-being of people and encourage pro-social behaviour through social, economic, health and educational measures, with a particular emphasis on children and youth, and focus on the risk and protective factors associated with crime and victimization" (United Nations, 2002, 4).

The underlying premise of CPSD is that certain interventions (ideally during the childhood years) may alleviate factors that can increase the risk of future criminality. When used in relation to at-risk children and youth, CPSD refers to targeted, social problem-solving strategies, actions, and provisions that minimize, eliminate, counter, or offset factors that put children and youth at risk of future offending or other deviant or antisocial behavior. As a social problem-solving approach to crime, CPSD attempts to remove criminogenic *risk factors* by replacing or countering them with *protective factors,* which are positive characteristics, conditions, or interventions that can counteract risk factors. As Farrington (2007, 606) writes, "the basic idea of risk-focussed prevention is very simple: identify the key risk factors for offending and implement prevention methods designed to counteract them."* Or as Savignac (2009, 3) puts it, "It is generally accepted that the risk of developing a life trajectory oriented towards delinquency is influenced by the number of risk factors to which a youth is exposed. By the same token, it may be suggested that as a youth is surrounded by protective factors, the risks of an orientation towards delinquency are diminished."

Coinciding with the delineation of risk factors into social environmental and personal, CPSD strategies are directed at one of two (complementary) targets: (1) a deleterious social environment or (2) personal risk factors. In other words, the protective factors delivered through CPSD interventions can either benefit the child indirectly or directly. Despite these conceptual differences, an ideal social problem-solving strategy is one that addresses both social environmental and personal risk factors.

An important foundation underlying CPSD principles and strategies is what the Search Institute calls *developmental assets*—the building blocks of healthy development of children and adolescents. Within the context of CPSD, these developmental assets are the factors that protect young people from the onset of delinquent and criminal behavior later in life. The Search Institute has identified 40 developmental assets for children, which can be broadly demarcated into *external* (social environmental) assets and *internal* (personal) assets. Among the external assets are support (e.g., loving and caring parents), empowerment (e.g., "children are welcomed and including throughout community life"), boundaries and expectations (e.g., children are well supervised by their parents), and constructive use of time. The internal assets critical to healthy child development are a commitment to learning, positive values (e.g., caring, integrity, honesty, responsibility),

---

* *A major challenge of risk-focused prevention is establishing which risk factors are causes and which are merely symptoms or correlates. For example, is substance abuse a cause of the problem or a symptom of a deeper problem? This is a key challenge because to be most effective, risk-focused, problem-oriented CPSD strategies must target the root cause of the problem.*

social competencies (e.g., interpersonal skills, peaceful conflict resolution), and a positive identity (e.g., strong self-esteem, sense of purpose). One of the goals of CPSD is to foster the developmental assets of at-risk children and youth, especially targeting those assets that are particularly weak or absent (and, as a result, places a child at risk of future delinquent and criminal behavior). To this end, the goal of CPSD is to transform a risk factor (e.g., poor parenting) into a protective factor (strong parenting).

Also central to CPSD strategies that target at-risk children and youth is the concept of *resilience*. Within the context of criminality and violence prevention, resilience is the construct used to describe the quality in children and youth who, although exposed to significant stress and adversity in their lives, do not succumb to criminal, delinquent, violent, or other antisocial behavior. In many respects, resilience is the culmination of the developmental assets (protective factors) in the life of a child; in theory, the more assets present, the more resilient the child. Thus, the protective factors delivered through CPSD interventions are meant to promote resilience within an at-risk child by fostering their developmental assets. For Farrington (2007, 604), "the fact that many children at risk have successful lives inspires the search for protective factors and individual resilience features that might inform prevention techniques."

According to Bedard (1995), within the context of child and human development, resilience is a "term used to describe a set of qualities that foster a process of successful adaptation and transformation despite risk and adversity." Everybody is "born with an innate capacity for resilience, by which we are able to develop social competence, problem-solving skills, a critical consciousness, autonomy, and a sense of purpose." The concept of resilience was first introduced into the adolescent health literature with a longitudinal study by Emmy Werner that began in the 1950s and ended in the 1980s. This research proposed that certain positive influences and institutions within the life of a child could mitigate high-risk behaviors during childhood that can be sustained into adolescence and adulthood. Specifically, her research showed that children brought up in poverty and who were considered at risk of engaging in delinquent behaviors, such as substance abuse or violence, were found to be resilient to these negative behaviors when positive factors such as a caring adult or effective schooling were present in their lives (as cited in Rink and Tricker, 2003, 1). In short, the presence of protective factors in the individual, the family, the school, and the community appear to alter or reverse predicted negative outcomes by fostering the development of resilience within children and youth.

According to the University of Hawaii's Center of the Family, three areas of strength that are common among resilient children are as follows: "(a) external supports and resources that provide safety and security: I have people I can turn to in times of need; (b) personal strengths—attitudes, beliefs, and feelings that allow them to bounce back and move forward: I am loved and I am lovable; and (c) social and interpersonal skills for interacting with others respectfully and responsibly: I can contribute and share responsibility" (Tom et al., 2009, 3). Based on prior research, Rink and Tricker (2003, 1) provide a more detailed list of the key protective factors that can contribute to resilience within children, youths, and adults, which is summarized in Table 3.1.

As intimated earlier, developmental assets, resilience, and prosocial behavior can either be nurtured through universally accepted positive social practices (loving parents, strong schools, integration into the local community, positive peer networks) or promoted through programs and services that are expressly developed to deliver protective factors. CPSD interventions are an example of the latter; as such, they are made up of specific strategies and programs that target at-risk individuals (especially children and youth living in poverty), groups (e.g., racial minority groups, homeless youth),

Table 3.1

Important Protective Factors Essential to Promoting Resilience

Family Assets	School Assets	Community Assets	Individual Assets
Positive adult role models	Connectedness to school	Connectedness to community	Positive peer group
Positive communication within the family	Supportive school environment	Positive and clear community norms and values	Problem-solving skills
Parental involvement in the youth's life	Participation in after-school activities	Effective prevention policies	Communication skills
Clear rules and consequences within the family and the school	Effective involvement in the school	Absence of weapons and firearms	Positive conflict resolution skills
Time with family			A positive sense of self
			Takes responsibility for own behaviors
			Empathy and sensitivity toward others

Sources: Scales, P. and Leffert, N., Developmental Assets, Search Institute, Minneapolis, MN, 1999; Hawkins, J.D. et al., The Seattle social development project: Effects of the first four years on protective factors and problem behaviors, in Preventing Adolescent Antisocial Behavior: Interventions from Birth through Adolescence, J. McCord and R.E. Tremblay, Eds., Guilford Press, New York, 1992, pp. 139–161, as cited in Rink and Tricker (2003, 1).

and communities (in particular, low-income, high-crime neighborhoods). At-risk children and youth are the primary focus of CPSD because, as criminological theory and research suggests, the foundation for delinquent and criminal behavior in the teenage and adult years is often laid during the first 10–13 years of a person's life. As discussed, it is also during the childhood years that resilience can best be promoted.

Some of the key principles underlying CPSD are summarized below.

Risk based: CPSD interventions should target those communities, families, children and youth that are at high risk of future criminal behavior, and serious and chronic criminal offending in particular.

Early intervention/focus on the family and parenting: Based upon their review of the literature, Duncan and Magnuson (2004, 101) contend that while the principles of developmental science suggest that "beneficial changes are possible at any point in life, interventions early on may be more effective at promoting well-being and competencies compared with interventions undertaken later in life." Furthermore, "early childhood may provide an unusual window of opportunity for interventions because young children are uniquely receptive to enriching and supportive environment... As individuals age, they gain the independence and ability to shape their environments, rendering intervention efforts more complication and costly" (Duncan and Magnuson (2004, 102–103). According to the International Centre for the Prevention of Crime (2008b, 81), early intervention programs "usually target families and children at risk of future involvement in offending, because of family circumstances or socio-economic background." There is a substantial body of evidence that early intervention in the lives of at-risk children can prevent delinquency, criminal offending, interpersonal violence, and other antisocial behavior that can emerge during adolescence, if not sooner. A significant emphasis of CPSD programs is "parent-focused interventions to support parents in the upbringing of very young children. These primary prevention strategies provide support for the personal challenges parents are facing, as well as assistance with coping with children's problematic or difficult behaviour" (International Centre for the Prevention of Crime, 2008, 81).

Problem-oriented/evidence-based approach/individualized: CPSD is guided by the problem-oriented philosophy, which means that the scope and nature of the intervention must be commensurate with the scope and nature of the risk factors. Thus, a risk-focused, social problem-solving approach to preventing the onset of criminal behavior in at-risk children and youth encompasses a scientific methodology that involves identifying, analyzing, and understanding risk factors, using rigorous (clinical assessment and research) instruments to better understand the scope and nature of the risk factors. Given recent research on the role of biological risk factors, the assessment stage may even include the use of medical technology, such as functional MRIs to identify any relevant impairment of the brain. Based upon the results of these assessments, evidence-based interventions (protective factors) that are best suited to addressing the risk factors and which are appropriate to the age and/or developmental level of the individual are designed and implemented. Indeed, the nature of a CPSD intervention is very much influenced by the age of the at-risk individual or group. Specifically, the approach and substance of a CPSD intervention is generally dictated by which of the following age groups the individual falls within: (1) infants (birth to 3 years old), (2) children (4–11 years of old), (3) adolescents (12–17 years old), and (4) young adults (18–25 years old). For infants, CPSD interventions target the parent, with particular emphasis on parental training (how to properly care for and nurture an infant) and support (financial, emotional, psychological, etc.). To maximize effectiveness, these programs and services should begin during the prenatal phase. CPSD interventions for children are directed at both the parent (training, support, etc.) and the child (preschool, addressing behavioral and psychological problems, social skills development, etc.). CPSD interventions for at-risk youth are primarily directed at the youth (remedial education, stay-in-school initiatives, job training, sports, and recreation); however, comprehensive approaches to help chronic young offenders (or those at risk of chronic offending) must also involve the parent and the youth's broader social support network. Finally, for older youth and young adults, the emphasis is on education, vocational training and placement, substance abuse, and intensive therapy for chronic offenders. In short, CPSD interventions should be highly individualized to the circumstances and developmental level of each at-risk person.

Flexibility: CPSD strategies can either seek to remove, eliminate, or minimize a particular risk factor. If a risk factor cannot be removed, then the intervention should include strategies that offset its negative impact. For example, if a child's main caregiver has poor parenting skills, a social environmental intervention would entail providing the parent with the education, skills, and support to become a more effective and nurturing caregiver (i.e., remove the risk factor). However, if the poor parenting persists (i.e., the risk factor cannot be removed), interventions should be delivered directly to the child to increase his or her resilience, which is meant to provide a protective barrier from the poor parenting (and other social environmental risk factors for that matter). Farrington (2007, 607) calls this type of protective factor a *moderator* in that it does not seek to remove the risk factor, but seeks to moderate or minimize the risk factor's impact.

Comprehensive: Because children and youth who are most at risk of future chronic and serious criminal behavior suffer from numerous personal and social environmental risk factors, effective CPSD interventions should attempt to address as many risk factors as possible. According to the 2001 report on youth violence by the U.S. Surgeon General, the "most highly effective programs combine components that address both individual risks and environmental conditions, particularly building individual skills and competencies, parent effectiveness training, improving the social climate of the school, and changes in type and level of involvement in peer groups."

Multi-institutional/multiagency: The delivery of a comprehensive array of problem-solving services often requires the interventions to be delivered (1) through multiple institutions (the family, the school, community, health-care facilities, etc.), (2) by different agencies and professionals, and (3) in an integrated, seamless, *wraparound* approach in which all service providers work in a coordinated and complimentary fashion. A major consideration in the development of CPSD interventions is the institution(s) through which services and programs can be delivered. There are essentially five institutions through which CPSD programs are delivered: the family, schools, the community, the health-care system, and labor markets. As inferred earlier, the institution emphasized in a targeted CPSD strategy will vary depending on the age group and risk factors. Programs targeting children are largely delivered through the family, the school, or the health-care system (for psychological and mental health issues). As children grow older, the relative importance of school- and employment-based interventions supersedes those of the family. Programs targeting youth are largely delivered through schools, the labor market, or a combination of the two. Because the neighborhood is a significant incubator of crime, it is also the target of community-based social developmental programs. This includes efforts to transform neighborhoods into socially cohesive, active, caring, and vigilant communities, which is often crucial to strengthening the capacity of local areas to prevent crime through informal social control and local programs. (Exploring the community as a CPSD institution is dealt with in greater depth in Chapter 5.)

Wraparound approach: The National Crime Prevention Centre of Canada (2012, 1–4) describes the wraparound approach as "… an intensive, individualized care management approach designed for children, youth and individuals with serious or complex emotional and/or behavioural problems. A comprehensive continuum of individualized services and support networks are adapted to meet the unique needs of individuals …" The wraparound approach is "designed to prevent fragmentation and 'gaps' in the services often encountered" by at-risk children, youth, and their families. "The approach also seeks to provide more extensive and proactive contact between the youth, his or her family, and other involved parties (e.g., court counsellor, social worker, etc.). The focus is on appropriately matching the youth's and family's needs to services …." Some of the key principles that guide the wraparound approach within the context of CPSD include

- "A collaborative, community-based interagency team (with professionals from youth justice, education, mental health and social services systems) designs, implements and oversees the project"
- A "comprehensive plan of care, which is updated continually, identifies the young person's unique strengths and weaknesses across domains, targets specific goals and outlines action plans"
- A case management approach in which "care coordinators" help participants create the comprehensive plan of care
- A support network (made up of family members, paid service providers, friends, and community members such as teachers and mentors), who "work in partnership to ensure that the young person's needs in all life domains are addressed with cultural competence." (Totten, 2008 as cited in National Crime Prevention Centre, 2012, 1–4)

High degree of fidelity in program implementation—Suffice to say, programs that are implemented with a high degree of fidelity are more apt to successfully reduce or eliminate criminogenic risk factors. In a review of literature on developmentally based interventions for at-risk boys and male adolescents, Bandy (2012, 8–9) writes, "Although few strategies or practices stood out as always effective, the most effective interventions tended to be structured, intense, high dosage, and facilitated by trained staff persons. For example, interventions that were manualized, met frequently on a scheduled basis, and were implemented by teachers, psychologists, or other trained professions were likely to have positive impacts. In contrast, programs that met less frequently, and those that were facilitated by peers or untrained staff, tended to less often result in positive impacts for boys" (Bandy 2012, 8–9). In their review of the literature entitled, *Proven Benefits of Early Childhood Interventions*, the RAND Corporation identifies three program features that appear to be associated with more effective interventions: well-trained caregivers, smaller child-to-staff ratios, and a high dosage level of services (RAND, 2005, 2).

The remainder of this chapter discusses specific CPSD strategies and programs, emphasizing those that have proven effective in addressing delinquency and criminogenic risk factors. First, social developmental interventions that are delivered directly to at-risk children and youth are discussed. This is followed by a description of interventions that

---

CASE STUDY 3.2

A COMPREHENSIVE, MULTIMODAL, MULTI-INSTITUTIONAL CPSD PROGRAM

One example of a comprehensive approach to reducing risk factors in children is the Families and Schools Together Program in the United States (Conduct Problems Prevention Research Group, 1992). The program integrates five intervention components designed to enhance family functioning, prevent academic failure, prevent substance abuse, and reduce the stress that parents and children experience from daily life situations. "The overall goal of the FAST program is to intervene early to help at-risk youth succeed in the community, at home, and in school and thus avoid problems including adolescent delinquency, violence, addiction, and dropping out of school" (MacDonald and Frey, 1999, 2).

The program incorporates in a complementary fashion, the following family- and school-based strategies that have been shown to work: (1) training for parents in family management practices; (2) home visits by program staff to reinforce skills learned in the training, promote a parent's self-efficacy, and enhance family functioning; (3) social skills coaching for children; (4) academic tutoring for children, three times per week; and (5) a classroom instructional program focusing on social competency skills coupled with classroom management strategies for the teacher.

Dodge (1993) reports that after 1 year of this intensive program, clear positive effects were evident for several of the intermediate behaviors targeted by the program (e.g., parent involvement in the child's education and developing the child's social competency skills), and significantly less problem behavior was recorded for children in the program compared to a control of those not in the program. Subsequent studies have shown that children participating in FAST have reported reductions in behavioral problems (bullying, hitting, stealing, and lying) and mental health problems (withdrawal and anxiety) as well as improvements in academic performance (see MacDonald and Frey, 1999, 13–14).

attempt to create a positive and nurturing social environment (by strengthening such key institutions as the family, the school, and the community) for at-risk children and youth. CPSD approaches for older youth and young adults are discussed in Chapter 4.

3.4.1 Interventions Targeting At-Risk Children and Youth Directly

Interventions that are delivered directly to at-risk children and youth are perhaps the most vivid examples of strategies that build personal resilience. Some of the dominant interventions that directly target at-risk children and youth are as follows: (1) cognitive–behavioral programs; (2) social competency and life skills development; (3) preventing and treating early antisocial behavior, aggression, delinquency, and related conduct problems; (4) youth mentoring; (5) enriched pre-school programs; and (6) intensive after-school/sports and recreational programs. Each of these CPSD approaches are discussed below.

3.4.1.1 Cognitive–Behavioral Approaches

In recent years, CBT has emerged as the "predominant psychological method of treating not only mental illness, but a broad spectrum of socially problematic behaviors including substance abuse, criminal conduct, and depression" (Thigpen, 2007, viii).

The use of CBT principles have proven beneficial in controlling conduct problems and modifying high-risk behavior among children, young people, and adults. Within the context of preventing delinquent or criminal behavior, CBT is frequently used with children and youth to ameliorate risk factors (e.g., conduct problems, anger issues, aggression, impulsivity) that can lead to future chronic and serious offending. CBT is also used as a basis for many recidivism prevention programs that treat delinquent, criminal, substance abusing, and violent behaviors. (See Chapter 4 for a discussion of cognitive behavioral approaches to reduce recidivism among adolescents and young adults.)

CBT is generally employed to help people identify and change problematic behavior by addressing patterns of cognition (thinking) that are dysfunctional as well as the beliefs or assumptions that underlie or compound such negative thinking. As such, CBT is premised on the understanding that "most people can become conscious of their own thoughts and behaviors and then make positive changes to them" (Clark, 2010, 22). In general, there are three phases that make up a CBT-based intervention. The first step is to identify irrational, negative, dysfunctional, or maladaptive thoughts (as well as underlying assumptions and beliefs) that may feed or trigger dysfunctional or antisocial behavior. The second step is to promote an understanding of how these patterns are dysfunctional, inaccurate, or simply not helpful to the individual. The third step is to replace these negative thinking and behavior patterns with alternatives that are more positive, self-affirming, and prosocial. Those undergoing CBT are often asked to practice positive *self-directed talk* to help erase the negative thoughts and beliefs they may have that leads to negative or self-defeating behaviors. For example, a student who is having problems in school may be the victim of repetitive negative thoughts, such as *I am stupid* or *I am a terrible student*. CBT encourages replacing these negative thoughts with more self-affirming ones, such as "I know my worst subject is math, so I should get help from a tutor." Other proven pedagogical techniques common to CBT are role-playing, behavioral and skills rehearsal, group discussion, behavioral modeling, and interactive exercises that help build important social competency and life skills (such as coping, problem solving, moral reasoning, impulse control) (Kendall, 1993). Assisting in the promotion of positive behaviors is *operant conditioning* or positive reinforcement. To help negate conduct problems within children, for example, parents are often encouraged to reward a child who is demonstrating good or compliant behavior through praise and/or material rewards.

From a preventative perspective, children with conduct problems can be taught how to use positive self-directed talk to avoid negative behavior while being praised and/or rewarded for good behavior. CBT can also be applied to help ameliorate other criminogenic risk factors, such as academic failure. As the Office of Juvenile Justice and Delinquency Prevention (OJJDP) (n.d.) points out, one of the most frequent reasons why students experience academic failure and dropout is not necessarily because of low intelligence but also because of a self-defeating attitude that can "influence students to behave in ways that reinforce these negative thoughts and increase their chances of actual failure." As such, effective "academic achievement programs directly target these negative thoughts and reinforce positive behavior by using CBT strategies delivered by teachers, mentors, tutors, peers, and school staff."

Proponents of biosocial criminology also view CBT favorably because it can affect brain functioning, especially if CBT-based interventions are sensitive to both neurological and social environmental risk factors. "In cases where risk factors are heritable or genetic, [CBT] programs can prevent crime through identifying environmental triggers that may increase criminal behavior." Regardless of the type of CBT approach used, it does "not seek to radically alter the individual's biology, but rather to improve functioning in the social world" (Rocque et al., 2012, 311).

In short, according to Thigpen (2007, viii), "CBT attempts to change negative behaviors by attacking, as it were, from both ends. Clients are not only taught more positive behaviors to replace their old ways of getting through life, they are also shown how to be more attuned to the thought processes that led them to choose negative actions in the past." As importantly, notes Milkman and Wanberg (2007, xiii–xiii), within the context of criminality and recidivism prevention, "a third focus is added to the traditional CBT focus on cognitive functioning and behavior: developing skills for living in harmony with the community and engaging in behaviors that contribute to positive outcomes in society."

Some of the early intervention social problem-solving programs and curricula used as case studies in this book—including Aggression Replacement Training (ART), FRIENDS for Life, and Multi-Systemic Family Therapy—incorporate CBT principles and techniques.

3.4.1.2 Social Competency Skills Development

According to Lösel and Bender (2012, 104), "social competence refers to three levels that interact: (1) cognitive competencies (e.g., effective social information processing adequate cognitions about self and others); (2) emotional competencies (e.g., age-appropriate development an expression of emotions); and (3) behavioral competencies (e.g., verbal and nonverbal communication and interaction skills)" (Lochman and Wells, 2002, 951). Various programs have been developed to train at-risk children and youth to modify their own behavior through techniques that enhance their *social competency skills*. Research suggests that programs attempting to alter behavior by enhancing social competency (or *social–cognitive*) skills among children and youth can reduce the onset of delinquent and criminal behavior. This is in line with research indicating that chronic and serious offenders are deficient in a number of areas necessary for social adaptation and prosocial behavior: they are impulsive and reactive, cannot control their anger, rely on aggression and violence to solve problems, are unnecessary risk takers and sensation seekers, do not consider the consequences of their actions before they act, have low levels of empathy, and lack interpersonal skills necessary for effective communication and basic interpersonal relationships.

Lösel and Bender (2012, 106) differentiate two traditional forms of social competency training: the first is behavior oriented and the second focuses on social–cognitive training. "Behavior-oriented programs teach children skills for getting in contact with others, making friends, accepting the rights of others, or expressing individual needs appropriately. Often, peers or other social models are used to promote these skills. In contrast, social-cognitive programs target basic cognitive skills for effective social problem solving, such as perspective-taking, self-control and anger management."

When used as a social problem-solving approach to address early-onset criminogenic risk factors, social competency training places particular emphasis on promoting critical thinking, problem solving, impulse control, anger management, peaceful conflict resolution, and deliberative decision making. Students are taught, for example, to identify and avoid their own risky or maladaptive behavior, to think before acting, to control impulses, to anticipate and consider the consequences of their actions (including the impact on others), to understand their feelings and emotions, to have empathy toward others, to cope with stress and anxiety, and to use nonaggressive, socially appropriate ways to achieve desired outcomes and solve interpersonal problems. Social competency training programs may also impart such basic social and life skills as making friends, acting in social settings, expressing one's self appropriately, dealing with peer pressure, and helping others (Goldstein et al., 1998; Office of the Surgeon General, 2001; National Institute on Drug Abuse, 2003; Lösel and Beelmann, 2003; Wasserman, et al., 2003a; Farrington, 2007).

Research into programs offering social–cognitive skills training demonstrates clear positive effects on current problem behaviors a child may be exhibiting as well as a range of future antisocial behaviors, such as delinquency, criminality, drug use, gang membership, and violence. In fact, social competency programs have been shown to be more effective at reducing substance abuse or gang membership among at-risk children and youth, compared with more narrow, instruction-based prevention programs (such as those focused on drugs or gangs), which do not include social competency training (see Wasserman et al., 2003a; Gottfredson et al., 2006; Farrington, 2007).

The University of Chicago Crime Lab (2012) contends, "A growing body of research demonstrates that social-cognitive skills predict success in school and the labor market, as well as improved health and reduced criminal involvement." The crime lab touts the benefits of social–cognitive skills training in school implying that one of the reasons the United States is not making "more progress in improving the long-term life chances of disadvantaged youth" is because "we devote relatively little attention, at least outside the earliest elementary-school grades, to addressing other important determinants of student success," in particular social–cognitive skills. Indeed, social competency programs should target at-risk youth because "children growing up in disadvantaged circumstances are at elevated risk of developing deficits in social-cognitive skills" (University of Chicago Crime Lab, 2012, 2).

Based upon a meta-analysis of the literature, Lösel and Beelmann (2003) carried out a systematic review of the effects of social competence training for children on antisocial behavior. Of the 55 randomized controlled experiments they reviewed, the "majority confirmed the benefits of treatment" (Lösel and Beelmann, 2003, 84). In other words, there was an improvement in social–cognitive skills and, to a lesser extent, the reduction of various types of antisocial behavior. "Well-implemented, cognitive-behavioral programs targeting high-risk youngsters who already exhibit some behavioral problems seem to be particularly effective" (Lösel and Beelmann, 2003, 102).

In short, "child skills training is an important and effective developmental approach to preventing crime" (Lösel and Bender, 2012, 103).

What contributes to the effectiveness of social competency skills training is not simply the substance of the programs, but the use of innovative and effective pedagogical techniques to convey the basic concepts and skills to children and youth. This includes cognitive–behavioral techniques (e.g., self-talk); interactive and experiential instructional techniques, such as role-playing (or *skills rehearsal*); behavior modeling (demonstration of skills by adult instructors or role models); problem-solving exercises (students are presented with problems and asked to solve them in both negative and positive ways); immediate feedback and praise; and homework that consists of applying the skills learned in a real-life setting.

As discussed, many theories and studies suggest that chronic and serious offenders are impulsive, reactive, imprudent risk takers who do not think through the consequences of their actions, have poor solving skills, and are unable or unwilling to identify the consequences of their actions or envision positive alternatives in the face of personal misbehavior, risky behavior, or adverse external conditions. Accordingly, important social competency and life skills taught to children and youth who are at-risk of future criminal and violent behavior also include the following: critical thinking and abstract reasoning (to recognize thoughts, feelings, and motives that generate problem situations), the self-recognition of conduct problems and high-risk behavior, the ability to anticipate and think through the consequences of one's actions before acting, and the ability to come up with a variety of alternative (positive) strategies to resolve misbehavior, risky behavior, or other problems and adverse conditions that may confront them.

3.4.1.3 Preventing and Treating Early Antisocial Behavior, Aggression, Delinquency, and Related Conduct Problems

Litschge et al. (2010) summarizes treatment effects for children and adolescence who display conduct problems based on a review of published meta-analytic studies. They conclude that there is "substantial variation in effect sizes" of the treatment programs. Yet, "the results seem to demonstrate evidence for equifinality." In other words, various treatment options do culminate in similar positive outcomes. As such, "practitioners who work with children and adolescents should be aware of the range of evidence-based treatments available for conduct problems" (Litschge et al., 2010, 21).

Interventions targeting conduct problems and aggressive behavior (or the preconditions thereof) often revolve around social competency skills training. According to Lösel and Bender (2012, 104), "Training for the prevention of antisocial development focuses on social skills/competencies that are particularly relevant for aggressive and delinquent behavior. For example, it aims to promote non-hostile modes of social perception and attribution, identification of own and others emotions, perspective-taking and victim empathy, self control and anger management, nondeviant attitudes, interpersonal problem solving in conflict situations, and communication skills." In their review of the literature, Litschge et al. (2010) conclude that social competency skills training shows moderate overall positive effects in affecting antisocial behavior and conduct problems among children, youth, and young adults. According to Doran et al. (2012, 758), "the inclusion of anger management and problem-solving components to CBT approaches appears to be particularly important in terms of minimizing aggression."

Another category of treatment interventions that have been implemented to treat conduct problems involve behavioral or cognitive–behavioral approaches. Such interventions target children and/or the parents of children and youth "with antisocial-related

CASE STUDY 3.3

SOCIAL COMPETENCY TRAINING FOR AT-RISK CHILDREN

Coping Power is a multicomponent social competency training program for children who exhibit or are at risk of conduct problems, in particular aggressive behavior. The theoretical basis for this program "assumes that aggression in children is the product of distortions in their social–cognitive appraisals" (they interpret situations or the actions and intentions of others negatively) and "deficiencies in their social problem solving skills," combined with parents who have deficiencies in their parenting skills and behaviors (Lochman and Wells, 2002, 945).

Given the assumption that the causes of conduct problems are rooted in both the child's social perceptions and social competency skills as well as the parent's parenting skills, the program includes components for both the child (those identified as aggressive or disruptive) and his or her parent. The component for children—which is offered to fifth and sixth graders, usually in an after-school setting—teaches coping skills to deal with anxiety and frustration, anger management skills, impulse control skills, and problem-solving skills (including peer-related interpersonal problem solving). To support this skill training, the child's component includes "a focus on behavioral and personal goal setting, awareness of feelings and associated physiological arousal, use of coping self-statements, distraction techniques and relaxation methods to use when provoked and made angry, organizational and study skills, perspective taking and attribution re-training, social problem solving skills, and dealing with peer pressure and neighborhood-based problems by using refusal skills" (Lochman and Wells, 2002, 951).

Parents are trained in such areas as "(a) identifying prosocial and disruptive behavioral targets in their children using specific operational terms, (b) rewarding appropriate child behavior, (c) giving effective instructions and establishing age-appropriate rules and expectations for their children in the home, (d) applying effective consequences to negative child behavior, (e) managing child behavior outside the home, and (f) establishing ongoing family communication structures in the home (such as weekly family meetings)" (Lochman and Wells, 2002, 951). Parents also learn how to support the social competency skills that children learn and to use stress management skills to remain calm and in control during stressful or irritating disciplinary interactions with their children.

In its full form, the program takes between 15 and 18 months to complete (a truncated version is also available that last about 12 months). The children's component consists of 34 group sessions. Each session is approximately 50 min in length and includes five children. Individual sessions between the trained facilitator and the child may also be held. The parent component consists of 16 group sessions in addition to periodic home visits and other forms of contact between the parent and a professional facilitating the training.

An experiment that tested Coping Power with preadolescent boys who were at risk of aggressive and disruptive behaviors concluded that the parent component of the Coping Power program "was instrumental in helping parents set more consistently clear expectations for boys' behavior and provide more consistent consequences for negative and positive behaviors. In a similar way, it is plausible that the child component of the Coping Power program assisted the boys in more carefully and accurately identifying the reasons for peers' and adults' reactions toward them" while helping them better manage "their escalating arousal and anger when experiencing problems in their social interactions" (Lochman and Wells, 2002, 964). Subsequent experiments (Lochman et al., 2006, 2009) that applied the Coping Power program showed statistically significant positive effects in reducing externalizing behaviors and school improving performance in school among at-risk (aggressive) children.

CASE STUDY 3.4

NURTURING SELF-REFLECTIVE PROBLEM SOLVING SKILLS IN CHILDREN AND YOUTH

Interpersonal cognitive problem solving (also called *I Can Problem Solve* or ICPS) was developed by Dr. Myrna Shure, a registered psychologist and professor at Drexel University in Philadelphia. The program was designed to reduce problem behaviors among children and youth with the ultimate goal being to increase the probability of preventing later, more serious problems.

The ICPS curriculum is usually delivered in a school setting, although there are complementary lesson plans for parents as well. The program takes about 10–12 weeks to complete, although a minimum of 6 weeks is sufficient to convey the core principles and skills. Specific lesson plans have been developed for children at the kindergarten, elementary, and secondary school levels. The curriculum begins with lessons on basic social skills and problem-solving language. The next module includes lessons that help students identify and become more attune to their own feelings and emotions as well as those of others. The goal is to help children learn to recognize other people's feelings in interpersonal problem situations and how they can influence the response of others through their own actions. The last module focuses specifically on promoting problem-solving skills, which includes identifying problem situations, formulating various options to solve the problem, evaluating the consequences of each solution, and choosing the most appropriate solution.

The ICPS curriculum incorporates a pedagogical approach that facilitates ongoing interaction between the instructor and the students (and among the students), as well as the use of age-appropriate games, role-playing, pictures, puppets, and group exercises. Many lessons encourage children to think about and solve real problems that they are encountering (or may encounter) in their lives. As part of the curriculum, parents may also be provided with exercises to help them think about their own feelings and become sensitive to those of their children. Parents also learn how to understand how their child may view a particular interpersonal problem and how to engage their child in the process of problem solving.

Research into and assessments of the ICPS program have been carried out since the mid-1970s. In general, the studies reveal that children who have taken the program were less impulsive, were less inhibited in the classroom, and exhibited better problem-solving skills following immediate completion of the program and after 1 year. A 5-year longitudinal study showed that 3–4 years after they had taken the program, children in the treatment group had better classroom behavior; more positive, prosocial behavior; healthier relationships with their peers; and better problem-solving skills compared to a control group. The evaluation results suggest that the program is most effective with respect to high-risk students than those from the general population (Shure, 1980, 1993, 1997; Shure and Spivack, 1979, 1982).

or disruptive behaviors" and include rational emotive behavior therapy, behavioral parenting training, parent treatment, and cognitive–behavior modification (Litschge et al., 2010, 23–24). With regard to behavioral and cognitive–behavioral treatments for antisocial children and adolescents, "the findings are nuanced and somewhat inconsistent but generally show that these treatments are moderately effective" and "seem to work best with older youth" (Litschge et al., 2010, 32). Most family-focused, group-based, and multimodal therapies produce moderate results in their effectiveness, especially with older youth. Furthermore, their results "show that parent-centered interventions seem to work better than those that focus on children or youth only" (Litschge et al., 2010, 32).

> This is theoretically and clinically plausible given that parents, as a result of their participation in the intervention, may be better equipped to identify and reinforce positive behavior. Parents may be able to correct and discourage inappropriate behavior as well. Having parents as "in-home reinforcers" of proper behavior may decrease the probability of a child or youth acting out. Therapies that focus on the child or youth only, although still helpful, may not be as effective as therapies that include parents as part of the intervention. In addition, children and youth who learn at an early age proper behavioral skills may be more likely to employ these abilities as they age. Thus, these newly learned skills may ultimately diminish the possibility of future behavior problems.
>
> **Litschge et al. (2010, 33)**

A pharmacological approach is another option in treating conduct problems among children and youth, especially when such behavior is caused or aggravated by psychological disorders, such as ADHD. Connor (2002) summarizes a number of studies that show a strong correlation between ADHD, on the one hand, and conduct disorders and early-onset aggression on the other. Connor also conducted a meta-analysis of 28 stimulant studies that assessed the effectiveness of three common medications: Adderall, methylphenidate, and Concerta. Among the 683 children with ADHD and aggression problems included in studies covered by this meta-analysis, the use of stimulants produced moderate to large effect sizes on aggression-related behaviors.

Programs that remove children and youth from violent environments and place them in more stable homes (e.g., foster care) is another technique to prevent the onset of aggressive and violent behavior. Similarly, mentorship programs that expose at-risk children to positive role models and mentors may offset the impact of any negative role models and behaviors.

3.4.1.4 Youth Mentoring Youth mentoring can be defined as a personal relationship between an adult and a young person in which the former helps to guide and contribute to the positive development of the latter. The dominant goal of youth mentoring programs is to positively impact on a young person's personal development in the holistic sense. This includes inculcating such adaptive functioning skills as strong self-esteem, self-sufficiency, and the ability to make positive life choices. Intertwined with this personal development goal is the fostering of prosocial values in children and youth. Clary and Rhodes (2006, 14) consider mentoring to be the "prototypical youth development approach." Mentoring is focused on not only improving the immediate life of a child and youth but also helping them make a successful transition to adulthood.

In theory, mentors provide a mentee with a number of protective factors, including a positive adult role model, friendship, advice, and emotional support. Davis and Garrison (1979, 8) write that there are many potential roles for a mentor, including coach, confidant, counselor, developer of talent, guardian, guru, inspiration, master, cheerleader, opener of doors, patron, role model, seminal source, and teacher. The impact of mentoring on young people does not necessarily stem from the activities undertaken by the pair, but the presence of a caring adult in their lives; someone who makes them feel special, respected, and listened to and someone who the child can confide in, look up to, learn from, and emulate. Perhaps the most beneficial outcome of mentoring programs is

CASE STUDY 3.5

ANGER MANAGEMENT PREVENTION AND TREATMENT PROGRAM

ART is a cognitive–behavioral anger management prevention and treatment program for children and youth. The goal of ART is to train program participants to understand and replace aggression and antisocial behavior with positive alternatives and the lesson plan is built on a three-pronged approach: (1) training in prosocial skills, (2) anger control training, and (3) moral reasoning training.

Social skills training is the behavioral component of ART and is intended to promote skills and competencies that can help avoid aggression when dealing with a conflict. The social skills taught in the program include basic social competencies (starting a conversation, introducing oneself, asking for help), understanding feelings and emotions (recognizing one's own feelings and emotions, expressing affection, dealing with fear), and alternatives to aggression (responding to teasing, dealing with an accusation, peaceful conflict resolution).

The anger control training component is meant to impart in children the skills and techniques necessary to understand and control anger and aggression. Students are taught how to recognize and control the "anger continuum," which includes recognizing triggers (external events and internal self-talk that can start the slide into and perpetuate anger and aggression) and cues (physiological signs that one is becoming angry). This component also provides students with practical skills and techniques that can reduce their anger, such as self-talk (positive statements that reinforce appropriate behavior), critical thinking (anticipating the consequences of one's actions and searching for positive alternative solutions), social skills (implementing the social skills taught in the first third of the curriculum), and evaluation (reflecting on the anger control continuum and assessing how well it was implemented).

The moral reasoning component trains program participants to use proper value judgments to overcome thinking and perception errors that might lead to aggression, such as self-centered thinking ("it's all about me"), assuming the worst ("it would happen anyways" or "they would do it to me"), blaming others ("it's their fault"), and mislabeling or minimizing ("it's not stealing, I'm only borrowing it" or "everybody else does it") (Goldstein et al., 1998).

Two studies measuring the impact of ART on incarcerated youth (ages 14–17) in New York in the 1970s indicated that those in the treatment group exhibited a higher level of skill in controlling their anger and aggression while in the correctional facility. They also exhibited fewer and less severe instances of problem behaviour compared to a control group. The research found these skills also transferred outside the correctional facility. Youth who underwent ART could better function in their communities in a prosocial manner compared to paroled youth who did not undergo the ART program. Based on these findings, the study's authors conclude, "ART is a viable intervention for aggressive, assaultive youths who are incarcerated. We have been able to demonstrate over the past 2 years that many of the youngsters who participate in a program of ART learn what to do instead of being aggressive, learn how to control their anger, and more frequently perceive value in choosing socially acceptable alternatives to resolve their problems" (Glick and Goldstein, 1987, 361).

A more recent assessment of the ART program implemented with children and youth in Norway with varying behavioral problems also produced positive results. According to the authors of this study, those in the "ART group indicated significant improvement following the intervention, both in terms of increased social skills and reduced behavioral problems; in contrast, informants in the comparison group did not generally indicate improvement" (Gundersen and Svartdal, 2006, 63).

that they foster connections between the youth and positive role models that have been shown to result in beneficial outcomes in youth, such as better functioning in emotional, behavioral, and academic areas (Grossman and Rhodes, 2002). A mentor can also offset criminogenic risk factors by imparting basic social competency and interpersonal skills, fostering a youth's bond to important institutions such as the school or the local community, helping with homework, or fostering self-worth through proficiency in sports or the arts. Another potential way in which mentoring might prevent crime is to reduce the opportunities for the youth. "Regular and lengthy meetings between mentors and mentees not only provide less time for the mentee to offend but might also disrupt their established relationships with delinquent friends. This would suggest that mentoring programs that had consistent and regular meetings between mentors and mentees would reduce the likelihood of crime" (Sullivan and Jolliffe, 2012, 212).

Youth mentoring programs have proliferated in recent years due to the increased need, which has been fuelled by the growing number of children living in single family homes (Tierney et al., 1995, 49), the lack of a stable and consistent father figure in the lives of children in single-parent households, and the lack of legitimate (male) role models, especially for children from minority groups living in disadvantaged environments. For Dubois et al. (2002, 160), "the significance attached to mentoring relationships as a protective influence suggests that programs may provide greater benefits to youth who can be considered 'at-risk' by virtue of individual and/or environmental circumstances." As Sherman (1997b, 21) writes, "mentoring provides the highest dosage of adult–child interaction of any formal community-based program. Compared to street workers and recreation program supervisors, mentors can develop much stronger bonds with juveniles at risk."

The positive impact of mentoring relationships in helping young people has been documented in studies and program evaluations. In general, research has found that mentors are able to "enhance social skills and emotional well-being, by improving cognitive skills through dialogue and listening…" (Rhodes, 2002, 35). In addition, "mentoring enhances young people's social capital, their knowledge of, and contacts with, a network of people who may be able to help them meet their goals" (Hamilton et al., 2006, 727). Moreover, "mentors can help adolescents with attachment/relationship issues and create strategies for coping with stress by acting as a sounding board and providing a model for effective communication" (Rhodes, 2002, 40). Researchers also conclude that the "guidance and support from an adult outside the home can lead to improvements in the quality of the parent–child relationship" (Rhodes et al., 2000, 1668). By taking an interest in a youth's schooling and demonstrating the importance of an education, mentors can help a youth value school more, have better attendance, and get better grades (Grossman and Tierney, 1998). By serving as positive role models, mentors may directly stimulate improvements in adolescents' self-perceptions, attitudes, and behaviors (Grossman and Rhodes, 2002, 201).

CASE STUDY 3.6

UNIVERSAL MENTORING PROGRAM

The largest, oldest, and most famous mentoring program in the world is Big Brothers/Big Sisters. The concept behind this mentoring program is simple enough: young boys or girls, especially those who are from a single-parent family or experience other depravations in their life, are matched with a nonrelated volunteer adult who serves as a mentor and positive, supporting, and caring role model. According to their website, both the volunteer and the youth are expected to make a commitment to meet two to four times a month for at least 1 year, with a typical meeting lasting 4 h. Big Brothers/Big Sisters match is carefully administered and supported by rigorous standards and trained personnel.

In the early 1990s, an assessment of the impact of the Big Brothers/Big Sisters program was undertaken through a study of 959 participating boys and girls, ages 10–16, living in eight cities in the United States (Tierney et al., 1995). Most of these children came from low-income households, while many were from families where the parents were divorced or separated or had a history of substance abuse and/or domestic violence. The research indicated that following an 18-month period, the young people who were mentored were 46% less likely than control group to begin using drugs, 27% less likely to begin to use alcohol, 32% less likely to hit someone, and 52% less likely to be truant from school. Those in the treatment group also performed better in school, were more likely to have higher-quality relationships with their parents or guardians than control youth, and were more likely to have higher quality relationships with their peers at the end of the study period than did those in the control group (Tierney et al., 1995, iv).

A recent study found that adults mentored as children through Big Brothers/Big Sisters are more likely to have a 4-year college degree; incomes of $75,000 or more; a strong relationships with their spouses, children, and friends; and a greater satisfaction with their lives when compared to adults who had similar profiles as children but who were not involved in the program (PRNewswire-USNewswire, 2009). All of the positive outcomes documented by these two students can serve as important protective factors against the occurrence of antisocial behaviors, including criminal offending and interpersonal violence, during adolescence and adulthood.

Big Brothers/Big Sisters is an example of a universal mentoring program that does not target a specific risk factor. Others have been designed to specifically address risk factors associated with delinquency, criminal offending, violence, and gang membership. In their review of research into mentoring programs, Welsh and Hoshi (2006, 184) write, "community-based mentoring is a promising approach to preventing crime." The authors temper this conclusion with the caveat that more studies are needed into mentoring programs to determine their impact on criminogenic risk factors.

Given the complex and ingrained nature of criminogenic risk factors, combined with the documented need to approach criminality and violence prevention through a multiagency, multidisciplinary, collaborative approach, youth mentoring has been implemented as one of several components of multifaceted intervention programs for at-risk young people. As Dubois et al. (2002, 158–159) note, "enhanced benefits generally have been expected to result when mentoring is linked to other supportive services." The Juvenile Mentoring Program (JUMP), which is described below, was not only designed as a criminality prevention program, but situates mentoring within a broader multimodal, multiagency approach.

CASE STUDY 3.7

MENTORING WITHIN THE CONTEXT OF A MULTIMODAL, MULTIAGENCY APPROACH TO CRIMINALITY PREVENTION

In the United States, the OJJDP developed and administered the JUMP, which was designed to provide one-on-one mentoring for youth at risk of delinquency, gang involvement, educational failure, or dropping out of school. Through the JUMP program, the OJJDP awarded 3-year grants to community organizations to support the implementation and expansion of collaborative mentoring projects. What made JUMP unique in the field of mentoring is that adult mentors were encouraged to work in partnership with other community agencies and institutions to help provide a multidimensional intervention that maximizes a comprehensive continuum of care for the youth they are serving (Office of Juvenile Justice and Delinquency Prevention, 1998a, 14). Typically, such coordination involves schools, medical service providers, mental health facilities, substance abuse treatment programs, and employment training and placement programs, among others. Many JUMP projects also supplemented their core mentoring activities with additional services for youth participants and their families, including parent support groups, self-help groups, and referrals to other community organizations (Office of Juvenile Justice and Delinquency Prevention, 1998).

One example of a JUMP-funded initiative was the Los Angeles-based RESCUE youth mentoring program. Developed and implemented by the Los Angeles County's District Attorney's Office and Fire Department, it targeted youth between the ages of 12 and 14 who displayed early signs of high-risk behavior. The district attorney's staff matched a young person with volunteer firefighters who served as mentors and helped the youth with their communication and conflict resolution skills, while providing training in fire prevention and first aid (Baldwin and Garry, 1997, 5).

In a meta-analysis that reviews 55 evaluations of the effects of mentoring programs on youth, Dubois et al. (2002, 187) conclude that their findings "provide support for the effectiveness of youth mentoring programs," especially for those suffering from social environmental risk factors. While their meta-analysis found "evidence of only a modest or small benefit of program participation for the average youth," those youth "from backgrounds of environmental risk and disadvantage appear most likely to benefit from participation in mentoring programs" (Dubois et al., 2002, 157). In contrast, "evidence of an overall favorable effect of mentoring is notably lacking under circumstances in which participating youth have been identified as being at risk solely on the basis of individual-level characteristics (e.g., academic failure)" (Dubois et al., 2002, 189). The positive effects of mentoring programs are enhanced significantly when best practices are utilized and "when strong relationships are formed between mentors and youth." These best practices include "ongoing training for mentors, structured activities for mentors and youth as well as expectations for frequency of contact, mechanisms for support and involvement of parents, and monitoring of overall program implementation" (187–188). Grossman and Rhodes (2002) found that youth–adult mentoring relationships that lasted a year or longer delivered more positive for the youth, while youth in mentoring relationships that were terminated after a very short time actually showed decrements in their functioning.

3.4.1.5 Enriched Preschool Programs According to Schindler and Yoshikawa (2012, 70), "One setting for prevention that has shown potential for successfully reducing early behavioral problems, later antisocial behavior, and societal costs related to criminal activity is preschool education. Preschool programs can be particularly effective CPSD interventions for at-risk infants and children for a number of reasons: they begin at a young age, they can enable the identification of risk factors at an early stage, they can provide a range of much-needed protective factors (education, social and life skills development, positive role models, peer networks), they allow children to experience social and educational settings at a young age, and they can free the parents to work toward their own personal development. "Preschool interventions have the potential to target several child and parent characteristics that are risk or protector processes related behavioral problems and crime," Schindler and Yoshikawa (2012, 70) contend. "Indeed, preschool intervention specifically designed to address relevant child processes, such as cognitive skills, behavioral problems, or executive functioning, have shown promising results." In their meta-analysis of preschool programs in the United States, Camilli et al. (2010) found their greatest impact was on cognitive outcomes but had a small positive impact on social skills as well.

Research shows that preschool programs are particularly effective when combined with other targeted interventions for at-risk families, such as home visitations and parenting skills training. Based on their review of the literature, Schindler and Yoshikawa (2012, 71) write, "a number two-generation preschool programs targeting parenting skills or offering comprehensive family services have successfully reduced rates of behavior problems and later crime." Research has also shown that preschool programs are particularly beneficial for children from high-risk environments. The conclusion of one study into preschool programs showed "the largest and most lasting academic gains" were "for disadvantaged children and those attending schools with low levels of academic instruction" (Magnuson et al., 2004, 2).

3.4.1.6 After-School Programs/Sports and Recreational Programs After-school programs—regardless of their content—should be considered an important crime and violence prevention intervention, especially for at-risk teenagers, for at least two reasons. First, the hours between 3 and 6 p.m. (on weekdays) are the period in which youth are most lacking in adult supervision. It is during this unsupervised time that youth are most apt to engage in unnecessary risk-taking and even delinquent and criminal activities. Within the field of criminology, "routine activities theory suggests that, when youth peer groups congregate away from adult authority, both opportunity for and motivation to engage in deviant acts increase" (Brown Cross et al., 2009). One American study found most arrests of youth for violent offenses occurred between 2 and 6 p.m. (Snyder et al., 1997). Braga (2003) reports that the majority of gun violence in Boston occurs immediately after school ends and during the weekend evening hours and also increases during summer months.

The Afterschool Alliance (2007) also notes that this "after-school gap" constitutes the "peak hours for teens to commit crimes, be in or cause car crashes, be victims of crime, and smoke, drink and use drugs." According to the National Center on Addiction and Substance Abuse at Columbia University (2003), the likelihood that a young person will experiment with drugs and alcohol can increase by as much as 50% due to a lack of adult supervision and boredom (as cited in Afterschool Alliance, 2007). Brown Cross et al. (2009, 393–394) summarize research indicating "a consistent relationship between

CASE STUDY 3.8

ENRICHED PRESCHOOL CHILD DEVELOPMENT PROGRAM

Head Start is probably the best-known preschool child development program in North America. It is also one of the most comprehensive. Head Start targets children aged 3–5 years old who have experienced some form of neglect, abuse, or deprivation. Participating children are offered a range of experiences to prepare them for academic learning and for positive social interactions with teachers and other students. Subsidized breakfast and lunch are also part of many Head Start programs. The daily preschool program is meant to offer a stimulating and enjoyable environment that encourages the adoption of positive social and learning skills and aims to bolster the self-esteem of children (and their parents).

Head Start is premised on the belief that disadvantaged children have multiple needs, including the need for intellectual stimulation and improved diet, health care, and support. Accordingly, the program emphasizes the development of multiple solutions that embrace education, social services, medical and dental care, nutrition, mental health services, and parent involvement. While much of the program is delivered outside the home, it is supplemented with home visits by teachers and other professionals. Head Start also targets parents, involving them in both an advisory and support capacity. Services are provided to parents to help them acquire literacy and job skills and develop strong coping and parenting abilities. Overall, the program aims to help families become self-sufficient (National Head Start Association, 2014).

Program evaluations by the U.S. Department of Health and Human Services (2002) show that the Head Start program delivers a number of protective factors for at-risk children. Compared to control groups, children who participated in a Head Start program demonstrated increased cognitive development, greater social and emotional competency, less aggressive behavior, and stronger literacy skills. Parents participating in the program showed fewer signs of depression, greater emotional support for their children, greater job stability, and better parenting skills relative to a control group of parents.

Longitudinal research indicates that adults who participated in the Head Start program as children were "significantly less likely" to have been charged with a crime compared to siblings who were not enrolled in the program (Garces et al., 2002, 1009). In another assessment using data from the National Longitudinal Survey of Youth, Deming (2009) compared the personal development of siblings years after one of them participated in a Head Start program. He found that those who attended Head Start showed stronger academic performance, were less likely to be diagnosed with a learning disability, were more likely to graduate high school and attend college, were less likely to suffer from poor health as an adult, and were less likely to commit a crime. Another much-publicized study (Puma et al., 2010) showed significant immediate benefits of the program, although these benefits were somewhat diluted once the children reached elementary school. The study concludes that while "Head Start has positive impacts on several aspects of children's school readiness during their time in the program," the cognitive benefits of the program were not sustained by the time the children reached grade 1. The reason for this *fading* effect, according to some, is the fact that children enrolled in the Head Start program tend to come from disadvantaged backgrounds and thus attend lower-quality public schools, which may undermine any advantage that the program would initially provide (Lee and Loeb, 1995).

the amount of time adolescents and young adults spend in unstructured socializing in the absence of authority figures and growth in delinquency and substance use."

After-school programs are particularly important because research shows that poor parental supervision of children and youth (especially those who suffer from other social environmental and personal risk factors) has been linked to youth violence. According to Fitzgerald (2010, 5), "the relationship between parental monitoring and youth violence has been demonstrated in a number of studies." More specifically, "the association between poor parental monitoring of the kinds of companions with whom youth spend time and subsequent violent behavior in youth has been noted in a number of studies." Based on data derived from a longitudinal study of boys in Montreal, Brendgen et al. (2001) found that poor supervision by parents of their sons helped turn aggressive behavior at ages 13–15 into violent delinquency at ages 16 and 17. This is because poor parental supervision presents aggressive youth with far greater opportunities "for deviant affiliations" with other aggressive peers, "implicitly paving the way for violent and delinquent behavior" (Brendgen et al., 2001, 302, as cited in Fitzgerald, 2010, 5–6).

In another study using 2006 survey data from a sample of students in grades 7–9 attending Toronto schools, Fitzgerald (2010, 5) found "a low level of parental monitoring is associated with a higher likelihood of youth violent delinquency, and this effect is stronger when youth attend schools where the prevalence of delinquency among the student population is high." This finding supports the hypothesis that the "negative influence of low parental monitoring is magnified when youth are also exposed to a pool of delinquent peers, and further suggests that the effectiveness of particular parenting strategies may vary depending on the environments to which youth are exposed" (Fitzgerald, 2010, 4). In a study conducted by Gibson (2012), "unstructured socializing with peers was the only factor that significantly influenced violent victimization risk across low, medium and high disadvantaged neighborhoods." Based on these research findings, the logical deduction is that keeping youth active in structured, adult-supervised, after-school activities reduces the opportunities to get into trouble.

The second reason why after-school programs may be a potent crime and violence prevention intervention is that they can be used as a platform to deliver a wide range of protective factors to children and youth, including tutoring, mentoring, community service, social competency training, as well as sports and other recreational and cultural activities. In other words, after-school programs consider time spent out of school for youth as a prime opportunity to nurture positive youth development (Perkins and Noam, 2007).

In sum, after-school programs constitute a significant crime and violence prevention strategy, because not only can they reduce the idle, unsupervised, unstructured time of young people but they can also delivery important protective factors to at-risk children and youth. Based on their review of the literature, Brown Cross et al. (2009, 394–395) conclude that the after-school programs "have shown promise in improving a range of youth outcomes, from academic performance to substance use and delinquency" especially those that are "highly structured programs that employ evidence-based practices..." (Brown Cross et al., 2009, 395). The Afterschool Alliance cites specific case studies of after-school programs that have demonstrated efficacy in reducing delinquent and criminal behavior, as well as some underlying risk factors, among participating youth:

- A study of after-school programs implemented as part of the California Juvenile Crime Prevention Demonstration Project in 12 high-risk communities found that crime and delinquency-related behavior among participants declined significantly after they completed the program. Vandalism and stealing declined by two-thirds; violent acts and carrying a concealed weapon fell by more than half as did police arrests of program participants (Afterschool Alliance, 2007).

- In New York City, after-school programs started by Boys & Girls Clubs in selected public housing developments saw significant drops in drug use, presence of crack cocaine, and police reports of drug activity among program participants. At the same time, parental involvement increased, compared to a control group of public housing developments (Afterschool Alliance, 2007).
- A study of the BEST (Better Educated Students for Tomorrow) after-school program in Los Angeles showed that children and youth participating in the program were 30% less likely to participate in criminal activities than those who do not attend the program. In addition, dropout rates among participants were 20% lower compared to the dropout rate for the LA school district as a whole (Afterschool Alliance, 2007).

Research and program evaluations also highlight the characteristics of after-school programs that can undermine their effectiveness. In particular, programs that are loosely structured "often show no effects, and in some cases, participants display worse outcomes than similar students who did not participate." In addition, large after-school programs "have been shown to be less effective in reducing problem behavior outcomes (e.g., delinquency and drug use) than those that serve fewer youth" (Brown Cross et al., 2009, 395). Brown Cross et al. (2009, 395) identify other challenges that after-school programs face, which are particularly pertinent in the context of at-risk children and youth. Because participation in after-school programs are voluntary, they have "traditionally struggled to maintain consistent attendance... Youth who are motivated to spend their after-school time socializing with friends in unstructured hanging out can easily avoid adult monitoring by not attending programs." More significantly, research shows that those youth who are most at-risk of antisocial, delinquent, criminal, and violent behavior as well as substance abuse are much less likely to become involved in after-school programs and are more likely to drop out if they do become involved. In other words, after-school programs tend to be dominated by low-risk young people who are not necessarily in great need of structured, adult-supervised after-school programs or the protective factors they deliver. Thus, after-school programs "will only reduce delinquency if they provide structured, supervised activities to youth who would otherwise be unsupervised and engaged in risky behavior."

Whether it is during the after-school hours or some other time during the day or week, sports, recreational, and leisure activities have long been seen as a potent strategy to prevent youth crime and delinquency. Included in this broad category are organized sports leagues, the arts (music, dance, acting, painting, etc.), drop-in community (recreation) centers, youth clubs, dances, scouting and wilderness programs, and community service activities.

Sports and recreation programs in particular have became "popular tools for crime prevention, particularly prevention aimed at so-called at-risk or high-risk minority populations," according to Hartmann and Depro (2006, 180). Developmentally based sports and recreation programs that aim to prevent crime have become quite popular for at least two reasons. "One is that these programs are relatively inexpensive and easy to implement. In an era of declining public resources for outreach and social intervention of any kind, sports-based programs have been viewed as a cost-effective way to implement policy. These initiatives are not only easily adapted to existing facilities and programming but also often attract funding and support from foundations, nonprofit organizations, and even corporate sponsorships." "The second reason has to do with long-held and deeply entrenched cultural beliefs about sports as a positive, progressive social force" (Hartmann and Depro, 2006, 181).

Like after-school programs generally, sports and other recreational programs for young people can provide constructive, adult-supervised, and enjoyable activities that reduce idle time, while delivering such protective factors as healthy physical fitness, proficiency in a particular activity, strong self-esteem, positive social interaction, community integration, and social competency skills. Research generally supports the crime prevention potential of sports and recreational programs for at-risk children and youth, especially if they are well structured, are under adult supervision, and incorporate CPSD principles and strategies that have shown to engage and benefit at-risk young people (King, 1988; Jones and Offord, 1989; Schinke et al., 1992; Graham, 1995, 30–31; Perkins and Noam, 2007). As the International Centre for the Prevention of Crime puts it (2010, 135), "Beyond their objective of diverting youth from the temptation of committing a crime, sports and cultural activities are seen to encourage self expression and esteem, life skills and social skills, and education…"

Perkins and Noam (2007) extol the benefits of sport-based programming that deliver "developmentally intentional learning experiences" for youth. When structured and delivered in such a purposive fashion, "sports-based youth development programs have an essential role to play in promoting healthy youth who contribute to society… In addressing the whole child within the multiple roles children play in their lives and not just their role as a player, these programs use multiple methods to address the needs of the whole child and foster a healthy and contributing young person" (Perkins and Noam, 2007, 81, 82).

The authors divide the developmental benefits derived from purposive sports programs into three categories. First, such programs provide opportunities for youth to develop positive relationships with other peers and adult role models. Second, program facilitators can identify and target specific knowledge, skills, and competencies that youth can learn and develop. Third, these programs can be tailored to the individual needs of the participating youth. For Perkins and Noam (2007), effective sport-based youth development programs are characterized by at least 12 traits:

- Physical and psychological safety
- Appropriate structure (clear methods of communication, appropriate pace of the sessions, and explicit rules and expectations that govern the behavior of youth, parents, coaches, officials, and organizers)
- Supportive and trusting relationships with adult role models
- Opportunity to belong (help youth foster friendships, positive peer networks, and positive group experiences)
- Positive social norms (inculcate sportsmanship, teamwork, cooperation, mutual reciprocation, abiding by rules, conflict resolution, etc.)
- Support for efficacy (promote skills, proficiency, athletic abilities, and self-improvement)
- Asset-based focus (build on youth's existing assets and strengths)
- Opportunities to foster cultural competence (rules and expectations are culturally relevant and respectful of population being served)

- Active learning ("interactive and reflective learning opportunities that engage multiple learning styles")
- Opportunities for recognition (of effort, improvement, and sportsmanship, as opposed to winning)
- Integration of family, school, and community efforts (Perkins and Noam, 2007, 78–82)

Despite the perceptible virtues and benefits of sports and recreation programs for at-risk youth, Hartmann and Depro (2006, 181–182) caution that there is a lack of reliable evidence that they directly contribute to the reduction of crime or criminal behavior. They cite other studies suggesting that these programs might have the potential to increase juvenile crime and delinquency by concentrating young people who are potentially at risk together, thus reinforcing antisocial tendencies and facilitating deviant peer-group subculture."

In addition to sports, arts programs "have shown promise with at-risk youth in terms of risk factor alleviation," especially for decreasing mental health symptoms, improving coping and social skills, and bolstering school attendance and academic achievement (Rapp-Paglicci et al., 2011, 113).

3.4.1.7 Preventing Mental Health and Substance Abuse Disorders
Given the statistics and other research findings that associate certain mental health disorders with criminal and violent behavior, the timely identification, diagnosis, and treatment of mental health problems among young people may reduce the risk of offending and their formal contact with the criminal justice system. Furthermore, early intervention programs and curriculum have been developed for children and adolescents that can help *prevent* the onset of certain mental health disorders.

In their meta-analysis of 13 studies, Cuijpers et al. (2005) showed the efficacy of different programs delivered to young people to prevent the onset of a variety of illnesses, ranging from psychosis to anxiety disorders. Common to many of these programs are such features as cognitive–behavioral principles (in particular self-talk), social competency skills training (emphasizing coping and problem-solving skills), positive attitudes (strong self-esteem and a positive outlook on life), as well as family and community support. Many programs and curricula do not require delivery by mental health professionals; indeed, most are designed expressly to be delivered by lay people, in particular teachers and parents.

Such preventative interventions can be particularly beneficial for children from high-risk environments because the programs promote personal resilience through coping and other social competency skills necessary to deal with a negative environment they often cannot always control. In short, preventive interventions help ensure that reactive, mental health-care *treatment* services in institutions (including correctional institutions) do not have to be provided later in life. Furthermore, the skills promoted by the program can potentially help stave off mental health problems that may contribute to criminal, violent, and other antisocial and self-destructive behaviors.

The prevention of substance abuse disorders is another key component of health-care policies and programs that contribute to the prevention of crime, delinquency, and violence. Substance abuse prevention programs for young people educate them on the dangers of drinking, smoking, and drugs (both legal and illegal), while promoting such relevant social competencies as critical thinking, problem solving, coping,

CASE STUDY 3.9

SOCIAL–COGNITIVE SKILLS TRAINING THROUGH AFTER-SCHOOL SPORTS PROGRAMMING

The Becoming a Man (BAM) Sports Edition, implemented in Chicago, is a "one-year program designed to remediate social-cognitive skill deficits among low-income adolescent male students." The program "focuses on developing skills related to emotional regulation, control of stress response, improved social-information processing, interpersonal problem solving, goal setting and attainment, and personal integrity. Another goal of this intervention is to impart a realistic, socially responsible view of adult masculinity to youth whose social environments often promote competing, more aggressive norms. The program is based on CBT principles—a variety of techniques that help individuals "identify, monitor, challenge, and change their thoughts and behavior..." (University of Chicago, Crime Lab, 2012, 2–3).

Over the course of the 2009–2010 school year, participants in the BAM program were offered a mix of in-school and after-school programming to develop social–cognitive skills. The in-school program entailed 27 1 h small group sessions that met once a week during the school day over an 8-month period. Each session was designed to develop a specific social competency skill and was "built around an explicitly articulated lesson." Students were also assigned homework to practice and apply that skill in a real-life setting. In addition, the program included after-school sports activities designed to reinforce some of the skills taught during the in-class sessions (e.g., conflict resolution) (University of Chicago, Crime Lab, 2012, 3).

This particular edition of BAM included an after-school sports component, involving activities "designed to reinforce conflict resolution skills and the social and emotional learning objectives" of the BAM curriculum and to increase program attendance. "Sports varied by school and included wrestling, martial arts, archery, weight lifting, boxing, and handball. This programming was provided by coaches trained in the overall goals of BAM and in social-emotional learning principles more generally" (University of Chicago, Crime Lab, 2012, 4).

An assessment of the program showed that participants "significantly increased school engagement and performance" during the year the program was offered and in the follow-up year. Researchers estimated that the improvements could potentially translate "into a 10 to 23 percent increase in graduation rates among those who completed the program." In addition, "The intervention also reduced violent-crime arrests during the program year by 8.1 per 100 youth, or 44 percent. Student surveys provide suggestive evidence that social-cognitive skills mediate these impacts." According to the study's authors, "the positive program effects provide the most rigorous, large-scale evidence to date that a social-cognitive skill intervention can improve both schooling and delinquency outcomes for disadvantaged youth" (University of Chicago, Crime Lab, 2012, 4). Moreover, "what is perhaps most remarkable about these findings" is the "relatively limited number of contact hours participants had in the program (about 13 sessions), and the low cost of the intervention ($1,100 per participant)." The "dollar-valued benefits to society range from 3 to 31 times the $1,100 per-participant program cost," which means "there may be considerable returns to society" by investing in similar social competency training programs from disadvantaged youth (University of Chicago, Crime Lab, 2012, 7).

CASE STUDY 3.10

CULTURAL ARTS-BASED SOCIAL COMPETENCY PROGRAM

Rapp-Paglicci et al. (2009, 2012) provide a description and assessment of the Prodigy Program, which "synthesizes two promising intervention modalities for positive youth development, namely, cultural arts and self-regulation skills." In particular, the Prodigy Program offers at-risk youth, ages 7–17, an opportunity to participate in classes comprising the visual, performing, musical, media, and theater arts. In addition, social competency (self-regulation) skills are modeled, taught, and practiced in the classes, including communication, anger management, conflict resolution, and problem-solving skills. Evaluations indicate that those who completed the program had reductions in mental health symptoms (depression, anxiety, etc.) and externalizing behaviors (aggression, disruptive behaviors, etc.). They also experienced increases in school-related measures (better grades in math and English, more consistent school attendance) and improved family functioning and communication (Rapp-Paglicci et al., 2009, 2012).

---

assertiveness, and resistance (to peer pressure and drug use). In his review of the literature, Greenwood (2006, 91) concludes:

> The approach to substance abuse prevention that has been identified as most promising utilizes psychosocial approaches that include training in personal, social, and resistance skills. The intent of these programs is to teach of the kind of generic skills for coping with life that will have a fairly broad application. By the mid-1980s, most of the studies testing the use of skills-training approaches began to demonstrate significant and large behavioral effects, showing reductions in experimental drug use ranging from 45 to 75 percent.

Botvin (1990) argues that those child- and youth-centered drug awareness, education, and prevention programs that research has shown to be "ineffective" are those that disseminate information about the effects of drugs; those that attempt to arouse fear about the risks of tobacco, alcohol, or drug use; and those that use moral appeals to teach students about the evils of drug use.

3.4.1.8 Education and Schools: Academic, Intellectual, and Cognitive Development
As a crime prevention institution, schools are second only to families in their potential contribution to reducing risk factors that give rise to delinquent, criminal, and violent behavior. As Gottfredson (1997, 1) writes:

> Schools have great potential as a locus for crime prevention. They provide regular access to students throughout the developmental years, and perhaps the only consistent access to large numbers of the most crime-prone young children in the early school years; they are staffed with individuals paid to help youth develop as healthy, happy, productive citizens; and the community usually supports schools' efforts to socialize youth. Many of the precursors of delinquent behavior are school-related and therefore likely to be amenable to change through school-based intervention.

This basic academic mandate of schools is now supplemented by its role in helping to positively socialize, feed, counsel, and even provide health-care services for children

CASE STUDY 3.11

PREVENTING AND TREATING ANXIETY IN YOUNG PEOPLE

FRIENDS for Life is a school-based anxiety prevention and treatment program that is meant to instill in children (ages 7–11 years) and adolescents (ages 12–16 years) the skills and capacities to effectively deal with fears, worries, anxieties, and depression. This is accomplished by building their psychological resilience, self-esteem, coping skills, and problem-solving skills, while promoting their ability to foster positive relationships with peers and adults. The long-term goal of the program is to "reduce the incidence of serious psychological disorders, emotional distress and impairment in social functioning by teaching children and young people how to cope with, and manage, anxiety both now and in later life" (Barrett, 2007, 4).

The program name (FRIENDS) is an acronym for the systematic lesson plan delivered by the curriculum (*F*eeling Worried?; *R*elax and feel good; *I*nner thoughts; *E*xplore plans; *N*ice work so reward yourself; *D*on't forget to practice; and *S*tay calm, you know how to cope now). The idea behind the acronym is to help children remember the strategies they can use to cope with stressful situations. The concept of friendships is also central to the program in that the curriculum "encourages children to (a) think of their body as their friend because it tells them when they are feeling worried or nervous by giving them clues; (b) be their own friend and reward themselves when they try hard; (c) make friends, so that they can build their social support networks; and finally (d) talk to their friends when they are in difficult or worrying situations" (Shortt et al., 2001, 526).

The FRIENDS for Life program is based on CBT principles. According to Paula Barrett, a psychologist who developed the program, children are "taught to be aware of somatic cues when they are feeling anxious, and learn relaxation techniques so as to eliminate tension, remain calm and think clearly. Children are also taught to recognize negative self-talk and challenge unhelpful thoughts in positive ways" (Barrett and Sonderegger, 2005, 42).

The program was designed for use in schools by teachers during normal class time. The curriculum consists of 10 regular sessions and 2 booster sessions. The first two sessions include an introduction to the program. The remainder of the sessions entail sequential steps in which the children learn to "feel confident and brave." These are also based on the FRIENDS acronym and are as follows:

- *F*eelings (understanding one's feelings and how others are feeling).
- *R*elaxation techniques (specific techniques to learn to relax in stressful situations).
- *I*nner thoughts (recognizing how our thinking or *self-talk* can promote anxiety or confidence).
- *E*xploring solutions and coping plans (fostering a specific coping plan for and by each child).
- *N*ice work! Now reward yourself (for positive reinforcement).
- *D*on't forget to practice (to inculcate the skills for use outside the FRIENDS group).
- *S*tay calm or smile (a summary of the skills taught in the entire program).

The curriculum is highly interactive; much of the learning is done in a small group context that encourages discussion and peer support. Each child is provided with a workbook in which he or she can complete exercises at home with a parent and a personal diary, which can be used to record thoughts, feelings, and emotions.

In addition to the curriculum implemented with children, FRIENDS for Life also includes a family skills component to nurture the ability of parents to help their child with the skills learned through the program (including practicing the skills at home) while encouraging a positive supportive family environment. In addition, the program also emphasizes peer support and peer learning; children are encouraged to learn from each other's experiences, to make friends, and to build their social networks, while parents are encouraged to facilitate their children's peer networks.

Through a number of studies, the program has proven effective in increasing coping skills, reducing anxiety symptoms, and preventing the onset of anxiety and depression for up to 36 months following initial exposure to the curriculum (Shortt et al., 2001; Lowry-Webster et al., 2003; Barrett et al., 2006).

and youth. Schools are also a key community institution in promoting young people's interest and proficiency in sports or other recreational and cultural activities. A wide range of additional services are available in schools that cater to those who are most at risk of criminal and violent offending, based on their behavior and academic performance, such as persistent truants, chronic academic under-achievers, bullies, victims, and those with conduct problems. Specialized services are also available to students that deal directly with such criminogenic risk factors, as substance abuse, violence, sex, and gang membership.

Gottfredson et al. (2006, 62) classify school-based criminality prevention into two broad categories: (1) "environmental-change strategies for school-based prevention (altering school or classroom environments)" and (2) "individual-change strategies for school-based prevention (changing the behaviors, knowledge, skills, attitudes, or beliefs of individual students)." Each category can be further divided into specific strategies that can foster school-based protective factors for students, such as academic success, bonding to school and to learning, and avoidance of high-risk attitudes and behaviors. These different strategies are summarized in Box 3.2.

Some of the most effective school-based programs targeting at-risk children and youth are implemented as part of larger strategies or philosophies that are intended to nurture a school climate conducive to minimizing both school-based (environmental) risk factors and personal (academic and behavioral) risk factors. How the school and classroom environment is organized and managed can make the learning process of students more effective and enjoyable, which can foster their attachment and commitment to their school and to education. In turn, this can mitigate such criminogenic risk factors such as academic underachievement, estrangement from schools, truancy, expulsion, and dropping out.

For criminologist Graham (1995, 27), effective schools are those where all students succeed in some way or another, where students have input into their own curriculum and school governance policies, where teachers and students like and trust one another, where rules are clear and are consistently and fairly enforced, and where schools accept full responsibility for not just teaching, but also looking after their students. Schools that successfully motivate, integrate, and reward their students, irrespective of academic ability, are more likely to contribute the most to preventing current delinquent and future criminal or violent behavior. Schools that have high rates of delinquency among students are generally those that, intentionally or unintentionally, segregate students according to academic ability, concentrate on academic success at the expense of social skills, categorize students as deviants or failures, and defer responsibility for the behavior and welfare of their students to outside agencies and institutions.

CASE STUDY 3.12

A COMPREHENSIVE DRUG USE PREVENTION INITIATIVE

The Midwestern Prevention Project (MPP) is a community-based, multicomponent, multiyear, universal substance abuse prevention program that was initiated in 1984 in Kansas City (and originally known as Students Taught Awareness and Resistance or STARR) and then replicated in Indianapolis. The program targets students in early adolescence (grades 7 and 8) because this age group is considered to be most susceptible to gateway drug use (i.e., alcohol, cigarettes, and marijuana).

The goal of the MPP is to help youth recognize the tremendous social and peer pressures to use drugs and to train them to acquire the skills in how to resist drug use. This comprehensive, scientifically developed drug prevention program includes components for the school, parents, the media, community groups, the private sector, and the local government. Each of these program components are introduced in sequence at a rate of one per year (for a total of 5 years), with the mass media component occurring throughout all the years.

The prevention messages and skills training are delivered though the school-based component of the program and are reinforced and supported by a consistent community norm against drug use through a system of coordinated, community-wide strategies that involve parents, the media, the wider community, and local governments. The underlying premise of this systematic, multimodal approach is that the more channels used in disseminating a prevention message, the greater the likelihood that positive behaviors will be adopted.

At the core of the school component is a specially designed curriculum that is integrated into classroom instruction by trained teachers over a 2-year period. During the first year, a 13-lesson curriculum is taught, followed by 5 booster lessons delivered in the second year. The curriculum focuses on increasing students' resistance skills and includes instruction on the consequences of drug use, resisting peer and other pressures to do drugs, problem solving in difficult situations, and assertiveness. Effective pedagogical techniques (i.e., behavioral modeling, role-playing, and discussion) are used alongside homework assignments designed to involve family members. To complement this curriculum, an anti-drug culture is promoted throughout the school (and community). This is accomplished through school-wide policies on drug use and student *skill leaders* who serve as role models for the skills being taught.

The parental program is initiated in the second year and involves parents in a number of ways to increase the impact of the program on their children. Parents are encouraged to participate in the school component by working with their children on homework assignments they are required to complete together. Parents are also encouraged to become involved in a school-based group that plans and implements strategies and activities that limit young people's accessibility to drugs, cigarettes, and alcohol, carries out fundraising projects, and helps school officials develop substance abuse policies. The parent component also includes two, 2 h training sessions that help them understand the program and the skills imparted to their children, how to support the skills taught through the program at home, how to effectively communicate with their children, and other techniques than can be used to help their kids avoid using and abusing substances.

The media component, which is introduced in the first year of the program, entails the use of the local media to introduce, promote, and reinforce the implementation and maintenance of the program and the drug prevention message. The media is used to increase exposure of the project and relevant substance abuse issues to youth and the community as a whole.

The community organizing component, implemented in years three through five, is meant to mobilize broad-based support for the program and its goals and to use local citizens to help oversee the implementation and maintenance of the program. Community organizing is carried out by parents and local leaders who are responsible for quality control, providing advice on the development of relevant health policies, helping to maintain community support for substance abuse prevention, and identifying funding sources.

The health policy component of the project involves the development and implementation of local public policies and bylaws on drugs, alcohol, and tobacco. These policies can include measures that create drug-free school zones and workplaces, restrict smoking in public places, restrict the display and availability of cigarettes and alcohol in retail stores, set up drug treatment facilities and services, and establish guidelines for referring young people to counseling and treatment programs.

Evaluations of the MPP have demonstrated positive results. Youth attending schools in communities where the program was fully implemented were less likely to smoke on a daily basis and there was also less use of marijuana and alcohol by youth in the treatment group within a year of completing the school-based training. Three years following completion of the program, youth in the treatment group continued to use less tobacco and marijuana than those in the control group, although the program's impact on alcohol consumption was not as strong at that point (Johnson et al., 1990; Chou et al., 1998).

Gottfredson et al. (2006, 72) identify four major "environmental-change" strategies that can increase a school's capacity to deliver protective factors to all students, but especially those who are at risk for future delinquent, criminal, and antisocial behavior:

1. Building school capacity to manage itself effectively and to manage discipline by establishing and enforcing school rules, policies, or regulations
2. Establishing norms or expectations for behavior
3. Changing classroom instructional and management practices to enhance classroom climate or improve educational processes
4. Grouping students in different ways to achieve smaller, less alienating, or otherwise more suitable microclimates within the school

For Gottfredson (1997, 10), school-based innovations begin by democratizing the "decision-making processes or authority structures" with a school. Specifically, the most effective capacity-building programs involve teams of staff, students, parents, and community members "engaged in planning and carrying out activities to improve the school. They can diagnose school problems, formulate school goals and objectives, design potential solutions, monitor progress, and evaluate the efforts." Programs and policies that enhance "the administrative capability of the school by increasing communication and cooperation among members of the school community" are also critical. Effective classroom management includes establishing expectations for behavior, consistently enforcing these rules, providing frequent and specific praise and encouragement to promote students' efforts and progress, using proven instructional techniques (interactive teaching, establishing clear objectives, frequent assessments to ensure comprehension, the use of audiovisual material, cooperative learning in a small group format to reinforce and practice what the teacher taught, rewards to teams

---

BOX 3.2

CATEGORIES OF SCHOOL-BASED PREVENTION STRATEGIES

Environmental change strategies (altering school or classroom environments):

"Managing schools and discipline"—"Interventions to change the decision-making process of authority structures to enhance the general capacity of the school."

"Establishing norms for behavior"—This involves "school-wide efforts to redefine norms for behavior and signal appropriate behavior through the use of rules."

"Managing classes"—"Instructional methods designed to increase student engagement in the learning process and hence increase their academic performance and bonding to the school," which includes "classroom organization and management strategies."

"Regrouping students"—"Reorganizing classes or grades to create smaller units, continuing interaction, or different mixes of students, or to provide greater flexibility in instruction."

Individual-change strategies (changing the behaviors, knowledge, skills, attitudes, or beliefs of individual students):

"Instructing students"—"These interventions provide instruction to students to teach them factual information, increase their awareness of social influences to engage in misbehavior, expand their repertoires for recognizing and appropriately responding to risky or potentially harmful situation, increase their appreciation for diversity in society, improve their moral character, etc."

"Behavior Modification and Teaching Thinking Strategies"—"Behavior modification strategies focus directly on changing behaviors," which include nurturing critical thinking skills in students so they avoid high-risk behaviors.

"Counseling and social work"—"Individual counseling, substance abuse, treatment, case management and similar group-based interventions ..."

"Mentoring, tutoring, and work-study experiences"—This includes one-on-one interaction between a young person and an adult that can include academic tutoring as well as "work-study" initiatives where students work at a job as part of their studies.

"Providing recreational, enrichment, and leisure activities"—"Activities intended to provide constructive and fun alternatives to delinquent behavior. Drop-in recreation centers, after-school and week-end programs, dances, community service activities, and other events are offered in these programs as alternatives to the more dangerous activities" (Gottfredson et al., 2006, 63–64).

---

for improvement), and the use of external resources such as parent volunteers, police officers, or professionals as instructors or teachers' aides.

Another effective school-wide philosophy that is particularly salient to delinquency, crime, and violence prevention is establishing norms and expectations for the behavior of students. According to Welsh (2007, 27), "school-based programs to prevent crime involve clarifying to students (and sometimes to teachers and others) what is and what is not acceptable behavior in schools, and targeting related risk factors for crime." Innovative and

CASE STUDY 3.13

A HOLISTIC APPROACH TO A POSITIVE SCHOOL CULTURE

Developed by educators in North Carolina's Charleston County School District, PATHE (Positive Action Through Holistic Education) is a holistic approach to promoting an overall positive school culture at the middle and high school levels, especially those that serve high numbers of minority students in impoverished areas. More a philosophy than a program, PATHE seeks to increase students' academic success, positive school-related experiences, attachment to their school, and commitment to their education, while reducing truancy, absenteeism, and school disorder. These objectives are to be achieved by encouraging mutual respect, cooperation, and a sense of belonging among all school members; improving communication between students, faculty, staff, and the school management; encouraging a high degree of student and staff participation in the governance of the school and school activities in general; providing clear, fair, and consistently enforced rules; and improving teachers' class management skills. Specific elements of the PATHE philosophy include the following:

1. Establishing teams of pupils, teachers, parents, school administrators, and representatives of community groups to review, revise, and implement positive changes in the curriculum and disciplinary matters
2. Identifying and diagnosing and strengthening school-wide academic weaknesses and discipline problems
3. Implementing innovative teaching techniques and student team learning to improve testing and study skills
4. Improving the sense of community and attachment of students, teachers, parents, and others to the school (extracurricular activities, peer counseling services, school pride campaigns, etc.)
5. Encouraging parents of children entering adolescence to recognize and acknowledge their emerging adult status and, in doing so, adopt a more conciliatory approach to the negotiation of rules and expectations, particularly with respect to the setting of boundaries to their newly emerging personal freedom
6. Helping students in their transition from school to career and postsecondary education, including training in skills for finding and keeping a job
7. Providing special academic and counseling services to pupils with academic or behavioral problems aimed at improving their self-efficacy, academic success, and bonds to the school and the wider community

An evaluation of the application of the PATHE philosophy in seven secondary schools in Charleston County from 1981 to 1983 showed that the students self-reported significantly less delinquent behavior and drug use, had fewer suspensions, and had fewer school punishments after the first year of the program. There were no similar changes for these variables among students in the control schools; in fact, in some schools, there was an increase in delinquency problems. Suspensions also declined significantly in the PATHE schools, although a similar decline was observed in a control school as well. Several indicators of the school climate targeted by the program (e.g., safety, staff morale, clarity of school rules, and effectiveness of the school administration) also changed for the better in the PATHE schools (Gottfredson, 1990, 1997; Graham, 1995, 28).

comprehensive efforts to communicate and enforce appropriate behaviors are particularly important to maintaining order in school, reducing student and teacher victimization, and even contributing to the academic success of students. This proactive approach to discipline, which includes rewarding good behavior, is viewed as more effective than reactive, punitive, sanction-based responses to bad behavior, such as detentions or expulsions.

The Department of Education in Nova Scotia, Canada, for example, has implemented Positive Effective Behaviour Supports (PEBS), which is concerned with "the development and implementation of comprehensive, school-wide positive behavioral interventions and supports, recognizing and rewarding positive behaviour, and proactively intervening to prevent disruptive behaviour from occurring (thereby minimizing the need for disciplinary responses)" (Nova Scotia Task Force on Bullying and Cyberbullying, 2012, 61). In this regard, PEBS "sets out clear expectations for student behaviour. Students are rewarded for positive behaviour" and "creating a better school environment" (Government of Nova Scotia, 2007, 46). Schools develop their own specific school codes of conduct, based upon the principles and behavioral standards outlined in the Provincial School Code of Conduct and Code of Conduct Guidelines.

The aforementioned environmental change strategies for school-based prevention are complemented by "individual-change strategies" that strive toward "changing the behaviors, knowledge, skills, attitudes, or beliefs of individual students" (Gottfredson et al., 2006, 62). Education negatively correlates with criminal behavior (i.e., a good education can protect against future criminal predispositions). As such, one of the most important CPSD interventions for enhancing the resilience of youth is intellectual and cognitive development through a strong formal education. Students who experience high academic achievement and feel attached to their schools are also less likely to engage in problem behaviors (Elliot and Voss, 1974; Hawkins and Lam, 1987; Gottfredson, 1988; Henggeler, 1989; Maguin and Loeber, 1996; Johnson et al., 2001; Gottfredson et al., 2006). As Welsh (2007) puts it, "general instruction of students is the most common school-based crime prevention strategy" and involves a wide range of functions: "to teach [students] factual information, increase their awareness of social influences regarding misbehavior, expand their repertoires for recognizing and appropriately responding to risky or potentially harmful situations, increase their appreciation for diversity in society, and improve their moral character" (Welsh, 2007, 27–28).

Intensive and individualized academic programs can be used successfully with at-risk students, including those with a low IQ, a learning disability, psychological disorders, a lack of attachment to schools and education, or other personal and social environmental problems that may block academic achievement and cognitive development. Particularly effective are educational strategies that begin with a diagnosis of behavioral, psychological, and cognitive problems and disorders, which are then followed by one or more of the following:

- The development of individual work plans with well-defined and realistic goals
- The use of specially trained teachers
- One-on-one tutoring support and/or a small group learning environment
- The application of effective, scientifically proven pedagogies (an interactive, experiential learning environment that includes constant feedback)
- Innovative and effective school and classroom management techniques
- The incorporation of social competency skills and cognitive–behavioral techniques into the learning environment (especially to change negative behaviors)
- The use of incentives to positively reinforce attendance and other positive behaviors

- The active involvement of parents in the child's education (including behavioral modeling by a parent, such as when a parent reads at home or furthers his or her own education) (Jurich and Estes, 2000; Gottfredson et al., 2006)

According to Boccanfuso and Kuhfeld (2011), programs that provide social competency skills training and targeted behavioral supports for students who exhibit chronic negative behavior are particularly important to promoting their academic success, while limiting misbehavior.

> Most notably, these programs typically involve program leaders engaging students in daily or weekly exercises to build social skills. These exercises, which generally are interactive, are designed to help students learn to listen, manage their anger, resolve conflicts, and practice and develop other social skills that can enable them to minimize instances of negative behavior. The other distinguishing feature of many of these programs is individualized behavioral support. Targeted behavioral support programs for at-risk students generally consist of small-group or one-on-one training sessions. Many effective behavioral supports also help students develop individualized anger management plans for dealing with the specific sources of stress or anger in their lives. These individualized interventions often involve trusted family members as well. By involving family members in these plans, targeted behavioral support programs educate family members about the sources of the student's negative behavior and help them to reinforce the lessons learned during training sessions.

Boccanfuso and Kuhfeld (2011, 4)

> Several character education and social-emotional learning programs have had significant, positive impacts on school safety by taking a preventive approach to violence and substance-related school offenses. Character education programs have been defined as programs that deliberately attempt to develop students' character by teaching core values … that help students to avoid negative behaviors. Social-emotional learning programs have been described as programs that aid the process through which children and adults acquire the knowledge, attitudes and skills to recognize and manage their emotions, set and achieve positive goals, demonstrate caring and concern for others, establish and maintain positive relationships, make responsible decisions, and handle interpersonal situations effectively.

Boccanfuso and Kuhfeld (2011, 5)

> A synthesis of results from existing rigorous evaluations of character education and social-emotional learning programs indicates that, in general, these programs have had significant, positive impacts on building social and emotional skills; adjusting behavior; reducing aggression and conduct problems; and increasing academic performance across grade levels, ability levels, racial/ethnic groups, and locales.

Boccanfuso and Kuhfeld (2011, 5)

Successful efforts to modify the behavior of at-risk students also rely on reinforcers, in particular praise and material rewards. One study examined a program that used positive reinforcements with high-risk youth to reduce tardiness and punishment, while increasing class preparedness, class performance, classroom behavior, and school attendance. Students met with program staff on a weekly basis and earned points, contingent upon their behavior, that could be cashed in for a class trip of the student's choosing. Frequent parent notification was also used. Students in the treatment group had significantly better grades and attendance at the end of the program than did those in the control group, although the positive effects did not appear until the students had been in the program for 2 years (Bry and George, 1979, 1980). Bry (1982) reports that in the year after the intervention ended, the treatment group of students displayed significantly fewer problem behaviors at school than did those in the control group; and in the 18 months following the intervention, the former group reported significantly less substance abuse and criminal behavior. Five years after the program ended, those in the treatment group were 66% less likely to have a criminal record than those in the control group.

Alternative schools are another example of how school-wide and student-focused strategies coalesce to help struggling students and at-risk youth realize academic success and other important personal developmental milestones. Alternative schools offer an enriched curriculum and specific philosophy that caters to students who have problems functioning in a traditional school setting. As such, they can also be considered a criminality and violence prevention measure insofar as they address academic failure and prevents students from dropping out or being expelled from traditional schools. Students targeted for alternative schools include those who have a high truancy rate, exhibit chronic and ongoing conduct problems, have been under long-term suspension from school, display little attachment to traditional schools, have dropped out of school, are at risk of dropping out of school, have acute psychological or mental health problems, or who simply have significant academic problems (including a learning disability). Alternative schools are particularly amenable to these youth because of the presence of several key characteristics. Steinberg and Almeida (2004, 7) cite the following key attributes of effective alternative schools:

- High academic standards transparently linked to future learning and work opportunities
- Small, caring environment with low teacher/student ratios
- Individualized flexible programs with high expectations and clear rules of behavior
- Opportunities for youth to catch up and accelerate knowledge and skills
- Innovative staff in multiple roles
- Operational flexibility/autonomy
- Opportunities for youth to participate and have voice in school matters
- Shared sense of community and mutual trust
- Parental involvement
- Links to community organizations

Within alternative schools, a team of professionals (teachers, psychologists, and counselors) is often assembled to help develop a specialized and individualized curriculum for these students based on their specific needs and abilities. The academic curriculum will frequently be complemented with social competency skills training, vocational skills training, and counseling for the student and his or her family. These schools are more flexible than traditional schools in that many students may be attending part-time. Some of the criteria used to judge the success of these schools is a high rate of graduation, job placement, or the student's successful return to his or her regular school.

In sum, schools that use innovative and effective school and classroom management strategies, as well as behavior modification and social competency skill training techniques for individual (at-risk) students, have shown positive effects. This includes increased academic performance and school attendance, greater attachment and commitment to their school, lower crime and delinquency rates, a reduction in antisocial and aggressive behavior, and lower rates of substance abuse. As Gottfredson et al. (2006, 145) conclude, "several school-based prevention strategies are effective for reducing crime…." Strategies that focus on changing the school environment are generally more effective than those focusing on changing individuals' attitudes, behaviors, or beliefs (the one exception is truancy and dropout, which are more effectively addressed through personal change strategies and material incentives for at-risk students). The most effective strategies are "school and discipline management interventions; interventions to establish norms and expectations for behavior; and instructional programs that teach social competency skills using cognitive-behavioral methods." Those school-based strategies that appear to be least effective are "instructional programs that do not use cognitive-behavioral methods; counseling, social work and other therapeutic interventions, and [unsupervised] recreation and leisure programs."

3.4.1.9 School-Based Bullying, Harassment, and Violence Prevention

As Farrington and Ttofi (2009, 8) write, "it is understandable why school bullying has increasingly become a topic of both public concern and research efforts," especially given the "serious short-term and long-term effects of bullying on children's physical and mental health." Victims of bullying may also be more apt to join gangs (for protection), which increases further exposure to violence. Those who are the instigators of chronic bullying or other forms of harassment or violence are also at risk of future delinquent, criminal, and violent behavior directly and indirectly (e.g., by being expelled from school).

Farrington and Ttofi (2009) conducted a review and meta-analysis of studies that examined the effectiveness of school-based programs designed to reduce bullying and victimization. As part of their review, they identified a broad range of approaches, which they grouped into the following categories:

* Whole-school antibullying policy—"the presence of a formal anti-bullying policy on behalf of the school"
* Classroom rules—"the use of rules against bullying that students were expected to follow"
* School conferences—"the organization of school assemblies during which children were informed about bullying"
* Curriculum materials—"the use of materials about bullying during classroom lessons"
* Classroom management—"an emphasis on classroom management techniques in detecting and dealing with bullying behavior"
* Cooperative group work—"the cooperation among different professionals (usually among teachers and some other professional groups) in working with bullies and victims of bullying"
* Work with bullies and victims—"individualized work (not offered at the classroom level) with children involved in bullying as victims or perpetrators"
* Work with peers—"the formal engagement of peers in tackling bullying" (e.g., peer mediation, peer mentoring, and "the engagement of bystanders in bullying situations")
* Improved playground supervision—"Some anti-bullying programs aimed to identify 'hot-spots' or 'hot-times' of bullying (mostly during playtime or lunchtime) and provided improved playground supervision of children"
* Disciplinary methods—"Some programs emphasized punitive methods in dealing with bullying situations"
* Nonpunitive methods—restorative justice (see Chapter 4 for a detailed description of restorative justice) and other nonpunitive methods to deal with young people involved in bullying

- Teacher training—to combat bullying and deal with its aftermath
- Parent training/meetings—information nights or educational presentations for parents and/or teacher–parent meetings that provide information about the antibullying initiative in the school
- Videos and virtual reality computer games—"the use of anti-bullying videos or virtual reality computer games to raise students' awareness regarding bullying" (Farrington and Ttofi, 2009, 63–65)

The authors conclude that the "results obtained so far in evaluations of anti-bullying programs are encouraging." Overall, the meta-analysis showed that "school-based anti-bullying programs are effective in reducing bullying and victimization (being bullied). On average, bullying decreased by 20%–23% and victimization decreased by 17%–20%." "The most important program elements that were associated with a decrease in both bullying and victimization," according to Farrington and Ttofi (2009, 6–7), "were parent training/meetings, disciplinary methods, the duration of the program for children and teachers and the intensity of the program for children and teachers" (Farrington and Ttofi, 2009, 66).

There is much agreement in the literature on school-based bullying prevention that the first step in effectively combating this problem is to foster a school culture that condemns bullying and other forms of harassment and violence, while promoting respect, tolerance, empathy, harmonious relationships, and peaceful conflict resolution. Schools must also foster within individual students the cognitive and behavioral capacity to resist harassing and violent behavior. This can be accomplished through curriculum and counseling that teaches relevant social competencies (such as empathy, self-control, anger management, and critical thinking); promotes beliefs favorable to nonviolence; increases knowledge about the harmful effects of bullying, conflict, and violence; and imparts tangible skills to students (and staff) to resolve conflicts peacefully. Specialized curriculum and intensive efforts should be dedicated to chronic bullies and violent students. More specifically, recommended strategies to reduce bullying, other forms of harassment, and violence in schools can be summarized as follows:

- Establishing a policy of zero tolerance toward bullying, harassment, and violence
- Establishing, communicating, and upholding clear, firm standards and boundaries regarding unacceptable behavior
- Communicating and consistently enforcing specific and clear policies and procedures that are school- and district-wide
- Training school officials and parents on how to identify and deal with bullying, harassment, and violence (and their root causes) in an effective manner
- Encouraging students to report incidents
- Implementing a comprehensive reporting system to track bullying and the interventions used with specific bullies and victims
- Providing counseling for students who have been bullied, harassed, or victimized in some other way as well as repercussions (and treatment) for those who instigated the harassment or violence
- Promoting vital relationships and communication between school staff and parents
- Ensuring the commitment of school staff, parents, and other key partners to all of the aforementioned

CASE STUDY 3.14

A SCHOOL-BASED BULLYING PREVENTION PROGRAM

The Olweus Bullying Prevention Program is a multilevel program designed to reduce and prevent school bullying in elementary, middle, and high schools. The program was developed and first implemented in Norway but has spread to other countries, including the United States, England, and Canada.

The main tactics used include increased awareness and knowledge about bullying, the involvement of all key stakeholders in designing and implementing the program (and bullying prevention in general), the development of clear rules against bullying, and providing support and protection to victims. The long-term goal of the program is to create a safe and positive school climate and to improve peer relations at school.

The program targets bullying at three levels: the school, the classroom, and the individual. The school level component begins with an assessment phases that gathers information on the nature and scope of bullying at a particular school (primarily through an anonymous questionnaire survey of students). This is followed by the formation of a committee (including administrators, teachers, counselors, health professionals, parents, and students) to coordinate the prevention program and the development of an adult based system for supervising students outside of the classroom (especially in areas where there is a high frequency of bullying).

The classroom-level component involves establishing clear and consistently enforced rules against bullying, as well as discussions and activities to reinforce antibullying strategies, values, and norms. This component also encourages parental involvement through meetings and discussion of the problem and efforts to address it. The individual-level component focuses on interventions with the bullies, victims, and their parents and is designed to ensure the cessation of the harassing behavior and to provide support to victims.

The program has been assessed in several studies in Norway, the United States, and England. In general, the findings were mixed with respect to reductions in self-reported bullying and victimization but are generally positive. More specifically, according to Crimesolutions.gov:

> In the original Norway study and the South Carolina replication, there were reductions in self-reported bullying and antisocial behaviors (theft, vandalism, and truancy). Only the Norway study demonstrated reductions in self-reported victimization and improved school climate, as well as teacher and peer reports of bully-victim problems. The outcomes in Norway were found in the first follow-up (8 months after baseline) as well as the second follow-up (20 months after baseline). South Carolina outcomes were significant only after one year of the program, and were not found after two program years. An English study also showed significant decreases in self-reported frequency of bullying. A second U.S. study in Seattle showed no overall effects on physical or relational victimization, however, both types of bullying victimization were significantly reduced among white intervention students, relative to white controls (Blueprints for Healthy Youth Development, Internet web site, Olweus Bullying Prevention Program).

A more recent evaluation of the program in Pennsylvania, which involved involving more than 70,000 students in 214 schools (Limber and Olweus, 2013, 2), found "large decreases" in student self-reports of being bullied and of bullying others. There were also "positive program effects related to students' attitudes about bullying (e.g., students' feelings when another student is being bullied, whether they thought they could join in bullying) and their reports of others' actions to address bullying (e.g., how much teachers or fellow students have done about the problem)."

Boccanfuso and Kuhfeld (2011) describe how proactive measures are increasingly replacing reactive, punitive approaches to controlling bullying, harassment, and violence on school campuses. Traditionally, zero-tolerance measures have been used to punish misbehavior because of the prevailing "belief among some educators and parents that a failure to strongly punish misbehavior sends a message that their school is not serious about the safety of students and staff. Some stakeholders use these policies out of concern that nonpunitive interventions may allow disruptive students to remain in the classroom and prevent other students from learning." Expulsion or other forms of punishment are still used to deal with students who display serious and/or chronic conduct problems, including interpersonal violence. Yet, Boccanfuso and Kuhfeld (2011) argue there are "several effective, nonpunitive alternatives to zero tolerance," which have been shown to reduce violent behavior in school while also having significant, positive impacts on student behaviors and even academic achievement in some cases. This includes initiatives that "take a largely preventive approach to violence and misbehavior" through (1) individual-based strategies (character education or social competency curriculum that focuses on changing students' behavior) and (2) school environment-based strategies (setting and enforcing standards for behavior, rewarding positive behaviors, creating a school environment that nurtures respect, empathy, and harmonious relationships) (Boccanfuso and Kuhfeld, 2011, 9).

CASE STUDY 3.15

SCHOOL-BASED PROGRAM TO PROMOTE POSITIVE BEHAVIORS

The School-Wide Positive Behavioral Interventions and Supports (SWPBIS) is a comprehensive, multitiered approach to controlling student conduct problems and school violence that has generated positive results based on rigorous evaluations. There are three tiers to this program, according to Boccanfuso and Kuhfeld (2011, 8). "The primary tier of prevention consists of defining and teaching behavioral expectations, rewarding positive behavior, providing a continuum of possible consequences for problem behavior, and collecting data for decision making purposes." The secondary tier "is designed for students who are at-risk for behavior problems or displaying early signs of behavior problems; it consists of targeted interventions that are consistent with the schoolwide behavioral expectations." The third tier of prevention is meant to support children with "more serious behavior problems; it includes more intense, individualized intervention, often with family or community involvement, as guided by a functional behavioral assessment" (Boccanfuso and Kuhfeld, 2011, 8). Evaluations of SWPBIS "have found a link between the use of this approach at the elementary school level and students' improved academic performance, better social behavior, and reductions in referrals to the principal's office for discipline problems" (Boccanfuso and Kuhfeld, 2011, 8).

Comprehensive school-wide programs that promote positive behavior through broad environmental-change policies, such as PATHE, PEBS, or SWPBIS, have shown to help minimize bullying, harassment, and violence. In addition, there are school-based programs that focus explicitly on preventing interpersonal violence through targeted policies and strategies.

3.4.2 Interventions Targeting At-Risk Young People Indirectly (Modifying the Social Environment): Promoting Stable Families and Effective Parenting

Because families play a critical role in nurturing well-adjusted, prosocial children, youth, and ultimately adults, they are a central institution through which CPSD programs and practices are delivered. In fact, parents are the single most important group of actors and the family is the most important institution in society when it comes to preventing future criminal and deviant behavior. Basic family practices in child-rearing matter enormously in protecting children from a future criminal life, and, as such, CPSD interventions at the family level often center around strengthening families as an institution by supporting good parenting practices. In this regard, the U.S. Department of Health and Human Services (2011, 20) identify the following five protective factors for parents that are key to a functional and caring family environment:

> Nurturing and attachment - Building a close bond helps parents better understand, respond to, and communicate with their children.

> Knowledge of parenting and of child and youth development - Parents learn what to look for at each age and how to help their children reach their full potential.

CASE STUDY 3.16

SCHOOL-BASED VIOLENCE PREVENTION PROGRAM IN AUSTRALIA

The James Busby High School in New South Wales implemented the "Peacemaker Program," which seeks to eliminate all forms of harassment, bullying, and violence from school life by modifying behavior through a school-wide culture of nonviolence and the teaching of nonviolent responses to conflictual situations. The program targets all students, their families, school staff, as well as the broader community in which the school is located. At the core of this program is training students, teachers, parents, and others in conflict resolution and peer mediation. A school atmosphere is also promoted that encourages student to seek mediation in difficult conflicts. In addition, training and support are provided to families to help them find solutions to problematic behavior that may be exhibited by their children. Efforts to embed antiviolence initiatives in the school's culture include enactment of an antiharassment policy, specific antibullying programs, and a restorative approach to bullies and violent offenders whereby they are taught to accept responsibility for and consequences of their behavior, apologize to the victim, and seek counseling or other remedial services so this behavior does not reemerge. Suspension and other forms of punishment may be used, but only as the last resort. According to one evaluation, during a 3-year period following implementation of the Peacemaker Program, suspensions from the school for violence were reduced by 33% (Mugford and Nelson, 1996, 20).

Parental resilience - Recognizing the signs of stress and enhancing problem-solving skills can help parents build their capacity to cope.

Social connections - Parents with an extensive network of family, friends, and neighbors have better support in times of need.

Concrete supports for parents - Caregivers with access to financial, housing, and other concrete resources and services that help them meet their basic needs can better attend to their role as parents.

Based upon their summary of the literature, Jain and Cohen (2012, 22) conclude, "different dimensions of family structure and functioning are associated with reduced problem behaviors or externalizing scores" among at-risk children and youth and those exposed to violence specifically. In particular, "family cohesion and lack of family conflict appear to reduce aggression from childhood to emerging adulthood for individuals who are otherwise prone" while parental monitoring, attachment, involvement, and support "have been associated with less frequent externalizing behaviors among adolescents and with fewer behavioral problems for youth exposed to violence."

In his meta-analysis of evaluations of crime prevention programs, Sherman (1997b, 1) argues that "family-based crime prevention" programs and services can directly address criminogenic risk factors, "with substantial success" and "given the normal disagreements among social scientists, the level of consensus about these conclusions is striking." Based on their own meta-analysis of parent training programs, Piquero and Jennings (2012, 90) conclude, "the majority were moderately effective in reducing childhood behavior problems." Parent training programs are particularly effective at reducing behavioral problems, "if they are implemented early on in a child's development" and if they "target a smaller more manageable number of children rather large-scale interventions." In short, their meta-analysis "provides support for continued use of parent training in preventing delinquency" (Piquero and Jennings, 2012, 97).

> The present research demonstrates policies should attempt to assist families in preventing antisocial and delinquent behavior by providing them with the resources needed to realize effective child development practices. Most of the studies demonstrated that childhood behavioral problems can be partially prevented or lessened with the implementation of the appropriate parent training programs. The same parenting programs have also produced many other benefits outside of crime reduction, including a higher pursuit of education, a decrease in pregnancies during teenage years, better financial security, and improved personal health… The evidence is clear: parent training programs are effective.
>
> **Piquero and Jennings (2012, 97)**

Based on their review of the literature, Farrington and Welsh (2002) conclude there are five types of family-based programs that have been found to be effective in preventing crime: (1) home visitation programs, (2) day care/preschool programs, (3) parent training (with younger children), (4) home/community parent training (with older children), and (5) multisystemic therapy. The remainder of this section describes effective family-based CPSD interventions, which are grouped into the following categories: teenage pregnancy prevention; home visitation; parental guidance, education, and skills training; family counseling and therapy; and family support.

3.4.2.1 Preventing Teenage Pregnancy In general, children born to teenage mothers are more likely to experience personal and social environmental criminogenic risk factors when compared to the general population. These risk factors increase when the mother is a single parent, lives below the poverty line, lacks a high school diploma, and has little or no social support networks. Thus, preventing pregnancies by single, teenage mothers is deemed an important crime prevention goal. Approaches to teenage pregnancy prevention are highly varied (and in many cases quite controversial) and include delaying sexual intercourse (abstinence), access to and the proper use of contraceptives, sex education (including education on risky sexual behaviors), social competency and skills training (focusing on increasing self-esteem, assertiveness, decision-making and communication skills), family planning advice, and incentives for young women to avoid risky sexual behavior and pregnancy and complete their education or become employed (Biemesderfer and Bustos, 1989; Hofferth, 1991; Graham, 1995, 18). There is widespread disagreement on what to do about teenage pregnancy, and this has contributed to the highly diverging approaches. Research consistently supports the effectiveness of the proper use of contraceptive methods in preventing pregnancy. Traditional sex education (human sexuality, reproduction, and contraception) does not appear to work, while there is inconclusive evidence as to the effectiveness on the promotion of abstinence to prevent unwanted teenage pregnancies (Blythe et al., 1981; Hofferth, 1991).

3.4.2.2 Home Visitation Programs At its most basic, a home visitation involves a professional who works with a parent in her home to help develop and support good parenting practices. These visits are most common during the mother's pregnancy and the child's infancy. The professional can be a nurse, social worker, educator, or psychologist, among others. The purpose of a home visit varies with each family (in part to individualize the service to the specific needs of the parent and child) but generally includes observing the parent and the child to identify good and bad parenting practices, providing information vital to parenting (caring for the child, nutrition, discipline, etc.), and providing emotional and moral support.

Studies have shown that home visitation programs can reduce such criminogenic risk factors as poor parenting practices (maltreatment, neglect, abuse) and mental illness among children and youth. Some programs have also contributed to a reduction in youth aggression and violence (Graham, 1995, 18; Sherman, 1997b, 11–15; Farrington and Welsh, 2006, 26–30; Zajicek-Farber, 2010). Based on a review of "four clearly defined, well-implemented, and methodologically rigorous home visitation programs," Piquero et al. (2008, 12) found that "this form of early intervention was effective in preventing child antisocial behavior and delinquency" primarily by providing parents "with the tools necessary to engage in effective child-rearing" (pp. 88–89). For Lawrence Sherman (1997b, 10), "Perhaps the most promising results in all areas of crime prevention are found in the evaluations of home visitation programs. While these programs are often combined with other institutional elements, such as preschool, there is a large and almost uniformly positive body of findings on this practice."

3.4.2.3 Parental Guidance, Education, and Skills Training Improving parenting skills through education, training, and support is a common CPSD intervention. These programs are especially important for parents with children who have behavioral problems or psychological disorders that are difficult to manage. In this vein, training is often geared toward providing parents with the skills to more effectively address troublesome and disruptive behavior of their children through proactive, evidence-based methods, such as positively reinforcing good behavior, setting limits, and effective supervision and discipline, while avoiding erratic, inconsistent, and counterproductive

---

CASE STUDY 3.17

TEENAGE PREGNANCY PREVENTION

Pregnancy prevention strategies developed and tested in Washington state high schools between 1978 and 1980 were premised on the belief that unprotected sex and unplanned and unwanted pregnancies among teenagers is mostly due to poor interpersonal communication and decision-making skills by women in this age group, and not to any underlying cognitive, psychological, or social deficits. The argument is that most teenagers lack the communication, negotiating, and decision-making skills necessary to prevent a pregnancy. As the program developers (Blythe et al., 1981, 503) note, one of the most difficult decisions that confront teenagers concerns whether to have sex. Even after making a personal decision on this subject, "teenagers who lack interpersonal skills cannot communicate the decisions to dating partners, parents, and health care professionals." Furthermore, teens may not get the kind of assistance from their parents that can help them through these difficult times, which is due in part to ineffectual communication between a parent and a child and the difficulty that many parents and children have in discussing sex with one another.

At the core of this pregnancy prevention program are education and training that stress effective interpersonal decision making and communication. Training is meant to promote the ability of young women and men to make decisions surrounding high-risk choices and effectively and assertively communicate these decisions. The program entailed 14 semi-weekly training sessions that lasted 1 h each. Both male and female teenagers were involved. The training began by providing a traditional sex education course. The students were then trained how to apply this information to making and communicating decisions that revolved around sex. For example, this could include decisions on using contraceptives (including how to use them or communicating the desire to use them to a partner) or deciding to abstain from having sex (and effectively communicating this decision to a partner). The training program used proven pedagogical techniques, such as having students role-play scenarios that involve decisions about having sex and how to assertively communicate these decisions.

Six months following the completion of this training, participating students indicated they had a strong commitment to reducing the possibility of an unwanted pregnancy, including using birth control. Program evaluations also showed that the training had an impact on the students' decision-making and communication skills within high-risk social situations (Blythe et al., 1981).

---

discipline, such as physical punishment. Other common goals of these training programs are to promote parents' skills in supporting the social competencies of their children, to bond with their children, to help them learn and succeed academically, to communicate effectively with their children, to resolve family problems, to help their children make friends, and to promote their children's self-esteem and empathy. For Savignac (2009, 12), parental training "uses a structured approach designed to: help parents identify positive and antisocial behaviors in their children, and use appropriate child-rearing techniques, improve family relations by strengthening ties of affection, and improve parental skills in such areas as problem-solving, family conflict and self-control." In their analysis of family-centered education and training programs, Farrington and Welsh (2007, 30–48) found that those that involved both the parent and the child showed desirable effects in improving parenting practices, reducing conduct problems among children, and bettering child–parent relationships.

CASE STUDY 3.18

THE NURSE–FAMILY PARTNERSHIP PROGRAM

The Nurse–Family Partnership Program provides home visits by registered nurses to first-time mothers. Their visits begin during pregnancy and continue through the child's second birthday (with decreasing frequency as the child grows older and the mother becomes more trained and independent). In addition to new mothers, the program also targets women who may be experiencing other risk factors (in particular, poverty, being unmarried, the absence of a father or support network, and a young age). The program was originally designed to tackle risk factors that contribute to conduct problems by a child.

The program has three primary goals: (1) to improve the outcomes of pregnancy by promoting more health-conscious behaviors by the expectant mother; (2) to improve the child's health, development, and safety by enhancing the quality of the care provided by the mother; and (3) to improve the mother's own personal development. The program also has two second-ary goals: to increase the family's support by linking them with health and social service agencies and to promote supportive relationships through a network of family and friends.

Registered nurses, who have received specialized training and who follow specific policies and protocols, visit a client family every 1–2 weeks on average. During the prenatal period, the nurses help the expectant mother maintain optimal health and a healthy lifestyle, through such services as dietary advice, plotting weight gains, ensuring regular checkups with a physician, helping to identify the signs and symptoms of pregnancy complications and other health problems, and helping the mother reduce or eliminate high-risk behavior (such as the use of cigarettes, alcohol, and drugs). Advice and training can also be provided to the mother to help her prepare for the delivery and caring of the child once it is born. Following delivery, nurses educate the mother on such basics as feeding and changing diapers, how to promote nurturing interactions with her child, how to anticipate and recognize health problems, and who to contact if her child becomes ill or injured. The nurses may also help the mothers with their own needs, such as solving problems in their lives, reducing the chance of future unwanted pregnancies, and assisting them with their education or employment. In addition to visits by a nurse, mothers can also receive free developmental screening and referral services for each child at various ages during the first 2 years of the child's life.

Assessments conducted of this program have shown very positive findings. In one study that evaluated the program in Elmira, New York, beginning in 1980, Olds et al. (1986) found that, compared to a control group of pregnant women, those participating in the program were more aware of the community services available to them, attended childbirth education classes more frequently, indicated that the fathers of their babies showed a greater interest in their pregnancies, and were more frequently accompanied by someone to the labor room. Expectant mothers who were smokers also made greater reductions in the number of cigarettes smoked than did smokers assigned to a control group. Teenage mothers involved in the program had babies who were on average heavier than the babies of adolescents in the control group. In a follow-up study, Olds et al. (1994) found that when the children were between 25 and 50 months of age, the homes of treatment group families had significantly fewer injuries and fewer instances of child behavioral or parental coping problems. During this period, children in the program made 35% fewer visits to the emergency room. A 15-year longitudinal evaluation (Olds et al. 1998) of the Elmira-based program found that compared with the control group, children that received a full range of home visitation services had significantly fewer instances of running away, far fewer sexual partners, consumed less alcohol, and had significantly fewer arrests and convictions.

CASE STUDY 3.19

TRAINING FOR PARENTS OF CHILDREN WITH CONDUCT PROBLEMS

The Oregon Social Learning Center is a "collaborative, multidisciplinary center dedicated to increasing the scientific understanding of social and psychological processes related to healthy development and family functioning." One of the center's areas of focus is "improving the strengths and decreasing the problems of youth ages 3 through 18 years, including studies tailored to children with conduct problems or delinquency, and children who have been abused or neglected by their parents."

As part of its mandate, the center administers the LIFT program, which stands for Linking the Interests of Families and Teachers. LIFT aims to prevent conduct problems, such as antisocial and aggressive behavior, oppositional defiant disorder, conduct disorder, involvement with delinquent peers, and drug and alcohol use in young school-age children (ages 6–11). The structured curriculum targets children with conduct problems and parents with poor or ineffectual parenting practices. It is administered in both the home and the school and encompasses 10 weeks of training for children (twice weekly) and 6 weeks of training for the parents (once a week). Each session lasts approximately 1 h.

LIFT is based on research findings suggesting that many antecedents of conduct problems derive from the interaction between children and their parents in the home setting (including poor parenting). As such, the parent training component of the program is concerned with the use of

- Effective child-rearing methods
- Setting limits and negotiating acceptable standards of behavior with their children
- Using positive, noncoercive methods of discipline
- Emphasizing the rewarding of positive behavior over the punishment of negative behavior
- Developing problem-solving skills
- Improving communication and interaction within the family
- Negotiating disagreements so that conflicts and crises do not escalate

Parents are also taught how to impart and reinforce basic social competencies with their children, such as helping their child make friends, resolving conflicts, and problem solving. The LIFT school component consists of teaching social competencies and problem-solving skills to the children, using proven pedagogical techniques (instruction in a small group format, group discussion, skill practicing, role-playing, rewards and incentives for good behavior).

A randomized clinical trial of the LIFT program, involving more than 600 children and their families, measured achievement according to three goals: a decrease in physical aggression of participating children, a decrease in the mother's aversive behavior during interactions with her child, and an increase in teacher ratings of the child's positive behaviors with peers. The preliminary results of the assessment showed that these goals were met, with some qualifications. Following 1 year after completing the program, children who were part of the LIFT program were less aggressive on the playground and showed a significant increase in positive behaviors with peers. The greatest advances were among children who had the highest level of behavioral problems before enrolling in the program. First graders who were in the program also showed reduced aggression, while their mothers displayed less aversive behaviors during family problem-solving discussions. Three years following their completion of the program, the first graders were less likely to display conduct problems at school, compared to a control group of children (Eddy et al., 2000).

3.4.2.4   Family Counseling and Therapy   As Graham (1995, 21–22) asserts, counseling and therapy services for families can be an important crime and violence prevention tool. Doran et al. (2012, 758) identify different forms of family therapies that can be applied to social environmental and personal criminogenic risk factors. These therapies are "typically designed to be delivered in the home and/or community" and are alternatives to individual therapy. Unlike one-on-one therapy, family therapies are designed explicitly to address risk factors at multiple levels (both within and outside the family environment) that contribute to antisocial and negative behaviors (of the children but also of the parents). For Savignac (2009, 14), "Family therapy aims to create more adaptive patterns of family interaction, reducing problem behaviors thought to be a result of family dysfunction." More specifically, family therapy programs are designed to "improve communication and interactions between parents and children, and resolve problems that arise, improve family functioning and improve parenting practices" (Savignac, 2009, 14).

Different variations of family therapies have been developed over the years for the treatment of youth substance abuse disorders, aggression, and delinquency (Doran et al., 2012, 758). Based on his analysis of the empirical literature examining different therapies for at-risk youth, Doran et al. (2012, 755) concludes the "evidence indicates that family therapy is more effective than individual therapy" for problem behaviors and youth substance abuse disorders in particular. Those family-based therapy approaches with the most empirical support, according to Doran and colleagues, are as follows:

> Multisystemic Therapy – An "intensive, in-home intervention designed as an alternative to secure placement for youth with severe social, emotional, or behavioral problems. Therapists are available to families at all times, and they work with caregivers to adjust the ecological context of problem behaviors."
>
> Functional Family Therapy – This "combines the family systems and social learning approaches" that focus on "increasing engagement and motivation for change before using behavioral techniques to develop healthier interaction patterns."
>
> Brief Strategic Family Therapy - A "structured, problem-focused therapy lasting 12 to 16 sessions over 3 to 4 months. Therapists observe family interactions and diagnose strengths and weaknesses, with a focus on issues linked to youth problem behaviors. Therapeutic techniques used include cognitive restructuring, conflict resolution, behavior management, and parenting skills training."
>
> Multidimensional Family Therapy – A "short-term approach that focuses on risk and protective behaviors for adolescent and family functioning." The therapist conducts "interventions with youth and caregivers individually and jointly; in joint sessions, family members try new ways of problem solving with active therapist guidance."

Doran et al. (2012, 755)

3.4.2.5   Family Support   According to Graham (1995, 25),

> In addition to financial assistance, other positive forms of family support include: child care services, emergency day-care and baby-sitting, health care, family planning advice, crisis intervention, and temporary shelter. Open access family centers which provide, playgroups, after-school clubs and remedial services such as debt counseling and family therapy, may also bear on the prevention of criminality and more isolated families can be targeted through outreach workers, who can offer more informal advice on, for example, nutrition, parenting and home management skills.

Services that support families are especially important during times of crisis (such as the loss of a job, family breakup, homelessness, as well as criminality or substance abuse in the family).

3.5   CRITIQUES OF AND CHALLENGES FACING CPSD

Notwithstanding the mostly positive evaluations of early CPSD interventions, they are not without their challenges, weaknesses, or limitations. One of the greatest challenges facing CPSD programs is inducing the involvement of high-risk parents in such programs. While some parents may welcome the programs, services, or advice, others may resent the implications of being targeted for such interventions or feel the services provided are not appropriate for their particular situations and refuse to participate. Others may refuse to participate for other reasons, apathy or conversely, a lack of time. Parents may also feel stigmatized by participating in these programs (Blyth and Solomon, 2009). According to the International Centre for the Prevention of Crime (2008, 82), "Without forethought, an early intervention programme may be perceived as patronising or degrading, stigmatising children and jeopardising the very success of the programme." Further, "social and educational approaches to prevention run the risk of criminalizing social policy, and potentially stigmatizing groups who are targeted for intervention. They have been seen as occupying 'an awkward space' between criminal justice and social and urban policy" (International Centre for the Prevention of Crime, 2010, 131).

In addition, some social problem-solving interventions do not appear to work, according to research. Prevention programs for children and youth that appear to be ineffectual include peer counseling and mediation, unsupervised recreational and leisure programs, and social competency instruction that does not use effective pedagogical techniques (Greenwood, 2006, 86–88).

Perhaps, the most ardent criticisms of CPSD is that it does not address immediate crime problems, especially when programs are geared toward young children (with that said, CPSD programs targeting high-risk teenage males can potentially have an immediate impact on crime and disorder problems). Despite the proven cost-effectiveness of CPSD programs (see Section 3.6), they can also be expensive to run and there is often a lack of funding for social intervention policies. Another critique is that research does not always support a direct connection between social developmental programs and reduced crime rates. There is also a shortage of professionals (especially those in the psychological and health-care fields) who are trained to test, diagnose, and treat the most at-risk children and youth. In practice, it is often very difficult to measure the effects of early interventions on later behavior, particularly criminality. There is a paucity of rigorous evaluations of CPSD programs, mostly because they require large investments of time and researchers must track the treatment and control groups from childhood into their teenage and adult years to determine if the interventions achieved their long-term goals.

3.6   CONCLUSION

CPSD truly personifies crime prevention given its focus is on preventing the onset of criminal behavior. The added benefit is that many of the recommended CPSD interventions for at-risk children can also potentially address the causes of a range of future antisocial behaviors. In addition, social competency and life skills programs that promote self-esteem and advance problem-solving and coping skills during childhood are touted as a way to prevent mental health problems that may emerge later in life (Freres et al., 2002; Lock and Barrett, 2003). Indeed, CPSD is largely based on Farrington's (2007) supposition that criminality is part of a larger syndrome of antisocial behavior that emerges in childhood and tends to persist into adulthood (i.e., the factors that put children and youth at risk of future offending are largely the same as those that put them at risk for other types of antisocial behavior and mental health problems). Thus, a risk-based CPSD program "that succeeds in reducing a risk factor for offending will in all probability have wide-ranging benefits in reducing other types of social problems as well" (Farrington, 2007, 607). This conclusion support the need for social practices and social problem-solving programs that are multimodal in scope (i.e., comprehensively address a number of risk factors that a child, family, or community may be experiencing).

As indicated in this chapter, the more risk factors in the life of a child or youth, the greater his or her risk of future offending as well as other antisocial and negative behaviors. Because of these multiple risk factors, and the fact that criminality does not arise from one cause or risk factor, CPSD interventions should ideally consist of comprehensive, multilayered strategies that attempt to address the full range of inter-secting factors that put a child or youth at risk of future offending (Wasserman and Miller, 1998). To this end, the many CPSD interventions discussed in this chapter are not mutually exclusively, but complementary. As importantly, social problem-solving interventions must be individualized to fit the circumstances of each at-risk child or youth. In their review of developmental crime prevention, Tremblay and Craig (1995) identified three key characteristics of effective development-based CPSD programs: (1) they lasted for a sufficient period of time (at least 1 year), (2) they were multimodal (i.e., multiple risk factors were targeted through multiple interventions), and (3) they were implemented during childhood (i.e., before adolescence).

At the very least, CPSD interventions should include strategies that (1) reduce, elimi-nate, or offset personal risk factors and strengthen personal developmental assets and (2) reduce, eliminate, or offset social environmental risk factors. This dichotomy of personal and social environmental risk and protective factors reflects the broader exis-tential debate on what has the greatest influence on an individual's behavior: human agency (in which individuals largely determine their own fate) and environmental/ structural forces (in which individuals' behavior and fate are predestined or at least significantly influenced by broader structural and social forces). From a pragmatic point of view, CPSD acknowledges that the causes of and solutions to criminal behavior are situated in the nexus of both human agency and social environmental forces. As Farrall et al. (2010, 547) state in the context of their discussion on offender's desistence from crime, human "agency is always exercised within the context of social structures...."

There is a substantial body of evidence that effective and early intervention in the lives of at-risk children and youth can prevent offending, victimization, and other prob-lems among young people. Table 3.2 summarizes some of the major types of preven-tive strategies that have demonstrated a reduction in risk factors.

In their review of successful crime prevention programs, Waller and Sansfaçon (2000, 6) hold out the following social developmental strategies as the most promising when intervening in the lives of at-risk children, youth, and their parents:

- Preschool and after-school remedial programs to increase the cognitive and social abilities of children
- Increasing support and assistance to parents
- Home visitations by professionals to help improve the parenting skills of young, single, low-income mothers
- Improving the cognitive and social skills of children and young people through at-home visits by teachers and structured recreational and cultural activities

Table 3.2
Overview of Major CPSD Strategies and Risk Factors Addressed

	Preventive Measures	Risk Factors Reduced
Family	Parenting programs Family support Preschool education Foster-parent training and supervision	Improve parental supervision Reduce family conflict Reduce early school problems Improve academic skills Improve family and youth relationships

School	School organizational change
	Whole-school antibullying
	Harassment, racism, sexism,
	  antidrug curriculum
	Mediation/conflict resolution
	  training
	Family–school links
		Improve school climate
		Reduce truancy, disruptive behavior
		Increase commitment and bonds
		Reduce bullying behavior
		Reduce antisocial attitudes and
		  behaviors, drug use
		Improve conflict resolution skills, reduce
		  escalation of conflict
		Improve parental/school support and
		  skills; reduce behavior problems

Community	Youth groups, centers, sports
	  and recreation
	Summer holiday programs
	Outreach youth workers
	Youth action groups
		Reduce risky behaviors, increase skills,
		  bonds
		Reduce antisocial behavior
		Reduce antisocial behavior, provide
		  support to at-risk youth
		Reduce local disorder, crime

Early adolescence
and peer groups
	Mentoring and education for
	  at-risk youth
	Drug education projects
	After-school programs,
	  homework clubs
	Gang prevention
		Improve general abilities to function and
		  develop good school, relations, and
		  leisure
		Reduce drug use
		Improve school attainment, reduce
		  unsupervised leisure time
		Reduce risks of recruitment and
		  offending, victimization

Later adolescence	Stay in school incentives
	Work skills training
	Teen parent programs
	Peer support programs
	Youth foyers and housing
	  projects
	Wraparound projects for
	  youths leaving care, custody
		Reduce dropout and unemployment
		Improve skills and qualifications
		Improve child-caring abilities and
		  education/work prospects
		Reduce isolation, homelessness
		Reduce risk of homelessness, crime, and
		  victimization
		Prevent homelessness, victimization, (re)
		  offending

Source: Shaw, M., Investing in Youth: International Approaches to Preventing Crime and Victimization, International Centre for the Prevention of Crime, Montreal, Quebec, Canada, n.d., pp. 21–22.

- Providing incentives to youth and adults to complete secondary studies by offering educational and financial assistance
- Improving the self-esteem and social integration capacity of children and young people
- Organizing school and after-school educational and recreational activities
- Working with families of first-time young offenders

In their meta-analysis of crime prevention experiments and project evaluations, Sherman et al. (1998) conclude that the following CPSD interventions targeting children and youth were effective or promising in reducing criminogenic risk factors:

Within the home:

- Frequent home visits to infants (ages birth to 2 years) by trained nurses and other professionals, which reduces child abuse and other injuries to infants
- Preschool and weekly home visits by teachers to children under the age of 5, which substantially reduces arrests when they are older
- Family therapy and parent training, which reduced such delinquency risk factors as aggression and hyperactivity

Within the school:

- Clarifying and communicating norms about behavior through rules, reinforcement of positive behavior, and school-wide initiatives (such as antibullying campaigns), which reduces crime, delinquency, and substance abuse among students
- Life, social competency, and coping skills training, such as stress management, critical thinking, problem solving, self-control, and emotional intelligence, which reduces delinquency and substance abuse
- Training or coaching in thinking skills for at-risk youth using rewards-based behavior modification techniques, which reduces substance abuse
- Innovative classroom management and instructional initiatives, such as those that group students into smaller units for cooperative learning or entail flexible and intensive instruction methods for underachieving or disruptive students, which reduces drug abuse and delinquency

Within the community:

- Community-based mentoring by Big Brothers/Big Sisters, which substantially reduced drug abuse in one experiment (although evaluations of other mentoring programs did not achieve the same impressive results)
- Community-based, supervised after-school recreation programs, which can reduce juvenile crime in the areas immediately around the recreation center.

CPSD is also lauded because it is a cost-effective social investment; a $1 investment in social developmental programs for at-risk children and youth can save $7–$10 in costs that are associated with welfare, social services policing, and prisons (Greenwood et al., 1998; Aos et al., 2004). Society can make no greater investment than funding education and related services for children, youth, and adults. According to a Statistics Canada (2004) study, "investment in human capital," such as education and skills training, is three times as important to economic growth over the long run as investment in physical capital.

3.7 DISCUSSION QUESTIONS AND EXERCISES

1. What do you believe to be more significant as far as the causes of criminality are concerned: social environment or personal risk factors?
2. What neighborhoods in your city have higher than average crime rates? What are the factors that contribute to these crime rates?

3. How would you define the concept of resilience? How does this relate to the concept of protective factors? Think about your own childhood and adolescence. What protective factors were present in your life growing up?
4. Identify organizations, agencies, and institutions in your city (or part of the city) that carry out problem-solving services that you think can be classified as crime prevention.
5. Conduct research into children and youth in your city who live in high-risk environments. What are the factors that put them at risk of future delinquency and criminal offending? What social problem-solving strategies would you implement that will provide them with protective factors and/or increase their resilience?

3.8 IMPORTANT TERMS

Anomie theory
At-risk
Control theory
Crime prevention institutions
Crime Prevention through Social Development
Criminality
Criminogenic conditions
Developmental assets
Developmental criminology
Differential association theory
Employment-based CPSD programs
Family-based CPSD programs
Mentoring
Protective factors
Resilience
Risk factors
Root causes of crime
Social learning theory
Social problem solving

FURTHER READING

Farrington, D., Childhood risk factors and risk-focused prevention, in *The Oxford Handbook of Criminology*, 4th edn., Maguire, M., Morgan, R., and Reiner, R., Eds., Oxford University Press, Oxford, U.K., 2007, Chap. 19, pp. 602–640.

Farrington, D.P. and Welsh, B.C., Family-based crime prevention, in *Evidence-Based Crime Prevention*, Sherman, L., Farrington, D., Welsh, C., and MacKenzie, D., Eds., Routledge, New York, 2002, pp. 22–55.

Gottfredson, D.C., Wilson, D.B., and Najaka, S., School-based crime prevention, in *Evidence-Based Crime Prevention*, Sherman, L.W., Farrington, D.P., Welsh, B.C., and MacKenzie, D.L., Eds., Routledge, New York, 2006, pp. 56–164.

Sherman, L.W., Family-based crime prevention, in *Preventing Crime: What Works, What Doesn't, What's Promising. A Report to the United States Congress,* Sherman, L.W. et al., Eds., National Institute of Justice, Washington, DC, 1997b, Chap. 4, pp. 1–43.

Wasserman, G.A., Keenan, K., Tremblay, R.E., Coie, J.D., Herrenkohl, T.I., Loeber, R., and Petechuk, D., Risk and protective factors of child delinquency, Child and delinquency bulletin series, U.S. Department of Justice, Office of Juvenile Justice and Delinquency, Washington, DC, April 2003, https://www.ncjrs.gov/pdffiles1/ojjdp/193409.pdf. Accessed August 15, 2013.

Welsh, B. and Farrington, D., Eds., Part I, Developmental crime prevention, in *The Oxford Handbook of Crime Prevention*, Oxford University Press, New York, 2012, pp. 23–154.

INTERNET RESOURCES

Center for the Study of Violence Prevention, University of Colorado at Boulder, Blueprints for Healthy Youth Development, http://www.blueprintsprograms.com/.

CrimeSolutions.gov (National Institute of Justice), http://www.crimesolutions.gov/.

National Head Start Association, http://www.nhsa.org/.

Office of Juvenile Justice and Delinquency Prevention, Model Programs Guide, http://www.dsgonline.com/mpg2.5/mpg_index.htm.

Promising Practices Network on Children, Families and Communities, http://www.promising-practices.net/programs.asp.

U.S. Interagency Working Group on Youth Programs, http://www.findyouthinfo.gov/evidence-innovation.

CHAPTER 4

CRIME PREVENTION THROUGH SOCIAL DEVELOPMENT FOR ADOLESCENTS AND YOUNG ADULTS

CONTENTS

4.1   LEARNING OBJECTIVES

By the end of this chapter, you should have a better understanding of the following:

- Factors that put adolescents and young adults at risk of criminality
- How these risk factors compare and contrast with those for children
- Characteristics of CPSD strategies for adolescents and young adults
- Common CPSD strategies for adolescents and young adults
- The main institutions through which CPSD interventions are delivered to adolescents and young adults
- Proactive, problem-oriented strategies to address youth gangs and violence
- Principles and strategies to prevent recidivism by young offenders
- Challenges that confront CPSD programs for adolescents and young adults

4.2   INTRODUCTION

This chapter discusses the application of CSPD to adolescents (13–17) and young adults (18–25). Young people spanning in age from the midteens to the early twenties are a particularly challenging group as far as preventing and treating criminal and delinquent behavior are concerned. Research and statistics show that these are the crime- and violence-prone years, especially for males. In fact, the field of criminology has expended considerable scholarship exploring *adolescence-limited criminality* or the *age–crime curve*, both of which are concerned with the question of why criminal offending peaks during adolescence and young adulthood and then declines with age. As the International Centre for the Prevention of Crime (2008, 14) notes, "young men of 15 to 24 are the age group with the highest rate of offending and victimisation worldwide."

Adolescents and young adults are susceptible to a number of heightened risk factors, compared to children, including peer pressure, less parental control and adult supervision, school truancy and expulsion, the onset of mental health problems, more exposure to violent images in the media, increased access to weapons, and greater opportunities to consume alcohol and drugs. Relative to children, teenagers and young adults are also much more resistant to change, especially if they have already begun engaging in high-risk, delinquent, and/or criminal behavior. The challenges to successful prevention and treatment interventions for adolescents and young adults are especially daunting if the young person has had to endure a number of untreated environmental and personal risk factors during his or her childhood. Many of the CPSD practices and programs that target children are no longer relevant during adolescence and adulthood. In fact, as far as addressing criminogenic risk factors during adolescence and young adulthood is concerned, there is as much emphasis on treatment (e.g., therapy, detox) as there is on prevention.

As far as criminal justice is concerned, in the United States and Canada, a *youth* or *juvenile* is considered to be under the age of 18. However, police-reported statistics for both countries indicate that a disproportionate number of criminal offenders and victims are young adults (Cooper and Smith, 2011, 3; Perreault, 2012, 13; Federal Bureau of Investigation, 2013). Many chronic and serious young adult offenders also continue to display criminogenic risk factors associated with adolescent offenders: immaturity, unnecessary risk taking, impulsivity, a lack of consequence anticipation, an underdeveloped sense of responsibility and moral sense, mental health and substance abuse disorders (SUDs), and negative peers (not to mention barriers to education and legitimate employment). This is not surprising given the research indicating that the prefrontal cortex of the brain—which is responsible for moderating cognitive and social behavior, personality expression, judgment, and decision making—is still developing up until the age of 25 (Yang and Raine, 2009). As reported in the *Daily Mail* newspaper in the United Kingdom, "adolescence no longer ends when people hit 18, according to updated guidelines being given to child psychologists in England and Wales. The new directive is designed to extend the age range that child psychologists can work with from 18 years old up to 25" and is based on research indicating that "the brain continues developing through and passed teenage years, well into a person's mid-twenties and thirties" (Woollaston, 2013). The implication for the field of crime prevention is that any comprehensive approach to address crime and violence by young people must incorporate strategies that target young adults who are involved in criminal offending or at risk of becoming involved. That is why this chapter focuses on both adolescents and young adults. Moreover, given the research and statistics that indicate a disproportionate amount of crime and violence is committed by a small pool of adolescent and young adult (male) offenders, this chapter also focuses on the application of crime and recidivism prevention theories and strategies to serious and chronic offenders.

How best to deal with the polarizing issue of delinquency, crime, and violence by young people has traditionally been characterized by "two complementary and often contradictory positions that view youth, on one hand, as young people who are developing and need protection, and on the other, as responsible persons who must answer for their actions" (International Centre for the Prevention of Crime, 2008, 14).

Many of the responses to youth crime and violence can be subsumed under these two broad categories. The premise that young people are maturing, developing, and in need of protection is the foundation for social problem-solving approaches that attempt to prevent the onset of criminogenic conditions during childhood and adolescence. For older youth and young adults who have been in trouble with the law and are at risk of chronic or serious offending, recidivism prevention (accomplished through the treatment of risk factors and the provision of opportunities for meaningful life experiences) can also be included under this social problem-solving category. The argument that young people must be responsible for their actions is a fundamental premise of both the criminal justice system (that seeks to suppress crime and violence through punitive sanctions) and alternative restorative approaches (in which offenders acknowledge their actions, the harms caused by them, and the need for reparations to victims).

The remainder of this chapter is concerned with exploring the theory and practice of social problem-solving approaches for preventing and treating delinquency, criminality, and recidivism among adolescents and young adults. It begins with an overview of youth development and criminogenic risk factors experienced by youth. It then summarizes the literature on preventing crime violence by youth and young adults. The remainder of the chapter explores developmentally based, social problem-solving preventative and treatment interventions for youth and youth at risk of serious and chronic offending in particular. This includes high school dropout prevention and recovery, initiatives targeting youth violence and gangs, youth outreach workers, youth (drop-in) centers, employment and labor markets, and recidivism prevention.

4.3 YOUTH DEVELOPMENT AND CRIMINOGENIC RISK FACTORS

To understand social problem-solving, development-based approaches to preventing and controlling delinquency and criminality by adolescents, one must first understand youth development. As Bonnie et al. (2012) write in their comprehensive report *Reforming Juvenile Justice: A Developmental Approach*, efforts to prevent and control criminal, delinquent, violent, and other antisocial behavior among youth must take into consideration the nature of adolescence. This includes acknowledging how they differ sociobiologically from adults, their ongoing maturation and development, and their greater predisposition for risky and antisocial behavior:

> Adolescence is a distinct, yet transient, period of development between childhood and adulthood characterized by increased experimentation and risk-taking, a tendency to discount long-term consequences, and heightened sensitivity to peers and other social influences. A key function of adolescence is developing an integrated sense of self, including individuation, separation from parents, and personal identity. Experimentation and novelty-seeking behavior, such as alcohol and drug use, unsafe sex, and reckless driving, are thought to serve a number of adaptive functions despite their risks. Research indicates that for most youth, the period of risky experimentation does not extend beyond adolescence, ceasing as identity becomes settled with maturity. Much adolescent involvement in illegal activity is an extension of the kind of risk-taking that is part of the developmental process of identity formation, and most adolescents mature out of these tendencies.

Adolescents differ from adults and children in three important ways that lead to differences in behavior. First, adolescents lack mature capacity for self-regulation in emotionally charged contexts, relative to adults. Second, adolescents have a heightened sensitivity to proximal external influences, such as peer pressure and immediate incentives, relative to children and adults. Third, adolescents show less ability than adults to make judgments and decisions that require future orientation. The combination of these three cognitive patterns accounts for the tendency of adolescents to prefer and engage in risky behaviors that have a high probability of immediate reward but can have harmful consequences.

Bonnie et al. (2012, 2)

Research into adolescent biology, neuropsychology, and brain development has facilitated a greater understanding of why unnecessary risk taking, antisocial behavior, delinquency, and criminality seem to crest during adolescence. Walsh and Beaver (2009, 91) cite the conclusions of the 2003 New York Academy of Sciences conference on adolescent brain development, which they argue provides "some key points relevant to the age–crime curve issue":

(1) Much of the behavior characterizing adolescence is rooted in biology intermingling with environmental influences to cause teens to conflict with their parents, take more risks, and experience wide swings in emotion. (2) The lack of synchrony between a physically mature body and a still maturing nervous system may explain these behaviors. (3) Adolescents' sensitivities to rewards appear to be different than in adults, prompting them to seek higher levels of novelty and stimulation to achieve the same feeling of pleasure.

White (2004, 4 as cited in Walsh and Beaver, 2009, 91)

The contribution that research into the nature of adolescence, adolescent behavior, and youth development has made to understanding unnecessary risk taking and antisocial behavior has inevitably contributed to a greater recognition of why criminal offending tends to peak during adolescence and young adulthood and the factors that contribute to delinquency and criminality by young people. A biological perspective is also integral to better understanding why males are disproportionately involved in antisocial, criminal, and violent behavior, especially during adolescence and early adulthood. According to Walsh and Beaver (2009, 92), it is during puberty that males have approximately 10 times more testosterone than females, and it is this pubertal testosterone surge that "facilitates behaviors such as risk taking, sensation seeking, dominance contests, sexual experimentation, and self-assertiveness, none of which are antisocial per se, but can easily be pushed in that direction in antisocial environments."

Consideration of these biological determinants during adolescence means that we can no longer rely solely on social environmental risk factors such as poor parenting, peer pressure, disadvantaged neighborhoods, the media, or video games to explain delinquency and criminality. Advances in the understanding of adolescence biological and neuroscience have already had a monumental impact on the American juvenile justice system: "The Supreme Court decision (Roper v. Simons, 2005) banning the death penalty for murders committed before age 18 relied heavily on data regarding the immaturity of the adolescent brain" (Walsh and Beaver, 2009, 93). (See Chapter 3 for more on biosocial criminology.)

The naturally occurring risk factors that can predispose adolescents to defiant, risk-taking, antisocial behavior are exacerbated by even more deleterious personal and social environmental risk factors that are introduced into their lives, often starting in prepubescence. Many of the criminogenic risk factors discussed in Chapter 3 are equally applicable to adolescents and young adults; indeed, serious and chronic juvenile and young adult offenders are often the product of (untreated) serious and chronic personal and social environmental risk factors that begin during childhood. Those most at risk of criminal behavior during adolescence and young adulthood not only continue to experience many of the same risk factors that were present during childhood but also encounter others that emerge as they get older. Box 4.1 summarizes the criminogenic risk factors for youth generated from the Communities that Care Youth

---

BOX 4.1

FACTORS THAT PUT ADOLESCENTS AT RISK OF DELINQUENT AND CRIMINAL BEHAVIOR

Individual Factors

- Rebelliousness
- Early initiation of antisocial behavior
- Early initiation of drug use
- Favorable attitudes toward antisocial behavior
- Favorable attitudes toward drug use
- Low perceived risks of drug use
- Sensation seeking
- Rewards for antisocial involvement

Peer Risk Factors

- Interaction with antisocial peers
- Friends' use of drugs

Community Risk Factors

- Low neighborhood attachment
- Neighborhood disorganization
- High rate of mobility (transience) and poor transitions (from place to place or school to school)
- Perceived availability of drugs

Family Risk Factors

- Poor family management
- Family conflict
- Family history of antisocial behavior
- Parental attitudes favorable toward drug use
- Parental attitudes favorable to antisocial behavior

School Risk Factors

- Academic failure
- Low commitment to school

Source: Arthur, M.W. et al., *Eval. Program Plann.*, 30, 199, 2007.

Survey, an epidemiological tool to assess a broad set of risk and protective factors among youth populations (Arthur et al., 2007, 199).

Generally speaking, juvenile offenders can be categorized into three groups. The first are youth who commit relatively minor criminal and delinquent acts and who are not at risk of continuing criminal offending into adulthood (i.e., *adolescent-limited offenders*). The second group is involved in minor antisocial and illegal activities, but who may be at risk for criminal behavior in the future. The third group is made up of a small number of youth who engage in serious, damaging, and persistent criminal activity, many of whom are at risk of continuing their criminal activities into the adult years (i.e., *life-course persistent offenders*). The first group is of lesser concern to crime prevention theories and practitioners because, by definition, they grow out of their anti-social behavior as they get older and mature. The second group is of concern to crime prevention theorists and practitioners because they are at risk of future offending (and because research shows that interventions are most effective when the first signs of antisocial, delinquent, and criminal behavior emerge or when they first come into formal contact with the criminal justice system). It is the last group of serious and chronic juvenile offenders; however, that most concerns those working in the field of crime prevention, because they make up a disproportionate amount of delinquency, crime, and violence within most societies (Prime et al., 2001; Farrington et al., 2006; Wikström et al., 2012) and are most at risk of continuing this criminal offending into adulthood.

4.4 PREVENTING CRIME AND VIOLENCE BY YOUTH AND YOUNG ADULTS: AN OVERVIEW

As intimated earlier, the disciplines of sociology, psychology, or biology are all limited in unilaterally explaining the age–crime curve; criminogenic risk factors that emerge during adolescence are the product of a combination of one's social environment, personality, and biological makeup. Those who are most at risk of life-course persistent criminal offending suffer from serious and chronic risk factors from all three categories.

There is an almost universal consensus in the literature that efforts to address serious and chronic offending by youth must go beyond the traditional criminal justice response; it must entail a comprehensive approach that incorporates three broad and complementary elements: (1) prevention (initiatives to prevent the onset of criminal and violent behavior by addressing root causes targeting high-risk children and youth), (2) intervention (social problem-solving initiatives targeting youth and young adults who have been in contact with the law to prevent recidivism and future violence), and (3) suppression (traditional and evidence-based enforcement and sanctions by police and the broader criminal justice system).

Traditionally, the most common response to crime and violence by adolescents and young adults is suppression by the criminal justice system, which focuses "on identifying persistent offenders and aggressively enforcing laws as they apply to these individuals." However, "critics suggest that these enforcement strategies alone have little effect on rates of crime and victimization…" (Bania, 2009, 103–104). As part of their longitudinal study of youth crime and delinquency in the United States, Thornberry et al. (2004, 12) provide a concise summary of a large body of research examining the impact of the traditional criminal justice approach on youth crime and violence. "The findings of these studies are quite consistent. In general, arrest has little impact on subsequent delinquent behavior, and when it does have an impact, it is most likely an increase in future delinquent behavior… In addition, those who are arrested and incarcerated as juveniles are subsequently more likely to be incarcerated as adults." Bania (2009, 103–104) concurs, asserting that a unilateral reliance on the criminal justice system to youth crime and violence "can lead to unintended consequences and counter-productive impacts on individuals and communities" and can create "a damaging cycle of release and imprisonment of young adults, especially young males." According to Welsh (2005, 23–24), "there is little empirical evidence or professional consensus on the ability of prisons to substantially reduce recidivism rates and improve public safety over the long term." Welsh also cites studies pointing to a number of "iatrogenic results" of punishment for young offenders, such as causing them to become more violent and exacerbating emotional trauma and other mental health problems common among incarcerated youth.

This is not to say that there is no role for enforcement and punitive approaches to youth crime and violence. However, an exclusive reliance on the traditional sanction-based juvenile justice system "represents an unsustainable approach in the prevention of juvenile violence (and juvenile crime in general)," Welsh (2005, 24) writes. According to Welsh (2005, 23–24), "A society that relies solely on punishing— in the form of incarceration— its young people who have come in conflict with the law cannot be said to be contributing to a sustainable future for its young people or the population at large."

The inherent limitations of the traditional criminal justice expose the need for alternative approaches that can complement and even replace enforcement and punitive sanctions in some circumstances. The need for a comprehensive approach is especially apparent in disadvantaged, high-crime, high-risk neighborhoods where residents are often confronted with a myriad of different problems that can give rise to criminal and violent behavior. In other words, any effort to address youth crime and violence at the neighborhood or citywide level requires a comprehensive, holistic, and strategic approach that prevents the problem from arising by addressing root causes, reduces opportunities for crime and violence to occur in a particular time and place, and provides treatment and other opportunities for young offenders to avoid recidivism while also relying on traditional and evidence-based police suppression and criminal justice sanctions.

In her report entitled *Youth and Gun Violence: The Outstanding Case for Prevention*, Shaw (2005, 6–7) identifies a range of social problem-solving interventions that collectively forms a comprehensive strategic plan to reduce gun violence by young men: Targeted support for high-risk children and youth:

- Early intervention home visiting, parental and family support programs
- Targeted and school-based educational and curriculum programs to change attitudes and behaviors to violence
- Conflict resolution, peace-building and peace-making training
- Cross-cultural youth life skills and leadership training
- Projects around gender and masculinity
- Mentoring programs to provide ongoing support
- Education, job training, microcredit, and job creation to provide alternative outlets for young people

Targeting high-risk areas, local communities, and the general public:

- Child and youth recreational and cultural programs
- School-based educational and curriculum programs to change attitudes
- Projects to strengthen community capacity
- Slum upgrading and urban renewal

- Public education campaigns to change attitudes, behavior, and social norms using creative media (Internet, film, music, etc.)

Targeting children and young men already using guns, exiting correctional systems, gangs, or militia:

- Education, job training, microcredit, and job creation to provide alternative economic outlets for young men
- Providing social, health, and economic support services
- Mentoring programs to provide ongoing supports
- Life skills and leadership training (Shaw, 2005, 6–7)

Notwithstanding the importance of a comprehensive approach to youth crime and violence, research shows that the most effective and long-lasting approach to controlling and reducing criminal behavior is a development-based, social problem-solving approach that either prevents the onset of criminal behavior by targeting at-risk children and adolescents or treats risk factors among young offenders (to prevent reoffending). The main objective of a developmentally based, social problem-solving approach to criminal offending by youth

---

CASE STUDY 4.1

COMPREHENSIVE STRATEGY FOR SERIOUS AND CHRONIC JUVENILE OFFENDERS

A holistic approach to youth crime and violence at the local level is epitomized by the Comprehensive Strategy for Serious, Violent, and Chronic Juvenile Offenders developed and published in 1993 by the Office of Juvenile Justice and Prevention in the United States (Wilson and Howell, 1993). This guide is meant to provide local communities with a strategic framework on how to address youth offending by "establishing a continuum of appropriate measures, from prevention to early intervention to graduated sanctions for juveniles who enter the juvenile justice system." The comprehensive strategy incorporates two main components: "Preventing youth from becoming delinquent through prevention strategies for all youth with a focus on those at greatest risk" and "improving the juvenile justice system response to delinquent offenders through a system of graduated sanctions and a continuum of treatment alternatives that include immediate intervention, intermediate sanctions, community-based corrections, and aftercare services" (Coolbaugh and Hansel, 2000, 1–2).

Central to this strategy is a preventative approach based on six principles for addressing criminogenic risk factors among youth. First, it must strengthen the family "in its primary responsibility to instill moral values and provide guidance and support to children." Second, it must support "core social institutions (schools, churches, youth service organizations, community organizations) in their roles to develop capable, mature, and responsible youth." Third, the strategy must promote "delinquency prevention as the most cost-effective approach to reducing juvenile delinquency." Fourth, it must intervene "immediately and effectively when delinquent behavior first occurs to prevent delinquent offenders from becoming chronic offenders or from progressively committing more serious and violent crimes." Fifth, the strategy must establish "a system of graduated sanctions that holds each juvenile offender accountable, protects public safety, and provides programs and services that meet identified treatment needs." Sixth, it must identify and control "the small percent of serious, violent, and chronic juvenile offenders who commit the majority of juvenile felony-level offenses" (Coolbaugh and Hansel, 2000, 2).

and young adults is to eliminate, reduce, or offset their personal and social environmental risk factors while nurturing their protective factors.

The field of CPSD for (at-risk) adolescents benefits greatly by scholarship into youth development. According to Bonnie et al. (2012), there are three broad conditions that are crucial to healthy adolescent development: "(1) the presence of a parent or parent figure who is involved with the adolescent and concerned about his or her successful development, (2) inclusion in a peer group that values and models prosocial behavior and academic success, and (3) activities that contribute to autonomous decision making and critical thinking..." (Bonnie et al., 2012, 2). The Search Institute provides a more comprehensive list of the "building blocks of healthy development—known as Developmental Assets— that help young people grow up healthy, caring, and responsible." These 40 developmental assets, which are broken into two broad categories—external assets and internal assets—are summarized below (Box 4.2).

BOX 4.2

SEARCH INSTITUTE'S 40 DEVELOPMENTAL ASSETS FOR ADOLESCENTS (AGES 12–18)

External Assets

Support
1. Family support
2. Positive family communication
3. Other adult relationships
4. Caring neighborhood
5. Caring school climate
6. Parent involvement in schooling

Empowerment
7. Community values youth
8. Youth as resources
9. Service to others
10. Safety

Boundaries and Expectations
11. Family boundaries
12. School boundaries
13. Neighborhood boundaries
14. Adult role models
15. Positive peer influence
16. High expectations

Constructive Use of Time
17. Creative activities
18. Youth programs
19. Religious community
20. Time at home

Internal Assets

Commitment to Learning
21. Achievement motivation
22. School engagement
23. Homework
24. Bonding to school
25. Reading for pleasure

Positive Values
26. Caring
27. Equality and social justice
28. Integrity
29. Honesty
30. Responsibility
31. Restraint

Social Competencies
32. Planning and decision making
33. Interpersonal competence
34. Cultural competence
35. Resistance skills
36. Peaceful conflict resolution

Positive Identity
37. Personal power
38. Self-esteem
39. Sense of purpose
40. Positive view of personal future

Source: Search Institute, Developmental assets for adolescents (ages 12–18), Search Institute, Minneapolis, MN, 2006, http://reachdevelopment.org/assets/40AssetsList.pdf

As discussed in Chapter 3, the developmental assets laid out by the Search Institute are, in essence, the factors that help protect youth from the onset of serious and chronic delinquency and criminal behavior. Canada's National Crime Prevention Centre (1995) succinctly articulates the developmental assets/protective factors specific to preventing criminal and delinquent behavior among adolescence ("what young people need to lead crime-free lives"):

- Young people need opportunities and responsibilities to go along with rights.
- They need a good education.
- Young people need to feel they are useful, appreciated, and of value.
- Young people need meaningful things to do.
- They need fair, clear, consistent, and meaningful consequences for their actions.
- Young people need a life free from abuse.
- They need both physical and emotional support.
- Youth need freedom from other types of harm.
- Young people need accurate, complete information.
- They need positive role models.
- Youth need a voice in what happens to them.
- Young people need a chance to be part of the solution.

For most young people, these protective factors occur naturally in their lives. For those who may come from more deleterious circumstances, these protective factors can be delivered through programs and services that expressly seek to fill those developmental voids that put young people at risk of antisocial behavior. One context for social problem-solving approaches to the prevention of adolescent crime and violence is youth development programs that are offered on a universal or targeted basis for at-risk youth. Perkins and Noam (2007, 76–77) define these developmental programs as "purposeful environments that provide beneficial, positive, and encouraging positive relationships with adults and peers that are sustained. At the same time, these programs provide an array of opportunities that enable youth to build their skills and competencies and enable them to become engaged as partners in their own development and their communities' development."

The remainder of this section discusses developmentally based, social problem-solving preventative and treatment interventions for youth and youth at risk of serious and chronic offending in particular. This includes high school dropout prevention and recovery, initiatives targeting youth violence and gangs, youth outreach workers, youth (drop-in) centers, employment and labor markets, and recidivism prevention.

4.5 HIGH SCHOOL DROPOUT PREVENTION AND RECOVERY

Given the strong correlation between dropping out of school, on the one hand, and criminal and violent behavior on the other, dropout prevention and recovery initiatives must be considered as significant crime and violence prevention initiatives. The protective factors delivered by successful dropout prevention and recovery programs are particularly potent "for individuals from troubled family backgrounds and low income neighborhoods" (Coelli et al., 2007, 1369). (See Chapter 3 for more information on the correlation between school exclusion and delinquent, criminal and violent behavior.)

According to Steinberg and Almeida (2004, 3), ameliorating the "dropout crisis" requires a dual response: the implementation of "dropout prevention strategies and dropout recovery efforts." This translates into "proactive strategies to stem the dropout tide by strengthening the holding and promotion power of high schools while also encouraging the development of a more diverse delivery system capable of offering programs that reach out to dropouts and engage them in studies that put them onto pathways to skills and credentials they need" (Steinberg and Almeida, 2004, 3).

Many of the recommendations for preventing students from dropping out focus on ensuring their academic success and nurturing their bonds to school, which includes individual student-centered strategies and those that focus on nurturing a school environment conducive to student success and school connectedness.

For Steinberg and Almeida (2004), efforts to keep at-risk youth from dropping out of school need to begin early (in elementary school) and should focus on ensuring student success by fortifying academic proficiency. In particular, there must be a greater emphasis on literacy at the school and district levels, which "is directed at improving instruction and student outcomes in the critical foundational skills of reading and writing." This approach is important to the overall academic success of students because as they begin grade nine, they "encounter literary texts in their English classes and textbooks in science and social studies that require fairly sophisticated reading and comprehension skills. This mismatch of students' skills with teacher and curricular expectations appears to be a key factor in the low promotion power and high dropout rates of many urban high schools" (Steinberg and Almeida, 2004, 4). Innovative and effective pedagogical approaches are also key to ensuring the academic success of struggling students and include "the creation of small learning environments both inside and outside the walls of current school buildings":

> A number of recent studies indicate that intentionally small high schools generally have higher achievement levels, higher graduation rates, and lower dropout rates than larger high schools, and they are safer as well... Qualitative studies provide clues as to how small schools getting the best results take advantage of their size in several critical ways. First and foremost, small schools that are effective with low-income and minority youth organize themselves around a clear academic focus and mission: they hold an explicit and transparent school-wide focus on critical literacy and numeracy skills required for students to succeed in college and in careers with advancement potential. The faculty take collective responsibility for students, working together to develop instructional methods, curricular themes, and performances of understanding that help young people connect school standards to real world standards. They also take advantage of their small size to increase personalization for students, through such practices as daily advisories or student/family advocates and mentors. Students get help managing life demands that may hinder learning, while simultaneously feeling pushed to meet high standards. The standards themselves are transparent: students know from day to day what they are working on and why.
>
> **Steinberg and Almeida (2004, 5)**

The National Association of School Psychologists recommends the development of prevention plans that are highly individualized to each student at risk of academic failure and dropping out.

> Schools can collect data about student performance and characteristics related to dropping out in order to identify potential problems early in the student's school experience and thus refer students for specific prevention efforts. Tracking student attendance, test scores, grades, behavior referrals, participation in activities, school attitudes and family participation in school events can provide information to identify students most at risk for later dropping out.

Prevention activities might include incentives and supports to improve attendance; programs to encourage parent involvement; early intervention for academic difficulties (such as peer tutoring programs); community and school-based mentorships; and partnerships with community business to connect school to work. Development of high school alternative programs that provide nontraditional approaches to vocational training and high school completion will also provide options for students who have not been successful in meeting the academic or social demands of the typical school program.

Hale and Canter (1998)

For Edwards (2008), efforts to reduce the number of students who drop out of school must be comprehensive. He outlines seven key principles that should guide schools in reducing the dropout rate:

1. Identify students at risk of dropping out as early as possible.
2. Examine school policies and procedures to determine how they impact those students who are most at risk of dropping out. Consider "how could modifications in policies and procedures have a positive impact on the success of ALL students?"
3. "Build strong community partnerships" and personalize the school by "making relationships between students and adults a priority."
4. Reduce social isolation of all students, but particularly those who are at risk of dropping out.
5. Manage student transitions "from year to year, from level to level, throughout the day."
6. Create options for at-risk students that allow them to receive the minimum number of credits to graduate (which includes "looking at extending the time for students to complete graduation requirements").
7. Build strong relationships between the school and parents ("overcommunicate, be proactive, work from the parents/family perspective").

The National Dropout Prevention Center/Network at Clemson University has identified 15 effective strategies that have most positive impact on the dropout rate:

School and Community Perspective

Systemic renewal, which entails "a continuing process of evaluating goals and objectives related to school policies, practices, and organizational structures as they impact a diverse group of learners"

School–community collaboration, in which "all groups in a community provide collective support to the school," which in turn promotes a "caring supportive environment where youth can thrive and achieve"

Safe learning environments, which enhance "positive social attitudes and effective interpersonal skills in all students"

Early Interventions

Family engagement, which has "a direct, positive effect on children's achievement and is the most accurate predictor of a student's success in school"

Early childhood education delivered in both a preschool setting and elementary grades

Early literacy development, especially for low-achieving students to "improve their reading and writing skills establish the necessary foundation for effective learning in all other subjects"

Basic Core Strategies

Tutoring to address "specific needs such as reading, writing, or math competencies"

Service learning, which "connects meaningful community service experiences with academic learning and promotes personal and social growth, career development, and civic responsibility and can be a powerful vehicle for effective school reform at all grade levels"

Alternative school, which "provides potential dropouts a variety of options that can lead to graduation, with programs paying special attention to the student's individual social needs and academic requirements…"

After-school opportunities, which can help with homework and fill the afternoon *gap time* with constructive and engaging activities

Making the Most of Instruction

Professional development for teachers especially those who work with youth at high risk of academic failure

Active learning, which "embraces teaching and learning strategies that engage and involve students in the learning process"

Educational technology, which can offer "some of the best opportunities for delivering instruction to engage students in authentic learning, addressing multiple intelligences, and adapting to students' learning styles"

Individualized instruction for struggling students that "allows for flexibility in teaching methods and motivational strategies" that consider the unique needs of each student

Career and technology education, such as school-to-work programs that recognize "youth need specific skills to prepare them to measure up to the larger demands of today's workplace" (Clemson University, National Dropout Prevention Center/Network, n.d.)

Material incentives have also shown some success in encouraging struggling students and at-risk youth from dropping out of school. One American study demonstrated that regular school attendance can be increased through the use of material incentives, such as bus passes and gift certificates (Brewer et al., 1995).

Schools that permanently exclude their most difficult students or ignore those who persistently fail to attend school may also be contributing to delinquent and criminal behavior. Thus, for Graham (1995), a critical crime prevention measure is reducing truancy and school expulsions. The days missed by students should be meticulously tracked, schools should be informed of persistent truants, greater efforts must be made to understand why such a high level of truancy exists for each of these students, and special reintegration programs should be devised to coax dropouts back into school (Graham, 1995, 27–28).

In addition to preventing students from dropping out or being expelled from school, there is also a great need for "a systemic approach to dropout recovery, the act of re-engaging students who have already left school…" (Rennie Center for Education Research & Policy, 2012, 1). As Steinberg and Almeida (2004, 6) write,

> For the foreseeable future, a large number of young people who have disconnected from school will need a way to reconnect to educational options that meet their needs. Disconnected older adolescents are among the most neglected and at risk of our young people. Three different and somewhat overlapping spheres of programming have long comprised a so-called "second chance" system:

CASE STUDY 4.2

COMPREHENSIVE PROGRAM TO REDUCE ACADEMIC FAILURE AND DROPOUT RATES

The goal of the Quantum Opportunity Program (QOP) is to overcome academic deficiencies and promote graduation among high school–aged youth with low grades and/or at risk of dropping out of school. A secondary goal is to foster more prosocial behaviors among the participating youth (Hahn et al., 1994). Disadvantaged youth, especially those at risk of academic failure and dropping out of school, are particular targets of the program. Using a comprehensive case management (wraparound) approach, QOP provides year-round services to participating youth over a 4-year period (generally grades 8–12). The services or "quantum opportunities" provided to students can be grouped into three areas: (1) academic activities (peer tutoring, help with homework, computer-based instruction), (2) school and community service (volunteering within the school or with community projects), and (3) a curriculum of developmental activities to reduce risky behavior and promote prosocial behavior (focusing on social competencies and life skills, as well as college and career planning) (Welsh, 2007, 24). Every year that students are enrolled in the program, they are expected to commit to 250 h in each of the three areas (Promising Practices Network, n.d.).

QOP also provides financial incentives, in the form of stipends, to students participating in each of the three aspects of the program. As an incentive for completing school and future postsecondary studies or job training, "students receive a stipend for each hour spent on QOP activities, and a bonus of $100 after completing 100 h of education, development, or service activities in a given year (for up to $300 total). The stipends and bonuses are placed in an interest-bearing Quantum Opportunity Account and held for approved use, such as college or job training" (Promising Practices Network, Quantum Opportunity Program, n.d.).

An evaluation of the original program, which was implemented in five American cities in the early 1990s, showed it had a positive effect on participating students. Compared to a control group, those in the treatment group dropped out of high school at lower rates, graduated at higher rates, and were more likely to be enrolled in a postsecondary institution. Compared to the control group, students in the treatment group also had better grades in their postsecondary studies, undertook more community service work, were more apt to view their lives as a success, were optimistic about their future, and were less likely to get in trouble with police (Hahn et al., 1994; Taggart, 1995; Schirm and Rodriguez-Planas, 2004).

Offering youth a reconnection to the educational system through alternative high schools where they can earn a diploma;

Providing youth with immediate help in entering the labor market through youth employment programs (e.g. Job Corps, Conservation Corps, YouthBuild), as well as through programs designed for unemployed and low-wage adults; and

Offering youth general literacy, English-language development, and GED certificates through community-based Adult Basic Education and community colleges programs.

The process of reengaging "out-of-school youth" begins with a full understanding why most students leave school, according to the Rennie Center for Education Research & Policy (2012, 2):

National research shows the principal factors of dropping out tend to be both academic and non-academic, and include disengagement from coursework, failure to succeed in school, social problems and family responsibilities, a lack of support services for non-academic needs, and infrequent attendance… Therefore, effective re-engagement strategies must address not only prior schooling, but also present solutions to the social, economic, and psychological barriers students may continue to face. This means accounting for student differences, employing distinct strategies with different subgroups, and offering learning opportunities that do not look like traditional school environments. Strategies may include evening courses, self-paced learning, partnerships with post-secondary institutions, earning credit for work experience, and flexible scheduling. Overall, there is a greater focus on creating individualized and supportive learning experiences where teachers and staff members act as caring mentors to advocate for each student's needs.

Rennie Center for Education Research & Policy (2012, 2)

Based on programs that address the needs of out-of-school youth implemented in the United States, the Rennie Center outlines some of the measures necessary to coaxing these youth to complete their education:

Maintain a focus on students' future after high school. Many students who leave high school before graduation do so because of financial obligations. In response, dropout recovery programs focus on youths' future after graduation by using real-world, career-oriented curricula. These programs also integrate or partner with youth employment programs and workforce preparation. Some programs partner with nearby community colleges to incorporate college-level coursework, thus maintaining a focus on future education opportunities.

Allow individualized and flexible academic programs. Out-of-school youth may have several non-academic reasons for leaving school, including pregnancy or childcare, incarceration, health problems, or caring for family members. To address returning students' needs, recovery programs offer flexible schedules and year-round learning, including open-entry and open-exit so youth may begin and finish programs at any time. They also may allow academic credit recovery and accelerated program options. A portfolio of options offers an increased range of program choices, such as online, early morning and evening classes, or dual enrollment with community colleges.

Take a needs-based and supportive approach. Previous negative school experiences may leave out-of-school youth with a lack of motivation, requiring immediate engagement and consistent encouragement to cultivate their initial optimism about returning to school. To do this, dropout recovery programs use needs-based assessments to properly identify and serve returning youth through a case management model. Staffing a program with committed adults is a key element of the work, and recovery programs include well-qualified and committed teachers who assist students in navigating the demands of school and life. These programs also incorporate clear codes of conduct and increase student and parental involvement in education.

Integrate or link to community organizations. Schools and districts are not designed to address the myriad non-academic needs of many out-of-school youth. Recovery programs use extensive support programs and wraparound services—typically through partnerships with community agencies, health centers, statewide services, or community colleges—to ensure all returning students are ready to learn. Many programs also partner with businesses in the surrounding community to provide job training and maintain a focus on post-high school careers.

Rennie Center for Education Research & Policy (2012, 2–3)

CASE STUDY 4.3

DROPOUT RECOVERY PROGRAM IN MASSACHUSETTS

The state of Massachusetts' Graduation and Dropout Prevention and Recovery Commission recommended that the state government conduct "active recovery, including reaching out to dropouts and providing them with support and alternative pathways to graduation" (Rennie Center for Education Research & Policy, 2012, 1). The result of this recommendation was the creation of the Massachusetts reintegration center (REC). Located in Boston, the REC is "a dropout recovery center that strives to re-enroll out-of-school youth through outreach, personal connections, and a variety of educational options that support students to graduation" (Rennie Center for Education Research & Policy, 2012, 7). Some of the premises upon which the REC operates include the following:

- Out-of-school youth, especially those who are a little older, are not comfortable returning to the school they left.
- Returning out-of-school youth benefit from nontraditional programs, settings, and educational options, yet they are often unaware of what options are available.
- Providing a range of options is essential to keeping reengaging students interested in continuing their education.
- Reengaging an out-of-school youth is a time-sensitive matter; students must be provided with viable options when interest is initially expressed.

The REC helps high school dropouts by providing them with a supportive environment that allows them to find a suitable alternative option to make up the credits they need to graduate. These options include

- Twilight school, a night school option where students can take up to two classes on two evenings per week for 15 weeks
- Summer review, a summer school option where a student can retake up to two classes 5 days per week for 6 weeks
- Online credit recovery, for students to retake courses they have failed and to acquire credit in new content areas
- REC recovery courses, which offer students the option to retake up to two courses they have previously failed with REC staff teachers, 2 days per week for 15 weeks

During the course of their alternative studies, or if a student chooses to return to school, the REC will offer follow-up and mentoring support. It also "has established relationships with community partners, such as mental health providers and child care centers that are able to provide non-academic wraparound services." In addition, the REC helps students prepare for and take the test required to obtain their grade 12 equivalency diploma (Rennie Center for Education Research & Policy, 2012, 8).

4.6 GANG PREVENTION AND INTERVENTION STRATEGIES

Young offenders tend to have friends who are also involved in delinquent and criminal activities. According to the U.S. Surgeon General's 2001 report on youth violence, "involvement with delinquent peers and gang membership are two of the most powerful predictors of violence" (12). In a Statistics Canada report examining parenting, school contexts, and violence delinquency, Fitzgerald (2010, 6) refers to studies indicating that "exposure to delinquent peers facilitates the development and enforcement of a subculture of peer violence and delinquency." Also citing the extant literature, Doran et al. (2012, 751–752) conclude, socializing "with antisocial peers strongly predicts both aggression and substance involvement." Wasserman et al. (2003a, 6–7) contend that three interdependent risk factors combine to account for chronic offending during the teenage years: (1) the individual's own antisocial tendencies, (2) the negative consequences of peer rejection that can result from these tendencies, and (3) the resulting deviant peer associations. Wasserman and colleagues believe that peer influence has an impact on delinquency in two ways: (1) it can initiate offending of relatively "late starters" and (2) it can lead to the escalation of serious offending among the "early starters."

Strongly related to the criminogenic risks posed by negative peer networks are gangs—perhaps the epitome of a negative peer network. Not surprisingly, there is a large body of research and statistics demonstrating that gang members are far more likely to be involved in criminal and violent behavior and are at a higher risk of violent victimization compared to youth who are not associated with gangs (Wortley and Tanner, 2004; Bania, 2009; Maher, 2010; McGarrell et al., 2013b). Youth involved in gangs account for a disproportionate amount of criminal offenses in the United States (especially serious and violent crime). For Brandt and Russell (2002, 25), "the intrinsic nature of gangs promotes violent behaviors." Rosenfeld et al. (1999) found that since the early 1990s, between a quarter and a third of all homicides in the United States were gang related. Based on the National Youth Gang Survey, the National Gang Center estimates that, between 2007 and 2011, the total number of homicides related to gangs averaged more than 1900 a year, which accounts for approximately 12% of all homicides annually during this period (National Gang Centre, n.d.).

Maher (2010, 312) cites a number of studies in the United States and the United Kingdom showing that gang members are far more likely to carry a weapon compared to other youth or young adults not in a gang, are more likely to have peers who carry a firearm, and are far more likely to be involved in a shooting as either a victim or an offender. In a study in Toronto, Wortley and Tanner (2004) found that 68.3% of individuals who self-identified as criminal gang members reported having carried a gun or a knife, compared to 11.2% of those not involved in a gang. Firearms also have a symbolic purpose for gang members. Maher (2010, 312) cites drive-by shootings—"one of the most publicised means of gang violence"—as a good example of a gang-specific weapon offense. Drive-by shootings tend not to result in a high rate of fatalities but serve important symbolic and functional purposes for a gang (to terrorize and deter rival gangs, to build status and reputation, for revenge, etc.).

While street violence "may be planned to promote and protect the gang's interests, such as targeting rival gang members or resources," the often impulsive nature of youth gang members also leads to a high degree of "spontaneous and opportunistic" violence. This can result in "intentional or unintentional harm to the general public from drive-by shootings, street gang cross-fire and mistaken identities" (Criminal Intelligence Service Canada, 2006, 23). As detailed in the following, there are a number of causes and aggravating factors behind gang violence:

- Conflict between competing gangs (this *out-group* conflict may be the result of expansion of one gang, encroachment on another group's territory, or competition over an illegal market)

- Conflict within a gang (this *in-group* conflict may result from individual rivalries or discipline; violence may also be perpetrated as part of the initiation of a new gang member)
- Substance abuse by gang members
- Active involvement in drug trafficking, especially when local drug markets are unstable (i.e., characterized by a high level of competition)
- Access to firearms and other weapons
- The existence of subcultural norms that promote violence, including the *code of the street* (or a *code of honor*) in which competition or interpersonal transgressions are responded to with violence due to "a hyper-inflated notion of manhood that rests squarely on the idea of respect" (Schmalleger, 2006, 233)

The personal and social environmental risk factors discussed in Sections 4.3 and 4.5 are also applicable when trying to understand the causes of gang violence as well as gang membership and formation. Thus, efforts to combat gang violence should include initiatives that prevent gang membership and gang formation. As McGarrell et al. (2013b, 34) write, "research indicates that targeted approaches to gang prevention and intervention are possible as there are identifiable risk factors that are predictive of gang membership and future criminality. These include factors such as critical life events that disrupt relationships, impulsivity and risk-taking, delinquent beliefs, lack of parental monitoring, peer delinquency, and negative peer relationships...."

The focus of most efforts to control youth gangs and related activities can be demarcated into two broad categories: (1) limiting gang membership either by preventing individuals from joining gangs or inducing the departure of gang-involved individuals (thereby preventing the formation or sustainability of gangs respectively) and (2) preventing, controlling, disrupting, and minimizing criminality and violence by gangs and individual gang members. In other words, broadly speaking, gang control measures "focus either on restricting the development of gangs or on restricting the criminal behavior of gangs" (Maher, 2010, 318). The prevention/intervention/suppression typology discussed in Section 4.4 is also applicable to combating gangs. Each of these strategies operates at "different points at which we could intervene to address the issue of youth gangs," according to Hastings (2010, 15). For example, prevention is primarily focused on discouraging children and youth from joining gangs, while intervention and suppression target those currently in gangs. Suppression refers to the targeting of gangs and gang members and the most serious and chronic offenders in particular. Prevention and intervention initiatives emphasize CPSD, while suppression is typically made up of traditional law enforcement approaches (arrest and punishment). In recent years, approaches have been developed that emphasize deterrence and/or incapacitation through "such mechanisms as special enforcement teams, civil injunctions applied specifically in gang territories, gang 'sweeps' by law enforcement task forces, and sentence enhancements for convicted gang members" (Maxson et al., 2014, 441). Other suppression tactics that have recently been applied to gang and gun violence are those that employ more innovative, evidence-based policing practices, such as CompStat, intelligence-led policing, and hot spot policing, to name just a few. (For more information on proactive, prevention-oriented policing strategies, refer to Chapter 7.)

Gang prevention initiatives can be delivered on a universal basis (e.g., school-based programs for all students without attempting to predict which youth are most likely to join a gang). These initiatives also target young people who are most at risk of joining gangs and focus on those factors that heighten the risk of gang membership (Office of Juvenile Justice and Delinquency Prevention, 2007; Maher, 2010, 318; Maxson et al., 2014, 441). Gang prevention principles and programs include many of the family- and school-based CPSD approaches discussed in Chapter 3. In the United States, schools have become central institutions through which gang awareness and prevention interventions are delivered. One of the most widespread school-based programs is Gang Resistance Education and Training (GREAT), a 9-week instructional program taught to secondary school students on a universal basis by trained, uniformed police officers. The goal of the program is to help youth develop positive life skills and social competencies, minimize risky behavior, resist peer pressure, resolve conflict, and make positive, prosocial choices while imparting facts about the consequences of gang involvement and drugs (Esbensen, 2004).

Other school-based prevention programs have focused specifically on violence and the heightened risk of youth becoming involved in violence through gangs. These programs typically raise awareness of the inherently violent nature of gangs and the detrimental impact of violence on individuals and communities. These programs also try to inculcate within students an understanding of how and why violence is initiated and how it can be avoided through critical thinking, peaceful problem solving, learning to understand the perspective of others, and conflict resolution skills.

Gang intervention strategies target gang-involved individuals with the goal of inducing them to leave a gang or at the very least to reduce their gang-related criminal and violent activity (Maxson et al., 2014, 441). Central to gang intervention strategies are efforts to help or even coerce individuals to leave a gang and abandon the gang lifestyle (Maher, 2010, 318). As Hastings (2010, 15) writes, "a great deal more attention needs to be paid to the issue of leaving gangs, especially for youth who are in custody. The concern is that leaving a gang or leaving custody do not, in and of themselves, assure successful insertion and integration into prosocial worlds. The failure to provide effective supports at this stage can leave the youth isolated and vulnerable to the appeals to returning to the gang." Broadly speaking, gang exit strategies take one of three forms. First, there is the social problem-solving approach that targets the risk factors that sustain an individual's involvement in a gang (e.g., treatment of mental health or SUDs, social and life skills training, access to crisis shelters, job training, and education). The second is a criminal justice (suppression) approach that seeks to remove an individual from a gang through incarceration. The third approach is a "deterrence supplemented with social service provisions" (McGarrell et al., 2013b, 34) model that persuades gang members to leave through a stick and carrot method, combining the threat of criminal justice sanctions (the stick) with the provision of meaningful alternatives to a gang lifestyle (the carrot), such as education and employment, as well as other social developmental initiatives (e.g., substance abuse treatment).

Gang violence intervention efforts can also include the application of situational crime prevention techniques. Such approaches do not address the root causes of gang violence. Instead, they attempt to prevent and control violence that may erupt between rival gangs and gang members by addressing the immediate proximate conditions that may create or facilitate opportunities for intergang violence to occur. (See Chapter 2 for more on the application of opportunity reduction measures to combat gang violence.) In addition to access control measures such as street closures described in Chapter 2, opportunity-reduction gang and violence intervention efforts can include conflict mediation and resolution. According to the International Centre for the Prevention of Crime, "methods of peaceful conflict

CASE STUDY 4.4

VIOLENCE EDUCATION AND GANG AWARENESS IN ILLINOIS

The Violence Education and Gang Awareness (VEGA) program was created in response to increasing gang violence in Illinois schools. One of VEGA's main goals is to stress alternatives to violence, with particular emphasis on nurturing conflict resolution skills among students. Consequences of joining gangs and consequences of gang violence are also explained to youth in the program. The program's main target group is fifth and sixth graders, and the program curriculum consists of five lessons delivered over five consecutive weeks, by trained police officers. The five VEGA lessons are as follows:

1. Gangs are a matter of choice: This lesson teaches students the facts about gangs and the consequences of gang membership.
2. Violence and its victims: This lesson assists students with discovering what causes conflicts and why violence is not always the right solution. It is emphasized through this lesson that the gang lifestyle is not glamorous.
3. The circle of violence: This lesson looks at sources of violence and conflict by discussing and analyzing how different ideas and feelings cause people to disagree. This lesson also illustrates that violence only escalates conflicts and problems instead of solving them.
4. Peacemakers, not peacebreakers: The importance of using problem-solving and prosocial skills is emphasized in this lesson. Students are taught to evaluate risks involved with a situation, and students are also taught to apply these problem-solving skills in order to resolve conflicts.
5. Thinking ahead—a look at tomorrow: The final VEGA lesson assists students with being able to understand and be empathetic to the effect people have on one another.

While students are the main targets of VEGA, police also invite parents and community members to participate in the program (Delaney, 2006, 259).

resolution have demonstrated their effectiveness" in the context of localized crime and violence problems around the world:

> Implemented in public places, within the family, on public transport, or within the justice system, conflict resolution approaches including mediation, legal disputes settlements, education in peaceful relationships, and citizenship, and conciliation, have multiplied in all regions, and have been the object of rigorous evaluation. A few examples: 11,000 people, mostly women, have been trained in conflict mediation in Brazilian favelas in the context of the PRONASCI programme. In Kingston, Jamaica, or in Chile, mediators intervene in those neighbourhoods where the most problems occur. In the United States, the use of "violence interrupters", initiated in Chicago and replicated in other cities, has helped reduce by half the number of retaliation shootings by street gangs. In France, social mediation has helped reduce conflicts by 90% and resulted in a 60% reduction in costs related to the destruction of public property.
>
> **International Centre for the Prevention of Crime (2010, IX–X)**

CASE STUDY 4.5

PULLING LEVERS *FOCUSED DETERRENCE STRATEGIES ON CRIME*

Braga and Weisburd (2012) provide a synopsis of the *pulling levers* focused deterrence strategy (also called the "deterrence supplemented with social service provisions" model) as well as a summary of their meta-analysis of studies assessing this strategy to date.

> A number of American police departments have been experimenting with new problem-oriented policing frameworks to prevent gang and group-involved violence generally known as the *pulling levers* focused deterrence strategies. Focused deterrence strategies honor core deterrence ideas, such as increasing risks faced by offenders, while finding new and creative ways of deploying traditional and nontraditional law enforcement tools to do so, such as directly communicating incentives and disincentives to targeted offenders. Pioneered in Boston to halt serious gang violence, the focused deterrence framework has been applied in many American cities through federally sponsored violence prevention programs. In its simplest form, the approach consists of selecting a particular crime problem, such as gang homicide; convening an interagency working group of law enforcement, social service, and community-based practitioners; conducting research to identify key offenders, groups, and behavior patterns; framing a response to offenders and groups of offenders that uses a varied menu of sanctions (*pulling levers*) to stop them from continuing their violent behavior; focusing social services and community resources on targeted offenders and groups to match law enforcement prevention efforts; and directly and repeatedly communicating with offenders to make them understand why they are receiving this special attention. These new strategic approaches have been applied to a range of crime problems, such as overt drug markets and individual repeat offenders, and have shown promising results in the reduction of crime.
>
> Based on our narrative review, we find that 9 of the 10 eligible evaluations reported statistically significant reductions in crime. It is important to note here that all 10 evaluations used nonrandomized quasi-experimental designs. No randomized controlled trials were identified by our search strategies. Our meta-analysis suggests that pulling levers focused deterrence strategies are associated with an overall statistically significant, medium-sized crime reduction effect.
>
> We conclude that pulling levers focused deterrence strategies seem to be effective in reducing crime. However, we urge caution in interpreting these results because of the lack of more rigorous randomized controlled trials in the existing body of scientific evidence on this approach.

Abridged from Braga, A.A. and Weisburd, D.L., *The Effects of "Pulling Levers" Focused Deterrence Strategies on Crime*, The Campbell Collaboration, Oslo, Norway, 2012, pp. 5–6.

The "violence interrupters" in Chicago were part of a broader strategy called Operation Ceasefire, which was implemented to reduce gang and gun-related shootings in that city. As Ritter (2009, 21) explains,

> CeaseFire's violence interrupters establish a rapport with gang leaders and other at-risk youth, just as outreach workers in a public health campaign contact a target community. Working alone or in pairs, the violence interrupters cruise the streets at night,

mediating conflicts between gangs. After a shooting, they immediately offer nonviolent alternatives to gang leaders and a shooting victim's friends and relatives to try to interrupt the cycle of retaliatory violence. Violence interrupters differ from community organizers or social workers. Many are former gang members who have served time in prison, which gives them greater credibility among current gang members. CeaseFire's message travels from violence interrupters to gang members, from clergy to parishioners, and from community leaders to the neighborhood through conversations, sermons, marches and prayer vigils. The message appears on banners at postshooting rallies, which are a major part of the program. The message is simple: "The killing must stop!"

Mediating settlements between rival gangs has the potential not only to control violence in a particular time and place but may also address the causes of the conflict itself.

To sum up this section, like other crime and violence problems, there is widespread agreement in the literature that the most effective approach to gangs and gang violence is a comprehensive one that combines prevention, intervention, and suppression techniques. According to Wyrick and Howell (2004, 20), the federal Office of Juvenile Justice and Delinquency Prevention (OJJDP) in the United States has "long advocated for comprehensive approaches to youth gangs that involve multiagency collaboration and a combination of prevention, intervention, and suppression efforts." By way of example, Pitts (2009, 32–34) outlines a comprehensive approach that relies on multiple strategies each of which targets different levels of (potential or current) gang membership:

1. Enforcement, intensive supervision and surveillance, and social interventions (exit programs) targeting core gang members and prolific violent offenders
2. Intensive problem solving (education, training, and employment) targeting younger members or those at risk of involvement in gangs
3. "Problem-oriented and social-educational interventions" (emphasizing "reintegration into, or support for participation in, mainstream educational, recreational and vocational activity"), which target those on the "periphery of gang involvement"
4. Universal "area/school-based social-educational/recreational youth and community interventions" directed toward "non-gang-involved children and young people, under pressure in gang-affected neighborhoods"

In 2006, Klein and Maxson identified and reviewed 59 gang response programs in the United States. Few were comprehensive and coordinated in that they incorporated prevention, intervention, and suppression approaches. The general findings of Klein and Maxson's meta-analysis also suggest that implementation has been uneven and the evidence of their impact on gang involvement and gang crime has been very limited (Klein and Maxson, 2006; Maxson, 2011). By 2013, as McGarrell et al. (2013b, 34) point out, three comprehensive approaches to gangs and gang violence had proliferated throughout the United States: (1) Boston's pulling levers strategy (Kennedy, 1997; Kennedy et al., 2001; Braga and Weisburd, 2012), (2) the Chicago CeaseFire (now CureViolence) intervention (Skogan et al., 2008), and (3) the so-called Spergel comprehensive model of gang prevention, intervention, and suppression (Spergel and Curry, 1993; Spergel, 2007). All three models are comprehensive in that they combine prevention, intervention, and suppression techniques in an integrated fashion and mobilize an array of resources, agencies, and institutions (police, other criminal justice agencies, neighborhood residents, families, social welfare agencies, community

CASE STUDY 4.6

MEDIATING GANG VIOLENCE IN CALIFORNIA

In San Mateo County, California, Bob Szelenyi, a street gang detective with the local police force became discouraged with the traditional enforcement response of arrests and incarceration to a 7-year war between two rival gangs, which includes stabbings, car bombings, and murder. "Everything I did as a street-gang detective never seemed to improve the quality of life in our community," he is quoted as saying. "We arrested people—they did their time, came out, and resumed with the same violent path. As a cop trying to make a difference, it was frustrating seeing the continuation of numerous young men getting permanently maimed, and even killed, as a result of gang violence."

In mid-1993, Szelenyi asked for and received a transfer to the community policing unit of the San Mateo Police Force, where he was trained in problem-oriented policing. He then applied his new-found skills to try and forge a lasting solution to the gang violence problem. His approach was to provide mediation between the rival gangs that would allow them to let them discuss and hopefully resolve their differences in a neutral environment.

Szelenyi first enlisted the help of a volunteer-based mediation agency called the Peninsula Conflict Resolution Center. He then approached probation authorities, which had court-ordered guardianship over gang members. With their help, he identified those from the rival gangs who were seen to be respected by and have authority over other gang members. To begin the mediation process, staff with the Peninsula Conflict Resolution Center set up separate meetings with members and leaders of the two rival gangs. The meetings were held in locations that were considered neutral territory for the gangs. Three mediators, two probation officers, and Szelenyi, in plain clothes, attended the meetings.

Probation officials persuaded their supervised gang members to attend the meetings, and Szelenyi even convinced the Sheriff's department to release a gang leader serving time in a county jail so he could attend. Police also petitioned a juvenile court judge to waive a clause of the gang members' probation prohibiting them from associating with one another, so that they could meet together without fear of court-ordered sanctions.

Over the course of four meetings with each gang, the mediators were able to persuade them to discuss what they perceived to be the causes of the intergang violence. As importantly, they were able to convince them of the harmful impact of the violence on the gangs, the gang members, their families, and communities while moving both groups toward some common ground that could form the foundation for a mediated truce. Eventually, the gang members expressed concern over the impact of the ongoing violence and resolved to try something new to stem the intergang warfare. This included a mutual agreement by leaders of both gangs to meet with their rivals. Each gang selected five members as their representatives and negotiators for the peace talks. Before the talks, the mediators once again met separately with each gang to ensure they were committed to the process and that they would negotiate sincerely. When these assurances were secured, the representatives of the two gangs met together with the mediators.

Each gang brought a list of items to be resolved. According to Szelenyi, "Respect was at the top of both lists… Each gang raised a lot of respect issues. They never [verbally] communicated with each other. They [communicated only] in warfare." Another issue that both groups agreed upon was "the need to put the past behind them." According to Szelenyi, "With the assistance of the mediators, they began conversing about all the issues that had been discussed at previous meetings, and the priorities that were on their respective lists. They spoke respectfully for about two hours. At the conclusion of the meeting, an agreement for peace was reached, and handshakes were exchanged. As a former street-gang detective, it was the most amazing thing I have ever witnessed."

Those gang leaders attending the peace talks agreed to a follow-up meeting and would bring along other members, who they would convince to support the truce. In attendance at this final meeting were 41 gang members from each side, all of whom agreed to abide by the conditions of the truce, such as refraining from crossing into each others' territories or defacing the rival gang's graffiti. They agreed to respect one other, and if "a confrontation arose, they would try to talk it through as opposed to using weapons."

While gangs still persist as a major criminal problem in San Mateo country, in the 4 years that followed the mediation efforts, there were no reports of violence between the two gangs. While isolated incidents between individual members in the two gangs still arise, they have not led to an all-out gang warfare. Szelenyi believes the mediation was successful for a number of reasons: "The timing was right, we never gave up, (the gangs) ended up trusting us, and they ended up believing that all we wanted to do was stop the violence" (Sampson and Scott, 1999, 27–29).

organizations, schools, etc.). The overarching approach of these three models is summarized by Chaterjee as such:

> These programs, together with targeted suppression, typically focused on medium to high-risk youths and utilize a multi-faceted approach including social skills/values development; they utilized clear, unambiguous and direct communication with the most serious gang members regarding consequences of violence, sought to provide youth with alternatives to criminal life style and put special emphasis on families, schools and communities. These programs utilized appropriately trained staff that understood the youths' perspective and experience. Most researchers agreed that a multi-agency, multifaceted approach to gang problems would be effective in almost all gang-related situations. Based on the stage and intensity of the problem, this effort would need to combine the most effective components: community mobilization, social intervention (crisis intervention, providing positive role models for youth, inter-gang mediation, counseling, assistance to leave gangs, and drug prevention and treatment), opportunity provision (for education and employment) and lastly, targeted suppression.

Chaterjee (2006, 51)

These three models have benefited from years of research into what works and what does not work in controlling gangs and violence and, as such, are very much evidence based. In their accounting of why certain gang prevention programs do not work in the United States, Spergel et al. (2014, 464) conclude, "It is likely that all the failed projects lacked implementation of an adequate, combined, community-based, inter-organizational, multi-strategy, and interdisciplinary street-based intervention model to address the youth gang program." In short, efforts to control gang problems, according to the U.S. Office of Juvenile Justice and Delinquency and Prevention, "must be comprehensive, long-term strategic approaches that contain the spread of gang activity, protect those youth who are most susceptible, and mitigate risk factors that foster gang activity." The four-pronged approach of effective antigang strategies promoted by the OJJDP includes "targeted suppression of the most serious and chronic offenders; intervention with youthful gang members; prevention efforts for youth identified as being at high risk of entering a gang; and implementation of programs that address risk and protective factors and targets the entire population in high-crime, high-risk areas" (Office of Juvenile Justice and Delinquency Prevention, Comprehensive Anti-Gang Initiative, n.d.).

CASE STUDY 4.7

COMPREHENSIVE COMMUNITY-WIDE APPROACH TO GANGS (THE SPERGEL MODEL)

In 1987, the OJJDP initiated the Juvenile Gang Suppression and Intervention Research and Development Program. Led by Dr. Irving Spergel, from the University of Chicago, the research entailed an assessment of existing agencies and programs dedicated to combating gangs and gang-related crime and violence in the United States. Based upon his review, Spergel concluded, "neither a single minded suppression nor a single-minded social-intervention approach has demonstrated success in reducing gang crime, especially gang violence" (Spergel, 2007, 25). Spergel and Curry (1993) argue that since the causes and proximate factors contributing to gang membership, gang existence, and gang activities are complex and multifaceted, an equally complex and multifaceted response is required. As a result of their research, in 1994, Spergel and his colleagues created the Comprehensive Community-Wide Approach to Gang Prevention, Intervention, and Suppression, commonly known as the "Spergel model" (Spergel and Curry, 1993; Spergel et al., 1994; Spergel, 1995). This model is one example of how a comprehensive, multiagency, multisectoral approach to addressing significant youth crime and violence problems can be pursued at the community level.

The Spergel model is premised on the social disorganization theory of crime and criminality and, more specifically, the premise that "gangs become chronic and serious problems in communities where key organizations are inadequately integrated and sufficient resources are not available to target gang-involved youth" (Public Safety Canada, n.d., 1). As such, according to Spergel et al. (2014, 452),

> The comprehensive gang program model required criminal justice and social agencies to integrate and collaborate on key elements of control and social development, with participation from local neighborhood groups. Focus was not primarily directed to strategies of general community development, political or social reform, community policing, inclusive youth socialization, or even mediation of conflicts between gangs. These strategies were subsidiary to reducing the gang problem through an integrated social development, control, opportunities provision, and interorganizational mobilization approach. The model required the development of a lead agency and a street team of police, probation officers, and outreach youth workers (some former gang leaders) – interacting and working together – targeting delinquent/criminal gang youth and youth at high risk of gang membership who were also involved in delinquent activity.

At the core of the Spergel model is a comprehensive approach to gangs, gang crime, and gang violence, executed through an integrated, multidisciplinary intervention team, composed of law enforcement agencies, probation agencies, social welfare agencies, street outreach workers, and community organizations. All are expected to work together to case manage individual gang members using five interrelated strategies: (1) community mobilization, (2) social interventions, (3) opportunity provision, (4) suppression, and (5) organizational change and development of local agencies and groups. The National Crime Prevention Centre of Canada (2008) summarizes the broad interventions delivered through the Spergel model as follows:

- Community mobilization: Mobilizing local residents, youth, community groups, civic leaders, and agencies to plan, strengthen, or create new opportunities or linkages to existing organizations for gang-involved and at-risk youth and coordinating programs and services as well as the functions of staff within and across agencies

- Social intervention: Providing programs and social services (via youth services agencies, schools, faith-based and other organizations) to gang youth and those at high risk of gang involvement; also, using outreach workers to actively engage gang-involved youth
- Opportunity provision: Providing and facilitating access to educational, training, and employment programs or services targeted to gang youth and those at high risk of gang involvement
- Suppression: Conducting suppression activities via formal and informal social control mechanisms and holding gang-involved youth accountable for their actions and behaviors, including close supervision or monitoring of gang youth by criminal justice agencies and also by community-based agencies, schools, and grassroots groups
- Organizational change and development: Facilitating organizational change and development to help community agencies better address gang problems through a team problem-solving approach that is consistent with the philosophy of community and problem-oriented policing; also, developing and implementing policies and processes that result in the most effective use of available and potential resources within and across agencies (National Crime Prevention Centre of Canada, 2008, 63–64)

This comprehensive model was piloted as the Little Village Gang Violence Reduction Project in Chicago, starting in 1992. As part of this project, the intervention team targeted approximately 200 hardcore gang members, ages 17–25, from two of the largest, most violent gangs in Chicago. The goal of the program was aimed at controlling violent or potentially violent youth gang offenders through surveillance and suppression activities by police, intensive supervision and monitoring by probation officials, and the delivery of social services (such as counseling, job training and referrals, and drug and alcohol treatment) to help gang-involved youth exit gangs and lead more prosocial lives (Spergel et al., 1999; Spergel, 2007).

Evaluations of the Little Village Gang Reduction Project found, over the course of 4 years, that serious gang violence (aggravated assaults and homicides) and other crimes committed by gang members targeted by the project were lower compared to members of gangs that were used as control groups. The project appeared to be effective in helping youth reduce their violent and criminal behavior—in part by diverting gang-involved youth into educational programs and employment—although these results were largely confined to older youth (the project did not seem to have a similar impact on younger gang members) (Spergel et al., 1999; Spergel, 2007).

Other notable principles and project evaluation findings of the Little Village Gang Reduction Project include the following:

- A "mobilized community is the most promising way to deal with the gang problem." A "community must first recognize the presence of a gang problem before it can do anything meaningful to address the problem." The community must also "systematically articulate and implement rationales for services, tactics, or procedures" and then must "organize effectively to combat the youth gang problem." In a "typical community, the mobilization process evolves through several stages before fruition" (National Gang Center, 2010, 2).
- While youth gang members must be held accountable for their criminal acts, they must at the same time be provided an opportunity to change or control their behavior (National Gang Center, 2010, 2).
- Youth gang intervention and control efforts require a thorough understanding of the complexity of gang activity in the context of local community life (National Gang Center, 2010, 2).

- Youth outreach workers, whose primary role was to build relationships with at-risk and gang-involved youth and then develop an intervention plan and find relevant services so they can adopt more prosocial behavior, were also considered critical to program success (National Gang Center, 2010, 21).
- A combination of various social interventions involving youth outreach workers and suppression tactics was more effective for chronically violent youths, while the sole use of youth workers was more effective for less violent youths (National Crime Prevention Centre, 2008, 65).

With some subsequent modifications, the Spergel model evolved into the OJJDP Comprehensive Community-Wide Gang Model. Beginning in 1995, this model was implemented and tested in five other sites in the United States. Since its initial pilot testing, the OJJDP has implemented this model in more than 25 urban and rural locations in the United States (Wyrick, 2005; National Gang Center, 2010).

One example of the OJJDP comprehensive model is the Gang Reduction and Intervention Program (GRIP), which was implemented in Richmond, Virginia. The neighborhood in which GRIP was implemented was a community of single-family homes and apartments that at the time was "transitioning from a middle-class to a working-class population, with an increase in Hispanic residents." Both traditional *homegrown* African-American gangs and Hispanic gangs with roots in the western United States and Central America were also present in the community (Office of Juvenile Justice and Delinquency Prevention, 2007, 9). According to the OJJDP (2007, 9), preventative activities implemented as part of the GRIP project were "aimed at the broad population of families and youth who are at risk of becoming involved in gang and delinquent activity" and included the following:

- One-stop resource center (an information and referral case management entry point to prevention services).
- Prenatal and infancy support.
- English as a second language for Hispanic residents.
- Spanish as a second language, with an emphasis on providing language skills to those serving the Hispanic population.
- Class action summer camp.
- Richmond school resource officers train the Class Action curriculum in target area schools under the auspices of the Gang Reduction Program.
- Public awareness programs and community events.
- School-based educational and family wraparound services.
- Sports and life skill activities and training.
- Theater group to showcase issues involving gang-involved youth.
- Gang awareness training to community and service providers.
- Hispanic liaison to link the program to local Hispanic residents.
- Mentoring/tutoring for youth at risk of gang involvement.
- Immigration services to Hispanic residents.
- After-school and summer programs for elementary and middle school youth.
- Arts and recreation for at-risk youth.

Intervention activities of the project were "supported by a multidisciplinary intervention team that conducts case-management activities, including street outreach to support gang-involved youth, with the goal of providing an alternative to gang membership." Interventions that specifically targeted gang-involved and other high-risk youth included the following:

- Job training development and placement through public/private partnerships
- Entrepreneurial training for at-risk youth
- Role modeling and mentoring
- Truancy and dropout prevention programs

- Mental health and substance abuse services
- Educational support and GED services
- Tattoo removal
- Community service projects (Office of Juvenile Justice and Delinquency Prevention, 2007, 9)

Other social developmental initiatives were offered to youth who were returning to the community from a correctional facility or another form of court-ordered supervision. These reentry initiatives were "closely tied to the multidisciplinary intervention team and include self-sufficiency skill training and job training and placement." Support services for these youth and young adults, including transportation, food, and other services, were also made available (Office of Juvenile Justice and Delinquency Prevention, 2007, 9).

> Law enforcement suppression and other policing activities undertaken as part of GRIP entailed "directed police patrols, community policing, community awareness, supporting increased law enforcement intelligence sharing, establishing a multiagency law enforcement and prosecution response to target gang leaders, increasing the number of school resource officers in target area schools, and expanding neighborhood watch teams in partnership with the Richmond Police Department and community members" (Office of Juvenile Justice and Delinquency Prevention, 2007, 9).

The evaluations of the Little Village project and other applications of the OJJDP comprehensive model revealed that project implementation was not without its challenges. It is highly ambitious and complex to implement, in part due to the comprehensive, multimodal, interagency approach combined with the need to mobilize local communities (which is a significant challenge in itself). Studies of the different comprehensive models that were applied produced mixed findings, which, according to McGarrell et al. (2013a, 34), is partially blamed on inadequate implementation of the theoretical model that neglected at least one of its five essential components.

4.7 YOUTH OUTREACH WORKERS

Within the context of comprehensive crime prevention programs, youth outreach workers have shown to be a particularly promising component of social problem-solving interventions for at-risk youth and young adults. This is particularly true of youth who are marginalized from mainstream society in some way, such as those who are homeless, have untreated mental health or substance abuse problems, are involved in gangs, or have a history of being difficult to serve or engage through mainstream agencies. "Projects which aim to support young people through difficult transitions, or those who may no longer be in education or work, have often used 'unattached' or outreach workers," according to the International Centre for the Prevention of Crime (2010, 136). In the United States, the title *street outreach worker* is commonly applied to this profession because the work "is not office-based or even institutional- or school-based, but occurs primarily in the targeted neighborhoods, at the street and home level (Arciaga and Gonzalez, 2012, 2). Outreach workers who journey and deliver services to marginalized and at-risk youth are crucial because "merely having programs available may not be adequate; outreach to the most seriously delinquent youth and their families may also be essential" (Thornberry et al., 2004, 14).

The primary roles of youth outreach workers are to build trusting relationships with at-risk youth, remove them from deleterious social environments, assist them in accessing relevant services and programs, and provide ongoing support, encouragement, mentoring, and a positive adult role model. According to Arciaga and Gonzalez (2012, 2), street outreach workers are frequently recruited from the neighborhoods in which they work, are sometimes former gang members or young offenders, and "are especially effective in working with marginalized youth mistrustful of authorities." Youth outreach workers are often in an ideal position to contact groups of marginalized youth where they naturally congregate, develop trusting relationships with individual youth as a precursor to helping them, identify their specific needs, and then connect them with the most appropriate local services and agencies without compromising the principles of trust and confidence (Graham, 1995, 3, 30). According to the National Gang Center (2010), evaluations of the OJJDP Comprehensive Community-Wide Approach to Gang Prevention, Intervention, and Suppression demonstrate the importance of the outreach component to that program's success. The outreach workers' responsibilities as part of this program include

- Identifying appropriate clients and recruiting them for the program (outreach workers are the intervention team's eyes and ears on the street and often constitute the primary recruitment tool for the program)
- Identifying youths' needs, strengths, and goals to help the intervention team develop a more comprehensive case management plan
- Referring program clients to service providers and then helping to manage this relationship
- Coordinating appropriate crisis responses to program clients following violent episodes in the community
- Coaching and providing role models for each youth
- Providing assistance to families in distress, ranging from accessing basic needs to helping resolve family conflicts
- Visiting clients who are incarcerated and helping to reconnect them to services when they are released from custody
- Resolving conflicts and/or mediating between clients, their families, other youth, and/or agencies
- Working with clients who are seeking employment (which may include helping with résumé writing and applying for jobs or job training programs)
- Conducting gang awareness presentations in schools (National Gang Center, 2010, 21)

Based on their research into street outreach workers (or *streetworkers*) in Manchester, England, Shropshire and McFarquar (2003, 12) list the following essential elements of an outreach program to combat gang cultures and gun violence specifically:

- Staff selection criteria: Streetworkers should already be known and trusted by young people and parents in the community and should themselves be from the community. They should ideally be in the age range 25–35 (much younger and they will not command respect with older members of the community and much older and they may not *connect* as well with this target group of young people). It is essential that they accept the need to work with close cooperation with all partner agencies including police and other criminal justice agencies and genuinely recognize the benefits thereof.
- Proactive outreach and nontraditional hours of working: Streetworkers should work nontraditional hours including evenings and weekends and be on call

24 h a day to talk to or meet with young people or concerned, anxious, or frightened parents.

- Outreach on the streets: Streetworkers should directly approach young people in the streets targeting unknown and unidentified young people in known problem areas as well as ensuring frequent contact with known gang-involved young people. Streetworkers should provide support to other youth workers working in gang-affected areas. Streetworkers should have clearly marked identifiable *streetworker* vehicles, not unmarked cars.
- Outreach in the schools: Streetworkers should liase directly with schools to identify and reach gang-involved, high-risk, and marginally gang-involved young people in order to keep them from causing problems in the classroom and ensure a safe environment is maintained in the school.
- Working with education welfare officers and excluded young people: Streetworkers should liase with education welfare officers when a young person from a gang-affected area is facing exclusion to ensure appropriate alternative provisions keep the young person off the streets thus limiting exposure to gang influences.
- Outreach in the home: Streetworkers should make regular visits to the homes of gang-involved or high-risk young people in order identify the needs of the young person's family and link them into the appropriate service provider agencies.
- Acting as an interface between statutory agencies and young people and families: Streetworkers should be on hand to assist social workers, youth offending team officers, probation officers, police officers, education welfare officers, and teachers on home visits to families of gang-involved young people.
- Conflict prevention, resolution, and mediation: Streetworkers intervene in crisis situations and assist police and other criminal justice agencies in cooling tensions between young people from rival factions.
- Working with incarcerated young people: In conjunction with probation and youth offending team officers, streetworkers should work with young people and, where appropriate, their families, during periods of incarceration to ensure there is a smooth transition from incarceration to life back in the community.
- Risk assessment and supervision: Streetworkers should liase with criminal justice agencies to ensure detailed assessments are carried out and support (youth outreach teams) and probation teams in implementing supervision orders (as cited in Chaterjee, 2006, 23–24).

As mentioned, outreach workers are most effective when used as part of a comprehensive, collaborative, multiagency, wraparound approach. According to Arciaga and Gonzalez (2012), "street outreach in the OJJDP Comprehensive Gang Model occurs inside the framework of a cooperative relationship with other agencies, including probation, law enforcement, social services, and schools." In particular, "outreach workers work closely with other agencies on a multidisciplinary Intervention Team, sharing information about gang-involved clients and their families with partnering agencies... The majority of an outreach worker's time is spent working directly with gang-involved clients, identifying their needs and goals, and reporting back to the Intervention Team" (Arciaga and Gonzalez, 2012, 2).

4.8   YOUTH-CENTERED AGENCIES

Youth centers, including drop-in centers, are quite varied in their mission and services offered. They may provide educational, supervisory, counseling, job training and placement, health services, and recreational services, all of which may help to prevent some young people from becoming offenders or involved in other antisocial behaviors. Some may also provide shelter and detox facilities. Ideally, they are intended to act as sanctuaries for youth who are trying to escape street life.

In the Canadian province of Quebec, a government-backed network of social problem-solving youth centers is in place that deals with at-risk youth and those who have been in formal contact with the criminal justice system.

CASE STUDY 4.8

RESIDENTIAL CENTER FOR AT-RISK YOUTH

Set up in the late 1960s, the House of Umoja is a nonprofit residential facility in Philadelphia for at-risk African-Americans between the ages of 15 and 18 years, including chronic offenders and gang members. The House of Umoja offers a variety of services, emphasizing a comprehensive approach to enhancing life skills and social competencies that lead to prosocial values, self-sufficiency, self-development, and positive community involvement. The House of Umoja operates like an extended family and emphasizes an environment that fosters a sense of togetherness and mutual trust, within the context of positive African cultural values (Umoja is a Swahili word that means *unity in the family*). While communicating a positive message of African-American heritage to black youth and the community at large, it also provides a range of services to youth and families in distress.

All youth who take refuge there sign a contract that requires them to obey the strict house rules, involves them in all aspects of the operation of the house (including chores), and requires their enrollment in school. Young people can receive individual counseling, advice on their educational needs, health checkups, and assistance in securing employment or vocational training. Youth are also encouraged to become involved in the various commercial enterprises run by Umoja, including a waste removal company, a printing company, a restaurant, a security institute, and a driving instruction enterprise. Members are expected to live independently after 6 months to 1 year of residence if family reunification is not a realizable goal (The House of Umoja, n.d.).

Following 3 years of research (from 1975 to 1977), Woodson (1981) found that the House of Umoja played a role in reducing gang-related deaths in Philadelphia during this period. According to Woodson (1981, 46), gang-related homicides "declined from an average of thirty-nine deaths per year to six in 1976 and to just one death in 1977." However, other gang prevention and enforcement initiatives may also have contributed to the reduction in gang-related homicides during this time (Howell, 1998, 287, as cited in Welsh and Hoshi, 2006, 174).

CASE STUDY 4.9

QUASI-GOVERNMENTAL CENTERS FOR AT-RISK YOUTH AND JUVENILE OFFENDERS IN QUEBEC

DeGusti et al. (2009, 6) point out that "historically, the province of Quebec has had a unique approach to youth justice. More than the other Canadian provinces, Quebec has promoted a child welfare/child protection approach to youth at risk of offending. Quebec has consistently espoused a social development philosophy where rehabilitation and reintegration are primary goals." This unique approach to youth crime and justice is reflected in the province's "third lowest police reported youth crime rate in Canada in 2006. In addition, it had the lowest youth charging rate in the country, and the lowest youth charging rate for violent crime" (DeGusti et al., 2009, 10).

Guided by this philosophy, the province of Quebec operates a network of youth centers or *centres jeunesse*. Located in communities across the province, the centers are quasi-governmental agencies, funded almost entirely by the provincial Ministry of Health and Social Services. They provide a range of services to young people (up to the age of 18) and "are responsible for both youth in need of protection as well as those in conflict with the law..." (DeGusti et al., 2009, 6–7).

Most of the *centres jeunesse* in the province "have embraced a differential clinical intervention approach" that provides a full and varied range of services to at-risk youth and young offenders, writes DeGusti et al. (2009, 7). "This often results in a case-by-case intervention strategy for chronic and persistent youth offenders" so that they "receive services on the basis of their dispositions and individual assessments during intake." This typically involves assigning youth workers to case manage the services being provided for the youth and their families. According to DeGusti et al. (2009, 8), almost all of the medium to large youth centers in Quebec also offer special programs to youth offenders in custody or under community supervision, which also emphasizes a wraparound, social developmental approach and includes coordinating cognitive behavioral treatment and social cognitive skill development. One study found that the Montreal youth center was effective in preventing recidivism among 76% of high-risk offenders referred to them, compared to a 47.7% recidivism rate of young offenders who were given open custody dispositions (Cournoyer and Dionne, 2007 as cited in DeGusti et al., 2009, 8).

4.9 LABOR MARKET APPROACHES TO CRIME PREVENTION

There is a complex relationship between labor markets and crime, according to Graham (1995, 37). Some common hypotheses underlying the relationship between property and other street crime and (un)employment are as follows:

- Those who commit property crime tend to be out of the labor force or (chronically) unemployed.
- Unemployed youth are more likely than those with jobs to be idle and to succumb to opportunities to commit offenses (*Note*: the highest unemployment rates and crime rates both tend to be among people between the ages of 16 and 25).
- Property crime, drug trafficking, and other revenue-generating offenses provide income that is lost through unemployment.

- Disadvantaged neighborhoods in which crime is so heavily concentrated are also characterized by persistently high jobless rates and a depressed local labor market and economy.
- The factors that contribute to chronic criminality are often the same that contribute to chronic unemployment (academic failure; poverty; untreated behavioral, psychological, and mental health problems; negative socialization process; lack of local opportunities; etc.).
- Chronic unemployment or underemployment can be a cause of poverty, high levels of stress, mental health problems, and family dysfunction, all of which can put children at risk of future criminal and violent behavior (Cantor and Land, 1985; Graham, 1995, 37; Sherman, 1997a, 11–12; Bushway and Reuter, 2006, 198–203).

Dominant etiological theories of criminality also appear to support the criminogenic effects of unemployment. The social control theory suggests that unemployment can contribute to delinquent and criminal behavior because the former can lessen legitimate ties to conventional society. Unemployment may also increase feelings of status frustration, which may lead to criminal behavior, according to the strain theory. The social disorganization theory is quite explicit that a lack of local jobs can increase neighborhood instability, which in turn creates a local environment conducive to fostering a negative socialization of young people and, ultimately, delinquency and criminality. Conversely, these theories would suggest that stable employment would help foster an individual's ties to conventional society and help avoid or alleviate status frustration or strain. A vibrant local labor market is also key to instilling neighborhood stability, which in turn helps suppress criminogenic conditions.

While the relationship between crime and unemployment is not clear-cut, employment-based programs, in particular job training and placements, are a common developmental approach for older youth and adults who are at risk of criminal offending, are convicted (and paroled) offenders, and/or are chronically unemployed. As Lawrence Sherman (1997a, 11) notes, "there is a long history of attempting to prevent the onset or persistence of criminality by engaging young people in the labor market for legitimate work." As a crime prevention strategy, a legitimate job not only removes the necessity for some to revert to crime to support themselves, but it also can help promote other prosocial behaviors and integrate people into legitimate society. According to John Graham (1995), gainful employment shows promise for keeping past and future potential offenders from engaging in crime when the following conditions are met:

- It provides a sense of commitment, attachment, and belief.
- The employee is satisfied with his/her job.
- The employee is suitably equipped to do the job, in terms of both ability and training.
- There are opportunities to use one's skills and learn new skills.
- The job has long-term prospects for the employee.
- The employee is assisted in the development of good relationships with other employees and learns the rules and standards that govern the organization or enterprise.
- The employee receives treatment for other risk factors (substance abuse, anger management problems, psychological disorders, etc.) that may jeopardize gainful employment.

- The employee has good rapport with supervisors and coworker.
- The employee regularly receives positive feedback on performance.
- There are opportunities for promotion and advancement (Graham, 1995, 38).

In a doctoral dissertation examining the long-term impact of employment on criminality among youth, Wang (2010, 66) found that *ladder jobs*—current employment that pays little, but improves the chances of a long-term career—demonstrates "a significant crime-decreasing effect." In contrast, a "dead-end job that pays comparatively well in the short-term" exhibits a crime-increasing effect for youth.

Some specific examples of employment-based CPSD initiatives include the following:

- Summer job or subsidized work programs for at-risk youth
- Apprenticeship programs
- Transitional services from school to work that prepare those without a high school diploma to enter the job market
- Pretrial diversions for adult offenders, which make employment training a condition of case dismissal
- Prison-based vocational training and education programs for convicted offenders
- Postrelease transitional employment assistance for convicted offenders
- Wage and work transportation subsidies
- Small business training and loans
- *Enterprise zones* for disadvantaged neighborhoods that provide no- or low-interest loans for budding entrepreneurs

Ideally, employment-based programs integrate education, job skills training, employment placement services, and strong support to participants throughout. One of the most well known of these comprehensive labor market programs is Job Corps.

According to Sherman (1997a, 11–12), "theoretical and empirical support for the crime preventive value of employment is generally quite strong in the longitudinal analysis of individual criminal careers" and "programs aimed at linking labor markets more closely to high crime risk neighborhoods and individuals could have substantial crime prevention benefits." However, in his review of research into employment as a crime prevention strategy, Sherman writes that "only Job Corps programs have demonstrated success at enhancing the employment experience of severely unemployable persons, and even that evidence is scientifically weak. No program has yet shown success in tackling the unemployment rates of high crime neighborhoods."

4.10   RECIDIVISM PREVENTION

In recent years, recidivism prevention has increasingly been viewed as a key pillar in crime and violence prevention strategies, policies, and programs. This is due in part to the statistics and research showing that a small number of adolescent and young adult offenders are responsible for a disproportionate amount of crime and violence (Prime, 2001; Farrington et al., 2006; Wikström et al., 2012). Moreover, many of these serious and chronic offenders do not desist once they are caught and/or released from custody. As part of a widespread survey of youth in custody in the United States, Sedlak and Bruce (2010) found that 85% have prior convictions. Only 5% of youth in custody have no prior involvement with the justice system.

CASE STUDY 4.10

COMPREHENSIVE JOB TRAINING, PLACEMENT, AND SUPPORT PROGRAM

In the United States, the federally funded Job Corps offers "a comprehensive array of career development services to at-risk young women and men, ages 16–24, to prepare them for successful careers. Through a nationwide network of campuses, Job Corps employs a holistic career development training approach which integrates the teaching of academic, vocational, employability skills as well as social and workplace competencies through a combination of classroom, practical and based learning experiences to prepare youth for stable, long-term, high-paying jobs" (U.S. Department of Labor, Job Corps website).

The mission of Job Corps "is to attract eligible young people, teach them the skills they need to become employable and independent, and place them in meaningful jobs or further education." The U.S. Department of Labor, the federal agency responsible for the program touts, "since its inauguration in 1964, under the *Economic Opportunity Act*, Job Corps has provided more than 2 million disadvantaged young people with the integrated academic, vocational, and social skills training they need to gain independence and get quality, long-term jobs or further their education." Job Corps helps individuals achieve their career objective by guiding eligible candidates through four sequential stages in a career path:

1. Outreach and admission (the applicant learns the nature of Job Corps, how it can help start a career, student responsibilities, and vocational training opportunities available at a particular Job Corps campus)
2. Career preparation (the student learns job search skills as well as personal responsibility skills for the workplace and creates and commits to a personal career development plan)
3. Career development (with the help of Job Corps staff and employers, the student learns, demonstrates, and practices work-related technical and academic skills, interpersonal communication and problem-solving skills, and social and personal management skills; the student also begins the job search process and prepares for independent living during this stage)
4. Career transition (with the support of Job Corps staff, the graduate obtains a job, finds a place to live, identifies transportation and family support resources required to continue working, continues to contact Job Corps for support, if needed, and responds to 13-week, 6-month, and 12-month survey requests) (United States Department of Labor, Job Corps, n.d.)

Federal Labor Department statistics show that during the first year after completing the program, Job Corps participants are one-third less likely to be arrested than nonparticipants. One evaluation found that 75% of graduates move on to a job or to full-time study. They also retain jobs longer and earn about 15% more compared to a control group. Furthermore, for every $1.00 spent on the Job Corps, $1.45 in savings accrues to society in the form of reduced crime, substance abuse, and welfare dependency as well as increased job productivity, income, and taxes (United States Department of Labor, Job Corps, n.d.; United States Department of Labor, 1995; Bushway and Reuter, 1997).

As Thornberry et al. (2004, 15) put it, although it is *never too early* to address factors that put children at risk of future criminal offending, it is also *never too late* to intervene to reduce the risk of recidivism among youth and young adults. The implication is that an exclusive reliance on punitive criminal justice sanctions to stop criminals from reoffending has proven to be inadequate; there needs to be a greater emphasis on the application of social problem-solving strategies to offenders to limit recidivism.

Recidivism prevention is concerned with helping juvenile and adult offenders desist from criminal and violent behavior. As indicated earlier, traditionally, this has been pursued through the use of punitive criminal justice sanctions—specifically, the incarceration of repeat offenders. In the postwar era, the American criminal justice system at both the federal and state levels has become progressively more punitive with respect to repeat offenders (epitomized by the "three strikes and you're out" laws adopted by many states). However, research has consistently shown the absence of a strong correlation between punishment or the threat of punishment, on the one hand, and a lower level of recidivism on the other (MacKenzie, 2006; Wilson et al., 2008; Lipsey, 2009; Petrosino et al., 2010; Sedlak and McPherson, 2010). Numerous studies have indicated that incarceration of juvenile offenders in particular fails to reduce reoffending, especially if the youth does not receive appropriate treatment interventions while in detention. In their meta-analysis of studies examining the effects of *formal system processing* of juvenile offenders, Petrosino et al. (2010, 6) found that traditional incarceration "does not appear to have a crime control effect. In fact, almost all of the results are negative in direction, as measured by prevalence, incidence, severity, and self-report outcomes."

Partially due to the results of studies that reveal the limitations of criminal justice approaches to controlling reoffending, the field of recidivism prevention has increasingly been characterized by social problem-solving approaches, emphasizing treatment, social reintegration, and the creation of positive, alternative opportunities to crime, in particular, education, job training, and employment. Social problem-solving approaches are particularly pertinent to preventing recidivism among offenders who have been incarcerated because, according to Lockwood et al. (2012, 380–381), "research has consistently revealed that released offenders, if unemployed and uneducated, would likely become recidivist offenders."

A theoretical underpinning of recidivism prevention is the concept of *desistence*, which in the context of criminology is the "process of abstaining from crime among those who previously had engaged in a sustained pattern of offending" (United Kingdom, Ministry of Justice, 2010, 1). Broadly speaking, desistence can occur in one of two ways. First, desistence can occur naturally, such as through the aging process, maturation, marriage, and/or strengthened ties to civil society. Second, it can be encouraged or induced through deliberate interventions that target criminogenic and recidivist risk factors among offenders. Whether it is naturally occurring or prompted by structured interventions, desistence is "a process of gradually decreasing offending, rather than a sudden one-off decision not to offend again, which is immediately put into effect" (Farrall et al., 2010, 547). Furthermore, desistence "seems to be related to both external/social aspects of a person's life (such as the supportiveness of those around them) as well as to internal/psychological factors (such as what they believe in and what they want from life)" (United Kingdom Ministry of Justice, 2010, 1).

The natural process of desistence is reflected in the well-documented *age–crime curve*, in which the majority of youth who are engaged in delinquency or criminality gradually withdraw from such behavior as they encroach upon and reach adulthood (whether this is due to biological factors, social causes, or a combination of both) (Moffit, 1993). As Verbruggen et al. (2012, 845) write,

> "In life-course criminology, transitions into adult roles such as employment, marriage or parenthood are considered to be of great importance in the process of desistance from crime (Sampson and Laub 1993; Laub and Sampson 2003). Transitions can lead to an increased embeddedness in a conventional society and stimulate maturity, responsibility, or a change in identity. Entering a (steady) job is considered one of the most important transitions. Getting a job not only provides a source of income but is also associated with numerous other factors that promote desistance."

Furthermore,

> Desisting from crime is a common, not a rare occurrence, even among recidivist offenders and has been shown in previous research to be linked to changes in offenders' life-styles. In particular, such research (beginning with Sampson and Laub's classic study of 1993) has emphasized the importance of attachment to pro-social sources of informal social control, notably by acquiring a stable partner, obtaining and remaining in suitable employment, and moving away from criminal friends. Additionally, the process of desistance has increasingly – and in our view rightly – been seen as intrinsically linked to the agency of the offender, with decisions to desist, or at least to try to change one's lifestyle, interacting with the offender's social setting and with opportunities to lead a more conformist life….

Farrall et al. (2010, 546–547)

According to the U.K. Ministry of Justice (2010, 1–2), the most important factors contributing to desistence from criminal behavior are the following: getting older and maturing, family and relationships ("forming strong and supportive intimate bonds to others"), sobriety, employment, hope and motivation to change one's life, something to give ("offenders who find ways to contribute to society, their community, or their families, appear to be more successful at giving up crime"), a connectedness "to others in a (non-criminal) community of some sort," not identifying as a criminal offender, and being believed in by others.

A second way that desistence from criminal offending can occur is through induced or *artificial* strategies that deliberately target the criminogenic and recidivist risk factors of offenders. A targeted, risk-based approach is central to the theory and practice of recidivism prevention or what can be called *assisted desistence*—"how organisations and people can help individuals caught in cycles of crime and punishment successfully move away from lives of crime" (United Kingdom Ministry of Justice, 2010, 1).

In his meta-analysis of studies assessing strategies to prevent recidivism by young offenders, Lipsey (2009, 124) groups such interventions into seven categories. Collectively, these categories include traditional criminal justice control or coercion approaches (surveillance, deterrence, discipline), alternative justice (restorative) programs, and social problem-solving, developmentally based, therapeutic interventions:

1. Surveillance: "Interventions in this category are based on the idea that closer monitoring of the juvenile will inhibit reoffending. The main program of this sort is intensive probation or parole oriented toward increasing the level of contact and supervision" (Lipsey, 2009, 133).
2. Deterrence: "Interventions in this category attempt to deter the youth from reoffending by dramatizing the negative consequences of that behavior. The prototypical program of this sort is prison visitation 'scared straight' type

programs in which juvenile offenders are exposed to prisoners who graphically describe the aversive nature of prison conditions" (Lipsey, 2009, 134).

3. Discipline: "The theme of these interventions is that youth must learn discipline to succeed in life and avoid reoffending and that, to do so, they need to experience a structured regimen that imposes such discipline on them. The main programs of this sort are paramilitary regimens in boot camps" (Lipsey, 2009, 134).

4. Restorative programs: "Programs of this sort aim to repair the harm done by the juvenile's delinquent behavior by requiring some compensation to victims or reparations via community service. They may also involve some form of direct reconciliation between victims and offenders" (Lipsey, 2009, 134).

5. Counseling and its variants: "This diverse and popular program approach is characterized by a personal relationship between the offender and a responsible adult who attempts to exercise influence on the juvenile's feelings, cognitions, and behavior. Family members or peers may also be involved and the peer group itself may take the lead role in the relationship." Within this broad category are a number of variants, including individual counseling, mentoring by a volunteer or paraprofessional, family counseling, short-term family crisis counseling, and group counseling led by a therapist (Lipsey, 2009, 134–135).

6. Skill building programs: "These programs provide instruction, practice, incentives, and other such activities and inducements aimed at developing skills that will help the juvenile control their behavior and/or enhance their ability to participate in normative prosocial functions." For Lipsey, the interventions that fall within this category include behavioral programs ("behavior management, contingency contracting, token economies, and other such programs that reward selected behaviors"), cognitive behavioral therapy, social skills training, challenge programs ("interventions that provide opportunities for experiential learning by mastering difficult or stressful tasks"), academic training (e.g., tutoring and GED programs), and job-related interventions (vocational counseling and training, job placement, etc.) (Lipsey, 2009, 135).

7. Multiple coordinated services: "Programs in this category are not organized around a primary service type or a combination of a few such service types but, rather, are designed to provide a package of multiple services which may be basically similar for all the participating juveniles or may be individuated with different juveniles receiving different services." The main intervention forms of this type, according to Lipsey, are case management ("a designated case manager or case team develops a service plan for each juvenile, arranges for the respective services, and monitors progress"), service brokerage ("referrals are made for the service or services deemed appropriate for each juvenile with a relatively minimal role for the broker afterwards"), and multimodal regimens ("a multimodal curriculum or coordinated array of services is provided to all participating juveniles, often occurring in a residential setting") (Lipsey, 2009, 135).

Based on his analysis of the literature, Lipsey concludes there are three categories of factors most strongly associated with effective recidivism prevention for juvenile offenders: (1) the type of treatment provided, (2) the quality and quantity of treatment provided, and (3) the characteristics of the youth receiving the treatment (Lipsey, 2009, 127). As far as the type of treatment is concerned, Lipsey's review of the literature concludes that interventions embodying *therapeutic* philosophies, such as counseling, cognitive behavioral treatment, and skills training, "were more effective than those based on strategies of control or coercion – surveillance, deterrence, and discipline" (Lipsey, 2009, 143–144).

Therapeutic programs based on cognitive behavioral treatment principles are widely supported by various studies that show their effectiveness in reducing recidivism and promoting prosocial behavior generally (Lipsey et al., 2001; Pearson et al., 2002; Landenberger and Lipsey 2005; Little, 2005; Wilson et al., 2005; Lipsey, 2009). (For an introduction to cognitive behavioral treatment principles as a crime prevention technique, refer to Chapter 2.) In its analysis of model programs for dealing with young offenders, the Office of Juvenile Justice and Delinquency Prevention (n.d.) writes, "the most widely used approaches to treatment in criminal justice today are variations of Cognitive-Behavioral Therapy." CBT-based interventions are appropriate for serious and chronic offenders because these individuals are often characterized by "distorted cognition, self-justificatory thinking, misinterpretation of social cues, deficient moral reasoning, schemas of dominance and entitlement, and the like ..."

According to Lipsey et al. (2001):

> Offenders with such distorted thinking may react to essentially benign situations as if they were threatening, for example, be predisposed to perceive comments others make about them as disrespectful or attacking. They may hold conceptualizations of themselves, others, and the world that justify antisocial behavior, for example, "nobody can be trusted," "everyone is against me," or "society doesn't give me a chance." Their behavior may be guided by dysfunctional assumptions and rules about how one should behave, for example, "you have to punish people for messing with you or they won't respect you," "you have to rebel against authority or they will break you." And they may have deficient cognitive skills for long-term planning, problem solving, and decision making that contribute to maladaptive and rigid behavior.

Lipsey et al. (2001, 145)

In response, Lipsey et al. (2001, 145) writes, "cognitive behavioral treatments for juvenile offenders are designed to correct dysfunctional thinking and behaviors associated with delinquency, crime, and violence."

> They employ systematic training regimens aimed at creating cognitive restructuring and flexible cognitive skills such that offenders develop more adaptive patterns of reasoning and reacting in situations that trigger their criminal behavior. For instance, CBTs may train offenders to monitor their patterns of automatic thoughts to situations in which they tend to react with violence. Various techniques are rehearsed for assessing the validity of those thoughts and substituting accurate interpretations for biased ones. Often role-play or practice in real situations is used to help consolidate new ways of coping with situations that tend to prompt criminal behavior. CBTs may focus on managing anger, assuming personal responsibility for behavior (for example, challenging offenders' tendency to excuse their behavior by blaming the victim, society, or other circumstances beyond their control), taking a moral and empathetic perspective on interpersonal behavior (for example, victim impact awareness), solving problems, developing life skills, setting goals, or any combination of these themes. A relapse prevention component is also often included, which teaches offenders strategies for avoiding or deescalating the precursors to offending behavior (for example, high-risk situations, places, associates, or maladaptive coping responses).

Lipsey et al. (2001, 145)

CASE STUDY 4.11

PREVENTING RECIDIVISM THROUGH MULTISYSTEMIC THERAPY

Multisystemic therapy (MST) is one example of a cognitive behavioral intervention for chronic, violent, or substance-abusing young offenders. The overarching goal of MST is to eliminate criminal and other types of antisocial behavior in both the short and the long term by addressing the multiple determinants of such behavior through a multimodal, therapy-based approach.

Within the context of MST, criminal and violent offending is viewed as having many causes; therefore, interventions focus on the multitude of factors influencing antisocial behavior. The specific treatment used is also dependent on the needs of the young person; it may include interventions that target the at-risk individual, his or her family, peers, school, community, or a combination thereof. Indeed, a multisystemic therapeutic approach is an example of a *social ecological* model of crime prevention (and health care) that views individuals as part of a network of interconnected social systems (the family, peers, school, neighborhood, social media networks, etc.). This social system (and its individual components) is viewed as the optimal platform through which problematic behaviors of a young offender can be addressed within the context of a therapeutic approach.

MST was developed in the late 1970s to address the limitations of existing services for serious juvenile offenders. In particular, the current treatment approaches were considered to be too narrowly focused (too much emphasis on treating the individual offender and not enough on modifying his or her social environment) and delivered in institutional settings (e.g., correctional facilities, psychiatric hospitals, residential treatment centers, outpatient clinics) that were too far removed from the youth's natural social environment. In other words, the existing treatment and *rehabilitation* programs were delivered in institutions that were too artificial for therapy to work, and most did not address the complexity of the needs of young offenders (i.e., they did not reflect the growing empirical evidence that serious delinquent, criminal, and antisocial behavior is greatly influenced by the complex interplay of individual, family, peer group, school, and neighborhood risk factors). Thus, if a youth's risk factors are grounded in his or her social environment, then this environment should be both the setting for therapeutic interventions and used to leverage more prosocial behavior from the young person. The implication is that the environment in which treatment is delivered is almost as important as the treatment itself; therapy can be more productive in the youth's *natural setting*, as opposed to an *artificial setting* such as a hospital, psychiatric institution, or correctional facility.

MST aims to promote changes in a juvenile offender by recognizing and addressing those social environmental and personal risk factors that are influencing the youth's problematic behavior. As such, an MST intervention is comprehensive and can include improving the parent's discipline practices, relationships between the youth and his parents, and the overall family environment; decreasing the youth's association with deviant peers; treating any behavioral, mental health, or academic problems; getting the youth involved in sports or other positive recreational activities; and developing a strong social support network. While the approach is comprehensive, the family is the primary locus for the intervention, and an important component of MST is to provide parents with the skills and resources needed to raise prosocial teenagers.

In the course of an MST treatment, a trained professional spends an average of 60 h over a 4-month period collaborating with a young person and his family in the development of a treatment plan. Treatment techniques include therapies and other remedies that studies have been shown to work. Despite the contribution of the therapist, the MST process is more family driven than therapist driven.

In a meta-analysis of studies examining MST treatments, Doran et al. (2012) concludes, "a strong evidence base shows that MST is effective" for SUDs and delinquent, aggressive behavior. "It produces better family, SUD, and criminal justice outcomes than usual services or individual therapy... and is more effective and cost-effective than hospitalization or incarceration" (Doran et al., 2012, 755).

With respect to the second variable that Lipsey contends is crucial to effective interventions with young offenders—the quantity and quality of treatment provided—he states that the higher the quality of the program, the bigger the effect it had on reducing recidivism. In other words, "the quality with which the intervention is implemented has been as strongly related to recidivism effects as the type of program, so much so that a well-implemented intervention of an inherently less efficacious type can outperform a more efficacious one that is poorly implemented" (Lipsey, 2009, 127). In contrast, Lipsey found that the duration and total hours of service of a particular program did not have a significant impact on reducing recidivism (Lipsey, 2009, 141). High-quality treatment programs—and CBT programs in particular—for young offenders are characterized by the following traits:

- The interventions are carefully documented in treatment manuals.
- Treatment providers are extensively trained and experienced.
- Fidelity to the treatment model is maintained through continuous supervision of the treatment providers.
- Evidence-based, interactive learning techniques, such as behavioral modeling, role playing, and cognitive restructuring, are used.
- Positive reinforcement (of compliant behavior) is emphasized (as opposed to punishment of negative behavior).
- Treatment is intensive, lasting 3–12 months (depending on need) and occupying 40%–70% of the offender's time during the course of the program.
- Interventions are conducted in the community as opposed to an institutional setting (Milkman and Wanberg, 2007, xxiv–xxv; National Association of Drug Court Professionals 2013, 43).

The research suggests that effective interventions for serious and chronic young offenders must be highly individualized to their unique circumstances. To this end, interventions that involve the assessment and treatment of offenders to prevent recidivism and encourage prosocial behavior are generally guided by the influential risk–need–responsivity model (Andrews et al., 1990; Andrews and Bonta, 2006). The three core principles of this model can be summarized as follows:

Risk: "The risk principle states that offender recidivism can be reduced if the level of treatment services provided to the offender is proportional to the offender's risk to re-offend" (Bonta and Andrews, 2007, 5). The higher the risk of reoffending, the greater the need for intensive treatment delivered as quickly as possible. Evidence-based, standardized risk assessment instruments have increasingly been used to assess an offender's likelihood of reoffending and "can reliably differentiate lower risk offenders from higher risk offenders" (Bonta and Andrews, 2007, 3).

Need: The criminogenic needs (risk factors) of the offender should be identified, assessed, and then targeted through the most appropriate interventions to reduce recidivism and encourage prosocial behavior (Bonta and Andrews, 2007, 5).

Responsivity: The offender's ability to learn from a rehabilitative intervention is maximized through "cognitive behavioral treatment and tailoring the intervention to the learning style, motivation, abilities and strengths of the offender … General responsivity refers to the fact that cognitive social learning interventions are the most effective way to teach people new behaviors regardless of the type of behavior" (Bonta and Andrews, 2007, 3, 5).

Lipsey (2009, 138) found that high-quality, therapeutic interventions are especially amenable to reducing recidivism among "higher-risk juveniles," that is, youth who have more risk factors and/or are involved in more chronic and serious delinquency and offending. This is particularly encouraging given this small group of serious and chronic adolescent and young adult offenders is responsible for a disproportionate amount of crime and violence.

4.10.1 Labor Market Approaches to Recidivism Prevention

Research has shown that unemployment or lack of gainful employment is considered a significant risk factor for reoffending. This is especially true of offenders who have been released from a correctional facility and who often encounter "incremental barriers to employment due to criminal history, lack of interpersonal skills, or lack of education and job skills" (Lockwood et al., 2012, 381). As discussed in Chapter 2, statistics and other research demonstrate that the majority of prison inmates have an education level below high school, are functionally illiterate, have minimal legitimate work experience, and few tangible job skills. It is not surprising then that incarcerated offenders are at a high risk of recidivism due to a lack of employability.

Conversely, "stable employment is an important predictor of postprison reentry success" (Zweig et al., 2011, 946). According to Lockwood et al. (2012), "at its most basic level, employment provides former prisoners with a consistent source of funding for necessary food, shelter, clothing, transportation, and other basic amenities. It also increases feelings of self-efficacy and self-sufficiency, building confidence in released prisoners that they can support themselves without needing to resort to criminal activities or reliance on family members or 'handouts,' and providing a new social network that supports positive behaviors and serves as a protective factor against future criminal activity" (Lockwood et al., 2012, 382–383). Accordingly, to help prepare inmates for release from correctional facilities, and to reduce the chances of reoffending, a number of corrections- and community-based programs exist that help educate and train offenders for employment and/or find them a job.

Lockwood and colleagues describe a number of studies showing inmates who completed an educational program while incarcerated had a higher employment rate and a lower recidivism rate compared to those who did not receive this education. In addition to job training, many correctional facilities operate work-release programs whereby inmates are granted day parole in order to be trained for or work at a legitimate job. In short, the "benefits of correctional education to the postrelease employment among offenders have been widely recognized." Studies have "found that prison education programs such as vocational training or work-release programs greatly enhanced access to a variety of job sectors for released offenders and that there was lower recidivism for those who were employed" (Lockwood et al., 2012, 381–382).

Based on recent research and program evaluations into employment-based programs for postrelease offenders, Rosen (2013) suggests "it is important for employment program administrators and service providers to consider three components in their program design to promote success at reentry:

- The kind of job training people receive in relation to available jobs in the community;
- The intensity of programs, since more intensive employment programs appeared to be more effective; and
- The use of paid wages in the program may also be an important component."

Providing transitional support, basic social competency skills training, and cognitive–behavioral therapy is also considered an important component in successful employment-based programs for postrelease offenders.

CASE STUDY 4.12

VOCATIONAL TRAINING AND PLACEMENT PROGRAM FOR INCARCERATED YOUTH

The Vocational Delivery System is one example of a corrections-based transitional employment program for incarcerated young adults. The program, which was implemented in two North Carolina juvenile detention centers for young men (ages 18–22), entails the following components: "(1) working individually with inmates to identify vocational interests and aptitudes, (2) developing individual plans of study for improving vocational skills, (3) providing the identified training as well as other needed services, and (4) helping inmates secure postrelease employment" (Lattimore et al., 1990, 5).

The program begins with the inmate undergoing a battery of tests administered by a trained vocational counselor to determine his employment interests and aptitudes. The results are discussed with the inmate and the two work to identify potential career paths based on the results of the tests. The inmate's correctional case manager will then help him develop a personal plan, which includes steps that need to be taken by the inmate to achieve his career goals. The case manager and the inmate will also discuss job opportunities in the chosen career with a job development specialist (who is responsible for prerelease employment assistance) and the Employment Security Commission (which assists the inmate in finding a job once he is released).

If employment prospects in the chosen career appear favorable for the inmate, the case manager will arrange for appropriate vocational training, along with other important preparatory and complementary education and counseling, such as completion of a grade 12 equivalent, the mandatory community reentry training program (which teaches job preparation skills, such as conducting oneself at a job interview), and counseling (e.g., substance abuse treatment). The case manager also works with the inmate to facilitate completion of the correctional plan, which includes such incentives as the designation of a parole date that is contingent upon the inmate's completion of the plan (a specified parole date is meant to facilitate postrelease employment placement since the employer now has a date as to when the inmate will be available for work). Once released, the inmate either begins the job identified prior to his release or continues to work with job placement specialists until suitable employment is found.

The results of one study that evaluated the Vocational Delivery System showed that those who participated in the program had a significantly lower recidivism rate upon release compared to a control group of inmates who did not participate in the program (Lattimore et al., 1990).

4.10.2 *Diversion from the Criminal Justice System to Community-Based Alternatives*

Diversion refers to formal and informal processes whereby an accused person is redirected from typical processing through the criminal justice system toward alternatives outside the criminal justice system. In particular, diversion is designed to enable an accused to avoid arrest, prosecution, conviction, and/or punishment. Often, the accused is allowed to escape any of the aforementioned items if he or she satisfies certain conditions of the diversion alternative. For example, an accused may avoid a criminal charge, conviction, or incarceration if he or she engages in some form of community service or completes a substance abuse program.

Common alternatives that offenders are redirected toward include restorative justice programs, specialty courts (for offenders with substance abuse or mental health disorders), and community service. Like the criminal justice system, community-based alternatives encompass a wide range of goals and processes. As such, an accused that has been diverted to a community-based alternative may be involved in one or more of the following: (1) an alternative justice process (e.g., victim–offender mediation), (2) treatment and rehabilitation (to ameliorate criminogenic risk factors), and (3) sanctions (e.g., community service, reparations to victims).

Diversion of an accused most often takes place at one of four points during the criminal justice process: upon contact (including arrest) by police, during initial postarrest detention, during the initial appearance of the accused before a judge, or during the trial (prosecution) of the accused.

From a recidivism prevention perspective, diverting an offender away from the criminal justice system carries a number of benefits for the accused and for society. These benefits are particularly potent when the accused is a young person who has no criminal record and is not at risk of serious and chronic criminal offending. It is for this group, as well as other vulnerable groups (such as those with mental health and SUDs), that diversion is employed as a harm reduction approach. In other words, the concept of diversion is based on the understanding that processing certain people through the criminal justice system may do more harm than good (to them and society). Given this, one major benefit of diversion is that it avoids the potential harms inflicted upon an accused that may result from a criminal charge, conviction, and record and the stigma that may result from an arrest and conviction, as well as the harmful effects of imprisonment.

A second major crime and recidivism prevention benefit of diversion is that the accused is redirected toward alternative processes, institutions, programs, or services that studies have shown can have a more positive effect compared to what is meted out through the criminal justice system. Specifically, an accused is often diverted toward alternative processes that provide treatment programs and services that can address criminogenic risk factors, such as a mental health or SUD, social competency deficits, a learning disability, or a lack of employable skills. In short, diversion can promote crime and recidivism prevention by facilitating access of an accused to programs and services intended to reduce the risk of reoffending.

By definition, alternatives to criminal justice processing are delivered in the community. From a crime and recidivism prevention perspective, the underlying justifications behind diversion to community-based alternatives are twofold. The first justification concerns "treatment that can be provided in communities, contrasted with what can be provided in jails and prisons" (Heilbrun et al., 2012, 351). Not only are there more appropriate programs and services available in a community setting, but these natural settings provide a more conducive therapeutic environment that is essential for the success of reintegration of offenders (compared to the artificial, adverse, counterproductive setting of a correctional facility, where the priorities are security and punishment). The second justification for community-based alternatives is that the actual process of reintegrating offenders into civil society and fostering positive social environments and networks is itself considered a powerful crime and recidivism prevention approach.

Diversion programs are also attractive because they can help lessen the load of overburdened courts and overcrowded correctional facilities while allowing the criminal justice system to focus on more serious offenders (Office of Juvenile Justice and Delinquency Prevention, 1999). Another important benefit of community alternatives is the savings in costs: processing an accused through the criminal justice system, including incarceration, is far more costly than community-based sanctions and alternatives. Moreover, the costs of providing needed treatment and other services to inmates while incarcerated in prisons often greatly exceed the costs of the same services being delivered in the community (Heilbrun et al., 2012, 351).

The remainder of this section discusses three common alternatives to formal criminal justice processes and sanctions to which offenders may be diverted: community service, restorative justice, and specialty courts.

4.10.2.1 Community Service Community service involves sanctions imposed by a court against an offender that are to be served in the community. Wermink et al. (2010) summarize the literature and report the findings of their own research in the Netherlands, both of which attempt to answer the same question: to what extent is community service "either more or less effective than imprisonment in mitigating recidivism?" (p. 327) To begin with, the authors note that there are contradictory theories regarding which is more effective in reducing crime and recidivism. Deterrence theory would suggest that imprisonment would result in a lower recidivism rate than community service because the prospect of jail time would serve as a greater discouragement to reoffend compared to community service (Wermink et al., 2010, 327). Conversely, dominant etiological theories of criminality, such as differential association and social learning theories, would suggest that prisons may promote recidivism because they are "schools of crime" where offenders meet each other and learn deviant attitudes and criminal techniques. These same theories would suggest that offenders have a far greater "differential opportunity" to surround themselves with prosocial, law-abiding individuals in the community, thereby promoting their own prosocial attitudes and behaviors. Moreover, labeling theory suggests that incarceration is more apt to "contribute to the development of a criminal career rather than prevent offenders from living a life of crime" because it can lead to social stigmatization and blocked employment opportunities that "progressively isolate offenders from the law abiding community thus fostering their return to committing criminal activities" (Wermink et al., 2010, 327).

Research tends to support those criminological theories that hypothesize about the crime and recidivism prevention benefits of community service compared to more punitive criminal justice sanctions like imprisonment. Citing the empirical literature, Wermink et al. (2010) indicate that recidivism rates of offenders assigned to community service are either no higher compared to those who have been incarcerated or in fact lower. Based on their own study that relied on a longitudinal analysis of the official records on more than 4000 adult offenders in the Netherlands, Wermink et al. (2010, 346) conclude, "offenders recidivate significantly less after having performed community service compared to after having been imprisoned. This finding holds for both the short- and long-term."

4.10.2.2 Restorative Justice   Restorative justice (RJ) is an alternative to the criminal justice system in which an offender, a victim, families, and other interested parties come together, through a "nonadversarial dialogue" (Bergseth and Bouffard, 2013, 1055) to apply problem-solving techniques to resolve and deal with the aftermath of a criminal offense (Marshall, 1996, 37). While it attempts to hold offenders accountable for their crimes, ostensibly, the focus of the restorative justice process is altruism: it focuses on the healing, reintegration, and restoration of the victim and the offender, as well as the broader community affected by a crime. Through a process of a face-to-face mediation guided by a trained facilitator, the offender acknowledges guilt and the harm caused by the offense and also expresses contrition, the victim articulates the pain and suffering caused by the offense, and reparations are negotiated. All of this is meant to build peace between the victim and the offender, repair the damage done by a particular offense, and restore the victim, the offender, and all others affected by a crime in part by reintegrating them into the community. Ideally, the restorative justice process not only delivers justice but, as importantly, contributes to safe and peaceful communities (Umbreit, 1994; Bazemore and Walgrave, 1999; Braithwaite, 1999).

Within the United States and Canada, restorative approaches are applied primarily to youth who are first-time offenders and whose offenses are relatively minor. Typically, a young person is diverted to a restorative justice process by police, a prosecutor, or a judge. A police officer may refer an accused to a restorative justice process as an alternative to the laying of charges. In this case, if the accused successfully completes the restorative justice process, no charges are laid. A prosecutor may also divert an accused after a charge has been laid, and if the accused successfully completes the restorative justice process, the charges are withdrawn. Finally, a judge may divert an accused after guilt has been established by the court. In this circumstance, the verdict is quashed if the accused successfully completes the restorative justice process.

There are four basic principles underlying a restorative justice approach:

1. Encounter, in which opportunities are created for victims, offenders, and community members who want to do so to meet to discuss a particular crime and its aftermath
2. Amends/restitution, whereby an offender takes steps to repair the harm he or she has caused
3. Healing/reintegration, whereby attempts are made to heal and *restore* the victim and offender
4. Inclusion, in which opportunities are provided for parties with a stake in a specific crime to participate in its resolution

These four principles are imbedded in the four stages that make up a restorative justice process:

1. Case referral and intake: The process is initiated when an accused is referred to a restorative justice mediation process by a police officer, by a prosecutor, or by a court.
2. Preparation for mediation: In this stage, a trained facilitator contacts the victim and offender, explains the process and goals of the mediation, seeks assurances that both are capable of making the mediation a constructive experience, ensures the offender accepts responsibility and the victim is emotionally prepared for the encounter, invites other parties affected by the offense, and schedules a date and time for the mediation to occur.

219

3. Mediation: It is during this stage that the parties meet to identify the injustice, rectify the harm, and establish reparations. During the mediation, both parties present their version of the events leading up to and the circumstances surrounding the crime: the offender tells his/her side of the story, apologizes, expresses remorse, and explains his/her behavior, while the victim discusses the personal dimensions of victimization and loss. The mediation concludes when the parties agree on the nature and extent of the harm and what is necessary to repair the injury to the victim.
4. Follow-up: It is during this final stage that the facilitator monitors whether the offender completes his or her end of the agreement. If the agreement cannot be successfully completed with the facilitator's intervention, the case may be returned to the police or the courts for further action.

According to Bergseth and Bouffard (2013, 1055), restorative justice programs "have increased in popularity because they hold promise for achieving several goals, including increased community and victim involvement in the justice process, greater victim and community satisfaction with the case outcomes, improved offender compliance with restitution, and increased perceptions of procedural fairness." The specific goals of a restorative justice process for the victim are healing, restoration, a reduction in fear, reintegration into the community, forgiveness of the offender, and satisfaction with the process and outcome. The goals as far as the offender is concerned is also healing, which is achieved through the fostering of prosocial behavior, positive socialization, and community reintegration, all of which should contribute to helping the accused desist from any future criminal activities. Equally important goals for the offender stemming from the process is an understanding of the impact of his or her offenses as well as his or her accountability for the offenses and the harms caused. The offender should also be satisfied with the alternative process and outcomes, including feelings of fair treatment.

As one can discern from the aforementioned principles and process, restorative justice is an approach to dealing with offenders that differs considerably from that of the traditional criminal justice system. This difference is based on a distinct philosophical approach to crime, victimization, and the subsequent responses of society. A fundamental underlying tenet of restorative justice is that criminal behavior is a violation of one individual by another; the victim is harmed, not the state. The implications of this tenet are twofold. First, the offender does not owe a debt to society, but to the victim. Second, the offenses and their resulting harm should be adjudicated privately by those parties most affected by the offense (the victim and offender) and therefore there is no involvement of the state. In many countries, restorative justice processes are administered by nongovernmental, nonprofit, community-based organizations (Zehr, 1990).

Another distinction of restorative justice is that those affected by crime should have the opportunity to participate fully in the response if they wish. This is not always the case during the traditional criminal justice process: offenders are represented by lawyers (who do most of the talking) and are not even required to take the stand during a criminal trial. A fundamental part of restorative justice is that offenders are required to accept responsibility for their actions and the harm caused. In other words, restorative justice does not attribute guilt; an offender must admit guilt to take part in the process. This is quite different from a criminal trial where the accused often does not admit guilt and is innocent until proven guilty. During a criminal trial, victims are represented by the state and often have very little say in how a criminal prosecution plays out. As Price (2001) writes, within the traditional criminal justice system, "Victims may be viewed, at worst, as impediments to the prosecutorial process—at best, as valuable witnesses for the prosecution of the state's case. Only the most progressive prosecutor's offices view crime victims as their clients and prioritize the needs of victims." The heightened focus on the victim is a particularly important characteristic of the restorative justice process.

The intended outcome of a restorative justice process is also quite different from that of the criminal justice system. In North America, the traditional retributive justice system focuses primarily on determining guilt or innocence (and to administer sanctions against the accused if found guilty). In contrast, restorative justice is not about retribution, but restoration: restoring the material and emotional losses suffered by victims, restoration of the offender in terms of socialization, restoring the relationship between the offender and victims, and restoration (reintegration) of offenders and victims in the community. The RJ process is said to help ensure justice through the healing process. As Braithwaite (2004, 28) states, "With crime, restorative justice is about the idea that because crime hurts, justice should heal." This is particularly pertinent with respect to victims, who may sometimes believe that the most severe punishment for offenders will bring them justice. However, punishment, vengeance, and retribution "cannot restore their losses, answer their questions, relieve their fears, help them make sense of their tragedy or heal their wounds. And punishment cannot mend the torn fabric of the community that has been violated" (Price, 2001).

In sum, restorative justice is not a program. "It is a different paradigm for understanding and responding to issues of crime and justice. Restorative justice takes its most familiar forms in victim-offender mediation (VOM) programs and victim-offender reconciliation programs (VORP). Other restorative justice responses to crime include family group conferencing, community sentencing circles, neighborhood accountability boards, reparative probation, restitution programs, restorative community service, victim and community impact statements and victim awareness panels" (Price, 2001).

Proponents of RJ argue that one of its goals is to prevent crime and recidivism, which in turn are achieved by "restoring offenders" (Braithwaite, 1999). The main conceptual underpinning of the recidivism prevention potential of restorative approaches is Braithwaite's reintegrative shaming theory. This theory maintains that if certain offenders—especially first-time young offenders who have strong bonds to their community—can be made to feel guilty about their actions, they can be deterred from committing further crimes. This is because feelings of guilt are an important precursor to remorse and restitution by the otherwise prosocial individual, which in turn can elicit forgiveness, acceptance, and ultimately reintegration within the community (Braithwaite, 1989; Bazemore, 1998). Reintegrative shaming avoids stigmatizing the offender by emphasizing that it is the delinquent or criminal act that is malevolent, not the person. This is in contrast to the counterproductive "disintegrative shaming," which labels the individual as a criminal offender and is often the outcome of the traditional criminal justice process (Braithwaite, 1989).

A number of studies have been conducted into restorative justice programs in the United States, Canada, Britain, and Australia that measure the extent to which youth and adults reoffend after participating in these programs. Many of these studies employ a control group of offenders who are processed through the traditional criminal justice system to compare recidivism rates. While some studies show mixed results or claim only modest reductions in the recidivism rates of offenders participating in a restorative process, more recent studies have demonstrated significant and meaningful reductions in reoffending, especially when compared to the recidivism rates of offenders processed through the criminal justice system. In other words, there is growing evidence that restorative justice programs are more effective in reducing reoffending compared to the traditional criminal justice system. The results of the many studies conducted into restorative justice programs have been the subject of at least three meta-analyses, summarized in the succeeding text. As Bergseth and Bouffard (2013, 1055) write, "Whereas individual evaluations have produced an inconsistent picture in terms of the effectiveness of RJ programs in recidivism reduction, meta-analyses have found consistent support for reduced recidivism among participants in programs that include restorative components…"

Latimer et al. (2005) analyzed data from studies that compared restorative justice programs to "nonrestorative approaches to criminal behavior" (127) and found that offenders who participated in restorative programs "were significantly more successful during the follow-up periods" in desisting from criminal offending (Latimer et al., 2005, 137). A meta-analysis of studies examining the impact of victim offender mediation on the recidivism of youth by Bradshaw et al. (2006) also provides empirical support for the effectiveness of restorative methods. In particular, an analysis of 15 studies found lower recidivism rates of those who participated in victim–offender mediation programs compared to offenders who were dealt with through traditional criminal justice responses.

Finally, Sherman and Strang (2007) undertook a meta-analysis of studies of restorative justice programs and concluded that in direct comparison to conventional criminal justice approaches, RJ "substantially reduced repeat offending for some offenders, but not all." Specifically, "the key finding is that RJ may work better with more serious crimes rather than with less serious crimes, contrary to the conventional wisdom" (Sherman and Strang, 2007, 68). As far as violent crimes are concerned, the authors identified "six rigorous field tests (that) found RJ reduced recidivism after adult or youth violence." This led them to conclude, the "success of RJ in reducing, or at least not increasing, repeat offending is most consistent in tests on violent crime… Whether we consider just randomized experiments, or include quasi–experiments as well, we find no evidence of increased repeat offending with RJ after violent crime. We also find, in some tests, substantial reductions in recidivism after violent crime" (Sherman and Strang, 2007, 68). The authors also identified five studies into RJ programs that "found reductions in recidivism after property crime," although "the use of RJ for property crime produces less consistency and magnitude of effects on recidivism than is found in RJ for violent crime" (Sherman and Strang, 2007, 4). Finally, the authors conclude the outcome of a RJ process was more effective in lower recidivism compared to incarceration (Sherman and Strang, 2007, 68).

4.10.2.3 Specialty (Problem-Solving) Courts

Specialty courts seek to help nonviolent, nonserious offenders through a problem-solving approach that attempts to ameliorate the personal issues that contributed to their formal contact with the criminal justice system. Although there are now various types of specialty or "problem-solving courts" serving both adults and juveniles, in the United States, the most common are drug courts, mental health courts, drinking-and-driving courts, and veteran's courts. Regardless of the target population served, these courts operate as an alternative to traditional criminal justice prosecution or sentencing. Instead of an adversarial approach that revolves around finding guilt and meting out sanctions, the goal of a specialty (or *problem-solving*) court is for the judge, police, prosecutor, defense counsel, and probation officers as well as social service, mental health, and treatment communities to work together to help offenders become law-abiding, productive citizens through a combination of treatment and judicial supervision (Sevigny et al., 2013, 191).

The first type of problem-solving court implemented in the United States was drug treatment courts, which "emerged spontaneously during the late 1980s and early 1990s in response to burgeoning drug offender arrests and prosecutions that overwhelmed the capacity of numerous courts to expeditiously process such cases" (Rossman et al., 2011, 1). The first drug treatment court was implemented in Dade County Florida in 1989 "to deal with drug-related crimes and drug-using offenders by offering court-monitored drug treatment to reduce both defendants' drug use and the constant recycling of such offenders through the court system" (Rossman et al., 2012, 9). Soon thereafter, drug courts began to proliferate throughout the United States. By 2013, according to the website of the National Associationof Drug Court Professionals, there were more than 2600 drug courts operating in the country. The popularity and success of drug courts spawned other forms of specialty courts, in particular those that focused on mental health disorders or served the unique difficulties faced by military veterans who came into formal contact with the law. Drug treatment and other specialty courts have been replicated in numerous other common law countries, including Canada, the United Kingdom, Australia, New Zealand, South Africa, Bermuda, and Jamaica.

Rempel et al. (2012, 166) succinctly summarize an adult drug treatment court as such:

> Adult drug courts seek to rehabilitate drug-involved offenders through a combination of community-based treatment and intensive judicial oversight. Although specific practices vary, all drug courts operate as specialized courts, hearing cases on a separate calendar presided over by a dedicated judge, who usually receives training in the pharmacology of addiction. Offenders enroll voluntarily, but upon agreeing to participate, they are ordered to treatment and are closely monitored through ongoing drug tests, meetings with court-affiliated case managers, and judicial status hearings. At these hearings, the judge and participants directly converse, and the judge responds to specific milestones or noncompliance with interim sanctions or incentives. Although the court ultimately directs the treatment process, through their regular interactions with the judge and case manager, drug court participants are invited to articulate their own needs, which may then be taken into account in selecting community-based programs and services. Program graduates have the charges against them dismissed or reduced, while those who fail receive a jail or prison sentence.

The goal of most drug courts is the cessation of substance abuse and other criminal activity, whether it is related or unrelated to addiction issues (National Association of Drug Court Professionals, 1997, 1). As Mitchell et al. (2012, 61) put it, the "drug court model combines drug treatment with the legal and moral authority of the court in an effort to break the cycle of drug use and drug related crime." Technically, according to the National Association of Drug Court Professionals, "a participant's progress through the drug court experience is measured by his or her compliance with the treatment regimen." As such, while desisting from drug use and criminal activity is the ultimate goal of most drug courts, "there is value in recognizing incremental progress toward the goal, such as showing up at all required court appearances, regularly arriving at the treatment program on time, attending and fully participating in the treatment sessions, cooperating with treatment staff, and submitting to regular (alcohol and other drug) testing" (National Association of Drug Court Professionals, 1997, 13). Moreover, according to Downey and Roman (2010, 4), "Unlike traditional treatment programs, becoming clean and sober is only the first step toward drug court graduation. Almost all drug courts require participants to obtain a GED, maintain employment, be current in all financial obligations (which often includes drug court fees) and child support payments if applicable, and have a sponsor in the community. Many programs also require participants to perform community service hours to make restitution to the community they have harmed." Defendants who successfully complete a drug court program typically receive a sentence of time served or probation.

Defendants targeted for drug court are usually nonviolent offenders whose formal contact with the criminal justice system is due primarily to their substance addiction (Downey and Roman, 2010, 4). Drug courts tend to focus on "high-risk, high-need" offenders, according to the National Association of Drug Court Professionals (2013, 5). In other words, drug courts target offenders "who are addicted to illicit drugs or alcohol and are at substantial risk for reoffending or failing to complete a less intensive disposition, such as standard probation or pretrial supervision." Offenders may be ruled ineligible due to prior offenses or behavior that suggests they cannot be managed safely or effectively in a drug court (National Association of Drug Court Professionals, 2013, 6).

The prototypical process of a drug court can be briefly described as follows. Shortly after arrest, an offender who appears to be eligible for participation in a drug court program is identified and screened for eligibility. Once it has been determined that the defendant meets the court's criminal justice and clinical eligibility criteria, he or she is given the option of participating in the drug court program or being processed in the traditional manner. If the arrestee chooses the former, he or she is offered to have her case heard in the drug court on the proviso that the charges will be reduced or dismissed upon successful completion of the program. A case management plan is then devised laying out the requirements and milestones that the defendant must meet to *graduate* from the program. The defendant is then referred to a mandatory treatment program for counseling and therapy. As described earlier, the defendant may also have to fulfill other basic stipulations as laid down by the court, such as obtaining a job. Throughout the process, a strict protocol of court supervision is imposed, which includes frequent drug testing and regular appearances before the drug court judge to ensure compliance with the case management plan (Downey and Roman, 2010, 4; Mitchell et al., 2012, 61). According to the National Association of Drug Court Professionals (2013), "Jail sanctions are imposed judiciously and sparingly" for drug court participants if they are found noncompliant. "Unless a participant poses an immediate risk to public safety, jail sanctions are administered after less severe consequences have been ineffective at deterring infractions. Jail sanctions are definite in duration and typically last no more than 3–5 days. Participants are given access to counsel and a fair hearing if a jail sanction might be imposed because a significant liberty interest is at stake" (National Association of Drug Court Professionals, 2013, 28).

As summarized below, the National Association of Drug Court Professionals (1997) identifies 10 key components of an effective drug court:

1. Drug courts integrate drug treatment services with justice system case processing.
2. Drug courts use a nonadversarial approach: prosecution and defense counsel promote public safety while protecting participants' due process rights.
3. Eligible participants are identified early and promptly placed in the drug court program.

4. Drug courts provide access to a continuum of alcohol, drug, and other related treatment and rehabilitation services.
5. Abstinence is monitored by frequent alcohol and other drug testing.
6. A coordinated strategy governs drug court responses to participants' compliance.
7. A drug court judge is the leader of the drug court team and plays an active role in the treatment process, including frequently reviewing treatment progress.
8. Monitoring and evaluation measure the achievement of program goals and gauge effectiveness.
9. Continuing interdisciplinary education promotes effective drug court planning, implementation, and operations.
10. Forging partnerships among drug courts, public agencies, and community-based organizations generates local support and enhances drug court program effectiveness.

One of the overriding goals of a drug court is to stop any future criminal offending by participants. To this end, the results of studies into drug courts have been generally positive. As Rempel et al. (2012, 166) write in their review of the literature, "To date, dozens of evaluations examined whether adult drug courts reduce official re-arrests or convictions, and most found that they do." However, they caution that "the results are not uniformly positive" and those studies that had greater rigor in their methodology tended to show more positive effects. In their review of the research, Downey and Roman (2010, 4–5) came to similar conclusions: "The vast majority of adult drug court evaluations have found that drug courts are associated with reduced recidivism." In a meta-analysis of 82 drug court evaluations, Schaffer (2011) found that participation in a drug court was associated with a lower recidivism rate compared to those processed through a traditional court process. In a 2012 article, Mitchell and colleagues systematically analyzed 154 evaluations of the effectiveness of drug courts in reducing offending. This included 92 evaluations of adult drug courts, 34 studies into juvenile drug courts, and 28 examining drinking-and-driving courts. Based on this analysis, the authors conclude: "Our results indicate that drug participants have lower recidivism than non-participants, but the size of this effect varies by type of drug courts" (Mitchell et al., 2012, 69). Adult drug courts appear to have the greatest impact on controlling recidivism and the relevant studies demonstrate "that any effect adult drug courts have on recidivism is not limited to the short term. Rather, the available research suggests that adult drug court participants have reduced recidivism during and after drug court treatment, and these effects appear to last at least 3 years post–drug court entry" (Mitchell et al., 2012, 68). While the evaluation results were not as robust for juvenile drug courts, the authors conclude, "Taken together, existing systematic reviews of drug court evaluations tentatively support the effectiveness of drug courts" (Mitchell et al., 2012, 62). A meta-analysis of studies examining the effectiveness of drug courts by Sevigny et al. (2013) found they "significantly reduced" the rate of incarceration of program participants compared to those in a treatment group. "However, drug courts did not significantly reduce the average amount of time offenders spent behind bars, suggesting that any benefits realized from a lower incarceration rate are offset by the long sentences imposed on participants when they fail the program."

The number of mental health courts has also multiplied in recent years. The goal of these problem-solving courts is to help ensure that people with mental health disorders who run afoul of the law (or are at risk of doing so) are provided with appropriate services and support to treat their disorders and prevent reoffending. The need for such courts had become abundantly clear, as Rossman and colleagues write:

> By the early 2000s, if not before, it became increasingly clear that the criminal justice system had become the primary public response to inappropriate behaviors by the mentally ill, and that persons with mental illness were over-represented within criminal justice populations … Many researchers and advocates assert that individuals with mental illness are trapped in a "revolving door" of the criminal justice system, cycling in and out of correctional facilities due to their mental illness and lack of treatment …Until the mid-1990s, most suspects with mental illness could expect to be processed by the criminal justice system in the same manner as suspects who were not experiencing mental health issues. However, justice system actors increasingly have sought solutions for balancing traditional objectives (e.g., public safety, punishment, incapacitation) with innovative responses designed to meet the special needs of this population.
>
> **Rossman et al. (2012, 1, 5–6)**

Like other specialty courts, mental health courts seek to do justice and contribute to public safety by replacing traditional court processing with a problem-solving approach that combines and balances the public health model (treating mental health disorders and co-occurring problems that contribute to criminal and antisocial behavior) with a criminal justice model (promoting the accountability and law-abiding behavior of accused persons). "Participants are identified through mental health screening and assessments and voluntarily participate in a judicially supervised treatment plan developed jointly by a team of court staff and mental health professionals. Incentives reward adherence to the treatment plan or other court conditions, non-adherence may be sanctioned, and success or graduation is defined according to predetermined criteria" (Council of State Governments, 2008).

Rossman et al. (2012, 13) cite some of the key features of a mental health court:

- Involved in the process are stakeholders from multiple fields (criminal justice, mental health, substance abuse, housing, and related fields).
- Participation by offenders is voluntary and requires their informed consent.
- Offenders are linked to community-based services (appropriate mental health treatment options are identified in the community and service-provision coordination for the offender is managed by a court-appointed case worker).
- The court is used to monitor the offender's compliance with his or her treatment process (a judge tracks his/her treatment through regular meetings and through communication with and reports from service providers).
- Both sanctions and incentives are used to encourage the offender's participation in treatment and court compliance.

Based upon a review of studies examining the effectiveness of drug courts, Rossman and colleagues (2012, 17–18) contend that, compared to control groups of substance-abusing offenders processed through a traditional court setting, participants in mental health courts "are more likely to engage in treatment" and may experience a decrease in substance abuse as well as an increased "level of functioning". However, "evidence of clinical improvement (e.g., reduction in mental health symptoms) is more ambiguous." The authors also found that the results of the studies "have also been mixed regarding criminal justice outcomes." Some studies showed "that mental health court participants had better criminal justice outcomes than similar comparison groups."

This includes spending less time in jail than other offenders with an identified mental illness who did not participate in a specialty court program. In addition, mental health court participants experienced fewer arrests than they did before participating in a specialty court (Rossman et al., 2012, 18–19). Steadman et al. (2011) examined the criminal justice outcomes of mental health court participants in four jurisdictions in California. Compared with a control group, participants in the mental health courts were less likely to be rearrested, less likely to use illegal substance, and spent fewer days incarcerated after their initial appearance before the court. "While these studies have shown positive impacts of mental health courts, other studies have been more equivocal," according to Rossman et al. (2012, 18–19). This includes studies that have "shown similar criminal justice outcomes for both mental health court clients and other individuals with mental illness processed more traditionally in terms of symptom reduction..." Despite the contradictory findings of different studies, Rossman et al. (2012, 18) conclude, "a consensus seems to be building in favor of mental health courts." In their own evaluation of mental health courts in the Bronx and Brooklyn, New York, Rossman et al. (2012, 141) found that court participants are "significantly less likely to recidivate, as compared to similar offenders with mental illness who experience business-as-usual court processing, although the extent of the impact differs across the two programs."

4.10.3 Community Reentry

The issue of offenders leaving prison and integrating back into society is a growing concern for the theory and practice of crime and recidivism prevention. This is especially true given the increase in the prisoner population in the United States in recent years, the large number of inmates who will inevitably be released from custody annually, and the relatively high rate of recidivism among those released from custody (Braga et al., 2009, 413–414).

Milkman and Wanberg (2007, xii) define prisoner reentry programs as those that "(1) specifically focus on the transition from prison to community or (2) initiate treatment in a prison setting and link with a community program to provide continuity of care." Like any recidivism prevention strategy, the key challenge in reentry programs is dealing with risk factors associated with recidivism, which tend to be more chronic and difficult to ameliorate for offenders who have been incarcerated. Moreover, time spent in custody may exacerbate these criminogenic risk factors while also making it difficult for offenders to readjust to the outside world. Readjusting to life outside prison is made even more challenging if a prisoner's risk factors have not been sufficiently addressed while in custody and/or there is a lack of social support as well as employment or educational opportunities for those being released.

The literature on prisoner reentry suggests there are three key programmatic variables that must be taken into consideration when attempting to reduce the rate of recidivism of offenders being released back into the community: (1) the treatment of risk factors, (2) community reintegration, and (3) supervision.

As already discussed in this chapter, studies have shown that the most effective way to treat risk factors associated with criminality and recidivism is through therapeutic interventions, especially those that emphasize cognitive behavioral techniques and social competency skills training. Community reintegration is essential to the successful transition of postrelease offenders as both theories and research indicate that desistence from criminal and recidivist behavior is heightened when an offender is reintegrated or *restored* within civil society. Successful community reintegration is contingent upon the availability of local treatment programs to help eliminate or minimize risk factors and the provision of such salient protective factors as positive personal support networks, access to housing, and the availability of meaningful opportunities for prosocial behavior, in particular employment and/or educational opportunities. Another important issue for consideration as far as community reintegration is concerned, according to Braga et al. (2009, 415), is "the communities to which ex-prisoners are returning. Former inmates generally return to urban communities with concentrated social, economic, and political stressors such as high unemployment, active drug markets, limited social services, high crime and endangered public health, and homelessness." Successful reentry initiatives must place a premium on steering postrelease offenders toward neighborhoods that provide social environments that are more conducive to nurturing prosocial behavior.

Recognizing the importance of appropriate service provision to offenders returning to their communities following incarceration, the U.S. Congress enacted the *Second Chance Act* in 2008 (and reauthorized by Congress in 2013). The purpose of the legislation is to help ensure a successful transition from prison or jail to the community by offenders, with particular emphasis on reducing recidivism. As part of the legislation, more than $250 million in grants was awarded to government agencies and nongovernmental organizations to support reentry programming for both adults and youth. In addition to effective case management by well-trained professionals, D'Amico et al. (2013, ES-4) summarize some of the reentry services provided to offenders by programs funded under the federal legislation:

- Mental health and substance abuse treatment services
- Education and training, including basic literacy, GED, and vocational training in fields such as culinary arts and health-care support
- Employment assistance, including one-on-one or group sessions on resume development, goal setting, interview preparation, and other job finding topics
- Cognitive behavioral therapy, including Moral Reconation Therapy and access to courses such as Thinking for a Change
- Prosocial services, including mentorship and courses on positive parenting, life skills development, communication skills, anger management, and other topics
- Housing assistance and/or other supportive services, such as placing participants in transitional housing and providing vouchers for housing expenses, transportation (bus passes), food, work, clothes, or other necessities

Two of the most significant obstacles to the successful reentry of offenders, according to D'Amico et al. (2013, ES-6), are the lack of safe and affordable housing and the shortage of mental health services.

The supervision of postrelease offenders by criminal justice officials and/or nongovernmental community organizations is also a key factor in preventing recidivism among postrelease offenders. The two aspects of supervision that appear to be most important in this regard are monitoring the offenders to ensure the conditions of their parole are adhered to and transitional support that facilitates a successful reintegration of the offender. As Braga et al. (2009, 415–416) write, "Proper postrelease supervision could reduce subsequent criminal offending through surveillance and by structuring released inmates lives so they are better connected to work, family, and support programs." Intensive monitoring and supervision of postrelease offenders contribute to recidivism prevention by increasing the ability of criminal justice officials and other key stakeholders "to detect violations and criminal behavior." As far as transitional support is concerned, "criminal justice agencies should work with public and private organizations to systematically reduce the risk of recidivism by assessing the public safety risk posed by each prisoner, developing in-prison and postrelease plans that reduces the risk, and, through a consortium of reentry services, provide returning prisoners 'concentric circles of support' by working with families, employers, and community organizations." An overarching concern in the successful reintegration of postrelease offenders is collaboration among all those who have a key stake in fostering their prosocial behavior. "Successful policies to reintegrate offenders into the community will require extensive collaboration among criminal justice organizations, human service agencies, and community partners supportive of returning prisoners and their families" (Braga et al., 2009, 416).

4.10.4 Punitive- and Deterrence-Based Approaches to Recidivism Prevention

Despite the generally positive results that have stemmed from treatment-based and restorative approaches to reducing recidivism, and despite the scant evidence that incarceration correlates with a reduction in reoffending, some jurisdictions have experimented with policies and programs that apply punitive sanctions to juvenile offenders in the hopes they will deter them from reoffending. Three of the most popular of these punitive- and deterrence-based recidivism prevention approaches are scared straight programs, correctional boot camps, and parental responsibilization policies.

4.10.4.1 Scared Straight Programs Petrosino et al. (2004, 7) describe *scared straight* programs as "organized visits to prison by juvenile delinquents or children at risk for criminal behavior" that are "designed to deter participants from future offending through first-hand observation of prison life and interaction with adult inmates." According to these researchers, deterrence is the primary theory underlying the crime and recidivism potential of scared straight programs. "Program advocates and others believe that realistic depictions of life in prison and presentations by inmates will deter juvenile offenders (or children at risk for becoming delinquent) from further involvement with crime." The initial scared straight program that began in New Jersey in the 1970s "featured as its main component an aggressive presentation by inmates to juveniles visiting the prison facility. The presentation depicted life in adult prisons, and often included exaggerated stories of rape and murder." While the crime and recidivism prevention goal of subsequent programs is still very much predicated on deterrence theory, they "are now sometimes designed to be more educational than confrontational." These more recent programs feature inmates as speakers who describe their life experiences and the current reality of prison life, while others include interactive discussions between the inmates and the youth visitors. Scared straight programs are popular not only because they "fit with common notions by some on how to prevent or reduce crime (by 'getting tough')," they can be quite inexpensive," and "they provide one way for incarcerated offenders to contribute productively to society by preventing youngsters from following down the same path" (Petrosino et al., 2004, 12).

Despite their popularity, scared straight programs do not appear to be effective in reducing delinquent and criminal behavior by youth, according to evaluations. In a meta-analysis of studies into programs that utilized this approach, Petrosino et al. (2004, 8) conclude, "they are likely to have a harmful effect and increase delinquency relative to doing nothing at all to the same youths. Given these results, we cannot recommend this program as a crime prevention strategy. Agencies that permit such

CASE STUDY 4.13

OFFENDER REENTRY PROGRAM IN BOSTON

Braga et al. (2009) describe and evaluate the Boston Re-entry Initiative (BRI), which helps "transition violent adult offenders released from the local jail back to their Boston neighborhoods through mentoring, social service assistance, and vocational development."

The BRI attempts its ambitious goal by developing individual plans to reintegrate them into society during their incarceration and, once released, continuing this work in the community through the focused attention of a mentor. Caseworkers and mentors draw on a variety of programs to support the transition, including social service assistance (such as substance abuse and mental health treatment) and vocational development (such as training, education, and resume development necessary to secure employment).

Within 45 days of entering the Suffolk County House of Correction, program participants attend a BRI panel session during which BRI participants are informed about institutional programs and community resources available to aid their successful reintegration and are informed that they will be held accountable for staying away from further criminal activity upon release to the community.

These panel sessions include representatives from criminal justice agencies, social service providers, and faith-based organizations who sit in a semicircle across from the new inmate participants. Each of the panel members addresses the inmates from the unique perspective of his or her organization. Representatives of social service and faith-based organizations describe the resources and support that they can provide to assist inmates with their transition back into the community, while they are both in the jail and postrelease. Representatives of prosecution, probation, and parole departments discuss the consequences that await the inmates if they are caught recommitting crimes upon their return to their neighborhoods, often providing information individualized for that month's participants. Collectively, they convey a unified message that the inmates have the power to choose their own destiny. At the same time, the panel serves to remind the inmates that they are not doing their time anonymously.

Following the panel, inmates are assigned jail-staff caseworkers and faith-based mentors from the community, who begin meeting and working with them immediately. Enrollments in education, substance abuse, and other institutional programs are coordinated in a "transition accountability plan" that includes a wide range of "wraparound" services customized to address their individual needs.

Community-based and government agency partners provide participants in the BRI with extensive case management and treatment programming to assist their successful transition to law-abiding and productive members of their communities. Each transition accountability plan charts out a recommended and coordinated regimen of treatment and supervision beginning at the House of Correction and continuing after release. These services address immediate issues, such as identification/driver's licenses, health insurance, shelter, transportation, clothing, and interim job, as well as long-term issues, such as substance abuse treatment, mental health treatment, education, career counseling, and permanent housing.

Faith-based organizations provide mentors to BRI-identified offenders both during their incarceration and postrelease. The mentors meet with the offenders while they are still at the House of Correction and develop a rapport with them. The mentors, with salaries paid by the Boston Police Department, also participate in the

development and implementation of the transition accountability plan. Mentors typically stay involved with BRI participants for 12–18 months after their release. If an
offender has conditional supervision with probation or parole following release, the
mentors will work with the offender's probation or parole officers. Also, the mentors provide the program partners with updated progress reports on the released
offenders.

An evaluation of the BRI found it "was associated with significant reductions—on the order
of 30%—in the overall and violent arrest failure rates" of program participants relative to a
comparison group of postrelease offenders that did not participate in the program. These
results led the authors of the study to conclude, "Not only is it possible to provide services
to this tough-to-reach population, it is possible to do so effectively." In recognition of its
success, the BRI was the recipient of the 2004 International Association of Chiefs of Police
Community Policing Award.

Abridged from Braga, A. et al., *J. Res. Crime Delinq.*, 46(4), 411–436, 2009.

programs, however, must rigorously evaluate them not only to ensure that they are
doing what they purport to do (prevent crime) – but at the very least they do not cause
more harm than good to the very citizens they pledge to protect."

4.10.4.2 Correctional Boot Camps Correctional boot camps are another response
to youth crime that employ mostly punitive measures. According to MacKenzie et al.
(2001, 127), at the core of boot camps are activities that resemble military basic training.

Participants are required to follow a rigorous daily schedule of activities including
drill and ceremony and physical training. They rise early each morning and are kept
busy most of the day. Correctional officers are given military titles, and participants
are required to use these titles when addressing staff. Staff and inmates are required
to wear uniforms. Punishment for misbehavior is immediate and swift and usually
involves some type of physical activity like push-ups. Frequently, groups of inmates
enter the boot camps as squads or platoons. There is often an elaborate intake ceremony where inmates are immediately required to follow the rules, respond to staff in
an appropriate way, stand at attention, and have their heads shaved. Many programs
have graduation ceremonies for those who successfully complete the program.

A survey of state correctional officials in the United States indicated that the major
goals of correctional boot camps are to rehabilitate the offenders, deter future crime,
lower recidivism, protect the public, and reduce costs. Boot camps are said to prevent
future delinquency, criminality, and recidivism of the inmates through a combination
of the following: changing their attitudes, values, and behaviors through *shock incarceration*, the use of group pressure to encourage conformity and a positive change
in attitude, instilling a strong work ethic, inculcating a respect for authority and the
law, and improving the physical condition and overall health of inmates (including an
abstinence from drugs) (MacKenzie et al., 2001, 128). The crime prevention goal of
correctional boot camps is also guided by the same theories that underpin all criminal justice sanctions: deterring future criminal behavior through punishment and by
shocking program participants.

The first generation of boot camps, which opened in the United States in the early
1980s, placed particular emphasis on the militaristic orientation (including physical
training and hard labor). Following evaluations that showed a lack of effectiveness in

reducing recidivism of those released from the camps, a second generation integrated more therapeutic programming, such as academic education, cognitive behavioral therapy, social competency skills training, and substance abuse treatment (Parent, 2003, 2).

Like incarceration in general, correctional boot camps for young offenders are highly controversial, according to MacKenzie et al. (2001, 128). The debate primarily involves questions "about the impact of the camps on the adjustment and behavior of participants while they are in residence and after they are released." Advocates of boot camps believe the goals, atmosphere, and tactics of the camps can achieve positive changes of and growth in participants, while critics argue "that many of the components of the camps are in direct opposition to the type of relationships and supportive conditions that are needed for quality therapeutic programming."

In a meta-analysis of studies examining correctional boot camps, MacKenzie et al. (2001) found "no overall significant differences in recidivism" between boot camp participants and a comparison group of offenders who received either community supervision (e.g., probation) or incarceration in a traditional correctional facility. In other words, "correctional boot camps are neither as good as the advocates assert nor as bad as the critics hypothesize." The authors speculate why boot camps do not reduce recidivism more effectively than traditional alternatives. "In our opinion, one possible reason boot camps are not any more or less effective than other alternatives is because they may offer no more therapy or treatment than the alternatives. That is, boot camps by themselves have little to offer as far as moving offenders away from criminal activities." In short, "a military atmosphere in a correctional setting is not effective in reducing recidivism" (MacKenzie et al., 2001, 139). An updated meta-analysis of studies into boot camps (Wilson et al., 2008, 3) reached similar conclusions: there was no difference in recidivism rates between participants in boot camps and those exposed to other criminal justice sanctions and that the defining militaristic feature of correctional boot camps "is not effective in reducing post boot-camp offending."

Similar conclusions have been reached by other studies that have reviewed the literature on correctional boot camps. According to a report prepared for the National Institute of Justice (Parent, 2003), correctional boot camp participants "reported positive short-term changes in attitudes and behaviors; they also had better problem-solving and coping skills." With few exceptions, however, "these positive changes did not lead to reduced recidivism. The boot camps that did produce lower recidivism rates offered more treatment services, had longer sessions, and included more intensive postrelease supervision" (Parent, 2003, ii). Some of the underlying reasons why the boot camps were not any more effective in reducing recidivism compared to other correctional approaches, including "low-dosage" effects ("the length of stay in boot camps—usually from 90 to 120 days—was too brief to realistically affect recidivism"), are the "absence of a strong underlying treatment model" and "insufficient preparation of boot camp inmates for reentry into the community" (Parent, 2003, 4). In their meta-analysis of correctional boot camps for youth, Wilson et al. (2005) also found that they were generally ineffective in preventing future criminal activity.

4.10.4.3 Parental Responsibilization Another punitive-based approach to youth crime and recidivism prevention is policies and programs that are intended to make parents "more aware of and responsible for their children's behavior" (International Centre for the Prevention of Crime, 2008, 81). Under this *parental responsibilization* approach, it is the parents that are targeted and bear most of the brunt of any sanctions meted out. The underlying premise of this strategy is the many theories and research evidence that situate the family, and parents in particular, as the most important institution in influencing whether children and young people adopt prosocial or antisocial behaviors. In her review of the literature, Parada (2010, 27) writes, "Some authors have observed that punishing parents for the criminality of their children reinforces the idea of a 'parenting deficit' that sees the root cause of youth criminality as developing within the domestic sphere." Making parents liable for the criminal or delinquent behavior of their children is also representative of the shifting of crime prevention responsibilities from the state to private citizens (Parada, 2010, 2).

However, unlike social problem-solving, family-based initiatives that aim to help parents become better caregivers, under parental responsibilization strategies, parents are coerced to become better parents and to exercise greater supervision over their children under the threat of state-imposed sanctions. These sanctions are enforced if a child or young person is in trouble with the law. According to Thurman (2003, 104), holding parents criminally responsible for the acts of their children is meant to accomplish the following goals. "First, it serves as punishment and motivation for the 'offending' parents to improve their parenting. Second, it may deter other parents from making the same mistake of 'bad' parenting."

According to the International Centre for the Prevention of Crime, this strategy has been adopted in a number of "common common law nations, where the definition of parental responsibility has been extended to include the idea that parents are liable for their child's delinquent acts."

> In the United States, certain state legislatures have created parental liability laws, which may instruct parents to attend counselling sessions or perform community service. There are also American municipalities that impose fines or parenting classes on parents whose children exhibit delinquent behaviour … Australian law compels parents to pay restitution for loss or injury caused by their children. … This trend has developed in other countries, such as the Netherlands, whereby a new Social Security Act requires welfare-dependent families with offending children to undergo intensive training; otherwise the family's welfare support will be reduced. Danish police may send "letters of concern" to parents with 10-13 year old children who have come to the attention of the police. Parents are expected to reply within eight days of receiving the letter; if they do not respond, their file is sent to the SSP, the combined service of the schools, social services, and the police.
>
> **International Centre for the Prevention of Crime (2008, 81)**

In Great Britain, "Parenting Orders" were created in 1998 as part of the *Criminal and Disorder Act*, brought in by the New Labour Government, which seeks to make parents more accountable for the delinquent and criminal behavior of their children. The government also gave the courts more powers to punish parents who "willfully neglect their parental responsibilities," which includes fines or attendance at counseling sessions or parental training courses (Home Office, 1997a, as cited in Goldson, 2002, 88). One assumption underlying New Labor's crime prevention strategies was that participation in family-based programs is nonnegotiable if the behavior of the most delinquent youth and their families is to be corrected. In other words, "coercive rather than voluntary engagement" of the most high-risk families is preferred, if not mandatory (Blyth and Solomon, 2009, 7).

Of course, this coercive strategy is highly controversial and has come under great criticism for what some see as a simplistic attempt to combat a complex problem. First, while it is true that the family and parents are critical to the positive socialization of children, this approach neglects to take into consideration all the other institutions in the life of a young person that can influence his or her behavior and development, such as schools, neighborhoods, peers, the media, and governments (i.e., it takes a village to raise a child). Second, "it has been suggested that this type of legislation negatively affects families mainly from disadvantaged socio-economic groups" (International Centre for the Prevention of Crime, 2008, 81) because these parents may have "few economic resources and consequently, less opportunity to provide their children with care and supervision" and are at risk of being unfairly punished (European Economic and Social Committee, 2008, as cited in International Centre for the Prevention of Crime, 2008, 81). Regardless of socioeconomic status, parents who are sanctioned under this approach could become highly resentful of the criticism of their parenting skills and their forced participation in parenting classes. As the ICPC (2008, 81) points out, "The effectiveness of parent training courses has also not been fully evaluated, but what does seem to be clear is that participation in a parenting course or family counseling is most successful when it is available on a voluntary basis." Finally, Thurman (2003, 10) argues that despite the availability of these laws in many American states, "few cases actually make it to a courtroom, which prompts questions about the feasibility of enforcing such laws."

Like the other punitive-based crime and recidivism prevention approaches described earlier, the parental responsibilization strategy is very much influenced by neoliberal ideology, which emphasizes a sanction- and deterrence-based approach. It is also reflective of neoliberal approaches to crime control by emphasizing the centrality of the family, as opposed to the state, in raising law-abiding children (Parada, 2010, 2). In turn, this is reflective of the importance that conservatives place on individuals being accountable for their own actions, and not relying on the domineering, interventionist *nanny state*.

4.11   CONCLUSION

The most important conclusion of this report is that youth violence is not an intractable problem. We now have the knowledge and tools needed to reduce or even prevent much of the most serious youth violence, with the added benefit of reducing less dangerous but still serious problem behaviors and promoting healthy development. Scientists from many disciplines, working in a variety of settings with public and private agencies, are generating needed information and putting it to use in designing, testing, and evaluating intervention programs. However, after years of effort and massive expenditures of public and private resources, the search for solutions to the issue of youth violence remains an enormous challenge.

Office of the Surgeon General (2001, 10)

In the intervening years since the Surgeon General's report on youth violence was written, we can be even more optimistic, albeit cautiously, about reducing crime and violence by adolescents and young adults. The rate of youth crime and violence has declined throughout much of the United States and other developed countries. However, we have yet to reach our full potential as far as initiatives to address this problem are concerned. While substantial progress has been made in recent years in applying effective, evidence-based, social problem-solving approaches to youth crime and violence, there continues to be significant challenges.

Some of the greatest challenges are identifying, reaching out to, and treating as many high-risk young people as possible—especially those who are at risk of serious and chronic offending. For some, this may be an unrealistic expectation, especially given the finite resources available at the governmental and nongovernmental levels. Even if such an ambitious, comprehensive outreach was possible, there are no guarantees that the most at-risk youth will agree to participate in such programs. One daunting hurdle to treating the criminogenic conditions of such youth is soliciting their involvement in developmental-based programs. The underlying reasons why this hurdle exists are complex, multifaceted, and individualized. One reason is that youth who are involved in antisocial, risky, delinquent, and/or criminal behavior often do not want to give up this lifestyle or leave the *subculture*. Others who do want to adopt a more prosocial lifestyle are often subject to intense peer pressure and/or suffer from a number of personal and social environmental risk factors that obstruct the realization of this desire. Still, others lack any trust in the programs, services, or sponsoring agencies, "which may come about due to negative experiences or distrust of adults due to family problems" (Resilience Research Centre, 2011, 7). Equally challenging is ensuring the commitment of high-risk youth to society's basic institutions, such as their family, schools and education, their community, and the labor market.

The challenges faced by social problem-solving, crime prevention interventions are magnified when they are applied to youth and young adults who have already become chronic and serious offenders and/or have been incarcerated. Based on a review of studies conducted between 1945 and 1967, sociologist Robert Martinson concluded that the research to date on most rehabilitation programs indicated that "with few and isolated exceptions, the rehabilitative efforts that have been reported thus far have had no appreciable effect on recidivism" (Martinson, 1974, 25). In the years since Martinson's pessimistic assessment, the positive effects of treating both adolescent and adult offenders have been well documented, and multiple studies point to the increased success that evidence-based interventions have on reducing recidivism. Based on her review of the literature, Doris MacKenzie (2012, 481) identifies the following interventions as effective in reducing recidivism: academic education, vocational education, cognitive skills programs, cognitive behavior and behavioral treatment for sex offenders, MST, drug courts, drug treatment facilities, and drug treatment in the community. In contrast, she argues that the following interventions have not been found to be effective in reducing recidivism: correctional boot camp for juveniles, correctional boot camps for adults, correctional institutions, community supervision for juveniles, domestic violence treatment with a feminist perspective, domestic violence treatment using cognitive behavioral treatment, electronic monitoring intensive supervision, life skills education, multicomponent work programs, psychosocial sex offender treatment, and residential treatment for juveniles (MacKenzie, 2012, 478–479). MacKenzie concludes that "no single explanation seems adequate to explain why some programs are not effective in reducing recidivism. Some possible reasons programs are not effective appear to be are: (1) they have a poor or no theoretical basis; (2) they are poorly implemented; (3) they focus on punishment, deterrence, or control instead of providing human service or rehabilitation; and (4) they emphasize the formation of ties or bonds without first changing the individuals thought process" (MacKenzie, 2012, 479).

In short, according to MacKenzie (2012), "none of the programs focusing on deterrence, punishment, or control were found to reduce future criminal activity" (479), while "studies of rehabilitation programs, on the other hand, do find that many are effective in reducing criminal activities" (481). Regardless of the evidence as to what works and what does not work in recidivism prevention, treating a young person who has become a serious and chronic offender so that he leaves a criminal lifestyle is far more difficult and far more costly than preventing such behavior from arising in the first place. This highlights the particular importance that must be placed on *preventing* the onset of criminal and violent behavior by addressing root causes through early intervention initiatives that target at-risk children. As detailed in Chapter 3, this is best accomplished through developmentally based interventions that deliver protective factors directly to children and youth who are at risk of serious and chronic offending with the goal of increasing their personal resilience in the face of criminogenic risk factors.

4.12 DISCUSSION QUESTIONS AND EXERCISES

1. What do you believe are the most significant factors that put youth at risk of delinquency, criminality, violence, and gang involvement?
2. How do risk factors for children differ from those of youth?
3. How do CPSD strategies for youth differ from those geared for children?
4. Identify organizations, agencies, and institutions in your city that deliver programs and services to youth that you think can be classified as crime prevention.
5. Research youth crime and violence in your city. Based on this research, identify and discuss the risk factors identified in this chapter that you believe are most pertinent in contributing to this problem. What social problem-solving strategies would you implement that will provide them with *protective factors* and/or increase their resilience?
6. Why do punitive- and deterrence-based approaches to youth delinquency and crime continue to proliferate given the body of research findings indicating they are ineffective?

4.13 IMPORTANT TERMS

Adolescence
Adolescence-limited criminality
Age–crime curve
Cognitive behavioral treatment
Community reentry
Community service
Correctional boot camps
Desistence
Deterrence
Developmental assets
Diversion
Dropout prevention
Dropout recovery
Drug treatment courts
Gangs
Mediation
Mental health courts
Mentoring
Parental responsibilization
Protective factors

Recidivism prevention
Reintegrative shaming
Restorative justice
Risk factors
Scared straight
Social competency skills training
Specialty (problem-solving) courts
Treatment
Victim–offender mediation
Youth centers
Youth outreach workers

FURTHER READING

Bergseth, K.J. and Bouffard, J.A., Examining the effectiveness of a restorative justice program for various types of juvenile offenders, *International Journal of Offender Therapy Comparative Criminology* 2012; 57(9):1054–1075.

Bonnie, R.J., Johnson, R.L., Chemers, B.M., and Schuck, J., *Reforming Juvenile Justice: A Developmental Approach*, National Academies Press, Washington, DC, 2012.

Heilbrun, K., Dematteo, D., Yasuhara, K., Brooks-Holliday, S., Shah, S., King, C., Dicarlo Bingham, A., Hamilton, D., and Laduke, C., Community-based alternatives for justice-involved individuals with severe mental illness: Review of the relevant research, *Criminal Justice and Behavior* 2012; 39(4):351–419.

International Centre for the Prevention of Crime, Strategies and best practices in crime prevention in particular in relation to urban areas and youth at risk, *Proceedings of the Workshop held at the 11th UN Congress on Crime Prevention and Criminal Justice*, Bangkok, Thailand, April 18–25, 2005, ICPC, Montreal, Quebec, Canada, 2007.

Lipsey, M.W., The primary factors that characterize effective interventions with juvenile offenders: A meta-analytic overview of effective interventions, *Victims and Offenders: An International Journal of Evidence-Based Research, Policy, and Practice* 2009; 4(2):124–147.

National Gang Center, *Best Practices to Address Community Gang Problems: OJJDP's Comprehensive Gang Model*, National Gang Center, Tallahassee, FL, 2010, https://www.ncjrs.gov/pdffiles1/ojjdp/222799.pdf.

Office of the Surgeon General, *Youth Violence: A Report of the Surgeon General*, Office of the Surgeon General, Rockville, MD, 2001, http://www.ncbi.nlm.nih.gov/books/NBK44294/.

Shaw, M., *Youth and Gun Violence: The Outstanding Case for Prevention*, International Centre for the Prevention of Crime, Montreal, Quebec, Canada, 2005, http://www.crime-prevention-intl.org/fileadmin/user_upload/Publications/Youth_and_Gun_Violence._The_Outstanding_Case_for_Prevention_ANG.pdf.

Steinberg, A. and Almeida, C., *The Dropout Crisis: Promising Approaches in Prevention and Recovery*, Jobs for the Future, Boston, MA, 2004.

Welsh, B.C., Public health and the prevention of juvenile criminal violence, *Youth Violence and Juvenile Justice* 2005; 3:23–40.

INTERNET RESOURCES

Clemson University. National Dropout Prevention Center/Network, http://www.dropoutprevention.org/effective-strategies.

Center for the Study of Violence Prevention, University of Colorado at Boulder, Blueprints for Violence Prevention, http://www.colorado.edu/cspv/blueprints/.

Helping America's Youth, Introduction to Risk Factors and Protective Factors, http://www.helpingamericasyouth.gov/programtool-factors.cfm.

National Association of Drug Court Professionals, http://www.nadcp.org/.

National Entry Resource Center (Justice Center: The Council of State Governments) http://csgjusticecenter.org/nrrc.

National Gang Center, http://www.nationalgangcenter.gov/.

Office of Juvenile Justice and Delinquency Prevention, http://www.ojjdp.gov/.

Office of Juvenile Justice and Delinquency Prevention, Model Programs Guide, http://www.dsgonline.com/mpg2.5/mpg_index.htm.

Promising Practices Network on Children, Families and Communities, http://www.promisingpractices.net/programs.asp.

Search Institute, http://www.search-institute.org/.

U.S. Department of Labor, JobCorps, http://www.jobcorps.gov/home.aspx.

The Violence Institute of New Jersey, University of Medicine and Dentistry of New Jersey, SourceBook of Drug and Violence Prevention Programs for Children and Adolescents, http://www.umdnj.edu/vinjweb/publications/sourcebook/about_sourcebook.html.

CHAPTER 5

COMMUNITY CRIME PREVENTION

CONTENTS

5.1 *LEARNING OBJECTIVES*

By the end of this chapter, you should have a better understanding of the following:

- The importance of community as a crime prevention institution
- Etiological theories of crime upon which community crime prevention (CCP) approaches are premised
- Essential element of CCP: community based, citizen participation, and collective action
- The community defense model and its essential elements (community based, citizen participation, collective action, behavioral modification/reinforcement, and informal social control)
- The community development model and its essential elements (community based, citizen participation, collective action, community building, social development, physical development)
- Challenges to and critiques of CCP

5.2 *INTRODUCTION*

This chapter examines community-based approaches to crime prevention. The United Nations defines *community, or locally based crime prevention*, as initiatives that aim to "change local conditions that influence offending, victimization and insecurity caused by crime, by leveraging initiatives, expertise and commitment of community members" (United Nations Office on Drugs and Crime, 2010, 13). This broad definition is reflective of the lack of consensus in the academic and professional literature on both the definition of community prevention and the types of initiatives that fall within it. At the very least, community crime prevention (CCP) can be demarcated into two distinct approaches: (1) the community defense model (also called the *immunological* model) that strengthens the capacity of the community to defend itself against crime primarily through opportunity-reduction measures and (2) the community development model (also called the *prophylactic* model) that seeks to prevent crime and criminality by eradicating its root causes through social developmental (social problem-solving) and community building measures (International Centre for the Prevention of Crime, 2008, 216).

While distinct conceptually, in practice, the two are complementary; together they reflect Welsh and Hoshi's (2006, 165) characterization of "community-based crime prevention" as some combination of situational crime prevention and developmental approaches. However, this chapter avoids vague conceptualizations of CCP that have the tendency to include any type of crime prevention strategy under this banner as long as it is implemented within or by a community. Instead, this chapter argues that the community is itself a crime prevention institution (like the family, the school, the labor market, and the police).

For crime prevention theorists and practitioners, the concept of community has traditionally been defined in spatial terms—the residential neighborhood. But community can also be defined in sociological terms as an organic unit of social organization characterized by enduring personal ties and a high level of social interaction and cohesion. A dominant etiological theory of crime underlying CCP is that the loss of the socially cohesive neighborhood has contributed to crime and disorder in Western societies. As such, the sociological concept of community forms the heart of a distinct crime prevention philosophy. Accordingly, this chapter emphasizes how the community must be viewed as an institution through which crime may be controlled and prevented at the local level. CCP fundamentally depends on the integration of people into a community through a socialization process that involves the inculcation of shared norms and values and the creation of an individual and collective consciousness that serves as the foundation for a communal approach to controlling, deterring, and preventing crime and criminal behavior. In one of the most comprehensive reports written on the theory and practice of crime prevention in the United States, principal author and criminologist Lawrence Sherman (1997c, 1) evoked the essential role that the institution of community plays in crime prevention:

> Communities are the central institution for crime prevention, the stage on which all other institutions perform. Families, schools, labor markets, retail establishments, police, and corrections must all confront the consequences of community life. Much of the success or failure of these other institutions is affected by the community context in which they operate. Our nation's ability to prevent serious violent crime may depend heavily on our ability to help reshape community life, at least in our most troubled communities.

The community defense model is geared toward preventing criminal opportunities by organizing local residents to keep a watchful eye out for suspicious activities or individuals. The theory behind this approach is that the implementation of crime prevention programs will mobilize residents around a shared control over private and public spaces. As an opportunity-reduction approach to preventing crime (see Chapter 2 for more detailed information on situational approaches to crime prevention), the community defense model is concerned with reinforcing or modifying the individual and collective behaviors of community residents to produce or strengthen a local social environment that can informally regulate itself, which includes preventing criminal opportunities from arising. In theory, informal social control, which is said to be a by-product of the socially cohesive community, is supposed to reduce the opportunity for crime and disorder through a vigorous enforcement of shared norms and standards that the community holds dear. It is hypothesized that the collective efforts of a cohesive, concerned, and vigilant neighborhood will contribute to the prevention of local crime and disorder problems. The crime prevention program that has become universally associated with the community defense model is Neighborhood Watch (NW).

The community development model promotes the physical, social, and socioeconomic development of a neighborhood, which includes a range of initiatives from organizing residents, economic development, beautification projects, graffiti removal, housing gentrification, and other types of physical development. Social problem-solving approaches (see Chapters 4 and 5 for more detailed information on CPSD) that address the root causes of crime through interventions that target at-risk children, youth, families, and entire neighborhoods can also be included in this community development category (if they are community based). A community development approach is said to help prevent crime in a number of ways: by addressing physical dilapidation and disorder problems that can contribute to a downward spiral of communities that invite more serious crime problems, through the development of local social cohesion and informal social control, and through social and economic developmental measures that address criminogenic risk factors.

The main difference between the community defense and community development models is that the former is concerned with reducing the opportunity for crime, while the latter attempts to address factors that contribute to the root causes of crime locally. Despite this demarcation, the two approaches share one element essential to CCP: the collective and proprietary efforts of residents to prevent and control crime and criminality at the local level.

In addition to sharing certain fundamental traits, the community defense and community development approaches to crime prevention are complementary, not only as a result of their different approaches to preventing local crime problems but also in that community development can be a prerequisite for the community defense model by fostering social cohesiveness and informal social control. Figure 5.1 depicts how community development can contribute to the efficacy of a community defense strategy, which, if successful, can contribute to the stability, health, and overall development of a neighborhood.

In summary, the neighborhood and the community have become a focal point for crime prevention for at least three reasons:

1. Crime prevention is premised on a community-based, citizen-driven process with the assumption being that private citizens play a major role in maintaining order in a free society and therefore should be encouraged to accept more responsibility for the prevention of crime.
2. The residential neighborhood is not only the place where many crimes (property, violent, drug trafficking, etc.) take place, but such crimes can have a significant destabilizing effect on neighborhoods.
3. The primacy of the *neighborhood* and the *community* cuts across all other approaches to crime prevention. Situational prevention measures involve managing the physical environment of the local neighborhood. Most developmental approaches to crime prevention take place at the neighborhood level, whether it is concerned with the local physical, social, or socioeconomic infrastructure. Most crime prevention initiatives work best when there is a strong sense of local social cohesion (i.e., a sense of community).

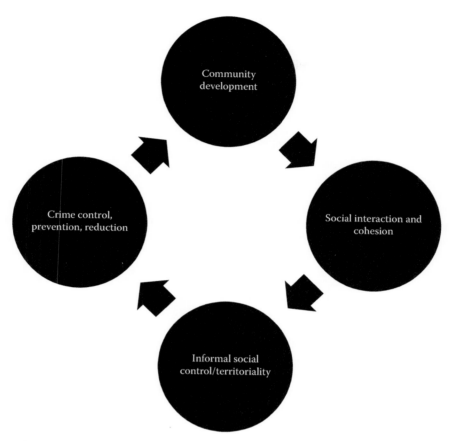

Figure 5.1
Symbiotic relationship between crime prevention and community development.

5.3   CRIME CAUSATION THEORIES UNDERLYING CCP

Within modern times, the almost universal homage paid to the ideal of community is surpassed only by the frequency of the eulogies that lament its passing. The inexorable loss of community has long been the refrain of social critics who argue that individualism has overtaken communalism and the ties that bind civil society together have slackened. Forrest and Kearns (2001, 2128) write that advanced Western societies display "all the hallmarks of a loss of cohesion, including social disorder and conflict, disparate moral values, extreme social inequality, low levels of social interaction between and within communities, and low levels of place attachment."

The historical basis for the contemporary version of this argument dates to the late nineteenth century. During a time of unparalleled urban growth and industrialization, influential social theorists such as Ferdinand Tonnies, Emile Durkheim, and Georg Simmel were suggesting that as Western societies became increasingly urbanized, industrialized, and modernized, informal and personal interactions between people were being replaced by legalistic and impersonal relationships. Modern urban society was creating weaker, more superficial ties between individuals, leading to social fragmentation and jeopardizing social cohesion and civil society. As industrialization progressed and cities grew, there was great concern that the sense of community that allegedly abounded in preindustrial society would disappear altogether. This proposition was sustained in the first half of the twentieth century by sociologists at the University of Chicago who believed that as the urban population increased in size, density, and heterogeneity, neighborhood residents became less socially engaged with one another and, as a result, less integrated in and attached to the local community (Wirth, 1938; Shaw and McKay, 1942). The result is that in modern society, "social ties are characterized as being weak, communal ties as being scarce," and the local community has "decayed, if not declined into oblivion" (Leighton, 1988, 353).

A dominant etiological theory of crime underlying CCP is that the loss of the socially cohesive community has contributed to crime and disorder within Western societies. The prevailing idea is that crime results from a breakdown in community life: the loss of community contributes to crime by undermining local informal social control. This theory of crime and disorder, first put forth by Wirth (1938), argues that the scale and complexity of mass society have robbed individuals in urban areas of *solidary* bonds. Communalism, which includes strong and enduring ties to fellow citizens, has weakened. The powerful ideology of individualism, whereby the rights and liberties of the individual supersede those of the collective society, has grown in strength and ushered in a growing culture of personal self-fulfillment, self-gratification, and extremely inward-looking perspectives (Lichterman, 1995).

The direct theoretical heritage of CCP can be found in the first half of this century, when social theorists at the University of Chicago articulated a relationship between delinquent behavior and the immediate social and physical environment (Shaw and McKay, 1942). Beginning in the 1920s, the Chicago School of Sociology studied the impact of local social conditions and neighborhood characteristics on young people in an attempt to explain deviant and delinquent behavior. Their analysis of where delinquents lived in Chicago showed a concentration in inner-city areas characterized by low rent and physical deterioration. In these areas, termed "zones of transition", there was also a rapid turnover of the local population, which led to a chronic problem of "social disorganization" that, in turn, undermined social cohesion, informal social control, and the positive socialization of children and youth. As a result of this social pathology and the weakening of local informal social controls, children and young people were ineffectually socialized, which gave rise to delinquency.

Hope (1995, 72) argues that the operation of urban markets, primarily in housing and employment, is a crucial context for the causes of local crime and violence problems. "Changes in the dynamics of the urban market, in which individual communities are located, thus have a major impact on their levels of crime and disorder, mediated by the employment and housing opportunities available to both current and prospective residents." Housing markets tend to differentiate people, reinforcing social division through segregation according to class, income, and race (Harvey, 1985). The lack of meaningful employment in inner-city neighborhoods—in part fuelled by the exodus of well-paying manufacturing jobs to the suburbs and then to other countries—has been cited as an important contributor to the complex underlying factors of crime and violence in inner-city neighborhoods: high levels of unemployment (especially among young men), poverty, despair, instability, a breakdown in social institutions, and marginalization.

Street level drug trafficking, and the violence this trade engenders, is particularly concentrated in inner-city, disadvantaged neighborhoods and carried out by groups

CASE STUDY 5.1

CRIME PREVENTION THROUGH COMMUNITY DEVELOPMENT IN CHICAGO

On the basis of their delinquency causation theories, the Chicago School sociologists formulated the *urban village model*. This community-based approach to social development operated on the following premise: because social disorganization is a primary cause of crime, efforts promoting strong, cohesive, and well-functioning communities that positively engage, supervise, and socialize young people can ameliorate crime and delinquency problems at the local level. This theory was tested through the Chicago Area Project (CAP), which began in the 1930s to address the problems of juvenile delinquency in some of the poorest neighborhoods in the city. CAP provided recreational programs for children and youth, began outreach work with delinquent youth, and worked to improve conditions in the neighborhood. The Chicago School's legacy for CCP is the importance of community organizing and empowerment, local collective action, informal social control, strong local institutions, as well as physical and social development in addressing local crime and disorder problems.

CAP originally consisted of approximately a dozen neighborhood organizations, each of which covered local populations of between 10,000 and 50,000 residents. The grassroots, self-governing groups were expected to raise funds; identify crime and disorder problems in their neighborhoods; organize the local population; nurture local leadership; develop and implement programs; provide local facilities to work with children and youth; help residents better understand the problems of children and youth; improve recreational, educational, and other community services for children and youth; assist local institutions and public officials expand and make more effective services for the community; and foster the physical and social development of the neighborhood.

CAP still exists today and continues to work toward improving the quality of neighborhood life, with particular emphasis on solving problems faced by young people and their families. As expressed on the CAP website, "the original mission of CAP has not changed since its inception: to work toward the prevention and eradication of juvenile delinquency through the development and support of affiliated local community self-help efforts, in communities where the need is greatest." The underlying philosophy of CAP is "that residents must be empowered through the development of community organizations so that they can act together to improve neighborhood conditions, hold institutions serving the community accountable, reduce antisocial behavior by young people, protect them from inappropriate institutionalization, and provide them with positive models for personal development."

Today, CAP and its many community-based affiliate groups are involved in a wide range of initiatives, such as recreational and sports programs (including summer camps) for children and young people, neighborhood development projects, mentoring, job training and employment, after-school remedial education, youth counseling, and alternative justice programs that divert young offenders away from the courts (Graham, 1995, 61; The Chicago Area Project, n.d.).

and individuals who are economically disadvantaged. For Fagan and Chin (1990, 13), the rapid growth of crack cocaine marketing and use in the United States beginning in the late 1980s "occurred in socially disorganized areas with few legitimate economic opportunities and strained informal social controls, conditions associated with increased rates of predatory and expressive violent crimes." Increases in violence associated with crack cocaine markets in America's inner cities resulted, in part, from "the erosion of formal and informal social controls in neighborhoods whose human, social, and economic capital has been depleted over the past two decades. High rates of residential mobility and declining capital investment have contributed to an ecology of violence in several inner-city areas. The emergence of a volatile crack market perhaps has benefitted from these processes and intensified them. The participation of generally violent offenders in the crack trade, coupled with decreased controls and increased crime opportunities in socially fragmented areas, may account for the increased violence in the crack market" (Fagan and Chin, 1990, 37).

Numerous contemporary studies have established that children who are raised in disadvantaged neighborhoods are at greater risk for delinquency, criminality, and violence, compared to children raised in relatively affluent families or neighborhoods. This is due, in part, because the former are more frequently exposed to norms favorable to criminality, which fosters a negative socialization, especially when regularly surrounded by successful criminal role models such as drug dealers or gang leaders (Sampson, 1985; Sampson and Lauritsen, 1994; Elliott et al., 1996; Office of Juvenile Justice and Delinquency Prevention, 1996; Sampson et al., 1997; Morenoff et al., 2001; Nicholas et al., 2005). Children living in socially disadvantaged neighborhoods are also at an increased risk of witnessing violence. According to Jain and Cohen (2012, 15–16), studies have linked this "to an increased risk for externalizing problem behaviors, including having higher rates of aggression, deviant behaviors and substance abuse." Children witnessing community violence are "also more likely to experience heightened internalizing psychosocial problems including Post-Traumatic Stress Disorder, depression and suicidal ideation" and are more apt to experience academic failure and to drop out of school. Stewart et al. (2002, 820) suggest that children in neighborhoods with a high rate of violence may "become desensitized to the pervasive neighborhood violence they witness" and may be more likely to "normalize" violence or become "desensitized to it."

In their broken windows metaphor, Wilson and Kelling (1982) articulate a hypothesized sequence of events that erodes the capacity of a community to invoke social control, which then contributes to a spiral of decline that invites crime. They argue that if a broken window is left unrepaired, the remainder of the windows would also soon be broken. The authors use the broken window as a metaphor; if disorderly and deviant behavior becomes unfettered or unaddressed by the local community and/or police, this can lead to the perception of social disorder and the concomitant breakdown of informal community control mechanisms. The authors contend that a cycle of urban decay can be initiated by the concentrated presence of local disorder problems and incivilities—such as a garbage-strewn street, a dilapidated building, or public drunkenness or drug use—which can then lead to the breakdown of informal social control and ultimately the social, physical, and economic destruction of neighborhoods. In their book on the broken windows theory, Kelling and Coles (1996, 20) describe how disorder and incivility problems can undermine the delicate social fabric that makes a neighborhood a community:

> ...disorderly behavior unregulated and unchecked signals to citizens that the area is unsafe. Responding prudently, and fearful, citizens will stay off the streets, avoid certain areas, and curtail their normal activities and associations. As citizens withdraw physically, they also withdraw from roles of mutual support with fellow citizens on the streets, thereby relinquishing the social controls they formerly helped to maintain within the community as social atomization sets in. Ultimately, the result for such a neighborhood ... is increasing vulnerability to an influx of more disorderly behavior and serious crime.

This theory has most commonly been used as a basis for a zero-tolerance enforcement approach by the police to crime that targets disorder and incivilities. However, the argument can be made that a negative spiral experienced by a neighborhood can only be truly reversed when there is a broad-based mobilization of residents who work toward the development of the community and the reinstatement of a sufficient level of informal social control that will help prevent incivilities, disorder, crime, and neighborhood decline.

In sum, theories of and research into neighborhood-level influences on crime are based on what Messner and Zimmerman (2012, 166) call "a fairly straightforward casual model of 'intervening effects': $X \rightarrow T \rightarrow Y$. Features of social structure X (e.g., concentrated disadvantage, population heterogeneity, residential instability) are depicted as causing relevant social processes T (e.g., the operation of informal controls, collective efficacy), which in turn are regarded as the approximate determines a levels of crime Y."

CASE STUDY 5.2

COMMUNITY ORGANIZING TO ADDRESS CRIME AND DISORDER PROBLEMS IN MINNEAPOLIS

The Hawthorne neighborhood in North Minneapolis was suffering from a number of problems, including drug trafficking, vandalism, burglary, litter, a derelict housing stock, the mismanagement of rental property, and local instability. As local crime and disorder problems escalated, homeowners moved from the neighborhood and the number of rental properties grew. Rental property owners then became part of the problem, allowing properties to fall into disrepair, failing to screen tenants, and even condoning drug trafficking and other criminal activity on their premises.

A consortium of local residents, community groups, a corporate foundation, as well as the police, city, county, and federal agencies came together to develop a comprehensive plan to combat crime and improve the neighborhood. Local residents were organized via neighborhood meetings and "block clubs," which served as a foundation to nurture local social cohesion and informal social control.

According to assessments of the community organizing efforts, "as the block clubs began to form, residents increasingly worked together to define neighborhood problems and to take ownership for resolving neighborhood issues." With the help of the CCP and Safety for Everyone Unit of the Minneapolis Police Department, residents were organized and trained to identify, record, and report suspected criminal activity on their blocks. Neighborhood residents also worked with faith-based groups to develop standards of conduct for the community. In response to one of these resulting community standards, the city of Minneapolis issued 300 "dirty collection" tags to properties where residents did not place their garbage in proper containers and allowed it to scatter around the yard. This enforcement had two direct results: first, commitment to enforce the community standards (i.e., informal social control) was demonstrated, and second, the garbage problem was addressed (which contributed to a more positive image of the neighborhood). The broader crime prevention strategy—which also included increased enforcement by the police, the use of city ordinances against problem homes, and greater cooperation among municipal departments—resulted in a significant decline in local drug trafficking, vandalism, and residential burglaries (U.S. Department of Justice, 2000, 24–29).

5.4 DEFINING CHARACTERISTICS OF CCP

There are two defining characteristics of CCP: It is community based and it entails the participation and collective mobilization of the local citizenry. (Partnerships can also be considered a defining characteristic of CCP; in fact, it is has become a key criterion in any crime prevention strategy [see Chapter 1].) These characteristics are fundamental to both the community defense and community development approaches to crime prevention.

5.4.1 Community Based

A community-based approach to crime prevention is predicated on the assumption that private citizens play a major role in maintaining order in a free society and therefore should be encouraged to accept more responsibility for ensuring safety and security. An underlying doctrine of CCP is that residents must become involved in proactive interventions aimed at reducing or precluding criminal opportunity from occurring in their neighborhoods (Lurigio and Rosenbaum, 1986, 19). As Jamieson (2008, 12) writes,

> It is largely taken for granted that communities have an important role to play in preventing crime and fostering community safety. Crime control agendas in most western democracies reflect this view and underscore the importance of community engagement and participation and partnerships. This expectation is based on the widely-held belief that many crime and community safety issues emerge from local, specific contexts and thus are rightfully "owned" at the community level. Locals experience crime problems first hand and thus have valuable knowledge that may be critical to the success of an intervention. Moreover, the long term success and sustainability of positive changes are seen as inextricably linked to the level of community involvement and ownership of strategies – particularly when institutional resources to address crime are scarce.

The Eighth United Nations Conference on the Prevention of Crime and the Treatment of Offenders espoused the central role of community through its promotion of "the safer communities" approach to crime prevention, which holds the following principles: The community is the focal point of effective crime prevention, the community needs to identify and respond to short- and long-term needs, crime prevention efforts should bring together individuals from a range of sectors to tackle crime, and strategies for preventing crime should be supported by the whole community (as cited in Department of Justice Canada, 1996, 1).

In the United States, the groundwork was laid for the future development of CCP scholarship and practice by the 1967 Presidential Crime Commission, which stressed the need for an active and involved citizenry in preventing crime. A key assumption of this report, and subsequent federal crime control policies, is that "the formal criminal justice system by itself cannot control crime without the help from neighborhood residents …." As such, the "community should play the central role in defining community crime prevention and that organized groups of residents are perhaps the best vehicle for responding to local crime" (U.S. Department of Justice, 1977, 3). In 1977, the U.S. Congress authorized the creation of the Law Enforcement Assistance Administration's Community Anti-Crime Program, which dispensed millions of dollars in grants to "assist community organizations and neighborhood groups to become involved in activities designed to prevent crime, reduce fear of crime, and contribute to neighborhood revitalization"

(U.S. Department of Justice, 1977, 1). For federal policy makers, the prevention and control of crime would now be shared between government and the citizenry through an implicit division of labor. This co-ownership was reflected in the preamble to the *Juvenile Delinquency Prevention Act* of 1974: "the responsibility for control, primary punishment, and rehabilitation of identified juvenile criminals remains with the court, but the responsibility for prevention has been given back to the community."

The centrality of the community to crime prevention has been reflected in government crime control agendas in other countries. In their 1993 report on crime prevention, the Canadian Standing Committee on Justice and the Solicitor General recommended that future federal crime control policies be premised on the belief that "crime occurs in communities and priorities concerning crime prevention are best determined at the local level" (Parliament of Canada, 1993, 33). One of the results of this report was the creation of the National Crime Prevention Centre, which includes a "community mobilization" funding component that helps local groups implement initiatives to deal with crime and victimization. In Australia, the National Community Crime Prevention Programme was established in 2004 to "increase the ability of Australian communities to recognise local crime problems and to pursue effective, locally organised, crime prevention initiatives." The program provides grants for "grass roots projects designed to enhance community safety and crime prevention by preventing or reducing crime and antisocial behaviour, improving community safety and security, and reducing the fear of crime" (Australian Government, Attorney General's Department). In England and Wales, a major national crime prevention strategy under the New Labour Government was the Safer Communities Initiative, which funded crime prevention projects at the local level with particular emphasis on promoting partnerships between community groups, the private sector, and municipal governments.

The implication of the role that the local community plays in crime control is profound: the philosophy of CCP espouses a partial transfer in responsibility for proactive, preventive efforts from the state to the citizenry. Shonholtz (1987, 46) writes that despite modern perceptions of crime control as the exclusive purview of the state, the (re-)emergence of crime prevention in the United States beginning in the late 1960s represented the type of responsibilities that for centuries had been carried out by local communities:

> ... historically Americans turned to community and religious institutions for the early settlement of conflict and promotion of community social values. In fact, swearing a police oath was considered in many communities to be a violation of individual moral responsibility and a sign that the community was lax in enforcing social norms. The Judeo-Christian base of American democratic thought stressed the responsibilities of individuals and the obligation of society in maintaining cooperative associations and support systems. Historically, civic justice has been understood to be a community undertaking, outside and separate from the more narrow and formal responsibility of the state's exercise of formal control.

Building upon social criticisms and etiological theories that locate the root causes of crime in the loss of the socially cohesive neighborhood, an underlying assumption of CCP is that the efficacy of efforts to prevent and control crime is contingent upon the existence of communal bonds at the local level. These localized bonds are commonly referred to as social cohesion or *a sense of community*. Bursik and Grasmick (1993) believe that for local neighborhoods to combat crime successfully, programs must provide for the development of strong networks of association among local residents and between residents and local institutions. Greenberg et al. (1985, 17) recommend that communities "develop programs that familiarize local residents with each other and with the neighborhood to help encourage intervention and reduce fear." For Mukherjee and Wilson (1987, 2), increasing social interaction, integration, and cohesion directly contributes to greater community safety:

> The most important element of community crime prevention appears to be to bring about social interaction, whereby residents of the community maintain a degree of familiarity with each other. Such interaction and familiarity should, in theory at least, make it possible to detect strangers in the community. And finally, crime prevention theory suggests that such interactions may lead to a cohesive neighborhood. The basic philosophy of community crime prevention is that social interaction and citizen familiarity can play an important role in preventing, detecting, and reporting criminal behavior.

In short, CCP theory is premised on the belief that both the problem of and the solutions to crime are strongly influenced by the sociological concept of community. While some may view the neighborhood as simply the spatial locale in which crime prevention programs are implemented, a socially cohesive community in and of itself forms the heart of a distinct crime prevention philosophy. Like the family, the school, or the labor market, the community is viewed as an *institution* through which crime is controlled and prevented.

5.4.2   Citizen Participation/Collective Action

Central to CCP is the participation of civic members, in most cases, neighborhood residents. In the broadest of terms, the International Centre for the Prevention of Crime (ICPC) outlined two ways that civil society can be involved in crime prevention: "public participation in defining local needs, including through local diagnoses of security, and public participation in implementing strategies" (International Centre for the Prevention of Crime, 2010, 115). More specifically, van Steden et al. (2011, 440–441) group the various forms of public participation in community safety programs into eight categories:

1. Passive surveillance: citizens acquire information on demand and pass their findings to the police or local authorities.
2. Active surveillance: citizens participate voluntarily in NWs.
3. Relational supervision: citizens make use of their interpersonal contacts to impose informal social control on undesired and antisocial behavior.
4. Conflict mediation: citizens are independent mediators in the resolution, for example, of a neighbor's quarrel.
5. Advising policy makers: citizens have an advisory role in shaping urban safety projects.
6. Shaping policy making: citizens are involved in directing policy formation.
7. Safety self-management: citizens install physical security measures to protect their property or hire a private security company at their own expense.
8. Vigilantism: citizens who take the law into their own hands.

As discussed in Chapter 1, one way to classify crime prevention strategies is to make a distinction between those that are individualistic in nature (e.g., target hardening, self-defense classes, avoiding certain parts of a city at night) and those that are collective in nature (e.g., NW, Block Parent, citizen patrols). Along the same vein, Schneider and Schneider (1978) categorize crime prevention approaches as either "private minded" or "public minded." The former is restricted to efforts that primarily self-protect the individual and his or her own home and assets from victimization, while the latter includes initiatives that help protect the entire community (which include looking out for one's neighbors and watching over public spaces).

Both individual (private-minded) and collective (public-minded) approaches are legitimate and important parts of CCP. However, an exclusive reliance on the former is often viewed as negative because it may serve to undermine the collective action, social cohesion, and informal social control underpinnings of CCP. As the U.S. National Advisory Council on Criminal Justice Standards and Goals (1973, 46) warns, while the retreat behind locks, bars, alarms, and guards may "be steps in self-protection, they can lead to a lessening of the bonds of mutual assistance and neighborliness" so crucial to CCP. More tersely, Newman (1972, 3) believes that "when people begin to protect themselves as individuals and not as a community, the battle against crime is effectively lost."

These observations all accentuate a central tenet of CCP: a collective response in which individuals act jointly to undertake crime prevention activities that they could not accomplish on their own (Barker and Linden, 1985, 15). Collective crime prevention programs follow the adage that there is strength in numbers—what we can't do individually, we can do collectively.

The argument that crime can best be controlled and prevented through efforts that transcend the capacity of the individual is reinforced by the role that social cohesion plays in crime prevention. CCP programs are not only dependent upon the presence of social cohesion, but some have argued that *collective* crime prevention programs can contribute to the cohesiveness of a block or neighborhood by promoting common goals and stimulating resident interaction and mutual helpfulness (Lewis, 1979; Dubow and Emmons, 1981; Lewis and Salem, 1981; Greenberg et al., 1985; Rosenbaum, 1986; Lewis et al., 1988; Enns and Wilson, 1999; van Steden et al., 2011). It is reasoned that efforts to encourage collective responses by local residents is the best way to counter "the disorganized community that is unable to exercise informal social control over deviant behavior" (Conklin, 1975, 99). According to van Steden et al. (2011, 435–436), civic participation in crime prevention initiatives may foster "social empowerment that can guarantee (feelings of) shelter, protection and belonging." To this end, "citizen participation is believed to reaffirm communal bonds, deepen democracy and transparency …." Skogan (1990, 16) argues that organized community groups have emerged as our primary hope for recapturing informal control and the destiny of threatened urban neighborhoods. According to Hope (1995, 66), a fundamental philosophy underlying CCP "is the communitarianism inherent in the legacy of Shaw and McKay—the belief that the solution to neighborhood crime problems can be achieved primarily through the self-help of residents … the common thread in all these efforts has been that residents should organize collectively to create or support institutions for dealing with crime problems that beset their residential space."

The importance of a collective effort was not lost on US policy makers. Early crime prevention project funding by the U.S. Department of Justice placed a priority on "programs and activities that are public minded in the sense that they are designed to promote a social or collective response to crime and fear of crime at the neighborhood level in contrast to private minded efforts that deal only with the actions of citizens as individuals or those that result from the provision of services that in themselves do not contribute to the organization of the neighborhood" (U.S. Department of Justice, 1977, 58). British government support for CCP during the 1980s was couched in similar terms: "protecting your own home is fine, but you will enjoy greater security if everyone around you is working on it" (Central Office of Information, 1989, 26, as cited in

Hope, 1995, 51). The importance of local collective efforts has also been empirically supported; in his analysis of a federally sponsored program to prevent juvenile crime in various neighborhoods in the United States, Fagan (1987, 57) contends that "community organizing was an essential element. Program activities could not be conducted without large cadres of residents volunteering their efforts."

CASE STUDY 5.3

MOBILIZING THE COMMUNITY TO SHUT DOWN PROBLEM PREMISES IN BROOKLYN

Sampson and Scott (1999, 26–29) describe the crime prevention efforts undertaken in the Clinton Hill neighborhood of Brooklyn, New York. The neighborhood is home to numerous local amenities, such as brownstone houses, a nice park, a college campus, retail shopping, a multicultural population, and strong social cohesion (exemplified by the existence of various block associations). However, the area also experienced a number of crime and disorder problems; in particular, abandoned and/or poorly maintained rental buildings, a high level of auto thefts and residential break-ins, muggings, and drug activity along a commercial corridor. The murder of a local convenience store owner in his shop was the final straw for residents. Due to its poor relationship with the police, the block associations reached out to the Neighborhood Anti-Crime Center, which is part of the Citizens Committee for New York City, a group that supports community self-help and civic action. In cooperation with an organizer from the committee, a meeting was scheduled to help residents work through a collaborative problem-solving process to address local problems. Invited to the meeting were a couple of community-oriented NYPD patrol officers who were well known to and trusted by local leaders.

Together, they identified several local privately and city-owned multiresidential complexes that were housing drug operations and/or addicts, which they believed were the source of many local problems. Staff with the Citizens Committee worked with the residents and local leaders on how to obtain more information to address the problem premises (e.g., conducting property research to identify landlords of problem premises), connect them with key stakeholders who could help (such as the district attorney's narcotics eviction unit and the city's public housing agency representative), and how their relationship with the New York City police could be improved so that they might work more collaboratively.

As part of their information-gathering process, the community leaders found that the police had been stymied in shutting down the drug houses because the landlords either colluded with the dealers or were unresponsive to pressure by the police and other government agencies. A combined enforcement and legal strategy was hatched, which included having community leaders put pressure on private owners and the city to clean up the drug houses. They also convinced the district attorney's office to press civil charges against landlords if they failed to clean up their properties and ensure that the properties were no longer being used for drug trafficking. City agencies also worked with the police to shut down the most egregious premises on code violations. Community leaders and the police also took one landlord to court, with the judge ordering him to clean up the property and ensure that it was crime-free to the best of his abilities. The judge also ordered the landlord to provide the police with keys to the premises so they could monitor whether the landlord had followed the judge's edicts. Eventually, the properties that were targeted were cleaned up and much of the illegal activity conducted within them was halted. According to one review of this community- and partnership-based effort, "closing the property made a huge difference in building the community's capacity to take on other problem buildings" (Sampson and Scott, 1999, 26–29).

5.5 COMMUNITY DEFENSE MODEL

The community defense model of crime prevention is characterized by a collective effort of neighborhood residents who regulate their local environment through the exertion of local informal social control. The theory underlying the community defense model is that local residents can be organized to act collectively in an effort to reduce the opportunity for crimes to occur by assuming a more vigilant and proprietary concern over their neighborhood. Simply put, the community defense approach presumes that "what seems most clearly needed to prevent most instances of crime and other antisocial incidents in neighborhoods is a caring and vigilant citizenry" (Lavrakas, 1985, 88). The theory is that once educated about the processes and benefits of a collective effort to fight crime, concerned residents will participate in local collective crime prevention undertakings or, at the very least, keep a watchful eye out for and report suspicious people or activities during their daily routines. In addition to the two aforementioned fundamental characteristics of CCP (community-based and citizen participation/collective action), the community defense model is distinguished by three other defining traits: informal social control, reinforcing or modifying behaviors of local residents, and situational crime prevention measures.

5.5.1 Informal Social Control

One implication of the shift in crime prevention responsibilities from the state to local communities is the increased importance of informal social control, which is said to prevent crime locally when exerted by private citizens acting collectively. The community defense model is concerned with reinforcing or modifying individual and collective behaviors of community residents to produce or strengthen a local social environment that can informally regulate itself, which includes preventing the opportunity for criminal and disorderly acts to occur. Informal social control is said to develop locally in one of two ways. It can develop *naturally* within a neighborhood, where there is a low rate of population turnover, where patterns of local association and interaction are well established, and where social cohesion is strong. Some have argued that informal social control can be *induced* in a neighborhood where it does not presently exist through the implementation of community development and crime prevention programs (Greenberg et al., 1985).

While formal social control is derived from state-imposed sanctions codified in written laws and regulations that are enforced by the police and the courts, informal social control is based on, and is said to restrict, crime and incivilities through community members' enforcement of local customs, common agreements, social norms, and unwritten rules that guide what they consider to be appropriate and accepted behavior for their neighborhood. Wilson (1975, 24) defines informal social control as "the observance of standards of right conducted in the public places in which one lives and moves, those standards to be consistent with, and supportive of, the values and life style of the particular neighborhood." Theoretically, neighborhoods with a strong sense of informal social control will not tolerate behavior that is contrary to established or conventional norms. As a response to undesirable behavior, the enforcement of local informal social controls includes the spontaneous and subtle (e.g., raised eyebrows, gossip, or ridicule), direct confrontation by individual community members (e.g., verbal reprimands, warnings, physical intervention), and the structured activities of local groups, such as NW or citizen patrols (Greenberg et al., 1985, 1; Rosenbaum, 1988, 327).

The intellectual history of CCP is replete with references to the role of informal social control. Explicit in the social disorganization theory of crime and deviance originated by the Chicago School of Sociology (Merton, 1938; Shaw and McKay, 1942) is the inability of local institutions to exert a positive socializing influence that can help regulate the behavior of residents (and outsiders). The concept of informal social control is also implicit in the writings of Jacobs (1961, 31–32), who insists that "the first thing to understand is that the public peace … is not kept primarily by the police, as necessary as police are. It is kept primarily by an intricate, almost unconscious, network of voluntary controls and standards among the people themselves …." For Skogan (1990, 12), local stability is contingent upon the capacity of a neighborhood to continually reproduce itself as a social system. Unstable social systems lack steering mechanisms capable of making midcourse corrections and the result is that neighborhoods slip into a perpetual cycle of decline. Informal social control represents one such steering mechanism.

As intimated earlier, an important prerequisite for informal social control (and hence successful crime prevention programs) is social cohesion. The essential elements of informal social control—residents' proprietary concern over their environment, increased vigilance, and a willingness to intervene in suspicious circumstances or disorderly conduct—are forged through a commitment and attachment to the neighborhood by individual residents, combined with a strong sense of social cohesion at the collective level. For Findlay and Zvekic (1988), the local crime control objective is advanced through cohesiveness, which, in turn, is established through the integration and socialization of community members that involves the inculcation of norms and values and the creation of a collective consciousness.

Numerous studies have postulated a causal relationship between social cohesion and informal social control, on the one hand, and lower rates of crime and disorder on the other. For example, research has indicated that crime and related problems are lower in areas where residents have a strong attachment to, and greater responsibility and control over, what happens in their neighborhood (Skogan and Maxfield, 1981; Greenberg et al., 1982; Taub et al., 1984; Taylor et al., 1984; Gatti and Tremblay, 2000), where there exists the perception that one's neighbors will provide assistance when needed (Fowler and Mangione, 1982; Newman and Franck, 1982) and where there is a willingness of residents to intervene in observed criminal activity (Maccobyet al., 1958; Clotfelter, 1980). Greenberg et al. (1984, 6) note that cohesive groups are better able to respond to threats by outsiders and are more likely to adopt protective actions compared to groups that are less cohesive. Research conducted by Gillis and Hagen (1983) suggests that bystanders are more likely to intervene in a criminal or violent altercation when the victim is a friend or an acquaintance and when the incident occurs in their own neighborhood.

A particularly important underpinning of CCP, according to Sampson et al. (1997, 919), is "collective efficacy," a concept that combines social cohesion with informal social control and that has been defined as "the linkage of mutual trust and the willingness to intervene for the common good" or the realization of "common values and the ability of groups to regulate their members according to desired principles"

(Crawford, 1999, 518). In a study of Chicago residents, Sampson and colleagues (1997) found that rates of violence were lower in neighborhoods characterized by collective efficacy, which led to the conclusion that the willingness of local residents to intervene for the common good depends in large part on conditions of mutual trust and solidarity. Maxwell et al. (2011) identify numerous subsequent studies that provide supporting evidence that neighborhoods with higher levels of collective efficacy have lower levels of violent crime.

In contrast to the aforementioned, Rohe (1985) writes that there is little strong evidence that the level of informal social control is related to crime rates. This position is also supported by a study carried out in English council estates by Hope and Foster (1992) who found that some high-crime areas also had high levels of informal social control.

5.5.2 Behavioral Reinforcement/Modification

As Orwellian as the aforementioned concept may sound, the community defense model is concerned with reinforcing or modifying the individual and collective behaviors of community residents. Crime is to be prevented—not by changing the behavior of the offender but rather by educating and modifying the attitudes and behaviors of potential victims who are in the best position to limit opportunities for their own victimization (Lewis and Salem, 1981). This is to be accomplished by producing or strengthening a local social environment that can informally regulate itself, including the regulation and reduction of criminal and disorderly behavior. In short, a principal goal of the community defense model is to motivate people to become involved in collective crime prevention programs and assume responsibility for protecting their local environment.

5.5.3 Situational Crime Prevention Measures

Reducing the opportunity for a criminal act to occur is the primary prevention strategy of the community defense model. As detailed in Chapter 2, criminal opportunities can be reduced in one of two ways: (1) through the management and/or design of the physical environment (e.g., target hardening, entry control, crime prevention through environmental design, etc.) or (2) by influencing the individual and collective behaviors of residents to minimize their vulnerability and that of others through both personal and collective measures. Either way, preventing the opportunity for a criminal event to transpire involves increasing the risk of detecting criminal opportunities and events and apprehending offenders. Within the context of the community defense model, increasing the risk of detection and apprehension as a means to reduce crime opportunities is contingent upon organizing residents through community safety groups or programs in which surveillance is key, such as NW or citizen patrols. The opportunity-reduction aspect of CCP is also contingent upon the presence of local informal social control, which can result in a willingness of residents to look out for one another, to watch over public and private spaces, to enforce local community values and standards, and to intervene in criminal acts (primarily by alerting the police).

CASE STUDY 5.4

CITIZEN PATROLS TO COMBAT PROSTITUTION IN VANCOUVER

The "Shame the Johns" campaign was originally organized in the West End of Vancouver, Canada, with the purpose of ridding the neighborhood of street prostitutes. The strategy of the loosely organized group of residents was to congregate around street walkers with the hope of scaring off their customers (the *johns*). Information, such as a license plate number, on any suspected john who was caught talking to a street prostitute was recorded and forwarded to the police. Participants often carried large signs and banners. Like the Guardian Angels, Shame the Johns was a confrontational approach to citizen patrols that often resulted in altercations with prostitutes. This group increasingly became well organized and made a series of submissions to municipal, provincial, and federal governments in Canada demanding that street prostitution be removed from the area "regardless of where it might end up" (Lowman, 1992, 7).

The community mobilization and resulting political pressure led to an extraordinary legal strategy by the provincial government: the issuing of civil nuisance injunctions against prostitutes. It was these injunctions that helped push many of the street prostitutes out of the West End and into other Vancouver neighborhoods, some of which subsequently formed their own version of Shame the Johns (Schneider, 2007a, 166–167).

5.5.4 Summary: The Theorized Process of the Community Defense Model

A theoretical premise of the community defense model is that the implementation of crime prevention initiatives will marshal the concern of residents into a collective effort that fosters an atmosphere of informal social control and promotes vigilance within their neighborhood. The collective and sustained effort of a cohesive and watchful neighborhood—in partnership with the police—is then expected to lead to the preclusion of or decline in local crime and disorder problems.

Conceptually, the community defense model incorporates five interdependent concepts: collective action, informal social control, crime prevention, behavior modification, and social cohesion. Figure 5.2 illustrates how the community defense model entails a positive and symbiotic interaction between crime prevention, community (social cohesion), and informal social control. Social cohesion is essential to the success of CCP due to its role as the foundation for informal social control and collective action. Once a social environment conducive to producing informal control has been created, the capacity to prevent crime and disorder is greatly enhanced. In turn, control over negative local forces increases the likelihood that local social cohesion (and hence informal social control) can be advanced. The engine that drives the interaction between these three variables, and which steers a neighborhood toward greater social cohesion and informal social control, is collective action. At the core of this tripartite relationship is the promotion or reinforcement of positive social behavior among community members that includes a commitment to working with one's neighbors to protect an area.

Figure 5.2
The theorized process promoted by the community defense model.

Thus, mobilizing neighborhoods around crime and disorder involves initiating or furthering a positive cycle by modifying the social behavior of neighborhood residents to achieve the interrelated objectives of social interaction, local integration, cohesion, informal control, and the prevention of crime. And it is the collective action of community members that directs this self-feeding spiral on a beneficial course. Dubow and Emmons (1981) were among the first to advocate the relationship between these central concepts and the importance of initiating a positive cycle between them. In their "community hypothesis," the authors emphasize the following theoretical tenets of the CCP cycle:

1. Neighborhood residents can be mobilized by community organizations to participate in collective action crime prevention projects.
2. Involvement in these activities creates a stronger community because people will take greater responsibility for their collective protection, and interactions among neighbors will increase.
3. An increase in social interaction and a stronger sense of community lead to more effective informal social control.
4. Therefore, aside from the direct effects of CCP activities in reducing crime or fear of crime, these activities may also reduce crime or fear by rebuilding local social control in the neighborhood.

Despite the inherent logic behind this theoretical process, there remains a Catch-22 in the CCP theory and practice: collective crime prevention projects are viewed as an important means of invoking or reproducing territoriality, social cohesion, and informal social control. However, research has shown that in order for a CCP program to be successfully implemented, it often requires these outcomes as prerequisites.

CASE STUDY 5.5

DEFENDING A SPOKANE NEIGHBORHOOD AGAINST CRIME AND DISORDER PROBLEMS

In the early 1990s, Spokane, Washington, began experiencing gang-related drug trafficking. One hard-hit area was the 1100 block of West First Avenue, an older area on the edge of the downtown core of the city. It was a poor neighborhood, with half of its residents living below the poverty level. The street was home to aging, deteriorating buildings, low-rent single-room occupancy hotels, government-subsidized housing, a bus terminal, a railway viaduct, bars and taverns, an adult video store, and what was deemed "an extremely active gang-run crack trade." According to Rick Albin, a member of the Spokane police force, "Gangs chose the West First area because of its proximity to cheap room rentals, the only Greyhound bus terminal, and because it was already a neighborhood where most of the low-income, special-needs and elderly residents had already 'given up' the street" (as cited in Sampson and Scott, 1999, 128).

Property crime, drug trafficking, violence, prostitution, gang-related problems were on the increase. Fear of crime also increased dramatically and many residents did not go out at night. Calls for police service rose from approximately 1,000 a year in the late 1980s to 3,300 in 1995. In August of 1996, six people were wounded as a result of two drive-by shootings.

In defense of their community, the police, led by Officer Albin, as well as municipal government departments, a local church, and residents collaborated on Project ROAR (Reclaiming Our Area Residences), which included numerous strategies to address the growing crime problems.

A community organizer was hired to mobilize local residents and help form a residential association in the public housing development, implemented NW committees, began a buddy system for people using the street at night, and organized neighborhood marches and social activities (including block parties, bingo nights, potluck dinners, and movie and music nights) to increase social interaction and cohesion.

Apartment building owners and hotel managers formed an association and agreed to better screen residents and implement more stringent security measures in their buildings, which included making design modifications to deter drug dealers and users.

Business owners formed a local steering committee and, along with other groups in the area, worked with the state's Economic Development Council to further economic opportunities on the street and surrounding areas and to install video surveillance cameras to monitor 20 high-risk blocks.

Safety audits were undertaken and safe design modifications were made by the city to public spaces while business owners applied CPTED principles to their properties. Among the physical modifications made were improvements to lighting in alleys (to deter drug trafficking and property crimes), fencing off the viaduct (where the dealers often hid their drugs), and implementing measures to restrict vehicular traffic (to cut down on motorists entering the street to buy drugs or sex). Community beautification initiatives, which included regularly removing litter and repairing and renovating dilapidated buildings, were also undertaken.

The police appointed a neighborhood resource officer (Officer Rick Albin), who was directed to work with residents and business owners to reduce crime and disorder problems and improve the local quality of life. The police also stepped up foot and bike patrols on the streets, and local businesses supplied them with pagers so they could be contacted directly by citizens for urgent problems. A community policing station was established in the public housing complex, which was staffed by police officers, community organizers, local citizens, and a legal intern provided by the district attorney's office. From that station, the police monitored the feed from the CCTV cameras that had been set up. The police also worked with the district attorney and parole officials to monitor offenders who had been released back into the community.

One assessment indicates that these initiatives resulted in a 75% decrease in violent crime and a 35% decrease in calls for police service on the block. The interventions also "successfully disrupted an entrenched and violent drug market that impacted the entire neighborhood. The strategies addressed each aspect of the problem: the circling of cars to buy drugs, the hiding of drugs in the viaduct, the lack of surveillance on the block, the lack of follow-up with offenders reentering the community, and the movement of evicted dealers from one apartment or hotel to another. And to replace the drug dealing and related crime, project participants initiated positive block activities and businesses" (McGarrell, 1998; Sampson and Scott, 1999, 128–131).

5.5.5 Neighborhood Watch

A crime prevention program that personifies the community defense model is Neighborhood Watch, whereby local residents make a commitment to be more vigilant in watching each other's homes and public spaces and report suspicious activities and people to the police. Whether it is known as Block Watch, Home Watch, Apartment Watch, Community Watch, or Neighborhood Watch, residents are organized and trained to conduct informal surveillance of their immediate surroundings as part of their daily routines. It is hypothesized that through NW membership and training, neighborhood residents will be more alert and responsive to suspicious people and behavior, which includes contacting the police. It "has been argued that visible surveillance might reduce crime as a result of its deterrent effect on the perceptions and decision making of potential offenders," Bennett et al. (2006, 438) write. "Hence, watching and reporting might deter offenders if they are aware of the likelihood of local residents reporting suspicious behavior and if they perceive this as increasing their risks of being caught."

In addition to its surveillance function, NW can also serve as a vehicle for other (situational) crime prevention initiatives, such as conducting safety audits, operating citizen patrols, disseminating suspicious activity and crime reports, providing property-marking services, and community advocacy (government lobbying) (Lab, 2004, 63). Property crime (in particular, residential burglaries, theft from auto, and theft of auto) is the overwhelming focus of NW, but local programs can be adapted to target other forms of crime that may predominate in a particular area, such as drug trafficking, prostitution, gang activity, or vandalism.

An NW group typically covers only a small area, usually a city block or an apartment building. NW programs are often administered and funded by the local police department, although no neighborhood resident who is a member of NW is paid. A minimum of two people are required to organize a block or apartment building and they are designated as the Block Captain and Co-Captain. The two are then trained by the local police and, armed with this knowledge, pamphlets, and NW identification cards, they canvass their neighbors, advising them of an upcoming meeting to discuss the fledgling NW program. The purpose of the initial meeting, often attended by police officers, is to educate NW members on the program, how to detect suspicious individuals or behavior, how and when to contact the police, and other measures that can make their home, their neighbor's homes, and surrounding public space safer. Following the meeting, the captain draws a map of the area covered by the new NW program, listing the names of participants, their addresses, and their phone numbers. The map is then submitted to the police and in some cases may be distributed to those involved in the NW group. After the NW captain completes all the necessary steps, two NW signs are posted in visible spots on the block or apartment building. Participants may also be given NW stickers that can be posted on the doors and windows of their homes.

Since the early 1980s, NW has been one of the fastest-growing community-based programs in North America. Based on his review of the U.S. Bureau of Justice Statistics national crime survey data on personal crime prevention behaviors, Freidman (1998) estimates that from 1992 to 1997, between 39 and 47 million Americans knew about an NW program or other anticrime activity in their neighborhood, while participation in an NW scheme was between 18 million and 19 million people. Findings from the 2000 British Crime Survey indicate that 27% of all households in England and Wales were members of an NW scheme (Sims, 2001).

Evaluations of the effectiveness of NW have produced mixed results. A number of studies have found that NW has had a positive impact on crime in areas where it was implemented. Lab (2004, 68) cites a number of evaluations of NW in the United States that demonstrate a positive impact, including reductions in burglary and purse snatchings in Detroit, lower crime rates in 11 of 15 Denver neighborhoods that had a program in operation, as well as "significant drops in burglary, larceny, auto theft, and total crime in an organized area of Cincinnati compared to the rest of the city." He also cites studies that report similar positive results in the United Kingdom, including recent programs that "significantly reduced the burglary levels in the experimental areas relative to the control neighborhoods." Lab (2004, 68) concludes, "Official crime records reveal a positive impact of neighborhood watch programs on crime. Most studies report a lower level of crime (particularly property offenses) in the target communities that control areas and/or decreases compared to preprogram levels." The main finding of a 2008 narrative review of 17 studies (covering 36 evaluations) found that "the majority" of NW schemes (19) was "effective in reducing crime, while only 6 produced negative results." The findings of an accompanying meta-analysis of 12 studies (covering 18 evaluations)" was that Neighbourhood Watch was followed by a reduction in crime of between 16 and 26 percent" (Bennett, et al., 2008, 7).

Despite this rosy picture, NW has also been the subject of much criticism, due partially to a number of evaluations that have shown it has failed to meet most of its objectives. One of the most extensive evaluations was conducted in nine Chicago neighborhoods (Rosenbaum et al., 1985). Surveys taken of households before and after the program was implemented showed that most areas did not realize any significant changes in victimization rates. One area exhibited a "marginally significant" decrease, while two other areas actually registered a significant increase in the number of victimizations per respondent over the study period. Mixed results from NW programs in different neighborhoods of the same city were also recorded in Minneapolis (Rasmussen et al., 1979) and in Washington, DC (Henig, 1984). Based on a review of four rigorous evaluations of NW in the United States, Sherman (1997d, 29) concludes that "the oldest and best-known community policing program, Neighborhood Watch, is ineffective at preventing crime."

A review of nine evaluations of NW programs in the United Kingdom (Husain, 1990) concludes that there is little evidence that the program prevented crime. Bennett (1990) reports no change in victimization for areas of London where the program had been implemented, while decreases were recorded for neighborhoods where no program was in effect. An assessment of NW in Ireland (McKeown and Brosnan, 1998) also found no appreciable impact where it was implemented. This conclusion is a micro-cosm of the findings of other studies indicating the failure of NW to realize both its process-oriented objectives (mobilizing communities, promoting surveillance, identifying and reporting suspicious activities to the police, undertaking complementary security measures) and its ultimate goals (lower crime and victimization rates):

> Indeed our analysis was virtually unable to isolate any benefits associated with the schemes for each of the variables measured: feeling safer, reduced risk of victimisation, taking security precautions because of the scheme, reporting suspicious activities to the [police]. This result may be attributable to the fact, expressed by participants themselves, that about two thirds of the schemes are inactive. However this would not explain why the active schemes also seem to have no impact. We can offer no explanation for this although we would suggest that some of the impacts which the schemes are expected to produce—such as reducing crime, increasing the sense of safety, reducing victimisation—may be too ambitious and disproportionate to the resources of a group of community volunteers who meet no more than once a month and often much less.

McKeown and Brosnan (1998, 106)

Other assessments and analyses also suggest that the failure of many NW schemes is due to problems in mobilizing and sustaining a sufficient number of residents to make an impact. Based on their research of NW at three test sites in the United States, McConville and Shepherd (1992) argue that it cannot be described as a success because there is a general lack of participation among residents, individual schemes quickly become dormant, and they have little impact on crime. Even on blocks where NW exists, according to Gillham and Barnett (1994, 25), an appreciable proportion of residents decline to become involved. Findings from the 1988 British Crime Survey indicate that of those households located on a block with an active NW program, the participation level was a mere 18% (Dowds and Mayhew, 1994, 1).

While a review of NW studies in the United States led Garofalo and McLeod (1989) to conclude that this program has had some modest success in reducing residential burglaries, the authors expressed skepticism about the potential for NW to have a sustained impact on crime because of the difficulty in maintaining citizen involvement. According to Garofalo and McLeod (1989, 337), NW does not appear to be effective in preventing crime, mobilizing residents, or building community because "most are not emergent, in the sense of being devised and initiated by residents on their own." The authors discovered in their survey of NW programs in the United States that the police usually play the lead role in organizing, educating, training, and motivating residents. "In short, Neighborhood Watch is generally not something created by residents in an area to meet their self-defined needs; rather it is a set of predefined rules, procedures and structures that the residents can either adopt or reject. As such, one may argue that the extensiveness of police involvement in forming and managing Neighborhood Watch programs is detrimental to the process of citizens developing their own solutions to their problems ..." (Garofalo and McLeod, 1989, 341).

The strategic approach of NW has also been criticized as ineffective in arousing a high level of participation because an active involvement of the citizenry is discouraged through the inherently passive nature of their *observe-and-report* function. While safety is of paramount concern in discouraging direct intervention in a criminal act by members of an NW group, this passive watch-and-report function may nonetheless dissuade a more active role of neighborhood residents in designing and implementing crime prevention programs. Slow response times by overburdened police officers to 911 calls placed by NW members can further erode citizen confidence and participation in local programs.

A critical factor in determining the success of NW (or any crime prevention intervention) is the extent to which the program has been effectively implemented; those that are successful may have been competently implemented and managed, including determined efforts to maximize the active participation of neighborhood residents in a local NW scheme. Those that failed to meet their goals may have been the victims of poor management, which minimizes participation. Other variables that may dictate the success of NW schemes are the levels of social cohesion, informal social control, and territoriality among residents where the program is being implemented. While some believe that NW and other community-based crime prevention programs can bring together residents and foster a sense of community (and hence territoriality), there are also those who would argue that NW will inevitably fail in neighborhoods where social cohesion and territoriality are not already in place (or cannot easily be developed).

5.5.6   CCP Organizations

Community-based organizations (CBOs) have become important vehicles through which local crime prevention services are delivered. These groups are also central to efforts to mobilize communities to reduce the opportunity for crime in public and private spaces. When one speaks of community-based crime prevention groups, it is in reference to nonprofit, nongovernmental organizations that are neighborhood based— founded, organized, governed, and run by neighborhood residents. Community organizations bridge the conceptual divide between situational (opportunity-reducing) and developmental-based (social problem-solving) approaches to crime prevention. Some may focus on reducing the opportunity for crime (e.g., Neighborhood Watch), some may carry out social problem-solving initiatives (e.g., the Chicago Area Project), while others may do both. In addition, some are single-issue groups, such as those that focus on local drug trafficking, prostitution, or problem homes, while others are broad-based organizations that incorporate crime prevention into a larger mandate, such as neighborhood associations (see Case Study 5.6 in this chapter).

Many of these community organizations are informal, nonhierarchical, and *ad hoc* in nature. They materialize on the scene quickly to address specific crime and disorder problems, often resist formalization (such as incorporating as a society), and disband soon after the worst part of their problems has subsided. Other groups become permanent fixtures in communities and incorporate as charitable societies with a board of directors and official members. The programs delivered by these groups are equally varied and include disseminating information, educating and training local residents, conducting security audits, administering NW or citizen patrols, implementing youth recreational or mentoring programs, providing substance abuse treatment, lobbying governments, running crime prevention or community policing offices, and advising the police, to name just a few.

The community organization not only represents an important vehicle to carry out crime prevention activities, but some argue it can be instrumental in promoting the social prerequisites essential for successful community safety initiatives (Skogan, 1990, 16). CBOs provide neighbors with opportunities to interact more frequently, and this social interaction, according to Rosenbaum (1988), should lead to a stronger feeling of integration into the community. In turn, this may promote for social cohesion, informal social control, and crime prevention. For Lewis et al. (1988, 135), the community organization plays a pivotal role in the recreation of a communal sensibility "for it can articulate the needs and interests of those who long for more of a sense of attachment and control."

CBOs represent an organized, collective approach to promoting community safety. On a continuum of organized, collective approaches to crime prevention, CBOs can be considered the culmination of a historical progression toward a more formal and institutional approach to crime prevention by local residents.

One of the crime prevention strategies increasingly being used by CBOs is civil remedies, which compel third parties to undertake measures to prevent or alleviate crime and disorder problems in their neighborhoods. Most often, these third parties are owners and/or managers of apartment buildings or rental homes that are being used for illegal purposes (drug trafficking, prostitution, etc.) or present a local disorder problem (raucous parties, buildings that have fallen into significant disrepair, etc.). In an article examining the role of community groups in undertaking civil remedies as a crime prevention technique, Roehl (1998, 241) writes that in the United States, "nuisance and drug abatement ordinances and municipal codes are the most common civil laws employed by community organizations, which may or may not work in concert with law enforcement, prosecutors and other government agencies. While civil remedy strategies are not without problems, community organizations report general success in their use."

5.5.7 The Community Crime Prevention Office

In recent years, CCP initiatives have increasingly been delivered through storefront offices, whether they are called community policing (see Chapter 7 for more information on community policing), community safety, or crime prevention offices. Neighborhood groups have been a driving force behind crime prevention offices. With that said, whether it is initiated by a community group or a police agency, most of these storefront offices require an active collaboration between the local community and the police (they are often staffed by a combination of police and civilians, including paid staff and volunteers).

These storefront offices can serve neighborhood residents in both a reactive and proactive manner: they provide visible outlets through which crime prevention services can be coordinated and delivered locally and provide a link between community members, crime prevention practitioners, and the police. Crime prevention offices encourage walk-in and phone-in traffic, take crime reports and tips from residents, coordinate specific crime prevention programs (such as NW), and disseminate literature with crime prevention tips. The offices also undertake crime prevention and community development projects that are not traditionally pursued by the police, such as social development initiatives that attempt to address the root causes of crime, as well as community beautification and development projects.

CASE STUDY 5.6

NEIGHBORHOOD IMPROVEMENT
ASSOCIATION IN DAYTON

Donnelly and Majka (1998) report on a case study that may very well represent one of the most successful community organizing efforts documented in the crime prevention literature. When crime problems began to intensify in Five Oaks, an inner-city, multiracial neighborhood in Dayton, Ohio, more than 400 residents attended a community meeting. Donnelly and Majka attribute the high turnout to the efforts of the Five Oaks Neighborhood Improvement Association (FONIA), a multi-issue group that was well known and respected by local residents and city officials and that already had in place a ready communication network, a strong leadership cadre, and a membership base that was used to recruit other residents through existing social networks. As part of an intensive outreach and communications strategy, "dozens of volunteers 'walked n' talked' every block in the neighborhood knocking on almost 1,800 doors, explaining the purpose of the meeting, and inviting residents to attend." A neighborhood newsletter, which is hand delivered on a monthly basis to all households, played up the meeting. Postcards were also mailed to every household reminding them of the meeting. FONIA also emphasized a decentralized approach to the community's role in addressing local crime problems. Organizers divided the neighborhood into numerous "mini-areas" and then selected captains for each mini-area, who used the same "walk n' talk" process to invite residents to attend a meeting in their mini-area. Each mini-area meeting discussed a proposed strategy developed by a consultant at a previous community-wide meeting, focusing on how it affected their area. Another community-wide meeting was eventually held, wherein issues and concerns discussed in each mini-area meeting were presented, with a view to arriving at a community-wide action plan. More than 300 residents attended this meeting.

While primarily concerned with safety issues, FONIA moved beyond the strict situational-based approach to crime prevention recommended by the consultant and, instead, adopted a more development-based philosophy that emerged from the mini-area meetings. Based on this resolution, committees of community members were established to deal with issues that were viewed as the causes of crime and other local problems, including those concerned with housing, physical environment, residential support services, security, social and recreational programs, and organizational development.

Despite the large turnout at the various community meetings, Donnelly and Majka note that the audience was still disproportionately made up of white homeowners. To ensure better diversity, FONIA amended its constitution to require greater representation from the diverse population on the board from each mini-area. In addition to effective community outreach and micro-level organizing, FONIA's success was also due to its long-standing external linkages. In particular, the neighborhood group was able to secure support and resources for its community safety initiatives from a sympathetic municipal government that had in place structures and resources that encourage citizen participation. FONIA also benefited from the genuine commitment of local residents to a healthy, inclusive, and racially diverse neighborhood (Donnelly and Majka, 1998).

CASE STUDY 5.7

COMMUNITY SAFETY OFFICE IN VANCOUVER

As of the summer of 2003, the Collingwood Community Policing Centre (CPC) was serving the south-central and southeastern portions of Vancouver, British Columbia. The population falling within this jurisdiction is demographically diverse, while the average income of residents is slightly below that for the city as a whole. Founded in 1994, and originally called the Joyce Street Crime Prevention Office, the Collingwood CPC was the first community-based crime prevention storefront office to be opened in Vancouver. In recent years, it formalized its long-standing partnership with the Vancouver Police to the point that it is now called a community policing center.

The office is run by a civilian coordinator, staffed by volunteers, and governed by a board of directors made up of community members. Among the many programs coordinated by the Collingwood CPC are Adopt-a-Block (garbage cleanups), Foot/Pooch/Bike Patrol (citizen patrols), Business Improvement Area Guardians (citizen patrols in the business district), Bike Rodeo (teaching bike safety to kids), Constable Chips (school visitation program), Court Watch (identifying and managing local chronic offenders), Garden Watch (community beautification through the promotion of private and public gardens), Growbusters (a tips line on local marijuana growing operations), It's All about M.E. and Senior Safe Tea (crime prevention education for seniors), Movie in a Park (free movies), Whistle Blower (provision of whistles to use in emergencies), and NW. Many of these programs are administered in conjunction with the Vancouver Police and/or other government agencies.

During an interview in the summer of 2003, the coordinator of the Collingwood CPC estimated that the office had more than 100 active volunteers. The success the Collingwood CPC has enjoyed in attracting volunteers and program participants is due to a number of reasons. It has more than 10 years of activism with the community and a history of strong and stable leadership. The office was founded by a group of long-time community activists and it has had the same coordinator since its founding. Board members, who are required to volunteer at the crime prevention office, are also active in the neighborhood in other capacities. The office undertakes regular needs assessments of the local population and then responds to these needs through appropriate programs and activities. The CPC actively recruits volunteers, including those from outside the community (such as university students) and recognizes the contribution by volunteers and program participants (including awards).

For this coordinator, the most critical factor influencing participation in CCP programs is "whether people care about their community." The key to working with and retaining volunteers in the CPC is "to keep them busy" and to provide them with tasks at their skill level but that will also allow them to learn and build new skills. The Collingwood CPC is also successful because the office is "more than crime prevention … we are also involved in skills development, job search, community development …. We often forget the human side. We need to help build human capacity." The CPC also benefits from a positive working relationship with the Vancouver Police Department (although not without the "occasional disagreement"). It also has strong support—financial and otherwise—from the local business community. This includes rent-free space in a well-resourced, highly visible, and accessible storefront office donated by a local real estate developer (Collingwood Community Policing Centre, n.d.; Schneider, 2007a, 136–137).

In addition to those crime prevention offices that cater to a spatially defined community (i.e., a neighborhood), Vancouver also has two crime prevention offices where the community being served is defined in ethnic terms. The two ethnic-based crime prevention offices are the Chinatown Community Policing Services Office and the Native Liaison Centre. These offices were formed to address the particular needs of these minority populations within Vancouver. The opening of these offices is the result of a joint effort between community members, the Vancouver Police, and various levels of government. The Chinatown office, for example, was initiated through a partnership between three levels of government, the police, and local Chinese groups (represented by the Chinese Benevolent Society). The board of directors consists of representatives of these partners. While it is located in Chinatown, its objective is to serve the Chinese and broader Asian communities in Greater Vancouver.

5.6 CRIME PREVENTION THROUGH COMMUNITY DEVELOPMENT

Some of the greatest challenges facing crime prevention practitioners stem from poverty and related ills that engulf some neighborhoods. It is no coincidence that crime and other threats to community safety are often most intense in these disadvantaged environments. Crime rate statistics, national victimization surveys, and scores of other studies show that crime is unevenly distributed within cities, with crime rates generally the highest in poor, inner-city neighborhoods. According to the Office of Juvenile Justice and Delinquency Prevention (1996), most of the serious violent juvenile crime in the United States is concentrated in a relative handful of neighborhoods. The same neighborhoods have homicide rates twenty times higher than the national average (Sherman et al., 1995). In their 2007 annual report, the Chicago Police Department pointed out that over half of all crime occurred in just 18 of the city's 77 designated communities, while just two of these communities accounted for more than 10% of the city's violent crimes (Chicago Police Department, 2008). For Sherman (1997a, 9), the entire rationale for the federal politics of crime prevention in America is largely "driven by the extreme criminogenic conditions of these relatively few communities in the U.S., areas of concentrated poverty where millions of whites and an estimated one-third of all African-Americans reside."

Pitts and Hope (1997, 38 and 40) write that, in Great Britain, citywide inequalities in crime reflect "the emergent distribution of the new poverty in Britain." British Crime Survey data for fiscal year 2004/2005 showed that one-third of all recorded crime took place in just 40 "high-crime areas." Although the survey results showed that the number of recorded offenses in these high-crime areas fell by a greater percentage than the rest of England and Wales between 2003/2004 and 2004/2005, the authors acknowledge that the property crime rate at both the individual and neighborhood levels still positively correlates with the socioeconomic status of neighborhoods. Households with an annual income of <£5000 were more likely to have experienced at least one burglary in the past year compared with households with a higher incomes and England and Wales as a whole, while neighborhoods with a high level of "physical disorder" were also at a greater risk of property crime (Nicholas et al., 2005, 52–53).

A series of studies undertaken by Statistics Canada in a number of cities in that country also reveals that crime and violence in urban centers are concentrated spatially within more socially disadvantaged, transient, inner-city neighborhoods. Savoie (2008, 7) sums up the findings of this Canadian research as such:

> Collectively, these studies support the notion that urban crime is not distributed equally or randomly. It is, instead, often concentrated in particular areas and associated with other factors related to the population and land use characteristics... These studies demonstrate major differences between the characteristics of high- and lower-crime neighbourhoods. When all other factors are held constant, the level of socio-economic disadvantage of people in a neighbourhood is the factor most strongly associated with the higher rates of violent and property crime in Winnipeg.

Savoie (2008, 7)

In short, concentrated in poor, inner-city neighborhoods are a multitude of adverse factors that simultaneously promote crime and criminogenic conditions: unemployment (especially among young males), poverty, a transient population, weak local institutions, family breakdown, a lack of social cohesion and informal social control, social instability, an overabundance of negative role models for children and youth, violence, access to weapons and drugs, and a relatively large substance-abusing population.

Within this context, one of the great challenges facing Western societies is alleviating those conditions that cause and contribute to crime and criminality within a city's poorest neighborhoods. The challenges inherent in promoting safety, security, and livability in disadvantaged neighborhoods can be especially daunting and have come to epitomize one of the greatest dilemmas in crime prevention today: poor, high-crime, inner-city neighborhoods are often in the most need of community safety programs, yet it is within these neighborhoods that such initiatives are most difficult to implement and sustain.

Crime prevention through community development is an approach that promotes the rebuilding and strengthening of a community for and by the people who live in it. Community development strategies work to strengthen the human and physical capital of neighborhoods by targeting its residents, housing, the local labor market, schools, recreational facilities, businesses, and the natural and built environment. Today's community development approaches to crime prevention owe much to the pioneering work of the Chicago School of Sociology and their landmark CAP.

For Rubin and Rubin (1992, 10), community development is intended to achieve five goals:

1. Improving the quality of life of community members as a whole through the resolution of shared problems
2. Reducing social inequities caused by poverty, racism, sexism, etc.
3. Exercising and preserving democratic values, as part of the process and outcome of community organizing and development
4. Personal self-development and efficacy
5. Social cohesion

For Ersing (2003, 261–262), empowering communities to achieve such developmental goals (or any goals) entails three principles: capacity building, collaboration, and community action. The first principle involves "building the competence or capacity of local residents and groups," which means "identifying the knowledge, talents, skills, and social networks of individuals, groups, and local organizations." Second, opportunities must be created for residents and local organizations to collaborate in resolving problems and effecting positive social change by harnessing the assets, skills, and resources of individuals and groups. The third principle "is the use of advocacy or social action as change strategies" that develop or shift power to those who are marginalized and do not participate in local policy- and decision-making processes. For Ersing, a vital community empowerment goal is to reduce the dependence of poor neighborhoods on external institutions and actors that traditionally play a major role in addressing local problems in these locales (Ersing, 2003, 261–262).

As a crime prevention strategy, community development falls most firmly within the social problem-solving category. In particular, through its emphasis on economic development, it can help address the root causes of criminality. Community development also emphasizes organizing residents, building a socially cohesive neighborhood, and empowering underprivileged groups or neighborhoods, which can also contribute to ameliorating the causes of criminal behavior. At the same time, community organizing and the fostering of social cohesion can lay the foundation for informal social control that is so critical to the community defense model. Even the physical development and beautification of neighborhoods, which are central to community development approaches, are an important CPTED strategy. According to Acosta and Chavis (2007, 651),

> The key components of community development that contribute to its ability to address crime are relationship building; the development of institutional, structural, and economic assets; engagement and collective action by citizens; and sustainable and institutionalized change. Relationship building creates an informal social network that influences citizen behavior and mediates some social conditions that contribute to crime, such as residential instability. Institutional, structural, and economic assets address negative community conditions over time, such as responsibility for neighborhood appearance, informal social control, attention to environmental deterrents to crime, and the promotion of workforce development and economic supports for families.

For the purposes of this chapter, a community-based developmental approach to crime prevention can take one of three (complimentary) forms:

1. Social (socioeconomic) development
2. Community building
3. Physical development

5.6.1 *Social (Socioeconomic) Development*

A community developmental approach to crime prevention addresses the social and economic factors that not only place neighborhoods and its residents at risk of high rates of crime and victimization but also foster the preconditions for criminal and delinquent behavior. Many of the social problem-solving strategies fall within the crime prevention through social development category discussed in Chapter 3 (and as such will only be dealt with briefly here). As Jamieson (2008, 17) notes,

> With the emergence of the concept of crime prevention through social development (CPSD) in the mid 1980s, community mobilization for crime prevention was integrated into the larger enterprise of addressing the "root causes" of crime. CPSD linked community mobilization for crime prevention to larger community development frameworks which focused on a broader vision of community safety and well-being and engaged a wider range of actors from both within and outside the community. Targeted interventions to address individual risk factors, integrated social policies and programs to reduce the structural inequalities that contribute to crime, and strategies to mobilize and engage communities in the enterprise of developing healthier and safer communities all came to the fore.

Within the context of community development, a social problem-solving approach to crime advocates greater public and private investments in (disadvantaged) neighborhoods, while emphasizing a comprehensive array of programs and services that can address criminogenic risk factors. Particular emphasis is usually placed on programs and resources targeting the most vulnerable families, such as young, single, undereducated mothers living in poverty who lack a strong social support network. Programs of this sort benefit children and young people *indirectly* by fostering a more positive and nurturing social environment (e.g., poverty alleviation, supporting good parenting practices and a stable family, adequate housing, strong local schools) and *directly* by fostering resilience within at-risk children and youth (through good nutrition, remedial tutoring, recreational programs, mentorship, social and life skills development, etc.).

From a community economic development perspective, social problem-solving approaches often involve initiatives that strive to bring greater economic prosperity to poor neighborhoods and their residents. Efforts to rescue neighborhoods with concentrated poverty and high crime rates require support for furthering local economic opportunities and reviving labor markets. This is generally accomplished by promoting small businesses as well as attracting companies and entrepreneurs to a neighborhood (through no- or low-interest loans, tax breaks, or technical support), establishing business cooperatives, subsidizing wages of employees, and setting up local entrepreneurial and job searching and training centers.

A social and economic development approach to CCP is premised on research that establishes a positive correlation between socioeconomic status and some of the most important prerequisites for CCP and safer neighborhoods: collective efficacy, an awareness and understanding of local issues, a financial stake in a neighborhood (i.e., home ownership), as well as local social integration, attachment, and cohesion. In other words, research shows that communities with a higher socioeconomic status will be more apt to initiate and sustain a community safety program, while individuals with a higher socioeconomic status are more likely to become involved in such initiatives (Merry, 1981; Skogan and Maxfield, 1981; Greenberg et al., 1982; Taub et al., 1984; Whitaker, 1986; Haeberle, 1987; Dowds and Mayhew, 1994; Skogan, 2004; Schneider, 2007a). As importantly, families and communities with a higher socioeconomic status generally have a lower victimization rate and are less likely to have the social conditions that ferment criminogenic risk factors.

CASE STUDY 5.8

COMMUNITY-BASED, SOCIAL DEVELOPMENTAL APPROACHES TO CRIME IN BRISTOL

Southmead is public housing estate in Bristol, England, that has long had a persistently high crime rate. During the 1950s, the Southmead housing estate was the focus of the Bristol Social Project, which attempted to reduce delinquency and other problems on the estate. Despite this program, the crime and delinquency rate remained stubbornly high throughout the 1970s and 1980s. Youth crime and delinquency, as well as drug use, were viewed as major contributors to the instability of the housing estate. During the late 1980s and 1990s, Southmead was a priority for the newly established Bristol Safer Cities Project, a Home Office-funded program that implemented a number of social, managerial, and environmental interventions that were directly or indirectly aimed at reducing crime and improving safety in the area. The many initiatives that have been implemented in Southmead to address crime and disorder are summarized in the following:

1. Southmead Sector Local Action Group: This group is the local strategic and coordinating vehicle for crime prevention and community safety efforts. The group has senior representatives from the police, city council, and the local health service and plays an important coordinating role among the various government and nongovernmental agencies providing services in Southmead.

2. Better Together (Southmead Family Project): Established in 1992, a multidisciplinary team identifies and works with at-risk youth, especially those from broken homes and those not attending or expelled from school or experiencing difficulty in their schooling. Summer activities are also coordinated for at-risk children and young people.

3. Southmead Day Nursery: The nursery provides traditional day-care services for children as well as intensive support and education for preschool children and their parents who have been identified as high risk by social workers.

4. Southmead Drugs Project: This grassroots organization provides treatment for those abusing substances. The project aims to reduce the harm caused by addiction and also helps clients with job training and employment placement (in conjunction with other local groups).

5. The Voice of Southmead: This organization began as a grassroots response by residents to the drug problems on the estate and combines a police enforcement approach with sports activities for at-risk children and youth.

6. Southmead Youth Sports Development: This initiative emerged from the desire of those involved in the Voice of Southmead to offer positive activities for young people and to help raise their self-esteem. Although focused on sports, the initiative also tries to meet other interests and needs of young people.

7. Team Mead: This program enables youth to legitimately ride motorbikes under adult supervision. The program currently works with teenagers aged 13–19, who are taken to sites outside Southmead three times a month.

8. Southmead Youth Centre: The center provides a range of activities for local at-risk youth (ages 13–19). The support programs offered include "leisure and personal development" (adventure activities, art, computer games, cultural activities, music; sports, dances), "relationships and emotions" (training and counseling on emotional well-being), "keeping safe" (responding to abuse, bullying, child protection, self-harm), "health issues" (drugs, nutrition, sexual health), and "employment and jobs" (careers advice and trends, help in preparing job applications and CVs and in job hunting).

9. The Ranch Adventure Playground: The playground caters to a younger age group (ages 7–15 years) than the Youth Centre and has indoor and outdoor facilities managed by full-time staff. It operates early evenings during the school year and all day during school holidays.

10. The Southmead On Track Programme: This program supports the social and academic development of at-risk children (ages 4–12 years). The focus is on engaging children and their families who are at a high risk of social exclusion, isolation, discrimination, and academic failure.

12. Southmead Federation for Learning: This is a network of groups and individuals that support lifelong learning through community education and training activities for adults and others who are not formally engaged in education.

13. Trymside Environmental Project: This project has promoted a number of environmental improvements and greening initiatives in cooperation with local schools and residents. The project employs professional gardeners who work with local residents.

14. The White Hall: This is a church-sponsored center that provides rooms and meeting places for a number of community development and youth outreach initiatives.

15. Southmead Community Centre: A long-established building that provides a limited range of recreational activities for older residents.

16. Southmead Shopping Centre Closed Circuit Television: This is a scheme originally funded by the Home Office that has enabled the installation of cameras around the main shopping and services area. The cameras are monitored at a centralized 24 h control center.

17. Neighborhood Renewal Programme: This is the local application of national and municipal government initiatives to regenerate the country's most disadvantaged areas. The goal of the program is to decentralize control of public services and resources so that they are more responsive and accountable to local development needs.

According to one evaluation report, there is sufficient evidence to conclude that criminal incidents decreased in the Southmead estate during most of the 1990s (and while the crime rate began to increase in 2000, the increase was not as large as that experienced by Bristol as a whole). Using the crime rate for the city of Bristol as a benchmark, Southmead moved from being an area with an above-average crime rate to one with a below-average rate. There was widespread agreement that conditions in Southmead had stabilized, that there was less disorder and incivility, and that those still causing trouble were a very small hard-core group of youth (Shaftoe, 2002).

5.6.2 *Community Building*

This category includes programs that focus on developing social cohesion in a neighborhood. This entails efforts to transform a spatial grouping of people (a neighborhood) into a socially cohesive group of residents who are bound by enduring personal ties and networks, a high level of social interaction, and common goals, norms, and values (Leighton, 1988, 359; Crank, 1994, 336–337). Writing in the *Encyclopedia of Community*, Briggs (2003, 246) defines community building as "a variety of intentional efforts to organize and strengthen social connections or build common values that promote collective goals (or both). Literally, community building means building more community (an interim goal) as a way of achieving some set of desired outcomes (safer neighborhoods, healthier children and families, better-preserved cultural traditions, more profitable businesses, etc.)."

Community building is central to crime prevention, at the very least because research has shown that neighborhoods with strong local social cohesion and collective efficacy are more likely to successfully mobilize around local social problems. Some of the essential "domains" of social cohesion, according to Forrest and Kearns (2001, 2129), are the existence of common values and objectives, participation in civic affairs, informal social control, tolerance, respect for difference, social solidarity, reductions in wealth disparity, acknowledgment of social obligations and willingness to assist others, strong social networks, a high degree of social interaction, and an attachment and commitment to where one lives. Similarly, activist communities are contingent upon trust and reciprocity among members, part of what Putnam et al. (1993) and Putnam (1995) refers to as "social capital." Without sufficient social cohesion or social capital, neighborhoods are deprived of a foundation upon which development strategies and vibrant community organizations can be built and sustained. A community development approach to crime prevention recognizes the importance of fostering and sustaining social cohesion and social capital within neighborhoods as a foundation for local collective problem solving and the broader goals of a healthy, self-governing, inclusive, politically efficacious community.

For crime prevention purposes, the goal of community building is to turn a neighborhood into a healthy, prosperous, well-functioning community, complete with a strong level of informal social control. Community building efforts revolve around groups, activities, and institutions that value a high level of local social interaction (through block parties, neighbor flea markets and yard sales, community gardens, etc.). Social interaction—in particular, positive interpersonal communications and face-to-face dialogue—has long been viewed as a principal community building tactic to foster social cohesion. One of the most effective (and enjoyable) ways to foster interaction and dialogue at the local level are neighborhood-based social gatherings, commonly referred to as block parties. As Walsh (1997, 46) writes, "celebrating the concept of living together" as neighbors and enjoying one another's company is a successful way to highlight the importance of community. Block parties give neighbors a chance to meet one another in a relaxed social setting and can be conveniently held in backyards, parks, schools, community centers, or on the street. Social gatherings can be structured to foster community building: potluck dinners promote cooperation, coordination, and sharing; games for children, youth, and adults can integrate exercises that build trust and teamwork; and in multicultural communities, social gatherings create the perfect opportunity to learn about different cultural traditions, thereby diffusing racial, ethnic, or religious stereotypes and divisions. Neighborhood social gatherings can come at the end of a community development activity, such as a meeting, a block cleanup, or a fund-raiser (Dobson, 2005).

Modifications to the physical environment have also been touted as a way to help build community. Architectural as well as urban planning and design theories propose that the physical environment can be designed to foster emotional attachments to a locality, defining the character and identity of a neighborhood, and encouraging social interaction and cohesion. According to Talen (1999), the home and neighborhood design philosophy called *new urbanism* attempts to build a sense of community through the careful design and integration of private residential space with surrounding public space. Social interaction is promoted by designing residences in such a way that people are encouraged to get out of their houses and into the public sphere. One way to achieve this is by limiting private space: lots and setbacks are small, houses are positioned close to sidewalks, and porches that face the street are encouraged. Personal space is, in a sense, sacrificed in order to increase the density of acquaintanceship and the nurturing of a vigorous community spirit. As far as density and scale are concerned, a sense of community can be promoted through small-scale, well-defined neighborhoods with clear boundaries and a natural center (preferably an inviting public space). When smaller scales are juxtaposed with increased residential density, face-to-face interaction is further promoted. Streets also have an overt social purpose in new urbanism and are designed to accommodate the pedestrian, to encourage street life, and to increase social encounters among residents. Public space is used for similar goals: neighborhood gathering places are encouraged, emphasizing parks and civic centers (Talen, 1999).

Specific urban design strategies can also be used to "create identity and a sense of pride for fragmented neighborhoods," writes urban planner Sherry Plaster (2002, 19–20). The design imperatives of *placemaking* include the use of names (which provides a sense of local identity), aesthetically pleasing functional features (e.g., clocks, parks, sidewalks, lighting, community rooms, transit stops), signage (for information and identification), landscaping and public art works (which increase the aesthetics of a locality), and historical landmarks (which link residents to a neighborhood's history). Dobson (2005) suggests that a distinctive community identity or "expression" can be achieved through such physical design features as community-made signs and markers that define a neighborhood's boundaries (residents in Seattle name their neighborhoods and then help design colorful street signs to mark the boundaries) or community-made signs that assert a strong sense of informal social control (residents of one Vancouver street have hand-painted signs that identify the street and ask motorists to slow down and watch for children playing).

5.6.3 Physical Development and Beautification

An attractive, clean, and well-maintained neighborhood can play a role in a broader strategy to resist crime and disorder. Physical deterioration is both a result of and a contributor to crime and disorder and sends a message to residents, outsiders, and especially potential offenders that no one cares. It can also undermine many of the

---

CASE STUDY 5.9

COMMUNITY BUILDING THROUGH ARCHITECTURAL DESIGN IN MARYLAND

In the Glendarden Apartments, a government-subsidized housing complex in Glendarden, Maryland, a planning and architectural team determined that one way to help address the high crime rate was to "totally redesign the complex, provide a comprehensive security program, and, most critically, involve the residents of Glendarden" (Tell, 1990, 209). Emphasis was placed on deterring drug trafficking and related crime through an architectural design that would help create a sense of community based on the residents' pride in their surroundings. To enhance a "neighbor-to-neighbor atmosphere and provide a bridge between residents and surrounding Glendarden community, a centrally located building was converted from residential use to a social services building" (Tell, 1990, 209). Also in the building was space for youth development activities, a day care, a health center, and a branch of the Glendarden Police Department.

While no estimates have been provided on the impact on crime, those involved in this project have cited a new attitude among residents toward their home and community and have adopted the slogan "Glendarden: Hope, Dreams, Reality" (Tell, 1990, 212).

CASE STUDY 5.10

BEAUTIFYING A BUS STATION IN DURHAM COUNTY, ENGLAND

Local government agencies and community groups in England's Durham County chose to reduce fear of crime at a bus station by cleaning and repairing it (which was carried out by offenders serving community sentences). The widespread perception of the centrally located and frequently used bus station was that it was "poorly maintained, an unpleasant place to be in, and a place where there was an increased risk of crime and antisocial behavior as compared to other areas of the city." This perception was supported by police statistics, which showed a high volume of criminal and disorderly acts taking place in and around the station. The beautification project was premised on the assumption that transforming the bus station into a "cleaner and more salubrious place would help to improve people's general perceptions of it, which would be likely to include the bus station's perceived safety." The beautification project concentrated on redecorating, repainting, and removing graffiti.

A survey of the general public revealed that the project achieved a degree of success in improving the public's perceptions of the bus station with regard to crime and antisocial behavior. The results of the interviews show a reduction in the perceived levels of overall crime in the vicinity of the bus station, a decrease in perceptions that one would be a victim of crime, and a decrease in the perceived likelihood of witnessing crime (Palmer et al., 2005).

---

essential prerequisites of CCP, such as a sense of neighborhood pride and attachment. Accordingly, physical community development initiatives—including beautification projects (flowers, gardens, murals, banners); repairing and maintaining dilapidated buildings, streets, parks, and other public spaces and facilities; razing abandoned buildings and replacing them with community gardens or parks; fixing potholes; removing garbage and graffiti; and towing away deserted cars—send out the message that people do care about their neighborhood. Clean, attractive, and well-maintained neighborhoods also promote a greater use of public spaces by residents, which increases natural surveillance opportunities (more *eyes and ears* on the streets).

5.7 COMPREHENSIVE COMMUNITY-BASED APPROACHES TO CRIME PREVENTION

The different strategies described in this chapter are complementary and, for best results in maximizing community safety, should be pursued simultaneously. A comprehensive approach to combating crime at the local level involves a wide range of suitable measures from each of the major crime prevention approaches (CPSD, situational, community defense and development, law enforcement, problem-oriented policing, etc.), which are delivered through a number of different institutions (the family, schools, places, labor markets, etc.), via a multiagency partnership approach that revolves around the mobilization and empowerment of the local community. Just as important, a comprehensive approach to CCP must be problem oriented, in that the solutions are appropriate for the crime and criminality problems experienced in a particular locale.

A comprehensive approach is especially important in those neighborhoods where crime and its underlying causes are endemic and strongly ingrained in the local social environment. This includes public housing complexes—government-subsidized, multi-residential housing developments that cater to low-income families—which are particularly challenging environments for the implementation of crime prevention programs. In addition to social environmental factors that provide a breeding ground for criminogenic conditions (poverty, overcrowding, a high proportion of undereducated single parents, a high rate of crime, including violence, drug trafficking, and gangs), the multiresidential makeup of most social housing makes crime prevention even more difficult (multiresidential developments are generally characterized by high rates of population turnover and lower levels of social cohesion, territoriality, and informal social control).

There are a number of factors affecting crime, community safety, and other quality-of-life issues in multiresidential social housing that must be taken into consideration when developing a comprehensive crime prevention plan for these environments. These measures, adapted from Fagan et al. (1998), are as follows:

> *Management*: Vigilant, motivated, dedicated, and caring managers (and staff) are essential to effective crime prevention in multiresidential, government-subsidized housing. Managers are key to ensuring the upkeep of the property, are responsible for overseeing security, serve as community leaders and organizers, are a conduit between tenants and the senior management of a government housing authority, and can play a major role in identifying and evicting problem tenants.

> *Admission and eviction policies*: Screening out potentially problematic tenants and the power to efficiently evict existing problem tenants are essential when addressing crime problems in multiresidential developments. Some social housing authorities, as well as private apartment building owners, screen out prospective tenants based on criminal history and drug-related offenses. In some cases, tenants are required to sign contracts stating that they agree to eviction if they lie on their tenancy application or are convicted of a criminal offense while living in the complex.

> *Tenant associations*: Some government-subsidized housing developments have tenant associations that can play an important crime prevention role. A tenant association can be a key player in mobilizing residents around local issues and in pressing housing management for appropriate services, resources, and policies. It can also act as a bridge between residents and the housing management, local police departments, social service agencies, and community organizations. A strong tenant association can contribute to community stability, cohesion, and activism, all of which have a significant impact on crime and community safety.

> *Physical design*: Few, if any, social housing complexes take crime prevention and safety into consideration when they are designed and built. A comprehensive approach to crime in these environments demands a spatial and physical design that can help reduce the opportunities for crime while promoting a sense of community among residents.

A sense of community: Like any neighborhood, the level of social cohesion in a social housing complex will go a long way in determining the ability of local residents to mobilize around crime problems. Public housing projects must battle a multitude of concentrated social and socioeconomic factors that frustrate social cohesion and informal social control (e.g., poverty, ethnic and racial heterogeneity, crime, lack of personal efficacy, high population turnover).

Residents perceptions: Residents' own perceptions of the housing complex in which they live can have a profound influence on their own level of vigilance and involvement in crime prevention activities. The length of residents' tenancy, their sense of belonging, and their connections to the larger community all affect their participation in community safety initiatives.

Policing: Some larger social housing authorities have their own police agencies or security personnel. Larger social housing projects without internal security often require special and intensified police attention. Whether it is an internal or external presence, the impact that the police can have in these environments is contingent upon a number of factors. These include their relationship with housing management and tenants, the perceptions of such environments by police officers, and the type of policing undertaken (ideally, the police should rely on a mix of law enforcement, problem-oriented policing, as well as community policing).

As importantly, for high-crime, high-risk, socially disadvantaged neighborhoods, a comprehensive approach to community-based crime prevention requires an integration of social developmental approaches (with emphasis on early interventions for high-risk families and children), education (increased resources for local schools, enhanced after-school tutoring and remedial help, increased dropout prevention and recovery), labor market approaches (job training and placement), community organizing (mobilizing and empowering local residents), community development (fostering social cohesion and community beautification), leadership training and development, and local economic (small businesses and entrepreneurial training) development.

5.8   CRITIQUES OF AND CHALLENGES TO CCP

Research and project evaluations have shown that applied CCP models have fallen short of the expectations set by their theoretical prescriptions. A host of empirical studies indicate that various CCP projects have had only modest or no impact on crime and fear of crime. Studies also reveal that CCP programs are often unable to engineer the social and behavioral preconditions (i.e., collective action, social interaction, territoriality) necessary to reach their objectives.

Three leading crime prevention scholars have conducted comprehensive reviews of the CCP program evaluation literature (Rosenbaum, 1988; Hope, 1995; Sherman, 1997d). Each of these authors has reached similar conclusions: a review of CCP program evaluations finds generally little evidence that local, collective crime prevention programs have achieved their desired impact. Rosenbaum (1988) concludes there is little hard evidence to assert that CCP is effective in reducing community crime

CASE STUDY 5.11

COMMUNITY BUILDING IN A COUNCIL ESTATE IN CHESHIRE

In 1976, the National Association for the Care and Resettlement of Offenders (NACRO), in combination with the Social and Community Planning and Research Agency of the British Government, began work in the Cunningham Road Housing Estate in Widnes, Cheshire. At the time, the public housing development had a population of 1600, half of which were under the age of 17 years. When the program started, the Cunningham estates had one of the highest crime rates in the area and vandalism was rife. Much of the estate was in a severe state of disrepair: "old houses were boarded up, others had broken windows; gardens were untended; fences were a jumble of corrugated iron, wire, and old boards. Shops were barricaded with steel shutters and daubed with graffiti. Streets and pavements were in poor condition." The tenants were demoralized, apathetic, and hostile to the housing management and the police (Geason and Wilson, 1990).

The two agencies embarked on a strategy that focused on nurturing residents' sense of local belonging, attachment, and responsibility, which in turn would (hopefully) spark an increased effort by residents to look after, improve, and protect their community. The team assembled for the project first consulted with tenants to have them identify and prioritize local problems. Through these consultations, the residents expressed their insecurity due to crime, incivilities, and vandalism, which they blamed on local youth. Residents also felt helpless to change things for the better, which stemmed in part from a high level of dissatisfaction with the poor repairs and maintenance record of the management of the Cunningham estate.

With assistance from NACRO and others, the tenants gradually began to overcome their feelings of helplessness and apathy. Community-wide meetings brought residents together for the first time, which helped nurture an increased level of social cohesion and empowered the tenants to negotiate and demand action from the estate management. A Residents' Association was established, which began lobbying the management for more timely and thorough maintenance and repairs. Their lobbying proved successful as roads, streetlights, and buildings were fixed, and a police officer was assigned to the estate at the request of tenants. The association also took the lead in addressing some of the causes of the youth problems on the estate by organizing recreational activities for young people. A playground was opened near the estate; a *play leader* was appointed, who organized mothers to help supervise and plan activities for the kids. The housing management allowed tenants to put personal touches on the exterior of their dwellings, such as painting their front doors, planting hedges, and erecting fences. The teenagers on the estate became involved by painting murals and planting trees, and a long-planned Youth and Community Centre opened nearby.

Although crime and vandalism did not disappear, these problems did decrease. Very little additional money was spent on the Cunningham Road project that was not already allocated to the area, although some was transferred from other budgets so that small repairs could be done quickly (Hedges, 1979; Geason and Wilson, 1990).

rates, encouraging collective action, or building community cohesion, a result he blames on theory failure, program implementation deficiencies, and the lack of reliable research findings:

> Perhaps the most important set of findings to emerge from these evaluations is that community organizing was unable to activate the intervening social behaviors that are hypothesized as necessary (according to informal social control and opportunity reduction models) to produce the desired changes in crime, fear and social integration. Specifically, the researchers reported very few changes in social interaction, surveillance, stranger recognition, crime reporting, home protection behaviors, feelings of control, efficacy and responsibility, satisfaction with the neighborhood and attitudes towards the police.
>
> **Rosenbaum (1988, 362)**

Hope (1995, 23) argues that "much of the effort to alter the structure of communities in order to reduce crime has not been noticeably successful or sustainable." Sherman (1997a, 33) states "there are no community-based programs of 'proven effectiveness' by scientific standards to show with reasonable certainty that they 'work' in certain kinds of settings."

The majority of studies examining participation in CCP suggests that such programs have had minimal success in initiating and sustaining the participation of neighborhood residents. The neighborhoods that are most reluctant to organize are those that are most in need of CCP programs: low-income, heterogeneous, transient, high-crime, inner-city neighborhoods (Podolefsky and Dubow, 1981; Lavrakas and Herz, 1982; Taub et al., 1984; Rosenbaum et al., 1985; Forst and Bazemore, 1986; Lindsay and McGillis, 1986; Fagan, 1987; Hope, 1988; Sherman, 1997c; Schneider, 2007a).

While the disappointing findings of CCP program evaluations have led some to argue that implementation failures have not allowed for a sufficient test of the CCP theory, the consistency of these research findings has forced researchers to call into question the very theoretical foundations of CCP. Lewis et al. (1988, 114) believe that "the theoretical underpinnings of this collective strategy are questionable in several respects and should be reconsidered." Skogan (1990, 170) contends it may be that "the theory upon which disorder and crime prevention programs are based is faulty."

Questions revolving around the theoretical foundations of CCP have stemmed from the inability of local crime prevention programs to spur a broad-based mobilization of residents. Rosenbaum (1986, 114) targets the sanguine assumption that given the opportunity to participate in NW, most citizens would find the program appealing and would become involved regardless of social, demographic, or neighborhood characteristics. Rosenbaum points out that most evidence indicates that if given the opportunity, residents in the majority of high-crime neighborhoods would not participate.

Some argue that community residents refrain from participating because their role will always be subservient to that of the police and policy makers. This problem is a legacy of the state-centered approach to crime control that dominated much of the twentieth century. It is also reflected in criticisms that the state and police agencies have failed to live up to the ideals of crime prevention and community policing, which emphasize a greater decentralization of decision-making power to communities (McPherson and Siloway, 1981; Garofalo and McLeod, 1989; Marx, 1989; Walker and Walker, 1993; Garland, 1996; Fielding, 2001; Miller, 2001; Pavlich, 2002). While CCP theory emphasizes a subordinate or partnership role for the state in local crime prevention, studies in the United States and Britain indicate that most CCP programs are planned, funded, administered, and controlled by the state. According to Gary Marx (1989, 503), since the early 1970s, CCP models in the United States have been funded and guided by federal agencies, organized and implemented by police forces, and evaluated by government policy makers and academics. This led him to characterize most CCP programs as "top-down outside expert model[s]." McPherson and Siloway (1981) made similar critiques in their evaluation of the U.S. Federal Community Anti-Crime Program initiative that allocated $30 million to fight crime through direct grants to community groups. The authors conclude that a heavy federal involvement in program planning and implementation rendered the local crime prevention initiatives ineffective.

King (1988) laments the centralizing tendencies within crime prevention initiatives in Great Britain where the Home Office maintains a direct control over funding and the broader policy agenda. Likewise, in his analysis of the Labour Party's crime prevention policies, Pavlich (2002, 120) argues that communities are provided with a "dubious managerial 'freedom'" to choose from a list of crime prevention programs prioritized by the government, while retaining "control over important funding decisions and monitoring the entire process through protocols, accountancy and evaluation." For Garland (1996), crime prevention is part of the neoliberal strategy of "governance at a distance," which simply represents another mode of exercising power. Under this new crime control model, the state does not diminish or become merely a nightwatchman. On the contrary, it retains all its traditional functions and takes on a new set of coordinating and activating roles, which "leaves the centralized state machine more powerful than before, with an extended capacity for action and influence" (Garland, 1996, 454). In their guidelines for citizen participation in community policing prepared for the Canadian government, Walker and Walker (1993, 18) put it quite simply: "A crucial question to ask regarding community policing programs is, how far the police are willing to go to share their authority with the citizen? At first glance, the answer would appear to be not very far at all."

In their critique of the U.S. Federal Community Anti-Crime Program, McPherson and Siloway (1981) contend that a top-down approach to crime prevention may limit community participation because the legalistic "conceptualization of the crime problem and crime prevention program at the federal level serves to limit the range of problem alternatives that would be considered in local programs." Programs formulated by governments and the police and then "sold" to community groups "may not be the ones the community would freely choose and as a result citizens may decide not to get involved" (McPherson and Siloway, 1981, 153–155). Lisa Miller (2001) concludes that a low level of participation by African-American residents in the Weed and Seed crime prevention program in a Seattle neighborhood may have stemmed from their perceptions that the lead organizers (mostly from federal and state government agencies) were out of step with their priorities and preferred strategies. As she states in her conclusion, the results of her study "highlighted the ways in which the original program reflected the priorities of national crime control agendas and local law enforcement goals more than a genuine interest in community revitalization and involvement" (Miller, 2001, 168). van Steden et al. (2011, 436–437) also point out that "considerable clashes of interest between the police and residential participants in local safety projects are not inconceivable. Police officers may view active citizens as troublesome "loudmouths" who only create problems, not solve them."

NW is perhaps the most vivid example of the control that the police agencies maintain over CCP programs. According to Garofalo and McLeod (1989, 337), NW does not appear to be effective in preventing crime, mobilizing residents, or building community because "most are not emergent, in the sense of being devised and initiated by residents on their own." The authors discovered in their survey of NW programs in the United States that the police usually play the lead role in organizing, educating, training, and motivating residents. "In short, Neighborhood Watch is generally not something created by residents in an area to meet their self-defined needs; rather it is a set of predefined rules, proce-dures and structures that the residents can either adopt or reject. As such, one may argue that the extensiveness of police involvement in forming and managing Neighborhood Watch programs is detrimental to the process of citizens developing their own solutions to their problems..." (Garofalo and McLeod, 1989, 341). For Pepinsky (1989), a primary problem with NW is that it turns management of neighborhood activity over to outsiders: the police. "It offers few opportunities for sustained interaction among residents."

The strategic approach of NW has also been criticized for being ineffective in encouraging greater participation because an active involvement of the citizenry is discouraged through the inherently passive nature of their *observe and report* func-tion. According to Garofalo and McLeod (1989, 337), "potential NW participants are not really asked to exercise a great deal of additional social control; they are asked to be more active in initiating social control by the police. While these messages may help to entice adoption of NW by people who are wary of making time commitments, it is not the kind of message that stimulates people to devote a great deal of effort to the solu-tion of neighborhood problems." Moreover, while the police stress the use of the 911 emergency system by local citizens, this system has become overloaded, which delays police response time and can further erode citizen confidence and participation in NW.

In short, according to Jamieson (2008, 22), "in practical terms, developing demo-cratic, inclusive processes and finding ways to equitably share power are enormous challenges. It takes time and adequate support to residents to allow them to participate effectively and develop confidence in their capacity …. Establishing the right structures and processes to enable community residents to be meaningful partners and equitably participate alongside services and agencies has proven challenging in many neighbor-hood regeneration efforts." More cynically, Carr (2012, 408) argues, "a true negotiated order where communities are equal partners in the coproduction of safety is illusory."

Greenberg et al. (1984) did not find that informal social control variables were predictive of differences in crime rates and concluded that there is little evidence that the level of informal social control is related to crime. According to Greenberg and colleagues (1984, 58–59), it may be that informal social control is effective in deterring crime only if it reaches some threshold level not reached in high-crime neighborhoods: "A strong ethnic identification or another binding force may be necessary for informal social control to reach that level." Similar findings were reported by Foster et al. (1993), who suggested that a significant obstacle to crime prevention initiatives in council estates in England was the instability of residential communities due in part to social heterogeneity. These studies suggest that the informal social control of public space will only be successful in stable environments where people have strong social, fam-ily, or ethnic ties through long periods of residence (Sampson, 1985). Unfortunately, this type of social cohesion is often not present in those neighborhoods that are most vulnerable to property, personal, and consensual crime.

Lewis (1979) rejects any crime prevention theory geared toward creating commu-nity. For him, "community is a context in which collective responses take place, not a consequence which can be manipulated through the implementation of a collective response." According to Skogan (1990, 170), most crime prevention theories focus on enhancing the capacity of communities to intervene and to extend the net of informal social control. "However, we have seen how difficult it is to engineer changes in subtle aspects of social relationships." He adds that for "whatever the reason, research does not suggest that theories emphasizing the role of social processes in informal crime control will steer organizing efforts in the right direction" (Skogan, 1988, 64). These indictments of CCP have led Rosenbaum (1987, 103) to question "whether collective citizen action is an effective strategy for controlling crime, reducing fear of crime and building a sense of community."

Stable, middle- and upper-middle neighborhoods have enjoyed greater success in implementing and sustaining effective crime prevention initiatives. For Crawford (1994), however, the community defense model of crime prevention that predominates in these neighborhoods is grounded in social conflict that involves the policing of, and interventions against, certain individuals and groups outside of that neighborhood. The territoriality promoted by opportunity-reduction programs like NW is imbued with a xenophobia that emphasizes the alien nature of outsiders, often overlaid by class-based and racial overtones, and the threat they pose to their neighborhood and its values (including property values). The opportunity-reduction approach to crime, according to Boostrom and Henderson (1983, 28–29), emphasizes the sanctity of private property and the responsibility of those with a stake in maintaining private property to the police those who have no such stake. Therefore, "this model reinforces the power of those who own property in our capitalist social structure and reinforces the traditional suspicion and fear they feel toward the propertyless."

Thus, critics charge that the community defense model is largely based on an inherent conflict between social groupings that revolves around socioeconomic cleavages, especially when they are manifested in the interrelated politics of identity, crime, and crime prevention (e.g., the propertied middle class as victims vs. the poor as offenders). This conflict between social groups is played out in spatial terms at the neighborhood level through opportunity-reduction crime prevention programs, which are largely carried out by the middle class to defend themselves, their property, and their shared identity (Schneider, 2007a). It is no wonder that collective, community-based situational crime prevention interventions are referred to as the community defense model. According to the ICPC (2010, 117), "it is the challenge of participatory crime prevention to reduce tendencies to blame or propose exclusionary approaches, and promote inclusionary approaches able to reinforce democracy and social inclusion. Developing inclusive and transformatory participatory methods and processes which avoid stigmatizing, blaming and encouraging vigilante punitive responses to crime, is a challenge for practitioners."

5.9   CONCLUSION

This chapter has provided a theoretical and empirical overview of CCP. The theory behind CCP proposes that the implementation of crime prevention programs will harness the shared concerns that neighborhood residents have over crime, which will then lead to their participation in local initiatives. The ascension in the popularity and theoretical currency of CCP can be attributed such instrumental actions as rational planning, proactive interventions, citizen involvement, and multi-institutional partnerships.

Citizen participation is central to the theory of CCP because it is asserted that only through collective efforts will a neighborhood be able to invoke such essential elements of CCP as surveillance, collective action, social cohesion, and informal social control.

Notwithstanding the critiques of CCP, van Steden et al. (2011, 435–436), believe there are a number of societal benefits accruing from citizen participation in crime prevention. There is a reduced criminal justice cost to governments. As Jamieson (2008, 20) argues, "the claim that community-based responses are more efficient and cost-effective than institutional ones is compelling to the state and individual taxpayers alike." CCP can also contribute to "the 'opening up' of professionals to the general public, better synergy in the flow of information between authorities and the public and, hence, improvements in the effectiveness of criminal justice processes." According to the ICPC (2008b, 18), "Crime prevention is essential to sustainable development, as is the prevention of problems linked to poverty, health, education, and urban development. In fact, vibrant communities are not possible without safety and social cohesion."

The popularity of CCP is also based upon its association with the highly idealized notion of community. Indeed, the normative basis for the CCP theory is the quest for *community* and the role its essential requisites—such as social interaction and cohesion, a shared identity, a sense of belonging among residents, collective efficacy, and informal social control—play in controlling crime and disorder at the local level. Within the praxis of CCP, the sociological concept of community is regarded as the essential resource to be mobilized in the battle against crime and the quest for the socially cohesive neighborhood has become a universal aspiration for many social theorists, practitioners, and policy makers dealing with the ills of modern societies. As Wilson (1976, 65) observes, unlike such words as state or government, the word community rarely seems to be cast in a disparaging light. The notion of a community-based approach to crime prevention speaks to the highest ideals of civic life, civil society, democracy, cooperation, and small-town morality. Simply put, "'Community' now reigns as the modern elixir for much of what allegedly ails American society" (Sampson, 2002, 213).

Despite the attractiveness and benefits of CCP, research indicates that many projects fail to reach both their substantive goals (i.e., a reduction in or prevention of crime) and their process-oriented objectives (e.g., widespread participation, social interaction, etc.). This is especially true in socially disadvantaged neighborhoods that are most in need of crime prevention initiatives. Participants in CCP initiatives tend to be in the middle- or upper-income range, well-educated, white, middle-aged, longer-term, home-owning residents who are socially integrated and committed to their neighborhood. As a result, CCP programs predominate in middle- and upper-income neighborhoods, while they are least likely to be found in low-income, transient, high-crime neighborhoods. The inability of CCP programs to effect the broad-based mobilization of residents, especially in disadvantaged neighborhoods, has forced some researchers to question the theoretical foundations of CCP.

5.10 DISCUSSION QUESTIONS AND EXERCISES

1. Do you believe it is realistic for private citizens to play a role in crime control?
2. How does CCP compare to situational and social developmental approaches? What do the three hold in common? What are their differences?
3. Should *community* be considered a crime prevention *institution*?

4. Identify and examine a crime prevention group in your city or town (or on the Internet). What type of crime or disorder problems does it address? What specific crime prevention strategies does it pursue? What are its strengths and weaknesses in terms of attracting participants? Mobilizing neighborhoods? Preventing crime from occurring?

5. Collective action is a key part of CCP. But the argument has been made that people are no longer rooted in their neighborhood (i.e., we have lost the sense of community in advanced Western societies). Do you believe there is still the potential to mobilize communities around crime? What are the obstacles to a more robust participation of private citizens and communities in crime control? What needs to be done to maximize the participation of private citizens in CCP initiatives?

6. The *implant* or *transplant* hypothesis raises important questions about the ability of disadvantaged neighborhoods to mobilize around crime. In your opinion, can social cohesion be nurtured in low-income, heterogeneous, high-crime neighborhoods? Can informal social control exist or be induced in neighborhoods that are characterized by a low level of social cohesion? Do you believe that the introduction of collective crime prevention programs can help foster social cohesion and informal social control? Do you believe that the introduction of crime prevention programs can promote a collective, active, and vigilant stand against crime and disorder by neighborhood residents?

7. There have been a number of criticisms of CCP. Research has also suggested that programs like NW do not work. What would you recommend to make crime prevention programs more effective in terms of attracting participants? Mobilizing neighborhoods? Preventing crime from occurring?

5.11 IMPORTANT TERMS

Citizen patrols
Collective action
Community
Community building
Community defense model
Community development model
Community organizing
Informal social control
Physical development/beautification
Neighborhood
Neighborhood watch (NW)
Social cohesion
Social development
Social interaction

FURTHER READING

Bureau of Justice Assistance, U.S. Department of Justice, Comprehensive Communities Program: A unique way to reduce crime and enhance public safety, Bureau of Justice Assistance fact sheet, Washington, DC: Bureau of Justice Assistance. December 2000, https://www.ncjrs.gov/pdffiles1/bja/fs000267.pdf (accessed January, 2013).

Crawford, A., Crime prevention and community safety, in *The Oxford Handbook of Criminology*, 4th edn., Maguire, M., Morgan, R., and Reiner, R., Eds., Oxford University Press, Oxford, U.K., 2006, Chap. 26.

Hope, T., Community crime prevention, in *Building a Safer Society: Strategic Approaches to Crime Prevention*, Tonry, M. and Farrington, D., Eds., University of Chicago Press, Chicago, IL, 1995, pp. 21–89.

Rosenbaum, D., Community crime prevention: A review and synthesis of the literature, *Justice Quarterly* 1988; 5:323–395.

Rosenbaum, D. and Schuk, A., Comprehensive community partnerships for preventing crime, in *The Oxford Handbook of Crime Prevention*, Welsh, B. and Farrington, D., Eds., Oxford University Press, New York, 2012, pp. 226–246.

Schneider, S., *Refocusing Crime Prevention: Collective Action and the Quest for Community*, University of Toronto Press, Toronto, Ontario, Canada, 2007.

Welsh, B.C. and Hoshi, A., Communities and crime prevention, in *Evidence-Based Crime Prevention*, revised edn., Sherman, L.W., Farrington, D.P., Welsh, B.C., and MacKenzie, D.L., Eds., Routledge, New York, 2006, pp. 165–197.

INTERNET RESOURCES

Australian Institute of Criminology, Crime and the Community, http://www.aic.gov.au/crime_community.html.

Maryland Community Crime Prevention Institute, http://www.dpscs.state.md.us/aboutdpscs/pct/ccpi/.

National Neighborhood Watch Institute (United States), http://www.nnwi.org/.

Neighborhood Watch (United Kingdom), http://www.neighbourhoodwatch.net/.

Neighborhood Watch Program (U.S. National Sheriff's Association), http://www.usaonwatch.org/.

Region of Waterloo (Ontario, Canada), The Community Safety and Crime Prevention Council, http://www.preventingcrime.net/.

PART III

ROLE OF GOVERNMENT AND POLICE IN CRIME PREVENTION

CHAPTER 6

THE STATE AND CRIME PREVENTION

CONTENTS

6.1 INTRODUCTION

Despite the importance of the private citizen and the local community in preventing crime, the state will always play a central and dominant role in crime prevention specifically and crime control generally. Not only are governments the caretakers of the criminal justice system, they are also responsible for a broad range of policy areas that can make a direct contribution to preventing crime and criminality, such as education and schools, child and family welfare, health care, subsidized housing, community development, recreation programs, and urban planning and design, to name a few.

County and municipal governments are in a particularly unique position with respect to crime prevention because, of all levels of government, they are the closest to private citizens and neighborhoods, have jurisdiction over local policing, and are engaged in a number of other policy areas that may have an impact on crime and its root causes. These local levels of government also represent the most important bridge between neighborhoods and community groups, on the one hand, and national and state/provincial governments on the other. Indeed, municipal and county governments can play a key role in building partnerships across governmental, nongovernmental, private sector, and community-based organizations and agencies.

It is beyond the scope of this chapter to document and describe the myriad of government policy and program areas that can potentially affect crime prevention and community safety. Neither is this the place to discuss how the criminal justice system can contribute to the prevention of crime. Instead, the purpose of this chapter is to explore the role of the state in initiating and supporting strategies that are expressly structured to prevent crime and criminality; that is, policies and programs that incorporate the proactive, problem-solving, inclusive philosophy of crime prevention. It will do so primarily by discussing the principles that should guide governments in promoting crime prevention and presenting case studies from around the world.

This chapter asserts that the four greatest roles the state can play in crime prevention are:

1. Implementing policies and programs that address the root causes of criminality, targeting at-risk communities, families, children, and youth
2. Supporting and helping neighborhoods and communities build capacity to undertake local initiatives to prevent crime

---

BOX 6.1

PRINCIPLES OF GOVERNMENT INVOLVEMENT IN CRIME PREVENTION

Government policies, programs, and funding should send a message that proactive strategies to prevent crime and the onset of criminal behavior are every bit as important as reactive (criminal justice) approaches and that everyone in society has a role to play in preventing and controlling crime.

Governments should empower local communities to play an active role in crime prevention, through policies, funding, and a decentralization of decision-making responsibilities. The broader context of the role of the state in local crime prevention capacity building is helping to create a civic society that is fully engaged in local governance and problem solving.

Relevant government departments, agencies, and institutions must work in an integrated and complementary fashion to address crime; representatives from government departments and agencies should adopt an interagency team approach to addressing chronic crime and disorder problems at the local level.

Governments must work in a collaborative fashion with other key partners (other levels of government, community groups, NGOs, health-care and educational institutions, the private sector, etc.) and should take a lead in assembling partnerships.

Governments should prioritize scarce crime prevention resources for neighborhoods and demographic groups that are at the highest risk of offending and victimization.

Governments should support research into the causes of crime; factors that put children, young people, and communities at risk; and evaluations of crime prevention policies, practices, and programs. Emphasis should also be placed on coordinating the dissemination of these findings to ensure the constant implementation of best practices.

Governments should develop and implement evidence-based policies and practices in the area of crime prevention and the criminal justice system generally while also encouraging research and experiments that contribute to a greater understanding of what works and what doesn't work in preventing crime and criminality. Governments must avoid policies and programs based on politics or ideology, especially when they have shown not to work to prevent crime.

---

3. Building capacity within government agencies to foster proactive, preventative, multiagency approaches to crime prevention
4. Complementing citizen-based preventative approaches to crime through the traditional criminal justice system

Box 6.1 provides more details on some of the principles that should guide governments in the field of crime prevention.

6.2   ROLE OF THE STATE IN CRIME PREVENTION

Contemporary crime prevention theory and practice arose as a critique of the criminal justice system and, in doing so put forth the proposition that the state can no longer be exclusively responsible for controlling crime. Despite the primacy of the individual citizen and the collective community in crime prevention theories and strategies, there will always be a role for the state in preventing crime. Governments are responsible for the broader crime-control agenda and are instrumental in setting the tone as to whether proactive, inclusive community-based crime prevention initiatives will be a priority.

Perhaps the most important role to be played by governments in preventing crime—whether at the national, state/provincial, or municipal level or whether it is policy, programs, or funding—is to promote social development and socioeconomic prosperity, focusing on the most vulnerable and marginalized segments of society. The state must take on a leadership role in helping those communities where there is a high concentration of crime and criminogenic risk conditions while targeting families and children who are most at risk of current and future offending. Governments have a wide range of tools and powers at their disposal to alleviate those factors that concentrate crime and its preconditions within neighborhoods, demographic groups, and families.

Governments must also ensure public safety policies and programs they adopt are scientifically informed. No longer can governments rely on politics, ideology, *mob rule*, or past practices as a basis to for public safety policies and programs. According to Konnerup and Gill (2012, 8), "There is a growing belief in the United States that interventions addressing social problems could be greatly improved if policy makers and managers supported interventions shown by scientific evidence to produce impact." Greenwood and Welsh (2012) suggest that state governments should establish evidence-based centers, which can provide training and technical assistance to agencies at the state, county, and municipal levels to help ensure effective policies and programs are implemented and evaluated.

The various roles that can be played by the state in preventing crime often depend on the level of government. This is due to the division of powers and responsibilities between the different levels of government as well as the resources available to each. A crucial role for national and state/provincial governments is the creation of laws and other policies that address directly crime (i.e., criminal laws, criminal justice policies and programs) and the root causes of criminal behavior (e.g., social welfare or educational policies and programs). National as well as state/provincial governments also have greater resources than municipal or county governments, and, as such, they need to assume a dominant role in funding crime prevention projects at the local and regional level. According to its 1993 report, *Urban Policies and Crime Prevention*, the United Nations Congress for the Prevention of Crime and the Treatment of Offenders urges, "Leadership and support by national governments are needed for cities who have limited resources and jurisdictional competence. National governments must pass legislation, create prevention councils, encourage research evaluation and training and maintain adequate financing" (United Nations, 1993, p. 1).

Leadership at the national level also includes developing a comprehensive, nationwide crime prevention strategy. As Graham (1995, 8) notes, Western European and Scandinavian countries, such as the France, Denmark, Sweden, Finland, and Belgium, have adopted national strategies and have coordinated their crime prevention work through national councils. Ideally, any national crime prevention plan should be constructed and implemented as part of a broader crime-control strategy that includes criminal laws and the criminal justice system. Not only is there a need for a comprehensive approach that couples complementary reactive and proactive strategies to crime, but problem-oriented crime prevention principles and responsibilities can also be incorporated into the criminal justice system. In Denmark, Sweden, and the United Kingdom, according to Graham (1995, 8), "specific policies

CASE STUDY 6.1

EVIDENCE-BASED LEGISLATION FOR YOUNG OFFENDERS IN CANADA

On April 1, 2003, the *Youth Criminal Justice Act* (YCJA) came into force in Canada, replacing the more punitive *Young Offenders Act*. The objectives and principles of the YCJA are very much informed by criminological literature on juvenile offending and the most effective approaches to dealing with both adolescent-limited juvenile offenders and those who are more serious and chronic offenders. In this context, the goals of the legislation include the following: establish clear and coherent principles to improve decision making in the youth justice system (which deal with youth 12–17 years old), distinguish between serious violent offenses and less serious offenses, divert less serious cases from the criminal justice system to alternative (restorative justice) processes, restrict the use of custody and reduce the high rate of youth incarceration, help to address the root causes of criminality among youth, and contribute to the effective reintegration of young people who have been in trouble with the law.

Part 1 of the legislation emphasizes the use of *extrajudicial* measures—diversion from the criminal justice system—for most youth who have conflicted with the law. This provision is based on the evidence that most of these young people are not serious and chronic offenders and are not at risk of future serious or chronic offending. As such, they should not be processed through the traditional criminal justice system (let alone be incarcerated or saddled with a criminal record). The objective of this part of the legislation is to increase the use of alternative measures for less serious offenses by strongly encouraging police and prosecutors to divert young offenders to community-based alternative processes. These alternative processes are inevitably restorative justice mediations, and the legislation requires each provincial attorney general to establish restorative justice processes for this purpose. Adhering to the principles of restorative justice, the legislation stipulates that there must be meaningful consequences for the young person, which includes admitting guilt, expressing remorse, apologizing, meeting face-to-face with victims, and repairing any harm done to the victim through reparations.

For more serious offenses, the legislation stipulates that young offenders can be ordered into custody, but the court must first consider and reject all reasonable alternatives to custody. The YCJA also provides youth court judges with alternative sentences: reprimand, intensive support and supervision order, attendance order, deferred custody and supervision, intensive rehabilitative custody, and supervision. Even if a young person is sentenced to custody, the YCJA emphasizes the importance of rehabilitation and reintegration into society.

The legislation requires a youth worker to help the young person plan for his/her reintegration, which sets out the most effective programs to maximize his or her chances for successful reintegration. The youth worker will also supervise and provide support and assistance to the young person upon release. *Reintegrative paroles* are emphasized for postrelease youth, which means that every period of custody is to be followed by a period of supervision in the community, as part of the sentence. The YCJA contains a list of mandatory conditions that apply to all young persons while under supervision and additional conditions can be imposed by judge. If a young person breaches a condition, a review will be held that can change conditions or return youth to custody.

In their assessment of the first 5 years of the YCJA, Bala et al. (2009, 132) conclude the YCJA has "succeeded in significantly reducing the rates and use of court and custody, without increasing recorded youth crime."

for preventing crime have been an explicit part of criminal justice policies for at least two decades." In Bulgaria and Hungary,

> ...the courts take responsibility not only for adjudication, but also for identify-
> ing and resolving the underlying causes of specific offences. Where an offender
> is found guilty of theft from the workplace, the employer will be issued with a
> directive to prevent such thefts from recurring. Failure to comply can result in the
> employer being penalized. Thus the courts, rather than merely punishing offenders
> and relying on the principle of general deterrence to prevent others from commit-
> ting similar offences, actively try to change the conditions and situations that gener-
> ate criminal behaviour.
>
> **Graham (1995, 8)**

At the local level, municipal and county governments generally have little influence over criminal law. However, they do have jurisdiction over local policing and, as such, can play a tremendous role in preventing crime and helping to empower the citizenry to do so through policies that promote community and problem-oriented policing. (For more on community and problem-oriented policing, see Chapter 7.) Further, as such, a police department that is not committed to crime prevention can undermine any such policies and programs established by a municipal or county government.

Yet, the role that municipal and county governments play in crime prevention tran-scends policing. Local governments are often responsible for a number of relevant policy areas (schools, recreational facilities, social housing, urban planning), can be a bridge between local communities and other levels of government, can play an important role in coordinating partnerships among different stakeholders, and can provide funding and other resources to build capacity at the neighborhood level. Local and regional governments must begin by building capacity within and across its own departments and agencies to internalize a proactive, preventative approach to crime. This includes ensuring that relevant departments and agencies pursue policies and programs that can contribute to the local government's mandate to prevent crime, whether it is the development of school board policies and programs for at-risk youth, the integration of CPTED principles into the work of the urban planning department, or ensuring that the department responsible for community centers and other recre-ational facilities is cognizant of their important role in addressing criminogenic risk factors among children and youth.

According to Homel (2010, 118), the critical role to be played by municipal govern-ments in crime prevention is also influenced by "the prevailing logic" that

> since most crime of immediate concern to communities is local (i.e. property crime,
> antisocial behaviour, vandalism, etc.) then the primary focus for preventive action
> should also be local. In practice this has meant that those promoting crime pre-
> vention action have generally turned to municipal governments as the principal
> resource for coordinating the delivery of the local preventive responses. This has
> been based on the assumption that municipal authorities are best placed to under-
> stand and reflect the particular needs and problems of their local community and
> are therefore also best placed to generate and/or deliver the most appropriate pre-
> vention interventions for their local communities.

The Institute for the Prevention of Crime at the University of Ottawa recommends assigning the responsibility of coordinating crime control and community safety to a specific unit within the municipal government. This unit, which would report to senior government officials (such as the mayor), would be mandated to

- Support the partnership structures in place and build strategic alignments with municipal elected officials, city managers, and other stakeholders
- Be a focal point for sharing strategic information and making the links between programs and projects
- Contribute to the analysis of crime and insecurity issues and trends
- Provide strategic and technical support to the development and implementation of municipal strategic vision, community safety policies, action plans, and projects
- Develop strategies to mobilize financial resources
- Develop indicators, monitor implementation of action plans and projects, report on the progress made to municipal authorities and other stakeholders
- Design communication strategies and tools (Institute for the Prevention of Crime, 2009, 13)

Given the importance of partnerships in crime prevention, municipal governments must play a leading role in bringing together the various key players to work in a coordinated, complementary fashion, whether it is to address a pressing problem in one neighborhood or a more permanent policy that is implemented on a citywide basis. As Sansfaçon (2004, 4) writes, because local governments do not have the same level of resources as central or regional governments, they have to "rely on implementing partnerships that bring together the police and the justice system, school and health-care administrators, and civil society organizations."

Municipal governments must also work to support and build capacity in local communities to help them spearhead crime prevention initiatives. This can begin with actions that demonstrate a government's commitment to and accommodation of an active citizenry empowered to undertake initiatives to prevent crime (and address other local problems). This includes providing community groups with funding and other necessary resources, facilitating access by community groups to local government decision makers and to knowledge and expertise, decentralizing some decision-making powers to community groups, fostering an integrated team approach in which community groups and nongovernmental organizations (NGOs) can work collaboratively with government agencies, and ensuring that local police are committed to the principles of crime prevention and community and problem-oriented policing. In short, according to the Institute for the Prevention of Crime (2009, 5), "Municipalities are the order of government most able to collaborate with local agencies and neighbourhoods to identify the needs for service and so tackle the multiple causes of crime in their areas most in need."

The broader context of the role of the state in building the capacity of communities is creating opportunities for an engaged civil society to take the lead in solving their own problems. In her guide for local governments on the effective implementation of community policing, Fisher-Stewart (2007, 7) writes, "Community policing is just the tip of a 'community' approach to the management of local government, defined by a philosophy that citizens should be involved in the day-to-day decisions that affect their lives." Governments must take the lead in creating an environment wherein everyone in society is encouraged to play an active role in building strong, vibrant, and healthy communities. In doing so, governments must work as equal partners with local

CASE STUDY 6.2

GOVERNMENT INNOVATIONS IN CRIME AND RECIDIVISM PREVENTION: PAYMENT BY RESULTS (AKA SOCIAL IMPACT BONDS)

In 2012, the City of New York joined a small but growing list of governments that applied the concept of *payment by results* to the criminal justice system. According to a *New York Times* article, Goldman Sachs, the Wall Street investment banking firm, "will provide a $9.6 million loan to pay for a new four-year program intended to reduce the rate at which adolescent men incarcerated at Rikers Island reoffend after their release" (Chen, 2012). The money from Goldman Sachs "will be used to pay MDRC, a social services provider, to design and oversee the program. If the program reduces recidivism by 10%, Goldman would be repaid the full $9.6 million; if recidivism drops more, Goldman could make as much as $2.1 million in profit; if recidivism does not drop by at least 10%, Goldman would lose as much as $2.4 million" (Chen, 2012).

The concept behind *payment by results* or *social impact bonds* is that a government pays a contractor "on the basis of the outcomes their service achieves rather than the inputs or outputs the provider delivers. It is suggested, by focusing reward on outcomes and providing minimal prescription as to how these outcomes should be achieved, payment by results models will drive greater efficiency, innovation and impact in tackling social problems" (Fox and Albertson, 2011, 397). "The social impact bond presents a new method of financing social outcomes via private investment," according to Fox and Albertson (2011, 397–398). "It is envisaged that the SIB will be used to raise capital for social projects in the way bonds are used for investment projects; a branch of national or local government will agree to pay for a measurable, social outcome and this prospective income is used to attract new funds to meet the up-front costs of the activity." The new funds could come from the private sector or a *social investor* (who may be an individual philanthropist or a charitable trust).

The scheme originated in the United Kingdom and while potentially applicable to many types of government services contracted out to private actors, in that country, it was most prominently seen as a tool in reforming criminal justice services and preventing recidivism among postrelease offenders specifically. The policy has been championed and implemented by the Conservative Party, which argues the following: "The principle of incentivising performance through payment by results, with success based on the absence of re-offending, should be introduced for prisons, the providers of community sentences and the providers of rehabilitation programmes—whether in the public, private or voluntary sector. With devolved responsibilities and new incentives, we can create a revolution in how offenders are managed, and drive down re-offending" (Conservative Party, 2009, 49 as cited in Fox and Albertson, 2011, 397).

In one application of a social impact bond to the UK criminal justice system, the Ministry of Justice signed a 6-year contract with Social Finance—which describes itself as a social investment bank to help the charitable sector respond to society's needs by facilitating greater access to investment—to reduce the reoffending of some 3000 adult male inmates who have been released from the Peterborough penitentiary. According to the Social Finance website, as part of the Peterborough Prison project, "experienced social sector organizations" were funded by Social Finance to provide "intensive support to 3,000 short-term prisoners over a 6 year period, both inside prison and after release, to help them resettle into the community. If this initiative reduces re-offending by 7.5%, or more, investors will receive from Government a share of the long term savings. If the SIB delivers a drop in re-offending beyond the threshold, investors will receive an increasing return the greater the success at achieving the social outcome, up to a maximum of 13%" (Social Finance, n.d.).

communities, empowering and guiding groups and individuals along a path of civic engagement and community building:

> Consider that *community partnerships* between law enforcement and citizens rarely, if ever, occur in isolation from other branches of local government. For such partnerships to grow and evolve, local governments must be willing to reach out to their citizens and actively engage them in the process of local government, whether that is community-oriented policing or economic development or public works or any other program or service a local government provides. In short, there must be a community-oriented philosophy that drives the whole local government and encourages collaboration and cooperation.

Fisher-Stewart (2007, 4)

Creating an environment that encourages an active citizenry and a collaborative approach to local problem-solving requires a decentralization of public resources and decision-making power to the community level. If governments are truly committed to empowering communities to take on an active role in controlling and preventing crime, they must be prepared to relinquish some power and give up some resources.

Governments also have an important role to play in reducing the opportunity for crimes to occur. This includes enacting bylaws that mandate safe design principles (and empowering urban planning and design staff to help promote safe design principles) as well as bylaws that make private organizations (e.g., property owners) "accountable for the crimes occurring at their locations" (Eck and Guerette, 2012, 369). According to Braga (2012, 317), "If municipalities can organize themselves to control the small number of risky places, risky times, and risky people who generate the bulk of the crime problems, they can more effectively manage citywide crime trends" (Braga, 2012, 317).

CASE STUDY 6.3

COMMUNITY ORGANIZING AND GOVERNMENT ACTION IN VANCOUVER

During the early 1990s, residents of Carolina Street in Vancouver, Canada, organized to protest a number of problem premises on their block, which evolved into a larger citywide campaign to force absentee landlords to accept a greater responsibility over their properties. One notorious slum landlord who owned a number of properties in East Vancouver was targeted by this informal collection of residents, which eventually became known as the Carolina Street Neighbourhood Group (at its peak, the group numbered around 60 people).

When no action was taken by the owner in response to the group's demands, they took their fight to the city council. In March 1992, the group proposed a bylaw authorizing the city to bill the landlord for visits to his houses by the police, the sanitation department, and the health department (Kines, 1992). Between 120 and 150 people attended the city council meeting to support the appeals of the organizers, prompting a veteran city councilor to comment that in his experience, "this was the very first time that a whole neighbourhood had shown up to raise hell" (*Vancouver Echo*, March 12, 1992). The ongoing effort of the Carolina Street Neighbourhood Group ultimately resulted in the bylaw and the suspension of the property owner's license to rent his premises located on this street (Box 6.2).

BOX 6.2

CRIME PREVENTION POLICY AND PROGRAM RECOMMENDATIONS FOR GOVERNMENTS IN CANADA

In 2003, the Canadian Forum for Crime Prevention, which advocates the adoption of scientifically based crime prevention policies and programs by all levels of government, made the following recommendations for federal, provincial/territorial, and municipal governments in Canada:

Federal Government

1. Assume responsibility for facilitating a national process aimed at developing a prevention vision and an action plan that is comprehensive, inclusive, and results oriented. The process must recognize the key roles played by local communities in crime prevention and give them an equal voice in the process.
2. Adopt legislation and implement policy to make crime prevention one of the four permanent components of crime policy and programming (along with policing, the courts, and corrections). Prevention must have a voice equal to that of the other three pillars in decision making. In practice, this requires the presence of a high-level Canadian crime prevention entity.
3. Create and disseminate evidence-based information on crime prevention. More specifically, they require annual victimization surveys in order to allow communities to better assess their needs and measure their progress, data on social indicators in local areas, increased levels of investment in research and innovation in crime prevention, increased levels of investment in public education on crime and prevention (special attention must be paid to the need to recognize the impact of poverty and other root causes of crime and victimization), and increased levels of technical assistance and support to local communities.
4. Raise the level of investment in crime prevention by reallocating 5% of annual spending in the area of criminal justice.

Provincial and Territorial Governments

1. Ensure the creation of an interministerial capacity for crime prevention that is responsible for planning and coordination and is accountable for results.
2. Require local governments to undertake crime and safety analyses on a regular basis and to develop prevention plans that target the identified problems. Adequate support must be provided to the local level to enable governments to meet this requirement.
3. Provide support to local communities, in the form of both investments in individual projects and core funding to local crime prevention councils.
4. Require that all policy decisions at the provincial and local levels be assessed for their potential impact on crime and victimization.
5. Raise the level of investment in prevention by reallocating 5% of justice spending to this area—an investment of a minimum of $5 per capita per year. This would allow provincial and territorial governments to match or exceed investments by the federal government in this area.

Local Governments

1. Create and support local crime prevention bodies. These councils should be linked to the mayor's office and be representative of both service providers and service users. Particular attention should be paid to the need to ensure the participation of youth and women and to reach out to representatives of aboriginal populations and other minority groups. Local governments must provide adequate financial support to these initiatives.
2. Develop and use (computer-based crime mapping) in order to facilitate the identification of needs and the targeting of investments (Canadian Forum for Crime Prevention, 2003).

The remainder of this chapter examines crime prevention policies and programs implemented by governments in different countries. The case studies are divided into two categories: (1) national and state/provincial governments and (2) local (municipal) governments.

6.3   CASE STUDIES: NATIONAL AND STATE/ PROVINCIAL GOVERNMENTS

6.3.1   United States

Within the realm of crime prevention and community safety, there is perhaps no government in the world that has developed more initiatives, provided more project funding, enacted more policies, and financed more research and published more reports on the subject than the U.S. Government. For more than four decades, the federal government has developed and implemented a number of crime prevention programs and policies (including legislation) and has provided billions of dollars in funding to government, law enforcement, NGOs, and researchers for crime prevention and community policing initiatives. The most active and sustained role of the U.S. Government in the realm of crime prevention has been through the funding of local projects and programs, which is administered mainly through various sections and divisions of the Department of Justice, such as the Office of Juvenile Justice and Delinquency Prevention (OJJDP), the Community-Oriented Policing Services Office, and the National Institute of Justice.

In the public policy arena, the initial thrust for crime prevention in the United States came from the 1967 Presidential Crime Commission Report, which asserted the need for an active and involved citizenry in augmenting the criminal justice system and in rectifying the social and environmental conditions that cause criminal and deviant behavior. In 1968, as a direct result of the Presidential Crime Commission, the Law Enforcement Assistance Administration (LEAA) was created as an agency in the Department of Justice to fund anticrime educational programs, research, and local initiatives. Beginning in the early 1970s, the LEAA financed and published a series of national evaluations of community crime prevention projects, most of which involved police and/or were based on opportunity-reduction strategies. In 1977, the U.S. Congress authorized the LEAA Community Anti-Crime Program to dispense $30 million to "assist community organizations and neighborhood groups to become involved in activities designed to prevent crime, reduce fear of crime, and contribute to neighborhood revitalization" (U.S. Department of Justice, 1977, 4). This funding was premised on federal crime-control policy, which asserted that "the formal criminal justice system by itself cannot control crime without the help from neighborhood residents in fostering neighborhood-level social controls" and that the "community should play the central role in defining community crime prevention and that organized groups of residents are perhaps the best vehicle for responding to local crime" (United States Department of Justice, 1977, 3).

A sample of past and current Department of Justice agencies and funding programs that include a strong crime prevention or community policing focus is summarized in the succeeding text. What is apparent when examining those federal programs that advocate crime prevention is that a community-based, proactive, and problem-oriented philosophy is viewed as one of many complementary approaches to tackling crime. In other words, as far as contemporary Department of Justice programs and program funding are concerned, the principles and strategies of crime prevention are integrated within a comprehensive approach to crime that includes traditional criminal justice responses.

Office of Justice Programs (OJP): According to its website, the OJP "provides innovative leadership to federal, state, local, and tribal justice systems, by disseminating state-of-the art knowledge and practices across America, and providing grants for the implementation of these crime fighting strategies." It does this by working "in partnership with the justice community to identify the most pressing crime-related challenges confronting the justice system and to provide information, training, coordination, and innovative strategies and approaches for addressing these challenges." The mandate of the OJP reflects the overall approach of the U.S. Government to crime prevention in that proactive, community-based initiatives should be pursued as part of a wide-ranging crime-control package. In its mandate and goals, the OJP also stresses two key aspects of crime prevention: partnerships with other justice agencies at the state, country, municipal, and tribal levels and an "evidence-based 'smart on crime' approach to criminal and juvenile justice" (Office of Justice Programs website).

Community Oriented Police Services (COPS) Office: The COPS office was created by the *Violent Crime Control and Law Enforcement Act of 1994*. The mission of COPS is to advance "the practice of community policing in America's state, local and tribal law enforcement agencies." It does so "principally by sharing information and making grants to police departments" to support community policing initiatives (Community Oriented Police Services website).

OJJDP: The mission of the OJJDP, according to its website, is to provide "national leadership, coordination, and resources to prevent and respond to juvenile delinquency and victimization. The OJJDP supports states and communities in their efforts to develop and implement effective and coordinated prevention and intervention programs and to improve the juvenile justice system so that it protects public safety, holds offenders accountable, and provides treatment and rehabilitative services tailored to the needs of juveniles and their families" (Office of Juvenile Justice and Delinquency Prevention, n.d.). The OJJDP seeks to accomplish this mandate by providing an array of research and applied project funding to states, local governments, and NGOs.

Project Safe Neighborhoods (PSN): PSN is a national strategy to reduce gun and gang violence by providing funding and coordination for local initiatives, disseminating evidence-based information for program development, and fostering the capacity of governments, police, and other criminal justice officials and local groups. Through the awarding of federal grants, PSN not only promotes a proactive, community-oriented, problem-solving, partnership-based approach but is also concerned with advancing traditional police enforcement techniques and the hiring and training of prosecutors.

Operation Weed and Seed: Operation Weed and Seed was launched in 1991 as both a systematic strategy and a funding program that aimed to "eliminate violent crime, drug trafficking, and drug-related crime from targeted high-crime neighborhoods" and to "provide a safe environment, free of crime and drug use, where law-abiding citizens can live, work, and raise families" (Roehl et al., 1996, 2). The program, which has also been referred to by the less colloquial "reclamation and stabilization," entailed a two-pronged strategy: "law enforcement agencies and prosecutors collaborated to 'weed out' drug trafficking, gangs, and violent crime through enforcement, which is joined or followed by a 'seeding' component that encompasses a social and community problem-solving approach, such as neighborhood revitalization, social developmental projects for at-risk youth, and drug treatment, among others" (Tien and Rich, 1994, 192). The program aimed to ensure a "strategic, coordinated approach to crime prevention and control" that required local authorities to "develop a comprehensive, multi-agency strategy to control and prevent violent crime, drug trafficking, and drug-related crime in targeted high-crime neighborhoods; to coordinate and integrate existing as well as new federal, state, local, and private-sector initiatives, criminal justice efforts, and human services, and to concentrate those resources in the project sites to maximize their impact on reducing and preventing violent crime, drug trafficking, and drug-related crime." In addition to providing funding, the role of the Department of Justice in this program involved convening and cochairing a steering committee in project communities. While the Weed and Seed initiative had a decidedly top-down approach to local crime problems (it is led by local Department of Justice attorneys), one of its goals was to mobilize residents in program sites (Roehl et al., 1996, 3).

Incentive Grants for Local Delinquency Prevention Programs: In 1992, the Congress enacted the Incentive Grants for Local Delinquency Prevention Programs, which provided funding for "collaborative, community-based delinquency prevention efforts." In particular, this initiative funded projects that incorporated the following principles:

1. Comprehensive and multidisciplinary approaches to tackling youth crime (including prevention, enforcement, and treatment)
2. A strong research base (through systematic risk assessments and ongoing data collection activities)
3. Community control and decision making ("local jurisdictions assess their own delinquency prevention needs and resources and then design and implement appropriate and sustainable initiatives that fit local conditions")
4. Evaluation (community members receive "the tools needed to assess program outcomes and monitor long-term changes in the prevalence of risk factors and adolescent problem behaviors in the community")
5. Long-term perspective (funded projects should take "a long-term perspective that fosters positive, sustained community change") (Office of Juvenile Justice and Delinquency Prevention, 1998b)

Comprehensive Communities Programs: Launched in 1994 by the Bureau of Justice Assistance, the Comprehensive Communities Program provided funding and other federal support for local projects that, as the name suggests, incorporated a comprehensive strategy to local crime problems. Rather than addressing a single issue (e.g., drugs, gun violence, property crimes) or pursuing a single approach (e.g., social developmental, neighborhood revitalization), the program funded projects that emphasized a strategic, comprehensive, multidisciplinary approach to targeting a wide range of crime and disorder problems that plague neighborhoods (although drug-related and violent crimes were a particular focus). The program's main goals were to "suppress violence and restore community well-being; initiate comprehensive planning and enhance intergovernmental and community relationships to focus on the problems and concerns of local residents; develop a comprehensive, multi-agency strategy within communities to identify the causes and origins of violence and to control and prevent violent and drug-related crime; use community policing and other efforts to encourage citizens to take an active role in problem solving; and coordinate federal, state, local, and private agency resources, and concentrate those resources on reducing violent and drug-related crime" (Bureau of Justice Assistance, 2001, 2). The two underlying crime prevention strategies of the Comprehensive Communities Program—community policing and community mobilization—were meant to further partnerships, collaboration, and shared problem solving at the local level. Communities were required to take the initiative to develop partnerships, to have an existing coordinating structure, and to develop community policing and crime prevention strategies. A few examples of the initiatives adopted as a result of program funding include community prosecutions, drug courts, crime prevention through environmental design projects, antigang initiatives, and community corrections (Bureau of Justice Assistance, 2001).

Comprehensive Strategy for Serious, Violent, and Chronic Juvenile Offenders: In 1993, the OJJDP published its "Comprehensive Strategy" (Wilson and Howell, 1993), which was meant to provide local communities with a strategic framework on how to systematically address youth offending by "establishing a continuum of appropriate measures, from prevention to early intervention to graduated sanctions for juveniles who enter the juvenile justice system." The comprehensive strategy incorporated two main components: (1) "preventing youth from becoming delinquent through prevention strategies for all youth with a focus on those at greatest risk" and (2) "improving the juvenile justice system response to delinquent offenders through a system of graduated sanctions and a continuum of treatment alternatives that include immediate intervention, intermediate sanctions, community-based corrections, and aftercare services." The strategy is based on the following principles for addressing criminogenic risk factors among youth:

1. It must strengthen the family "in its primary responsibility to instill moral values and provide guidance and support to children."
2. It must support "core social institutions (schools, churches, youth service organizations, community organizations) in their roles to develop capable, mature, and responsible youth."
3. It must promote "delinquency prevention as the most cost-effective approach to reducing juvenile delinquency."
4. It must intervene "immediately and effectively when delinquent behavior first occurs to prevent delinquent offenders from becoming chronic offenders or from progressively committing more serious and violent crimes."

5. It must establish "a system of graduated sanctions that holds each juvenile offender accountable, protects public safety, and provides programs and services that meet identified treatment needs."
6. It must identify and control "the small percent of serious, violent, and chronic juvenile offenders who commit the majority of juvenile felony-level offenses" (Coolbaugh and Hansel, 2000).

More recent federal initiatives that promote a preventative approach to crime and public safety include the following:

- The *Second Chance Act of 2007* and the *Second Chance Reauthorization Act of 2013*, which attempt to reduce recidivism among postrelease offenders by providing resources and support for their successful reintegration (see Chapter 4 for more information on this legislation and recidivism prevention in general)
- The Justice and Mental Health Collaboration Program, created by the *Mentally Ill Offender Treatment and Crime Reduction Act of 2004*, the purpose of which is to facilitate collaboration among the criminal justice, juvenile justice, mental health treatment, and substance abuse systems to increase access to treatment for offenders with mental health disorders
- The establishment of federal specialty courts, including drug courts, mental health courts, and veterans courts (see Chapter 4 for more information on specialty courts)
- The creation of the Center for Faith-based and Neighborhood Partnerships in the Department of Justice, which works to support community-based and faith-based organizations address local social problems
- The National Forum on Youth Violence Prevention, which is mandated to enhance the capacity of local governments and communities to more effectively prevent youth and gang violence
- The Responsible Fatherhood initiative, which promotes strategies that encourage support for fathers and families in order to address the problem of broken families

6.3.2 Pennsylvania

According to a 2007 report by researchers with the Prevention Research Center for the Promotion of Human Development at Pennsylvania State University,

> For over a decade, Pennsylvania has been a national leader in confronting youth problem behaviors in a progressive and proactive fashion, investing heavily in supporting local community prevention coalitions and the use of proven-effective models for preventing youth violence and aggression, delinquency and youth substance abuse. Since 1998, the Pennsylvania Commission on Crime and Delinquency (PCCD) has invested over $60 million in implementing more than 140 effective prevention programs in more than 100 Pennsylvania communities. Community priorities are guided by local data based on a public health model of reducing known risk factors associated with violence and delinquency and promoting positive youth development.
>
> To further support the positive impact of this investment, PCCD has also made a commitment to providing training and technical assistance to these communities to ensure that the programs are implemented with the highest quality and fidelity, and that thoughtful planning is undertaken to ensure that programs are sustained beyond PCCD grant funding.

Chilenski et al. (2007, 4)

In their article on US states that have implemented evidence-based juvenile justice programs, Greenwood and Welsh (2012) write, "The experiences of the two most progressive states—Connecticut and Pennsylvania—offer many lessons for policy makers and practitioners in other states." One lesson from Pennsylvania is the strategy of promoting and supporting model programs, at the local level, which research has shown to work in reducing criminogenic risk factors among children and youth. These model programs include many documented in this book: Communities that Care, Promoting Alternative THinking Strategies (PATHs), the Olweus Bullying Prevention Program, Big Brothers/Big Sisters, Families and Schools Together (FAST), the Nurse-Family Partnership Program, the Multidimensional Treatment Foster Care, the LifeSkills Training program, Multisystemic Therapy, and the Functional Therapy program (Chilenski et al., 2007). (See Chapter 4 for a description of many of these programs.)

Chilenski et al. (2007, 66) conclude, "these case studies demonstrate, communities and the Commonwealth have benefited from PCCD's investment in proven-effective prevention programs. The reduction in delinquency, substance use, and related risk factors seen by these sites is testament to the potential of evidence-based prevention programs to reduce violence and delinquency in Pennsylvania."

6.3.3 Canada

A 1993 report by the Parliamentary Standing Committee on Justice and the Solicitor General recommended that national policies should support the principles of community crime prevention, recognizing that "crime occurs in communities and priorities concerning crime prevention are best determined at the local level" (Parliament of Canada, Standing Committee on Justice and the Solicitor General, 1993, 33). This report led to the National Strategy on Community Safety and Crime Prevention, which was meant to "provide a policy framework for the implementation of crime prevention interventions in Canada" (Public Safety Canada, 2007, 1).

The objectives of the National Strategy are to "promote partnerships between governments, businesses, community groups, and individuals to reduce crime and victimization; to assist communities in developing and implementing community-based solutions to local problems that contribute to crime and victimization; to increase public awareness of, and support for, crime prevention, and to conduct research on crime prevention and establish best practices" (Treasury Board of Canada Secretariat, RPP 2004–2005, n.d.). One should note the nuanced description of its mandate and goals: there is no national crime prevention strategy per se, just a national strategy to promote crime prevention projects by providing funding and by promoting certain crime prevention principles, such as partnerships or crime prevention through social development.

The National Strategy is based on the belief that the most effective way to reduce crime is to focus on the factors that put individuals at risk of criminal behavior. Thus, it emphasizes the development of community-based responses to addressing risk factors that can lead to criminal behavior, with a particular emphasis on young people and aboriginal people.

The National Strategy is administered by the National Crime Prevention Centre (NCPC), a federal agency created in 1998 that oversees the planning, development, and implementation of federal policies and programs related to crime prevention. The mission of the NCPC, according to its website, is to "provide national leadership on effective and cost-efficient ways to both prevent and reduce crime by addressing known-risk factors in high risk populations and places." Further, "The NCPC's principles are that, to produce optimum results, crime prevention interventions should: be integrated with the activities of other programs and services, build on the knowledge of known risk and protective factors and use evidence-based practices, be focused on specific priorities, and be measurable" (Public Safety Canada, National Crime Prevention Centre, n.d.).

Since its inception, the primary function of the NCPC has been to act as a federal funding agency for crime prevention projects. The NCPC administers a number of different funding streams, each of which has a specific focus and mandate in furtherance of the agency's overall goal in promoting effective crime prevention strategies in the country. The largest funding program is the Crime Prevention Action Fund, which provides "time-limited grant and contribution funding that supports evidence-based crime prevention initiatives in communities." In recent years, under the Conservative Government, other funding priorities include those that "support initiatives that clearly target youth in gangs or at greatest risk of joining gangs" (Youth Gang Prevention Fund), "enhance the security infrastructure of communities targeted by hate crimes" (Communities at Risk: Security Infrastructure Program), and support the development and implementation of programs to "address known risk and protective factors to reduce offending among at-risk children and youth, and high risk offenders" in aboriginal communities (Northern and Aboriginal Crime Prevention Fund) (Public Safety Canada, Crime Prevention Funding Programs website). (Chapter 4 provides a description of the developmentally based approaches to young offenders and at-risk youth in the province of Quebec.)

6.3.4   United Kingdom

In 1960, the Cornish Committee on the Prevention and Detection of Crime was established by the Home Office. In a report issued 5 years later, the committee promoted the role of citizens and communities in crime control and recommended the establishment of crime prevention units and specialists within police departments. The report also encouraged police to work more closely with other government ministries and agencies to combat crime (Newburn, 2007, 567). Following this report, the Home Office established the *Standing Conference on Crime Prevention*, an advisory body made up of representatives from the national and municipal governments, the police, NGOs, and the private sector. The goal of the Standing Conference was to encourage the involvement of all sectors of British society in the prevention of crime. The conference convened a number of working groups, which led to a series of crime prevention demonstration projects, most of which were based on opportunity-reduction principles (Geason and Wilson, 1988).

The emphasis on a multisectoral, inclusive approach to crime prevention and community safety was preceded by the distribution of an influential circular to all police forces and local authorities in England and Wales (Newburn, 2007, 567). Commenting on the circular, the University of the West of England writes,

> It was the first explicit statement by the government of the view that crime prevention "must be given the priority it deserves and must become a responsibility of the community as a whole". What had previously been identified as primarily a police task

was now seen as something for local authorities and the general public to be actively involved in. Unfortunately, the Circular was not immediately backed up by additional government funding, the official view being that crime prevention could be supported through existing programs and resources.

University of the West of England (2004a)

The mid-1980s marked the beginning of a flurry of crime prevention policies and programs initiated by the New Labour Government, some entirely focused on crime prevention, while others placed it within the context of larger community and social development schemes. This period also witnessed the central government's move away from its exclusive focus on opportunity-reduction to one that integrated social developmental approaches. Central to this approach was early intervention initiatives targeting at-risk families and children.

In 1986, the British Government set up an Interdepartmental Ministerial Group on Crime Prevention, with the prime minister serving as its first chairperson. That same year, the Home Office launched the so-called Five Towns Initiative, which established demonstration projects in Bolton, North Tyneside, Wellingborough, Croydon, and Swansea. Funded for 18 months by the national and local governments, the initiative included the hiring of crime prevention coordinators for each town. The coordinators were tasked with overseeing crime prevention projects and reported to a committee composed of local agencies and representatives from the community. Financial support from the British Government eventually dried up, but the results of the initiative were so encouraging that funding from other sources was obtained to continue the work (Geason and Wilson, 1988; Newburn, 2007, 568).

Emerging from this initiative in 1988 was the Safer Cities program whereby the Home Office provided funding for 20 pilot projects implemented at the local level. While the Home Office determined which projects were funded, the priorities and activities were determined locally through a multiagency steering committee. During the first phase of the Safer Cities program, which ran from 1988 to 1995, funding was provided to more than 3600 projects that targeted a wide range of local crime problems, including residential and commercial burglaries, domestic violence, vehicle crime, shoplifting, disorder and incivilities, and fear of crime. The majority of the projects entailed situational crime prevention measures, such as the approximately 375 burglary reduction schemes that employed target hardening as their predominant prevention strategy. Research showed that between 1990 and 1992, the number of residential burglaries decreased in areas where these initiatives were implemented. A cost–benefit analysis found that the residential burglary projects prevented 56,000 burglaries and saved £31 million—the cost of the entire Safer Cities program (Eckblom et al., 1996; Welsh and Farrington, 1999; Gant and Grabosky, 2000, 22–23; University of the West of England, 2004a).

Around the same time, government-subsidized housing estates in England and Wales became a particular focus of crime prevention initiatives spearheaded or supported by municipal governments and the central government (Geason and Wilson, 1988; University of the West of England, 2004a; Newburn, 2007, 568).

In 1988, Crime Concern was launched with Home Office funding as a semiautonomous government agency mandated to support the development and implementation of community-based crime prevention initiatives. Today, Crime Concern UK is an independent nonprofit agency that, according to its website, specializes in "community safety for the public sector and loss prevention and building security for the private sector." Their services include "crime reduction" (crime and disorder audits, managing crime reduction projects), "community engagement" (identifying community priorities), "antisocial behavior" (combating violence and disorder, youth diversionary projects), "priority offenders" (working with offenders in the community, drug intervention programs), and "reducing fear of crime" (fear of crime audit and surveys) (University of the West of England, 2004a; Crime Concern, n.d.).

During the late 1980s and the 1990s, situational measures that emphasized CPTED and the installation of closed-circuit televisions (CCTVs) in public spaces became a dominant plank in central and local government crime-control strategies. In 1994, the Department of the Environment in conjunction with the Welsh Office produced an influential circular entitled *Planning Out Crime*, which offered advice to local government authorities and private-sector developers on design measures that should be considered in new residential and commercial real estate developments as well as public spaces. During the same period, the British Government worked with local authorities to apply CPTED principles and physical security technology to public housing estates (University of the West of England, 2004a).

In 1998, the Labour Government brought in the *Crime and Disorder Act*. This legislation included provisions that obligate all municipalities to plan, implement, and evaluate a local crime reduction strategy through Crime and Disorder Reduction Partnerships that involve the police and other criminal justice agencies, other relevant government departments, and community and business groups. These local strategies, which were to operate in 3-year cycles, had to include research into local crime problems, the establishment of priorities, and the development, publication, and execution of a crime prevention plan. In addition, local authorities were required under the legislation to keep crime and disorder issues in mind when considering other public policy matters. This legislation was controversial for its "parenting orders," which sought to make parents more accountable for the delinquent and criminal behavior of their children and gave the courts more powers to punish neglectful parents. Participation in family-based programs was often nonnegotiable for high-risk families with youth who were constantly in trouble with the law (Blyth and Solomon, 2009). (This approach is reflective of the so-called parental responsibilization strategy for controlling juvenile crime and delinquency, which is discussed in Chapter 4.)

The *Crime and Disorder Act* also established the Social Exclusion Unit in the Prime Minister's Office, which was mandated to coordinate different social policy areas of the British Government to combat poverty and integrate disadvantaged and marginalized communities into the mainstream (Sansfaçon and Welsh, 1999). In September 1998, the Social Exclusion Unit published a report on disadvantaged neighborhoods that laid a foundation for a national urban renewal strategy. This strategy envisioned four key outcomes for such neighborhoods: better education, better health, lower unemployment, and less crime. The report set out a three-pronged approach to implementing the strategy:

1. National policies, such as welfare reform, to deal with the underlying causes of social exclusion
2. Development and implementation of local crime prevention and community development programs to test promising ideas for turning around disadvantaged neighborhoods
3. Expedient policy development process involving 18 multiagency teams to issues plaguing poor, marginalized areas (International Centre for the Prevention of Crime, 2001, 13)

In 1999, the Labour Government announced its Crime Reduction Programme (CRP), an ambitious 3-year initiative that included specific steps and programs to be undertaken and crime reduction targets to be achieved in the short to medium term (some of these programs were new, while others already existed and were incorporated into the program). According to Homel et al. (2004, v), the CRP was created with three goals in mind:

1. Achieve a sustained reduction in crime.
2. Improve and mainstream knowledge of best practice.
3. Maximize the implementation of cost-effective crime reduction activity.

The CRP was to provide a "road map for guiding long-term investment strategies for the government in its continuing effort to drive down crime," and to achieve this goal, the program "worked through an array of 20 separate but linked crime reduction initiatives of varying scale organised around five broad themes, or mechanisms." These five themes were

1. Working with families, children, and schools to prevent young people from becoming offenders in the future
2. Tackling crime in communities, particularly high-volume crime such as domestic burglary
3. Developing products and systems that are resistant to crime
4. More effective sentencing practices
5. Working with offenders to ensure that they do not re-offend (Homel et al., 2004, v–vi)

Homel and colleagues (2004, v) write that the national CRP has been called "the most ambitious, best-resourced and most comprehensive effort for driving down crime ever attempted in a Western developed country." What is unique about this initiative, compared to those in other developed countries, is the specification of clear national targets in crime reduction. This included a 30% reduction in vehicle crime by 2004, a 25% reduction in residential burglaries by 2005, and a 14% reduction in robberies by 2005 (Homel et al., 2004, vii). While the CRP was introduced by the central government, much of the work necessary to achieve its objective would be carried out at the local level, primarily through the Crime and Disorder Reduction Partnerships that were mandated by the *Crime and Disorder Act* (Homel et al., 2004, vi). More than 1300 projects, at a total cost of £400 million, were implemented as part of the CRP, with most of the funds being dedicated to installing CCTV systems (Bullock and Tilley, 2003, 148–150). The CRP also stressed evidence-led crime reduction strategies "with a special focus on promoting innovation, generating a significant improvement in knowledge about effectiveness and cost-effectiveness, and fostering progressive mainstreaming of emerging knowledge about good practice" (Dhiri et al., 2001, 179, 181, as cited in Welsh, 2007, 34). To this end, various initiatives were implemented to promote evidence-led and cost-effective interventions in the field of public safety, including funding randomized experiments and evaluations of crime prevention programs. It also led to the creation of the Centre for Criminal Justice Economics and Psychology at the University of York, the mandate of which is to advance evaluation research assessing the economics of different crime prevention strategies (Welsh, 2007, 35).

In February 2001, the Home Secretary unveiled *Criminal Justice: The Way Ahead*, a 10-year crime reduction plan that promised a more coordinated social developmental approach to crime prevention. According to the Home Office, the plan represented "… a coordinated attack across Government on the causes of crime." In addition to the Home Office, other British Government departments, such as those responsible for education, employment, health, and regional governments, "are now spending billions each year on programmes which will have a direct impact in the short, medium and long term on crime rates: initiatives like Sure Start to improve the life chances of pre-school children; or the £600 million that DfEE [Department for Education and Employment] is spending on tackling school truancy and exclusion; or the £900 million DETR [Department of the Environment, Transport and the Regions] is investing in turning around England's most deprived neighbourhoods, for whom high crime is one of the worst problems" (Secretary of State for the Home Department, 2001, 7). According to the 2001 plan, the Labour Government also vowed to allow local police to accredit private security companies to carry out some policing duties, such as patrolling crime-ridden housing estates and "working under police co-ordination to deliver improved community safety." The role of the private security industry is placed within the context of how private and public police "can be coordinated to make the most effective contribution to making safer communities" (Secretary of State for the Home Department, 2001, 14).

In September 2002, the Crime Warden program came into effect. Crime wardens are meant to operate as community-based adjuncts to the police, providing "a highly visible, uniformed, semi-official presence in residential and public areas, town centres and high-crime areas with the aim of reducing crime and fear of crime." Wardens are to help police (and community members) on a range of local concerns including crime, antisocial behavior, and minor nuisance problems. Where they are unable to provide immediate help, they are required to report the incident to the appropriate authority and ensure that the matter is satisfactorily addressed. The overall goal of the Crime Warden program is to reduce street crime by reducing crime and fear, deterring antisocial behavior, fostering social inclusion, and promoting community development, although the role of the wardens will also be dictated by the specific needs of each community (BBC News, 2003).

In 2008, the Home Office released the Youth Crime Action Plan, which has as its goal a 20% reduction in youth entering the criminal justice system for the first time. It plans to accomplish this goal through a "triple-track" approach of "enforcement and punishment where behaviour is unacceptable, non-negotiable support and challenge where it is most needed, and better and earlier prevention." As far as prevention is concerned, the plan calls for more assessment services to identify children and youth most at risk for future chronic offending, more services for youth who receive permanent expulsion from school, expanding programs that link police to schools, aligning the hours of youth centers to times when young people are likely to offend, providing more support for parents of first-time young offenders, increasing interventions for families with children at risk of offending (including the expansion of home visitation programs), and ensuring a greater availability of intensive foster care programs for at-risk children and youth (Home Office, 2008, 4–7).

In 2011, the Coalition Government issued its policy report *A New Approach to Fighting Crime*. The report identified the importance of engaged and active communities (helping "the public become more involved in keeping communities safe" in part by encouraging "the public to participate in Neighbourhod Watch schemes and volunteer as special constables…") (Home Office, 2011, 5). It also pledged to "prevent crime in the first place by tackling the risk factors that can drive it across society: from poor parenting and education to dealing with drug abuse and problem drinking" (Home Office, 2011, p. 6). New initiatives to combat youth crime and violence include those that attempt to "nip bad behaviour in the bud - raising standards of discipline in schools by strengthening and simplifying teachers' powers. We will also issue statutory guidance to extend head teachers' powers to punish school pupils who misbehave on their way to or from school" (Home Office, 2011, 10).

6.3.5 *France*

Since the beginning of the 1980s, the national government in France has been at the forefront in the development and implementation of progressive crime prevention strategies that are guided by such principles as social problem solving (addressing the root causes of crime), inclusion (reaching out to and involving at-risk youth and offenders), and intergovernmental coordination (partnerships between the various levels of governments to coordinate policy both horizontally—across ministries and agencies within one government level—and vertically—between local governments and the central government). The French crime prevention model was one of the first to "focus on addressing the problems experienced by disaffected community members (e.g. young people, immigrants, unemployed, etc.) by striving to integrate them in to their local communities thereby reducing the potential risk of them participating in crime." These efforts should be spearheaded by local governments, but with the participation of other governmental, nongovernmental, and private sector entities (Homel, 2010, 119).

In 1981, following a rash of riots, vandalism, and crime by young people in Paris and Lyon, the government embarked on a concerted national effort to address the causes of crime and disorder problems, especially those committed by young people. In the spring of 1982, the French prime minister established the Mayors' Commission on Security, a body composed of mayors from the four main political parties to formulate recommendations on how best to prevent crime and delinquency. The commission's report, entitled *Face à la Délinquance: Prévention, Répréssion, Solidarité* (Dealing with Delinquency: Prevention, Repression, Solidarity; Bonnemaison, 1983), criticized the traditional criminal justice approach as insufficient and recommended that greater emphasis be placed on addressing the root causes of crime and delinquency problems, stressing flexibility and adaptation to local circumstances. Changes to public policies on housing, education, and employment should also be made to prevent the marginalization of young people. Local crime prevention strategies should bring together all the key partners, including local government agencies responsible for policing, the judicial system, social services, public health, education, youth and sports, culture and housing, and representatives of local communities, nonprofit organizations, the private sector, and trade unions (University of the West of England, 2004b).

The Commission's recommendations laid the foundation for the National Council for the Prevention of Crime, chaired by the prime minister and made up of representatives from relevant central government departments. At the regional level, Departmental Councils for the Prevention of Crime were formed, chaired by the chief administrator for each region, with the chief judicial officer as vice chairperson. The mandate of the regional councils was to coordinate the implementation of national crime prevention policies at the regional and local levels, in part by integrating and coordinating relevant policies and programs within and between national government departments.

The Mayors' Commission on Security also led to the creation of an innovative system of contracts between the central government and local governments (*Contrat de Ville*). The contracts were meant to both symbolize and solidify the partnerships between various levels of government in addressing crime. Each contract must include an action plan that identifies the scope, nature, and causes of local crime problems and a strategy to be implanted at the local level (emphasizing a partnership approach). Signing a contract often leads to funding from the French Government and a commitment of resources and support from relevant national ministries.

Under the *Contrat de Ville*, local crime prevention initiatives are to be developed and coordinated by the *Conseils Communaux de Prévention de la Délinquance* (Community Crime Prevention Councils). Chaired by the mayor, a council is meant to bring together a range of people and agencies from within and outside government, including elected politicians; officials from the police and the judiciary; officials responsible for schools, health care, and housing; and representatives of voluntary organizations, social workers, trade unions, and the private sector (International Centre for the Prevention of Crime, 2001, 13–14; Chalom et al., 2001, 30). According to Chalom et al. (2001, 31), the councils "were originally designed to integrate the twin currents of punishment and prevention. Over the years, they have abandoned the first area and focused on prevention through social development."

Since 1989, the contracts between cities and the central French Government have been administered through a national interministerial agency—*Delegation Interministerial de la Ville* (DIV). The DIV coordinates the interests of national ministries when working with municipal governments and helps the Community Crime Prevention Councils with research, program development, and priority setting. In 1993, the DIV laid out five priorities that should be addressed in the city contracts: parental responsibilities, prevention of reoffending, prevention of drug addiction, help and support to victims, and safety in high-crime, disadvantaged neighborhoods.

In 1994, the French Government augmented its crime prevention policies by introducing the *Contrat local de sécurité* (local security contract). This initiative targeted neighborhoods and districts that were experiencing chronic problems in terms of poverty, unemployment, access to housing, and crime. The contracts are based on the notion that local security is achieved through prevention, traditional criminal justice sanctions, and the reintegration of offenders back into the community and French society. While sanctions are mostly the responsibility of the justice system, the contracts emphasize common ownership of the crime problem and the importance of civic responsibility (so that prevention and reintegration are seen as the responsibility of everyone in the community). According to Lenoir (2010, 123), this "contractualization is often seen as a guarantor for the initiation of action within an integrated approach to crime prevention, bringing together the various partners" and "also facilitates the local design and delivery of prevention through the co-financing of safety audits, local observatories, professional training, and positions for prevention strategy coordinators who contribute to cooperative and sustainable prevention governance."

The local security contracts are embedded within the larger city contracts and emphasize an interagency coordination (involving schools, housing authorities, employment and youth services, among others) in such priority areas as adult education; drug abuse prevention and treatment; facilitating access to police and other justice agencies by the public; greater support for victims; ensuring security in sensitive areas such as shops, public transportation, and schools; and a range of youth-centered development initiatives (job creation and training, parent support, and sports and cultural programs that meet local and cultural needs). Youth from disadvantaged areas with high levels of unemployment are given jobs arising from the local security contracts. This includes employment as social agents to work on prevention and security issues at the local level and local security assistants, who are attached to police departments (Graham, 1995, 9; Sansfaçon and Welsh, 1999; Chalom et al., 2001, 30; International Centre for the Prevention of Crime, 2001, 13–14; Homel, 2010, 119).

By 1995, 214 contracts involving over 750 communities and 1300 districts in France had been signed (Chalom et al., 2001, 30), and by 2010, a total of 415 had been signed (Lenoir, 2010, 122). By way of example, a security contract signed with the City of Marseilles, which ran from 1994 to 1998, focused on at-risk youth and set out five crime prevention priorities: ensuring youth complete school; employment and job training; fighting substance abuse; participation in recreation, culture, and sports; and urban renewal and improvement of housing for the disadvantaged.

6.3.6   The Netherlands

Contemporary crime prevention policies and programs in the Netherlands can be traced to the 1984 *Roethof Report*, which advocated for greater involvement of private citizens and businesses in crime prevention and the promotion of interagency cooperation at the local level. The *Roethof Report* led to the influential 1985 Dutch Government plan entitled *Society and Crime* (Roethof, 1984), which recommended that responsibility for crime prevention and community safety not just be in the hands of police and criminal justice authorities but all members of Dutch society. It also advocated that government and other sectors apply both situational and social developmental crime prevention principles (University of the West of England, 2004c; Willemse, 1994, 34–35).

As a result of these recommendations, an interdepartmental committee of the Dutch Government was established in 1985. The committee was responsible for administering funds that would subsidize approximately 200 social developmental pilot projects. After 5 years of testing, the results were deemed satisfactory enough for funding to continue, and the focus was widened from social development (where the emphasis was on working with at-risk youth) to include opportunity-reduction strategies. In addition, a new emphasis was placed on fostering local informal social control, through, for example, the introduction of neighborhood watch schemes (Willemse, 1994, 35).

A crime prevention directorate was set up in the Ministry of Justice, the purpose of which was to promote coordination across different government departments in fostering crime prevention at a local level, help police efforts in this area, deliver victim assistance services, and regulate the private security industry. Ministries throughout the Dutch Government were encouraged to develop policies and programs for at-risk youth, the chronically unemployed, and young people from ethnic minority groups (United Nations, 1993, 16; University of the West of England, 2004c).

In 1996, the Dutch Government developed the Major Cities Policy to respond to growing problems in many of its larger cities, such as unemployment, family breakdown, decaying neighborhoods and public spaces, drug addiction, and crime. Modeled after the French *Contrat de Ville*, agreements were drawn up between the national government and cities to work as partners to strengthen the social and economic bases of cities in three broad areas: employment and education, public safety, and quality of life and care. The contracts ensured funding from the national and local governments for the development of strategies and programs targeting priority concerns. Like the French contracts, the premise of this approach is that solutions to crime problems must be shared among different levels of government, different departments within one government, and between government and private actors. Any community safety plan developed under the auspices of the contract would emphasize a community-based, strategic, problem-oriented, multiagency approach that targets the causes of crime through a number of complementary measures. The contract must spell out specific achievement targets as well as the measures to be undertaken to achieve these targets. As part of the Major Cities Policy, the Ministry of Justice spearheaded the opening of neighborhood justice offices in five Dutch cities to work in problem-oriented ways with local residents. The offices were meant to provide accessible, quick, and direct action to deal with local street crime, nuisances, and conflicts and offer information, legal advice, and conflict mediation for local disputes (Willemse, 1994, 43; International Centre for the Prevention of Crime, 2001, 14, 44).

In 1999, the Integral Program on Safety and Security (IPSS) was launched. This program emphasized coordination across different government departments and incorporated an intergovernmental division of labor whereby local governments are responsible for developing and implementing prevention policies and programs, while the central government supports these initiatives through funding, training, program development assistance, and evaluation. Priority areas for the IPSS have included youth and safety, drug-related nuisance problems, street violence, safe and secure living environments, robberies and muggings, vehicle-related crime, and traffic safety (International Centre for the Prevention of Crime, 2001, 14). Some of the initiatives that have since emanated from the IPSS include

- Funding of comprehensive community crime prevention plans
- Expansion of the neighborhood justice offices to other locales
- Juvenile delinquency action plans, which aim to enhance the security of schools, lower the dropout rate, strengthen parental abilities, and provide immediate interventions for at-risk youth
- Outreach programs for youth from minority ethnic groups
- Promotion of the Secured Housing Police Label, an accreditation program for market and social housing that meets safe design requirements for prevention of burglaries (Netherlands Ministry of Justice, 2001)

6.3.7 Commonwealth of Australia and the State of New South Wales

In its 2006 state plan, the government of the state of New South Wales pledged to reduce crime and recidivism as well as levels of antisocial behavior over a 10-year period. The targets established in the plan include a 15% reduction in the number of residential burglaries, a 10% reduction in the number of violent crimes, and a 10% reduction in the proportion of offenders who reoffend within 24 months of their original offense. A Crime Prevention Framework was developed to achieve these goals (New South Wales Government, 2008, 3). A Crime Prevention Steering Group, which is made up of senior management from the Department of Premier and Cabinet, the Attorney General's Department, and the New South Wales Police Force, was established to oversee the implementation of this strategy. One of the mandates of the steering group is to ensure that there is collaboration among government agencies in planning, funding, and carrying out crime prevention and reduction strategies (New South Wales Government, 2008, 3).

Central to the state government's crime reduction and prevention strategies are municipal councils, which are required to develop crime prevention plans for their jurisdictions.

These plans are submitted to the attorney general for approval as Safer Community Compacts. If approved, the local councils can access funding from the state government to help implement their plan. The local plans are expected to be carried out by Crime Prevention Partnerships, which are "formal partnership[s] between local council and local representatives of the NSW Police Force, relevant NSW Government agencies (and may include the Departments of Housing, Education and Training, Community Services, Health, and the Office of Liquor, Gaming and Racing), local transport companies, and other agencies as relevant and appropriate." The Crime Prevention Partnerships are chaired by the NSW Police Force Local Area Commander and are "tasked with developing Crime Prevention Partnership Action Plans which align their local crime prevention and reduction objectives with the extended targets" jointly set by the Crime Prevention Steering Group and the respective municipal councils (New South Wales Government, 2008, 5–6).

The statewide crime reduction framework also advocates the involvement of community groups and private citizens in planning and carrying out strategies at both the state and local levels. Nongovernment organizations are "given an opportunity to participate in crime prevention planning by inviting them to Steering Group meetings on a regular basis." At the local level, "Community Safety Precinct Committees are the vehicle through which the NSW Police Force and Government agencies consult with the community and other key stakeholders on crime prevention and community safety issues" (New South Wales Government, 2008, 7).

While the states and territories have primary responsibility for the criminal justice system in Australia, in 1997, the Australian Government established the National Crime Prevention Programme, which, according to Welsh (2007, 35), is notable for embracing "the notions of using evidence on what works best and contributing to the state of science on crime prevention through evaluations...." Funding programs include the National Crime Prevention Fund as well as the *Proceeds of Crime Act*, which "provides a scheme for tracing, restraining and confiscating the proceeds of crime against Australian law" some of which is "returned to the Australian community to fund anti-crime initiatives." These initiatives include "graffiti prevention reduction and/or removal, youth diversion programs, security infrastructure, community programs, people trafficking and labour exploitation as well as funding election commitments" (Australian Government, 2011). Established in 2004, the National Community Crime Prevention Programme provides "funding for grass roots projects designed to enhance community safety and crime prevention by: preventing or reducing crime and anti-social behaviour, improving community safety and security, and reducing the fear of crime" (Australian Government, 2011).

6.4 CASE STUDIES: MUNICIPAL GOVERNMENTS

As mentioned, municipal governments are extremely important players in crime prevention and local safety for a number of reasons: they are the level of government closest to communities, they are responsible for local policing and law enforcement, they have jurisdiction over other policy areas that can impact crime and its causes, and they are well positioned to identify, coordinate, and mobilize the key partners that must be involved in community safety initiatives. Some of the key principles and responsibilities of a local government's involvement in crime prevention and community safety are summarized in Box 6.3. The remainder of this chapter describes examples of municipal government action in the area of crime prevention.

BOX 6.3

KEY PRINCIPLES AND RESPONSIBILITIES OF LOCAL GOVERNMENT INVOLVEMENT IN CRIME PREVENTION AND COMMUNITY SAFETY

Strong leadership by local politicians, senior police officers, and other municipal government officials in advocating a problem-oriented, preventative approach to local crime problems.

Develop and undertake safety audits.

Identify and prioritize crime hot spots and the neighborhoods most vulnerable to crime and the causes of criminality.

Develop citywide and local crime prevention action plans, including those that fundamentally address criminogenic risk factors.

Help communities build capacity to prevent crime through funding, program development and implementation support, training and skills development, etc.

Provide funding and other crucial resources (office space, translation, training) needed by community groups.

Connect private citizens and NGOs with higher levels of government.

Initiate and facilitate partnerships that cut across jurisdictional boundaries both horizontally (with local communities, across local government departments, and with other municipal governments) and vertically (with state/provincial and federal governments).

Assign the responsibility for coordinating crime prevention and community safety to a specific unit within the municipal organization, and provide adequate and sustained resources for that purpose.

Ensure that the community and key stakeholders develop a shared vision of the challenges related to crime and insecurity, including (1) the municipality, school boards, housing, social services, the police service, NGOs and neighborhoods and (2) collaboration across all orders of government including tripartite agreements.

Facilitate the emergence of a strategic plan, on crime prevention and community safety that is city wide and articulates specific objectives, strategies, priorities, partners, and dedicated resources.

Make safety a crosscutting priority in the city's general strategic plan.

Sources: International Centre for the Prevention of Crime, The role of Local Government in community safety, Bureau of Justice Assistance, Department of Justice, Washington, DC, 2001, pp. 21–33, http://www.ncjrs.gov/pdffiles1/bja/184218.pdf; Institute for the Prevention of Crime, Making cities safer: Action briefs for municipal stakeholders, Institute for the Prevention of Crime, University of Ottawa, Ottawa, Ontario, Canada, 2009, p. 12.

6.4.1 United States

6.4.1.1 San Antonio, Texas   The Greater San Antonio Crime Prevention Commission, which was created by a municipal bylaw, has 29 members who are appointed by the mayor and confirmed by city council for 2-year terms. The commission's membership includes representation from elected city officials, the business sector, health care, education, the police, the justice system, the military community, the media, faith-based groups, community service groups, and neighborhood associations. The commission is chaired by an elected councilor appointed by the mayor and "is charged with developing and recommending to the City Council and Police Department a results-oriented, community-wide action plan that focuses on crime prevention and early intervention. The Commission develops a workable plan to significantly reduce crime and fear in the City; involves all relevant sectors in developing the plan; and develops a long-term vehicle to address the issue of crime" (City of San Antonio, n.d.).

When it was established, the commission had four main priorities:

1. "To" *promote a greater community awareness and community involvement in prevention activities* by creating the Business Crime Council of South Texas, establishing a city department to assist in setting up neighborhood associations, and increasing police community activities
2. "To" *establish social, educational, and recreational services for youth* by offering a range of services, mainly from 3 to 6 p.m.; establishing a parenting skills development program; and committing funds to renovate or build over 60 community centers, parks, and playgrounds
3. "To" *increase young offenders' sense of responsibility* by launching a pilot project to rehabilitate nonviolent offenders, strengthening community service programs as an alternative to traditional court solutions, and passing a bylaw on mandatory school attendance during the day
4. "To" *reduce street violence through the prevention of domestic violence and promotion of greater cooperation among the various levels of law enforcement* by setting up a unit to coordinate responses to domestic violence, providing more training for police officers, and increasing services for victims and offenders (United Nations Crime and Justice Information Network, 1995)

The members of the commission are divided into working committees, each of which deals with a particular issue, such as violent crime, neighborhood safety, at-risk families, and crime prevention for businesses. Having representatives of the media on the commission, combined with intensive outreach by the public information committee of the commission, helps promote the commission's work to the public and encourages public participation in the process (United Nations, 1993, 19–20).

6.4.1.2 Gainesville, Florida   In 1986, after a spate of armed robberies of convenience stores, the Gainesville City Council passed a bylaw that attempted to reduce the opportunity for such crimes in the future. Based on research into situational crime prevention, the bylaw required convenience stores to limit the amount of cash in the till (and post visible signs to that effect), keep on site a time-release drop-safe for cash, provide better lighting in their parking lots, ensure that staff have a clear view of the street and parking lot from the store (which includes removing posters from windows that obstruct sight lines into and out of the store), install closed-circuit cameras, and train clerks in robbery prevention and other emergency procedures. In 1987, the city adopted another ordinance that required stores to have two employees on duty between 8:00 p.m. and 4:00 a.m. (stores could avoid this requirement if they had a prevention plan in place that reduced robberies by 50%) (United Nations, 1993, 27; Sampson and Scott, 1999, 169). According to one evaluation, these ordinances resulted in a decline in convenience store robberies in Gainesville from 97 in 1986 to 39 in 1987, 29 in 1989, and 18 in 1990. Over this same time period, convenience store robberies remained largely unchanged throughout the rest of Florida (United Nations, 1993, 27).

6.4.1.3   Joliet, Illinois   In Joliet, Illinois, police were confronted with an all-too-common problem: drug trafficking out of multiresidential rental properties owned by absentee landlords who cooperated little with police. At the behest of police, Joliet's City Council passed an ordinance requiring all landlords to cooperate with police once they had been notified that criminal activity was suspected on their properties. If the property owners or landlords did not cooperate, they could be forced to vacate the property. To complement this ordinance, police trained landlords to screen prospective tenants, identify problem tenants, and draft and enforce leases that allowed landlords to evict tenants if illegal activity was conducted on their premises. An assessment of these civil remedies indicated that they "had a positive effect on the community by reducing the number of calls-for-service and by increasing the quality of life in the neighborhood" (Center for Problem-Oriented Policing, 2000) (Box 6.4).

6.4.2   Canada

6.4.2.1   Toronto, Ontario   In 1999, a municipal Task Force on Community Safety produced a comprehensive community safety plan for the City of Toronto. Chaired by two city councilors, the task force included representatives from police, school boards, neighborhood crime prevention groups, businesses, agencies working to prevent family violence, ethnocultural groups, organizations working with at-risk families, youth-led organizations, and groups serving people with disabilities. In putting together its plan, the task force undertook extensive consultations, including a survey sent out to more than 6500 people and community organizations in Toronto, interviews with city council-ors, 20 public meetings, consultations with experts (to discuss best practices in the crime prevention field), the circulation of an interim report for input, and a conference attended by about 250 people to discuss the draft recommendations (City of Toronto, 1999).

The final report, *Toronto, My City, A Safe City: A Community Strategy for the City of Toronto*, describes the extent of the city's crime problems (primarily by examining police-recorded statistical data), discusses what is known about the root causes of crime, sets out its vision for a safe city, and outlines 35 recommendations (including identifying the municipal department that should take the lead in implementing each recommendation) (International Centre for the Prevention of Crime, 2001, 37–38).

The recommendations made in the Community Safety Strategy report are demar-cated into four categories (strengthening neighborhoods, investing in children and youth, policing and justice, and information and coordination). These recommenda-tions are summarized in the following:

1. Strengthen Neighborhoods
   a. Increase the use of neighborhood safety audits.
   b. Ensure that the city responds quickly and consistently to recommendations arising from safety audits.

BOX 6.4

USE OF CIVIL REMEDIES BY MUNICIPAL GOVERNMENTS IN THE UNITED STATES

Municipal governments across the United States have increasingly relied on civil remedies to both prevent and respond to crime and disorder problems. Mann (1992, 1809) defines a civil remedy as "an action taken by an authoritative body—a legislature, a court, or an administrative agency—to enforce compliance with prescribed conduct or to impose a cost for failure to comply." For Mazerolle and Roehl (1998, 1), civil remedies (also called civil sanctions) are "procedures and sanctions, specified by civil statutes and regulations, used to prevent or reduce criminal problems and incivilities. Civil remedies generally aim to persuade or coerce non-offending third parties to take responsibility and action to prevent or end criminal or nuisance behavior." Within this context, civil remedies have most frequently been used to force property owners and landlords to take steps to control criminal and nuisance problems, such as drug trafficking, prostitution, frequent loud parties, or the presence of strewn garbage on their property. Local governments in California and British Columbia, Canada, used civil remedies to prevent suspected gang members and prostitutes, respectively, from congregating in certain places. As used by a government authority, a civil remedy can include health code or fire safety bylaws, municipal abatement statutes, or even civil suits. The penalties accruing from civil remedies can include fines, physical repair and cleanup requirements, the closure of properties, eviction of tenants, the removal of (rental or liquor) licenses, more intensive tenant screening, and legally binding promises to maintain drug- and nuisance-free properties. As a prevention tactic, civil remedies can also include youth curfews; injunctions against gangs, drug traffickers, or prostitutes; bans on alcohol advertising, public telephones, or cigarette machines; and restrictions on bars and liquor stores (Mazerolle and Roehl, 1998, 1). Civil remedies and bylaw enforcement can be more effective than criminal sanctions because they can be used more proactively, efficiently, and quickly. For example, it is often difficult to criminally convict a property owner for drug trafficking that occurs on his premises, if the owner is turning a blind eye to the problem. However, civil remedies against the owner can be used to close the property, while just the threat of such measures can be a powerful tool to *persuade* the owner to ensure that no illegal activity is taking place on the property. Moreover, unlike a criminal trial where the state has to prove beyond a reasonable doubt that an individual is guilty of a criminal offense, in a civil court, the burden of proof on the state is much less onerous and there is also an onus on the defendant to prove his/her innocence. According to Brunet (2002, 74), civil suits can also be pursued by nonstate actors (e.g., neighborhood residents) and "are a relatively inexpensive and easy to implement."

c. Make public buildings and spaces safer.

d. Improve pedestrian safety.

e. Encourage property owners and landlords to manage and maintain their buildings in a manner that promotes community safety.

f. Decrease the number of *problem premises*, including a faster response to complaints by citizens and police and a decrease in crimes related to these properties.

g. Continue supporting safety initiatives for the private sector, such as TaxiWatch, Transit Community Watch, and Business Watch.

h. Expand the Drug Abuse Prevention Community Grants Program.

i. Ensure that community safety is a major focus in the city's new official plan by making public safe design principles a criterion for development proposals.

2. Invest in Children and Youth
   a. Coordinate child and youth violence prevention policies and programs across the city.
   b. Coordinate substance abuse policies and programs in schools.
   c. Improve parenting supports; promote the expansion of parenting skills education to libraries, schools, and workplaces, with an emphasis on high-risk families.
   d. Expand the city's *one-on-one* school-based mentoring program.
   e. Increase quality recreation for at-risk children, youth, and families.
   f. Maintain and expand the number and range of self-defense classes provided in the city's community centers.
   g. Continue to support and expand youth employment initiatives that combine job training and employment creation with community safety enhancement, such as the Graffiti Transformation, Drug Ambassador, and Job Corps programs.

3. Policing and Justice
   a. Expand, intensify, and ensure the success of Community Police Liaison Committees as the primary way to involve citizens in problem-oriented policing, ensure that these committees reflect the demographic diversity of the areas they represent, and provide outreach to marginalized groups.
   b. Expand precharge diversion programs for young offenders.
   c. Where needed, refer offenders in alternative justice programs to drug abuse treatment and other supports.

4. Information and Coordination
   a. Develop a comprehensive database on citywide crime prevention and community safety resources.
   b. Promote research in and evaluation of crime prevention.
   c. Promote and award excellence in community crime prevention.
   d. Expand the Breaking the Cycle of Violence Grants program.
   e. Ensure that city staff who work with citizens on safety concerns are adequately supported.
   f. Establish a *City Watch Program* to assist frontline staff in parks, streets, and driving vehicles in observing and reporting suspicious activities to police or to the appropriate authorities.
   g. Ensure that community and personal safety is integrated into the proposed social development plan, with an emphasis on vulnerable communities and neighborhoods.
   h. Make community safety a corporate policy with an accountability structure for the city council (City of Toronto, 1999).

6.4.2.2 Waterloo Regional Government, Ontario In 1993, the Waterloo Region Crime Prevention Council was established. The mission of the Council, according to its website, is to "mobilize the efforts of community in reducing and preventing crime, victimization and fear of crime; increasing safety; and fostering the well being of everyone." The specific goals of the Council are to "1. Research new and creative ways to deal with crime, 2. Address root causes of crime, 3. Develop a team approach to promote citizen support and involvement, and 4. Engage in public education" (Waterloo Region Crime Prevention Council, 2008, 5). The council is made up of 30 members who represent a wide range of key stakeholders, including police, neighborhood associations, schools and school boards, the Canadian Mental Health Association, victims services groups, local correctional institutions, public health, government social services agencies, and the John Howard Society, among others. The council carries out much of its work through committees, which include a Community Relations Committee, the Advisory Group on Research and Evaluation, the Municipal Partnership Task Force, the Violence Prevention Plan Implementation Committee, and the Waterloo Region Integrated Drugs Strategy Task Force. The day-to-day operations of the council are coordinated by an executive director. The council issued a community-based plan for 2010–2104, which outlined priority directions, goals, and actions to be taken.

6.4.2.3 Vancouver, British Columbia   One of the innovations undertaken by the City of Vancouver to tackle crime and other local problems is the Neighbourhood Integrated Service Teams (NISTs). Each NIST is composed of municipal staff from different departments and agencies who work in an integrated and coordinated fashion to address problems within each of the city's official communities. The mission statement of NIST is "To lead, to provide and to facilitate integrated community-based service delivery." According to the City of Vancouver, more than 200 city employees work on 16 teams, each of which represents a particular area of the city. Initiated in 1994, the NIST program takes advantage of the network of city powers, expertise, facilities, and services that already exists in communities, including police and fire departments, planning, inspections, garbage collection, engineering services, schools and the school board, the health department, city legal services, permits and licenses, the liquor control board, libraries, and the recreation department. The teams are expected to work with residents to help solve problems relating to a wide range of quality-of-life issues, including sanitation, crime, drug trafficking, problem houses, noise, physical and infrastructure problems. A NIST is particularly useful when a local problem arises that may involve more than one city department. In 1997, the Institute for Public Administration of Canada awarded the City of Vancouver its Innovative Management Gold Award for the NIST program and, in 2003, the program garnered the City of Vancouver a United Nations (UN) award for *Innovation in Public Service* (City of Vancouver, n.d.).

6.4.3 United Kingdom

6.4.3.1 Borough of Brent   Brent is one of 33 London boroughs. Crime rates in the borough were higher than the national average and were concentrated in poor social housing developments, some of which had significant crime and disorder problems, such as street robberies, residential burglaries, drug- and alcohol-related crime, and violence (International Centre for the Prevention of Crime, 2001, 35–36).

Based on the requirement of the *Crime and Disorder Act* that compels local governments to conduct safety audits and produce a crime prevention plan every 3 years, the Borough of Brent (2000) created a strategic plan entitled *A Crime and Disorder Reduction and Community Safety Strategy for Brent 1999–2002*. The report was produced through a partnership between the local council and the police, the probation service, and health authorities serving the borough. A safety audit compared Brent's crime levels with neighboring boroughs, highlighted hot spots, and examined trends in burglary, robbery, violence, sexual offenses, young offenders, domestic violence, racial incidents, victimization of the elderly, disorder, road injuries, drug and alcohol problems, and fear of crime. Approximately 10,000 copies of a summary of the safety audit were sent to the public, community groups, and business associations. The full audit was available in police stations, libraries, and medical clinics. Following release of the audit, public forums were held to discuss the safety audit and help craft a strategic plan.

The resulting strategic plan prioritized 15 crime reduction targets for the borough, outlined the action plan for each target, and set out performance measures to assess the effectiveness of each. The top priority was burglary reduction, with the target being a minimum 6% reduction (from 1998 figures) in 12 months and 12% after 36 months. Other priorities included reducing youth victimization (especially within the racial minority communities), domestic violence, road injuries, and drug and alcohol abuse problems (International Centre for the Prevention of Crime, 2001, 35–36).

Based on the plan, Brent implemented burglary reduction initiatives, began a mentoring program for young people, bolstered its neighborhood watch program, set up accredited community safety training courses for citizens, and implemented a targeted policing initiative for high-crime areas using crime mapping technology. Between 2002 and 2005, further crime prevention initiatives were undertaken in Brent, including

- Establishing a warden program in the town center, parks, and social housing developments
- Establishing Safer Neighbourhood Teams, consisting of a police sergeant, two police officers, and three police community support officers who are mandated to "deal with local quality of life and crime issues in consultation with communities"
- Implementing CCTV systems in crime hot spots
- Enhancing burglary prevention programs for businesses
- Instituting an arson reduction plan, emphasizing the removal of abandoned vehicles in high risk areas
- Establishing an antisocial behavior team, made up of police and other local government officials
- Implementing initiatives to address domestic violence, including a full-time domestic violence coordinator, a domestic violence directory to help women at risk find support, training for staff to identify those at risk, and a sanctuary project that allows victims to remain safely in their own homes
- Implementing antidrug programs, including a local ad campaign targeting youth, funds to support local groups providing positive alternatives to drugs, and drug treatment programs for youth
- Implementing projects that engage socially excluded youth
- Establishing a Children's Support Panel, which works with at-risk children ages 8–13 through a support worker who helps parents develop a plan to support their family by accessing government and nongovernmental services (Borough of Brent, 2005, 7–11)

6.4.4 France

6.4.4.1 Aix-en-Provence The city of Aix en Provence agreed to a *Contrat de Ville* with the national government in 1994 to develop delinquency and drug prevention strategies and improve housing, transport, education, and health services in an attempt to address the social problems that gave rise to local crime and delinquency problems. A Community Crime Prevention Council was formed, and a comprehensive safety audit was undertaken to identify the causes, symptoms, and facilitators of local delinquency problems. Based on this research, the city developed an action plan that included such priorities as the provision and enhancement of social, cultural, and sports facilities and policies for young people, the prevention of child abuse and neglect, greater support for parents of at-risk children, prevention of substance abuse, and greater support and aid for victims of crime (International Centre for the Prevention of Crime, 2001, 45).

The subsequent action plan outlined 42 separate strategies that the city would carry out to achieve its priorities. Each strategy identified "the specific problem, the objectives set, the agreed action, the partners responsible for implementation, methods of finance, evaluation, and target dates. The prevention of school violence, for example, involves measures to reduce absenteeism and school exclusion, early identification of behaviour problems, use of alternative disciplinary measures, and educational support." Other initiatives include a greater emphasis on community policing and the recruitment of social mediation agents to mediate conflicts and develop creative solutions to problems that may arise between different groups, such as storeowners and young people (International Centre for the Prevention of Crime, 2001, 45–46).

6.4.5 *Australia*

6.4.5.1 Brisbane In Australia, cities and towns across the states of Victoria, South Australia, and Queensland have developed crime prevention strategies since at least the mid-1990s. Brisbane, the capital of Queensland, recognized a number of social issues concerning young people that contribute to local crime, vandalism, and disorder problems. These issues include a growing number of homeless youth, the social exclusion of racial minority youth, substance abuse, the migration of a large number of indigenous youth from rural areas to Brisbane, and youth gangs (International Centre for the Prevention of Crime, 2001, 38).

Recognizing that the city suffers from a lack of transport, social services, recreational and cultural opportunities, and facilities designed to meet the needs of young people, between 1995 and 1997, the City of Brisbane undertook a project to identify, analyze, and address difficulties experienced by youth in *major centers* (public sites where young people gathered, such as shopping malls, beaches, and parks). The initial aims of the project were to develop guidelines for the design and management of the major centers "to take into account the needs of young people, the reduction of community conflict, enhancement of cultural development, and maintenance of centre viability" (Heywood et al., 1998b, 10). The project took as its starting point the importance of recognizing the legitimate place of young people in civic life and their inherent right to have access to public spaces.

Based on research that included consulting with at-risk youth in Brisbane, a 1998 report made the following recommendations:

- Each major center should develop a youth and community participation strategy.
- The city council should develop a consolidated youth policy from its existing programs and activities (specific youth policies should address the provision of sport and recreation infrastructure, like libraries, and skate parks, cultural and community development programs, and health and employment strategies).

- The city council should establish a youth communication strategy (including a media-based program that presents positive images of young people to the community).
- There should be greater consultation with young people in the design of public and private space frequented by youth (including privately owned shopping malls).
- Youth and community facilities should be expanded in major centers and include informal meeting places, sports and recreation facilities, social and cultural infrastructure, libraries, and youth information services.
- A community youth liaison manager and youth worker should be hired.
- Police and local authorities should discuss how to police public and community spaces in ways that understand the problems of marginalized youth (Heywood et al., 1998a, 2–3).

Based on its research and recommendations, Brisbane's City Council began developing strategies, policies, and programs, which included designing "public spaces that were more inclusive and relevant to the needs and interests of young people" (International Centre for the Prevention of Crime, 2001, 39).

6.4.6 Africa

The Safer Cities Programme is a UN Habitat initiative that was launched in 1996 at the behest of African mayors who wanted to address urban violence. With support from the UN, the Safer Cities Programme provides support to local authorities by

- Strengthening their capacity to address urban safety issues and reduce delinquency, violence, and security problems
- Promoting crime prevention initiatives, implemented in collaboration with central and local governments, criminal justice agencies, the private sector, and NGOs
- Encouraging the exchange of knowledge, expertise, and good practices among cities
- Developing and implementing crime prevention, capacity-building programs focusing on three main areas: at-risk groups, situational prevention, and reform of the criminal justice system

The Safer Cities Programme followed a structured process designed to nurture local crime prevention capacities, which entailed

- Mobilizing key partners who can contribute effectively to the reduction and prevention of crime
- Creating a local safety coalition led by a public figure and supported by a technical coordinator
- Rigorously assessing crime problems through safety audits
- Developing a local strategy that includes a detailed plan of action
- Implementing the action plan (which includes a broad range of short- and long-term prevention initiatives)

Municipal governments are the primary recipient of UN support and are expected to play a central role in coordinating the activities aimed at reducing crime (United Nations, Habitat, n.d.).

One African city where the Safer Cities Programme was implemented was Nairobi, Kenya, which was experiencing significant local crime problems that were exacerbated by institutional weaknesses within the criminal justice system, including corruption. Following a 1999 request for technical assistance, the Safer Cities Programme established the Safer Nairobi initiative, a citywide strategy to be implemented by Nairobi's City Council. As part of the development of the strategy, a victimization survey was undertaken, and consultations were held in 2004 with various key stakeholders, including residents associations, business associations, antipoverty groups, police, and women's groups. The four pillars of the Safer Nairobi strategy were (1) social developmental interventions targeting at-risk groups; (2) situational measures, stressing safe design modifications; (3) improved law enforcement; and (4) community mobilization and good governance. Public awareness campaigns were also launched, such as a Safety Audit Night Walk and a public rally, to raise the profile of and engage city residents in the initiative (United Nations Habitat, Safer Cities Programme, Best Practices, n.d.).

6.4.6.1 Johannesburg, South Africa

In postapartheid South Africa, the control and prevention of crime have become a national priority, and a large portion of the government's focus and resources has been allocated to the restructuring of the criminal justice system. However, it is acknowledged that efforts to reduce crime must go beyond the police and law enforcement and include preventive interventions directed at the social and economic factors that contribute to crime. In Johannesburg, which has some of the country's highest crime rates, maintaining order through policing is increasingly complemented by community-based solutions to crime.

The Greater Johannesburg Safer Cities strategy, which was developed by the Metropolitan Council, led to the implementation of a range of crime prevention programs in collaboration with other government agencies at the local, provincial, and national levels. This includes the police, the business sector, and community groups. The process that led to this Safer Cities project consisted of a strategic and problem-oriented approach that involved detailed crime diagnoses (including ongoing victimization surveys), strategy development (which flows from the diagnostic work and focuses on addressing the causes of crime, making environments less conducive to crime, developing a culture of crime prevention, supporting preventative policing and law enforcement, and providing information and tools for assisting victims and preventing victimization), and developing partnerships (between agencies to work collaboratively to address the priorities identified in the victimization survey).

In recognition of the serious threat of crime to the city, a crime prevention forum was established by the council in 1996, the result of which was the creation of a task force to consider proposals for crime prevention programs, to develop a coordinated strategy to prevent the duplication of services, and to foster cooperation among the stakeholders in the community. The task force recommended establishing an umbrella body comprising representatives of the local government, provincial departments, political parties, and business, labor, religious, and community organizations. This group, which became known as the Anti-Crime Network, drafted and implemented a local crime prevention strategy that included several initiatives. Some of the projects that were initiated or assisted by the network are summarized in the following:

- *Operation safety*: This includes community police forums, as well as Operation *Vimba*, a program to encourage people to report crimes.

- *Thou shalt not commit crime*: Groups such as Christians Against Crime, Religion Against Crime, the Police, and the Departments of Education, Culture, and Welfare, along with the Council, developed social developmental programs for at-risk families.
- *Local jobs for local people*: Along with the city council, the network helped produce a local economic development program that focused on job creation and training.
- *Life after prison*: Programs have been developed to reintegrate offenders who have been released from prison back into the community, which includes job training as well as support for communities who are leery about reintegrating the offenders.
- *Victim support center*: A victim support center, run on a volunteer basis, was established. There are also programs that offer assistance to women and children who have been the victims of family violence or left homeless.
- *Anticrime news*: The council launched a media campaign to publicize the various crime prevention initiatives, with the goal of gaining the support and participation of the community (Meek and Bowen-Willer, 1998, 31–33).

6.5 CONCLUSION

Since the end of the Second World War, the nature and scope of the state's role in crime control in the United States and other developed countries can be divided into two periods. The first period persisted up until around the early 1970s, when the state's jurisdiction over crime was unchallenged, fuelling the steep growth of the criminal justice system. The second period was characterized by an ever-expanding role of nonstate actors in crime control, including private citizens, NGOs, community groups, and the private sector.

As the case studies presented in this chapter demonstrate, governments throughout the world—whether at the national, regional, or local level—appear to have encouraged a greater role of private actors in crime prevention and policing and are pursuing more proactive and preventive approaches to crime problems. Numerous governments have created new departments, agencies, and bureaus and have established funding for crime prevention initiatives. While this funding is nowhere near what is allocated to most country's criminal justice systems, it does represent some commitment by governments to a proactive, preventative approach that mobilizes nonstate actors.

To some, the openness of government to crime prevention, and a greater role of nonstate actors in crime control, is a recognition of the limitations of the state and government agencies (and not just criminal justice agencies) in controlling crime, the need for a partnership among all relevant sectors of society, and the importance of assuming a more proactive, preventive approach.

Some critics, however, take a more cynical view of why governments have been receptive to crime prevention. Garland (1996) asserts that the philosophy of crime prevention represents a decentralization of crime-control responsibilities, which he deems is part of a broader "responsibilisation strategy" of governance in the postwar period, whereby governments partially devolve responsibility for crime control to private citizens and organizations while persuading them to act appropriately. This decentralization is a reflection of the rise of a neoliberal ideology in many advanced Western societies that advocates a smaller role for the state in society and, more pointedly, "the dismantling of the welfare state and its perceived perpetuation of a culture of dependency" (Crawford, 1997, 299). Community crime prevention coalesces perfectly with this neoliberal ideology through their shared advocacy of individual responsibility and self-reliant communities. Pavlich (2002, 104) believes that these right-wing beliefs helped propel the ascendancy and currency of crime prevention because "the political logic underlying community crime prevention derives from an advanced neo-liberal discourse that has substantively eroded the previously dominant 'social welfare' governmental rationalities" and which instead valorizes the free market, individual initiative, moral self-responsibility, and community self-reliance as the most effective means to solving (local) social problems.

Despite this apparent commitment to community crime prevention, legitimate questions have been asked as to whether governments are, in fact, willing to give up power and control to nonstate actors. The centralized control that the state and police agencies exercise over local crime prevention projects has also been cited as a factor limiting citizen participation. (For more detailed critiques regarding how the state has undermined citizen participation in community crime prevention, see Chapter 5.)

Governments have also been criticized for failing to place proactive crime prevention policies, programs, and funding at the same level as the criminal justice system. In 1995, the UN Crime and Justice Information Network contended that while many national governments have taken some initial steps to promote proactive policies and programs to prevent crime, no one government "has implemented all these necessary steps. Much remains to be done for these logical approaches to reach their potential, in order to reduce crime in a sustainable way." The same conclusion can be applied today; while national governments throughout the world continue to pursue policies and programs that enlist the principles of crime prevention, these efforts pale in comparison to the massive amount of resources committed to the (largely reactive) traditional criminal justice system. Indeed, there is no doubt that the criminal justice system will continue to be the primary instrument used by the state to address crime and will consume the vast majority of government resources dedicated to crime control.

One of the greatest challenges facing governments in their efforts to control and reduce crime is the allocation of finite resources between the criminal justice sector and other extrajudicial sectors, initiatives, and groups that are increasingly critical to preventing crime and fostering community safety directly (e.g., neighborhood watch programs and recidivism prevention programs) and indirectly (schools, community development, social welfare policies and programs, etc.). "It is a question of balance between pre-crime prevention and post crime reaction. It must be based on evidence as to what works to get effective and cost-efficient crime reduction" (Institute for the Prevention of Crime, 2009, 8).

6.6 DISCUSSION QUESTIONS AND EXERCISES

1. Identify and discuss crime prevention initiatives that have been undertaken by national and state/provincial governments that affect the city or town in which you live.
2. Identify and discuss the crime prevention initiative(s) undertaken by your local government. What policies and programs has it enacted? To what extent does it follow the principles laid out in this chapter?

3. How can governments better promote crime prevention in disadvantaged communities in your city or town?
4. Rudolph Giuliani, the former Mayor of New York, has persistently claimed that the precipitous fall in the city's crime rate was the direct result of the zero-tolerance policies he enacted while he was mayor of the city. Research and critically analyze the claims he has made.
5. In your opinion, why do government resources dedicated to the criminal justice system still greatly exceed those dedicated to the prevention of crime and criminality?

FURTHER READING

Caledon Institute of Social Policy, Crime prevention from the ground up: Municipal crime prevention initiatives, Caledon Institute of Social Policy, Ottawa, Ontario, Canada, February 2001, http://www.caledoninst.org/Publications/PDF/1-894598-50-4.pdf (accessed June, 2007).

Canadian Criminal Justice Association, Safer communities: A social strategy for crime prevention in Canada, *Canadian Journal of Criminology* 1989; 31(4):360–579.

Homel, P., Nutley, S., Webb, B., and Tilley, N., Investing to deliver: Reviewing the implementation of the UK Crime Reduction Programme, Home Office Research, Development and Statistics Directorate, London, U.K., 2004.

Institute for the Prevention of Crime, Making cities safer: Action briefs for municipal stakeholders, Institute for the Prevention of Crime, University of Ottawa, Ottawa, Ontario, Canada, 2009, http://sciencessociales.uottawa.ca/ipc/eng/MCS_actionbriefs.asp.

International Centre for the Prevention of Crime, The role of local government in community safety, Bureau of Justice Assistance, Department of Justice, Washington, DC, 2001, http://www.ncjrs.gov/pdffiles1/bja/184218.pdf.

Justice Center, *Lessons from the States: Reducing recidivism and curbing corrections costs through justice reinvestment*, The Council of State Governments, New York, April 2013, https://www.bja.gov/Publications/CSG_State-Lessons-Learned-Recidivism.pdf.

Linden, R., *Primer on Municipal Crime Prevention*, Federation of Canadian Municipalities, Ottawa, Ontario, Canada, 2000, https://www.fcm.ca/Documents/reports/Primer_on_Municipal_Crime_Prevention_EN.pdf.

United Nations, Twelfth United Nations Congress on crime prevention and criminal justice, Salvador, Brazil, 12–19 April 2010, Making the United Nations Guidelines on crime prevention work, Vienna: United Nations Office on drugs and Crime, Working paper prepared by the Secretariat, 2010, http://www.unodc.org/documents/crime-congress/12th-Crime-Congress/Documents/A_CONF.213_18/V1053828e.pdf.

CASE STUDIES

City of Newcastle [Australia]. *City of Newcastle Crime Prevention Plan*. The City of Newcastle, Newcastle, 2001. www.newcastle.nsw.gov.au/__data/assets/pdf_file/0017/5552/crime_prevention_plan.pdf (Accessed February 21, 2014).

Crime Prevention Ottawa [Canada], Internet web site, http://www.crimepreventionottawa.ca/en (Accessed July 12, 2014).

Lake Macquarie City Council [New South Wales, Australia]. *Crime Prevention Plan, 2009–2011*. Lake Macquarie City Council, 2009. http://www.lakemac.com.au/downloads/Lake%20Macquarie%20Crime%20Prevention%20Plan%202009-2011.PDF (Accessed June 19, 2014).

National Crime Council. A Crime Prevention Strategy for Ireland: Tackling the Concerns of Local Communities. The Stationary Office, Dublin, 2003. www.irlgov.ie/crimecouncil/downloads/CrimePrevention.pdf (Accessed September 11, 2014).

New South Wales Government [Australia]. Preventing Crime. Internet web site www.crimeprevention.nsw.gov.au/ (Access May 30, 2014).

Waterloo Region [Ontario, Canada] Crime Prevention Council, Internet web site http://www.preventingcrime.net/, (Accessed September 1, 2014).

Zimring, F.E., *The City that Became Safe: New York's Lessons for Urban Crime and Its Control*, Oxford University Press, New York, 2011.

CHAPTER 7

POLICING AND CRIME PREVENTION

CONTENTS

7.1 *LEARNING OBJECTIVES*

By the end of this chapter, you should have a better understanding of the:

- Historical roots of crime prevention and community policing
- Evolution of modern policing and its implications for community-based and problem-oriented policing
- Theory underlying community policing and problem-oriented policing
- Contemporary factors that gave rise to the philosophies of community- and problem-oriented policing
- Distinguishing characteristics of community policing and problem-oriented policing
- Similarities and differences between community- and problem-oriented policing
- Practical application of community- and problem-oriented policing
- Other recent innovations in policing and their relationship with crime prevention
- Critiques of community policing, problem-oriented policing, and other recent models

7.2 INTRODUCTION

> Police departments are the sleeping giants of prevention. They are powerful tools that need to be redeployed from reacting to bad things to preventing them.

Jim Jordan
Director of Strategic Planning, Boston Police Department
(as cited in Hicks et al., 2000, 3)

This chapter explores the role of policing and police agencies in crime prevention. Particular emphasis is placed on how the principles of crime prevention are reflected in community- and problem-oriented policing (POP).

Since the creation of the London Metropolitan Police in the early nineteenth century, police have become society's principal instrument of crime control. For Sir Robert Peel, the driving force behind the London Police, there are two main philosophical tenets of policing. First, police should focus on preventing crime. Second, crime control and order maintenance ultimately rest in the hands of the public, so when combating crime the police operate as an extension of the public. More than 150 years later, these two principles have coalesced to form the foundation of community-based and problem-oriented policing.

Community policing advocates that police agencies and their individual members forge strong partnerships with local communities, empowering citizens, and neighborhoods to help prevent crime. While conceptually distinct, problem-oriented policing is also viewed as a central tenet of community policing through its emphasis on a proactive, problem-solving approach to crime and disorder problems.

The adoption of a community policing philosophy has far-reaching implications for police agencies; it represents a significant departure from the modern, paramilitary model that characterized policing during much of the twentieth century, which includes a fundamental shift in power from the police executive to the frontline constable and to the communities served. And while few police forces can truly say they have achieved all the high ideals of this lofty policing philosophy, there is no doubt that community- and problem-oriented policing have had a major impact on policing throughout North America and the developed world.

The theory and practice of community poling arose around the same time that the currency of crime prevention was on the rise. This is no coincidence as the two synergistically informed one another, leading to a number of common traits. In particular, both seek to address the underlying causes of crime problems, require active involvement by community residents, require partnerships beyond law enforcement to be effective, and are approaches or philosophies, rather than programs (Bureau of Justice Statistics, 1997).

Overall, studies into community- and problem-oriented policing have shown them to be effective in accomplishing their goals and in helping to reduce and control crime in areas where they have been implemented with a high degree of fidelity. However, the theory of both has been criticized as being too utopian for most police departments; as such, in practice, few police departments have fully implemented these philosophies, especially the one tenet of organizational change that entails the transfer of power from police executives to frontline officers and the communities they serve.

This chapter begins by providing a brief history of policing in western society, which must be understood in order to locate the roots of community policing (and crime

CASE STUDY 7.1

INTEGRATION OF COMMUNITY- AND PROBLEM-ORIENTED POLICING PRINCIPLES IN THE CALGARY POLICE SERVICE

The Calgary Police Service, located in Alberta, Canada, reports that it has made a number of changes to its policing and organization, reflecting the principles of community- and problem-oriented policing. Early in its 2006–2008 Business Plan, the police service emphasized that it is "dedicated to the concept of community policing, both philosophically and operationally. We focus primarily on crime prevention, crime detection and apprehension, and traffic safety. The tools that we use are: positive community relations, education, problem-solving and use of current technology to analyze conditions, project trends and deploy resources" (Calgary Police Service, 2006, 3).

The International Centre for the Prevention of Crime (2002, 30–31) summarizes the major changes the Calgary Police Service has made in its move toward a community-oriented policing model:

- Strengthening connections with Calgarians and enhancing its relationship with its many diverse communities
- Addressing the demographic, social, economic, and technological changes taking place in Calgary and the rest of the world
- Working with the City of Calgary departments and community partners on homelessness and other pressing social issues
- Maintaining its focus on the youth by addressing the many challenges the youth face

Working with the Community:

- Many community partnerships have been established resulting in improved police response to issues like children at risk, prostitution, and domestic violence.
- Relationships with Calgary's diverse communities have been strengthened through the establishment of advisory committees and increased police involvement. Key to the success of these relationships is the involvement of both frontline officers and senior management.
- There are increased opportunities for the public to provide feedback and input into decision making.

Organizational Restructuring:

- The entire organization was restructured based upon feedback from communities and staff.
- Work areas were reorganized to directly link intervention and prevention with investigation, enforcement, and prosecution, helping to integrate proactive policing.
- Decision making now involves people at all levels of the organization.
- Employee recruiting, training, promotions, and transfer systems now are aligned with community needs and expectations.
- The recruiting process aims to increase the diversity of members within the service. New police facilities have been developed locating police services within communities, strengthening ties, and reinforcing a community-based approach.

Problem-Oriented Approach:

- The police service has shifted from a reactive force to a proactive, strategic service.
- A more holistic approach to problem solving has been adopted, strengthening both intervention and prevention efforts.
- Police priorities are determined with the community, so the issues of most concern are addressed.
- New programs have been developed in response to emerging problems or issues (e.g., stalking, high-risk offenders) (International Centre for the Prevention of Crime, 2002, 30–31).

prevention). Following this historical overview, this chapter defines, describes, compares, and contrasts community- and problem-oriented policing. Other recent innovations in policing that satisfy the central tenets of crime prevention will also be discussed. These innovations go by such monikers as hot spot policing, CompStat, broken windows policing, predictive policing, third-party policing, and intelligence-led policing. Challenges and critiques of all of these models of policing will then be presented.

7.3 RETRACING THE ORIGINS OF COMMUNITY POLICING: A BRIEF HISTORY OF POLICING IN WESTERN SOCIETIES

To understand the nexus between policing and crime prevention, one must examine policing in historical terms, for the roots of crime prevention and community policing can be traced back centuries, (only to be ignored for much of the twentieth century and then rediscovered beginning in the 1970s).

It is possible to locate the origins of public policing and law enforcement to the adjunctive role the military played in civil society in some early western civilizations. This was true of the Roman Empire, which relied on the Roman legions to maintain law and order, or the fourteenth-century France, where a military corps operating under the command of the Constable of France (the *connétablie*) protected the roads from highway robbers. Despite these early precedents, most other forms of state-imposed social control (including enforcement and punishment) were not directed toward grievous acts that occurred between private citizens, but rather toward maintaining obedience and loyalty to the monarchy and, to lesser extent, the Church (Lab, 1997, 2).

7.3.1 Early Policing in England

For centuries, most western countries had no state agency to intervene on behalf of a crime victim, and the earliest responses to acts that would today constitute a criminal offenses were left to the individual, the family, and the local community (Lab, 1997, 2). As Stevens (2005) writes in *A Brief Guide to Police History*,

> In the beginning, there was "kin policing," with its penchant for blood feuding and traditions of tribal justice. Many pre-civilized villages or communities are believed to have had a rudimentary form of law enforcement (morals enforcement) derived from the power and authority of kinship systems, rule by elders, or perhaps some

form of totemism or naturism. Under kin policing, the family of the offended individual was expected to assume responsibility for justice by capturing, branding, or mutilating the offender.

In England, long before the Industrial Revolution, rural villages maintained order through cooperative practices that relied on volunteers to help protect the community and one another. One common practice, referred to as *watch and ward*, rotated the responsibility for keeping vigil over the town, particularly at night, among the able-bodied male citizens. Should a threat be identified, a call for help would be made (a *hue and cry*), and it was then up to the other night watchmen or the community at large to mobilize, apprehend, and even punish an offender (Lab, 1997, 2–3).

As the decades passed, this communal approach to policing became more formalized in England. King Alfred the Great (who ruled from 871 to 899) decreed that it was the various *thanes* (landowners) who were responsible for policing, which included delivering criminals to the king for punishment and settling civil disputes. The arrangement was based on the concept of the *King's peace*, whereby the sovereign assured his subjects' peace and security in return for their loyalty. The responsibility for policing villages and countrysides was passed along to the commoners who, in later years, were organized into a *tithing*. The membership of tithings (which literally meant *10 people*) was generally made up of 10 homesteads. All adult males were obligated to be a member of a tithing, and in doing so, they had to take an oath (a *mutual pledge* or *frankpledge*) that they would not engage in any behavior that broke the law, harmed another person (outside the family), and betrayed the norms and customs of the village. The tithing also acted as a pledge for the behavior of all its members, guaranteeing that offenders within their jurisdiction would be delivered to the thane or, in later years, the court (failing that the tithing might be liable to compensate an injured party). The head of this group was called a *tithingman*. In some areas, 100 tithingmen came together to form a *hundred*, which elected one representative who was called a *reeve*. The reeve essentially became a judicial authority for those in the *hundred*, dealing with lawbreakers, handling complaints, and mediating disputes (Trojanowicz et al., 1998, 29; Stevens, 2005).

By the tenth century, law enforcement professionals began to emerge in England. Unpaid, part-time constables were appointed by nobility to supervise different tithings, which included mobilizing men and quarter mastering the necessary resources (horses, weapons, etc.). The *hundreds* were further organized into groups of 10, each of which was called a *shire*. A shire was supervised by a *shire-reeve*, who was empowered by the monarchy to maintain order over a particular district or county and was given law enforcement and judicial powers. At first, the shire-reeve (the forerunner to the latter-day sheriff) was elected by the parish (a church district). Eventually, he was appointed by the Crown (Palmiotto, 2000, 3). As such, he was no longer accountable to the local people, but to the king. This was one of the very first steps along the path whereby the state began to take responsibility for policing, law enforcement, and crime control.

In 1285, King Edward proclaimed the Statute of Winchester, which made it the duty of all citizens to keep the king's peace and, as a result, had the right and responsibility to arrest a suspected offender. The statute codified into law the requirement that all villages in the Kingdom adopt a system of surveillance and policing. In effect, this royal order formalized the *watch and ward* system, requiring all able-bodied men, acting under the supervision of a constable, to take turns guarding the gates and patrolling the town at night. Increasingly, the wealthier men in the villages compensated commoners to perform their policing duties (Stansfield, 1996, 25; Palmiotto, 2000, 3–4).

In short, policing and crime prevention in England before the Industrial Revolution relied on social ties that existed naturally within the community and emanated from one's communal responsibilities. Civic justice was understood to be a community undertaking, outside and separate from the more narrow and formal social control that was exercised by the state (the monarchy), which was concerned with ensuring that taxes were collected, rebellions were crushed, and the absolute power of the monarchy remained intact.

This community-based, voluntary system of civic justice persisted in England until the late seventh century, when the shift in responsibility for policing, law enforcement, and crime control from the local citizenry to the state began to accelerate. The passage of the *Highwayman Act* in 1692 set up a new form of policing by establishing the practice of paying bounty to individuals for the capture of thieves and the recovery of property. By the mid-1700s, these bounty hunters (or *thief takers*) were organized under the control of English magistrates and were paid through a finder's fee levied against the recovered property (Lab, 1997, 3). A similar system was used during wartime when maritime *privateers* were licensed by the Crown to pillage the merchant ships of enemy countries.

The dramatic social changes that resulted from the Industrial Revolution in the late eighteenth century accelerated even further the evolution toward the state's control over law and order. As the British population expanded and as villages grew into cities, crime and civil unrest increased, leading to calls for a more formal and permanent system of policing and law enforcement. One of those who pushed for reforms was the magistrate and author Henry Fielding, who believed that while crime control was the responsibility of everyone, a dedicated police force was required for the modern city. As the magistrate for Bow Street in London, Fielding established and supervised the Bow Street Runners, a small group of plainclothes, salaried constables whose job it was to bring criminals to justice. Over the years, the Bow Street Runners grew in number, patrols became commonplace in London, and mounted patrols expanded to the rural areas to curb thefts from trains and carriages (Palmiotto, 2000, 4–5).

During the early part of the nineteenth century, the need for a more formal and dedicated police force in London was becoming increasingly apparent. Concern over public safety was growing as theft, prostitution, and alcohol-related street violence, along with countless other crime and disorder problems, were on the rise. A spate of vicious murders and riots finally spurred the British government to embark on the creation of a government-run, citywide police force for London. In 1829, Sir Robert Peel, the Home Secretary in the British Cabinet, won parliamentary approval for his bill to create the London Metropolitan Police Force, the world's first modern police agency.

A true visionary, Peel—along with Charles Rowan and Richard Mayne, the first co-commissioners of the London Metropolitan Police—touted the prevention of crime as a basic principle underlying police work. As part of their nine principles of policing (see Box 7.1), they also stressed that crime control and order maintenance ultimately rest in the hands of the public and that the police are simply an extension of the public (symbolized by the famous quote "the police are the public, and the public are the police"). In the early days of the London Metropolitan Police, the paid constables—who wore three-quarter-length royal blue coats, white trousers, and top hats and were armed with a truncheon—had no greater power, rights, or duties than other citizens (Dempsey, 1994, 5). The only difference was that they were hired to give their full attention to maintaining law and order. The personification of Peel's

---

BOX 7.1

NINE PRINCIPLES OF POLICING, AS COMPILED BY THE CREATORS OF THE LONDON METROPOLITAN POLICE

1. To prevent crime and disorder, as an alternative to their repression by military force and by severity of legal punishment.
2. To recognize always that the power of the police to fulfill their functions and duties is dependent on public approval of their existence, actions and behavior, and on their ability to secure and maintain public respect.
3. To recognize always that to secure and maintain the respect and approval of the public means also the securing of the willing co-operation of the public in the task of securing observance of laws.
4. To recognize always that the extent to which the co-operation of the public can be secured diminishes, proportionately, the necessity of the use of physical force and compulsion for achieving police objectives.
5. To seek and preserve public favor, not by pandering to public opinion, but by constantly demonstrating absolutely impartial service to law, in complete independence of policy and without regard to the justice or injustices of the substance of individual laws; by ready offering of individual service and friendship to all members of the public without regard to their wealth or social standing; by ready exercise of courtesy and friendly good humor; and by ready offering of sacrifice in protecting and preserving life.
6. To use physical force only when the exercise of persuasion, advice and warning is found to be insufficient to obtain public co-operation to an extent necessary to secure observance of law or to restore order; and to use only the minimum degree of physical force which is necessary on any particular occasion for achieving a police objective.
7. To maintain at all times a relationship with the public that gives reality to the historic tradition that the police are the public and that the public are the police; the police being only members of the public who are paid to give full-time attention to duties which are incumbent on every citizen, in the interests of community welfare and existence.
8. To recognize always the need for strict adherence to police executive functions, and to refrain from even seeming to usurp the powers of the judiciary or avenging individuals or the state, and of authoritatively judging guilt and punishing the guilty.
9. To recognize always that the test of police efficiency is the absence of crime and disorder, and not the visible evidence of police action in dealing with them (as cited in CIVITAS, n.d.).

policing model, which Chalom (2001, 7) writes, "is the foot patrol, which was supposed to counter public disorders while bringing the police closer to the community."

Did You Know?

Police officers with the London Metropolitan Police are named *bobbies* after Sir Robert Peel and the police force's *Scotland Yard* nickname derived from the location of its original headquarters in an old palace in London that was built for Scottish royalty.

7.3.2   Early Policing in North America

The origins of policing and community safety in the United States and Canada during colonial times roughly paralleled that of their mother country. Private citizens were expected to keep the peace in most early towns and villages. A night watch established by a town meeting in Boston in 1636 may have been one of the earliest forms of community-based policing, while similar nighttime patrols or *watch and ward* systems were being implemented in larger towns, such as New York, Philadelphia, Toronto, and Quebec City. Philadelphia is credited with advancing the evolution of citizen-based policing "by organizing the city into ten patrol areas, each with a constable who recruited citizen volunteers to keep the watch with him" (Trojanowicz et al., 1998, 32). Following on the heels of the creation of the London Metropolitan Police, American cities on the eastern seaboard, such as New York, Boston, Baltimore, Cleveland, and Philadelphia, also witnessed the creation of dedicated police agencies. In the west, the so-called frontier justice was enforced by local sheriffs who often relied on citizens to form posses that were, at times, nothing more than vigilante mobs.

During their colonial years, the most populous portions of Upper and Lower Canada were amply garrisoned with British troops and local militias. As in Britain, magistrates were appointed for most areas of Upper and Lower Canada and had the powers of police, judge, and jury. As the country expanded westward during the latter part of the nineteenth century, lawlessness reigned in the absence of any government presence, which was epitomized by whiskey forts that traded cheap rotgut liquor with local Indian bands in exchange for valuable buffalo pelts (contributing to both the decimation of the native and buffalo population). The trading posts became a serious political issue for the Dominion government in Ottawa, which decided to create a new paramilitary police force to be dispatched westward. This accomplished the dual objectives of bringing law and order to the Northwest Territories, while establishing the Dominion government's sovereignty over the land. On May 3, 1873, Prime Minister John A. MacDonald introduced a bill into the Canadian Parliament that led to the creation of the North West Mounted Police. Unlike most other countries in the world, the large-scale settlement of a vast region of Canada was accompanied by a professional police force to maintain order and stability.

7.3.3   Policing in the Twentieth Century

During the late nineteenth and early twentieth centuries, a number of significant changes in how western societies responded to crime and deviance emerged. As industrialized societies became more populated, urbanized, and complex, the state assumed more and more responsibility for crime control, which in turn was delegated to state-run agencies (the police, the courts, correctional facilities, etc.). And while governments in most western countries assumed the responsibility for ensuring public safety and security prior to the rise of *welfare state*, the growth and intractability of the state-imposed criminal justice system following World War II were unprecedented. The result was that the formal social control apparatus of the state (the criminal justice system) increasingly eclipsed and usurped the community-based system of informal social control that had been in place for centuries.

Unfortunately, the earliest police forces in America's largest cities were notoriously corrupt, primarily because power was instilled in precinct captains who were politically appointed by crooked ward bosses who ran the precincts. According to Fisher-Stewart

(2007, 2), this *political era* of policing in America, which lasted until the 1930s, was marked by graft and corrupt behavior on the part of the police. The result was that "many Americans did not trust the police who were seen as in the pockets of big-city political machines." Further, city policemen in America differed from their British counterparts in that they carried a firearm, thus "giving them a very definite power over the average citizen." This power was routinely abused as "police ruled largely by physical coercion."

The 1930s marked the so-called *reform era* for policing in America as a number of measures were undertaken at the local, state, and federal levels to increase professionalism and decrease the level of police corruption and brutality. Police forces were given autonomy from the ward bosses, police executives were hired and promoted based on merit, higher education standards were expected of recruits, more rigorous screening and training of police officers were put in place, professional standards were created for the conduct of individual police officers, and a military discipline and hierarchical organizational structure was adopted with power being centralized in police management "to ensure compliance with standard operating procedures and to encourage a professional aura of impartiality" (Community Policing Consortium, 1994, 5).

The advent of the new professional law enforcement agency, however, also marked a period wherein police forces were moving away from the community-based and proactive policing philosophy envisioned by Sir Robert Peel. The centralization of power in police executives meant that the frontline constables had less discretion in their daily duties and were now accountable not to the community they served but to their superiors in the police force. Police managers also assigned "officers to rotating shifts and moved them frequently from one geographical location to another to eliminate corruption," which meant that police officers were no longer rooted in one particular community (Community Policing Consortium, 1994, 5).

The sprawling cities of the twentieth century also required the need for the roaming patrol car, which physically (and symbolically) removed police officers from the communities they served and made Peel's cherished *beat cop* almost extinct. As Manning and Stoshine put it, the "patrol car, in widespread use by the 1920s, changed the mode of policing from foot patrols to motor patrols, thereby reducing face-to-face contact between police and the citizenry." The widespread availability of residential telephones, combined with police two-way radio systems, meant that citizens, who before had to seek out the beat cop in their neighborhood, could now contact police simply by placing a telephone call (Manning and Stoshine, 2002, 1194).

Moreover, as cities continued to grow in size—in terms of both population and geographic scope—and as crime increased, police agencies were becoming largely reactive and incident driven, leaving few resources for a preventive, proactive approach to crime problems. The advent of the 911 public emergency systems in the 1960s, combined with the growing crime rate of that decade and the finite resources of police, only contributed to the reactive, incident-driven nature of the police. It also exacerbated the limited interaction between citizens and police, outside of their responses to calls for service. According to the Community Policing Consortium,

> By the 1970s, rapid telephone contact with police through 911 systems allowed them to respond quickly to crimes. Answering the overwhelming number of calls for service, however, left police little time to prevent crimes from occurring. As increasingly sophisticated communications technology made it possible for calls to be transmitted almost instantaneously, officers had to respond to demands for

assistance regardless of the urgency of the situation. Answering calls severely limited a broad police interaction with the community. The advent of the computer also contributed to the decrease in police contact with the community. Statistics, rather than the type of service provided or the service recipients, became the focus for officers and managers. As computers generated data on crime patterns and trends, counted the incidence of crimes, increased the efficiency of dispatch, and calculated the rapidity and outcome of police response, rapid response became an end in itself.

Community Policing Consortium (1994, 6)

As police agencies grew in size and adapted the *professional* model of policing, they became centralized, bureaucratic, hierarchical, and paramilitary organizations. At the same time, they were less and less part of a community's response to peace, security, and order and more and more preoccupied with advances in internal structure and operations, the narrow responsibility of law enforcement, and the belief that the professional police officer knew best and community involvement in crime control was perceived as unnecessary (Goldstein, 1979; Community Policing Consortium, 1994, 6).

7.3.4 Crisis in Policing

Despite the proliferation of the professional, high-tech, incident-driven, rapid-response policing model, by the late 1960s, the crime rate continued to skyrocket throughout North America. This prompted accusations that the state-controlled criminal justice system, and the police in particular, could no longer be considered the exclusive or even the most effective institution to control crime in complex, modern societies. At the same time, *race riots* were rocking American cities, with some blaming police for setting the conditions that led to the civil unrest (due to systematic racial profiling and the enforcement of Jim Crow laws in the south) or by failing to prevent the riots from occurring in the first place (President's Commission on Law Enforcement and Administration of Justice, 1967). The police appeared to be estranged from and grossly out of touch with the communities they were supposed to be serving and were even seen as adversaries by some communities. This was especially true among many in the African-American community, who viewed police as simply another repressive, racist tool of the state that was deployed to maintain an unjust and discriminatory society (Fisher-Stewart, 2007, 3). Criticisms of law enforcement agencies in the United States could no longer be ignored when they were being made by middle-class, white college students protesting the Vietnam War, who also became victims of disproportionate responses by police. As Braga (2008, 8) writes, "The tactics used in law enforcement responses were viewed as draconian, and there was a public outcry over police forces that resembled and acted like 'occupying armies' rather than civil servants." The uncovering of massive corruption in the New York City Police Departments in the early 1970s also served to undermine the public's confidence in police.

By the late 1960s, the principles of community policing and crime prevention, which accompanied the creation of the London Metropolitan Police Force, began to reemerge as options to address the crisis of legitimacy that was engulfing police. Within the public policy arena, the initial groundwork for a new vision of policing in America was laid with the 1967 Presidential Crime Commission Report, which asserted the need for an active and involved citizenry in helping police address local crime problems.

Eventually, the US federal crime-control policy recognized that the "community should play the central role in defining community crime prevention and that organized groups of residents are perhaps the best vehicle for responding to local crime" (U.S. Department of Justice, 1977, 3). It also became clear that the police needed to reestablish a positive relationship with the communities they served.

During the 1970s, police agencies in America began embarking on initiatives that sought to bring them back into the community fold, while supporting local crime prevention efforts. This included establishing community relations units, school liaison officers, foot patrols, and Neighborhood Watch schemes. While initiatives like foot patrols did not result in any significant impact on crime rates, early research suggested that they did help increase people's perceptions that their neighborhoods were safer, while their opinions of police improved (Kelling et al., 1981).

In 1979, University of Wisconsin law professor Herman Goldstein introduced the concept of *problem-oriented policing*, which would also prove to have a major impact on the theory and practice of policing. Goldstein adroitly encapsulated a major problem in policing that accompanied its modernization and professionalization: police agencies became increasingly preoccupied with how they were doing their work (e.g., the organization and management of a police agency) and seemingly less concerned with the effectiveness of their work (i.e., crime control). In other words, while police agencies were becoming more efficient, they appeared to be less effective at controlling the upward spiraling crime rate. Police had lost touch with a major foundation of policing: to best address criminal problems, one must try to ameliorate the underlying cause or at least the facilitating factors (Goldstein, 1979). The strategy of problem-oriented policing conceived by professor Goldstein provided a new paradigm that was built on the basic tenets of crime prevention: determining the scope and nature of a crime problem and then formulating an appropriate response, stressing solutions that are individualized to the specific circumstances of the problem. Goldstein's work contributed to a tidal wave of police introspection and helped usher modern policing into a new era that placed far more emphasis on a proactive, problem-solving approach to crime.

As the millennium drew to a close, police forces throughout the world were complementing their predominant incident-driven law enforcement model with a more proactive, community-based, problem-solving approach. With that said, police agencies continue to dedicate far more resources to traditional, incident-driven, reactive law enforcement compared to proactive, community-based crime prevention and problem-oriented policing approaches.

7.4 COMMUNITY- AND PROBLEM-ORIENTED POLICING: AN OVERVIEW

The philosophies of community policing and problem-oriented policing materialized in response to deficiencies in modern policing. And while community- and problem-oriented policing are mutually conducive, they actually arose as a critique of and a correction to different problems that plague the so-called professional policing model, which contribute to their conceptual distinctiveness (Sherman and Eck, 2006, 298).

Mastrofski (1991) argues that community policing emerged as an articulation of a police reform movement that addressed a number of interrelated problems that threatened police legitimacy: the inability of police to control crime and disorder, the limitations inherent in an overwhelming emphasis on law enforcement (as opposed to a broader *peacekeeping role*), and the alienation of many communities from local police agencies. According to Stone and Travis (2011, 4–5), the advent of community polic- ing and a greater focus on a problem-solving approach to crime "marked an epochal shift" from the professional crime-fighting model of policing that was criticized as "too hierarchical in its management, too narrow in its response to crime," and "deliber- ately removed from communities." Moreover, "it reinforced pernicious biases deeply entrenched in the wider society. Both good and bad police work was performed in that mode, but it was hardly professional." In short, the organizing framework for policing up until the 1980s was not professionalism at all, "but rather a technocratic, rigid, often cynical model of policing" (Stone and Travis, 2011, 5).

The dimunition of police legitimacy, combined with the renewed importance placed on the public's role in preventing crime and a more problem-oriented approach to con- trolling crime in general, demanded that new approaches to the delivery of policing services be incorporated into modern policing.

First and foremost, these new approaches required some attempts by police to reconnect with the communities they served through greater consultation, coopera- tion, coordination, and communication. As such, the philosophy of community polic- ing, has most concertedly sought to redress the modern police force's estrangement from the communities it served.

In contrast, problem-oriented policing arose from the crisis of police effectiveness at "preventing and controlling crime" (Sherman and Eck, 2006, 299). The strategies that had become dominant in the arsenal of police as part of their reactive, incident-driven, law enforcement, crime-control approach—random patrolling, hiring more police offi- cers, tougher laws, rapid response, etc.—were simply not proving effective in stemming rising crime rates and solving crime problems. They were largely reactive, responding to the same problems and the same offenders, while relying on rigid, inflexible, and short-term solutions (i.e., processing offenders through the criminal justice system).

Thus, when comparing the defining characteristics of the two policing philosophies, problem-oriented policing is concerned with directing police attention to the causes of crime problems, while community policing emphasizes a strong partnership between the police and the public. As Sherman and Eck (2006, 299) put it, "where the core concept of community policing was community involvement for its own sake, the core concept for problem-oriented policing was *results*: the effect of police activity on public safety, including (but not limited to) crime prevention."

Despite these conceptual and practical differences, the two policing philosophies are highly complementary, and problem-oriented policing has become an important part of the broader community policing paradigm. According to Braga (2008, 12–13), "community-oriented police officers use problem solving as a tool, and problem- oriented departments often form partnerships with the community."

The remainder of this chapter explores the definitions and characteristics of each of these distinct but complementary approaches to policing.

7.5 COMMUNITY POLICING

First and foremost, community policing is about the relationship between police and the communities they serve. Specifically, it intends to promote a closer relationship between the police and the community, emphasizing an active partnership in identifying and solving local crime and disorder problems. For Robert Trojanowicz and colleagues, central to community policing is the idea that

> ... police officers and private citizens working together in creative ways can help solve contemporary community problems related to crime, fear of crime, social and physical disorder, and neighborhood conditions. The philosophy is predicated on the belief that achieving these goals requires that police departments develop a new relationship with citizens in the community, allowing them the power to set local police priorities and involving them in efforts to improve the overall quality of life in their neighborhoods. It shifts the focus of police work from handling random crime calls to addressing community concerns.
>
> **Trojanowicz et al. (1998, 3)**

Fielding (2005) succinctly defines community policing as a "style of policing in which the police are close to the public, know their concerns from regular everyday contacts, and act on them in accord with the community's wishes" (as cited in Glaser and Denhardt, 2010, 310). Furthermore, given its strong emphasis on community participation (and its implicit critique of the passive role of citizens in crime control), community policing engages citizens and other private actors as "coproducers" of public safety (Skolnick and Bayley, 1988).

Community policing is not a technique, a tactic, a program, or a single unit within a police department. Rather, it is a philosophy as to how police are to deliver their services to the public, within the broader context of how best to address crime and disorder problems. In theory, community policing has a number of profound implications for the delivery of policing services:

- The community policing mandate, as it reflects the broader goals of community crime prevention, is to support citizen-based initiatives and reinforce the informal social control mechanisms of the local community (Wilson and Kelling, 1982).
- The goal of community policing is much more than simply enforcing laws; it is about contributing to the broader safety, security, and health of a community.
- Community policing emphasizes a proactive, problem-oriented approach that strives to address the causes and facilitators of local crime problems in order to prevent such problems from emerging, continuing, or worsening. A problem-solving approach means that police seek out solutions that are most appropriate to the problem, which may entail alternatives to the criminal justice system (Goldstein, 1987, 15).
- Community policing requires a transformed organizational structure that is intended to result in greater responsibility, autonomy, and discretion for front-line constables (Skolnick and Bayley, 1988). Police officers are responsible for a wide range of activities geared toward solving neighborhood crime and disorder problems, in partnership with community members. Community policing is often accompanied by a spatial decentralization that, at the very least, involves establishing community policing stations in different neighborhoods. The composition of a police agency should also better reflect the demographic and social composition of the communities it serves (Leighton, 1991, 10).

In short, the advent of community policing entails sweeping and comprehensive changes to police departments operating under the professional model. It "requires changes to every part of policing, including its supervision and management, training, investigations, performance evaluation, accountability and even its values" (Stone and Travis, 2011, 4). In the words of one former senior English police officer,

> Implementing community policing is not a simple policy change that can be effected by issuing a directive through the normal channels. It is not a mere restructuring of the force to provide the same service more efficiently. Nor is it a cosmetic decoration designed to impress the public and promote greater cooperation. For the police it is an entirely different way of life. It is a new way for police officers to see themselves and to understand their role in society. The task facing the police chief is nothing less than to change the fundamental culture of the organization (as cited in Stone and Travis, 2011, 4).

The defining characteristics of community policing can be grouped into three categories that collectively distinguish it from the hierarchical, incident-driven, centralized model that has characterized public (*professional*) policing for much of the twentieth century:

1. *Partnerships*: Collaboration with the communities served by police and other third parties (including other government agencies) in addressing crime and disorder problems
2. *Problem oriented*: An analytical process that is applied to crime problems, which entails defining the problem, identifying contributing causes, and then applying the most appropriate problem-solving strategy (which may fall outside the criminal justice system)
3. *Organizational restructuring*: A transformation of the traditional organizational structure and culture of police agencies

Each of these major themes is addressed in detail on the following pages.

7.5.1 Partnerships

While there is no universally accepted definition of community policing, Leighton (1991, 3) suggests that its defining principle is a full partnership between the community and the police in identifying and ameliorating local crime and disorder problems. Community policing emphasizes that such problems are the joint property of the police and the public, and both are to become coproducers of order and civility (Wilson and Kelling, 1982; Schneider, 1987). This is no simple matter, as Liederbach et al. (2008, 272) note, for "one of the central problems for police administrators and other proponents of community policing has been the integration of community concerns and the activities of street-level officers, and the issue of how police can successfully work with citizens to reduce crime has been a primary focus of community-era reforms since the inception of the movement."

The police–community partnership is achieved through an interactive, cooperative, and reciprocal relationship that entails a genuine bonding of interests; close, mutually beneficial ties; and a pooling of resources (Skolnick and Bayley, 1988, 27). A police force must be seen as part of—not separate and isolated from—the public. For Friedmann (1992), what characterizes community policing is an unprecedented, genuine reaching out to the community. At the practical level, this means that police need to take into account the needs and priorities of the community they serve and work with citizens and organizations as equals. In other words, community policing imposes a new responsibility on the police to devise ways to sincerely work as equal partners with the public in policing and crime prevention. For Skolnick and Bayley (1988, 5), "community policing should be said to exist only when new programs are implemented that raise the level of public participation in the maintenance of public order."

CASE STUDY 7.2

PARTNERSHIP-BASED COMMUNITY POLICING IN WISCONSIN

West 6th Street in Racine, Wisconsin, was considered one of the worst blocks in town. Drug trafficking, gang activity, violent crime, litter, abandoned cars, and derelict properties all contributed to the decline of this low- to moderate-income area. Many residents were also losing faith in the ability of police to control crime in the neighborhood, which compounded an already strained relationship that included rock-throwing confrontations between unruly crowds and police officers.

In response, a joint police–community action group was formed to organize area residents and to direct policing, crime control, and other neighborhood priorities. Through these partnerships, a variety of collaborative problem-solving approaches were initiated that involved cracking down on gangs, drug trafficking, litter, absentee landlords who violated building codes, and other local problems. The partnership evolved into the West 6th Street Association, a formal organization made up of police, local residents, churches, and businesses that became one of the strongest neighborhood advocacy organizations in the city.

The police department also embarked on a partnership with local business leaders to purchase houses located near the center of criminal activity and renovate them for use as community policing offices. Police also developed better working partnerships with other city and county agencies to combine resources and utilize the powers of these other agencies to address the local crime and disorder problems.

To help residents access needed government services, the police offered space in its neighborhood-based office to a number of governmental and nongovernmental social service agencies, including a family welfare agency, the health department, the state probation and parole agency, and a reading tutoring service for children and adults.

These partnership-based initiatives, along with more intensive policing, helped contribute to a decrease in property crime, drug trafficking, violent crime, and calls for service. There was also an increase in home ownership, an increase in the number of local businesses in the area, and an improvement in the physical appearance of the neighborhood (U.S. Department of Justice, 1999, 30–36).

Some of the components or themes essential to a fruitful partnership between the police and the communities they serve (and hence central to community policing) include the following: effective two-way communication; commitment to community empowerment, informal social control, and collective efficacy; responsive and accountable to the community; and multiagency cooperation.

7.5.1.1 Effective Two-Way Communication A productive and symmetrical partnership between police and community members is very much contingent on effective communication and dialogue between the two. Skolnick and Bayley (1988, 6) stress that it is important to remember that the words *community* and *communicate* share a common origin; community-based policing suggests active communication with the public. Communication between the police and the public must be two-way; the public must be encouraged to play its traditional role of providing information to police on local problems but should also be empowered to provide input into policing priorities and strategies. The advent of community policing has meant that many police agencies now employ a community consultation process as a strategy to solicit input from local residents (Weiler, 1993). Consultation mediums include public meetings, victim surveys, neighborhood liaison officers, race relations departments, and community policing offices. Two-way communication also means having the police keep the public informed as much as possible of its priorities, strategies, and progress on serious and prolonged cases (without jeopardizing operations).

The Community Policing Consortium (1994, 15–16) discusses some of the various examples of communication that should occur between the police and the public under the rubric of community policing:

> For the patrol officer, police/community partnership entails talking to local business owners to help identify their problems and concerns, visiting residents in their homes to offer advice on security, and helping to organize and support neighborhood watch groups and regular community meetings. For example, the patrol officer will canvass the neighborhood for information about a string of burglaries and then revisit those residents to inform them when the burglar is caught. The chief police executive will explain and discuss controversial police tactics so that community members understand the necessity of these tactics for public and officer safety. The department management will consult community members about gang suppression tactics, and every level of the department will actively solicit the concerns and suggestions of community groups, residents, leaders, and local government officials. In this police/community partnership, providing critical social services will be acknowledged as being inextricably linked to deterring crime, and problem solving will become a cooperative effort.

Dialogue, as opposed to technical reports and memos, would be the preferred mode of communication. In their dialogue with community members, police should emphasize conversation and avoid lecturing. Police officers should continually enter into reflective dialogue with community members and listen with sincerity and empathy. As Skolnick and Bayley (1988) argue, "community policing in practice involves not only listening sympathetically but also creating new opportunities to do so." Police would ensure that they speak the same language as the communities they serve. This would mean avoiding technical jargon or legalese and relying on language (including slang) and other forms of communication familiar to and understood by community members.

CASE STUDY 7.3

MASS COMMUNICATION BY POLICE IN CHILE

In 1997, police in Chile set up a community radio station to communicate with and educate the public. The station broadcasts daily bulletins on crime problems but also delivers educational information on a diverse range of issues such as drug abuse, alcoholism, family violence, and delinquency. "Program content is based on the sharing of experience and focuses on prevention and educating the public through an interactive process designed to foster positive relations with the community and respect for individual rights" (Chalom et al., 2001, 22).

7.5.1.2 Commitment to Community Empowerment, Informal Social Control, and Collective Efficacy For communities to be equal partners with police, and as a way to ensure that the ideals of community-based crime prevention are achieved, community policing agencies should work to reinforce the informal social control and collective efficacy mechanisms of local communities (see Chapters 1 and 5 for a description of informal social control and collective efficacy) (Wilson and Kelling, 1982). Community policing must help nurture or reinforce local norms and behaviors that facilitate the ability of communities to informally regulate their own environment. Community policing recognizes that the police cannot impose a lasting order on a community from the outside; instead, they are one of many resources a community can turn toward to help empower them to solve local problems. In theory, community policing can help support informal social control and collective efficacy by helping to empower residents to take a proprietary interest over their neighborhood. In their study exploring the role of policing in promoting local collective efficacy, Sargeant et al. (2013, 170) found that "police are most likely to enhance CE when they foster a sense of effectiveness, use inclusive and partnership-oriented strategies and when they implement strategies in a manner that encourages perceptions of police legitimacy. Moreover, if police can maintain or cultivate a sense of empowerment among community residents, they are more likely to foster CE."

7.5.1.3 Responsive and Accountable to the Community One way to empower communities is to provide them with greater input into policing policies, priorities, and processes. For Chalom et al. (2001, 43), "police forces must go beyond mere consultation to set up formal mechanisms for partnership between the police and local communities." This includes providing the public with the powers to actually help set policing priorities. As an extension of its commitment to the ideals of crime prevention, community policing requires the police agency and its individual members to be responsive and accountable to the communities it serves. In this respect, the public is viewed not only as the partners of police but also as their clients and even their bosses. Under the banner of community policing, a police agency can be judged as to whether the needs of the community are being appropriately served, mechanisms are in place to ensure a police force is accountable to the communities it serves, communities have a say in policing and community safety policies and programs, and the police force makes sure there is sufficient transparency to allow a reasonable awareness and scrutiny of the organization. A further implication is that individual police officers are no longer exclusively accountable to their supervisors but also to the people they serve. To this end, the priorities and the strategies of the police department and the individual police officer are influenced by the needs and interests of their constituents and not just the dictates of the police management.

7.5.1.4 Multiagency Cooperation The partnership approach that underlies community policing extends beyond the public to include government agencies. A multiagency approach entails police working as a team with other government agencies to jointly solve problems through a mutually compatible division of labor. The argument is that through the pooling and coordination of different yet complementary areas of expertise, powers, resources, and approaches, a multiagency team approach can address crime and disorder problems in a more problem-oriented, comprehensive, long-term, and permanent fashion. It is also a more efficient model for the delivery of services to the public by reducing overlap and duplication by government agencies (U.S. Conference on Mayors, 1999).

This intergovernmental team approach is a recognition that certain crime problems and their underlying causes are complex and multifaceted enough to warrant a multi-faceted approach that cannot be delivered exclusively through one government agency (the police or otherwise). As Fisher-Stewart (2007, 10) notes, the police

> ... do not have the resources or skills to deal with all the root causes of crime. They are not equipped to solve the causes and problems of poverty or unemployment. They are not psychologists or counselors who can uncover the reasons for spousal or child abuse. They are not educators who can give people hope for a productive life. These larger societal issues are best handled by agencies set up to address those problems with input from the citizens they serve... While the police are not equipped to deal with the root causes of crime, community policing can enable the police to create bridges to the agencies charged with dealing with those root causes. Law enforcement officers can serve as ombudsmen, providing a critical link to public and private organizations that offer help.

Solutions to addressing the causes or even the symptoms of a crime problem may also fall under the jurisdiction of different government agencies. An intergovernmental team approach reflects the problem-oriented principles inherent in community policing; government agencies other than police may have more appropriate powers, resources, and expertise to solve certain crime problems or criminogenic risk factors. For example, public health agencies or fire departments have the powers to close down houses that are being used for drug trafficking for health or fire code infractions. The use of non-criminal legal powers that are available to other government bodies to help address crime problems (often referred to as *third-party policing*) is a recognition of the limits of police powers. Further, according to Braga and Weisburd (2006, 6), "third party policing recognizes that much social control is exercised by institutions other than the police and that crime can be managed through agencies other than the criminal law." Cherney (2008, 632) believes that third-party policing is part of a much broader role of community police officers: he uses the term *harnessing capacity* to refer to how police facilitate the coproduction of public safety by leveraging all available resources to combat crime.

As Chalom et al. (2001, 19) note, the interagency partnerships between police and other government bodies are deemed so important when addressing local crime problems that in the United Kingdom, such cooperation has been legislated into law. "The Crime and Disorder Act adopted in 1998 stipulates that municipal governments and the 43 regional police forces covering the country must work together to develop local strategies to reduce crime and insecurity. Such strategies must involve other groups such as the healthcare sector and the justice system." The act also ensures that the public is not left out as any intergovernment strategies and must be based on "a thorough local analysis of public security which has been validated by consultation with local citizens."

In some places, police have also partnered with private-sector security companies. One of the ground-breaking, public–private policing partnerships in Canada was forged through the Edmonton Police Force's Co-operative Policing Program, which began in 1982. Edmonton Police provide a 3-day training course for private security personnel on the laws pertaining to public policing and private security, including the powers of arrest, *Criminal Code* offenses, writing reports, and giving court testimony. This program was developed, in part, to respond to the time-consuming process of rewriting

> ## CASE STUDY 7.4
>
> ### COMMUNITY ACTION TEAMS IN SALT LAKE CITY
>
> In each of Salt Lake City's seven districts, the municipal government set up Community Action Teams (CATs), neighborhood-based problem-solving units, made up of staff from different municipal, county, and state government agencies. The various CATs include representatives from the police department (including peace officers, community mobilization specialists, and youth and family specialists), the Probation and Parole Office, the Prosecutor's Office, Child and Family Services, Housing and Zoning Enforcement, Parking Enforcement, the Health Department, and Animal Control. Launched in 1995, the original goal of the teams was "to create a mechanism for unified response to juvenile crime issues— the kind of response that the police or other agencies, acting alone, could not make."
>
> CATs were also a first step by Salt Lake City's municipal government toward a community governance philosophy "where the citizens have to take ownership in keeping their neighborhoods clean and safe by working with government instead of relying on government to do everything for them" (U.S. Conference on Mayors, 1999). As the CATs matured, they began addressing a broad range of issues from parking and code enforcement to serious public safety issues, including drive-by shootings, criminal gangs, and drug houses. CATs meet weekly to collaborate on developing and implementing comprehensive solutions to specific problems in a district, to provide services expediently to residents and businesses, and to serve as a conduit between neighborhood residents and government agencies (e.g., youth workers assigned to CAT help link at-risk youth to appropriate government services) (U.S. Conference on Mayors, 1999; International Centre for the Prevention of Crime, 2001, 43).

reports submitted by security guards to conform to police standards. Report writing by private security personnel in Edmonton is now accepted by the courts (Murray and McKim, 2000, 11). In addition, once a month, intelligence meetings are held where police and private-sector security managers discuss crime problems, trends, repeat offenders, and potential solutions in their jurisdictions. The result of this enhanced cooperation and coordination, according to Murray and McKim (2000, 11),

> ... is a savings of police resources, better outcomes from cases, and, because of better understanding of their role and responsibilities, less conflict and greater respect between the two groups. By recognizing that private security has a separate responsibility and a contribution to make in its own right, and by providing training difficult to obtain elsewhere, the Edmonton Police Service has improved the effectiveness of both police and private security and improved service to the public.

The Edmonton Police Service claims that the partnership is successful, not only because it saves police resources but also because these private security officers gather and share pertinent information with police counterparts (Police Futures Group, n.d., 14–15).

7.5.2 Restructuring of the Police Organizational Hierarchy and a Reenvisioning of Police Culture

In theory, community- and problem-oriented policing necessitates a paradigmatic shift in the traditional hierarchical organizational and power structure of a police department (and police culture). Community- and problem-oriented policing flourishes in an organizational structure that imparts greater responsibility and autonomy to frontline street constables to work with local communities and apply problem-oriented crime prevention strategies. The implication is that decision-making power is shifted from police management to the frontline constables, providing them with the power and discretion to make decisions without having to constantly consult with (and defer to) police management. Community policing envisions a police structure that is much less hierarchical, and this flatter profile allows frontline constables to exercise such decision-making powers (Guyot, 1991). The focus on problem solving has wider implications for the police organization, according to Sampson and Scott (1999, 1). This shift from "a reactive, incident-driven model of policing to a proactive, problem-solving approach" demands "wholesale change in police organizations, and a move away from a command-and-control model."

Community policing also dictates a rethinking of police culture. In particular, the culture of the *thin blue line*—an attitude among police that has symbolically served to separate them from civilian society—is to be replaced with Sir Robert Peel's original vision of the integration of police in civil society: "the police are the public, and the public are the police." This shift in the police culture is also reflected in more partnerships with the communities served by police, an increase in multiagency collaboration (*third-party policing*), a greater accountability of police to their constituents, greater use of creative crime problem-solving techniques, police officers who are more reflective of the communities they serve, and an heightened emphasis on police as peace officers (and not just law enforcers).

CASE STUDY 7.5

ORGANIZATIONAL CHANGES AT THE LONDON METROPOLITAN POLICE

During the 1990s, the London Metropolitan Police returned to its roots with a renewed emphasis on community- and problem-oriented policing principles. According to the International Centre for the Prevention of Crime (2002, 30), the "roles of most police ranks changed as decision-making around programs and policies were devolved to lower levels of the organization, de-centralizing command in the process. This meant that Divisions and front-line police officers had more flexibility in how they addressed problems in their jurisdiction; more staff were transferred to operational posts; civilians replaced police in non-operational posts (allowing more police officers to work in the field); the hierarchy was flattened where possible, and specialists units were closed and police members transferred to patrol and community policing duties." Other changes were made to internal functions within the department to support and promote a more community-based approach to policing by divisions and individual police officers. "Training and personnel functions were devolved to divisions," allowing each division to determine its own training needs. "Performance pay was introduced and supported by a new appraisal system that reinforced a community-based, problem-oriented style of policing. New promotion exams were developed, again reflecting the sort of skills needed to deliver community-oriented, partnership policing services." Finally, "police resources, including budgets, were strongly linked to neighborhood delivery of services."

Some of the implications of a revamped organizational structure and a reenvisioning of police culture include a decentralization of decision-making power, police officers who are more reflective of the communities they serve, and police as peace officers (not simply law enforcers).

7.5.2.1 Decentralization (Police as Part of the Community)

Decentralization has three implications: (1) power is decentralized from police management to the frontline constable to make decisions, in tandem with community members; (2) the police constable is expected to be become an integral part of the community he or she serves; and (3) there is a decentralization of police facilities (from the centralized police headquarters to neighborhood-based community policing offices).

For Friedmann (1992), a police force must be seen as part of, not separate and isolated from, the general public. Community policing means that police departments must create and develop a new breed of line officer; one who can exercise enough autonomy to solve local problems and to help empower communities to solve their own problems. For Trojanowicz et al. (1998, 2), community policing "requires freeing some patrol officers from the isolation of the patrol car and the incessant demands of the police radio, so that these officers can maintain direct, face-to-face contact with people in the same defined geographic (beat) area every day." According to the Community Policing Consortium (1994, 13–14), "decentralization is about increasing the visibility and accessibility of police officers to community members. In turn, increased police presence is said to establish trust and serves to reduce fear of crime among community members, which, in turn, helps create neighborhood security."

The *police constable as a generalist* model also stresses more long-term assignments of police personnel to specific neighborhoods while fostering their ability to assume responsibility for a broad range of local crime and disorder issues. The community policing officer (CPO) has responsibility for a specific beat or a well-defined geographical area that is "small enough so that the officer can get around the entire beat area often enough to maintain direct contact." The significance of stationing a CPO permanently in a specific beat area rests on allowing the officer to "co-own that particular piece of turf" and to increase "his or her formal and informal (face-to-face) contact, communication, and problem-solving partnerships with members of the community" (Trojanowicz et al., 1998, 5). The CPO is mandated to develop "imaginative ways to address the broad spectrum of community concerns which exist in every community." In effect, the CPO "acts as the police department's outreach specialist to the community, serving as the people's link to other public and private agencies that can help. The CPO not only enforces the law, but begins, supports, and facilitates community-based efforts aimed at local concerns. The CPO allows people to set day-to-day, local police priorities in exchange for their cooperation and participation in efforts to police themselves" (Trojanowicz et al., 1998, 4).

When police officers are integrated into a community, they are not only in a position to work closely with community members, thus helping to implement proactive, problem-solving, individualized partnership-based solutions to specific problems. They are also in a better position to understand the local norms, values, and priorities and help residents informally regulate their neighborhood. Another implication of the organizational changes envisioned by community policing is a geographical decentralization of many functions, including management and resource deployment, so that those with responsibility for frontline policing are closer to the *consumers* of their services (Leighton, 1991, 496).

CASE STUDY 7.6

DECENTRALIZED COMMUNITY POLICING IN JAPAN

Despite an increase of more than 15% in crime in the past 25 years, Japan is still an industrialized country with a low crime rate. Many cultural factors are credited with this low crime rate, including the concept of honor, responsibility to the community, and informal social control. The country's unique system of community policing may also be a factor. Rather than concentrating police forces in a few large stations, the Japanese policing system features a highly decentralized network of community police stations. This decentralized style of policing is largely carried out by the *koban* system, which consists of small neighborhood-based police stations, located in strategic spots, which is meant to increase their visibility and accessibility to the public and to promote cooperation between citizens and the police. Also called *police boxes* because of their small size, *koban* literally means three to four police officers standing watch in rotation. There are more than 15,000 of these micro neighborhood policing stations in Japan, including the *Chuzaisho* (residential police box), which is typically located in rural areas and is operated by one community officer, who also lives in the facility. This epitomizes one philosophy of the koban system, which is that police officers are first and foremost "members of the community who [are] paid to look after the welfare of fellow-citizens, performing a civic duty seen as incumbent upon every citizen" (Chalom et al., 2001, 7).

All graduates of the national police academy must serve several years in these mini–police stations. Emphasis is placed on integrating the police officer into the community and establishing strong ties with community members. Foot patrols are emphasized and, in addition to responding to calls for service, officers are expected to focus on proactive crime prevention and other community services. In this context, they are expected to work in conjunction with citizen groups to address local issues, keep constituents informed of local crime problems and other issues, participate in community meetings, help resolve disputes among residents, organize events for young people, and serve as a liaison between citizens and local government agencies. Police officers are also required to visit each family and business in the neighborhood they serve at least twice a year, to provide and solicit information on their security and safety needs. Particular attention is paid to visiting seniors (Chalom et al., 2001, 23; Leishman, 2007).

The power shift inherent in a decentralized community policing system also has important implications for the flow of information within a police organization. Given the need for greater input from the community, information and direction must flow upward from the community to the police organization, with the patrol officer serving as a conduit between the clients of the police organization and the senior management of the organization. An important consequence of this upward flow of information is that senior managers are now the recipients of relevant information that helps set policing policies and priorities, as opposed to the downward flow from senior management that is characteristic of the hierarchical, paramilitary structure of most police organizations. According to Leighton (1991, 495), "much of the success of policing depends on how well its personnel operate as information managers who engage in 'interactive policing' by routinely exchanging information on a reciprocal basis with community members through close formal contacts and numerous informal networks."

7.5.2.2 Police Reflective of the Community Ideally, the composition of a police agency committed to community policing should reflect the demographic and social composition of the communities it serves. This includes the greater representation of women as well as visible and ethnic minorities (Leighton, 1991, 495).

7.5.2.3 Police as Peace Officers (Not Simply Law Enforcers) A central objective of a community-oriented police force is to help foster safety, security, peace, and civility. The enforcement of laws only partially achieves these goals. A community policing philosophy asserts that police cannot define their role strictly as law enforcers and must broaden their mandate beyond a narrow focus on crime incidents. As Kelling and Moore (1988, 2, 4) contend, "during the 1950s and 1960s, police thought they were law enforcement agencies primarily fighting crime." In the community policing era, the police function is much broader and includes "order maintenance, conflict resolution, provision of services through problem solving, as well as other activities." According to the Community Policing Consortium (1994, 15),

> ... this broadened outlook recognizes the value of activities that contribute to the orderliness and well-being of a neighborhood. These activities could include: helping accident or crime victims, providing emergency medical services, helping resolve domestic and neighborhood conflicts (e.g., family violence, landlord-tenant disputes, or racial harassment), working with residents and local businesses

---

CASE STUDY 7.7

WOMEN-RUN POLICE STATIONS IN SAO PAULO, BRAZIL

In an effort to address violence against women in Brazil, the Sao Paulo State Council on the Status of Women, with the support of the Brazilian Bar Association and various nongovernmental women's groups, obtained support from the Brazilian government, the City of Sao Paolo, and the police to create police stations run exclusively by female police officers and civilians. The underlying idea was that women who were victims of violence would be more receptive to laying a complaint with a female police officer because she would be treated more fairly and empathetically. The long-term goal was to encourage and increase reporting by abused women, increase arrests and convictions, and ultimately reduce and prevent violence against women.

Beginning in 1985, the new police stations were empowered to not only take complaints and investigate reports of abuse but also provide victimized women with emergency shelter, arrange for support services such as counseling, and organize antiviolence workshops for abusive male partners.

The result of the initiative was an increase in the reporting of violent assaults against women; the number of cases reported to the women's police station in San Paolo rose from 2000 in complaints in 1985 to over 7000 in 1989. The new, all-female police station was deemed such a success that it was replicated in Rio de Janeiro in 1987. Although estimating the scope of violence against women is difficult (let alone attributing such changes to these new police stations), between 1987 and 1989 there was a 63% reduction in threats against women and 37% fewer rape cases. By the start of the new millennium, there were 70 all-female police stations throughout Brazil (Eluf, 1992; Chalom et al., 2001, 22; Hicks et al., 2000, 37).

to improve neighborhood conditions, controlling automobile and pedestrian traffic, providing emergency social services and referrals to those at risk (e.g., adolescent runaways, the homeless, the intoxicated, and the mentally ill), protecting the exercise of constitutional rights (e.g., guaranteeing a person's right to speak, protecting lawful assemblies from disruption), and providing a model of citizenship (helpfulness, respect for others, honesty, and fairness).

Most of these services are already provided by municipal police forces, given that they are expected to be the first response to many of society's ills. Community policing simply advocates that these broader functions not be secondary to enforcement of (criminal) laws.

The expanded role for police in society envisioned by the theory of community policing is predicated on the realization "that crime incidents cannot be solved in isolation—separate from each other and separate from their relationship to the social context" (Trojanowicz et al., 1998, 98). Community policing officers are seen as peacekeepers, professionals who help maintain those factors that promote the creation of safe, healthy, vibrant communities. Community police forces help create and foster local standards and norms that nurture a sense of peace, order, and vitality within local environments. This perspective is very much influenced by the field of *peacemaking criminology*, which holds that governments, their criminal justice agencies, and private actors can best solve crime and criminal behavior by working together to alleviate social problems and human suffering (Pepinsky and Quinney, 1991).

7.6 PROBLEM-ORIENTED POLICING

While community- and problem-oriented policing are conceptually distinct, the latter is a vital ingredient in the former. This is especially true because community policing is touted as policing philosophy that has in its sights a more effective approach to controlling crime and ensuring safe and healthy communities. Problem-oriented policing is perfectly aligned with community policing in that it contributes to such goals through its efforts to solve the underlying causes of local crime and safety problems via a partnership approach with community members and other key partners.

The concept of problem-oriented policing was first proposed by Herman Goldstein (1979) who argued that police must be involved in changing the conditions (i.e., solving the problems) that give rise to criminal behavior and criminal acts. The advent of problem-oriented policing in the 1980s represented a profound shift from the so-called professional model that simply responded to criminal incidents by arresting criminal offenders or deterring them through random patrols. According to Clare et al. (2010, 7), "Goldstein advocated that to achieve this shift in focus, policing practices need to meet a number of objectives, including: (a) being more specific about the nature of individual problems, involving research, analysis, and interpretation of current and previous police responses, (b) assess the adequacy and effectiveness of these approaches within the context, (c) undertake a comprehensive exploration for novel, alternative responses to existing problems, and (d) select the most suitable response(s) and implement them."

Compared to traditional policing, the methodology underlying problem-oriented policing requires the identification of crime problems "in more precise terms, researching each problem, documenting the nature of the current police response, assessing the adequacy of existing authority and resources, engaging in a broad exploration of alternatives to present responses, weighing the merits of these alternatives, and

---

CASE STUDY 7.8

COMMUNITY POLICING AND MARGINALIZED YOUTH IN FRANCE

Hicks et al. (2000, 16) describe how the National Police in France moved beyond a strict role as law enforcers to reach out to marginalized youth in the country:

> Relations between the National Police and young people, particularly in underprivileged areas, have become increasingly strained over the years. A need existed to renew dialogue between these groups without setting aside the role of the national police as authority figures and their responsibility for applying the law.

> For several years now, the National Police have operated youth recreation centres (Centres de Loisirs Jeunes, CLJ) which provide places where young people can gather for sports and recreational activities. These activities are guided and supervised by National Police personnel assisted by auxiliary police personnel (on national service) and public safety assistants (youth employment positions). The centres are run in close partnership with, and as a complement to, other social organizations.

Their role is to

> Act as the association-based extension of the work performed by the National Police with young people, particularly in sensitive or problem areas

> Assist in establishing dialogue with young people by helping them discover other aspects of the work of the National Police and its personnel

> Foster youth integration and prevent delinquency by using recreational and sports activities supervised by volunteers as means of communicating messages regarding respect for community life, behavioural standards and the importance of personal effort

> Participate in the ongoing training of police officers through which these personnel can discover new kinds of relationships with young people

> Work towards positive changes in the relationships between youth groups and the police

> Since 1982, police have also participated in the project Ville, Vie, Vacances (City, Life, Vacation) which, during school vacations, offers youth from difficult neighborhoods a variety of activities aimed at keeping them active, introducing them to new environments and helping them to develop values of citizenship.

---

choosing from among them" (Goldstein, 1979, 236). The application of this problem-solving methodology is exemplified by the SARA model, which has developed a cult following among many police agencies in the United States and abroad. Weisburd et al. (2010, 141) describe the four sequential phases of SARA as follows:

> "Scanning" is the first step and involves the police identifying and prioritizing potential problems in their jurisdiction. After the potential problems have been identified, the next step is "analysis," which involves the police thoroughly analyzing the identified problem(s) using several data sources so that appropriate responses can be developed. The third step, "response," has the police developing and implementing interventions designed to solve the problem(s). Finally, once the response has been administered, the final step is "assessment," which involves evaluating the impact of the response.

The elements of the SARA model are described in more detail in Box 7.2.

BOX 7.2

THE SARA PROBLEM-SOLVING MODEL

1. Scanning:
   a. Identify problems of concern to the public and the police.
   b. Prioritize problems.
   c. Collect as much information from as many sources as possible on a problem.
   d. Set objectives for reducing or preventing the scope and harm of the problem.
2. Analysis:
   a. Analyze the collected data with the goal of understanding the nature, scope, symptoms, impact, aggravating factors, and underlying causes of the problem.
   b. Identify and understand the events and conditions that precede and accompany the problem.
   c. Develop a working hypothesis about why the problem is occurring.
   d. Understand how the problem is currently addressed and the strengths and limitations of the current response.
   e. Search for solutions that have been implemented for similar problems in the past or in other jurisdictions.
   f. Identify resources that may be of assistance in developing a deeper understanding of the problem.
   g. Encourage the participation of all key partners (especially community members) to help analyze the problem from their perspective.
3. Response:
   a. Mobilize key partners and resources.
   b. Brainstorm interventions, identifying the possible outcomes and pros and cons of each.
   c. Choose among the alternative solutions.
   d. Outline the response plan and identify those who need to be involved in implementing the solution.
   e. Articulate the goals for the intervention.
   f. Identify relevant data to be collected during the intervention for evaluation purposes.
   g. Carry out the planned strategies.
4. Assessment:
   a. Determine whether or not the plan was implemented effectively and appropriately.
   b. Determine whether the goals were attained.
   c. Identify any new strategies needed to augment the original plan.
   d. Learn what methods are effective in dealing with particular problems.

Sources: U.S. Department of Justice, *Excellence in Problem-Oriented Policing: The 1999 Herman Goldstein Award Winners*, National Institute of Justice, Washington, DC, 2000a, http://www.ncjrs.gov/pdffiles1/nij/182731.pdf; U.S. Department of Justice, *Excellence in Problem-Oriented Policing: The 2000 Herman Goldstein Award Winners*, U.S. Department of Justice, National Institute of Justice, Washington, DC, 2000b, http://www.ncjrs.org/pdffiles1/nij/185279.pdf, pp. 2–3; Eck, J.E. and Spelman, W., *Problem-Solving: Problem-Oriented Policing in Newport News*, Police Executive Research Forum, Washington, DC, 1987; Patrick, M., *Proving the SARA Model: A Problem Solving Approach to Street Crime Reduction in the London Borough of Lewisham*, InfoTech Enterprises Europe, London, U.K., 2002; Center for Problem-Oriented Policing, *The SARA Model*, 2008a, http://www.popcenter.org/about/?p=sara.

Some have recommended that an *M* (for *maintenance*) be added to the ending of the SARA acronym. This means that efforts should be taken by those implementing a problem-solving approach to ensure that positive results are maintained over the short and long terms (without regular interventions by police), by those affected by the problem, (concerned community members, and other key stakeholders).

The remainder of this section discusses some of the principal characteristics of problem-oriented policing: problem solving (addressing causes of crime problems), research and analysis (a better understanding of crime and its causes), and flexibility in applying solutions (alternatives to the criminal justice system).

7.6.1   *Problem Solving (Addressing the Causes of Crime Problems)*

Traditional policing has been criticized for only dealing with the symptoms of crime problems and, as such, ignores the factors that give rise to a particular criminal event or the deeper problems that promote criminal behavior. As its name suggests, problem-oriented policing focuses as much as possible on applying solutions that can best eliminate a problem on a long-term basis or at least reduce the harm caused by a particular problem.

The terms *problem-oriented* and *problem-solving* have been used interchangeably; however, there is an important distinction between the two. "In its broadest sense, the term 'problem-oriented policing,' as used by Goldstein, describes a comprehensive framework for improving the police's capacity to perform their mission. Problem-oriented policing impacts virtually everything the police do, operationally as well as managerially" (Scott, 2000, 45).

The more narrow term *problem-solving* refers to the ultimate goal on the problem-oriented process: solving a crime problem; that is, addressing its causes and aggravating factors. This problem-solving methodology begins with a complete understanding of the scope and nature of a single criminal act, a series of criminal act, and even criminal behavior (through exhaustive information gathering and analysis), identifying symptoms, aggravating factors, and causes. It then entails implementing measures that can solve the identified problem, so it does not continue or at least reduces its frequency and/or harm. While an ideal solution addresses the symptoms and aggravating factors, a problem-solving approach is most potent when it ultimately focuses on the root cause of the problem. The application of a problem-solving approach is particularly relevant to chronic, ongoing crime and disorder issues that cannot be sufficiently addressed through a traditional criminal justice response.

As part of a problem-solving approach to crime and disorder issues, Scott (2000, 6) cautions that efforts by police to identify factors that contribute to or even cause a particular crime problem should not be confused with the broader goals of criminality prevention (crime prevention through social development), which is to eliminate the root causes of criminal behavior. "Associating problem-oriented policing with a search for 'root causes' is misguided," Scott contends. "Problem-oriented policing looks for the deepest underlying conditions that are amenable to intervention, balancing what is knowable with what is possible. Many of what are commonly thought of as 'root causes' are beyond the police's capacity to change" (Scott, 2000, 6).

Despite those who believe police do not have the mandate or resources to address the root causes of criminality, some police forces have successfully embarked on social problem-solving interventions. According to the International Centre for the Prevention of Crime (2008, 184), "some police services have developed initiatives to increase their active involvement with youth, exercising a mentoring role. This includes youth capacity-building

CASE STUDY 7.9

APPLYING SARA TO CRIME AND DISORDER PROBLEMS IN A SHOPPING CENTER IN DELTA, CANADA

In 1988, the Sunshine Village Shopping Centre was built in the Municipality of Delta, British Columbia. This strip mall experienced few crime or disorder problems until 1989 when the Elite Video Arcade opened. Soon thereafter, the Delta Police started receiving numerous complaints regarding vandalism, litter, graffiti, thefts, and other delinquent behavior in and around the mall. At first, the problems that police were responding to were isolated within the arcade. As the owners ignored these problems and gradually lost control over their young clientele, the conflicts between different groups of youths spilled into the parking lot. Drug transactions and sales of stolen property began to occur in the arcade. At the same time, the vacancy rates at the mall increased as stores around the arcade closed. As a result, the mall began to lose revenue. A security guard service was implemented but the aforementioned problems continued to fester. The nearby residential community began to feel the impact, and residents presented a petition to city council and police to take action.

Initially, the Delta Police Service implemented two conventional approaches: Operation Blackjack, a surveillance operation, and zero tolerance, which entailed increased police patrols of the mall and immediate vicinity. Both strategies were largely unsuccessful and unsustainable. It was decided that a longer-term solution was needed.

Scan and Analyze. Constable Mike Sheard, of the Delta Police, was assigned to tackle the problem. He began by analyzing crime statistics and police reports, conducting on-site interviews, and attending meetings with mall administrators, the arcade owners, and community groups. He discovered that the problems began to erupt 9 months after the arcade opened, which also was when the interior layout of the arcade was redesigned. Originally, there were 25 video machines around the perimeter of the inside of the arcade, providing good sight lines that helped staff keep an eye on the patrons. Few problems were occurring at this time. The owner then greatly increased the number of machines to 44, which necessitated design changes inside the arcade. A new wall was also erected and the amount of lighting was reduced. The design changes and increased number of machines reduced sight lines for staff, making it more difficult to monitor patrons and to spot illegal or disorderly acts.

Constable Sheard reviewed the interior layout and use of the arcade and found numerous problems, including a lack of natural surveillance, poor management, no control of interior spaces, and entrapment areas. He reviewed the research on arcade designs that can either lead to or minimize problems. Attempts were made to convince the arcade owner to correct the problems by removing the extra 19 video machines and the new wall and return the lighting to original levels. The owner refused, arguing that there was insufficient proof that these features were responsible for the problems in the mall.

Constable Sheard then contacted the original architects of the mall and officials in the municipal government's planning department. Together they undertook a study of arcade crime with the help of criminology students at a local university. The study compared the Elite Arcade with two other arcades in the municipality and six video arcades in neighboring cities and found that certain designs accompany low-problem video arcades. The results were brought to the city hall where a public presentation was made by the students to the council. The arcade owner was summoned to the city hall to hear the study results. He then agreed to make changes to his arcade.

Respond. The recommended interventions to address the crime and disorder problems in and around the arcade included the following:

- Limiting the number of people in the arcade at any one time
- Setting up machines only around the periphery of the arcade to provide for better visibility
- Removing tinted or reflective film on the arcade's windows to ensure a clear view into and out of the arcade
- Providing ample lighting levels inside the arcade
- Providing ample lighting for access routes and parking areas throughout the mall
- Restricting the hours of operation for the arcade to those of the other mall businesses
- Using in-house or contracted security staff within the arcade
- Posting and strictly enforcing rules in the arcade as to acceptable behavior
- Enforcing age restrictions with the arcade's clientele (12–18 years of age only)
- Controlling access to restrooms

Assess and Maintain. Upon implementation of the recommendations, police calls for service to the mall were reduced initially by 151% from 1990 to 1991 and a further 5% in 1992. This rate remained consistent for the 6 years following the implementation of the strategies. Some displacement effects were anticipated and did occur; in particular, there was some increased illegal and delinquent activities around nearby parks, but this was handled through a combination of conventional policing responses (increased enforcement of park bylaws) and community crime prevention (recruiting more volunteers for citizen patrols). Displacement of some youth from the arcade to the local boys' and girls' club was anticipated and promoted due to the provision of adult-supervised activities.

Additional public confidence in this community initiative was demonstrated when over 2000 people signed a petition to the city council asking to have the video arcade hours extended. They wanted the arcade to operate during the same hours as the other mall stores to accommodate parents dropping off their kids at the arcade while they went shopping.

The Elite Video Arcade project provided the catalyst for developing a sustainable way to tame video arcades that become crime generators. After the changes were implemented, Constable Sheard worked with city planners to begin drafting new municipal bylaws for video arcades in future development. These were adopted by the council in 1992. The video arcade bylaws have since become a working model for other communities. In the past 2 years, copies of the Delta video arcade bylaws were requested by municipalities across North America.

In 1997, Constable Sheard won a Herman Goldstein Award for Excellence in problem-oriented policing for his work on this project (Centre for Problem-Oriented Policing, 1997; Constable Mike Sheard, personal communication).

through various activities (economic, recreational, or sports). The goal is to stimulate a sense of responsibility and provide youth with better socio-economic opportunities."

7.6.2 *Research and Analysis*

A problem-solving approach to crime is built on a process whereby the scope and nature of the problem are assessed through the gathering and analysis of relevant information. When applying the SARA model to particular crime problems, the *scanning* phases refer to research, while *assessment* refers to the analysis of information collected during the scanning phase. The data gathering phases involve collecting as

CASE STUDY 7.10

GRAFFITI PREVENTION AND SUPPRESSION IN SAN DIEGO

Officers in the Mid-City Division of the San Diego Police used a problem-oriented approach to address a common problem in southern California: graffiti and tagging by street gangs. Police were sensitive to the concerns of the public who, during public meetings with San Diego police, expressed great consternation over the widespread graffiti problem. Police then went to "great lengths to document the dimensions of the problem by surveying the community, counting the number of sites defaced, analyzing patterns of vandalism, and noting the prevalence of different types of graffiti."

In their attempts to address the problem, police sought to better understand the motivations of the graffiti vandals. They consulted with experts, read research papers, and even discovered numerous websites that promote graffiti tagging (whereby taggers boast about their graffiti, showcase their work through digital photos, find out about the best tagging locations in a city, and locate stores with spray paint and other supplies). In conjunction with youth probation authorities, the San Diego Police even had 10 convicted taggers that participate in a focus group that was facilitated by a psychologist to ascertain their motivations. Those participating in the session gave the following reasons for tagging: the need for attention and acceptance (by one's peers), the thrill of risk taking, competition, and the absence of adult role models in their lives. After working with the taggers for 3 months, the psychologist provided the following explanations as to why these youth were involved in graffiti tagging: lack of intimate adult interaction and direction, lack of self-discipline, poor self-esteem, unresolved life trauma, and impulsiveness.

The police officers also studied reports on effective responses to graffiti elsewhere and incorporated what they learned into their local response.

In developing their plan, police did not go it alone; they emphasized a collaborative approach with other key partners, including schools, juvenile probation authorities, counselors, the juvenile court, governmental and nongovernmental youth service agencies, and nonprofit community groups. The result was a comprehensive and multipronged, problem-solving strategy that targeted both active taggers and potential future taggers. Specifically, six solutions were pursued to stop graffiti tagging (all of which fell outside formal criminal justice interventions):

1. *Counseling.* Ten chronic taggers received professional counseling by social workers. The youth set personal goals to help them stop tagging and met the counselors every week to discuss ways to meet these goals. As a motivation to attend, the counseling counted toward the community service they had to perform as a penalty for their past vandalism.
2. *Paint-outs.* Young offenders on probation for tagging were made to clean up graffiti with bimonthly *paint-outs* at heavily tagged sites. The paint-outs used the same color as the graffiti, based on a national study indicating that a graffiti site covered with paint the same color as the graffiti was 10 times less likely to be retagged.
3. *Adopt-a-block.* Community members volunteered to monitor cleanup sites and quickly paint over those sites that were retagged.
4. *Murals.* Junior high school students were recruited to paint murals on heavily tagged walls. The students worked with teachers, local businesses, and residents to paint murals that reflect positive images of the community. This strategy was based on research indicating that murals are less likely to be tagged.
5. *Handler program.* San Diego Police officers helped supervise young offenders who were on probation for graffiti-related offenses. If they contravened any of their

probation sanctions, they would be sent back to their probation officer and/or ordered to perform paint-outs in the neighborhood or some other form or community service.

6. *Joint patrol.* Police helped initiate and coordinate *Kids in Control*, a bike team made up of local youths who join bike police patrols of highly tagged sites. An ancillary benefit of the joint bike patrol is that it enhanced the relationship between youth and police officers, while teaching young people how to work with police to solve problems.

After the strategy was implemented, a 90% reduction in tagging in the Mid-City area was recorded. Three of the ten chronic young offenders who had received counseling stopped painting graffiti altogether, while the murals that had been painted remained graffiti free (Center for Problem-Oriented Policing, Herman Goldstein Awards, 2000).

much (relevant and high quality) information as possible from as many sources as possible to ensure the analysis phase is fruitful possible (i.e., helps ensure an understanding of the scope and nature of the problem). (Refer to Chapter 8 for more detailed information on what is involved in collecting information as part of the problem-oriented crime prevention process.) The problem-solving police officer is expected to spend a greater amount of time collecting more information and new sorts of information to solve the problem, compared to the traditional *occurrence report* that would be submitted following a call for service. New forms of information to be collected include those typically generated in the early phase of any crime prevention project, such as the findings of safety audits, surveys of community members, expert opinion, statistical data, and a review of the literature.

Sampson and Scott (1999, 76) describe an "ingenious scheme" concocted by problem-oriented police officers in San Diego to collect information to help them learn more about the graffiti tagging subculture. Police officers "posed as a video production crew seeking to do a documentary on tagging, and they invited several known taggers to a 'preproduction interview.'" Over the next 4 months, the police officers worked undercover in these roles "during which they learned a lot about taggers' methods and motives. They learned that tagging crossed all ethnic and economic lines and involved both males and females, ranging in age from 10 to 25. This knowledge later helped them develop their education-and-awareness campaign, particularly that part of it targeting younger school children" (Sampson and Scott, 1999, 76).

The problem-solving approach also encourages police officers and their partners to employ critical and analytical thinking skills in order to identify and solve the causes and facilitators of particular crime and disorder problems. This analytical process differs from the traditional reactive, incident-driven model where police generally follow a routinized approach to crime problems (search for, arrest, and prosecute the offender). Goldstein (1990, 36–37) describes the analysis stage as

… an in-depth probe of all of the characteristics of a problem and the factors that contribute to it—acquiring detailed information about, for example, offenders, victims and others who may be involved; the time of occurrence, locations and other particulars about the physical environment; the history of the problem; the motivations, gains and losses of all involved parties; the apparent (and not so apparent) causes and competing interests; and the results of current responses.

The analytical component in problem-oriented policing also requires that a crime problem be examined in a context that is much broader compared to traditional policing when only the circumstances specific to a particular criminal occurrence are

CASE STUDY 7.11

ADDRESSING CRIMINOGENIC RISK FACTORS BY POLICE IN DENMARK

Hicks et al. (2000, 14) report on the Dog Sledge Project, which was initiated in 1993 through a coordinated effort of the Copenhagen police and social welfare and school authorities in Denmark.

"It aimed to reduce existing and future criminal activity among at-risk children and youth involved in street gang activity. Forty-seven participants (13 to 21 years of age) were drawn from Copenhagen to participate in a series of program elements composed of four phases.

- Phase I: The existing gang network was used as a vehicle to promote positive behaviour. Participants were recruited via home visits, divided into 5 to 7 groups with each group assigned a police officer— their 'Bonus Pater' (Good Parent)— to provide mentoring on a 24 hour basis. Other social services such as employment, education, and housing for participating youngsters and their families were also provided.
- Phase II: A contract was signed outlining conditions for participation including: staying out of crime, attending school/alternative education and other criteria. While failure to comply with the conditions could result in exclusion from the program, police officers found that immediately confronting unacceptable youth behaviour was effective due to the trust established through the ongoing mentoring.
- Phase III: Participants received training in team and individual skills (e.g., first-aid, map and compass reading, etc.) necessary for a dog sledge tour in Greenland. Participants also engaged in various community activities to generate better relations with local residents; this included a Christmas fund-raiser in a local shopping center that helped acquire funds for the trip to Greenland.
- Phase IV: After project completion, participating youth were referred to established neighborhood youth clubs.

Among the children and youth in the program, there was a 60 percent reduction in criminal activity. Of 47 participating youth, 34 attained employment or continued their education following completion of the program. An evaluation of the program identified the following elements as key to its success: group therapy, use of police officers as mentors, recruitment methods and general activity programs (the Greenland tour itself was considered expensive and an unnecessary overkill).

Key aspects of this program were replicated in a 1997 Job Motivating Program that aimed to reduce crime among at-risk ethnic minority youth. This initiative targets youth from ethnic minority families who are poorly integrated into Danish society and who live under difficult socio-economic conditions. The aim of the project was to provide greater social stability for at-risk ethnic minority youth through increased opportunities to engage in education, employment, and self-esteem building" (Hicks et al., 2000, 14).

considered. This broader context is especially important if attempts are being made to address the root causes of a particular problem. For example, a problem-solving investigation into a rash of residential burglaries on one street may be expanded to understand the design characteristics of the victimized homes (compared to those not victimized) or even look at social factors that may be giving rise to such problems (such as a high proportion of young, unemployed males in the neighborhood).

7.6.3   Flexible Solutions (Alternatives to the Criminal Justice System)

A problem-solving approach that seeks the most appropriate solutions means that each crime problem must be treated in a highly individualized fashion. Further, the intervention must be appropriate to the scope and nature of the problem and should avoid a standardized, *cookie-cutter* approach that predominates in the traditional criminal justice. Thus, a problem-oriented approach often entails interventions that do not involve the criminal justice system. Problem-oriented police officers should have the option, except when a serious crime has been committed, to choose not to enforce the law if another alternative appears more effective in addressing the problem. The search for the most appropriate solution, combined with the need for alternatives to the criminal justice system, necessitates that police officers think more creatively. Alternatives to the criminal justice system are limited only by the imagination of those involved in solving a crime or disorder problem (Goldstein, 1987, 15; 1990, 102–147).

In the past few years, community-based restorative justice processes have become a common alternative to the criminal justice system, especially for first-time young offenders. In Canada, police are not only mandated to refer nonserious cases involving youth to restorative justice processes, but some police forces have developed and implemented their own models.

7.7   ASSESSING THE EFFECTIVENESS OF COMMUNITY- AND PROBLEM-ORIENTED POLICING

The ultimate test for community- and problem-oriented policing is whether it has achieved the theoretical goals that have been set out for it. As Sherman and Eck (2006, 298) note, it is difficult to evaluate community- and problem-oriented policing because in practice they both involve a great many "variations and possible combinations of police activities." Notwithstanding these methodological limitations, studies and program evaluations have provided some evidence as to the effectiveness of community policing in regard to (1) the adoption of this philosophy by police departments, (2) the extent to which it has buttressed relationships and joint problem solving with local communities, and (3) the extent to which community- and problem-oriented policing have been effective in preventing and controlling crime and disorder problems.

A key determinant of the impact of community- and problem-oriented policing is whether they have become standard practice within police agencies. For Scott (2000, 32),

> The problem-oriented policing movement can be said to have succeeded once police agencies have integrated the problem-solving operational strategy of police work into their operations at least as completely as they have the other operational strategies of preventive patrol, routine incident response, emergency response, and criminal investigation. It will have succeeded too once the imbalance between policing's "means" and "ends" has been altered to better reflect a direct concern on the part of police administrators and researchers with the substantive aspects of police business.

CASE STUDY 7.12

RESTORATIVE JUSTICE AS CARRIED OUT BY POLICE IN CANADA

In Canada, the *Young Criminal Justice Act* codifies into law the use of extrajudicial measures by police, prosecutors, and judges, when dealing with most young people who come into formal contact with the law. The act requires police to consider all options, including informal alternatives to the court process, before laying charges. (For a more detailed overview of the YJCA, see Chapter 6.)

In 1996, the Royal Canadian Mounted Police (RCMP) began the Community Justice Forum (CJF), which involves a victim–offender mediation process that strives for a consensual or negotiated solution. Within the framework of restorative justice, RCMP officers use their discretionary powers to defer certain cases to a local CJF process. The mediation is conducted by a RCMP-trained facilitator who guides participants through a restorative justice process (listening to the experiences of the victim, offender, and other key stakeholders in the process; directing discussion so that victims can express the harm they have suffered, while offenders acknowledge the impact of their behavior; helping participants communicate how they believe the harm can best be resolved and what reparations should be made, and coming to a consensus-based resolution). If a consensus is reached, the RCMP facilitator closes the CJF by formalizing the agreement and deciding upon follow-up measures to ensure adherence to the agreement.

While no study has been conducted as to measure the effectiveness of the CJF in terms of recidivism of youth who had been through the process, an assessment of participant satisfaction with the process and outcomes of the CJFs was undertaken. This study found that participants were highly satisfied: 96% indicated that they felt the CJF process was *very* or *quite* fair, while 91% felt that the outcome was *quite* or *very* fair; and 97% of victims rated the fairness of the agreement reached with the offender as *quite* or *very* fair, while 77% of offenders rated it either *quite* or *very* fair. The study's results also showed that 98% of offenders who took part in a CJF process understood the consequences of their actions and the need for them to take responsibility for their actions. Eighty-five percent of all participants stated that the offenders complied with agreement conditions (Chatterjee, 1999; Hicks et al., 2000, 48).

It is nearly impossible to quantify the number of police agencies that have bought into and follow the principles of community- and problem-oriented policing, "much less to gauge the precise nature and quality of those efforts" (Scott, 2000, 39–40). There is evidence to suggest that while the professional police model still persists and incident-led, reactive policing involving traditional methods of arrest and prosecution still predominates, many police agencies have recognized the importance of community- and problem-oriented policing and have integrated such principles and strategies into their operational fold. According to U.S. Bureau of Justice Statistics' estimates, in 1997 approximately 79% of municipal law enforcement agencies in the United States had full-time community policing officers, 59% actively encouraged officers to engage in problem-solving projects in their patrol areas, while 35% included problem-solving efforts as part of their evaluation of patrol officers. In addition, 68% of municipal police departments reported that they had met with community groups and formed partnerships to address local crime problems (Reaves and Goldberg, 1999). The results of Law Enforcement Management and Administrative Statistics Survey indicated that approximately 22,000 police officers practiced community policing in the United States in 1997. That number rose more than fivefold by 1999 (as cited by the Office of Community-Oriented Policing Services, 2003, 1).

Given that the "core concept of community policing was community involvement for its own sake" (Sherman and Eck, 2006, 299), one central evaluation criterion is the extent to which community policing initiatives have resulted in the mobilization of the public. In their meta-analysis of studies examining community policing, Sherman and Eck (2006, 315) conclude that the "evidence against the effectiveness of police organizing communities into neighborhood watches is consistent and relatively strong." A study by the Vera Institute into Innovative Neighborhood-Oriented Policing projects in eight US cities found that all sites "experienced extreme difficulty in establishing a solid community infrastructure on which to build their community policing programs." In other words, researchers found that police were generally unable to "organize and maintain active community involvement in their projects" and those who became involved was generally confined to a small group of dedicated activists (Sadd and Grinc, 1994, 31, 33). These conclusions are consistent with other studies, summarized in Chapter 5, that demonstrate the difficulties in mobilizing communities around crime prevention.

In contrast, Skogan et al. (1999) provide evidence that citizen participation in the ambitious Chicago Alternative Policing Strategy (CAPS) has been one of the program's "most significant successes" (p. 6). Under this strategy, patrol officers in five districts were divided on a rotating basis into beat teams and rapid-response teams. The former spent much of their time applying community policing and crime prevention principles in active collaboration with community groups. In each district, a civilian advisory committee was formed to give advice to police commanders, identify local priorities, plan and execute policing and crime prevention strategies, and help mobilize resources. One of the regular features of CAPS was the police-sponsored monthly beat meetings, which were open to the public, where police and community members discuss local crime problems and how they can be addressed. Citizen participation in CAPS was deemed a success based on the widespread awareness of the program among the city's residents and the high level of attendance at monthly neighborhood-based meetings. According to the researchers,

> Actual involvement in the program remains constant, but high. During the first 11 months of 1998, an average of 234 beat community meetings were held each month, and attendance averaged 6,000 persons. Yearly attendance has grown from 59,000 in 1995 to over 66,000 in 1998. During the 47-month period between January 1995 and November 1998, a total of about 250,000 Chicagoans attended a meeting.
>
> **Skogan et al. (1999, 7)**

Studies also show that "community policing strategies that entail direct involvement of citizens and police, such as police community stations, citizen contract patrol, and coordinated community policing, have been found to reduce fear of crime among individuals and decrease individual concern about crime in neighborhoods." In addition, community policing has been shown to improve "citizens' judgments of police actions," leading Braga and Weisburd (2006, 14–15) to state, "clearly, community policing has been a strategic innovation that has helped bridge the police confidence gap in minority communities."

Research into the impact of community policing strategies on crime and victimization rates is mixed. In their review of the literature, Braga and Weisburd (2006, 14–15) conclude, "In general, broad-based community policing initiatives have been found to reduce fear of crime and improve the relationships between the police and the communities they serve." With that said, the authors conclude that "unfocused" community policing tactics, such as "foot patrols, storefront offices, newsletters, and community meetings," do not reduce crime and disorder problems (Braga and Weisburd, 2006, 13). For Connell et al. (2008, 130), evaluations of community policing indicate that this approach "reduces disorder and increases positive community-police relations; second, community policing initiatives increase the positive attitudes that police officers have both toward their jobs and toward the community." However, the impact of community policing on crime reveals mixed results. They cite an analysis of Cordner (2001), who after reviewing 60 studies, "found that a slight majority of studies reported decreases in the crime rates after the implementation of some type of community policing model."

In their review of the evaluation literature concerning drug enforcement, Mazerolle et al. (2007) write, "The major trends from the community policing evaluations were: (1) Community policing appeared to be effective in dealing with drug problems, such as dealing and drug offenses; (2) community policing also appeared to have success addressing associated crime problems, such as property, violence, and/or disorder-related offenses and [calls for service]; and (3) improvements in quality of life, fear of crime, and satisfaction with the community often resulted from interventions." In contrast, the Vera Institute's study of the Innovative Neighborhood-Oriented Policing projects—which applied community policing principles to reducing demand for illegal drugs in eight American cities—found that "these forays into community policing produced only minimal, and often transient, effects on drug trafficking, drug-related crime, and fear of crime" (Sadd and Grinc, 1994, 35). In his analysis of crime statistics from 164 American cities in which community policing strategies had been implemented by the local police force, Macdonald (2002, 592) concludes that the implementation of a community policing strategy had "little effect on the control or the decline in violent crime."

The evaluation research suggests that problem-oriented policing is effective in dealing with a wide range of specific crime and disorder problems, from residential and commercial thefts and convenience store burglaries to gang violence, graffiti, and other forms of vandalism by youth, prostitution, street-level drug trafficking, and alcohol-related violence in pubs and clubs (see Sherman and Eck, 2006, 319–321; Braga, 2008). In their review of evaluation findings, Sherman and Eck (2006, 319) found that problem-oriented policing was particularly successful when targeted at crime and disorder hot spots; in five studies that were reviewed, all but one reported "substantial and significant reductions in target offences at the places receiving the treatment, compared to control places." They conclude that "there is considerable evidence based on strong evaluations that problem-oriented policing is an effective way to reduce crime," and while there is still the need for much research, the principle of problem-oriented policing is sound conceptually.

Braga and Weisburd (2007, 12) argue that while the rigor of evaluation designs varies, "problem-oriented policing, when appropriately focused on specific crime problems, has been found to be effective in preventing crime." They go on to cite literature that shows "problem-oriented policing to be effective in controlling a wide range of specific crime and disorder problems." This includes burglaries in apartment complexes, prostitution, convenience store robberies, and alcohol-related violence in pubs and clubs.

The outcome of a meta-analysis by Weisburd et al. (2010) of a limited number of rigorous evaluations of problem-oriented policing also supports its overall effectiveness. According to the authors, "the central conclusion of our review is that POP as an approach has significant promise to ameliorate crime and disorder problems broadly defined. The most successful studies in this review covered problems that ranged from parolee recidivism, to violence in hot spots, to drug markets." Their meta-analysis "supports the overall commitment of police to POP but suggests that we should not necessarily expect large crime and disorder control benefits from this approach" (Weisburd et al., 2010, 164).

7.8   CHALLENGES TO AND CRITIQUES OF COMMUNITY- AND PROBLEM-ORIENTED POLICING

While community policing has been enthusiastically touted as the vision of the future for police agencies across the world and has greatly influenced the operations of thousands of police organizations, legitimate concerns have been raised as to whether it will ever be accorded equal status and resources as the traditional incident-driven, law enforcement, arrest and prosecute model. This aspiration may be unrealistic, given the continued need for police to respond to calls for service from the public and the finite resources available to apply labor-intensive problem solving, not to mention the reluctance of many police agencies to fundamentally reorganize their internal power structures and hierarchies. This has led some to fear that community policing is simply another *flavor of the day* and will be replaced by some other trendy policing model in the future. Others contend that the mantra of community policing is repeated by police departments simply to create the impression that they are on the cutting edge of their profession (i.e., as a cynical public relations ploy). A "downside" of community policing, as written by Goldstein (1994, viii), is that police departments are free to employ this label without "concern for its substance. Political leaders and, unfortunately, many police leaders hook onto the label for the positive images it projects, but do not engage or invest in the concept. The meaning of community policing, as a result, is diluted, with consequences that are confusing and troubling for those seriously interested in effecting meaningful change in the police." As Bayley (1988, 225) rightly argues, the implementation of community policing has been "very uneven" because, "although widely, almost universally, said to be important, it means different things to different people ... Community policing on the ground often seems less a program than a set of aspirations wrapped in a slogan."

Others accuse police management of pursuing community crime prevention and community policing principles as a ploy to transfer crime-control responsibilities to the public and other government agencies, in part to save money. In an analysis of the shift to community policing as part of a broader top-down organizational change occurring within the RCMP during the 1990s, Clarke (2002, 17) contends that the changes "had less to do with citizen empowerment and police responsiveness. Instead decentralization represented a quick fix for the achievement of budgetary reductions." Community policing, and its emphasis on leveraging nonpolice resources to combat crime, is another example of what Mazerolle and Ransley (2005, 23) call the "neo-liberal, governed-at-a-distance, risk-managing approach" to crime control. The future viability of community policing is also questioned in the post-911 environment in which so many law enforcement resources have been shifted to the war on terror.

Given the minimal success that police have enjoyed in mobilizing the local community around crime issues, some have questioned whether community policing and crime prevention are the best way to allocate scarce policing resources. The underlying argument here is that police should focus on their law enforcement mandate and let other sectors of society solve the problems that give rise to crime and criminality (see Liederbach et al., 2008, 272).

Some would say that in its theoretical prescriptions, community policing is a utopian aspiration that can never truly be achieved by the modern police force. According to Braga and Weisburd (2007, 18), "while all major American police agencies report some form of community policing as an important component of their operations (Bureau of Justice Statistics, 2003), the police have been generally resistant to its adoption. This is not surprising since community policing involves the most radical change to existing police organizations." The idea of flattening a paramilitary hierarchical organization and transferring powers from senior executives to frontline personnel is naive and poses a number of threats to the professional police model (including controlling corruption and abuse by individual officers).

Problem-oriented policing is saddled by the critique that it can be very resource intensive (although if it does solve a reoccurring problem, it can be considered quite cost-effective in that it avoids future calls for police services). A problem-solving approach can also be difficult for the average police officer to implement, especially without the proper skills and training (Eck and Spelman, 1987; Braga and Weisburd, 2006). Based on their research, Braga and Weisburd (2006, 18) state that when applied by the average police officer, "problem analysis is generally weak and implemented responses largely consist of traditional enforcement activities. Problem-oriented policing as practiced in the field is but a shallow version of the process recommended by Goldstein (1990)." For Tilley (2010, 186), the systematic application of the SARA model of problem-oriented policing often falls short of the "demanding processes of specific problem identification, detailed analysis for causal pinch-points and careful trialling and the adaptation of thoughtfully chosen interventions." The superficial or inadequate application of SARA may lead to a "pseudo-POP", which may undermine the effectiveness of problem-oriented policing. In short, "the ideal of POP has been difficult to achieve in practice" (Cherney, 2008, 632).

In his analysis of entries for the Herman Goldstein Award for Problem-Oriented Police, Scott (2000, 140–141) discerned a wide range of variance in adherence to POP's principles. The police who submitted entries "continue to frequently use the criminal justice system, but usually more selectively and in conjunction with alternative responses. The police are willing to use informal and noncoercive response alternatives in addition to formal and coercive measures." With that said, the use of "Problem analysis remains generally weak, with most analysis serving merely to substantiate the existence of the suspected problem rather than to develop a more insightful understanding of why it is occurring." Conspicuously, the absentees from "many good problem-solving initiatives" are police executives and midlevel managers.

Perhaps the greatest obstacle to a police department's embracing of community- and problem-oriented policing is that implementation in its ideal form requires "profound changes within the police organization" (Community Policing Consortium, 1994, vii).

As mentioned, there may very well be great resistance by senior management to decentralize decision-making power to the patrol officer and the community. This apprehension may not simply stem from power hungry and micromanaging police executives but from their notoriously conservative and change-resistant demeanor (Braga and Weisburd, 2006, 2). For Fisher-Stewart (2007, 4), the structured chain of command inherent in paramilitary police departments is not exactly amenable to "allowing law enforcement officers the latitude to respond creatively to problems that come before them and engage in problem-solving efforts directly with residents...." In fact, decentralized decision making inherent in community- and problem-oriented policing "represents very different, and perhaps at times, an unfamiliar and uncomfortable way of doing things" within many police forces.

Chalom et al. (2001) identify the challenges that accompany another major paradigm shift for police—actively working with communities as equal partners in crime prevention. "Citizens are generally used as information sources rather than engaged as partners in producing public safety. Officers prefer law enforcement strategies to developing and implementing alternative problem-oriented responses," according to Cherney (2008, 632). Community policing may also underestimate "the resistance of the police organizations towards community consultation and participation":

> The traditional method of gathering and controlling information, the difficulty in understanding political and social issues, the overly centralized command structure of many police forces, the absence of accountability to civilian authorities, isolation of the police and a poor public image and lack of public confidence by a large segment of society, are all obstacles to the development of effective partnerships between the police and the community.
>
> **Chalom et al. (2001, 47)**

Police agencies have come under fire for failing to relinquish greater control over local crime issues and for failing to live up to one ideal of community policing and crime prevention—a decentralization of decision-making power to communities (McPherson and Silloway, 1981; Garofalo and McLeod, 1989; Marx, 1989; Walker and Walker, 1993; Garland, 1996; Fielding, 2001; Miller, 2001; Pavlich, 2002). The reluctance of police agencies to share control over crime prevention and policing may stem from the perception among police agencies that to give up absolute control over crime issues would be to compromise their power within society, not to mention a potential reduction in their resources.

The advent of community policing was supposed to create a *new breed* of police officers, while providing the type of benefits that would be welcomed by frontline police officers, such as greater discretion and increased decision-making powers to solve local crime problems (Lurigio and Rosenbaum, 1994, 148). In their review of studies chronicling the impact of community policing on frontline police officers, Lurigio and Rosenbaum (1994, 148) found that "community policing has exerted a positive impact on the police." Individual police members "have reported increases in job satisfaction and motivation, a broadening of the police role, improvements in relationships with co-workers and citizens, and greater expectations regarding community participation in crime prevention efforts." In contrast, research conducted in eight American cities that assessed the Innovative Neighborhood-Oriented Policing projects found that "the level of enthusiasm for community policing among patrol officers in all eight sites was weak at best. Even in those cities where community policing is at present nothing more than an experimental unit, patrol officers generally had serious doubts about its potential for success." The researchers observed that patrol officers were "particularly resistant to the transition to community policing because community policing seeks to redefine their role and the way they perform their duties" (Sadd and Grinc, 1994, 35). Liederbach et al. (2008, 286) suggest that it may be most appropriate to view any resistance by individual police members to community-oriented policing "as a by-product of a traditional police culture that continues to hold sway over police officers." In particular, they may resist this approach because it "represents a fundamental departure from the aggressive, no-nonsense approach to crime fighting that has long been recognized as a hallmark of police culture."

7.9   OTHER RECENT INNOVATIONS IN POLICING

While community policing "was one of the first new approaches to policing to emerge in this modern period of police innovation" (Braga and Weisburd, 2007, 3), other emergent techniques, strategies, and models have been touted as innovations that enhance police effectiveness. This includes hot spot policing, CompStat, broken windows policing, and intelligence-led policing. Collectively, like community- and problem-oriented policing, these new models have helped oriented police to a more preventative approach to crime control.

7.9.1   Hot Spot Policing

Hot spot policing is a place-based strategy that concentrates police resources in a small spatial area that "has a greater than average number of criminal or disorder events, or an area where people have a higher than average risk of victimization" (Eck et al., 2005, 2). Hot spot policing relies primarily on traditional law enforcement strategies (e.g., the patrol function) and to a lesser extent situational crime prevention tactics. Sherman and Weisburd (1995) first examined this approach in Minneapolis, arguing that the preventative aspects of the patrol function may be more effective if it focused on high-crime areas: if "only 3 percent of the addresses in a city produce more than half of all the requests for police response," then "concentrating police in a few locations makes more sense than spreading them evenly through a beat" (Sherman and Weisburd, 1995, 629). According to Braga and Weisburd (2007, 6–7), hot spot policing "does not demand that the police change their strategies, but requires that they focus them more carefully at places where crime is clustered."

Hot spot policing is relevant to crime prevention because, theoretically, a concentration of police resources in any one location can more effectively maximize the deterrence function of a police presence. According to Ratcliffe et al. (2011, 798), "a refocusing on place, location-specific crime prevention can add to general offender deterrence with options to prevent potential offenders from committing crime at a specific location." Nagin (2010, 313) argues that for deterrence to work, there must be a strong perception by the potential offender of the prospect of detection, and hot spot policing "is probably effective because it tangibly and directly increases apprehension risk at the hot spot by substantially increasing police presence."

In a meta-analysis of studies evaluating hot spot policing operations, Braga et al. (2012) found that 80% of the studies that tested hot spot policing interventions

> ... reported noteworthy crime and disorder reductions. The meta-analysis of key reported outcome measures revealed a small statistically significant mean effect size favoring the effects of hot spots policing in reducing citizen calls for service in treatment places relative to control places. The effect was smaller for randomized designs but still statistically significant and positive. When displacement and diffusion effects were measured, unintended crime prevention benefits were associated with the hot spots.

These results led the authors to conclude, "The extant evaluation research provides fairly robust evidence that hot spots policing is an effective crime prevention strategy. The research also suggests that focusing police efforts on high-activity crime places does not inevitably lead to crime displacement and crime control benefits may diffuse into the areas immediately surrounding the targeted locations" (Braga et al., 2012, 6). There is some research indicating that the effects of hot spot policing may be limited. Ratcliffe et al. (2011) found that police foot patrols implemented in Philadelphia neighborhoods with high violent crime rates resulted in a significant reduction in the level of violent crime in the short term. However, this reduction was not sustained over a long term. Sorg et al. (2013) summarize the findings of this research as such: intensive foot patrols by police can reduce street crime, but the effects do not last after police strength is reduced to normal.

7.9.2 CompStat

In general, CompStat consists of regular performance meetings among police management from various districts who, based on up-to-date crime data, analysis of crime trends and patterns, and geospatial mapping, determine and deploy police resources and crime-control efforts in a timely and strategic manner. Another a key part of CompStat is holding the police supervisors accountable for the delivery of crime reduction strategies in their jurisdiction (Silverman, 2006). According to Golden and Almo (2004, 9), the CompStat process began in New York in the early 1990s

> ... as a part of a new philosophy to use data for management and planning. Local precinct commanders and their supervisors analyze data— presented on maps that show where crimes are occurring— and use it to determine appropriate responses to emerging crime problems. They must then defend their strategies at weekly CompStat meetings at police headquarters. This process helps the NYPD identify where in the city crime, including gun crimes, is a problem, target appropriate resources to those areas, and hold local precinct commanders accountable for results.

For Willis and Mastrofski (2012, 75), CompStat encompasses "four crime reduction principles: (1) accurate, timely information made available at all organization levels; (2) selection of the most effective tactics; (3) rapid focused deployment of people and resources; and (4) relentless follow-up and assessment. Fundamental to this approach is the delegation of decision-making authority to precinct commanders with territorial responsibility." For the Bureau of Justice Statistics (2008, 2), "CompStat integrated many of the lessons learned from previous experimentation: a scientific analysis of crime problems, an emphasis on creative and sustained approaches to solving the crime problems, and strict management accountability. In many ways, CompStat introduced the era of smart policing."

CompStat can be used not only as a traditional reactive enforcement strategy but also as an important proactive, predictive, preventative tool. To this end, it incorporates many principles of crime prevention (proactive identification and response to pressing crime problems), community policing (decentralizing decision making to middle managers), and problem-oriented policing (identifying and then responding to the causes of crime problems for long-term solutions). It also incorporates other important policing innovations, including crime mapping, hot spot policing, crime analysis, and intelligence-led policing.

According to Silverman (2006), while New York and other American cities have seen decreases in crime and violence after their police departments adopted CompStat, the evidence on its impact on crime is limited, in part because CompStat has usually been introduced alongside other policing strategies, such as hot spot policing.

7.9.3   Intelligence-Led Policing

A timely and effectively response to individual criminal acts (the theft of a car) and ongoing criminal conspiracies (e.g., a drug trafficking network) requires the collection and analysis of information. Within the realm of law enforcement, the term *intelligence* refers to "information that has been analyzed and refined so that it is useful to policy-makers in making decisions…" (Federal Bureau of Investigation, n.d.). Criminal intelligence information can be used both on a tactical level (for an isolated criminal event or investigation) or on a strategic level (to help develop long-term forecasts and allocate resources). Whether it is used on a tactical or strategic level, criminal intelligence information is used "to direct police resources with the aim of reducing and preventing (serious) crime, and disrupting criminal activities" (Verfaillie and Vander Beken, 2008, 534–535).

For Ratcliffe and Guidetti (2008, 111), intelligence-led policing is "an information-organizing process that allows police agencies to better understand their crime problems and take a measure of the resources available to be able to decide on an enforcement tactic or prevention strategy best designed to control crime." The relevance for crime prevention is that intelligence-led policing "advocates a proactive approach: decision makers want to be informed about significant and emerging challenges and threats to anticipate, plan and take appropriate preventive action, and target their crime control efforts better. The key objective is then for law enforcement agencies to develop proactive or future-oriented law enforcement action, i.e. to develop plans and tools that can aid decision makers in the assessment of criminal goals, objectives and intentions" (Verfaillie and Vander Beken, 2008, 534–535). Along the same proactive lines, intelligence-led policing helps police approach and prioritize potential crime problems according to risks and threats posed. As the International Centre for the Prevention of Crime (2008, 181) puts it, intelligence-led policing is "a way of understanding crime, not merely in terms of incidents, but also in terms of probabilities, influenced by the quality of the information available. It is based on the principle that in order to evaluate risks, it is necessary to have the right information."

7.9.4   Broken Windows (Order Maintenance) Policing

The broken windows theory of Wilson and Kelling (1982) (see Chapter 2 for more details on this theory) has influenced a number of police forces in the United States.

Wilson and Kelling (1982) theorized that police could prevent crime and community decline by targeting minor offenses and disorder problems. Those who subscribe to this theory advocate an approach that targets low-level, highly visible, and/or destabilizing crime problems, incivilities, and disorderly acts as a means to restore order and ameliorate an environment that fosters crime. According to Hinkley and Weisburd (2008, 503), broken windows or order maintenance policing entails "a series of methods that focus on reducing decline through police crackdowns on minor offenses and disorder." Such methods have included "issuing citations and arrests for disorderly behavior, loitering, and any number of other disorders and minor crimes that the police are likely to ignore in standard policing practices." Problem-oriented policing can also be used as part of order maintenance strategies to "get at the root causes of these types of social disorders and/or to attack physical disorders, such as dilapidated buildings and abandoned lots, through strategies such as code enforcement and community development" (Hinkley and Weisburd, 2008, 503). According to Braga and Weisburd (2007, 12–13), "the available empirical evidence on the crime control effectiveness of broken windows policing is mixed," and it "remains unclear whether police departments that engage a broad-based broken windows policing strategy actually reduce crime."

CASE STUDY 7.13

INTENSIVE DISORDER ENFORCEMENT IN NEWARK, NEW JERSEY

Informed by broken windows theory, police in Newark, New Jersey, undertook a systematic strategy to reduce crime and disorder problems in various hot spots in the city, which included the following:

1. To reduce loitering and disruptive behavior, drug sales, and street harassment, police conducted *street sweeps*, which were intended to confront groups of four or more people who may be creating a public hazard. Loiterers were first warned using an amplified speaker from a police car and then by search and arrest.
2. Police foot patrols were increased to disperse unruly groups of youths and enforce criminal laws and municipal ordinances.
3. Radar checks were implemented to enforce traffic regulations.
4. Bus checks were organized where police rode on or boarded buses to check for potential crime or disorder problems.
5. Roadblocks were set up to deal with motor vehicle offenses but also included searches for drugs, weapons, and parole violations.

Other actions undertaken to reduce disorder problems included intensifying city services, such as increasing the speed of repair to buildings, making structural improvements, improving garbage collection, and keeping the streets and other public spaces clean. The youth convicted of petty offenses and sentenced to community hours were assigned to some of these activities (Graham, 1995, 65).

7.10   CONCLUSION

While crime prevention theory places the utmost importance on the mobilization of local communities and other nonstate actors to prevent crime, the role of police in preventing and controlling crime remains paramount. According to the International Centre for the Prevention of Crime (2008, 179),

> Among all the public authorities in the criminal justice field, the police are still perceived to be primarily responsible for prevention policies, even if other institutional stakeholders are involved and can legitimately claim an important role. Police services are generally seen as the "natural" crime prevention actors and this is generally underlined by national governments. However, their prevention role does not seem to be clearly defined, and most conceptual frameworks on the role of the police do not specifically deal with prevention, even if there are numerous areas of overlap.

The relevance of police to local crime prevention has been augmented by the philosophies of community- and problem-oriented policing, unarguably the most widely touted policing models to emerge in recent times. Both represent a reemergence, renewal, and revitalization of the philosophical, organizational, and operational approach to urban policing developed by Sir Robert Peel. In a 1997 monograph entitled *Crime Prevention and Community Policing: A Vital Partnership,* the National Crime Prevention Council cites what community policing and crime prevention have in common:

1. "Each deals with the health of the community": Both "acknowledge the many interrelated issues that generate crime. They look to building health as much as curing pathological conditions."
2. "Each seeks to address underlying causes and problems": While short-term and reactive measures are necessary to help crime control, "they are insufficient if crime is to be significantly reduced. Looking behind symptoms to treat the causes of community problems is a strategy that both, at their best, share in full measure."
3. "Each deals with the combination of physical and social issues that are at the heart of many community problems": "Community policing and crime prevention both acknowledge that crime-causing situations can arise out of physical as well as social problems in the community … Both approaches examine the broadest possible range of causes and solutions."
4. "Each requires active involvement by community residents": The chief task of crime prevention practitioners, law enforcement and civilian alike, is to enable people "to make themselves and their communities safer, by helping them gain appropriate knowledge, develop helpful attitudes, and take useful actions."
5. "Each requires partnerships beyond law enforcement to be effective": "Crime prevention efforts involve schools, community centers, civic organizations, religious groups, social service agencies, public works agencies, and other elements of the community. Experience in community policing documents the need for similar partnerships both to reach people and to solve problems."
6. "Each is an approach or a philosophy, rather than a program": "Neither community policing nor crime prevention is a 'program,'—that is, a fixed model for delivery of specific services. Rather, each is a way of doing business. Each involves the development of an institutional mindset that holds community paramount and values preventive and problem-solving efforts in all of the organization's business. Each can involve a wide range of programs and other initiatives" (Bureau of Justice Assistance, 1997).

As detailed in this chapter, other innovations in policing in recent years have buttressed police effectiveness in controlling crime, while also internalizing some of the key precepts of crime prevention. This includes problem-oriented policing, hot spot policing, CompStat, broken windows policing, and intelligence-led policing. Using a matrix published by Clarke and Eck (2005, 9), Table 7.1 summarizes and contrasts these different policing models.

As Table 7.1 indicates there are important differences in each of these policing models, yet, as detailed below these innovations in policing have a number of common elements, many of which are emblematic of crime prevention.

Place based: A common denominator in many new policing strategies is a focus on places as opposed to offenders. While hot spot policing is the most obvious, a critical element of CompStat is examining crime trends and patterns in specific locales. CompStat and community policing are both influenced by place-based strategies insofar as police decision making is decentralized to officers and supervisors working in different neighborhoods.

Risk based: As discussed in Chapter 1, crime prevention very much operates on a risk-based approach. Most of the policing philosophies and strategies introduced in recent years also operate on a risk-based approach. Indeed, hot spot policing, CompStat, intelligence-led policing, and broken windows policing are all about responding to and minimizing risks, especially in a place-based context. As Beck (2009) writes, "risk-based deployment has been demonstrated to effectively address the main goals of police deployment: allocate police resources when and where they are needed to prevent or deter crime through a strong police presence and to ensure the ability to respond rapidly by proactively positioning resources when and where they are likely to be needed in order to ensure a timely response" (Beck, 2009). In short, "when police departments focus their efforts on identifiable risks, such as crime hot spots, repeat victims, and serious offenders, they are able to prevent crime and disorder" (Braga and Weisburd, 2007, 11–12). This risk-based or actuarial approach to crime control and community safety is also reflective of another important trend in policing: "concern with allocating organizational resources more efficiently and effectively, sometimes referred to as a 'new managerialism.'" For example, "under CompStat, we would expect to see structures designed to streamline and monitor management's decision-making processes and enhance the strategic use of limited police resources" (Willis and Mastrofski, 2012, 76).

Problem oriented: One of the most influential innovations in policing in recent years is problem-oriented policing. Indeed, this philosophy influences and permeates almost all the other advances made in policing in recent years. To truly maximize the effectiveness of such strategies as intelligence-led policing, hot spot policing, community policing, or CompStat, police cannot simply rely on limited crim-control methods, such as deterrence or the arrest of offenders. These strategies are increasingly being replaced or complemented by a problem-solving orientation that places a premium on analyzing the scope, nature, impact, and causes of the problem and then finding long-lasting solutions that are individualized to each problem and the circumstances surrounding it.

Predictive: Central to many of the aforementioned policing strategies is the concept of prediction. Hot spot policing, intelligence-led policing, and CompStat are all concerned with predicting where and when crimes will occur, based in part on analyzing and extrapolating past data. Personifying this principle is *predictive policing*, which entails "taking data from disparate sources, analyzing them and then

Table 7.1
Differences between Problem Oriented Policing and Other Strategies

	Focus	Objective	Rationale	Method	First Steps
Problem-oriented policing	Specific, recurring crime problems	Remove the causes of these problems	Prevention is more effective than enforcement.	Undertake focused action research (SARA)	Identify problems requiring attention
Community policing	Public–police relations, organizational changes, problem solving	Proactive prevention of crime and social disorder and increased public confidence in and support of police	Support is critical for police effectiveness. Organizational changes are essential to maintain changes; problem solving is a central method to dealing with crime and social disorder issues.	Build trust by contacts with residents and community meetings, enacts organizational changes to support efforts, and engages in problem solving	Appoint a community officer for the neighborhood, identify problems requiring attention, and identify organizational changes necessary to support efforts
Broken windows	Deteriorating neighborhoods	Halt slide of neighborhood into serious crime	Nip trouble in the bud.	Policing incivilities/ order maintenance	Identify a deteriorating neighborhood
Intelligence-led policing	The process of collecting, analyzing, and disseminating intelligence	Base policing strategies and tactics on sound intelligence	Action only effective when based on sound intelligence.	Promote the intelligence cycle of collection, evaluation, collation, analysis, and dissemination	Development of data gathering, processing, and dissemination
CompStat	Acute short-term geographic crime patterns	Reduce crime hot spots	Fewer hot spots reduce overall crime.	Computerized hot spot identification and intensive patrols and enforcement	Build crime mapping and geographic accountability

Source: Clarke, R. and Eck, J., Crime Analysis for Problem Solvers in 60 Small Steps, Office of Community Oriented Policing, Washington, DC, 2005, p. 9.

using results to anticipate, prevent and respond more effectively to future crime" (Pearsall, 2010, 16). One of the more exhaustive and sophisticated predictive policing programs was piloted in Santa Clara, California, which "uses an earthquake aftershock model to determine where future crimes will occur. Similar to the predictability of an aftershock after an earthquake, the models predicts that there will be 'aftercrimes' after an initial crime" (Santa Cruz Police Department, 2011). What makes the Santa Clara model unique is the use of a considerable amount of data and sophisticated statistical (algorithms) techniques to analyze the data (Pearsall, 2010, 18). Crime and location data dating back many years are entered into a complex algorithm that generates a prediction about where crimes are likely to take place on a certain day and time. Police officers are then provided with these forecasts before beginning their shifts and are assigned to use their "proactive time" between 911 calls to patrol those areas (de Leon, 2013).

Computer-driven quantitative crime analysis (advanced analytics as a policing tool): Many of the policing innovations in recent years rely on "sophisticated statistical techniques for assessing risk and predicting dangerousness, and the implementation of innovative risk-based crime control strategies" (Willis and Mastrofski, 2012, 84). Intelligence-led policing, CompStat, hot spot policing, and predictive policing all rely to some extent or another on gathering, quantifying, and analyzing relevant data (and not just crime data) and then making decisions based on the data (indeed, CompStat is short for *comprehensive computer statistics*).

Evidence based: Like crime prevention in general, many of the advancements in policing in recent years have been informed by empirical evidence (including what works) as well as sound theories. For Braga and Weisburd (2007, 8), "evidence based policing argues that it is understandable that standard models of policing had failed because successful strategies must be based on scientific evidence. This approach calls for the development of such evidence, and in particular for the expansion of controlled experimental studies of policing practices."

Collaboration and partnerships "(third-party policing)": One of the most profound changes in crime control and policing in recent years is the increased role of individuals, groups, and agencies outside the criminal justice sector and policing in particular. Of course, the defining tenet of community policing is a partnership between the policing and the communities they serve. But the advent of *third-party policing* goes beyond that. According to Braga and Weisburd (2007, 6), "third party policing asserts that the police cannot successfully deal with many problems on their own, and thus that the failures of traditional policing models may be found in the limits of police powers. Using civil ordinances and civil courts, or the resources of private agencies, third party policing recognizes that much social control is exercised by institutions other than the police and that crime can be managed through agencies other than the criminal law." Collaboration with other actors is also highly relevant to problem-oriented policing, according to Cherney (2008, 632):

> Relevant to promoting innovative problem-solving is the willingness of police to engage third parties in furtherance of crime control. Harnessing such capacities is critical to POP given that many public safety problems the police have to address require some level of partnership with external agencies. One reason for this is that many factors that lead to crime have very little to do with the police directly, but instead originate in the functioning of other institutions and the capacity of actors within those settings to assert effective social control.

This includes, for example, people who act as place managers, handlers or guardians, whose action or inaction can create opportunities for crime. Hence, drawing upon the crime control capacities of external parties as a core aspect of problem analysis and response is essential to the effectiveness of POP in practice ... A key requirement is that police act as effective brokers of public safety, engaging third parties through the use of various levers that facilitate cooperation in crime prevention and link the internal social control capacities of external institutions to crime reduction outcomes.

Increased accountability: Community policing helped usher in a new era of police accountability to the public and to the communities police serve. CompStat has also made police supervisors more accountable for the districts and/or line functions they are responsible for. As Stone and Travis (2011, 12) write, "the CompStat accountability process, in which chiefs in headquarters hold precinct and other area commanders accountable for continuing reductions in crime and achievement of other goals, is now a staple of police management in most large departments." Whether it is community policing, CompStat, or numerous other ways, "police agencies are now routinely accountable for their ability—or inability—to reduce the volume of crime" (Stone and Travis, 2011, 12).

Despite generally positive assessments of spatially concentrated policing models, such as broken windows and hot spot policing, they have also been subject to vociferous critiques. In particular, they have been characterized as nothing more than a mask for traditional, punitive policing that overwhelmingly focuses on impoverished neighborhoods and systematically harasses and abrogates the civil rights of the poor and marginalized minority groups through indiscriminate and repressive law enforcement tactics (Kochel, 2011).

7.11   DISCUSSION QUESTIONS AND EXERCISES

1. Mastrofski (1991) argues that community policing emerged due to a number of interrelated problems that threaten the legitimacy of police in the eyes of the public and politicians. Do you think this loss of legitimacy still exists with respect to policing today?
2. Do you believe that any police force can truly satisfy the theoretical ideals of community policing, such as the transfer of power from police management to the frontline constable?
3. Some have argued that police forces must not simply focus on law enforcement but should help address a wide range of problems, including those that give rise to crime and criminality. Yet, the multiagency approach that is advocated by community policing means that police officers can rely on other professionals who may be better suited to address such causal problems. Within the context of this multiagency approach to community policing, do you believe that police should stay focused on what they do best (enforcing the laws, responding to calls for service, arresting offenders) and allow their partners to focus on the social problems that give rise to crime?
4. Search the Internet for other examples of community-based and problem-oriented policing.
5. Research and discuss how the police department in your city or town has incorporated the principles of each community-based and problem-oriented policing.

7.12   IMPORTANT TERMS

Community policing
CompStat
Harnessing capacity
Hot spot policing
Incident-driven policing
Intelligence-led policing
Law enforcement
Peacekeeping (peacemaking)
Predictive policing
Problem-oriented policing
Professional policing model
SARA
Third-party policing

FURTHER READING

Bureau of Justice Assistance, *Understanding Community Policing: A Framework for Action,* Bureau of Justice Assistance, Office of Justice Programs, Department of Justice, Washington, DC, 1994, https://www.ncjrs.gov/pdffiles/commp.pdf.

Capobianco, L., Key developments, issues, and practices: The role of the police in crime prevention, Background Paper prepared for the *International Crime Prevention Centre's Seventh Annual Colloquium,* Oslo, Norway, November 8–9, 2007, http://www.crime-prevention-intl.org.

Hicks, D.C., Denat, F., and Arsenault, B., *Inspiring Police Practices: Crime Prevention Partnerships,* International Centre for the Prevention of Crime, Montreal, Quebec, Canada, 2000.

International Centre for the Prevention of Crime, *The Role of the Police in Crime Prevention, Tool Kit,* ICPC, Montreal, Quebec, Canada, 2002.

Kappeler, V.E. and Gaines, L.K., *Community Policing: A Contemporary Perspective,* 6th edn., Anderson Publishing, Cincinnati, OH, 2012.

National Crime Prevention Council, *Crime Prevention and Community Policing: A Vital Partnership,* Bureau of Justice Statistics, Department of Justice, Washington, DC, 1997, http://www.ncjrs.gov/txtfiles/166819.txt.

Sherman, L. and Eck, J., Policing for crime prevention, in *Evidence-Based Crime Prevention,* revised edn., Sherman, L.W., Farrington, D.P., Welsh, B.C., and MacKenzie, D.L., Eds., Routledge, London, U.K., 2006, Chap. 8, pp. 295–329.

Stone, C. and Travis, J., *Toward a New Professionalism in Policing, New Perspectives in Policing,* Harvard Kennedy School, Program in Criminal Justice Policy and Management, National Institute of Justice, Cambridge, MA, 2011.

INTERNET RESOURCES AND CASE STUDIES

Australian Institute of Criminology, http://www.aic.gov.au/criminal_justice_system/policing.html.
Centre for Problem-Oriented Policing, http://www.popcenter.org/.
Chicago's Alternative Policing Strategy (CAPS), https://portal.chicagopolice.org.
Community-Oriented Policing Services Office (U.S. Department of Justice), http://www.cops.usdoj.gov/.
Policing.com, http://www.policing.com/index.html.
Problem-Oriented Policing Projects (candidates for and winners of The Herman Goldstein Award), http://www.popcenter.org/library/awards/.

PART IV

PLANNING, IMPLEMENTING, AND EVALUATING A CRIME PREVENTION PROJECT

CHAPTER 8

CRIME PREVENTION PROJECT, PHASE ONE
Planning

CONTENTS

8.1   *LEARNING OBJECTIVES*

By the end of this chapter, you should have a better understanding of the following:

- The importance of planning crime prevention activities, including conducting research to identify crime and disorder problems
- The stages involved in planning a crime prevention project
- How the planning process (in particular the research and analysis stages) epitomizes the problem-oriented approach to crime prevention
- The importance of involving community members and other key stakeholders in the planning process
- The skills necessary to undertake and assemble a crime prevention plan

8.2   *INTRODUCTION*

Chapters 8 through 10 explore the steps involved in planning, implementing, and evaluating a community-based crime prevention project. These steps are grouped into four phases, which are summarized as follows:

1. Phase 1: Planning—plan the crime prevention project:
   a. Research (safety audit): Identify and describe the community and its crime and disorder problems.
   b. Analysis: Examine the research findings, separating causes from symptoms and facilitators.

   c. Crime prevention plan: Develop strategic interventions that are commensurate with the scope and nature of the identified problems.

   d. Evaluation plan: Prepare an evaluation plan and carry out *pretest* evaluation research before implementing the crime prevention plan.

2. Phase 2: Implementation—implement the crime prevention plan.
3. Phase 3: Monitoring and evaluation—monitor and assess the implemented strategies to ensure they reach their objectives and are as effective as possible.
4. Phase 4: Modify—based on the ongoing monitoring and evaluation, modify the plan (if necessary) to maximize success.

These four phases are not necessarily followed in sequential order; there can be overlap. In particular, as indicated earlier, the evaluation plan should be developed during the project planning phase, and the first part of the evaluation (the collection of *pretest* data) should actually be implemented before the crime prevention plan is carried out. The monitoring and evaluation of the crime prevention initiatives should permeate all stages of the crime prevention process. As indicated in Figure 8.1, the crime prevention process is ongoing and success often involves continual planning, action, learning, adaptation, and modification.

That an entire chapter is dedicated to planning a crime prevention project shows how important this phase is. Complex crime problems cannot be prevented through ad hoc, spontaneous, arbitrary measures based on gut feelings or *common sense*. What is first required is a systematic plan, which is the product of such essential steps as identifying and analyzing local crime and disorder problems, mobilizing community members, brainstorming around possible solutions, selecting the most appropriate interventions, building a team that will carry out the interventions, and documenting all the aforementioned in a planning report.

While crime prevention plans can be developed for certain demographic groups (e.g., women, children, youth, the elderly, the disabled), this chapter focuses largely on crime prevention planning for the residential neighborhood.

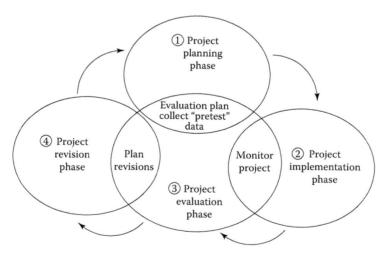

Figure 8.1
The (overlapping) phases of the crime prevention project process.

8.3 CRIME PREVENTION PLAN AS A STRATEGIC PLAN

The goal of the planning phase is to identify and examine local crime and disorder problems and then develop a strategic plan that will address these problems. Thus, any significant crime prevention project must be preceded by a strategic planning process.

Strategic planning (verb): An applied, action-oriented process that guides the implementation of a project

Strategic plan (noun): A report (blueprint) that is the final product of a planning process

---

The strategic planning process personifies the problem-oriented approach to crime prevention. This phase involves two basic tasks: (1) identifying, researching, and analyzing the scope and nature of current and potential crime and disorder problem(s) and (2) developing solutions that are most appropriate to addressing these problems.

8.4 KEY STAGES IN PLANNING A CRIME PREVENTION PROJECT

Planning a crime prevention project is every bit as important as implementing it. To truly satisfy its problem-oriented methodology, a crime prevention project should be guided by a well-thought-out plan.

The Institute for the Prevention of Crime at the University of Ottawa provides one framework for crime prevention planning that includes five elements: (1) understanding the problem and developing a vision, an action plan, and responsibility centers; (2) concentrating resources; (3) relying on evidence-based approaches; (4) assuring adequate and sustained supports; and (5) informing and engaging the public. The IPC explains that the planning process should start with a clear definition of the nature and size of problem, the factors that contribute to it, and an idea of how prevention could improve the problem. From this point, an action plan is developed that identifies goals and milestones (Hastings, 2013, 3).

The remainder of this chapter discusses the key steps in the crime prevention planning phase, which are summarized in Box 8.1. The planning phase (as well as subsequent phases) reflects a number of fundamental principles of crime prevention that have been emphasized throughout this book: the use of a problem-oriented methodology, relying on an evidence-based approach (implementing *best practices*), a collaborative, team approach and ensuring the process is controlled by (or at least involves) those most affected by the problems being addressed.

8.4.1 Stage 1: Environmental Scan—Define and Understand the Community, Identify Community Members and Other Key Stakeholders, and Assess Community Capacity and Readiness

Within the context of community crime prevention planning, an *environmental scan* consists of defining and gathering basic information on the community that will be

CASE STUDY 8.1

COMPREHENSIVE, COMMUNITY-BASED CRIME PREVENTION PLANNING AND IMPLEMENTATION MODEL

Communities that Care (CTC) is a comprehensive, community-based crime prevention planning model developed and tested in the United States. While this approach was initially developed to address youth crime and violence, it represents a generic model that provides local communities a blueprint and the infrastructure to "engage in multi-level, multi-sectoral prevention planning and implement evidence-based programs" (Flynn, 2008, 84):

> As an operating system for youth prevention and promotion, CTC mobilizes community leaders, organizations, and grassroots members to tailor prevention planning, implementation and evaluation to local needs. Training and technical assistance support community leaders and ordinary citizens as they mobilize resources, research risk and protective factors, and implement validated intervention programs on an ongoing, long-term basis.
>
> **Flynn (2008, 85–86)**

CTC is implemented in five sequential phases:

1. Assessing community readiness to undertake collaborative prevention efforts
2. Mobilizing and organizing community residents and other key partners
3. Conducting an assessment of community problems, risk factors, and causes
4. Developing an action plan, which includes adapting evidence-based policies, practices, and programs
5. Implementing and evaluating the action plan (Flynn, 2008, 84)

According to Flynn (2008), CTC is based on several important crime prevention and community mobilization principles: "providing guided mobilization and empowerment of the local community," a comprehensive approach to addressing existing problems and risk factors by relying on multiple strategies and interventions, collaboration among all stakeholders, a proactive approach to local problem solving, addressing multiple problems and risk factors within the community, and "implementing, with a high degree of fidelity, prevention programs that are tested and effective (i.e., evidence-based)" (Flynn, 2008, 85).

One of the hallmarks of the CTC model is the support and training provided to community organizers and residents from experienced and certified facilitators. The CTC structure includes training workshops, manuals, and other tools that help guide community members through each stage of the process.

When applied specifically to at-risk youth, CTC uses a problem-solving approach to prevent the onset of such antisocial, risky, and problematic behaviors, as violence, delinquency, dropping out of high school, and substance abuse. CTC is designed to help community members identify, understand, and address risk factors that confront youth collectively and to develop programs that address these risk factors. CTC is theoretically derived from social developmental models concerned with strengthening protective factors that promote positive youth development while deterring young people from high-risk situations and problematic behaviors. These protective factors include promoting young people's constructive involvement in and attachment to their local neighborhood and nurturing the social competencies and life skills needed to effectively deal with problematic circumstances and behaviors (Arthur et al., 2010).

BOX 8.1

KEY STAGES IN THE CRIME PREVENTION PLANNING PROCESS

Stage 1: Environmental scan—define and understand the community, identify community members and other key stakeholders, and assess community capacity and readiness

Stage 2: Initial community outreach—holding a community-wide meeting

Stage 3: Research—collect information on local crime and disorder problems

Stage 4: Conduct research—collect information by administering research instruments

Stage 5: Collate and analyze the collected information

Stage 6: Develop the crime prevention plan

Stage 7: Draft an evaluation plan—determine how the crime prevention strategies will be monitored and evaluated

Stage 8: Prepare the crime prevention planning report

Stage 9: Disseminate a (draft) crime prevention plan

Stage 10: Modify the crime prevention plan (if necessary)

Stage 11: Finalize the crime prevention plan

Stage 12: Seek funding and *in-kind* resources to support the crime prevention activities

Stage 13: Collect pretest evaluation data

---

the focus of the strategic plan. One of the very first steps in this stage is to define and better understand the community in terms of spatial boundaries, demographic characteristics, community leaders, community groups, local institutions, private-sector businesses, and governmental or nongovernmental organizations (NGOs) that are located in or serve the community. In addition to defining and better understanding the community, one of the ostensible goals of this stage is to identify a community's capacity to mobilize around and effectively address crime and disorder problems (by identifying assets and resources that can be used to this end while also understanding any limitations and obstacles that must be overcome). As the first stage of a local crime prevention planning process, an environmental scan should accomplish the following steps:

1. *Determine the spatial boundaries (i.e., the geographic scope) of the neighborhood that is to be targeted by the plan.* Because most crime prevention plans are developed and implemented at a geospatial level (e.g., citywide or for a neighborhood, a block, an apartment complex, a park, a school, etc.), the spatial boundaries of the community should be well defined. Defining the spatial

boundaries not only allows planners to focus their work, but it helps identify community members, local groups, resources, and institutions that must be mobilized for both the planning and implementation stages.

2. *Compile a comprehensive and up-to-date mailing list of neighborhood residents.* One task that will prove useful throughout the project planning and implementation process is the compilation of a comprehensive list of residents in the neighborhood, including names, addresses, e-mail addresses, and phone numbers. At the very least, a mailing list (snail mail and/or e-mail) should be prepared. This list will be essential to organizers when reaching out to and mobilizing community members in the project planning and implementation stages.

3. *Identify the demographic characteristics of neighborhood residents.* The demographic makeup of the neighborhood must be understood and taken into consideration when planning and implementing a crime prevention project. Demographic characteristics influence the scope and nature of local crime and disorder problems (e.g., a large population of young males often translates into a higher crime rate). Local demographic characteristics will also influence the crime prevention strategies to be implemented and the type of outreach to be undertaken. Some important local demographic traits that should be documented in the planning stage include the following:

   a. Age breakdown (average age; different age groups; the size of local crime-prone age groups, such as young males; the size of particularly fearful or vulnerable groups, such as seniors or women)
   b. Gender breakdown
   c. Socioeconomic status (average income level, education, different socioeconomic groups in the neighborhood, local unemployment rate)
   d. Racial and ethnic composition (including different languages spoken)
   e. Household composition (the average number of people in a dwelling, their relationship to one another, the number of single-parent families)
   f. Tenure of residence (the proportion of homeowners vs. renters)
   g. Population turnover (the number and proportion of people moving in and out of the neighborhood on an annual basis)

   This demographic information is often collected through government census surveys and is usually available through the public library or municipal government sources.

4. *Identify the different (demographic) groups that exist within the neighborhood.* Within many neighborhoods, one may find numerous smaller communities, which can be defined by ethnicity, nationality, race, mother tongue, socioeconomic status, age, sexual preference, and even hobbies. Identifying all the different groups that make up a neighborhood is important because, as mentioned earlier, this information can be vital to understanding the scope and nature of crime and disorder problems. Community outreach strategies and the crime prevention plan itself may also have to be adapted to different demographic communities in the neighborhood. A better understanding of these different communities can help identify local crime and disorder problems that may be unique to or prioritized by each. In addition to crafting outreach messages that can be tailored to each community, any strategy that hopes to effect a broad-based mobilization of neighborhood residents should

include efforts to win over those who are seen as influential leaders within each of the different groups in a neighborhood.

5. *Identify local businesses, governmental agencies, NGOs, and institutions.* Organizers should also identify all of the organizations and institutions located within the neighborhood or that serve the neighborhood. This includes private-sector businesses, government agencies, NGOs, neighborhood associations, schools, community centers, day-care centers, after-school programs, sports and recreational clubs, group homes, social service providers, and places of worship. The goal of this step is to identify local assets and resources that can play a potential part in planning and implementing a crime prevention strategy. It is important to identify local groups and institutions because they can also be used to reach out to and involve residents in crime prevention activities. Local schools, community centers, day cares, and youth recreational centers or sports leagues are also key institutions through which (social developmental) crime prevention interventions can be delivered.

6. *Identify government agencies that have jurisdiction over and can contribute to crime prevention planning and project implementation.* Police and other government agencies have an important role to play in any crime prevention plan. Police, in particular, should be involved early in the planning process; they are a source of information on local crime and disorder problems, they can facilitate outreach to community members, and they can be instrumental in helping to develop and implement a crime prevention plan. Other relevant government agencies and institutions include social welfare agencies, the fire department (essential partners in shutting down problem premises), the local health department, urban planning (to address public design problems that may promote crime or to help with community development), engineering, schools, as well as community and recreation centers. Elected officials who represent the neighborhood should also be identified, as they can be a key resource in connecting organizers with relevant government departments, mobilizing resources, and locating funding.

By the end of stage 1, organizers should have the following:

- A list of residents, including contact information
- Information on the demographic characteristics of the neighborhood
- An understanding of the different demographic groups that exist within the neighborhood
- A list of local public sector, private sector, and NGOs (including names of key contacts within each)

8.4.2 Stage 2: Initial Community Outreach—Holding a Community-Wide Meeting

Once organizers have conducted some preliminary research and garnered a basic understanding about the neighborhood to be targeted by the crime prevention plan, the next step is to reach out to and involve community members and other individuals, groups, and agencies that are affected by or can contribute to the planning, implementation, and/or evaluation of the crime prevention project. The information collected in stage 1 will contribute to efforts to conduct an outreach campaign that invites neighborhood residents and other key partners to an initial public meeting. The goals of this meeting can include any of the following:

- Providing some initial information on the local crime and disorder problems (often a presentation by police)
- Alerting local residents to and educating them on the crime prevention planning process
- Soliciting input from community members on their perceptions of local crime and disorder problems and measures needed to address these problems
- Enlisting the involvement of community members in the planning process
- Discussing the next steps that should be taken following this meeting
- Formation of action groups, the most important being one that will collect information to identify and analyze the local crime and disorder problems

The initial community meeting represents the start of an ongoing effort to reach out to and mobilize community members and other key partners. Given the importance of community support for local, collective crime prevention strategies, organizers must constantly strategize about how to maximize participation in the planning and implementation process. The initial public meeting is a start because it is here that organizers can determine who attended and who did not (including which local communities from the neighborhood were represented at the meeting and which were not). From here, organizers can develop strategies to solicit the participation of those who did not attend the meeting. (Tactics to organize neighborhoods and maximize participation in crime prevention projects are dealt with in more detail in Chapter 9.)

By the end of stage 2, organizers should have

- Developed an outreach strategy (for the initial community meeting), which includes specific strategies for different demographic groups in the neighborhood
- Reached out to those in the community (primarily to promote the meeting)
- Held an initial community-wide meeting
- Solicited input from community members on their perceptions of local crime and disorder problems
- Educated community members on the planning process
- Determined the next steps that should be taken following this meeting (with input from neighborhood residents, the police, and other key partners)
- Formed action groups, the most important being one that will collect information to identify the local crime and disorder problems
- Reflected on the effectiveness of the outreach strategy (based on how many and who attended the community meeting), with a view to determining its strengths and weaknesses vis-à-vis maximizing the participation of residents in the future

---

8.4.3 Stage 3: Research—Collect Data on Local Crime and Disorder Problems

The goal of the research stage is to identify and analyze the scope and nature of the crime and disorder problems in the neighborhood. As discussed throughout this textbook, a problem-oriented approach to crime prevention requires a comprehensive and rigorous enumeration of local crime problems. The research stage can also be used to collect information and perspectives (from local residents and groups) on how these problems can best be addressed.

Also called *safety audits*, the research component of the planning phase can be as short as one community meeting where participants provide input; or it can be quite extensive, requiring the drafting of a research proposal and the use of numerous data-gathering methods and instruments. The nature and extent of the research will be dictated by a number of factors, including the size of the neighborhood (spatially and by population), available resources and expertise, and the desire of the planning committee and community members.

Paramount in the research process is the collection of reliable and accurate information. Information that does not accurately depict the true nature, scope, and causes of local crime problems will undermine any subsequent crime prevention plan to the point that it may be entirely misguided and ineffectual (succinctly summarized by the adage *garbage in, garbage out*). Some things that organizers should consider before undertaking research are summarized in Box 8.2.

According to Husain (2007), research into crime and disorder problems at the local level can make a significant contribution to the effective planning and implementation of crime prevention activities. In particular, these *safety audits* can serve to

- Enable the information, energy, and resources of different organizations and communities to be pooled to build a comprehensive composite picture
- Help organizations with differing perspectives on which problems should be given the highest priority
- Reveal the complex linkages between social and economic factors and other factors and mobilize agencies to participate in preventive action providing the basis for effective problem solving and enabling the right balance to be struck between alternative approaches and activities

---

BOX 8.2

SOME TIPS TO CONSIDER BEFORE COLLECTING INFORMATION

- Plan the research in a methodical and systematic fashion (prepare a research proposal; determine what data will be collected, how it will be collected, who will be the sources of the information, and how the data will be used to inform a crime prevention plan).
- Involve community members in the research process; they should take the lead in identifying and defining local crime and disorder problems.
- Engage professionals—police, professional researchers, students, and urban planners—to help design and carry out the research.
- Consider using a number of complementary research *instruments* and sources (e.g., a victimization survey, review of police statistics, safety audits, observations of the physical environment, interviews with *experts*).
- Make sure that as part of the research and analysis stages, efforts are made to determine the causes of the problems in the community.

- Promote partnerships and community involvement
- Build the capacity of local stakeholders through development of skills and knowledge
- Reveal the distinctive characteristics of crime problems in a particular area, enabling solutions to be tailored to local needs
- Shed light on which measures and services have previously worked well and provide a baseline against which change and achievement can be measured
- Provide the foundation for strategies that are effective in preventing crime and improving the quality of life for citizens (Husain, 2007, 12)

8.4.3.1 Involving Community Members and Other Key Partners in the Research Process

Given the importance of involving neighborhood residents in the planning process, one of the first tasks organizers must undertake is to solicit their participation in the research. This entails getting neighborhood residents involved in both providing and collecting information. The initial community meeting is the perfect opportunity to seek input and to form a research action group.

When involving neighborhood residents in data collection, organizers will want to follow the principles of participatory action research (PAR), an approach to conducting local research that engages and empowers residents to identify, examine, and understand issues that affect their lives. A PAR approach combines research, social investigation, local knowledge and experience, education, and collective action by community members to address neighborhood issues and problems (Hall, 1981, 7). The word *participatory* represents a decentralizing and democratizing thrust in social research that recognizes the importance of ensuring that the principal researchers and decision makers are those who are affected by the issue or problem and have control over how to intervene. Unlike traditional scientific approaches to local social problem solving, where state technocrats or professional researchers define the process, collect and analyze the data, and generate knowledge, under PAR the community's interests are identified and defined as the starting point. Community members also determine the focus of knowledge generation, data collection and analysis, and action that must be taken to manage, improve, or solve their problem situation (Todhunter, 2001). Under a PAR approach to data gathering, police, other criminal justice officials, and professional researchers serve as technical consultants. The *action* component of PAR indicates that the research is intended to address local issues or problems and to contribute to needed changes based on the desires and direct involvement of group participants.

When research is carried out by people affected by local issues or problems, they become engaged in a "collective, self-reflective enquiry." Through the acquisition and control of knowledge, understanding, and indigenous problem solving, this enquiry contributes to their own empowerment (Todhunter, 2001). Thus, PAR facilitates the education of local residents (as people gather and analyze information about a problem or issue), fosters collective action (as people work together to gather information and learn that they share the same problem), and promotes capacity and community building (as people work to solve the problem collectively) (Rubin and Rubin, 1992, 156).

By the end of stage 3, project organizers should have assembled a research action team made up of local community members as well as professionals that will be responsible for collecting information to identify local crime and disorder problems.

BOX 8.3

RESEARCH PLAN VS. THE CRIME PREVENTION PLAN

As part of a crime prevention project planning process, two types of plans will be prepared: a research plan and a crime prevention plan. The two can be distinguished by their sequence in the planning process (the research plan comes first) and their respective goals (the former is a plan on how to *collect* information on local crime problems, while the latter is a plan on how to *address* the problems identified in the research).

In other words:

- The research plan answers: What must we do to identify, describe, and analyze the crime and disorder problems (as well as capacities and assets) of the community?
- The crime prevention plan answers: What must we do to alleviate the crime and disorder problems identified in the research?

8.4.3.2 Plan the Data Collection (Draft a Research Proposal)

One of the first tasks of the aforementioned research team will be to put together a data collection plan. Just as the implementation of a crime prevention project is planned, so too the research be planned (Box 8.3). Central to the research planning stage is a proposal that will guide the data collection.

A research proposal may not be necessary but it is recommended if organizers want to comprehensively and rigorously identify local crime and disorder problems. A research proposal can also be submitted to external agencies for funding to conduct the research.

The purpose of a research proposal is to provide a blueprint for the data collection and analysis; it should outline the objectives of the research (what is the research intended to accomplish?), the methods used (how will information be collected to satisfy the research objectives?), sources of information (from where and whom is the information collected?), as well as a work plan that will provide a step-by-step framework for the research (when will each step in the research process be undertaken?).

A research proposal may be as simple as a safety audit checklist, which can be used to examine design issues that may promote the opportunity for crimes to occur. A structure of a more detailed research proposal is provided in Box 8.4. Despite the number of headings, a research proposal does not have to be longer than 10 pages.

The research plan can be summarized in a matrix that lists each research objective, the variables to be examined for each, the sources of information for each objective and variable, and the methods and instruments that will be used to collect the data on each variable. A sample research design matrix is provided in Table 8.1.

8.4.3.2.1 Research Methods and Instruments Once a research proposal has been written and a decision has been made as to which methods will be used to collect information, the next step is to identify or draft the research *instruments*, which are used to record the information that will be gathered. Two commonly used instruments for crime prevention research are a victimization survey questionnaire and a safety audit checklist. Another research method that can be used is observation.

BOX 8.4

RECOMMENDED STRUCTURE OF A RESEARCH PROPOSAL

1. *Introduction.* The introduction should identify and succinctly summarize the subject that is the focus of the research. The introduction should work as an abstract of the whole document; the reader should know from the very first paragraph what this proposal is about.

2. *Background.* This section should be used to provide a background of the community, based on the preliminary research conducted in stages 1 (preliminary research) and 2 (initial community meeting). The purpose of the background is to provide some information to help contextualize the research objectives and methods. This section can begin by broadly describing the community (e.g., its spatial boundaries, demographic characteristics) and then focusing more narrowly on what is known about local crime problems.

3. *Research objectives.* This section answers the question: What is it that this research is meant to accomplish? Every research project should have one overarching goal, which is stated at the beginning of this section (e.g., The goal of this research is to comprehensively identify and examine the nature and scope of the crime problems being experienced by this neighborhood as well as the assets and resources available to address these problems). This should be followed by a list of subobjectives, which are more specific goals that systematically and collectively satisfy the overarching goal. The subobjectives of the research should be listed in a logical fashion; for example, describe the neighborhood; identify and examine its crime and disorder problems; identify (and separate) symptoms, causes, and facilitators; indentify local assets and resources; and draft a crime prevention plan.

4. *Variables to be measured.* A variable is something you can measure through research. For the purposes of crime prevention research, variables are indicators of the nature, scope, causes, symptoms, and facilitators of local crime and disorder problems. The purpose of the research is to gather as much information as possible on those variables that are reflective of the local crime and disorder problems (i.e., that help address the research objectives). Some typical variables that are measured to determine the nature and scope of local crime problems are as follows:
   - Crime rate (recorded by police)
   - Victimization rate (based on a survey of community members)
   - Calls for police service
   - Types of local crime and disorder problems
   - Fear of crime
   - Feelings of safety and security among residents
   - Local design issues that may create crime opportunities
   - Behavior and actions of residents that may create crime opportunities
   - Social factors that may be causing criminal behavior
   - Factors that may facilitate (or aggravate) local crime and disorder problems

5. *Research methods and sources.* If the research objectives articulate *what* information is to be collected and examined, the research methods section describes *how* this information will be collected and from what sources. It is important to be as specific as possible in listing sources and how data will be collected from each of them.

Note: Do not confuse research objectives with research methods; the former is what the research will address (e.g., crime problems in a particular community), while the latter is how you will collect information on these problems (e.g., survey, interviews, review of police data, observation).

a. Typical research methods (and sources) for collecting data on local crime problems include the following:
    -   Victimization survey (of community residents)
    -   Focus groups (with community members)
    -   Interviews (with residents, local leaders, police, experts, etc.)
    -   Review police-recorded information (crime rate statistics, calls for service, occurrence reports, etc.)
    -   Observation (of the physical environment or the behavior of local residents)
    -   Review of media sources (e.g., newspapers)
    -   Review of literature (books, reports, etc.) that has information relevant to the issues to be examined as part of the research (including research conducted and strategies implemented in similar environments)

b. Ideally, the research should use more than one of the aforementioned methods because they are complementary. For example, focus groups with community members complement a questionnaire survey because the latter is administered to people individually and the results provide a general overview of the extent of a crime problem. In contrast, a focus group gathers information from people in a group format and is often used for a more in-depth discussion and analysis.

c. The variables can be measured quantitatively or qualitatively. A quantitative measurement involves numbers or statistical data that have been collected through surveys (e.g., the local victimization rate is determined by collecting data through a door-to-door survey) or is adapted from existing statistical data (e.g., calls for service data maintained by police). A qualitative measurement often provides more in-depth information on a particular variable, explaining why or how something has occurred. For example, quantitative information from a victimization survey can indicate how many break-ins occurred on a particular block during the past year, while qualitative research tries to answer how the break-ins occurred or why the break-and-enter rate is so high on one block but low on another. In general, how or why a crime problem occurs cannot be answered through descriptive statistics; one must pursue more in-depth, explanatory information, which can be gathered through interviews or focus groups with residents, police or experts, observation, press clippings, as well as *open-ended* questions on a victimization survey. In short, quantitative information provides a broad statistical overview of crime and disorder problems, while qualitative information provides a more in-depth description and analysis of the problems.

6. *Work plan*. A work plan lays out the major phases and individual steps required to complete a research project. The work plan can include all the major phases and steps involved in the research process and should include dates when each phase and step will be completed.

Victimization survey questionnaire: A victimization survey gathers information on the scope and nature of crime and disorder problems from neighborhood residents, based on their experiences and perceptions. Broadly speaking, a victimization survey questionnaire should include four major sections:

1. Introduction: Introduce the questionnaire and its goal to the survey respondent.
2. Background: Demographic information to be provided by survey participants.

Table 8.1
Sample Research Design Matrix

Objective	Variables	Source of Information	Methods and Instruments
Determine the scope of local crime problems.	Crime rate, calls for police service, and victimization rate	Police, neighborhood residents, the media	Review of police occurrence reports and other statistics, door-to-door survey using a victimization questionnaire.
Determine the nature of local crime problems, focusing on property crimes.	Types of crimes occurring (determining which crimes are most frequent and any other descriptive info on each crime type)	Police, neighborhood residents, experts (e.g., criminologists), the media, other government agencies	Review of police occurrence reports and other statistics, door-to-door survey using a victimization questionnaire, public meetings and focus groups, interviews.
Determine the spatial distribution of crime, including crime hot spots.	Crime rate, calls for police service, and victimization rate	Police, other government agencies, neighborhood residents, experts, observation, the media	A crime map of the local neighborhood; spatially map out police calls for service or crime incidents to identify distribution of crime problems and hot spots.
Determine the causes and facilitators of the current crime problems.	Demographics (number of residents in crime-prone years, 13–25), socioeconomic status (income level, poverty level, etc.), local drug abuse addicts, physical design, etc.	Police, neighborhood residents, experts, observation, census agency or municipal government, the media, social workers/government welfare office, day-care facilities, schools, teachers, community centers	Review of police occurrence reports and other statistics, door-to-door survey using a victimization questionnaire, public meetings and focus groups, interviews, spatial crime map, review of census data, observation of the physical and spatial design of the community (using a safety audit checklist).
Predict future crime problems. Determine the causes of future crime problems.	Demographics (number of child entering crime-prone years, 13–25), socioeconomic status (income level, poverty level, etc.), at-risk children and youth, local drug abusers/addicts, physical design, etc.	Police, neighborhood residents, experts, observation, census agency or municipal government, social workers/government welfare office, day-care facilities, schools, teachers, community centers	Review of police occurrence reports and other statistics, door-to-door survey using a victimization questionnaire, public meetings and focus groups, interviews, review of census data.

(Continued)

Table 8.1 (Continued)
Sample Research Design Matrix

Objective	Variables	Source of Information	Methods and Instruments
Determine local resources and assets to be used for crime prevention purposes.	Level of social cohesion Existing institutions (schools, day care, community centers, youth sports/recreation programs, boys'/girls' clubs), family support networks, existing crime prevention programs, and local available funding	Residents, other key partners (police, schools, community centers, etc.), community groups	Using interviews, physical observation of the neighborhood survey, identifying the local resources that can be used to address crime and disorder problems.

3. Crime and victimization: Information on whether a survey participant has been victimized and, if so, when and what type of crime. This section can also solicit opinions from respondents on what they believe to be the most significant crime and disorder problems in the neighborhood, the causes and facilitators of these problems, and what problems should be prioritized in the crime prevention plan.

4. Solutions: As part of a crime prevention planning process, a victimization survey should also ask respondents how they think the identified problems can best be addressed. This should include questions that help identify local and external resources and assets that can be used to address the identified problems. This section (or another section) of the questionnaire can also be used to ask participants if they would like to become involved in crime prevention activities in the neighborhood (which would be followed by a section that records contact information).

To maximize the validity and reliability of survey, its implementation should be as rigorous as possible (if not, the findings may not be accurate, much to the detriment of a crime prevention plan that is predicated on these findings). The validity and reliability of any data collection method is contingent upon the extent to which the overall research is planned. Steps should also be taken to ensure that the sum of all the people surveyed is representative of the community targeted by the crime prevention plan. Ideally, this would mean trying to get a questionnaire to every resident in the community. However, this is often impractical (unless focusing on a small spatial area). Instead, a questionnaire survey is usually administered to a *sample* of residents (a relatively small number of people who are representative of the greater population). If the sample is representative (and large enough), the findings can then be extrapolated to the community as a whole. The easiest way to select a sample is by choosing every 3rd, 5th, or 10th household in the neighborhood (using the comprehensive list of addresses compiled in the early stages of the planning process).

Some key issues to consider when planning a questionnaire survey are as follows:

- How many people will be surveyed?
- How can a sample of residents be drawn that is representative of the community?
- Who will be administering the questionnaire? Will the questionnaire be self-administered, or will questions be asked by those conducting the survey?

- Will the survey be conducted by telephone, mail, e-mail, the Internet, or door to door (or all of the aforementioned)?
- Is the questionnaire well constructed? Are the questions simple, straightforward, and unbiased?
- Is the questionnaire focused? Does it only include questions that directly contribute to collecting information that satisfies the research objectives
- Does the questionnaire need to be translated into other languages?

Physical environmental safety audits: A physical environmental safety audit is a systematic analysis of a physical environment (lighting, building design, landscaping, signage, garbage, current security measures, etc.) that is conducted to identify physical environment design features that may help create the opportunity for a crime to occur in a particular time and place. This type of safety audit is also referred to as a threat and risk assessment because it helps determine the threat and risk of crimes occurring in a particular setting. A safety audit administered at the neighborhood level is mostly geared toward gathering information on crime and disorder problems that can be addressed through opportunity-reduction approaches and crime prevention through environmental design (CPTED) in particular. Some general questions to include on such a checklist are as follows:

- Are there visible signs of crime and/or disorder problems at this location?
- What types of problems are being experienced at this location?
- Is the area clean? Graffiti free? Vandalism free?
- Is the location well maintained? Are necessary repairs quickly made?
- What is it about the design of this location that promotes or inhibits crime?
- What types of security measures have been adopted in the area?
- What design changes can be made to make this location safer and less vulnerable to crime?

Crime hot spots should be subject to particularly detailed safety audits, in combination with information gleaned from other sources. Photographs should also be taken of locations with unsafe design principles (and incorporated into the crime prevention plan).

Observation: Observation is another method that can be used to research local crime and disorder problems. Inherent in the administration of a physical environmental safety audit checklist is observational research. Observational research can potentially gather information on other relevant crime and crime prevention variables. First, observational research can be used to study group processes and personal interactions within a neighborhood. As indicated in Chapter 5, community crime prevention is contingent upon the level of social interaction and cohesion in neighborhoods. Researchers can determine if these important prerequisites are present by watching how people interact at the local level and answering the following questions:

- Do people seem familiar with one another?
- Are people friendly toward one another?
- Do people make an effort to talk to one another?
- Does the interaction cut across race, ethnicity, age, etc.?
- Do people take pride in their homes and their neighborhood?
- Do residents display a strong commitment and sense of belonging to the neighborhood?
- Are there active neighborhood groups?

Observational research can also be used to determine the crime prevention behaviors of and measures undertaken by community members as well as the extent to which they appear to be vigilant in protecting their neighborhood (e.g., by conducting informal surveillance). Some questions that observational research (as well as interviews, surveys, and focus groups) can answer are as follows:

- What crime prevention and personal safety measures have residents undertaken?
- To what extent are these measures *private* (those undertaken by residents that simply protect themselves and their assets) or *public* (those that contribute to the safety of neighbors and include vigilance over public spaces)?
- To what extent does there appear to be an atmosphere of territoriality and informal social control? Do neighborhood residents report suspicious people or activities to police? Are they protective of public spaces?

8.4.3.2.2   Existing Sources of Data for Crime Prevention Planning   It may be possible for crime prevention planners to avoid having to collect their own information; in other words, salient data may be already available at the neighborhood level. Key sources of data on crime that may already exist include the following:

Police-reported crime data: Police departments regularly keep statistics on local crime problems, which often can be broken down on a neighborhood level.

Victimization surveys: Local police departments, government agencies, or university researchers may conduct their own victimization surveys from time to time. In the United States, the federal Bureau of Justice Statistics conducts a national victimization survey on an annual basis, the results of which may help local crime prevention planners.

Self-reported crime surveys: Criminologists and government researchers often conduct anonymous surveys of the general public or subsets (e.g., youth) to identify whether individuals have been involved in crime (or have used illegal substances in the recent past).

Crime mapping: Most local police departments spatially map out crime data, and these maps should be available to local community groups for crime prevention planning purposes.

8.4.3.2.3   Collecting Information for a Social Problem-Solving Approach to Crime   Victimization surveys and safety audits typically include only information on crime and disorder problems; they do not address local social conditions that may give rise to current and future criminal behavior. As such, if the goal is to develop a comprehensive and future-oriented crime prevention plan, organizers should not simply collect information that identifies *existing* crime problems. Attempt should also be made to identify social problems that contribute to existing and *future* crime and criminal behavior. As Husain (2007, 2) writes, "A safety audit needs to examine not just crime and victimisation, but their linkages with socio-economic factors and existing services, as well as the wider political and institutional context in which problems occur." Identifying local social problems can even anticipate and prevent future crime problems by identifying at-risk children and youth. In general, this social research entails identifying problems and risk factors at two levels: the community level and individual/family level.

Community level: At the community level, risk factors that may promote delinquent and criminal behavior should be identified and examined. Ideally, much of this information can be collected during the environmental scan. Four groups of community character-istics should be examined as part of this research:

1. *Socioeconomic status/local economic conditions.* Low socioeconomic status and poor local economic and employment conditions may contribute to imme-diate or future criminal and delinquent problems. Some research questions to be asked to gauge the socioeconomic status and local economic conditions of a neighborhood include the following:
   - What proportion of the local population lives below the poverty line?
   - What is the average education level of residents?
   - What is the proportion of renters to homeowners?
   - What is the extent of the local population turnover (i.e., local stability)?
   - What are the unemployment levels?
   - What are the local job conditions like?
   - How are local businesses doing?
   - What is the environment like for local businesses?
   - Are there adequate social services available to residents?
   - Is there adequate social (community) support for at-risk families?

2. *Social capital.* As discussed in Chapter 5, neighborhoods with high crime rates often lack social cohesion, informal social control, and collective efficacy. Some research questions that can be asked to gauge a neighborhood's level of social cohesion and informal social control include the following:
   - What is the extent of local social interaction?
   - To what extent do neighbors know and look out for one another?
   - To what extent do residents have a strong commitment and sense of belonging to the neighborhood?
   - Are there existing neighborhood groups? How active are they?
   - Are local problems regularly addressed through collective action, or are they left untended?
   - Are there any community events that bring together residents on a regular basis?
   - Are there adequate community-based facilities for people to meet and socialize?

3. *Local institutions.* As detailed in Chapter 3, the presence or absence of strong local institutions, such as schools, cultural and recreational organizations and facilities, community groups, and places of worship, can greatly influence whether a community has a preponderance of criminogenic risk factors or protective factors. For example, strong schools and ample recreational facilities and activities are integral to childhood development and help keep youth out of trouble. Some research questions to be asked to gauge the extent to which local institutions exacerbate or minimize criminogenic risk factors include the following:
   - What local institutions exist in the community?
   - Are they sufficiently resourced? How stable are they?
   - To what extent are they involved in fostering the health, vitality, and secu-rity of the community (in part by reducing local criminogenic risk factors)?
   - To what extent do they offer services to the most at-risk individuals, fami-lies, and groups in the community?
   - What role do these institutions play in efforts to control and prevent local crime and disorder problems?

4. *Physical environment.* As discussed in Chapter 2, the physical and built environment of a neighborhood can promote or hinder criminogenic risk factors. Some research questions to be asked to gauge the extent to which the physical environment promotes or inhibits crime include the following:

- Does the design of the neighborhood promote social interaction, cohesion, community attachment, and the positive socialization of children and youth?
- Does the design take into consideration the needs and wants of children and youth?
- To what extent are the buildings, homes, and roads in good physical shape?
- What are the local housing conditions like?
- Are the parks, schools, and other public spaces clean and well maintained?
- How clean is the in general
- Is there much graffiti or vandalism in the neighborhood? Are graffiti and vandalism addressed quickly?

Individual/family level: In addition to identifying conditions at the community level, a social problem-solving crime prevention plan should also address families whose children are involved in delinquent and/or criminal behavior or at risk of developing such behavior. A number of standardized instruments currently exist that can be used to identify and assess at-risk children, youth, and families. These instruments should be administered by trained professionals (such as psychologists), which highlights the need for professional help when assessing and addressing complex social environmental and personal risk factors. Notwithstanding the importance of identifying the most at-risk families and young people, organizers need to approach this research cautiously to avoid stigmatizing families and to protect the privacy of those deemed at risk. While professionals such as social workers, teachers, and police are sources of information on at-risk families and young people, they are often not in a position to release any information that may compromise privacy.

By the end of stage 3, organizers should have planned the research, which includes drafting a research proposal and individual research instruments.

Before data are collected, the research plan should be tested by administering the research instruments on a limited basis (with neighbors, friends, coworkers, etc.). Revisions should be made to the research plan and the instruments if necessary.

For a comprehensive crime prevention plan, researchers should gather information from a wide array of sources (police, neighborhood residents, businesses, community leaders, government officials, professionals, the physical and built environment). The research plan (just like the final crime prevention plan) should include information on current crime and disorder problems and potential future problems (by identifying high-risk children and youth).

Finally, each *member of the community-based research team* should receive some form of training, no matter how informal. This training should emphasize how best to avoid bias in collecting information and ensuring that all researchers follow the same procedures to ensure uniformity. Faculty at a local college or university can conduct the training as part of their larger contribution to the research process.

8.4.4 Stage 4: Conduct Research—Collect Information by Administering Research Instruments

Once the research proposal and research instruments have been finalized, information on local crime and disorder problems (as well as risk factors) can be collected. Some tips that should be heeded when collecting data include the following:

- Be true to the research proposal and the steps laid out in the work plan; do not deviate from the objectives or methods, unless absolutely necessary.
- Try to make sure the research team is representative of the target community; it is especially important that all the different ethnic groups are represented.
- Throughout the research process, begin an informal analysis of the information being collected: What appear to be the major local crime and disorder problems? What are the causes of these problems? What are the aggravating factors? Is there a discernable pattern or trend emerging? Are there particular crime *hot spots* in the neighborhood?

By the end of stage 4, local organizers should have collected information that identifies the current and potential crime and disorder problems in the community, as well as suggestions from residents and others on potential solutions to these problems.

8.4.5 Stage 5: Collate and Analyze the Collected Information

Once all the steps laid out in the research work plan have been completed and organizers are confident that sufficient information has been collected to satisfy the research objectives laid out in the proposal, the data should be analyzed. It is during this stage that the *raw data* will be turned into *meaningful information* that will help discern the community's crime and disorder problems, their causes and facilitators, trends and patterns, hot spots, etc.

To facilitate the analysis, all the collected data must first be collated. This can be accomplished by pooling the data gathered from all sources according to each of the research objectives. For example, if one research objective is to estimate the number of break-ins for a neighborhood, this estimate can be derived by examining a combination of police-recorded calls for service and the results of a victimization survey. Most research objectives will require information from more than two methods and sources. If the focus of a crime prevention plan is drug trafficking in a park, for instance, results from a safety audit conducted at the park, an examination of police-recorded crime data (arrests, occurrence reports), and interviews with police, park officials, users of the park, and local residents should be collated and analyzed together.

The Institute for the Prevention of Crime (2009, 17–18) states that an analysis of local crime problems entails collecting and examining information on

- Victim or target characteristics
- Offender characteristics
- Patterns of the location of offenses
- Times when offenses are committed
- Involvement of alcohol and drugs
- Opportunity factors (such as inadequate lighting or inadequate supervision of apartment buildings)
- Distinctive methods of committing the crimes

In their guide for crime analysts, Clarke and Eck (2005, 70) suggest that to fully understand local crime problems, local researchers should "ask whether it meets the test of a good newspaper story. Does it adequately answer what, where, when, who, why, and how?"

> What happened? "This entails spelling out the sequence of events and the actions of those involved …."
>
> Where did it happen? In what part of the neighborhood did the crime or crimes take place? This facilitates the spatial mapping of crime and helps to identify crime hot spots that may require particular attention.
>
> When did it happen? This includes the day of the week and time (although this information is often difficult to obtain for certain crimes). This information can also benefit crime prevention plans (e.g., during a particular time, perhaps a target needs to be *hardened* or activities for idle youth should be implemented).
>
> Who was involved? This includes identifying the potential offender, victim, and witnesses.
>
> Why did they act as they did? "It is important to understand the specific benefits that a particular kind of crime brings to the offender."
>
> How did the offender carry out the crime? "Crime can be thought of as a process, with several steps from initiation to completion, rather than a circumscribed act occurring at a specific point in time." Understanding how a crime was carried out helps identify means to prevent similar crimes in the future.

Clarke and Eck (2005, 70)

The goals of the analysis stage can also be organized as follows:

1. *Identify and prioritize crime and disorder problems.* The first step in the analysis is to list, as comprehensively as possible, the community's crime and disorder problems identified in the research. These problems should then be prioritized. The priorities are usually the problems that are causing the community the most harm. Alternatively, some crime prevention plans prioritize problems that can be addressed relatively quickly and easily (a strategy that provides some momentum, a sense of accomplishment, and sends a positive message to community members). Some questions to be answered as part of this analysis are as follows:
   - What are the crime problems being experienced by this neighborhood?
   - What crime problems are occurring most frequently?
   - What problems have residents identified as the most pressing?
   - What problems are causing the community the most harm, in terms of severity (e.g., violent crimes), the number of people affected, financial costs, or the frequency of occurrence?
   - What problems can be addressed relatively quickly and easily?
2. *Examine salient characteristics, patterns, and trends.* Characteristics and patterns can be deduced by analyzing the types of crimes committed, the target of crimes, the location of crimes, the physical characteristics of the locations victimized, and the characteristics of the victims. Identifying the characteristics and patterns can help determine what type of intervention is most appropriate for the problem. As Linden (1996, 2) writes, "Knowledge of the manner in which offences are typically carried out is useful in trying to prevent them. If we know that break and enters in an area are unforced apartment entries rather than forced single-family dwelling entries, we can infer something about the factors involved in the offence (such as poor key control in apartments), which then

have implications for prevention." Understanding trends in crime patterns is also critical to any analysis of local crime problems. When identifying trends, one should pay particular attention to whether crime is increasing or decreasing over time in the neighborhood, which includes identifying specific types of crimes that are increasing or decreasing (Institute for the Prevention of Crime, 2009, 16).

3. *Identify and examine the location of crimes, including a spatial distribution of crime in the neighborhood.* It can be very instructive to look at how (different types of) crime problems are spatially distributed, which includes determining the existence of any *hot spots*. Spatial crime mapping can facilitate an analysis of the types and extent of crime problems within a particular locale while helping connect these problems to any local factors that may be causing and/or facilitating the problems (e.g., a crack house, unsupervised youth, an abandoned building). Police may be able to provide a crime map (digital or had copy) for a local area. If that is not possible, a crime map can be created using statistical data provided by police (containing addresses) and/or data collected through a victimization survey. This information is plotted on a large map of the neighborhood using colored pushpins (each color representing a different type of crime). Linden (1996, 11–12) also emphasizes the importance of knowing the time at which most offenses are committed. "You should analyze crime patterns by time of day, month, and even season. For example, many cottage break-ins happen in the winter when cottages are unoccupied. An increase in minor crimes by young people between 4:00 and 6:00 p.m. suggests a need for supervised after-school recreation."

4. *Identify causes, symptoms, and facilitating factors.* The analysis should determine the causes of the crime problems because any future interventions should, as much as possible, target causes. What is important in the analysis stage is to separate the *causes* of the crime and disorder problems from the *symptoms* and *facilitators* (those factors that simply create opportunities for the problems to occur or worsen).

From a situational perspective, a criminal opportunity may be caused by a lack of security precautions in a particular building or by poor design of the physical environment. The cause of violent altercations or vandalism may be traced to a local bar. Perhaps a nearby house that is dealing drugs may be cited as the cause of a rash of local residential burglaries. The *causes* of local crime and disorder problems may also be defined as *social* in nature (poverty, lack of affordable housing, dysfunctional families, a lack of local recreational facilities for youth, etc.). The point is that crime prevention planners must determine how they want to define the cause of the problem. If they are simply going to apply situational measures as part of their crime prevention plan, then they would define the cause of a problem as a lack of security in a building, the unsafe design of a park, or the lack of proper lighting in a pathway. Ambitious crime prevention planners, who are intent on addressing the root causes of local criminal behavior, would dig much deeper in their analysis; they would attempt to identify the offenders behind the crimes, understand what has contributed to their criminal behavior, and then work to address their criminogenic risk factors.

In short, the analytical stage is complicated by how a particular problem is defined (as a symptom of a deeper problem, a facilitator, or the cause). For example, are drugs and drug abuse the cause of local break and enters, or are they simply symptoms of deeper local social problems that should be addressed? Some in the neighborhood may simply want to focus on reducing the opportunity for a crime to take place, and as such, they limit their definition of the *cause* of a problem as poor lighting or a lack of access control measures. These are important and difficult choices that this community must grapple with as it develops its crime prevention plan (see Box 8.5).

5. *Discern the characteristics of offenders.* As mentioned earlier, if possible, the analysis of collected data should try to identify and understand the characteristics of offenders, such as age, race, ethnicity, sex, previous criminal history, and motivation. Knowledge about offender characteristics can be particularly informative for social development interventions that are directed toward treating offenders or preventing (young) people from becoming offenders in the first place. This information can be difficult to obtain. However, even when no suspects have been identified, educated hypotheses can be formulated about their characteristics. For example, a rash of break and enters may suggest there is an addict population nearby (Linden, 1996, 11).

6. *Identify community resources and assets that can be mobilized and community strengths that can be leveraged.* The analytical stage of the crime prevention planning process should always be geared toward identifying appropriate

---

BOX 8.5

IDENTIFYING, ANALYZING, AND DELINEATING SYMPTOMS, FACILITATORS, AND CAUSES OF LOCAL CRIME PROBLEMS

The following example illustrates how the collation and analysis of information from different sources can separate symptoms from facilitators and root causes. Local research found that the most significant local crime problem is residential break and enters (*symptoms*). Interviews with local businesses found a hardware store had recently been doing a brisk business in tools that are commonly used for residential burglaries: crowbars, screwdrivers, channel-lock pliers, bolt cutters, and hammers (*facilitators*). The group's safety audit indicated that there are a number of factors that can also be classified as facilitators, such as design problems in the neighborhood (an alley running in back of the houses), inadequate security within the burglarized homes (no deadbolt locks, easily breakable windows, etc.), as well as poor street lighting and overgrown shrubbery (which provides plenty of concealment opportunities for offenders). During the course of a meeting with police, the group was informed that a rental home just a block away is a significant distributor of crack cocaine. While the group does not have a lot of information on the offenders, they hypothesized that many of those behind the daytime burglaries are attempting to feed a drug addiction (*cause*). Following their analysis, but before the crime prevention plan is finalized, the planning group (or the community as a whole) must determine how they will address the break-and-enter problem. Will they just implement measures that reduce the opportunity for the crimes to take place in their neighborhood (through situational measures)? Will they work with the hardware store to restrict sales of hardware to minors? Will they take measures to try and have the local crack house shut down? Will they take a role in trying to help the offenders with their substance abuse problems? Will they pursue all of the aforementioned strategies?

interventions that can address the identified crime problems. The analysis should take into consideration the capacity of the neighborhood to address such problems (and, by extension, what external resources will be needed). To this end, some key questions that crime prevention planners must ask are as follows: What resources will be needed to effectively overcome the identified problems? To what extent does the neighborhood possess the necessary resources? What resources need to be obtained from external sources? Through what institutions should the interventions be delivered? What improvements need to be made to these institutions so they can effectively deliver these interventions? What key partners should be involved in developing and implementing the solutions? One cautionary note: while it is important to always be thinking about possible solutions to problems, conclusions should not be reached or interventions fully developed until the crime problems, causes, facilitates, priorities, etc. have been fully examined.

By the end of stage 5, organizers should have collated and analyzed all the collected data. This includes prioritizing local crime and disorder problems and separating root causes from facilitating factors. This analysis provides the foundation to develop crime prevention interventions.

8.4.6   Stage 6: Develop the Crime Prevention Plan

The crime prevention plan is the culmination of the preceding research and analysis stages. The plan should be structured in a report format that, at the very least, includes (1) research findings, (2) analysis of the collected information (characteristics, patterns, causes, facilitators, etc.), and (3) strategies that will address the identified problems. As emphasized throughout this chapter, these three parts of the report are critically interconnected (reflecting the problem-oriented approach to crime prevention); the results and analysis of the research will dictate the contents and approaches of the crime prevention strategy.

The crime prevention plan can establish crime reduction goals, outline different options to achieve these goals, recommend preferred strategies, and identify individuals, groups, agencies, and institutions that should be involved in implementing these strategies. The costs of such interventions should be detailed (as should other resources that may be needed) and a work plan and time line should be included.

The same group that was tasked with collecting and examining the data should also take the lead in developing the plan and drafting the report. However, this stage should be very transparent and inclusive; great emphasis should be placed on soliciting as much input as possible from neighborhood residents and other key partners in drafting the report.

The steps involved in pulling together the crime prevention plan can be grouped under three categories:

1. The community's (existing and potential) problems
   - Identify, describe, and examine crime and disorder problems.
   - Separate symptoms and facilitators from causes.
   - Identify and examine factors that may give rise to future criminal behavior and crime problems.
   - Prioritize the community's crime and disorder problems.

2. Current responses to identified problems
   - What are the current responses (if any) by the neighborhood, police, and/ or other actors?
   - What are the pros and cons of the current responses?
   - If the current responses are not working effectively, why?
   - What can be done to build upon current responses?
3. Strategies to address the community's crime and disorder problems
   - Determine the crime priorities that will be addressed (list in descending order).
   - Determine the intended *reach* of the interventions (i.e., just address symptoms and facilitators or also tackle root causes of local criminal behavior).
   - Set realistic and tangible crime reduction objectives (e.g., reduce break and enters by 25%, help a group of homeless youth get off drugs).
   - Develop individual, yet complementary strategies that will address each of the (prioritized) crime problems and satisfy the crime reduction objectives.
   - Determine the level of intervention for each crime problem:
     - Begin broadly by identifying the overall approach (social developmental, situational, community mobilization, law enforcement, etc.).
     - Identify the institutions through which the crime prevention interventions will be delivered (families, preschool, schools, community centers, police, labor markets, etc.).
     - Develop specific, tangible strategies that can best address the problem (e.g., target hardening, CPTED, intensive preschool programs, recreational facilities for youth, substance abuse counseling, community beautification).
   - Learn how other communities have dealt with similar problems (surf the Internet, talk to police or other local government officials, visit the library, etc.); do not reinvent the wheel, but do not just apply an *off-the-shelf* model regardless of how well it has worked in other jurisdictions (i.e., adapt it to the particular circumstances identified in the research and analysis stages).
   - If possible, ensure the crime prevention plan is comprehensive in that it uses the five main pillars already discussed: social developmental, situational, community crime prevention (both community defense and development approaches), policing, and recidivism prevention.
   - Hold community meetings to allow residents to brainstorm around specific strategies (be creative and innovative, do not stifle input, learn from the successes and failures of other communities).
   - Debate and discuss these options in a thoughtful and deliberative way.
   - Decide on the most appropriate strategy (ideally through agreement and consensus).
   - Work out the specific steps and activities that must be undertaken.
   - Determine which institutions and key partners should be involved in implementing the strategy.
   - Prepare a work plan, which is a step-by-step process in the implementation of the crime prevention plan.
   - Document all the aforementioned in a crime prevention plan.

Any effort to come up with a crime prevention plan must be built on a thoughtful deliberation of the salient issues by key stakeholders. Mathews (1994, 136) uses the term "deliberative democracy" to refer to a process of public dialogue where people concentrate "on carefully defining and, if need be, redefining problems before moving onto solutions."

Deliberative dialogue is premised on the belief that the ideal democracy is one where everyone assembles for a full discussion of salient issues, which are explored and debated in depth and where action-oriented decisions are reached through a democratic process (Fishkin, 1995, 34). The deliberation process includes awareness raising, information gathering and dissemination, education, understanding, brainstorming, choice making, and judgment. It involves a statement of individual and community values and aspirations, a problem definition, a discussion of and reflection on potential solutions to problems, the choice of the most appropriate option, the group's acceptance of the consequences of this action, and the resolve to act. Those people who are affected by the issue under deliberation or by the consequence of the action are the main participants in a public dialogue. Mathews (1994, 41) believes that public dialogue is ultimately action oriented; that is, something must come out of the discussion.

At the neighborhood level, a structured deliberative discussion can employ the techniques of *study circles*, which are small groups of people who meet over a period of days, weeks, or even months to deliberate on important public issues. Study circles are organized to ensure that all participants have an equal say and to help the group explore complex issues through an informed and thoughtful deliberation process. A typical study circle progresses from a session on personal experience (How does the issue affect me?) to sessions providing a broader perspective (What are others saying about the issue?) and concludes with a session on action (What can we do about the issue?). Study circles attempt to help citizens gain *ownership* of public issues, a recognition that there can be a connection between personal experiences and public issues, a deeper understanding of their own and others' perspectives and concerns, and a discovery of common ground among opposing viewpoints or groups. An important part of the study circle process is educating participants so they can engage in a more thoughtful discussion and make informed judgments. Prior to the study circle, participants are encouraged to read materials or watch educational videos about the issue under discussion. Throughout the process, participants are presented with information on the issues from different perspectives, giving them a range of realistic choices, with the pros and cons of each spelled out to help them arrive at a decision and formulate an action plan (Sinclair, 1994).

8.4.7 Stage 7: Draft an Evaluation Plan—Determine How the Crime Prevention Strategies Will Be Monitored and Evaluated

Ideally, the project evaluation plan should be designed at the same time the crime prevention plan is being designed. This evaluation plan can then be incorporated into the overall crime prevention planning report. This is particularly important if the planning report is being used to request funding from an external agency (most crime prevention project funders require an evaluation plan). (See Chapter 10 for more information on planning and designing an evaluation plan.)

8.4.8 Stage 8: Prepare the Crime Prevention Planning Report

All of the results of the crime prevention planning phase should now be documented in a report that can be used as a problem-oriented action plan to guide the community in addressing its identified crime and disorder problems. The action plan should be written in a report format that is systematic, logically ordered, comprehensive,

CASE STUDY 8.2

A DELIBERATIVE DIALOGUE AROUND CRIME, POLICING, AND COMMUNITY SAFETY

A study circle format was employed by the Vancouver Police Department (VPD) and the Vancouver Police Board, which cohosted a community *deliberative dialogue* session on March 27, 2004. According to the Vancouver Police website, the deliberative dialogue session "allowed the VPD and the Police Board to hear what matters to the community" in order to "prioritize the top safety issues in Vancouver." When combined with input from police members, the results of the session were used "to develop a comprehensive plan to improve community safety" and to contribute to the development of a new Vancouver Police Strategic Plan for 2004–2008 (Vancouver Police Department, 2004). Participants were invited from each of the 23 official neighborhoods that make up the city of Vancouver. Along with members of the Vancouver Police Board and senior management of the VPD, this session brought together 103 participants "with diverse backgrounds and perspectives from all over Vancouver" (Vancouver Police Department, 2004). Two weeks before the session, participants were sent reading material that included an overview of the policing situation in Vancouver, crime statistics, and a series of relevant media articles. The session took place from 9:00 a.m. to 4:30 p.m. The participants were randomly seated at 19 (circular) tables of 8 people each. Each table included a representative from either the Vancouver Police Board or the VPD and a facilitator. The participants took part in nine conversations throughout the day, each of which had a different (although overlapping) theme, including various service delivery options for the future of policing in Vancouver. The session closed with participants reflecting on their experiences participating in the session.

These nine themes, including some sample questions asked in each, were as follows:

1. *Community safety issues in Vancouver*: How do the media stories reflect your daily reality? What are the top community safety issues from your perspective? Why?
2. *Root causes of crime*: What are the root causes behind the top community safety issues in Vancouver?
3. *Vancouver—the safest major city in Canada by 2008*: In 2008, what would the new headlines and images be?
4. *Service delivery—strategic option A*: The VPD should deploy the majority of available police officers on the street to eliminate street disorder.
5. *Service delivery—strategic option B*: The VPD should dedicate more of its resources to deal with perceived root social causes of crime such as inadequate parenting, poverty, addiction, and youth at risk.
6. *Service delivery—strategic option C*: The VPD should deploy more of its personnel conducting analysis of general and specific crimes, thereby allowing for a more strategic approach to addressing crime issues.
7. *Service delivery—strategic option D*: The VPD should allocate more of its resources to developing community policing centers and working in partnership with the community to address safety and crime concerns.
8. *Service delivery—common ground*: What ideas from any of the four strategic options (or any other) do we agree would best address the root causes and improve community safety in Vancouver?
9. *Deliberative dialogue closing words*: Your experience today; one idea, feeling, commitment, or learning you are taking with you.

According to the document produced from this session, "over 3800 comments, thoughts and ideas were expressed by the participants and recorded by the police representatives during the deliberative dialogue session" (Vancouver Police Department and the Vancouver Police Board, n.d., 6).

yet concise and easy to read. While there is no one way to write a report, there are some important principles to follow:

- Write economically, use action-oriented nouns, and avoid technical jargon.
- Make sure the report flows logically:
  - Begin by introducing and summarizing the report.
  - Provide a background of the community (brief history, spatial boundaries, demographics).
  - Identify and analyze the crime and disorder problems.
  - Discuss different options to address these problems.
  - Outline the plan (including objectives, specifics strategies, and a work plan).
- Use numbered headings and subheadings throughout.

(*Note*: If the plan is being submitted for funding from a particular agency, this agency may require a specific format for the plan.)

Clarke and Eck (2005, 106) stress the importance of telling a "clear story" when presenting the results of a crime analysis:

> The purpose of your work is to help people make better decisions. To assist decision-makers, you must tell a clear story that leads from an important question to possible answers and then to effective actions. To communicate effectively you need to know who your audience is and the questions they want answered. Your story has to address their particular needs...

> Do not simply recount what you did to detect, analyze, respond, or assess. This is tedious and does not help people make actionable decisions from your work. You must translate your analytical work into a story that addresses the needs of your audience.

A clear story for a crime prevention plan entails four elements:

1. What is the scope and nature of the problem(s)? (Research)
2. What are the causes behind problem? (Analysis)
3. What, if anything, is currently being done to address the problem? (Current responses)
4. What more should be done to address the problem? (Future responses)

Generally speaking, there are four parts to a report that documents the crime prevention plan (which capture all of the aforementioned):

1. *Introduction*. Introduce the report; summarize the substance of the following three sections.
2. *Community profile (spatially and nonspatially)*. Describe the target community, spatially, geographically, historically, and demographically; make note of its problems, deficiencies, and weaknesses as well as its strengths, resources, and assets.
3. *Crime and disorder problems*. Describe and analyze the research findings (scope, nature, and causes of the problem), making sure to prioritize problems and separate symptoms from causes.

BOX 8.6

RECOMMEND CRIME PREVENTION REPORT STRUCTURE

---

1. Title Page
2. Executive Summary
3. Introduction
4. Research Design
    a. Research objectives
    b. Research methods
    c. Research questions
5. Background: Community Profile
    a. Geographic location
    b. Spatial layout
    c. Demographic characteristics
    d. Problems/weaknesses/deficiencies
    e. Strengths/resources/assets
6. Findings and Analysis: Crime and Disorder Problems
7. Crime Prevention Plan (Recommendations):
    a. Crime reduction objectives
    b. Specific strategies, approaches, and programs (including broad approaches, institutions, and specific measures)
    c. Key partners (who is to be involved)
8. Work Plan
9. Appendices:
    a. Evaluation plan
    b. Outreach and communications plan
    c. Research instruments

---

4. *Current responses.* List and summarize the current responses (if any), their pros and cons (asking why they are not working effectively), and what can be done to build upon current responses.
5. *Crime prevention plan.* List the crime prevention strategies to be pursued to address the identified problems.

A more detailed recommended structure of a crime prevention plan is provided in Box 8.6.

By the end of stage 8, organizers should have developed a comprehensive crime prevention plan (in a report format), which includes a number of approaches and specific strategies that are commensurate with the nature and scope of the problems identified and analyzed in previous stages. This report should also include an evaluation plan.

8.4.9 Stage 9: Disseminate a (Draft) Crime Prevention Plan

Once the crime prevention plan has been completed, it should be disseminated as widely as possible, especially among neighborhood residents. Copies of the report should also be circulated to all key partners and stakeholders. If necessary—and if resources permit—the report should be translated into other languages that predominate in the neighborhood. While the report will be the main source of information on the crime prevention plan, efforts should be made to disseminate the information through other sources, such as public meetings or the Internet.

8.4.10 Stage 10: Modify the Crime Prevention Plan (if Necessary)

One of the objectives of the crime prevention planning report is to solicit final feedback from neighborhood residents. Many people within the community will not have attended the meetings where the crime prevention strategies were developed. As such, there should be at least one final attempt to get as much public input into the plan as possible. While this may prolong the planning process, the consultation stage is an important part of the ongoing effort to involve community members in local problem solving. Input from other key partners outside the community (e.g., police or other relevant government agencies) should also be solicited.

8.4.11 Stage 11: Finalize the Crime Prevention Plan

A deadline should be established for final community input into the report. When that deadline has been met, the report should be finalized and circulated.

8.4.12 Stage 12: Seek Funding and In-Kind Resources to Support the Crime Prevention Activities

Once the crime prevention plan has been finalized, funding can be sought to help implement its recommendations. In some instances, the crime prevention activities may require minimal external resources, relying entirely on volunteer support (such as Neighborhood Watch). For complex crime problems and ambitious crime prevention strategies, there will be a need for some type of funding. Some questions organizers need to ask in relation to crime prevention project funding include the following:

- What is the amount of funding needed to carry out the project(s)?
- What resources are already available?
- From where can additional funding be secured? Public sector? Private sector? Private foundations?
- What steps must be taken to maximize chances of receiving funding?
- What sources can possibly provide *in-kind* resources (e.g., office materials or furniture, food and refreshments for volunteers)?

There are a number of sources of funding for community-based crime prevention projects. Some tips on maximizing success in any fund-raising efforts include the following:

- Be prepared! Have a plan! Have a vision!
- Begin at the community level by soliciting donations from local residents and businesses (which demonstrates that the plan has community support; this is important when soliciting funding from external agencies or foundations).
- Consider incorporating a local organization with charitable status, which will help with donations.

- Solicit *in-kind* donations locally; for example, approach a local accountant for free technical assistance in bookkeeping or ask a local supermarket or restaurant to provide food for volunteers.
- Be prepared to use the crime prevention planning report as a basis to seek funding; tailor the plan to the particular focus of the funding agency.
- Find out if the local or state/provincial government has established any funding programs (work through elected representatives).
- Apply for funding from government sources, private foundations, or businesses. As far as businesses are concerned, focus on companies that may have branches in the community (e.g., banks, insurance companies, restaurant chains). Appeal not only to their philanthropy but also their self-interest. Promise the company that all crime prevention information packets to be circulated around the community will contain the logo of the company and will acknowledge its support.
- Ensure that the proper forms are completed thoroughly and accurately.
- Ensure that the proposal meets the funding criteria of the agency.

8.4.13   Stage 13: Collect Pretest Evaluation Data

If the crime prevention project is to be evaluated using a *pretest/posttest design*, stages 1 and 2 of the evaluation plan (detailed in Chapter 10) should begin before any of the crime prevention strategies are implemented.

8.5   EXERCISE

Develop a crime prevention plan for a real community. The community you choose can be defined anyway you like: one building (e.g., apartment, commercial building, hospital), one residential or retail block, a park, a school, an industrial site, or an entire neighborhood. Alternatively, you can define your community in nonspatial terms (e.g., seniors, women, an ethnic group, the mentally ill, public transit riders).

In drafting your plan, you need to undertake a multistep, problem-oriented process (an abbreviated version of what was laid out in this chapter) that includes the following:

1. Identifying and defining your community (including its assets and liabilities)
2. Conducting research to identify crime and disorder problems in that community
3. Analyzing your research findings (including separating causes from contributing factors, isolating priorities, and identifying the existing resources within the community to address these priorities)
4. Documenting this information in a crime prevention plan (report)

8.6   IMPORTANT TERMS

Crime mapping
Crime prevention plan
Crime prevention planning
Focus groups
Observational research
Participatory action research

Pretest/posttest research
Random sample
Research instruments
Research methods
Safety audit
Strategic planning
Study circles
Victimization survey

FURTHER READING AND INTERNET RESOURCES

Crime Prevention Project Process

British Columbia, Community Crime Prevention Guide, Government of British Columbia, n.d., Victoria, British Columbia, Canada, http://www.criminaljusticereform.gov.bc.ca/en/what_you_can_do/crime_prevention_single_page.pdf.

Linden, R., *Building a Safer Community: A Community-Based Crime Prevention Manual*, Department of Justice, Ottawa, Ontario, Canada, 1996.

National Youth Network, Planning a successful crime prevention project, *Youth in Action Newsletter*, Office of Juvenile Justice and Delinquency Prevention, U.S. Department of Justice, No. 1, April 1998, http://www.ncjrs.gov/pdffiles/94266.pdf.

United Nations Office on Drugs and Crime, *Handbook on Planning and Action for Crime Prevention in Southern Africa and the Caribbean Regions*, United Nations Office on Drugs and Crime, Vienna, Austria, 2008, http://www.unodc.org/documents/justice-and-prison-reform/CPhandbook-120109.pdf.

COLLECTING INFORMATION ON LOCAL CRIME AND DISORDER PROBLEMS

Research Process

Clarke, R. and Schultze, P., Researching a problem, Problem-oriented guides for police, problem-solving tool series no. 2, Office of Community Oriented Policing Services, Washington, DC, 2004, http://www.popcenter.org/tools/pdfs/researchingproblem.pdf.

Safety Audits

Metropolitan Action Committee on Violence against Women and Children, METRAC's community safety audits, http://www.metrac.org/programs/safety/safety.htm#institutional.

New York State Police, School Safety Audit Checklist, http://www.scnus.org/local_includes/downloads/9160.htm.

The Toronto Housing Company, Site Safety Audit, Three Laxton Ave, http://de.ryerson.ca/de_courses/CJUS500/flash/toronto_audit.pdf.

Victimization Surveys

Linden, R., Appendix B: Sample questionnaire, Building a safer Canada: A community-based crime prevention manual, Department of Justice, Ottawa, Ontario, Canada, 1996, http://ww4.psepc-sppcc.gc.ca/en/library/publications/general/community/criteria.html#AppendixB.

Statistics Canada, General Social Survey—Victimization, http://www23.statcan.gc.ca/imdb/p2SV.
pl?Function=getSurvey&SDDS=4504.

U.S. Census Bureau, National Crime Victimization Survey questionnaire, http://www.bjs.gov/
index.cfm?ty=dcdetail&iid=245.

U.S. Department of Justice, Conducting community surveys: A practical guide for law enforcement agencies, http://www.bjs.gov/content/pub/pdf/ccspglea.pdf.

ANALYZING DATA

Clarke, R. and Eck, J., *Crime Analysis for Problem Solvers in 60 Small Steps*, Office of Community
Oriented Policing, Washington, DC, 2005, http://www.popcenter.org/learning/60steps/.

Tilly, N., Ed., Analysis for crime prevention, in *Crime Prevention Studies*, Vol. 13, Criminal Justice
Press, Monsey, NY, 2002, http://www.popcenter.org/library/crimeprevention/volume_13/.

CRIME PREVENTION PROJECT, PHASE TWO
Implementing a Crime Prevention Project

CONTENTS

9.1 LEARNING OBJECTIVES

By the end of this chapter, you should

- Understand and learn practical skills essential to implementing and sustaining a community-based crime prevention project
- Understand the challenges in implementing local crime prevention projects
- Deliberate on some of the more contentious issues involved in the implementation of crime prevention projects

9.2 INTRODUCTION

This chapter focuses on the second phase of the crime prevention process: implementing the plan. It is not the intention of this chapter to describe the substantive aspects of crime prevention strategies (e.g., social developmental, situational, community mobilization, restorative justice, and community policing) as these have been examined in Chapters 2 through 7. Instead, this chapter discusses some of the key factors that must be considered for the successful implementation of a crime prevention project. In particular, the topics addressed in this chapter are as follows:

Mobilizing the neighborhood (effective community-organizing strategies)

- Community outreach and communication
- Micro-level organization
- Reaching out to and involving those who do not become active
- Leadership
- Working with volunteers
- Partnerships and team building

Determining the type of organization that will carry out the crime prevention activities.

Sustaining crime prevention initiatives and activities over time.

Box 9.1 provides a summary of tips for successfully implementing local crime prevention projects. As with Chapter 8, this one focuses on implementing a crime prevention project at a neighborhood level.

BOX 9.1

TIPS FOR SUCCESSFULLY IMPLEMENTING LOCAL CRIME PREVENTION PROJECTS

- Ensure phase one has been effectively carried out.
- From the outset of the planning process, build strong support in the neighborhood.
- Strive for a broad-based mobilization of the community: ensure all (demographic) groups are represented in the crime prevention organization and activities; reach out to and involve individuals who are seen as leaders of these different groups.
- Set realistic expectations for the number of community members and other volunteers who will be willing to actively participate; make sure the planned activities do not exceed the level of resources.
- For large community-based crime prevention projects, organize at the *micro* (block) level as much as possible.
- Reach out to and communicate with community members frequently through different mediums; however, emphasize personal contact as much as possible; make sure the medium and the message are appropriate and appeal to different (demographic) groups.
- Cherish community members and others who volunteer their time; make them feel wanted and useful; provide adequate training; ensure the tasks assigned to individual volunteers are suited to their abilities and time constraints; reward them periodically.
- Deliver crime prevention activities through established and reputable organizations and institutions.
- Utilize a team approach; identify and involve all the key stakeholders within and outside the community early in the planning phase; establish linkages between the local planning group and other institutions, government agencies, and community organizations early in the planning phase; have them become formal partners in the initiative; develop solutions that take advantage of the unique (and complementary) resources, expertise, powers, etc.
- Ensure there is strong, motivational, and committed local leadership (which is as representative of the community as possible); nurture leadership among community members.
- Make the crime prevention activities enjoyable; try to work in a social component; plan and implement the activities around families, children, and youth (potluck dinners, bike rodeos, self-esteem parties for children, sports events for multiracial team building, etc.).
- Ensure there is a strategy in place to sustain the crime prevention activities over time.

9.3 MOBILIZING THE COMMUNITY: OBTAINING COMMUNITY SUPPORT FOR AND PARTICIPATION IN THE CRIME PREVENTION ACTIVITIES

As with the planning phase, the successful implementation of community-based crime prevention projects depends on the support and participation of those affected by the interventions as well as other key partners (e.g., the police, other government agencies, schools, and recreation centers). As indicated in Chapter 8, throughout all four phases of the crime prevention project process, efforts must continuously be made to mobilize neighborhood residents, which means providing them with control over (or at least significant input into) the planning and implementation phases and then sustaining that participation to the extent that they are integral to and *own* the project, its goals, and its strategies.

One of the greatest challenges faced by crime prevention organizers is initiating and sustaining participation by neighborhood residents in local groups, projects, and activities. This is the case even when residents express great concern over crime problems, are supportive of the crime prevention initiatives being implemented, and are provided with input into and control over these initiatives. This chapter outlines some key principles, strategies, and tips to help organizers achieve the most important foundation of a local crime prevention initiative: the participation and mobilization of community members.

As discussed in Chapter 5, the neighborhoods that are the most difficult to organize are those that have the greatest need for crime prevention programs: low-income, transient, high-crime, inner-city neighborhoods. And while local crime prevention programs must continuously strive to involve as broad an array of local residents as possible, the research findings also show that participants are overwhelmingly drawn from a narrow group of residents characterized as white, well-educated, middle-class homeowners with a strong attachment to their neighborhood and involvement in a number of volunteer groups and activities (Merry, 1981; Skogan and Maxfield, 1981; Greenberg et al., 1982; Taub et al., 1984; Haeberle, 1987; Dowds and Mayhew, 1994; Schneider, 2007a).

Studies into community crime prevention suggest that what is lacking among non-participants are those demographic and sociopsychological traits that appear to play a crucial role in driving participation in community crime prevention programs. In particular, nonparticipants are disproportionately characterized by a low socioeconomic status, a lack of social interaction with their neighbors, and little attachment to their neighborhood. Factors at the collective neighborhood level that militate against a broad-based mobilization of community members include a high population turnover, ethnic and socioeconomic heterogeneity, widespread poverty, and a lack of social interaction and cohesion. Research has also shown that local crime prevention groups and activities can undermine their own community mobilization efforts through weak, ineffectual, and inappropriate outreach and communication; a lack of strong leadership; inadequate resources; and programs that do not appeal to the needs of community members (Schneider, 2000, 2007a). These research findings should not discourage efforts to initiate crime prevention projects in those neighborhoods that are most in need; instead, they simply illuminate the necessity of an intensive and strategic organizing effort.

The goal of a local crime prevention organizing strategy is not to *fully* mobilize a neighborhood around crime or other related problems, as this would be almost impossible. Instead, the goal is to ensure that there is broad-based support among local residents, that a sufficient number of people are involved so as to make achievement of the ultimate goals of the initiative attainable, and that participants are representative of the community as a whole. Emphasis should also be placed on increasing the opportunities for the involvement of those who are underrepresented in community-based activities (the poor, the socially excluded, youth, racial minorities, new immigrants, single mothers, etc.). This is especially true of crime prevention and community development projects implemented in disadvantaged neighborhoods that have a strong social problem-solving component (Box 9.2).

BOX 9.2

GETTING PEOPLE INVOLVED, ACCORDING TO THE CITIZEN'S HANDBOOK

- Ask members to invite others (e.g., friends, family members, and neighbors).
- Go to where people are. Go to the meetings of other groups and to places and events where people gather; this is particularly important for involving ethnic groups, youth groups, seniors, and others who may not come to you.
- Look for ways to collect names, addresses, and phone numbers. Have sign-in sheets at your meetings and events. At events organized by others, ask people to add their names, addresses, e-mail addresses, and phone numbers to petitions and requests for information. In return, hand out an issue sheet or an explanation of how your group is attempting to address an issue.
- Door-knocking is the oldest and best outreach method.
- Create detailed membership lists, including entering name, address, day and evening phone and fax numbers, priorities for local improvement, occupation, personal interests, special skills, times available, what the person would be willing to do, and what the person would not be willing to do. Membership lists can also form the basis of a telephone tree, a system for getting messages out to large numbers of people.
- Generate newsletters and leaflets. Newsletters keep group members in touch. Because most neighborhood groups deliver to all residents whether members or not, a newsletter helps attract new people (Dobson, 2005).

9.3.1 Community Outreach and Communication: Intensive, Varied, Personal, and Appropriate

Community outreach encompasses efforts to raise awareness of, support for, and participation in crime prevention groups and activities. Communication refers to both the message and the medium through which the crime prevention activities are *sold* to neighborhood residents. Both are absolutely critical to mobilizing communities around crime prevention (a *build it and they shall come* mindset will doom most local projects or groups). Effective communication with a target population is characterized by the following:

- Frequent and personal contact between organizers and community members
- Providing an ample amount of notice for events (followed up by reminders as the event draws near)
- The use of varied mediums (flyers, posters, public service ads, telephone, e-mail, websites, social media, face-to-face contact, and news media coverage)
- Ensuring that the medium and the message are appropriate to the target population

In short, successful community outreach is characterized by frequent communications with the target population, using a variety of mediums (but stressing personal contact), and ensuring that both the medium and the message are appropriate to the target population.

In developing an outreach and communication strategy, local organizers must have a strong understanding of their community (which should have been an outcome of the environmental scan and research conducted in the planning phase). Successful community organizers are those who are familiar with the demographic makeup, concerns, and needs of the community as a whole and those of the different groups that make up the larger community. Organizers need to take into consideration education and literacy levels, linguistic and cultural backgrounds, perceptions of and concerns over local crime and disorder problems, previous victimization, and the level of neighborhood attachment that exists among residents. Ensuring communications are appropriate to the different target populations often means using different messages, ensuring they appeal to and address the unique concerns and needs of the different groups. For example, opportunity-reduction, community defense strategies, such as Neighborhood Watch (NW), which stress surveillance, territoriality, protecting one's assets, and reporting suspicious people or activities, may appeal to socially integrated, middle-class homeowners who have assets worth stealing (which helps to explain why this demographic group is so overrepresented among NW participants). However, NW is less appealing to, for example, the first-generation immigrant family that is less integrated into the neighborhood, or the poor single mother who owns few assets and may be more concerned with keeping her children out of gangs.

Communication failures by crime prevention groups were blamed for a high rate of cynicism among the poor and ethnic minority residents in the Tees Valley of Britain about the benefits of local crime prevention programs (Safe in Tees Valley and the Home Office, 2003). A survey of nearly 1000 residents found that less than a third from minority ethnic groups could recall any crime prevention campaign, compared to half of those who classified their ethnicity as "white British". As the program director of the crime prevention group, Safe in Tees Valley stated in a media interview, "If we expect members of ethnic minorities to improve their security by changing their behavior, then we have to reach them with the right prevention message, delivered in the right way" (*BBC News*, 2004).

One characteristic of successful community outreach strategies is face-to-face dialogue between organizers and community members. Because dialogue has historically been the main form of communication at the local level (Young, 2001, 36), it should also be the communicative basis upon which people are mobilized to build community and address local problems. Face-to-face dialogue is especially important for mobilizing neighborhoods because, as research has shown, personal contact is often the most effective way to solicit participation in local collective action, especially when carried out by trusted and motivational local leaders or members of the potential participant's social network. Personal contact may be the most effective outreach strategy because of its affective–emotional basis, which avoids the more impersonal, pedantic, and technical traits of reports, mail-outs, e-mails, etc. Indeed, dialogue stands in contrast to social guidance models of governance that stress the technical aspects of written communication, a legacy of the positivist tradition of "objectified, systematized knowledge that exists independently of any person who expresses these ideas" (Daly, 1978, 199). Dialogue, whether on a one-to-one basis or in a group context, is the method of communication that best facilitates the collection and sharing of information, personal experiences, opinions, and perspectives and is the optimal means by which people can spark ideas and generate possible solutions to local problems. While face-to-face dialogue should be emphasized, written and electronic communication, the Internet and social media can be used to reach larger audiences more efficiency (Box 9.3).

BOX 9.3

ROLE OF SOCIAL NETWORKING MEDIA IN LOCAL CRIME PREVENTION PROJECTS

Much has been written about the role of social media in mobilizing people to support certain causes, whether it is the election of Barak Obama as president or the mobilization of disenchanted protestors during the *Arab Spring*. No doubt social networking media—including Facebook, Twitter, Myspace, Instagram, and blogs—has revolutionized the art and science of communicating with, educating, and mobilizing people. Social media is an effective organizing tool because it can reach hundreds if not thousands of people in real time, provides a central (virtual) *meeting place* and communication tool, and can facilitate an inclusive and interactive conversation among interested people.

Some tips on using the power and unique nature of social networking media for local crime prevention groups and projects include the following:

- Set up a Facebook group dedicated to a particular crime prevention group or activity (e.g., NW).
- Use social media to communicate criminal acts that have immediately or recently taken place.
- Use social media to organize urgent community safety initiatives (e.g., to find a lost child, to respond to a series of robberies or sexual assaults).
- Use social media to provide important updates on ongoing crime prevention projects and activities or simply to communicate crime prevention tips.
- Use social media to reach young people, to attract them to the cause, and/or to inform them of ongoing (developmentally based) events and activities they can participate in.
- Use social media to educate young people on how to use social media and the Internet safely and securely (how not to victimize others or be victimized).
- Ensure crime prevention organizers and local police engage in a two-way conversation with local constituents through social media.
- Compile membership lists (e.g., NW) through social media sites, like Facebook.
- Use social media sites to solicit feedback from community members on current crime prevention projects and initiatives.
- Send out *tweetalongs* (through Twitter) that communicate to others activities undertaken during the course of a particular crime prevention event (e.g., a citizen patrol, local safety audit, and a youth event).
- Send or post photos of local sites where there is a particular need for safe design improvements.
- Don't sent out too many messages or *tweets*; the important ones may get ignored.
- Link to other social media sites (on crime and crime prevention tips) that community members may find useful and educational.

9.3.2 Organize at the Micro Level

Another common denominator in successful local mobilization efforts is targeting a numerically small and spatially concentrated population. Focusing at a micro level appears to contribute to successful organizing because it facilitates intensive communication and allows organizers to personally contact residents on a repeated basis. In other words, concentrating on a limited and spatially confined area facilitates an intensive, personal, and repeated outreach by a limited number of organizers that would not be possible with a larger population.

Research into local social movements emphasizes the importance of organizing at the micro level. Small citizen groups, according to Fowler et al. (1979), are much more effective crime prevention vehicles than large neighborhood-, city-, or region-wide organizations. In his *Citizen's Handbook*, Dobson (2005) writes that when trying to mobilize a large neighborhood or community, organizing should be carried out on a block-by-block basis, which can then be used as the foundation for a larger organizing effort:

> Resident organizers find block reps for every block in the area. A block can either be a block of houses on opposite sides of the same street, an apartment block, co-op, or condominium complex. Block reps get to know everyone on their block, then introduce everyone to one another. When neighbours first meet, they are often surprised and delighted to discover how many interesting people live on their own block. Once residents know one another, they can elect a block rep. Block reps then elect neighbourhood reps, who can form an area coordinating committee. Neighbourhood reps can also elect area reps, who can form a city coordinating committee.
>
> **Dobson (2005)**

According to Perkins et al. (1990, 90), there are several reasons why the block is an important organizational focus for community crime prevention: Its boundaries are less ambiguous to local inhabitants; residents are more likely to know one another; neighbors share common concerns that affect their neighborhood; social interaction, social cohesion, and informal social control are more likely to flourish through face-to-face interaction; and the small settings allow for a more intensive recruitment effort by community organizers.

9.3.3 *Reach Out to* Communities within a Community

Local organizers must always ensure that participants in neighborhood groups and activities are demographically representative of the community as a whole. Use the information gathered in the planning process to identify the different communities in the neighborhood. Then, identify someone who may be a well-known and respected leader of that community and make a concerted effort to attract his or her support. These individuals can be invaluable in providing information that will help identify issues of concern to different groups within the community as well as how best to reach out to and involve these community members.

9.3.4 *Reach Out to Those Who Typically Do Not Become Active Locally*

A special effort must be made to involve those in the neighborhood who are disproportionately underrepresented in crime prevention groups and activities. These are often individuals and groups who are socially excluded from many of the opportunities and benefits of mainstream society. Shorthand terms such as social exclusion, social isolation, alienation, marginalization, or disenfranchised are used to denote a by-product of "what can happen when people or areas suffer from a combination of linked problems such as unemployment, poor skills, low incomes, unfair discrimination, poor housing, high crime, bad health and family breakdown" (Office of the Deputy Prime Minister, 2004, 4). Marginalization is characterized by a social and physical detachment and isolation and by a lack of supportive and sustaining relationships with others (Bloom and Kilgore, 2003, 440). Social isolation, according to Duncan (1999, 9), refers to the segregation of poor people from middle- and upper-income citizens, resources, activities, and opportunities; in other words, "it keeps the haves out of contact with the have-nots."

Efforts to involve marginalized groups must include the greater goal of integrating them into the community and *mainstream* society. A lack of integration in and attachment to a neighborhood in which one lives is a major reason why people do not become involved in local collective action (and is also cited as a cause of criminal behavior). According to Flint (2002, 261), "the willingness of people to act communally for the good of a neighborhood is related to their sense of local attachment and belonging and the way they view their own role within the community." The challenge is: What can be done to help marginalized, socially isolated groups and individuals buy a stake in the community in which they live? At the very least, efforts to integrate those who are socially isolated and excluded need to be sincerely asked why they do not take part in local group activities or why they shy away from other forms of social interaction. They should also be asked: What would make you feel more welcome in the community? What would it take to get you more involved? What is your hope and desire for your community, especially as it relates to your own life?

The extent to which residents are integrated locally also depends on their ability to identify with others who make up the local community or neighborhood group. The more strongly one identifies with other members of a community, the greater the chance that local integration, a sense of belonging, and group participation will occur. Research into civic participation, collective action, and social movements, including community crime prevention, indicates that those who become involved tend to identify with the larger group (and not just the issues addressed by the group) (Pratkanis and Turner, 1996). Including those who are locally and socially isolated can begin with efforts to help them identify with others in the neighborhood, especially those active in local groups and activities. Responsibility for the goal of integrating the poor and socially isolated into the local community falls on the shoulders of those more affluent, empowered, and civic-minded residents, who can help provide (local) support networks for disadvantaged and marginalized residents.

One of the most useful ways that affluent members of society can promote greater social inclusion among the poor and marginalized is to help them climb the socioeconomic ladder. For neighborhood groups, this means working with other key partners (including governments) in tangible ways to directly address the immediate and long-term needs of their most vulnerable neighbors. The lesson for a community development approach to crime prevention is clear: to be successful, inclusive community organizing in disadvantaged neighborhoods must strive to address the immediate material needs of the most impoverished residents through both short-term problem solving and long-term personal socioeconomic development.

Intensive efforts to draw new immigrants into local multicultural social networks are particularly important because of the difficulty they may experience in adjusting to a new society, culture, and language. The integration of refugees and other immigrants into existing multicultural social networks is also central to a broad-based mobilization of disadvantaged neighborhoods, not only because many find themselves settling in such neighborhoods, but also because exclusive ties to an ethnic community may lead people to withdraw from civic engagement in the larger multicultural community.

CASE STUDY 9.1

COMBATING SOCIAL ISOLATION THROUGH THE FAMILY PARTNERS PROGRAM

Bloom and Kilgore (2003) describe the US-based Family Partners Program, which is run by the Beyond Welfare group. Through this program, middle-class families help socially integrate and better the lives of those less fortunate by volunteering to help socially disadvantaged families to emerge from poverty. Volunteers are expected to not only establish a peer relationship with these struggling families but also help them develop a plan to move out of poverty; help them access community services; provide support when dealing with government agencies, schools, and other institutions; and simply be a supportive friend.

In their research into this program, Bloom and Kilgore found that volunteers undertook many practical activities, such as babysitting, giving driving lessons, providing transportation, donating clothes, helping with home repairs, and accompanying them when they attend school, legal, or social service meetings. In addition to reducing the social isolation that people living in poverty often experience, this program also endeavors to spur middle-class volunteers to examine and move past any biases they may have toward people living in poverty and to increase their understanding of the challenges that poverty presents to individuals and the community at large. All of these ancillary goals are meant to help motivate and sustain the participation of the middle class in eradicating poverty (Bloom and Kilgore, 2003, 434–435).

Neighborhood groups can play a leading role in integrating and acculturating immigrants into their new society. Individuals, families, and community organizations can help educate and acculturate new immigrants while introducing them to political, social, and economic institutions as well as the government, community, health-care, and social services available to them. Community organizers can solicit help from nongovernmental organizations that offer settlement and other social services to immigrants. Neighborhood-based social gatherings are another way to integrate new immigrant families into the local communal fold, especially when such events revolve around children. Because children often integrate and acculturate faster than their parents, the social networks they establish with their peers from other races and ethnicities can serve as a springboard to integrate parents and older siblings into the local community.

Special outreach efforts should also be made to involve and empower first-generation women of color. In describing her unsuccessful struggles to engage immigrant Chinese women in English classes at the YWCA, Marilyn Callahan (1997, 179–180) learned that they in fact "did not wish to learn another language." She also learned other valuable lessons:

> Their children were bilingual, they themselves did not work outside the home, and they had a large, close circle of friends and family, none of whom spoke English. While there were likely other reasons for their disinterest, I learned a fundamental lesson: that successful community developers begin by listening to the needs of others and moving at their pace, in their directions, using their methods. I also learned that outsiders, particularly those from dominant cultures, often do not understand the realities of women of colour who cope daily with gender and race both within and outside their culture.

If youth are to become civically engaged, they must develop attachments to their community, local institutions (such as the family and the school), and society; they must be provided with genuine and meaningful opportunities to participate in and serve their community; they must have a voice in what happens to them; they must have a chance to be part of the solution; and they must have an impact on the problems that concern them. Young people must be made to feel that they are useful and of value, not in a paternalistic or patronizing way, but in a spirit that genuinely recognizes and respects the experiences and knowledge that they can bring to help solve local problems (Smith, 1993; National Crime Prevention Centre, 1995; Pearson and Voke, 2003). As a means to achieve both developmental and social integration goals, particular attention should be paid to those youth who are most disadvantaged, those at risk of chronic offending, those who have been in trouble with the law, and those who are from first-generation families, racial minority groups, and aboriginal groups. In his research into youth crime on English council estates, Purdue (2001, 2218) observed that while youth are widely perceived as the source of problems on the estates, they were largely absent from any decision-making structures. This contributed to difficulties in determining and addressing their needs and deprived decision makers of perspectives on how these needs could be met to help avoid delinquency problems. White (2000, 66–67) writes that a "greater democratization of decision-making at the neighborhood level" should incorporate the input of young people, including young offenders, directly into the decision-making process, especially decisions that affect their lives. "This can be done both on an *ad hoc* basis, and through institutionalization of youth advocacy, youth policy and youth participation through local government bodies." Youth councils have been enacted in numerous jurisdictions as adjuncts to the governance of schools, community centers, youth drop-in facilities, and city councils. By creating opportunities for input from the perspective of young people, youth councils represent an ideal operational nexus for the combined principles of decentralization, development, empowerment, and integration.

According to the International Centre for the Prevention of Crime (2008, 82), "many prevention initiatives targeting young people are encouraging greater involvement by youth themselves, to help develop their independence and decision-making capacities, and help them take an active, responsible part in social life." The National Crime Prevention Council (1997) in the United States agrees, writing "youth should be involved in planning and carrying out strategies to prevent violence in their communities. They contribute a valuable perspective on the problem as they build skills that will help them make positive contributions to their neighborhoods."

The participation of youth in project planning and implementation should not be a token or secondary to that of adults. Their active participation is essential given their experiential qualifications, direct exposure to youth crime and violence, proximity to other youth, in-depth understanding and use of social media, and the importance of peer-based interventions. This qualifies youth to play numerous roles: "they join task forces of planning coalitions, volunteer in community-based prevention projects, mediate conflicts in schools and the community, perform in prevention-focused programs for younger children, counsel peers, and organize neighborhood antidrug and anticrime events" (National Crime Prevention

Council, n.d.). One example of a youth-led violence prevention initiative in the United States is Teens on Target:

> ... a peer education program established by Youth Alive in partnership with Oakland, California's Unified School District and Pediatric Spinal Injury Service. Formed after two high school students were shot by peers, the program trains high-risk students to advocate violence prevention by educating and mentoring their peers and younger children on gun violence, drugs, and family conflict. The youth arrange trips to local hospital emergency rooms to give their peers a first-hand look at violence's impact on victims.

National Crime Prevention Council (1995, 255–256)

Some of the key prerequisites to involving youth in crime prevention programs are not that much different than those used to attract and involve adults: effective outreach, sufficient training and support, providing meaningful opportunities, and valuing and rewarding participation (National Crime Prevention Council, 1997).

Parents and other role models can encourage youth to become involved civically and politically by setting an example. Schools can help out by offering civics classes and providing *service learning* options where students get credit for volunteering. There should also be an increase in the "quality and quantity of activities in schools that support engagement skills including oral reports, persuasive debate, discussion, and group service activities" (Pearson and Voke, 2003, 26). Schools should lead by example through the creation of a democratic environment in which civic ideals can best be imparted by giving students the opportunities to provide input into school administration, policies, and curriculum (Pearson and Voke, 2003, 26).

Young people who have not finished school or do not go on to receive postsecondary education should not be forgotten. One project that targets the latter group is the Philadelphia-based Youth VOICES, in which young adults who do not go on to post-secondary education attend a 6-week summer academy, located at a university, where they "work to identify and define an issue of interest to their peers that concerns their community." As part of this academy, the group "develops a strategy for addressing the problem, determines timelines, and builds partnerships to address the problem with community-based organizations, businesses, and others." This program has the added benefit of exposing young people to the university environment, including students and professors who assist them in their projects, which may lead to their future enrollment (Pearson and Voke, 2003, 5).

White (2000) suggests that cultural activities such as dance, art, music, storytelling, computer games, and fashion embody skills and activities that can help integrate at-risk young people into their local community. Because young people, and especially young offenders, know the streets, they are also in a good position to be knowledgeable about safety and security issues and can be employed in novel ways as agents of public safety (White, 2000). For Smith (1993), a national youth service program is an effective way of providing young people with constructive ways to contribute to society and to be rewarded for their work. Selected work in public service should be rewarded through various benefits, such as education scholarships, school credit, gift certificates, unemployment compensation, or cash bonuses. In France, young people undertaking national service have been recruited by schools as mentors and "recreational counselors" and also help monitor schoolyards to protect students against bullies and other forms of victimization (Pitts and Hope, 1997, 47).

9.3.5 Leadership

Successful community organizing is characterized by enthusiastic, active, and motivational organizers who are known and respected by local residents. Leadership, writes Dobson in the *Citizen's Handbook*, is a skill, and like any other skill, it is learned, not inherited, and it takes practice. Good community organizers do not tell other people what to do but help others take charge. They do not grab the limelight but nudge others into it. "They are not interested in being 'The Leader,' but in trying to create more leaders. They recognize that only by creating more leaders can an organizing effort expand" (Dobson, 2005). They know how and when to delegate and then allow their colleagues to carry out the tasks in their own way. Some situations require working together to reach a consensus. Other situations require a rapid decision with little chance for consulting others. A strong leader must be able to determine when different decision-making processes are most appropriate.

Effective leaders must be able to communicate the broader purpose of the group and foster a shared identity and meaning for those involved. Leaders inspire trust and confidence among group participants and do so by helping them understand the group's overall purpose and strategies and how each member of the group personally contributes to achieving key goals and by constantly communicating with and providing information and feedback to all those involved.

For Purdue (2001), community leaders not only require pragmatic organizational skills and expertise in the issues being addressed but must also inspire others to follow and articulate a wider "moral vision" that includes a sense of justice and equality. Community leaders, especially within poor, marginalized neighborhoods, must be agents of change. The entrepreneurial side of the community organizer includes "an ability to cope with risk and uncertainty; creativity in solving problems through divergent thinking," and having a competitive streak that still prizes collaboration. Community leaders must be able to raise funds while being efficient in the use of available resources. Leaders are "quick to spot an opportunity to turn contingencies to their advantage" and will learn from their mistakes without dwelling on them. They are willing to work within the available conditions (without being too conformist), which include taking advantage of the existing political opportunity structure. Community leaders have a plan and try to stick to the plan but work in enough flexibility to move in a different direction if that plan does not seem to be working. They integrate new ideas into their thinking and then experiment with and learn from these ideas. Community leaders must create a network of partnerships and strategic alliances with other neighborhood groups and external agencies and act as key point of contact between them. They must also be able to run democratic meetings, facilitate complex deliberative discussions, and help guide meetings toward tangible, action-oriented results (Purdue, 2001, 2215–2217).

9.3.6 Working with Volunteers

One of the most challenging tasks for community organizers is working with volunteers. Much of the time spent by community organizers may be consumed by planning, coordinating, and supervising volunteer-based activities. Effective leaders keep volunteers committed to and working on the cause. Some tips for successfully working with volunteers include the following:

- Make sure the roles and responsibilities for volunteers are clear and fully understood by them.
- Provide initial and ongoing training to make sure volunteers understand the goals and objectives of the cause and that they have the skills necessary to perform the tasks assigned to them.
- Understand the needs of volunteers; be cognizant of their time constraints.
- Realize the skill level of volunteers; make sure the work provided to them is at their physical and intellectual level. Also try to make the work volunteers perform meaningful to them; at least some of the work assigned should contribute to the volunteer's personal, educational, or career development (this is most applicable to young people).
- Communicate frequently with volunteers and ensure that the communication is not one way; create opportunities for volunteers to provide their own views and opinions.
- Show volunteers that they are valued and that their efforts are recognized. Show appreciation for work well done. Respect all contributions, no matter how small. Give thank-you notes and other tokens of appreciation. Arrange a monthly social event. Give out certificates, special awards, or prizes (especially for special efforts). Solicit gift certificates from local businesses as rewards (National Youth Network, 1998; Dobson, 2005).
- Have the police department cosponsor volunteer appreciation events, with a senior police official personally providing awards and other acknowledgments to volunteers.
- If the funds are available, consider a paid position in the community group that is responsible for coordinating volunteers.

9.3.7 *Partnerships and Team Building*

Successful crime prevention programs require a team approach that integrates a number of appropriate and complementary resources, expertise, and discipline, which collectively can attack current and potential crime and disorder problems from a number of different angles.

While community members should have ultimate control over crime prevention strategies, their *experiential* expertise often needs to be complemented with *processed* expertise and resources. This means involving professionals who have a particular expertise or resources that are conducive to addressing a specific problem.

For many crime problems, a partnership between a neighborhood crime prevention organization and the police is critical. Community organizers need to communicate their interest in working with police as partners, rather than merely demanding increased services (Feins, 1983, 28). Community groups should also be patient and empathetic when it comes to working with police, who may not perceive the problems of that particular community as a priority, especially when they have to deal with the city as a whole.

9.4 DETERMINING THE TYPE OF ORGANIZATION THAT WILL CARRY OUT THE CRIME PREVENTION ACTIVITIES

One of the key issues that must be addressed in any collective, community-based initiative is the nature of the organization through which people will become involved. As discussed in Chapter 5, community-based organizations (CBOs) are nongovernmental organizations that are founded, organized, governed, and run by local residents (sometimes in tandem with outside professionals and experts). CBOs help foster collective action by identifying issues of concern, stimulating public interest, bringing individuals together, and generating resources for program implementation.

Many CBOs are quite ephemeral and *ad hoc*, emerging and dissipating concurrent with an individual crime or disorder problem. Others are formed as long-term ventures and, in some neighborhoods, mature into local institutions. In their efforts to advance crime prevention programs, CBOs are central to mobilizing and involving local residents. According to Bennett (1995, 74), community groups and crime prevention organizers may be a more important influence on participation in community crime prevention than the salient issue of crime. Studies of community activism and crime prevention programs indicate that relatively few individuals volunteer to become involved. "More generally, individuals are recruited through face-to-face encounters with acquaintances or with community organizers."

There are two basic issues that should be taken into account when considering the organization that will coordinate local crime prevention activities:

1. *Will the organization be formal or informal?* That is, will it be a formal organization—complete with a board of directors, charitable status, and an internal hierarchy—or will it operate in a more informal, *ad hoc* way? Informal organizations materialize on the scene quickly to address specific crime and disorder problems, resist formalization (such as incorporating as a society), do not have a hierarchical structure, and often disband soon after the worst part of their problems subside. The strengths of informal groups are that there is less internal bureaucracy and they are much more flexible and nimble in addressing local issues. The disadvantage is that without any formal structure or acknowledged leadership, informal groups are more likely than formal groups to dissolve into chaos and anarchy.

    Formal organizations are often incorporated bodies with a board of directors, a division of labor, registered members, and charitable status. The extent to which a CBO becomes a formal organization is most dependent on the nature, severity, and complexity of the issue being addressed (severe and complex issues often require formal organizations). A formal organization that is incorporated with charitable status also helps with fund-raising. It is generally recommended that local crime prevention initiatives, especially those that are comprehensive in scope, be pursued through a formal organizational structure. With that said, Dobson (2005) advises that community groups have as little structure as possible:

    > The right amount is just enough to address their goals. In an attempt to become legitimate, many small groups decide they need more structure. Unfortunately, this can lead to spending more time on the needs of the

organization than on the reason for getting together…. Grassroots organizations seem to work better with a flat structure as free as possible of boards,
directors, and chairs. Flatness, or the absence of an organizational hierarchy, does not mean the elimination of individual roles or responsibilities. It
does mean the end of people with over-riding authority over other people's
work. Citizen's groups must avoid the common mistake of involving small
numbers of people heavily. They should strive to involve large numbers of
people lightly. Flat organizations, which emphasize horizontal connections,
seem to be the best bet for involving large numbers of people lightly.

The most formal community-based crime prevention organizations have paid
staff. Even a single, part-time staff member can greatly enhance the effectiveness of a community group. A paid staff member can maintain momentum
in pursuing the mandate of the group while fostering the regular contact that
is necessary to sustain community participation and for the durability of the
program overall (Feins, 1983, 35).

2. *Should the crime prevention activities be delivered through an existing multi-
issue organization, or should a new group, dedicated to crime prevention,
be founded?* There are some who believe that crime prevention strategies
can most effectively be delivered through existing multi-issue community
organizations, such as a neighborhood association. Existing groups may be
especially productive in maximizing local participation. According to Linden
(1996, 15):

> One of the best methods of mobilizing citizens is to use existing commu-
> nity groups. Although crime prevention may not be the major focus of these
> groups, many of their members will likely participate in prevention activities
> when their organization is involved. In addition, public support will be more
> likely if a group with a reputation for success sponsors the program. These
> groups are also aware of the needs and resources of the community.

Feins (1983, 25) suggests, "Anyone wishing to start a crime prevention program should first look to established neighborhood organizations. Members
of neighborhood-based organizations can suggest that the issue of crime be
added as one of their concerns." An organization with a history or track record
of benefiting the neighborhood in areas other than crime and safety is a more
promising vehicle for anticrime activity because its very reputation for success
can potentially help keep the crime prevention efforts going.

Existing organizations may have resources that can be applied to crime
prevention. Volunteer and/or staff resources developed for other issues can be
applied to anticrime efforts. While concern about crime may lead some residents to become active in the neighborhood for the first time, there are also
those who place a higher priority on other issues or who may not be as concerned about crime. An organization with a broad mandate that addresses a
number of local issues may be the only way to get them involved in crime prevention efforts. Because local crime problems are causally connected to larger
community issues (such as poverty or the lack of youth-centered activities),
a multi-issue organization may be better placed to address crime as part of
a broader community development plan. Indeed, especially suitable to crime
prevention activities are organizations with a community development focus,

as crime prevention is fundamentally premised on development, whether it is community, social, economic, or human development. An existing community organization with strong neighborhood support also has in place a system of communication that can serve as a vehicle to mobilize residents around community safety issues (Feins, 1983, 25–27).

The downside of having a multi-issue community organization carry out crime prevention activities is that these activities may take a backseat to other issues.

9.5 SUSTAINING A CRIME PREVENTION PROGRAM AND ACTIVITIES OVER TIME

Crime prevention projects can be difficult to maintain. People become bored with watching and patrolling. The more successful the program is at reducing crime, the more difficult it is to keep people involved; as crime problems lessen, people begin to slacken their efforts. This is particularly problematic because crime and disorder problems can easily reemerge without sustained preventative efforts and vigilance.

Crime prevention programs must therefore be structured for durability, which includes integrating maintenance strategies into the crime prevention plan. Inventive ways must be found to keep community members and volunteers involved over time (Box 9.4). Most techniques center on volunteer appreciation, as already discussed in Section 9.3.6. Newsletters are a common method of keeping people informed and of reinforcing success (Feins, 1983). To help sustain active participation in the NW program in Seattle, a maintenance program for Block Captains was devised. It had four elements: (1) a short questionnaire, to help captains identify problems and areas needing follow-up;

BOX 9.4

SUMMARY OF MAINTENANCE TECHNIQUES FOR CRIME PREVENTION PROGRAMS

For Watch Captains, Patrol Leaders, etc.	For Watchers, Patrollers, etc.
Regular contacts from program (leaders or staff)	Neighborhood events, such as fairs or picnics
Phone chain or captains' network	Volunteer recognition
Awards for highest rate of households involved	Meetings with films or speakers
Personal visits	Regular contacts from captain
Steering committee of captains	Leadership development
Evaluation and technical assistance	Meetings with other blocks and organizations
Organizing of adjacent blocks/buildings	Activities around other neighborhood issues
Advanced formalized training	Community organization newsletter

Source: Feins, J., *Partnerships for Neighbourhood Crime Prevention*, U.S. Department of Justice, National Institute of Justice, Washington, DC, 1983, p. 41.

---

(2) personal visits to Block Captains by NW coordinators, to talk about problems with turnover, training, or leadership and to help develop solutions to them; (3) a network of Block Captains, to coordinate efforts on adjacent blocks or to aid in organizing their respective blocks; and (4) a neighborhood-wide meeting of captains, to acquaint them with each other and with new police personnel in the area (ABT Associates, 1976, as cited in Feins, 1983, 40).

9.6 CONCLUSION

Successful crime prevention organizing is characterized by strong, motivational leaders who target a small number of residents through intensive communication and personal, multiple contacts that appeal to both crime concerns and a sense of community. These elements of success are mutually reinforcing: intensive communication and multiple and personal contact is often only possible when directed at a small number of people, given the reality of finite resources and a limited number of organizers. The presence of simply one of these factors may not result in high levels of participation. The presence of all, while certainly not guaranteeing success, may have significant influence on the levels of participation in crime prevention groups and activities. These organizational success stories also corroborate Hope's (1995) contention that when comparing the participation of individuals from different socioeconomic groups, the privileged will become involved in crime prevention programs on their own, given their stake in the community. The less privileged will also become involved, although a much more concerted effort must be made to attract them and sustain their participation. Once involved, community organizers must work to sustain active participation by community members and their commitment to the cause, which is the most important element in any community crime prevention project. Organizers must have strong leadership skills, must constantly work to show they value those who are volunteering, and must constantly work maintenance strategies into a crime prevention plan that ensures the sustainability and vitality of the group over a period of time.

9.7 DISCUSSION QUESTIONS AND EXERCISES

1. Identify community-based crime prevention groups in your city or town and analyze the structure and mandate of these groups *vis-à-vis* the organizational characteristics discussed in this chapter.
2. Deliberate on some of the more contentious issues involved in the implementation of a community-based crime prevention project. For example, should such projects be implemented by an organization dedicated to crime prevention or a multi-issue group, such as a neighborhood association?
3. In your opinion, what crime prevention project implementation issues have not been covered or downplayed by this chapter?
4. Think of some creative ways to initiate and sustain a community crime prevention organization or project, including ways that funds can be raised, ways to actively engage community members, ways to sustain the group over time, and ways to use social media.

9.8 IMPORTANT TERMS

Communications
Communication mediums
Community outreach
Integrated service teams
Leadership
Mobilization
Social (networking) media
Volunteers

FURTHER READING AND INTERNET RESOURCE

See Chapter 8.

CHAPTER 10

CRIME PREVENTION PROJECT, PHASES THREE AND FOUR

Evaluating and Adjusting the Crime Prevention Plan

CONTENTS

10.1   LEARNING OBJECTIVES

By the end of this chapter, you have a better understanding of

- The importance of evaluating a crime prevention project
- The general principles and methods of a project evaluation
- The steps required of a project evaluation
- Some of the basic skills to evaluate a crime prevention project
- How to write an evaluation proposal and an evaluation report
- When and how to modify the crime prevention activities, based on the evaluation as well as other input

10.2   INTRODUCTION

This chapter explores the steps involved in phases three and four of the crime prevention project: evaluating and modifying the project. This chapter begins by describing the principles of a project evaluation generally and then outlines the basic steps necessary for a rigorous, fruitful, and accurate assessment of a crime prevention project. Conducting a project evaluation need not be intimidating; it can be a straightforward process that produces meaningful results, if a few general rules and principles are followed.

A project evaluation involves collecting, analyzing, and disseminating information to determine if a project or strategy is doing what it was intended to do. Evaluations are considered an integral part of crime prevention projects, and most government agencies or private foundations that provide funding for such projects require an evaluation component. Rigorous project evaluations are also important because they contribute to a better understanding of what works and what does not work in the crime prevention field. (The evidence-based foundation of crime prevention is very much reliant on project evaluations. See Chapter 1 for more information on the importance of scientific evidence to the theory and practice of crime prevention.)

Ideally, organizers should begin planning and designing the evaluation at the same time they are developing the project itself (i.e., during the planning phase). This is especially true if a *pretest/posttest* methodology is being used because there is a need to collect information on certain variables (e.g., crime and victimization rates) before the project is implemented. The same variables are measured again at some predetermined point after the project has been implemented to see if there have been any changes and, if so, to determine if the project was responsible for these changes.

While there are different evaluation models, most have one thing in common: they are based on comparisons. This may involve comparing certain variables before and after the implementation of a project or comparing the actual performance of a project to its predetermined objectives.

10.3 PHASE THREE: OVERVIEW OF CRIME PREVENTION EVALUATIONS

A project evaluation is a research process that involves collecting, analyzing, and disseminating information in order to determine a project's impact and/or whether it has met its objectives. Ideally, evaluations should assess both the implementation of the project (called the *process or formative* evaluation) and the actual effect of the program (called the *impact, outcome,* or *summative* evaluation). When most people think of evaluation, they usually think of an *impact evaluation,* which is meant to address such questions as

- How successful has the project been?
- Has the project met its objectives?
- Has the project made a difference? If so, how much of a difference can be attributed to this project (as opposed to other factors)?
- What are the factors behind the success of the project?
- What factors may have inhibited the success of the project?
- What modifications should be made to improve the effectiveness of the project?

A *process evaluation,* on the other hand, focuses on whether a project has been implemented effectively. A process evaluation is as important as an impact evaluation because how a project is implemented can determine its success or failure. In other words, if an impact evaluation determines that a project has not met its objectives, it may be because it was implemented ineffectively, which can be revealed by the process evaluation. Some questions that are answered in a process evaluation include the following:

- Was the project implemented according to plan? Was it implemented competently and effectively? Was it implemented in a manner that would help achieve its ultimate goals?
- Were there sufficient resources available for proper implementation?
- What influence did the project implementation have on project outcomes? To what extent did the project implementation impact on the ability of the project to meet (or not meet) its objectives?
- What were some of the factors involved in the implementation of a project that contributed to its success (or lack of success)?
- What specific problems were encountered as part of the implementation that may limit the impact of the project?

10.3.1 Why Evaluations Are Important for Crime Prevention

Monitoring and assessing a crime prevention project is an integral part of the implementation process. This is because the findings of an evaluation can

- Determine if a project is working or not
- Facilitate an assessment of the impact of different approaches to crime problems, determining if they are effective and which can best maximize community safety
- Help identify and understand problems that impede crime prevention strategies while potentially providing some direction on how these problems can be overcome
- Pinpoint where modifications and improvements should be made
- Benefit other crime prevention project organizers (i.e., what to do and what not to do)
- Be used to determine if crime prevention resources are being distributed effectively and appropriately
- Contribute to the growing body of knowledge on what works and what does not work in crime prevention, which in turn contributes to developing and implementing more effective strategies
- Help determine whether a crime prevention strategy should be funded and/or implemented in other locations, thereby ensuring a more efficacious allocation of scarce resource

10.3.2 When the Evaluation Process Should Begin

There is often a misconception about when the evaluation process begins. Because one has to wait until a project has been implemented for a period of time before any conclusion can be made as to whether it has had any impact, the typical thinking is that the evaluation process begins long after the project has begun (or at the end of the project). In fact, an evaluation should be planned and designed during the project planning phase (phase one). The reasons for this are threefold:

1. Efforts to develop an evaluation plan force organizers to think more clearly, systematically, and specifically about what they want their crime prevention project to achieve.
2. Evaluation research often requires ongoing data collection throughout the life of a project, which means constant monitoring, scrutiny, and assessment.

Given this, developing an evaluation plan before the project is implemented should help organizers determine what to monitor while prompting them to continuously assess the project, beginning at the point it is initially implemented.

3. If organizers are going to evaluate the impact of a crime prevention project, they need to collect information on relevant (crime and safety) variables before the project has been implemented.

10.3.3 Who Should Conduct the Evaluation?

Traditionally, a neutral party who has no connection to the project should conduct the evaluation. This helps ensure it is as objective as possible. For community-based groups, this may mean engaging the services of professional researchers (such as university professors, students, or private-sector consultants) to conduct a project evaluation. The advantage of this option is that the assessment will more likely be conducted in a rigorous and unbiased manner and, as such, there is more confidence in the accuracy of the findings. The disadvantage is that research carried out by professionals can be costly. Walker et al. (2001, 21) list some circumstances where it may be necessary to have an expert conduct a project evaluation:

- The evaluation design uses a large number of data collection methods that need detailed comparison and analysis.
- The evaluation requires the gathering and analysis of complex statistics.
- Organizers are not clear as to what kind of information will be most helpful or how to collect this information.
- A detailed analytical report of the findings is expected, and organizers have no idea what this means, let alone what is involved.
- Project organizers believe they do not have the expertise, resources, or neutrality to conduct the evaluation.

Governmental agencies, such as the police or city auditors, may agree to evaluate a project or, at the very least, lend support to the research. This is particularly likely if the community is selected as the site for a pilot program that may be considered for wider use in the future (Taylor, 1998). A third option is to have people from another community undertake the evaluation (this can be done on a reciprocating basis). This option eliminates costs and can help ensure an objective evaluation; however, the evaluation may not be conducted as rigorously compared to one carried out by research professionals.

For many community crime prevention projects, it will fall to those implementing the project to conduct the evaluation. While there may appear to be a perceived conflict of interest in such a self-evaluation, organizers can avoid problems of bias by ensuring that the evaluation process follows all the rules laid out in this chapter, is as transparent as possible, and incorporates some form of oversight or at least an audit by a research professional (or the project funders). Even if neutral research professionals are unable to take a lead role in a project evaluation, at the very least, they may be able to play the role of technical consultants, which can include quality control, ensuring an objective assessment, and training community members on evaluation research. To keep down the evaluation costs or workload for external researchers, an arrangement can be made where they take the lead in planning and implementing the evaluation, but responsibilities are gradually handed over to the project organizers.

Ultimately, crime prevention organizers must remember that their goal in conducting an evaluation is not to *prove that* the intervention has been successful but rather to *determine if* it has been successful. Project organizers who are undertaking a project self-evaluation must be able to put distance between themselves and the project and fulfill the role of the independent, objective, neutral observer.

This chapter operates on the assumption that those who are planning and implementing the crime prevention project will also be taking the lead in monitoring and assessing the project.

10.4   EVALUATION METHODOLOGIES

There are many different ways to evaluate a project, although most have one thing in common: they are based on comparisons. For example, different evaluation models involve comparing

- Certain variables before and after the implementation of a project
- The actual performance of a project to its predetermined objectives
- The performance of a project against ideal standards
- A *treatment* group with a *control* group (e.g., comparing variables in a neighborhood where a crime prevention project has been implemented against variables in a similar neighborhood without one)

This section examines three evaluation models that are commonly used assess crime prevention projects: (1) before and after (pretest/posttest) comparison, (2) planned versus actual performance comparison, and (3) comparing a treatment group with a control group. It is important to note that in the course of a project evaluation, these different models are often combined.

10.4.1   Pretest/Posttest Comparison

One of the most common approaches to evaluating a crime prevention project is to measure the variables that are the target of the intervention (e.g., the number of burglaries, fear of crime, victimization rate, and overall crime rate) before it has been implemented and then measuring the same variables after the project has been operating for some time. By measuring variables before and after a project has been implemented, the evaluation can determine the impact, if any, the project has had on these variables. The basic steps involved in this evaluation approach are as follows:

1. Select the variables to measure (which will be dictated by the goals of the crime prevention plan).
2. Collect information that measures the variables before the project has been implemented (e.g., the number of burglaries that have occurred in a neighborhood during a 1-year period before the crime prevention strategy was implemented).
3. Collect information that measures the same variables at some point after the project has been implemented (e.g., the number of burglaries that have occurred in the neighborhood during a 1-year period after the crime prevention strategy was implemented).

4. Compare the two sets of data to determine if there has been any change in the variables (e.g., how many burglaries occurred in the neighborhood during the year preceding project implementation compared to 1 year after the project was implemented).
5. Identify any other factors that may account for changes in the variables (e.g., increased police patrols). Researchers call this *controlling for extraneous variables.*
6. Draw conclusions as to whether the planned strategies have affected the variables (to what extent are the strategies responsible for changes, if any, in the variables?).

10.4.2 Planned versus Actual Performance

This evaluation approach makes a comparison between what organizers wish the project to accomplish and what it actually did accomplish. In other words, a project is assessed against the objectives that were laid out during its planning phase. If the evaluation reveals that the project has reached its predetermined objectives, then the project is generally considered a success. The basic steps involved in this evaluation model include the following:

1. As part of the project planning phase, set objectives for the crime prevention strategy that will be implemented (e.g., to reduce residential burglaries by 50% in the year following the implementation of the plan).
2. Select variables that are good indicators of these objectives (e.g., the number of residential burglaries).
3. Collect information that measures these variables at some point after the project has been implemented (e.g., conduct a victimization survey and/or ask police for crime rate data for the neighborhood).
4. Compare actual performance with the planned objectives.
5. Identify and analyze any other factors that may account for changes in the variables being measured.
6. Draw conclusions based on the analysis (i.e., did the implemented strategies have any effect on the variables being measured and, if so, did they change to the extent that the objectives were met?).

10.4.3 Comparison between Treatment and Control Groups

The impact of a crime prevention project can also be evaluated by comparing the treatment group with a control group. Within the context of a local crime prevention project, a *treatment* or *test* group can be a street where a neighborhood watch (NW) program is being implemented, a park that has been redesigned using crime prevention through environmental design (CPTED) principles, or a group of children from a high-risk environment that is taking part in a mentoring program. The *control group* is a similar street, park, or group of children, respectively, that have not been subject to any comparable crime prevention interventions and, therefore, can be used as a comparative benchmark to determine if the interventions in the treatment group were actually responsible for any changes in variables being measured. Using this approach, data collection and analysis methods implemented with the treatment group are replicated with the control group, with the same variables measured for both groups.

The *controlled experiment* method is not used on its own; it is frequently in combination with either of the two previously discussed evaluation approaches to help maximize the accuracy of their findings. In particular, a control group is used because it helps determine whether any changes in the variables being measured in the treatment group can be attributed to the crime prevention strategies being implemented. For instance, if burglaries decreased on a street where NW was implemented (the *treatment group*) and also decreased on a similar street where no NW scheme was implemented (the *control group*), this may indicate that the decline on the NW street may have been the result of something other than the NW scheme (e.g., stepped-up police patrols for both streets). If a control group was not used as part of the evaluation, it could be erroneously assumed that the changes in the variables measured for the treatment street were the result of the NW scheme.

The basic steps involved in this evaluation approach are as follows:

1. Determine if the *pretest/posttest* or *planned versus actual performance* (or both) evaluation method will be used.
2. Select the appropriate variables to measure.
3. Identify a control group that is similar to the treatment group for comparative purposes and ensure no similar crime prevention interventions are being made with respect to the control group that may affect the variables being measured.
4. Collect data that measure the variables for both the treatment and control groups before the project is implemented.
5. Collect data that measure the variables for both the treatment and control groups at some point after the interventions have been implemented.
6. Analyze the data from both the treatment and control groups (this first involves examining the pretest/posttest data for each group, determining if there has been any change in the variables being measured for either group, and then comparing the changes in the variables, if any, between the two groups).
7. Identify other factors that may account for changes in the variables (if any) in both the treatment and control groups.
8. Draw conclusions based on the analysis (i.e., did the intervention in the treatment group influence the variables being measured?).

10.5 IMPORTANT VARIABLES TO MEASURE

To determine whether a crime prevention project has met its objectives, certain *variables* must be measured. A variable is something that can be measured through research and can provide an accurate indicator of a project's objectives (e.g., the number of burglaries in a neighborhood is a variable that can be measured to assess a crime prevention strategy that has as its goal a reduction in residential burglaries). The purpose of the evaluation research is to measure any change in a variable that might have been influenced by a planned intervention. Some typical variables that can be measured as part of the evaluation of a community-based situational crime prevention project are listed in Box 10.1 on the following page. These are divided into *output variables* (which measure *intermediate* objectives that are necessary for a project to meet its ultimate goals) and *impact variables* (the ultimate goals of the

BOX 10.1

TYPICAL OUTPUT AND IMPACT VARIABLES MEASURED IN A NEIGHBORHOOD-BASED OPPORTUNITY REDUCTION CRIME PREVENTION PROJECT

Output variables

- Participation in the crime prevention project or individual activities
- Ability of residents to recognize suspicious people/activities
- Number of residents using streets and public spaces
- Interaction by and cohesion of residents
- Extent to which informal social control and territoriality exists in the neighborhood
- Extent to which residents report suspicious people or activity to police

Impact variables

- Crime rate (police-recorded occurrences, such as the number of burglaries and assaults)
- Victimization rate (victim-reported occurrences)
- Monetary costs of crime incidents
- Fear of crime
- Calls for police service
- Feelings of safety and security among residents
- Satisfaction with the crime prevention activities

crime prevention project). The output goals are ones that help achieve the ultimate (impact) goals. For example, if the crime prevention initiative is the implementation of an NW program, then before the ultimate impact goals of reducing a particular crime problem can be achieved, the program must satisfy a number of *intermediate* (output) goals. For an NW scheme, these output goals include signing up neighborhood residents as members, ensuring they are carrying out the surveillance responsibilities of the NW program, ensuring they are notifying police and their neighborhoods if they see suspicious activities occurring, etc.

These are only a few examples; the variables to be measured will depend on the nature of and specific objectives set for the crime prevention project. Variables to be measured for a social developmental project for at-risk children and youth will be different (and a little more complex) than variables that are to be measured for a situational crime prevention initiative. For example, the variables measured to determine if a social competency program for children exhibiting early signs of aggression is working could include self-esteem, empathy, impulsivity, the ability to work cooperatively in teams and groups, friendship-making skills, anger management skills, and problem-solving skills. If the project evaluation research encompasses a long-term (longitudinal) perspective, then the variables measured would be reflective of whether the children in the program were involved in criminal, delinquent, and violent behavior when they were older. (Chapter 2 identifies the many variables that would be measured in an evaluation of a CPSD initiative.)

A careful analysis and interpretation of the evaluation findings includes ensuring that factors other than the crime prevention project did not contribute to any changes in the variables being measured. This means that any conclusion on how a planned intervention influenced the variables being measured must take into consideration plausible alternative explanations for any changes in the variables. No conclusion should be reached as to the impact of the planned intervention until the other plausible explanations are ruled out. In short, the evaluation must establish a direct cause–effect relationship between the crime prevention initiative and any changes in the variables being measured. This is why the use of a control group is so important in an evaluation; its central role is to control for the variables being measured by helping isolate the impact (if any) the interventions had on the treatment group.

10.6 RESEARCH METHODS AND INFORMATION SOURCES

To measure those variables that will provide an indication of the impact of a crime prevention project, one or more research methods should be employed. There are a number of research methods that can be used to collect information for a crime prevention project evaluation (e.g., interviews, focus groups, surveys, and observation). These methods are no different from the ones used during the research stages of the project planning phase described in Chapter 8. In fact, information collected during the crime prevention project planning phase to determine the scope and nature of the problems to be addressed is generally the same information to be used as part of the evaluation (in this case, it becomes the *pretest data*). One then uses the same research methods at some point after the crime prevention project has been made to collect information on the variables being measured.

10.7 STEP-BY-STEP GUIDE TO CARRYING OUT AN EVALUATION

Planning and implementing a project evaluation involve a number of steps, most of which take place during the crime prevention project planning and implementation phases. The evaluation plan should be designed during the project planning phase, and *pretest data* should be collected before the crime prevention project is implemented. During the project implementation phase, organizers and evaluators should be collecting information that constantly monitors, assesses, and scrutinizes the project, its implementation, and its results. At some predetermined point in the life of the project (or if the project has a finite life, at its conclusion), the *posttest data* gathering should begin.

The remainder of this chapter provides a step-by-step guide to planning and implementing a project evaluation (summarized in Box 10.2 on the following page). This guide focuses on how to conduct an *impact evaluation* and does not provide information on a *process evaluation*. The evaluation plan outlined below entails seven stages. Note that stage 1, the planning stage, is the lengthiest of all the stages. That is because it is important that the evaluation be rigorously planned before data are collected.

Designing an evaluation need not be an intimidating experience. In essence, it comes down to addressing the following questions:

- What?—What are the project's objectives? What variables will be measured?
- Where?—From where will information be collected (i.e., sources)?

BOX 10.2

KEY STAGES AND STEPS IN A PROJECT EVALUATION

Stage 1: Plan the evaluation:

  i. Determine the overall evaluation approach (identify the treatment neighborhood if the pretest/posttest approach is used).
  ii. Determine the objectives of the crime prevention project.
  iii. Identify the variables to be measured (based on the objectives set for the crime prevention project).
  iv. Determine the sources of information.
  v. Determine the research methods.
  vi. Construct the research instruments.
  vii. Select the sample.
  viii. Anticipate problems and other factors that may influence the evaluation.
  ix. Put together a work plan.
  x. Estimate the evaluation costs (if any) and put together a budget.
  xi. Draft the evaluation plan and submit to funding agencies (as part of the project plan).

Stage 2: Collect pretest information.

Stage 3: Implement and monitor the project.

Stage 4: Collect posttest information.

Stage 5: Collate and analyze the data.

Stage 6: Compile the final evaluation report.

Stage 7: Disseminate the evaluation findings.

- How?—How will the information be collected (i.e., research methods)?
- When?—When will the evaluation and its major tasks be conducted (i.e., work plan)?
- Who?—Who will be conducting the evaluation? Who can assist? Who can provide funding?

10.7.1 Stage 1: Planning and Designing the Evaluation

Planning, designing, and implementing an evaluation before the project is implemented will help with the gathering of valid and reliable data. An evaluation plan should be developed during the project planning process, and *pretest* information should be collected for evaluation purposes before the project is implemented. As indicated in Chapter 8, stage 10 of the project planning phase is when the evaluation is planned and designed. This evaluation plan can then be incorporated into the overall crime prevention planning report. Chances of receiving funding for a crime prevention project are improved if organizers can show that they intend to carry out a rigorous evaluation. Also, a key step in any evaluation is gathering as much background information as possible about the project (objectives, methods, key partners, and work plan) and its context (problems addressed, community in which it is being implemented, etc.). The project organizers should already have collected this information during the project planning phase. The key steps in the planning stage of the evaluation phase are as follows:

1. *Determine the overall evaluation approach*: The first step in planning a project evaluation is deciding on how the research is to be carried out (the evaluation design). It is recommended that a combination of the three aforementioned research approaches (pretest/posttest, planned versus actual performance, treatment and control group comparisons) be used to maximize the accuracy of the evaluation. (The steps and examples detailed below assume that all three methods are used.)

2. *Determine the objectives of the crime prevention project*: To carry out an evaluation that compares the planned and actual performance of the project, one simply has to refer to the project objectives established during the crime prevention planning phase. The evaluation plan allows organizers to revisit the objectives set for the crime prevention project to ensure that they are realistic, specific, and measurable. If objectives were not set during the planning phase, then now is the time to do so. For the purposes of the evaluation, the objectives should be

   a. Reflective of what the crime prevention project is to achieve.
   b. Realistic (are the objectives achievable?).
   c. Specific (e.g., don't set out to vaguely measure *local crime problems*; instead, set objectives related to a specific crime problem, such as residential burglaries).
   d. Precisely established (incorporate specific milestones) so that they are measurable through the collection of information (e.g., reduce the burglary rate by 50% in a year following the implementation of the NW scheme).

   The objectives to be measured as part of the evaluation can include both *output objectives* and *impact objectives*. For a truly comprehensive and more rigorous evaluation, a *process evaluation* should also be conducted to determine if the project was implemented in an effective manner. This includes assessing project *inputs* (determining if the quality and quantity of resources were appropriate and adequate) and project *activities* (determining what interventions were implemented and if they were carried out in an effective and competent manner).

3. *Identify the variables to be measured*: Once the project objectives have been determined, the variables to be measured for each objective need to be identified. The variables to be selected will flow directly from the objectives. To help identify measurable variables for each objective, a simple matrix can be used. Table 10.1 provides an example of one such matrix, using the implementation. and evaluation of an NW program as an example. Note that objectives 1–4 are *output or intermediate* objectives, while the last two are the *outcome or impact* objectives (the ultimate goals of the program).

4. *Determine the sources of information*: The next step in the evaluation planning stage is to determine the sources from which information will be collected to measure the identified variables. For each objective, information can be collected from one or more sources. For example, information on a neighborhood burglary problem can be obtained from police crime statistics and a victimization survey of residents. Table 10.2 shows how the project evaluation matrix can be used to list the sources of information to measure each variable.

Table 10.1
Crime Prevention Project Evaluation Matrix
(with Objectives and Variables)

Objective	Variable
Output Objectives and Variables	
1. Involve at least 70% of the houses on their block in the NW program.	Number of households attending the NW meeting or number of names on the NW map
2. Increase the ability of participating residents to recognize strangers and suspicious people and activities.	Recognition of strangers and recognition of suspicious people and activities
3. Increase the awareness and knowledge of security measures by participating residents.	Awareness and knowledge of proper safety and security measures
4. Increase the participating residents' familiarity with one another.	Residents' familiarity with one another
Impact Objectives and Variables	
5. Reduce the rate of break and enters, and theft from autos.	Break and enters, and theft from autos
6. Increase feelings of safety and security and decrease the fear of crime among participating residents.	Safety and security of residents and fear of crime

5. *Determine the research methods:* Once a decision has been made as to the sources of information to be collected, how the information will be collected—that is, the research methods to be used—should be determined. The research methods are generally dictated by the sources of the information to be used. For example, given that a main source of information on local crime problems is neighborhood residents, there are different data gathering options available, including a questionnaire survey, focus groups, interviews, or a combination thereof. Once again, it is recommended that more than one method be used. The three aforementioned methods are complementary, and together they can help maximize the completeness and accuracy of the information required to determine the scope of the crime problem and the effectiveness of the crime prevention project. A survey that is circulated among residents produces quantitative (statistical) information (e.g., number and percentage of residents who have been victimized). This method is complemented by a focus group, which is better at soliciting in-depth, qualitative information through an interactive discussion involving a number of people. In addition, focus groups can be used to elaborate on answers provided in the survey. Interviews can also provide more in-depth information and complement focus groups because the interview is conducted on a one-to-one basis. In choosing the method to be used, such factors as the costs and time involved in employing the method should be considered. Table 10.3 shows how a column added to the evaluation planning matrix identifies the research methods to be used for each objective, variable, and source of information.

6. *Construct and test the research instruments:* Once a decision has been made as to the research method(s) that will be used, questions that will be posed to research participants must be drafted. This can range from jotting down a few questions to ask neighbors to constructing a formal research *instrument*, such

Table 10.2
Crime Prevention Project Evaluation Matrix (with Objectives, Variables, and Information Sources)

Objective	Variable	Source of Information
Output Objectives and Variables		
1. Involve at least 70% of the houses on their block in the program.	Number of names on the sign-up sheet, number of households attending the NW meeting	NW sign-up sheet, attendance at the NW meeting, survey of residents, number of members of NW Facebook group
2. Increase the ability of residents to recognize strangers and suspicious people and activities.	Recognition of strangers, recognition of suspicious people and activities	NW members (as well as nonmembers on the treatment street and control street for comparison purposes)
3. Increase the awareness and knowledge of security measures by participating residents.	Awareness and knowledge of proper safety and security measures	NW members (as well as nonmembers on the treatment street and control street for comparison purposes)
4. Increase the participating residents' familiarity with one another.	Residents' familiarity with one another	NW members (as well as nonmembers on the treatment street and control street for comparison purposes)
Impact Objectives and Variables		
5. Reduce the rate of break and enters, and theft from autos.	Break and enters, and theft from autos	Police crime statistics, residents (NW members as well as nonmembers on the treatment street and control street for comparison purposes)
6. Increase feelings of safety and security and decrease the fear of crime among participating residents.	Fear of crime and safety and security of residents	NW members (as well as nonmembers on the treatment street and control street for comparison purposes)

as a survey questionnaire. Once again, when writing the specific questions to be posed to respondents, the objectives and variables should be used as a guide. Furthermore, it is always a good idea to test the research instruments before they are finalized and implemented. One example of a questionnaire that can be circulated among residents (in both the treatment and control groups) to evaluate an NW program is provided at the end of this chapter (see Appendix: Crime Prevention Survey).

7. *Select the sample:* Collecting information from a representative sample of the community targeted by the interventions is essential to the accuracy of an evaluation. The *sample* is made up of those who will take part in the research and represents a portion of the broader community that is affected by the crime prevention project (the *population*). If a control group is used, a similar sample is also selected from this population. Based on the research findings drawn from these samples, generalizations are then extrapolated to the populations as a whole. Because the research findings are extrapolated from the *sample* to the *population*, it is crucial that the sample be as representative of

Table 10.3

Crime Prevention Project Evaluation Matrix (with Objectives, Variables, Information Sources, and Research Methods)

Objective	Variable	Source of Information	Research Method
1. Involve at least 70% of the houses on their block in the program.	Number of names on the sign-up sheet, number of households attending the NW meeting	NW sign-up sheet, attendance at the NW meeting, number of members of NW Facebook group	Review NW sign-up sheet, count attendance at NW meeting, survey or interview residents
2. Increase the ability of residents to recognize strangers and suspicious people and activities.	Recognition of strangers, recognition of suspicious people and activities	NW members (as well as nonmembers on the treatment street and control street for comparison purposes)	Observations, interviews, survey, focus groups
3. Increase the awareness and knowledge of security measures by participating residents.	Awareness and knowledge of proper safety and security measures	NW members (as well as nonmembers on the treatment street and control street for comparison purposes)	Observations, interviews, survey, focus groups
4. Increase the participating residents' familiarity with one another.	Residents' familiarity with one another	NW members (as well as nonmembers on the treatment street and control street for comparison purposes)	Observations, interviews, survey, focus groups
5. Reduce the rate of break and enters, and theft from autos.	Break and enters, and theft from autos	Police crime statistics, residents (NW members as well as nonmembers on the treatment street and control street for comparison purposes)	Review of police stats, interviews, survey
6. Increase feelings of safety and security and decrease the fear of crime among participating residents.	Fear of crime and safety and security of residents	NW members (as well as nonmembers on the treatment street and control street for comparison purposes)	Observations, interviews, survey, focus groups

the population as possible. A sample that is not representative may produce evaluation findings that are inaccurate. In general, the larger the population, the smaller (in proportion) the sample has to be to ensure a given level of accuracy. For example, if the population is 10, then the sample must be 10 to ensure accuracy. If the population is 100,000, then 384 people are needed to obtain a level of accuracy (Walker et al., 2001, 51–53; see p. 53 for a useful table on how to determine a sample size from a given population). For most neighborhood-based crime prevention project evaluations, a sample group can be chosen simply by listing all the addresses of residents and then selecting every fifth or tenth address (depending on the required sample size).

8. *Anticipate problems and other factors that may influence the evaluation:*
Before a project evaluation is undertaken, it is important to identify any

limitations or obstacles that may impede it. By acknowledging the limitations and anticipating potential problems, researchers may be able to overcome them before they occur or at least minimize their impact when they do materialize. Potential problems that evaluators may face include limited or no access to information and a lack of resources. In addition, evaluators should try to identify other factors that may influence the variables to be examined. For example, organizers should determine if there are any other police programs, crime prevention projects, community development projects, or major changes occurring in the treatment and control areas being examined and determine how these may influence the variables being measured (e.g., how they may affect the number of burglaries being committed).

9. *Construct a work plan, including a time line*: The evaluation work plan should be drafted at the same time the work plan for the crime prevention project is being developed. If the evaluation is going to use a pretest/posttest comparison, it is especially important that evaluators determine when the *pretest and posttest* information gathering will be conducted.

10. *Estimate the evaluation costs (if any) and put together a budget*: Once a work plan has been constructed, evaluators should be in the position to identify the evaluation expenses and put together a budget. This step is particularly important if a proposal for funding is going to be submitted to an external agency. Funders require at least an overview of the evaluation and estimates of its cost, including a breakdown of individual expenses. If the evaluation plan is being submitted along with the project plan, the evaluation budget should be integrated with the overall budget (with evaluation expenses separate from the project implementation expenses).

11. *Draft an evaluation plan*: Once all the aforementioned steps have been completed, an evaluation plan can be finalized. Box 10.3 provides an example of the structure of an evaluation plan.

10.7.2 Stage 2: Pretest Information Collection

Once the evaluation design has been finalized, approved (and funded), the pretest data can be collected. This is done prior to the implementation of the project. Using the research methods laid out in the evaluation plan, evaluators begin collecting information that will measure the variables identified in the plan. Once the pretest information collection stage is finished, it is important to summarize and analyze the findings. Note that information collected during the research stage of the project planning phase can often be used as pretest data.

It is important that research participants be told that their input is confidential and will be treated as such. This means not attributing any comments to an identified person and protecting all the data collected by storing paper files in a locking file cabinet and all electronic data in a password-protected computer.

10.7.3 Stage 3: Implement and Monitor the Project

Once the pretest information has been collected and the project implementation stage begins, it is important to conduct some form of ongoing monitoring, at the very least, to determine if the project has been implemented as planned and is running smoothly.

BOX 10.3

CRIME PREVENTION PROJECT
EVALUATION PROPOSAL OUTLINE

Title Page

Covering Letter (if submitted to a funding agency)

Table of Contents

Introduction: Introduce the proposal and its contents.

Background: This section provides a context for the evaluation. What is being evaluated? What is the history behind this project? Provide a description of the proposed crime prevention project and the community where it will be implemented.

Research Objectives: This section identifies the goals of the project evaluation. Why is the evaluation being conducted? What are the goals of this project evaluation? What is the evaluation to achieve? How will the evaluation results be used?

Evaluation Design: This section documents the decisions made in the evaluation planning stages (steps i–x). What are the objectives of the crime prevention project? What overall evaluation approach will be used? What research methods will be used? What variables will be measured? What are the research methods and sources of information? What is the sample to be used? Will a control group be used? If so, describe the control group and how it is similar to the treatment group. (These can all be summarized in a matrix.)

Scope and Limitations: This section makes clear the parameters for the project evaluation. What is the geographic scope of the evaluation (what neighborhoods are to be covered)? What limits are being placed on the evaluation (e.g., will focus only on residential burglaries)? What factors may limit the evaluation? What obstacles to the evaluation are anticipated? Are there any other factors that may influence the variables to be measured?

Work Plan and Time Line: This section details the evaluation tasks to be carried out, who will be carrying them out, and when they are to begin and end (including when the pretest/posttest data collection will take place).

Budget: This section estimates the costs of the evaluation (if submitting to a funding agency). Include any financial and in-kind resources already available for the evaluation.

Appendix: An appendix can include any information too detailed to include in the body of the plan and may also include the research instruments to be used as part of the evaluation.

This ongoing monitoring also helps with the process evaluation (i.e., scrutinizing the actual implementation of the project).

10.7.4 Stage 4: Posttest Information Collection

Typically, posttest information is collected at three points in the life of a project: (1) at some predesignated point after the project has been implemented (a reasonable period in which its impact can be felt), (2) at the immediate conclusion of the project (if there is a conclusion), and (3) at some future time following the conclusion of the project. The period of time covered by the posttest information collection should equal the

449

period of time used for the pretest data collection for a fair comparison. For example, if the pretest data consisted of the total number of calls for police service for the year prior to the project start date, then calls for police service should be collected for the year following program implementation.

It is very important that the posttest research be conducted exactly as the pretest research was conducted. In other words, the same methods, data sources, and instruments must be used; those completing a questionnaire or participating in a focus group should be the same as those who did so in the pretest phase.

10.7.5 Stage 5: Collate and Analyze the Data

Once the posttest data collection stage is complete, the accumulated information can be collated and analyzed. The first step is to assemble all the information that has been collected. Collating the data is also the first step in analyzing the data because it helps identify patterns that have emerged from the evaluation research. To make the analysis manageable, evaluators should focus on one project objective at a time. The analysis is complete when enough information has been produced to determine whether all the project objectives have been achieved.

As indicated at the beginning of this chapter, the analysis of the data (and the determination of whether the project objectives had been achieved) is largely based on the following comparisons:

Comparing pretest and posttest data. One can first analyze the data by comparing the findings from the pretest and posttest stages to determine if the project has had any impact on the variables being measured. A determination then must be made as to whether these changes have moved in a direction that satisfies the corresponding objective of the crime prevention plan. In addition to noting the *direction* of change in the measurement of a variable, the analysis should also note the *extent* of such change. In other words, if there is a change in the number of residential burglaries from the pretest to posttest periods, the analysis identifies the direction of the change (did the number increase or decrease?) and the extent of the change (calculated as a percentage).

Comparing the actual performance of a project to its predetermined objectives. Calculating the direction and extent of the changes in the variables being measured will determine if the change moved in the right direction and was significant enough to meet the goals established in the crime prevention plan or project evaluation. Thus, central to any analysis of evaluation results is whether the project has met its predetermined objectives, as laid out in the crime prevention plan (e.g., decrease residential burglaries by 50%).

Comparing a treatment group with a control group. If a control group was used as part of the evaluation, the analysis will involve comparing any changes that occurred in variables between the two groups. If the variables changed in the treatment neighborhood in the direction predicted in the objectives, while the variables did not change in the control neighborhood, a conclusion can be drawn that it was the crime prevention intervention that caused the change (although one must first make sure there were no other factors that could have caused the changes in the treatment group). If the variables in both groups changed in the same direction, evaluators must determine if (1) the crime prevention project was unsuccessful or (2) something other than the crime prevention project impacted the variables in both the treatment and control groups. Use of a control group is indicative of a critical aspect of the analysis phase: isolating the impact (if any) of the intervention (i.e., how the crime prevention project caused a change in the variables being measured). As discussed earlier, this entails determining if it was the crime prevention project, and not something else, that may have resulted in changes in the variables being measured. This means that evaluators must identify all other explanations for the change in the variables.

10.7.6 Stage 6: Compile the Final Evaluation Report

The final stage in the evaluation process is to take the evaluation findings and analysis and present them in a report format. An example of an evaluation report is presented in Box 10.4. Some tips on writing an evaluation report include the following:

- When describing and analyzing the findings, refer to the project objectives. Group the description and analysis under each objective. Structure the description and analyses so that they address the project objectives.
- Try to be comprehensive, yet as concise as possible. Include only information and analyses that are relevant to the evaluation.
- Use tables, graphics, and maps to summarize and analyze the data. Maps are especially useful for evaluating crime prevention projects because they allow for a spatial analysis of crime rates, participation in the program, etc.
- Combine the *statistical* information with *qualitative* information. In other words, back up statistics with quotes from research participants and observations by researchers.
- As with the proposal, ensure that there is a good flow to the report: (1) Summarize the evaluation design, (2) describe the findings, (3) analyze the findings, (4) draw conclusions from the analysis, and (5) recommend a future direction (including modifications) for the project.

BOX 10.4

PROPOSED OUTLINE OF AN EVALUATION REPORT

Title Page

Table of Contents

Introduction—Introduce the report, its purpose, and its structure.

Project Background—Provide information on the project being evaluated, such as how the program got started, where it is being implemented, and the objectives of the project.

Evaluation Design—Outline project objectives and evaluation objectives, research methods, and sources of information; describe scope and limitations of evaluation.

Evaluation Findings and Analysis—Describe the research findings (statistics, quotes, observations, etc.); analyze the findings (What do the descriptive findings mean? Did the variables change between the pretest and posttest periods? What direction was the change? What was the scope of these changes? To what extent did the project result in changes to the variables? What other factors may have contributed to changes in variables measured?).

Conclusions and Recommendations—Based on the description and analysis of findings, draw the final conclusions: Did the project impact on the variables? Has the project reached its objectives? Can it be considered a success? If so, why? If not, why? What can be done to improve upon the project?

10.7.7   Stage 7: Disseminate the Report and Solicit Feedback

Once the evaluation report has been written, it should be disseminated. Recipients of the report should include research participants and other community members, any agency that is funding the project, the police and other relevant government agencies, and other groups in the community. Following the release of the final evaluation report, feedback should be solicited, both formally and informally. Taylor et al., (1998) recommends a meeting among community members and other key partners that should:

- Be based upon an informed understanding of the contents of the report
- Be preceded by distributing a synopsis of the findings
- Be facilitated to prevent the session becoming an assault on the evaluator if the report is critical
- Not assign blame to anyone who may have inhibited the effectiveness of the program
- Be constructive and positive by explaining weakness(es) but also offer solutions through recommendations
- Allow stakeholders to respond to the findings of the report by focusing on actions for improvement rather than justifying past behaviors
- Be structured rather than a free for all (Taylor et al., 1998)

10.8   PHASE FOUR: MODIFYING THE PROJECT

The final phase of the crime prevention project is where the results of the evaluation, as well as feedback from the evaluation report, are used to make modifications to the crime prevention interventions. Few projects are ever perfect, so inevitably some modifications will be made, even if they are minor. In many respects, the evaluation report represents a reconstituted version of the original plan.

10.9   EXERCISES

1. Search the crime prevention literature and the Internet for evaluations of crime prevention projects. Determine if the evaluation design is sufficiently rigorous. Compare and contrast this evaluation design with that outlined in this chapter.
2. Prepare an evaluation plan for the crime prevention project that resulted from the plan devised (as part of the exercise in Chapter 7).

10.10   IMPORTANT TERMS

Control group
Impact evaluation
Open-ended question
Outcome evaluation
Output evaluation
Pretest/posttest
Process evaluation
Project evaluation
Qualitative data

Quantitative data
Research participant
Self-evaluation
Treatment group
Variables

APPENDIX: CRIME PREVENTION SURVEY

This questionnaire is being circulated to people who live in this neighborhood to solicit their experiences with and perceptions of local crime problems. Your answers are anonymous and confidential; please do not include any identifying information. Please circle the appropriate number. The results of this survey will be used to develop effective crime prevention activities for this neighborhood.

10.A VICTIMIZATION/FEAR OF CRIME

1. Has your household been broken into for the purposes of a burglary in the past six (6) months?

Yes	1
No	2
Don't know	88

2. Has your car been broken into for the purposes of a burglary in the past six (6) months while parked on this block?

Yes	1
No	2
Don't know	88

3. How safe do you feel being out alone in your neighborhood at night?

Very Safe	Somewhat Safe	Somewhat Unsafe	Very Unsafe	Don't Know
1	2	3	4	88

4. How safe do you feel in your home at night?

Very Safe	Somewhat Safe	Somewhat Unsafe	Very Unsafe	Don't Know
1	2	3	4	88

10.B CALLS FOR POLICE SERVICE

1. Have you called for police in the last six (6) months?

Yes	1
No	2
Don't know	88

10.C SOCIAL INTEGRATION, COHESION, AND TERRITORIALITY

1. How frequently do you and your neighbors get together for social events?

Often	Sometimes	Rarely	Never	Don't Know
1	2	3	4	88

Please indicate whether you believe each of these statements is true or false:

2. I really feel like a part of this neighborhood. True False
3. If I were sick, I could rely on a neighbor in my building to run an errand for me. True False
4. If I had to be away, I know that a neighbor would keep an eye on my apartment. True False
5. I try to keep an eye out for suspicious people or activities around my home. True False
6. I can tell a stranger apart from a resident of this block. True False

10.D AWARENESS OF AND PARTICIPATION IN SAFETY AND SECURITY MEASURES

What crime prevention activities have you undertaken in the last six (6) months?

7. I make sure all doors and windows of my home and car are locked. [ ]
8. I participate in neighborhood watch. [ ]
9. I had a security check of my home. [ ]
10. I have marked my valuables with an engraver. [ ]
11. I watched a neighbor's apartment while they were away. [ ]
12. I reported suspicious person/activities to the police. [ ]
13. I helped someone who was a victim of crime. [ ]
14. Others (please specify). [ ]
15. Please provide any other comments or observations you may have regarding crime or crime prevention efforts on this block. Please include any comments you may have on what you believe is causing local crime problems as well as solutions to these problems (use the back of this page if necessary).

Thank you for taking time to complete this questionnaire

FURTHER READING AND INTERNET RESOURCES

Tilly, N., Ed., Evaluation for crime prevention, *Crime Prevention Studies*, Vol. 14, Lynne Rienner Publishers, 2002, http://www.popcenter.org/library/crimeprevention/volume_14/.

Walker, G., Walker, C., Johnson, C., and Savageau, J., *You Can Do It: A Practical Tool Kit to Evaluating Police and Community Crime Prevention Programs*, National Crime Prevention Centre, Ottawa, Ontario, Canada, 2001, http://www.ottawapolice.ca/en/resources/publications/pdf/you_can_do_it_evaluation_toolkit.pdf.

Walker, G., Walker, C., Johnson, C., and Savageau, J., *You Can Do It, Part Two: An Evaluation Resource Workbook*, National Crime Prevention Centre, Ottawa, Ontario, Canada, 2002, http://www.ottawapolice.ca/en/resources/publications/pdf/crime_prevention_program_evaluation_resource_workbook.pdf.

Walker, G., Walker, C., Johnson, C., and Savageau, J., *Crime Prevention Performance Indicators*, self-published, n.d., http://www.ottawapolice.ca/en/resources/publications/pdf/crime_prevention_performance_indicators.pdf.

REFERENCES

Abt Associates, Exemplary project validation report: Project candidate: Seattle Community Crime Prevention Program, Abt Associates Inc., Cambridge, MA, 1976.

Acosta, J. and Chavis, D., Build the capacity of communities to address crime, *Criminology & Public Policy* 2007; 6(4):651–662.

Adams, E., *Healing Invisible Wounds: Why Investing in Trauma-Informed Care for Children Makes Sense*, Justice Policy Institute, Washington, DC, 2010.

AfterSchool Alliance, Afterschool programs: Keeping kids and communities safe, AfterSchool Alliance, Washington, DC, No. 27, 2007a. http://www.afterschoolalliance.org/researchIBList.cfm (accessed August 20, 2012).

AfterSchool Alliance, Afterschool programs: Making a difference in America's Communities by Improving Academic Achievement, Keeping kids safe and helping working families, Afterschool Alliance, Washington, DC, 2007b.

AfterSchool Alliance, Evaluations backgrounder: A summary of formal evaluations of afterschool programs' impact on academics, behavior, safety and family life, Afterschool Alliance, Washington, DC, 2011.

Agnew, R., *Pressured into Crime: An Overview of General Strain Theory*, Roxbury, Los Angeles, CA, 2006.

Agnew, R., *Why Do Criminals Offend? A General Theory of Crime and Delinquency*, Roxbury, Los Angeles, CA, 2005.

Alvesalo, A., Tombs, S., Virta, E., and Whyte, D., Re-imagining crime prevention: Controlling corporate crime? *Crime, Law and Social Change* 2006; 45(1):1–25.

Andrews, D.A. and Bonta, J., *The Psychology of Criminal Conduct*, LexisNexis, Newark, NJ, 2006.

Andrews, D.A., Bonta, J., and Hoge, R.D., Classification for effective rehabilitation: Rediscovering psychology, *Criminal Justice and Behavior* 1990; 17:19–52.

Aos, S., Miller, M., and Drake, D., *Benefits and Costs of Prevention and Early Intervention Programs for Youth*, Washington State Institute for Public Policy, Olympia, WA, 2004.

Arciaga, M. and Gonzalez, V., Street outreach and the OJJDP comprehensive Gang model, *OJJDP National Gang Center Bulletin*, Office of Juvenile Justice and Delinquency Prevention, Washington, DC, 2012.

Arthur, M.W., Briney, J.S., Hawkins, J.D., Abbott, R.D., Brooke-Weiss, B.L., and Catalano, R.F., Measuring risk and protection factors in communities using the communities that care youth survey, *Evaluation and Program Planning* 2007; 30:197–211.

Arthur, M.W., Hawkins, J.D., Brown, E.C., Briney, J.S., Oesterle, S., and Abbott, R.D., Implementation of the communities that care prevention system by coalitions in the community youth development study, *Journal of Community Psychology* 2010; 38(2):245–258.

Atkins, S., Husain, S., and Storey, A., The influence of street lighting on crime and fear of crime, Crime Prevention Unit Paper 28, Home Office, London, U.K., 1991.

Atlas, R., Other side of CPTED, *Security Management* 1991; 35(3):63–66.

REFERENCES

August, G.J., Egan, E.A., Realmuto, G.M., and Hektner, J.M., Parceling component effects of a multifaceted prevention program for disruptive elementary school children, *Journal of Abnormal Child Psychology* 2003; 31:515–527.

August, G.J., Hektner, J.M., Egan, E.A., Realmuto, G.M., and Bloomquist, M.L., The early risers longitudinal prevention trial: Examination of 3-year outcomes in aggressive children with intent-to-treat and as-intended analyses, *Psychology of Addictive Behaviors* 2002; 16:27–39.

Australian Government, Attorney-General's Department Crime Prevention, Australian Government Crime Prevention Initiatives, 2011. Available at: http://www.crimeprevention.gov.au/Pages/default.aspx (accessed January 13, 2014).

Australian Government, Attorney-General's Department, National Community Crime Prevention Programme, http://www.crimeprevention.gov.au (accessed July 21, 2014).

Australian Institute of Criminology, National Community Crime Prevention Programme, http://www.aic.gov.au/crime_community/crimeprevention/ncp.html (accessed July 21, 2014).

Bala, N., Carrington, P.J., and Roberts, J.Y., Evaluating the youth criminal justice act after five years: A qualified success, *Canadian Journal of Criminology and Criminal Justice* 2009; 51(2):131–167.

Baldwin, G.J. and Garry, E.M., Mentoring—A proven delinquency prevention strategy, *OJJDP Juvenile Justice Bulletin*, 1997;1–8. https://www.ncjrs.gov/pdffiles/164834.pdf (accessed June 2011).

Bales, W.D. and Piquero, A.R., Assessing the impact of imprisonment on recidivism, *Journal of Experimental Criminology* 2012; 8:71–101.

Bandura, A. and Walters, R.H., *Adolescent Aggression*, Ronald Press, New York, 1959.

Bandura, A., *Social Learning and Personality Development*, Holt, Rinehart and Winston, New York, 1975.

Bandura, A., *Social Learning Theory*, General Learning Press, New York, 1977.

Bandura, A., *Social Learning through Imitation*, University of Nebraska Press, Lincoln, NE, 1962.

Bandy, T., What works for male children and adolescents: Lessons from experimental evaluations of programs and interventions publication, *Child Trends Fact Sheet* August 2012, Publication No. 2012–22. http://www.childtrends.org/wp-content/uploads/2013/01/Child_Trends-2012_08_20_WW_MaleChildrenAdol.pdf (accessed November 2013).

Bania, M., Gang violence among youth and young adults: (Dis)Affiliation and the potential for prevention, *Institute for the Prevention of Crime Review* 2009; 3:89–116.

Barclay, P., Buckley, J., Brantingham, P.J., Brantingham, P.L., and Whinn-Yates, L., Preventing auto theft in suburban Vancouver commuter lots: Effects of a bike patrol, in *Preventing Mass Transit Crime*, Clarke, R.V., Ed., Crime Prevention Studies, Vol. 6, Criminal Justice Press, Monsey, NY, 1996, pp. 133–161.

Barker, I. and Linden, R., *Community Crime Prevention*, Ministry of the Solicitor General Canada, Ottawa, Ontario, Canada, 1985.

Barrett, P. and Sonderegger, R., Anxiety in children—FRIENDS program, in *Encyclopedia of Cognitive Behavior Therapy*, Freeman, A., Ed., Springer, New York, 2005, pp. 42–45.

Barrett, P.M., Farrell, L.J., Ollendick, T.H., and Dadds, M., Long-term outcomes of an Australian universal prevention trial of anxiety and depression symptoms in children and youth: An evaluation of the friends program, *Journal of Clinical Child and Adolescent Psychology* 2006; 35(3):403–411.

Barrett, P.M., Friends for Life: Introduction to FRIENDS, 2007, http://www.friendsinfo.net/downloads/FRIENDSintrobooklet.pdf (accessed May 2009).

Bayley, D.H., Community policing: A report from the devil's advocate, in *Community Policing: Rhetoric of Reality*, Greene, J.R. and Mastrofski, S.D., Eds., Praeger, New York, 1988, pp. 225–238.

Bazemore, G. and Walgrave, L., *Restorative Juvenile Justice: Repairing the Harm of Youth Crime*, Criminal Justice Press, Monsey, NY, 1999.

Bazemore, G., Building community and nurturing justice: A review of the community justice ideal, *Contemporary Justice Review* 2000; 3(2):225–234.

REFERENCES

Bazemore, G., Crime victims and restorative justice in juvenile courts: Judges as obstacle or leader? *Western Criminology Review* 1998; 1(1), http://wcr.sonoma.edu/v1n1/bazemore.html (accessed July, 2014).

BBC News, Call for crime message re-think, *BBC News World Edition*, August 30, 2004, http://news.bbc.co.uk/2/hi/uk_news/england/tees/3610102.stm.

BBC News, Police recruit support officers, *BBC News World Edition*, May 5, 2003, http://news.bbc.co.uk/2/hi/uk_news/wales/south_east/2944692.stm.

Beck, A., *Prisoners of Hate: The Cognitive Basis of Anger, Hostility, and Violence*, HarperCollins Publishers, New York, 1999.

Beck, C., Predictive policing: What can we learn from Wal-mart and Amazon about fighting crime in a recession? *The Police Chief* 2009; 76(11):18–24.

Bedard, B., Fostering resilience in children, ERIC Digest. Clearinghouse on Elementary and Early Childhood Education, August 1995, http://resilnet.uiuc.edu/library/benard95.html.

Bell, M.M. and Bell, M.M., Crime control: Deterrence and target hardening, in *Handbook on Crime and Delinquency Prevention*, Johnson, E.H., Ed., Greenwood Press, Westport, CT, 1987, pp. 45–68.

Bennett, S., Community organizations and crime, *Annals of the Academy of Political and Social Science* 1995; 539:72–84.

Bennett, T., *Evaluating Neighborhood Watch*, Gower, Aldershot, U.K., 1990.

Bennett, T., Holloway, K., and Farrington, D.P., Does neighborhood watch reduce crime? A systematic review and meta-analysis, *Journal of Experimental Criminology* 2006; 2(4):409–529.

Bergin, T., *The Evidence Enigma: Correctional Boot Camps and Other Failures in Evidence-Based Policymaking*, Ashgate, Burlington, VT, 2013.

Bergseth, K.J. and Bouffard, J.A., Examining the effectiveness of a restorative justice program for various types of juvenile offenders, *International Journal of Offender Therapy Comparative Criminology* 2012; 57(9):1054–1075.

Berrueta-Clement, J.R., Schweinhart, L.J., and Barnett, W.S., *Changed Lives: The Effects of the Perry Preschool Program on Youths Through Age 19*, High/Scope Press, Ypsilanti, MI, 1984.

Berry, G., Briggs, P., Erol, R., and van Staden, L., *The Effectiveness of Partnership Working in a Crime and Disorder Context: A Rapid Evidence Assessment*, Home Office, London, U.K., 2011.

Biemesderfer, S.C. and Bustos, P.D., Youth at-risk: Targeting teen-agers for pregnancy prevention, *State Legislative Report* 1989; 14(10):1–8.

Bierman, K.L., Coie, J.D., Dodge, K.A., Greenberg, M.T., Lochman, J.E., McMahon, R.J., and Pinderhughes, E.E., Initial impact of the fast track prevention trial for conduct problems. The high-risk sample, *Journal of Consulting and Clinical Psychology* 1999; 67(5):631–347.

Blackburn, R., *The Psychology of Criminal Conduct*, Wiley, Chichester, U.K., 1993.

Bloom, L.R. and Kilgore, D., The volunteer citizen after welfare reform in the United States: An ethnographic study of volunteerism in action, *Voluntas: International Journal of Voluntary and Nonprofit Organizations* 2003; 14(4):431–454.

Blueprints for Healthy Youth Development, Olweus bullying prevention program, http://www.blueprintsprograms.com/evaluationAbstracts.php?pid=17ba0791499db908433b80f37c5fbc89b870084b (accessed July 21, 2014).

Blyth, M. and Solomon, E., Introduction, in *Prevention and Youth Crime: Is Early Intervention Working?*, Blyth, M. and Solomon, E., Eds., The Policy Press, Bristol, U.K., 2009, pp. 1–7.

Blythe, B.J., Gilchrist, L.D., and Schinke, S.P., Pregnancy prevention groups for adolescents, *Social Work* 1981; 26(6):503–504.

Boccanfuso, C. and Kuhfeld, M., Multiple responses, promising results: Evidence-based, non-punitive alternatives to zero tolerance, child trends: *research to results briefs*, #2011-09, Washington, DC, 2011.

Bonnemaison, G., *Face à la Délinquance: Prévention, Répression, Solidarité* (Dealing with Delinquency: Prevention, Repression, Solidarity). Rapport au Premier Minister. Commission Des Maires Sur La Securite, Paris, 1983.

Bonnie, R.J., Johnson, R.L., Chemers, B.M., and Schuck, J., *Reforming Juvenile Justice: A Developmental Approach*, National Academies Press, Washington, DC, 2012.

Bonta, J. and Andrews, D.A., Risk-need-responsivity model for offender assessment and rehabilitation, Public Safety Canada, Ottawa, Ontario, Canada, 2007.

Boostrom, R.L. and Henderson, J.H., Community action and crime prevention: Some unresolved issues, *Crime and Social Justice* 1983; 19:24–30.

Bor, W., McGee, T.R., and Fagan, A.A., Early risk factors for adolescent antisocial behaviour: An Australian longitudinal study, *Australian and New Zealand Journal of Psychiatry* 2004; 38:365–372.

Borough of Brent, *A Crime and Disorder Reduction and Community Safety Strategy for Brent 1999–2002*, Borough of Brent, London, 2000.

Borough of Brent, Strategy 2006–2008, Borough of Brent, 2005, http://www.brentbrain. org.uk/brain/braincf.nsf/Images/crime_strategy_2005/$file/crime_strategy_2005.pdf (accessed February, 2008).

Botvin, G.J. and Eng, A., The efficacy of a multicomponent approach to the prevention of cigarette smoking, *Preventive Medicine* 1982; 11:199–211.

Botvin, G.J., Schinke, S.P., Epstein, J.A., Diaz, T., and Botvin, E.M., Effectiveness of culturally focused and generic skills training approaches to alcohol and drug abuse prevention among minority adolescents: Two-year follow-up results, *Psychology of Addictive Behaviors* 1995; 9(3):183–194.

Botvin, G.J., Substance abuse prevention: Theory, practice, and effectiveness, in *Drugs and Crime*, Tonry, M. and Wilson, J.Q., Eds., University of Chicago Press, Chicago, IL, 1990.

Bowers, K.J., Johnson, S.D., and Hirschfield, A.F., Closing off opportunities for crime: An evaluation of alley-gating, *European Journal on Criminal Policy and Research* 2004; 10(4):285–308.

Bozeman, B. and Feeney, M.K., Toward a useful theory of mentoring: A conceptual analysis and critique, *Administration & Society* 2007; 39(6):719–739.

Bradshaw, W., Roseborough, D., and Umbreit, M.S., The effect of victim offender mediation on juvenile offender recidivism: A meta-analysis, *Conflict Resolution Quarterly* 2006; 24(1):87–98.

Braga, A., Papachristos, A., and Hureau, D., *The Effects of Hot Spots Policing on Crime*, Campbell Collaboration, Oslo, Norway, 2012.

Braga, A., Piehl, A., and Hureau, D., Controlling violent offenders released to the community: An evaluation of the Boston reentry initiative, *Journal of Research in Crime and Delinquency* 2009; 46(4):411–436.

Braga, A.A. and Weisburd, D.L., Police innovation and crime prevention: Lessons learned from police research over the past 20 years. Paper presented at *The National Institute of Justice (NIJ) Policing Research Workshop: Planning for the Future*, Washington, DC, 2007.

Braga, A.A. and Weisburd, D.L., Police innovation and crime prevention: Lessons learned from police research over the past 20 years, paper presented at the *National Institute of Justice (NIJ) Policing Research Workshop: Planning for the Future*, Washington, DC, November 28–29, 2006.

Braga, A.A. and Weisburd, D.L., The effects of "pulling levers" focused deterrence strategies on crime, The Campbell Collaboration, Oslo, Norway, 2012.

Braga, A.A., High crime places, times, and offenders, in *The Oxford Handbook of Crime Prevention*, Welsh, B.C. and Farrington, D.P., Eds., Oxford University Press, Oxford, U.K., 2012, pp. 316–336.

Braga, A.A., *Problem-Oriented Policing and Crime Prevention*, 2nd edn., Criminal Justice Press, Monsey, NY, 2008.

Braga, A.A., Serious youth gun offenders and the epidemic of youth violence in Boston, *Journal of Quantitative Criminology* 2003; 19(1):33–54.

Braithwaite, J., *Crime, Shame and Reintegration*, Cambridge University Press, Cambridge, U.K., 1989.

Braithwaite, J., Restorative justice and de-professionalization, *The Good Society* 2004; 13(1):28–31.

Braithwaite, J., Restorative justice: Assessing optimistic and pessimistic accounts, in *Crime and Justice: A Review of Research*, Tonry, M., Ed., University of Chicago Press, Chicago, IL, 1999, pp. 1–127.

Brantingham, P.J. and Faust, F.L., A conceptual model of crime prevention, *Crime and Delinquency* 1976; 22(3):284–296.

REFERENCES

Brantingham, P.L. and Brantingham, P.J., Anticipating the displacement of crime using the principles of environmental criminology, in *Theory for Practice in Situational Crime Prevention*, Smith, M.J. and Cornish, D.B., Eds., Crime Prevention Studies, Vol. 16, Criminal Justice Press, Monsey, NY, 2003, pp. 119–148.

Brantingham, P.L. and Brantingham, P.J., Burglar mobility and crime prevention planning, in *Coping with Burglary*, Clarke, R. and Hope, T., Eds., Kluwer-Nijhoff, Boston, MA, 1984, pp. 77–95.

Brantingham, P.L. and Brantingham, P.J., Crime pattern theory, *Environmental Criminology and Crime Analysis*, Wortley, R. and Mazarolle, L., Eds., Willan Publishing, Portland, OR, 2008, pp. 78–93.

Brantingham, P.L. and Brantingham, P.J., Environmental criminology: From theory to urban planning practice, *Studies on Crime and Crime Prevention* 1998; 7(1):31–60.

Brantingham, P.L. and Brantingham, P.J., Nodes, paths and edges: Considerations on the complexity of crime and the physical environment, *Journal of Environmental Psychology* 1993; 131:3–21.

Brantingham, P.L. and Brantingham, P.J., *Patterns in Crime*, MacMillan, New York, 1981.

Brantingham, P.L. and Brantingham, P.J., Situational crime prevention in practice, *Canadian Journal of Criminology* 1990; 32(1):17–40.

Brendgen, M., Vitaro, F., Tremblay, R.E., and Lavoie, F., Reactive and proactive aggression: Predictions to physical violence in different contexts and moderating effects of parental monitoring and caregiving behavior, *Journal of Abnormal Child Psychology* 2001; 29(4):293–304.

Brennan, P.A., Mednick, B.R., and Mednick, S.A., Parental psychopathology, congenital factors, and violence, in *Mental Disorder and Crime*, Hodgins, S., Ed., Sage, Newbury Park, CA, 1993, pp. 244–261.

Brewer, D.D., Hawkins, J.D., Catalano, R.F., and Neckerman, H.J., Preventing serious, violent, and chronic juvenile offending: A review of evaluations of selected strategies in childhood, adolescence, and the community, in *A Source Book: Serious, Violent, and Chronic Juvenile Offenders*, Howell, J.C., Krisberg, B., Hawkins, J.D., and Wilson, J.J., Eds., Sage, Thousand Oaks, CA, 1995, pp. 611–641.

Brezina, T., Adolescent maltreatment and delinquency: The question of intervening processes, *Journal of Research in Crime and Delinquency* 1998; 35:71–99.

Bridgeland, J.M., DiIulio, J.J., and Morison, K.B., *The Silent Epidemic: Perspectives of High School Dropouts*, Civic Enterprises, Washington, DC, 2006.

Brisbane City Council, Visible ink: Brisbane City Council's youth strategy 2004–2008, Brisbane City Council, Brisbane, Queensland, Australia, n.d.

Brown, B. and Altman, I., Territoriality and residential crime: A conceptual framework, in *Environmental Criminology*, Brantingham, P.J. and Brantingham, P.L., Eds., Sage, Beverly Hills, CA, 1981, pp. 55–76.

Brown, B.B., Residential territories: Cues to burglary vulnerability, *Journal of Architectural and Planning Research* 1985; 2(4):231–243.

Brown Cross, A., Gottfredson, D.C., Wilson, D.M., and Rorie, M., The impact of after-school programs on the routine activities of middle-school students: Results from a randomized, controlled trial, *Criminology & Public Policy* 2009; 8(2):391–412.

Browning, K. and Loeber, R., Highlights of findings from the Pittsburgh youth study, Fact Sheet No. 95, Office of Juvenile Justice and Prevention, U.S. Department of Justice, Washington, DC, 1999.

Brunet, J.R., Discouragement of crime through civil remedies: An application of a reformulated routine activities theory, *Western Criminology Review* 2002; 4(1):68–79.

Bry, B.H. and George, F.E., Evaluating and improving prevention programs: A strategy from drug abuse, *Evaluation and Program Planning* 1979; 2:127–136.

Bry, B.H. and George, F.E., The preventative effects of early intervention on the attendance and grades of urban adolescents, *Professional Psychology* 1980; 11:252–260.

Bry, B.H., Reducing the incidence of adolescent problems through preventive intervention: One- and five-year follow-up, *American Journal of Community Psychology* 1982; 10:265–276.

REFERENCES

Bullock, K. and Tilly, N., Analysis: Lessons from the crime reduction programme, in *Mainstreaming Problem-Oriented Policing*, Knutsson, J., Ed., Crime Prevention Studies, Vol. 15, Criminal Justice Press, Monsey, NY, 2003, pp. 147–181.

Bureau of Justice Assistance, Comprehensive communities program: Program account, *BJA Bulletin*, Bureau of Justice Assistance, U.S. Department of Justice, Washington, DC, 2001, http://www.ncjrs.org/pdffiles1/bja/184955.pdf (accessed July 21, 2014).

Bureau of Justice Statistics, Criminal victimization in the United States, 1985, U.S. Department of Justice, Washington, DC, 1987.

Bureau of Justice Statistics, Reducing crime through intelligence-led policing, National Institute of Justice, Bureau of Justice Statistics, Washington, DC, 2008, https://www.ncirc.gov/documents/public/reducing_crime_through_ilp.pdf (accessed July 21, 2014).

Bursik, R.J. and Grasmick, H., *Neighborhoods and Crime: The Dimensions of Effective Community Control*, Lexington Books, Lanham, MD, 1993.

Bushway, S. and Reuter, P., Labor markets and crime risk factors, in *Preventing Crime: What Works, What Doesn't, What's Promising. A Report to the United States Congress*, Sherman, L.W. et al., Eds., National Institute of Justice, Washington, DC, 1997, Chap. 6.

Bynum, T.S. and Purri, D.M., Crime and architectural style: An examination of the environmental design hypothesis, *Criminal Justice and Behavior* 1984; 11(2):179–196.

Calgary Herald, Police smash credit card ring: Calgary focus of massive investigation, *Calgary Herald*, February 1, 2002.

Calgary Police Service, 2006–2008 business plan, Calgary Police Service, Calgary, Alberta, Canada, 2006, http://www.calgarypolice.ca/news/pdf/2006-business-plan.pdf (accessed March, 2008).

Callahan, M., Feminist community organizing in Canada: Postcards from the edge, in *Community Organizing: Canadian Experiences*, Wharf, B. and Clague, M., Eds., Oxford University Press, Toronto, Ontario, Canada, 1997, pp. 181–204.

Camilli, G., Vargas, S., Ryan, S., and Barnett, W.S., Meta-analysis of the effects of early education interventions on cognitive and social development, *Teachers College Record* 2010; 112(3):579–620.

Campbell Collaboration Crime and Justice Group (accessed February 1, 2014). http://www.campbellcollaboration.org/crime_and_justice/index.php.

Canadian Criminal Justice Association, Safer communities: A social strategy for crime prevention in Canada, *Canadian Journal of Criminology* 1989; 31(4):360–579.

Canadian Federation of Municipalities, CSCP08.2.06: National action to prevent crime and enhance community safety. *2008 Annual Conference Decision: Category "A"*; Resolution Adopted, 2008, http://www.crimepreventionottawa.ca/uploads/files/initiative/cscp06.2.06nationalactionpreventcrime.pdf (accessed October, 2013).

Canadian Forum for Crime Prevention, Forum on evidence-based crime prevention for Canada agenda for safer Canada, Waterloo Region, Ontario, Canada, December 4–6, 2003, http://www.socialsciences.uottawa.ca/ipc/pdf/reports_4-3-3.pdf (accessed April, 2005).

Canadian Press, Police say Calgary headquarters of counterfeit credit card operation, *Canadian Press Newswire*, January 31, 2002.

Cantor, D. and Land, K.C., Unemployment and crime rates in the post-World-War-II United States: A theoretical and empirical analysis, *American Sociological Review* 1985; 50(3):317–332.

Caplan, M., Weissberg, R.P., Grober, J.S., Sivo, P.J., Grady, K., and Jacoby, C., Social competence promotion with inner-city and suburban young adolescents: Effects on social adjustment and alcohol use, *Journal of Consulting and Clinical Psychology* 1992; 60:56–63.

Carr, P.J., Citizens, community, and crime control: The problems and prospects for negotiated order, *Criminology and Criminal Justice* 2012; 12:397–412.

Carter, D.L., Measuring quality: The scope of community policing, in *Quantifying Quality in Policing*, Hoover, L.T., Ed., Police Executive Research Forum, Washington, DC, 1996, pp. 73–94.

Catterall, J.S., *On the Social Cost of Dropping Out*. Center for Education Research, Stanford, CA, 1985.

REFERENCES

Center for Problem-Oriented Policing, Belmont Neighborhood Violence Reduction Project, Charlotte-Mecklenburg Police Department, Charlotte, NC, submission to the Herman Goldstein Award Program, 2005, http://www.popcenter.org/library/awards/goldstein/2005/05-04(F).pdf (accessed July 21, 2014).

Center for Problem-Oriented Policing, Cruising abatement project: Reducing street cruising and related crime, Santa Ana Police Department, Santa Ana, CA, submission to the Herman Goldstein Award program, 1997, http://www.popcenter.org/library/awards/goldstein/1997/97-60(F).pdf.

Center for Problem-Oriented Policing, Graffiti prevention and suppression—Winning project, San Diego Police Department, San Diego, CA, submission to the Herman Goldstein Award program 2000, http://www.popcenter.org/library/awards/goldstein/2000/00-28(W).pdf.

Center for Problem-Oriented Policing, Repairing neighborhoods with partnerships, Joliet, IL, Police Department, submission to the Goldstein Awards 2000, http://www.popcenter.org/library/awards/goldstein/2000/00-12(F).pdf (accessed July 21, 2014).

Center for Problem-Oriented Policing, Surrey street standards tackling anti-social behaviour, Surrey Police, U.K., submission to the Herman Goldstein Award Program, 2003, http://www.popcenter.org/library/awards/goldstein/2003/03-51(F).pdf (accessed July 21, 2014).

Center for Problem-Oriented Policing, The Chula Vista residential burglary reduction project, Chula Vista Police Department, Chula Vista, CA, submission to the Herman Goldstein Award Program, 2001, http://www.popcenter.org/library/awards/goldstein/2001/01-12(F).pdf (accessed July 21, 2014).

Center for Problem-Oriented Policing, The Elite Arcade: Taming a Crime Generator, Herman Goldstein Awards, http://www.popcenter.org/library/awards/goldstein/1997/97-12(F).pdf (accessed July 21, 2014).

Center for Problem-Oriented Policing, The Hopwood Triangle: Revitalizing a depressed neighbourhood in Lancashire, submission to the Herman Goldstein Awards 2004, http://www.popcenter.org/library/awards/goldstein/2004/04-23(F).pdf (accessed July 21, 2014).

Center for Problem-Oriented Policing, The key elements of problem-oriented policing, 2008b, http://www.popcenter.org/about/?p=elements (accessed July 21, 2014).

Center for Problem-Oriented Policing, The SARA model, 2008a, http://www.opcenter.org/about/?p=sara (accessed July, 2009).

Center for Problem-Oriented Policing, The transient enrichment network (TEN-4) Fontana Police Department, Fontana, CA, submission to the Herman Goldstein Award Program, 1998, http://www.popcenter.org/library/awards/goldstein/1998/98-20(F).pdf (accessed July 21, 2014).

Center for the Study of Violence Prevention, Institute of Behavioral Science, University of Colorado, Boulder, http://www.colorado.edu/cspv/.

Central Office of Information, *Practical Ways to Crack Crime*: The Handbook, Central Office of Information, London, 1989.

Chalom, M., Léonard, L., Vanderschueren, F., and Vézina, C., Urban safety and good governance: The role of the police, International Centre for the Prevention of Crime and Habitat (Safer Cities Programme), Montreal, Quebec, Canada, 2001, http://mirror.unhabitat.org/pmss/listItemDetails.aspx?publicationID=1337 (accessed July 21, 2014).

Chambers, R.W., Gainesville convenience store security measures ordinance: A review and analysis, Assets Protection Systems Associates, Largo, FL, 1988.

Chatterjee, J.A., *Gang Prevention and Intervention Strategies*, Royal Canadian Mounted Police, Ottawa, Ontario, Canada, 2006. http://publications.gc.ca/collections/collection_2007/rcmp-grc/PS64-38-2007E.pdf (accessed July 21, 2014).

Chatterjee, J.A., Report on the evaluation of RCMP restorative justice initiative: Community justice forum as seen by participants, Royal Canadian Mounted Police Research and Evaluation Branch, Ottawa, Ontario, Canada, 1999, http://www.rcmp-grc.gc.ca/pubs/ccaps-spcca/restor-repara-chaterjee-eng.htm (accessed July 21, 2014).

Chen, D., Goldman to invest in city jail program, profiting if recidivism falls sharply, *New York Times*, August 2, 2012. p. A14.

Cherney, A., Harnessing the crime control capacities of third parties, *Policing: An International Journal of Police Strategies & Management* 2008; 31(4):631–647.

Chicago Area Project, n.d. www.chicagoareaproject.org (accessed July 21, 2014).

Chicago Police Department, 2007 annual report: A year in review, Chicago Police Department, Chicago, IL, 2008. https://portal.chicagopolice.org/portal/page/portal/ClearPath/News/Statistical%20Reports/Annual%20Reports/07AR.pdf (accessed July 21, 2014).

Chilenski, S.M., Bumbarger, B.K., Kyler, S., and Greenberg, M.T., Reducing youth violence and delinquency in Pennsylvania: PCCD's Research-Based Programs Initiative, Prevention Research Center for the Promotion of Human Development, Pennsylvania State University, University Park, PA, 2007.

Chou, C.P., Montgomery, S., Pentz, M.A., Rohrbach, L.A., Johnson, C.A., and Flay, B.R., Effects of a community-based prevention program on decreasing drug use in high-risk adolescents, *American Journal of Public Health* 1998; 88(6):944–948.

Cisneros, H.G., Defensible space: Deterring crime and building community, U.S. Department of Housing and Urban Development, Washington, DC, 1995. http://www.huduser.org/periodicals/cityscpe/spissue/ch2.pdf (accessed July 21, 2014).

City of Newcastle, Crime prevention plan, The City of Newcastle, New South Wales, Australia, 2001, http://www.newcastle.nsw.gov.au/ (accessed June, 2005).

City of San Antonio, Boards and commissions agendas, n.d., http://epay.sanantonio.gov/BoardComm/ (accessed May, 2009).

City of Toronto, Toronto. My city. A safe city. A community safety strategy for the City of Toronto, Task Force on Community Safety, Toronto, Ontario, Canada, 1999, http://www.city.toronto.on.ca/safety/sftyrprt.htm (accessed October, 2003).

City of Vancouver, Beach Neighbourhood East (500 Pacific Street) CD-1 guidelines, City of Vancouver, Vancouver, British Columbia, Canada, 1996.

City of Vancouver, Neighbourhood Integrated Service Teams (NIST), n.d. http://www.city.vancouver.bc.ca/nist/nis_teams.htm (accessed January, 2002).

CIVITAS (The Institute for the Study of Civil Society), Principles of good policing, http://www.civitas.org.uk/pubs/policeNine.php (accessed July 21, 2014).

Clare, J., Brantingham, P., and Brantingham, P., Problem-oriented policing approaches to outdoor Cannabis growing, Prepared for Research and National Coordination Organized Crime Division Law Enforcement and Policy Branch Public Safety Canada, Ottawa, report no. 005, 2010, http://publications.gc.ca/collections/collection_2012/sp-ps/PS4-92-2010-eng.pdf (accessed July 21, 2014).

Clark, P., Preventing future crime with cognitive behavioral therapy, *NIJ Journal* 2010; 265:22–25.

Clarke, C., Between a rock and a hard place, RCMP organizational change, *Policing: An International Journal of Police Strategies and Management* 2002; 25(1):14–31.

Clarke, R. and Eck, J., *Crime Analysis for Problem Solvers in 60 Small Steps*, Office of Community Oriented Policing, Washington, DC, 2005. http://www.popcenter.org/library/reading/PDFs/60steps.pdf (accessed July 21, 2014).

Clarke, R.V. and Cornish, D.B., Modeling offender's decisions: A framework for policy and research, in *Crime and Justice: An Annual Review of Research 6*, Tonry, M. and Morris, N., Eds., University of Chicago, Chicago, IL, 1985, pp. 147–185.

Clarke, R.V. and Goldstein, H., Reducing theft at construction sites: Lessons from a problem-oriented project, in *Analysis for Crime Prevention*, Tilly, N., Ed., Crime Prevention Studies, Vol. 13, Criminal Justice Press, Monsey, NY, 2002, pp. 89–130.

Clarke, R.V. and Goldstein, H., Thefts from cars in center city parking facilities: A case study in implementing problem oriented policing, in *Problem-Oriented Policing: From Innovation to Mainstream*, Knuttsson, J., Ed., Crime Prevention Studies, Vol. 15, Criminal Justice Press, Monsey, NY, 2003.

Clarke, R.V., Introduction, in *Situational Crime Prevention: Successful Case Studies*, 2nd edn., Clarke, R.V., Ed., Harrow and Heston, Albany, NY, 1997, pp. 2–43.

Clarke, R.V., Situational crime prevention: Its theoretical basis and practical scope, in *Crime and Justice: An Annual Review of Research*, Tonry, M. and Morris, N., Eds., University of Chicago Press, Chicago, IL, 1983.

Clary, E.G. and Rhodes, J.E., *Mobilizing Adults for Positive Youth Development: Strategies for Closing the Gap Between Beliefs and Behaviors*, Springer, New York, 2006.

Classen, R., Restorative justice—Fundamental principles, paper presented at *UN Alliance of NGOs Working Party on Restorative Justice*, 1996, http://peace.fresno.edu/docs/rjprinc.html (accessed July, 2014).

Clayton, R.R., Cattarello, A.M., and Johnstone, B.M., The effectiveness of drug abuse resistance education (project dare): Five year follow-up results, *Preventive Medicine* 1997; 25:307–318.

Clemson University, National Dropout Prevention Center/Network, n.d. Available at: http://www.dropoutprevention.org/effective-strategies (accessed December 1, 2013).

Clotfelter, C.T., Explaining unselfish behavior: Crime and the helpful bystander, *Journal of Urban Economics* 1980; 8:196–212.

Cloward, R. and Ohlin, L., *Delinquency and Opportunity*, Free Press, New York, 1960.

Coelli, M., Green, D.A., and Warburton, W., Breaking the cycle? The effect of education on welfare receipt among children of welfare recipients, *Journal of Public Economics* 2007; 91(7–8):1369–1398.

Cohen, A., *Delinquent Boys*, Free Press, Granville, NY, 1955.

Cohen, L.E. and Felson, M., Social change and crime rate trends: A routine activity approach, *American Sociological Review* 1979; 44:588–608.

Colins, O., Vermeiren, R., Vreugdenhil, C., Van den Brink, W., Doreleijers, T., and Broekaert, E., Psychiatric disorders in detained male adolescents: A systematic literature review, *Canadian Journal of Psychiatry* 2010; 55:255–263.

Collingwood Community Policing Centre, n.d. http://www.collingwoodcpc.com/ (accessed February, 2007).

Community Oriented Policing Services, Community Oriented Policing Services web site (accessed January 29, 2014). Available at: http://www.cops.usdoj.gov/Default.asp?Item=35.

Community Policing Consortium, Understanding community policing: A framework for action, Bureau of Justice Assistance, Department of Justice, Washington, DC, 1994. https://www.ncjrs.gov/pdffiles/commp.pdf (accessed July 21, 2014).

Conduct Problems Prevention Research Group, A developmental and clinical model for the prevention of conduct disorder: The fast track program, *Development and Psychopathology* 1992; 4:509–527.

Conklin, J.E., *The Impact of Crime*, MacMillan, New York, 1975.

Connell, N.M., Miggans, K., and McGloin, J.M., Can a community policing initiative reduce serious crime? A local evaluation, *Police Quarterly* 2008; 11(2):127–150.

Connor, D.F., *Aggression and Antisocial Behavior in Children and Adolescents: Research and Treatment*, Guilford Press, New York, 2002.

Conservative Party, *Prisons with a Purpose: Our Sentencing and Rehabilitation Revolution to Break the Cycle of Crime*, The Conservative Party, London, U.K., 2009.

Coolbaugh, K. and Hansel, C.J., The comprehensive strategy: Lessons learned from the pilot sites, *Juvenile Justice Bulletin*, Office of Juvenile Justice and Delinquency Prevention, U.S. Department of Justice, Washington, DC, March 2000, https://faculty.unlv.edu/mccorkle/www/Comprehensive%20Strategy%20Lessons%20Learned.pdf (accessed July 21, 2014).

Cooper, A. and Smith, E.L., Homicide trends in the United States, 1980–2008: Annual rates for 2009 and 2010, U.S. Department of Justice, Office of Justice Programs, Bureau of Justice Statistics, Washington, DC, 2011.

Copeland, W.E. et al., Which childhood and adolescent psychiatric disorders predict which young adult disorders? *Archives of General Psychiatry* 2009; 66(7):764–772.

Corcoran, T.B., Effective secondary schools, in *Reaching for Excellence: An Effective Schools Sourcebook*, Kyle, R.M., Ed., U.S. Government Printing Office, Washington, DC, 1985.

REFERENCES

Cordner, G. and Biebel, E., *Research for Practice: Problem-Oriented Policing in Practice*, National Criminal Justice Reference Service, Washington, DC, 2003. https://www.ncjrs.gov/pdffiles1/nij/grants/200518.pdf (accessed July 21, 2014).

Cordner, G.W., Community policing: Elements and effects, *Critical Issues in Policing: Contemporary Readings*, Dunham, R.G. and Alpert, G.P., Eds., Waveland, Prospect Heights, IL, 2001, pp. 493–510.

Cornish, D.B. and Clarke, R.V., Opportunities, precipitators, and criminal decisions: A reply to Wortley's critique of situational crime prevention, in *Theory for Practice in Situational Crime Prevention*, Smith, M.J. and Cornish, D.B., Eds., Criminal Justice Press, Monsey, NY, 2003, pp. 41–96.

Correctional Services Canada, Task force report on the reduction of substance abuse, Correctional Services Canada, Ottawa, Ontario, Canada, 1991.

Council of State Governments, Lessons from the States: Reducing recidivism and curbing corrections costs through justice reinvestment, Council of State Governments Justice Center, New York, 2013. http://csgjusticecenter.org/jr/kansas/media-clips/lessons-from-the-states-reducing-recidivism-and-curbing-corrections-costs-through-justice-reinvestment/ (accessed July 21, 2014).

Council of State Governments, Mental health courts: A primer for policymakers and practitioners, The Department of Justice, Bureau of Justice Assistance, Washington, DC, 2008.

Crank, J., Watchman and community: Myth and institutionalization, in Policing, *Law and Society Review* 1994; 28(2):325–351.

Crawford, A., Crime prevention and community safety, in *The Oxford Handbook of Criminology*, 4th edn., Maguire, M., Morgan, R., and Reiner, R., Eds., Oxford University Press, Oxford, U.K., 2007, pp. 866–909.

Crawford, A., Questioning appeals to community within crime prevention and control, *European Journal on Criminal Policy and Research* 1999; 7:509–530.

Crawford, A., *The Local Governance of Crime: Appeals to Community and Partnerships*, Clarendon Press, Oxford, U.K., 1999.

Crawford, A., *The Local Governance of Crime: Appeals to Community and Partnerships*, Oxford: Clarendon Press, 1997.

Crawford, A., The partnership approach to community crime prevention: Corporatism at the local level? *Social & Legal Studies* 1994; 3(4):497–519.

Crime Concern, n.d. http://www.crimeconcern.org.uk/ (accessed July 21, 2014).

Crimesolution.gov., Parenting with love and limits, n.d., https://www.crimesolutions.gov/ProgramDetails.aspx?ID=189 (accessed July 21, 2014).

Criminal Intelligence Service Canada, Annual report on organized crime, 2006, Criminal Intelligence Service Canada, Ottawa, Ontario, Canada, 2006.

Crowe, T.D., *Crime Prevention through Environmental Design: Applications of Architectural Design and Space Management Concepts*, Butterworth, Boston, MA, 1991.

Cuijpers, P., Van Straten, A., and Smit, F., Preventing the incidence of new cases of mental disorders: A meta-analytic review, *The Journal of Nervous and Mental Disease* 2005; 193(2):191–125.

Daly, K.W., Planning theory in search of an audience, in *The Structural Crisis of the 1970s and Beyond: The Need for a New Planning Theory*, Goldstein, H.A. and Rosenberry, S.A., Eds., Virginia Polytechnic Institute and State University, Blacksburg, VA, 1978, pp. 192–201.

Davis, R. and Garrison, P., Mentoring: In search of a taxonomy. Thesis submitted in partial fulfillment of the requirements for the Degree of Master of Science, Massachusetts Institute of Technology, Boston, MA, 1979.

DeGusti, B., MacRae, L., Vallée, M., Caputo, T., and Hornick, J.P., Best practices for chronic/persistent youth offenders in Canada: Summary report, Canadian Research Institute for Law and the Family and Centre for Initiatives on Children, Youth and the Community, Ottawa, Ontario, Canada, 2009. http://www.publicsafety.gc.ca/cnt/rsrcs/pblctns/prstnt-ffndrs/index-eng.aspx (accessed July 21, 2014).

Delaney, T., *American Street Gangs*, Pearson Prentice Hall, Upper Saddle River, NJ, 2006.

de Leon, J., Seattle police turn to computer software to predict, fight crime, *Seattle Times*, February 27, 2013. http://blogs.seattletimes.com/today/2013/02/seattle-police-turn-to-computer-software-to-fight-crime/?utm_medium=referral&utm_source=t.co (accessed July, 2014).

Deming, D., Early childhood intervention and life-cycle skill development: Evidence from head start, *American Economic Journal: Applied Economics* 2009; 1(3):111–134.

Dempsey, J.S., *Policing: An Introduction to Law Enforcement*, West, St. Paul, MN, 1994.

Department of Justice Canada, A statistical analysis of the impacts of the 1977 firearms control legislation, Research, Statistics and Evaluation Directorate, Department of Justice Canada, Ottawa, Ontario, Canada, 1996.

Department of Justice Canada, Canada's youth criminal justice act: A new law—A new approach, Department of Justice, Ottawa, Ontario, Canada, 2003.

de Souza Briggs, X., Community Building, in *Encyclopedia of Community: From the Village to the Virtual World*, Vol. 1, Christensen, K. and Levinson, D., Eds., Sage, Thousand Oaks, CA, 2003, pp. 246–250.

Dhiri, S., Goldblatt, P., Brand, S., and Price, R., Evaluation of the United Kingdom's Crime Reduction Programme: Analysis of costs and benefits, in *Costs and Benefits of Preventing Crime*, Welsh, B.C., Farrington, D.P., and Sherman, L.W., Eds., Westview Press, Boulder, CO, 2001, pp. 179–201.

Dishion, T.J., Patterson, G.R., and Kavanagh, K.A., An experimental test of the coercion model: Linking theory, measurement and intervention, in *Preventing Anti-Social Behavior: Interventions from Birth through Adolescence*, McCord, J. and Tremble, R.E., Eds., Guilford Press, New York, 1992.

Ditton, J., Nair, G., Hunter, G., and Phillips, S., *Street Lighting and Crime: The Strathclyde Twin Site Study*, Criminology Research Unit, Glasgow University, Glasgow, Scotland, 1992.

Dobson, C., *The Citizen's Handbook*, Vancouver Citizens' Committee, Vancouver, British Columbia, Canada, 2005, http://www.vcn.bc.ca/citizens-handbook/ (accessed September, 2003).

Dodge, K.A., Effects of intervention on children at high risk for conduct problems, paper presented at the biennial meeting of the *Society for Research in Child Development*, New Orleans, LA, March 1993.

Donnelly, P.G. and Majka, T.J., Residents' efforts at neighborhood stabilization: Facing the challenges of inner-city neighborhoods, *Sociological Forum* 1998; 13(2):189–213.

Doran, N., Luczak, S., Bekman, N., Koutsenok, I., and Brown, S., Adolescent substance use and aggression: A review, *Criminal Justice and Behavior* 2012; 39:748–769.

Dowds, L. and Mayhew, P., Participation in neighbourhood watch: Findings from the 1992 British Crime Survey, *Home Office Research and Statistics Department: Research Findings*, 1994; 11:1–4.

Downey, P.M. and Roman, J.K., *A Bayesian Meta-Analysis of Drug Court Cost-Effectiveness*, The Urban Institute, Washington, DC, 2010. http://www.dccrimepolicy.org/costbenefitanalysis/images/12-10-Bayesian-Cost-Benefit-Drug-Court_2.pdf (accessed July 21, 2014).

DuBois, D.L, Holloway, B.E., Valentine, J.C., and Cooper, H., Effectiveness of mentoring programs for youth: A meta-analytic review, *American Journal of Community Psychology* 2002; 30(2):157–197.

Dubow, F. and Emmons, D., The community hypothesis, in *Reactions to Crime*, Lewis, D.A., Ed., Sage, Beverly Hills, CA, 1981, pp. 167–181.

Duke, D.L., School organization, leadership, and student behavior, in *Strategies to Reduce Student Misbehavior*, Moles, O.C., Ed., U.S. Department of Education, Washington, DC, 1989.

Duncan, C.M., *Worlds Apart: Why Poverty Persists in Rural America*, Yale University Press, New Haven, CT, 1999.

Duncan, G.J. and Magnuson, K., Individual and parent-based intervention strategies for promoting human capital and positive behavior, in *Human Development Across Lives and Generations: The Potential for Change*, Chase-Landsale, P.L., Kiernana, K., and Friedman, R.J., Eds., Cambridge University Press, New York, 2004, pp. 93–138.

Dwyer, J., *Subway Lives: 24 Hours in the Life of the New York City Subway*, Crown, New York, 1991.

467

D'Amico, R., Geckeler, C., Henderson-Frakes, J., Kogan, D., and Moazed, T., Evaluation of the Second Chance Act (SCA): Adult demonstration 2009 grantees, Interim report, National Institute of Justice, Department of Justice, Washington, DC, 2013.

Early, K.W., Chapman, S.F., and Hand, G.A., Family-focused juvenile reentry services: A quasi-experimental design evaluation of recidivism outcomes, *Journal of Juvenile Justice* 2013; 2(2):1–22.

Eck, J.E. and Guerette, R.T., Place-based crime prevention: Theory, evidence and policy, in *The Oxford Handbook of Crime Prevention*, Welsh, B.C. and Farrington, D.P., Eds., Oxford University Press, Oxford, U.K., 2012, pp. 354–383.

Eck, J.E. and Rosenbaum, D.P., The new police order: Effectiveness, equity, and efficiency in community policing, in *The Challenge of Community Policing: Testing the Promises*, Rosenbaum, D.P., Ed., Sage, Thousand Oaks, CA, 1994, pp. 3–23.

Eck, J.E. and Spelman, W., Problem-solving: Problem-oriented policing in Newport news, Police Executive Research Forum, Washington, DC, 1987.

Eck, J.E. and Weisburd, D., Crime places in crime theory, in *Crime and Place*, Eck, J.E. and Weisburd, D., Eds., Willow Tree Press, Monsey, NY, 1995.

Eck, J.E., Assessing responses to problems: An introductory guide for police problem-solvers, Problem-oriented guides for police problem-solving tools series, No. 1, Office of Community Oriented Policing Services, U.S. Department of Justice, Washington, DC, 1999. http://www.popcenter.org/tools/pdfs/AssessingResponsesToProblems.pdf (accessed July 21, 2014).

Eck, J.E., Chainey, S., Cameron, J.G., Leitner, M., and Wilson, R.E., Mapping crime: Understanding hot spots, National Institute of Justice, Washington, DC, 2005. https://www.ncjrs.gov/pdffiles1/nij/209393.pdf (accessed July 21, 2014).

Eck, J.E., Preventing crime at places, in *Evidence-Based Crime Prevention*, Sherman, L.W., Farrington, D.P., Welsh, B.C., and MacKenzie, D.L., Eds., Routledge, New York, 2002, pp. 241–294.

Eck, J.E., Preventing crime at places, in *Evidence-Based Crime Prevention*, Sherman, L.W., Farrington, D.P., Welsh, B.C., and MacKenzie, D.L., Eds., Routledge, New York, 2006, pp. 241–294.

Eckblom, P., Law, H., Sutton, M., and Wiggins, R., Safer cities and domestic burglary, Home Office Research Study, No. 164, Home Office, London, U.K., 1996.

Eckblom, P., Proximal circumstances: A mechanism based classification of crime prevention, *Crime Prevention Studies*, Vol. 2, Criminal Justice Press, Monsey, NY, 1994, pp. 185–232.

Eckblom, P., The private sector and designing products against crime, in *The Oxford Handbook of Crime Prevention*, Welsh, B.C. and Farrington, D.P., Eds., Oxford University Press, Oxford, U.K., 2012, pp. 384–403.

Eckblom, P., Towards a discipline of crime prevention: A conceptual framework, Home Office Research and Statistics Directorate, London, U.K., 1996.

Eddy, J.M., Reid, J.B., and Fetrow, R.A., An elementary school-based prevention program targeting modifiable antecedents of youth delinquency and violence: Linking the interests of families and teachers (LIFT), *Journal of Emotional and Behavioral Disorders* 2000; 8(3):165–186.

Edwards, S., *The Principal's Role in Dropout Prevention: Seven Key Principles*, National Dropout Prevention Center/Network, Clemson University, Clemson, SC, 2008. http://www.dropoutprevention.org/sites/default/files/uploads/webcast/slides_20080226.pdf (accessed July 21, 2014).

Ekblom, P. et al., *Safer Cities and Domestic Burglary*. Home Office Research Study, No. 164, Home Office, London, U.K., 1996.

Ekici, N., Ozkan, M., Celik, A., and Maxfield, M., Outsmarting terrorists in Turkey, *Crime Prevention and Community Safety* 2008; 10(2):126–139.

Elliot, D. and Voss, H., *Delinquency and Dropout*, DC Health, Lexington, MA, 1974.

Elliott, D.S. and Menard, S., Delinquent friends and delinquent behavior: Temporal and developmental patterns, in *Delinquency and Crime: Current Theories*, Hawkins, J.D., Ed., Cambridge University Press, New York, 1996, pp. 26–67.

REFERENCES

Eluf, L.N., A new approach to law enforcement: The special women's police stations in Brazil, in *Freedom from Violence: Women's Strategies from around the World*, Schuler, M., Ed., United Nations Development Fund for Women, New York, 1992.

Embry, D.D., The good behavior game: A best practice candidate as a universal behavioral vaccine, *Clinical Child and Family Psychology Review* 2002; 5(4):273–297.

Enns, C. and Wilson, J., Sense of community and neighbourliness in Vancouver suburban communities: The picket fence project, *Plan Canada* 1999; 39(4):12–15.

Ersing, R., Community empowerment, in *Encyclopedia of Community*, Vol. 1, Christensen, K. and Levinson, D., Eds., Sage, Boston, MA, 2003, pp. 261–264.

Esbensen, F.-A. and Osgood, D.W., National evaluation of G.R.E.A.T, National Institute of Justice Research in brief, Washington, DC, November 1997.

Esbensen, F.-A., Evaluating G.R.E.A.T.: A school-based gang prevention program, U.S. Department of Justice, Office of Justice Programs, National Institute of Justice, Washington, DC, 2004. https://www.ncjrs.gov/pdffiles1/198604.pdf (accessed July 21, 2014).

European Economic and Social Committee, Opinion of the European Economic and Social Committee on the prevention of juvenile delinquency: Ways of dealing with juvenile delinquency and the role of the juvenile justice system in the European Union, *Official Journal of the European Union* 2006; 49(9):75–82.

European Forum for Urban Safety, Guidance on local safety audits: A compendium of international practice, European Forum for Urban Safety, Paris, France, 2007.

Exum, M.L., Kuhns, J.B., Koch, B., and Johnson, C., Examination of situational crime prevention strategies across convenience stores and fast-food restaurants, *Criminal Justice Policy Review* 2010; 21(3):269–295.

Fagan, J. and Chin, K.L., Violence as regulation and social control in the distribution of crack, in *Drugs and Violence: Causes, Correlates and Consequences*, De La Rosa, M., Lambert, E.Y., and Gropper, B., Eds., National Institute on Drug Abuse Monograph Series #103, National Institute on Drug Abuse, Washington, DC, 1990, pp. 8–43.

Fagan, J., Dumanovsky, T., Thompson, J.P., and Davies, G., Crime in public housing: Clarifying research issues, *National Institute of Justice Journal* 1998; (235):2–9. https://www.ncjrs.gov/pdffiles/jr000235.pdf (accessed July, 2014).

Fagan, J., Neighborhood education, mobilization, and organization for juvenile crime prevention, *The Annals of the American Academy of Political and Social Sciences* 1987; 494:54–70.

Farrall, S., Bottoms, A., and Shapland, J., Social structures and desistance from crime, *European Journal of Criminology* 2010; 7(6):546–570.

Farrington, D., Coid, J., Harnett, L., Jolliffe, D., Soteriou, N., Turner, R., and West, D., Criminal careers up to age 50 and life success up to age 48: New findings from the Cambridge Study in delinquent development, Home Office, London, U.K., 2006.

Farrington, D.P. and Loeber, R., Transatlantic replicability of risk factors in the development of delinquency, in *Historical and Geographical Influences on Psychopathology*, Cohen, P., Slomkowski, C., and Robins, L.N., Eds., Lawrence Erlbaum, Mahwah, NJ, 1999, pp. 299–329.

Farrington, D.P. and Ttofi, M.M., *School-Based Programs to Reduce Bullying and Victimization*, Campbell Systematic Reviews, Oslo, Norway, 2009. http://www.campbellcollaboration.org/news_/reduction_bullying_schools.php (accessed July 21, 2014).

Farrington, D.P. and Welsh, B.C., Effects of improved street lighting on crime: A systematic review, Home Office Research Study, No. 251, Home Office, London, U.K., 2007.

Farrington, D.P. and Welsh, B.C., Family-based crime prevention, in *Evidence-Based Crime Prevention*, Sherman, L.W., Farrington, D.P., Welsh, B.C., and MacKenzie, D.L., Eds., Routledge, New York, 2002, pp. 22–55.

Farrington, D.P. and West, D.J., Criminal, penal and life histories of chronic offenders: Risk and protective factors and early identification, *Criminal Behaviour and Mental Health* 1993; 3:492–523.

Farrington, D.P. and West, D.J., The Cambridge study in delinquent development: A long-term follow-up of 411 London males, in *Criminality: Personality, Behaviour and Life History*, Kerner, H.J. and Kaiser, G., Eds., Springer-Verlag, Berlin, Germany, 1990, pp. 115–138.

469

Farrington, D.P. et al., Risk and protective factors, in *Oxford Handbook of Crime Prevention*, Welsh, B.C. and Farrington, D.P., Eds., Oxford University Press, Oxford, 2012, pp. 46–69.

Farrington, D.P., Childhood aggression and adult violence: Early precursors and later-life outcomes, in *The Development and Treatment of Childhood Aggression*, Pepler, D.J. and Rubin, K.H., Eds., Erlbaum, Hillsdale, NJ, 1991, pp. 5–29.

Farrington, D.P., Childhood risk factors and risk-focused prevention, in *The Oxford Handbook of Criminology*, 4th edn., Maguire, M., Morgan, R., and Reiner, R., Eds., Oxford University Press, Oxford, U.K., 2007, pp. 602–640.

Farrington, D.P., Early predictors of adolescent aggression and adult violence, *Violence and Victims* 1989; 4:79–100.

Farrington, D.P., Implications of criminal career research for the prevention of offending, *Journal of Adolescence* 1990; 13:93–113.

Farrington, D.P., Loeber, R., and Van Kammen, W.B., Long-term universal outcomes of hyperactivity-impulsivity attention deficit and conduct problems in childhood, in *Straight and Devious Pathways from Childhood to Adulthood*, Robins, L.N. and Rutter, M., Eds., Cambridge University Press, Cambridge, U.K., 1990, pp. 62–81.

Farrington, D.P., Loeber, R., and Ttofi, M., Risk and protective factors for offending, in *The Oxford Handbook of Crime Prevention*, Welsh, B.C. and Farrington, D.P., Eds., Oxford University Press, Oxford, U.K., 2012, pp. 70–88.

Farrington, D.P., Multiple risk factors for multiple problem violent boys, in *Multi-problem Violent Youth: A Foundation for Comparative Research on Needs, Interventions and Outcomes*, Corrado, R.R., Roesch, R., Hart, S.D., and Gierowski, J.K., Eds., IOS Press, Amsterdam, the Netherlands, 2002, pp. 23–34.

Farrington, D.P., Predictors, causes and correlates of male youth violence, in *Youth Violence*, Vol. 24, Tonry, M. and Moore, M.H., Eds., University of Chicago Press, Chicago, IL, 1998, pp. 421–447.

Farrington, D.P., *Psychological Explanations of Crime*, Aldershot, Dartmouth, U.K., 1994.

Farrington, D.P., Stepping stones to adult criminal careers, in *Development of Antisocial and Prosocial Behavior*, Olweus, D., Block, J., and Radke-Yarrow, M., Eds., Academic Press, New York, 1986, pp. 359–384.

Fazel, S., Gulati, G., Linsell, L., Geddes, J.R., and Grann, M., Schizophrenia and violence: Systematic review and meta-analysis, *PLoS Medicine* 2009; 6(8). http://www.ncbi.nlm.nih.gov/pmc/articles/PMC2718581/pdf/pmed.1000120.pdf (accessed July, 2014).

Federal Bureau of Investigation, Crime in the United States, Table 38: Arrests, By Age, 2012, 2013 (accessed February 20, 2014). Available at: http://www.fbi.gov/about-us/cjis/ucr/crime-in-the-u.s/2012/crime-in-the-u.s.-2012/tables/38tabledatadecoverviewpdf.

Federal Bureau of Investigation, Intelligence defined, n.d., http://www.fbi.gov/about-us/intelligence/defined (accessed May 19, 2013).

Feins, J., Partnerships for neighbourhood crime prevention, National Institute of Justice, Washington, DC, 1983.

Felner, R.D. and Adan, A.M., The school transitional environment project: An ecological intervention and evaluation, in *14 Ounces of Prevention: A Casebook for Practitioners*, Price, R.H., Cowen, E.L., Lorion, R.P., and Ramos-McKay, J., Eds., American Psychological Association, Washington, DC, 1988, Chap. 9.

Felson, M. and Clarke, R.V., *Opportunity Makes the Thief: Practical Theory for Crime Prevention*, Police Research Series Paper 9, Vol. 98, Home Office, London, U.K., 1998.

Felson, M., Routine activities and crime prevention in the developing metropolis, *Criminology* 1987; 25(4):911–931.

Felson, R. and Staff, J. Explaining the academic performance–delinquency relationship, *Criminology* 2006; 44(2):299–320.

Fennelly, L., Designing security with the architects, in *Handbook of Loss Prevention and Crime Prevention*, Fennelly, L., Ed., Butterworths, Boston, MA, 1982, pp. 23–41.

Fielding, N., Community policing: Fighting crime or fighting colleagues? *International Journal of Police Science and Management* 2001; 3(4):289–302.

470

REFERENCES

Findlay, M. and Zvekic, U., *Analysing Informal Mechanisms of Crime Control: A Cross-Cultural Perspective*, United Nations Social Defence Research Institute, Rome, Italy, 1988.

Fisher, B. and Lab, S.P., *Encyclopedia of Victimology and Crime Prevention*, SAGE Publications, Thousand Oaks, CA, 2010.

Fisher, B. and Nasar, J., Fear of crime in relation to three exterior site features: Prospect, refuge, and escape, *Environment and Behavior* 1992; 24(1):35–65.

Fisher, R. and Kling, J., Leading the people: Two approaches to the role of ideology in community organizing, *Radical America* 1987; 21(1):31–45.

Fisher-Stewart, G., *Community Policing Explained: A Guide for Local Governments*, Office of Community-Oriented Policing Services, U.S. Department of Justice, Washington, DC, 2007.

Fishkin, J., *The Voice of the People: Public Opinion and Democracy*, Yale University Press, New Haven, CT, 1995.

Fitzgerald, R., Parenting, School contexts and violent delinquency, Crime and Justice Research Paper Series, Statistics Canada, Canadian Centre For Justice Statistics, Ottawa, Ontario, Canada, 2010. http://www.statcan.gc.ca/pub/85-561-m/85-561-m2010019-eng.pdf (accessed July 21, 2014).

Flint, J., Return of the governors: Citizenship and the new governance of neighbourhood disorder in the UK, *Citizenship Studies* 2002; 6(3):245–264.

Flynn, R., Communities that care: A comprehensive system for youth prevention and promotion, and Canadian applications to date, *International Prevention of Crime Review* 2008; 2:86–106.

Forrest, R. and Kearns, A., Social cohesion, social capital and the neighbourhood, *Urban Studies* 2001; 38(12):2125–2143.

Forst, M. and Bazemore, G., Community responses to crime, *Journal of California Law Enforcement* 1986; 20(3):100–105.

Foster, J., Hope, T., Dowds, L., and Sutton, M., *Housing, Community and Crime: The Impact of the Priority Estates Project*, Her Majesty's Stationary Office, London, U.K., 1993.

Fowler, F.J. and Mangione, T.W., *Neighborhood Crime, Fear and Social Control: A Second Look at the Hartford Program*, U.S. Department of Justice, Washington, DC, 1982.

Fowler, F.J., McCalla, M.E., and Mangione, T.W., *Reducing Residential Crime and Fear: The Hartford Neighborhood Crime Prevention Program*, U.S. Department of Justice, Washington, DC, 1979.

Fox, C. and Albertson, K., Payment by results and social impact bonds in the criminal justice sector: New challenges for the concept of evidence-based policy? *Criminology and Criminal Justice* 2011; 11:395–413.

Franklin Learning Systems, Inc., The Impulse Control Board Game. Facilitator Handbook. *Franklin Learning Systems*, Westport, CT, 2007.

Freidman, W., Volunteerism and the decline of violent crime, *Journal of Criminal Law & Criminology* 1998; 88(4):1453–1474.

Freres, D.R., Gillham, J.E., Reivich, K.J., and Shatté, A.J., Preventing depressive symptoms in middle school students: The Penn resiliency program, *International Journal of Emergency Mental Health* 2002; 4:31–40.

Friedmann, R.R., *Community Policing: Comparative Perspectives and Prospects*, St. Martin's Press, New York, 1992.

Gabor, T., Crime displacement and situational crime prevention: Toward the development of some principles, *Canadian Journal of Criminology* 1990; 32(1):41–74.

Gabor, T., The crime displacement hypothesis: An empirical examination, *Crime and Delinquency* 1981; 27:390–404.

Galaway, B. and Hudson, J., Eds., *Criminal Justice, Restitution, and Reconciliation*, Criminal Justice Press, Monsey, NY, 1990.

Gant, F. and Grabosky, P., *The Promise of Crime Prevention*, 2nd edn., Research and Public Policy Series, No. 31, Australian Institute of Criminology, Canberra, Australian Capital Territory, Australia, 2000.

Garces, E., Thomas, D., and Currie, J., Longer-term effects of head start, *The American Economic Review* 2002; 92(4):999–1012.

REFERENCES

Gardiner, R., *Design for Safe Neighborhoods*, U.S. Department of Justice, Washington, DC, 1982.

Garland, D., The limits of the sovereign state. Strategies of crime control in contemporary society, *The British Journal of Criminology* 1996; 36(4):445–471.

Garofalo, J. and McLeod, M., Improving the use and effectiveness of neighborhood watch programs, National Institute of Justice, Washington, DC, 1988.

Garofalo, J. and McLeod, M., The structure and operations of neighborhood watch programs in the United States, *Crime and Delinquency* 1989; 35(3):327–344.

Gatti, U. and Tremblay, E., Civic community as a factor of containment of violent crime: A criminological study of Italian regions and provinces, *Polis* 2000; 14(2):279–299.

Geason, S. and Wilson, P.R., Designing out crime: Crime prevention through environmental design, Australian Institute of Criminology, Canberra, Australian Capital Territory, Australia, 1989.

Geason, S. and Wilson, P.R., Preventing car theft and crime in car parks, Australian Institute of Criminology, Canberra, Australian Capital Territory, Australia, 1990.

Geason, S. and Wilson, P.R., Preventing graffiti and vandalism, Australian Institute of Criminology, Canberra, Australian Capital Territory, Australia, 1990.

Geason, S. and Wilson, P.R., Strategies for crime prevention, in *Crime Prevention: Theory and Practice*, Australian Institute of Criminology, Canberra, Australian Capital Territory, Australia, 1988.

Gibson, C.L., Unpacking the influence of neighborhood context and antisocial propensity on violent victimization of children and adolescents in Chicago, Report Submitted to the National Institute of Justice, Washington, DC, Award No: 2009-IJ-CX-0041, 2012.

Gillham, J.R. and Barnett, G.A., Decaying interest in burglary prevention, residence on a block with an active block club and community linkage, *Journal of Crime and Justice* 1994; 17(2):23–48.

Gillis, A.R. and Hagen, J., Bystander apathy and the territorial imperative, *Sociological Inquiry* 1983; 53(4):449–460.

Glick, B. and Goldstein, A.P., Aggression replacement training, *Journal of Counseling & Development* 1987; 65(7):356–362.

Golden, M. and Almo, C., *Reducing Gun Violence: An Overview of New York City's Strategies*, Vera Institute of Justice, New York, 2004. http://www.vera.org/pubs/reducing-gun-violence-overview-new-york-citys-strategies (accessed July 21, 2014).

Goldson, B., Youth crime, the 'parenting deficit' and state intervention: A contextual critique, *Youth Justice* 2002; 2(2):82–99.

Goldstein, A.P., Glick, B., and Gibbs, J.C., *Aggression Replacement Training: A Comprehensive Intervention for Aggressive Youth*, Research Press, Champaign, IL, 1998.

Goldstein, H., Foreword, in *The Challenge of Community Policing: Testing the Promises*, Rosenbaum, D.P., Ed., Sage, Thousand Oaks, CA, 1994, pp. viii–x.

Goldstein, H., Improving policing: A problem-oriented approach, *Crime & Delinquency* 1979; 25(2):236–243.

Goldstein, H., *Problem-Oriented Policing*, Temple University Press, Philadelphia, PA, 1990.

Goldstein, H., Toward community-oriented policing: Potential, basic requirements, and threshold questions, *Crime and Delinquency* 1987; 33(1):6–30.

Goode, W. and Smith, T.J., *Building from the Ground Up: Creating Effective Programs to Mentor Children of Prisoners*, Public/Private Ventures, Philadelphia, PA, 2005.

Gottfredson, D.C., An empirical test of school-based environmental and individual interventions to reduce the risk of delinquent behavior, *Criminology* 1986; 24:705–731.

Gottfredson, D.C., Changing school structures to benefit high-risk youths, in *Understanding Troubled and Troubling Youth*, Leone, P.E., Ed., Sage Publications, Newbury Park, CA, 1990.

Gottfredson, D.C., Gottfredson, G.D., and Hybl, L.G., Managing adolescent behavior: A multiyear, multischool study, *American Educational Research Journal* 1993; 30:179–215.

Gottfredson, D.C., School-based crime prevention, in *Preventing Crime: What Works, What Doesn't, What's Promising. A Report to the United States Congress*, Sherman, L.W. et al., Eds., National Institute of Justice, Washington, DC, 1997, Chap. 5. https://www.ncjrs.gov/works/ (accessed July 21, 2014).

Gottfredson, D.C., *Schools and Delinquency*, Cambridge University Press, New York, 2001.

Gottfredson, D.C., Wilson, D.B., and Skroban, N.S., School-based crime prevention, in *Evidence-Based Crime Prevention*, Sherman, L.W., Farrington, D.P., Welsh, B.C., and MacKenzie, D.L., Eds., Routledge, New York, 2006, pp. 56–164.

Gottfredson, G.D., *American Education—American Delinquency*, Center for Social Organization of Schools, Johns Hopkins University, Baltimore, MD, 1988.

Gottfredson, M.R. and Hirschi, T., *A General Theory of Crime*, Stanford University Press, Stanford, CA, 1990.

Government of Nova Scotia, Helping kids, Protecting communities: Response to the Nunn Commission, Government of Nova Scotia, Halifax, Nova Scotia, Canada, 2007. http://www.novascotia.ca/just/nunn_commission/_docs/NunnResponse.pdf (accessed July 21, 2014).

Graham, J., *Crime Prevention Strategies in Europe and North America*, Helsinki Institute for Crime Prevention and Control, affiliated with the United Nations, Helsinki, Finland, 1995.

Grasmick, H.G., Jacobs, D., and McCollom, C.B., Social class and social control: An application of deterrence theory, *Social Forces* 1983; 62:359–374.

Greenberg, M.T., Kusche, C.A., Cook, E.T., and Quamma, J.P., Promoting emotional competence in school-aged children: The effects of the paths curriculum, *Development and Psychopathology* 1995; (7):117–136.

Greenberg, M.T., The PATHS project: Preventive intervention for children, Final Report to the National Institute of Mental Health, Washington, DC, (Grant # R01MH42131), 1996.

Greenberg, S.W., Rohe, W.M., and Williams, J.R., *Informal Citizen Action and Crime Prevention at the Neighborhood Level: Synthesis and Assessment of the Research*, National Institute of Justice, Washington, DC, 1985.

Greenberg, S.W., Rohe, W.M., and Williams, J.R., Neighborhood conditions and community crime control, *Journal of Community Action* 1983; 19(5):39–42.

Greenberg, S.W., Rohe, W.M., and Williams, J.R., Neighborhood design and crime: A test of two perspectives, *Journal of the American Planning Association* 1984; 50:48–61.

Greenberg, S.W., Rohe, W.M., and Williams, J.R., *Safe and Secure Neighborhoods: Physical Characteristics and Informal Territorial Control in High and Low Crime Neighborhoods*, National Institute of Justice, Washington, DC, 1982.

Greene, J.R., Community policing and organization change, in *Community Policing: Can It Work?*, Skogan, W.G., Ed., Wadsworth, Belmont, CA, 2004, pp. 30–54.

Greenwood, P.W. and Welsh, B.C., Promoting evidence-based practice in delinquency prevention at the state level: Principles, progress, and policy directions, *Criminology & Public Policy* 2012; 11(3):491–492.

Greenwood, P.W., *Changing Lives: Delinquency Prevention as Crime-Control Policy*, University of Chicago Press, Chicago, IL, 2006.

Greenwood, P.W., Model, K., Rydell, C.P., and Chiesa, J., *Diverting Children from a Life of Crime Measuring Costs and Benefits*, Rand Corporation, Santa Monica, CA, 1998.

Greenwood, P.W., Prevention and intervention programs for juvenile offenders, *The Future of Children* 2008; 18(2):185–210.

Grossman, J.B. and Rhodes, J.E., The test of time: Predictors and effects of duration in youth mentoring relationships, *American Journal of Community Psychology* 2002; 30(2):199–219.

Grossman, J.B. and Tierney, J.P., Does mentoring work? An impact study of the big brothers/big sisters program, *Evaluation Review* 1998; 22:403–426.

Gundersen, K. and Svartdal, F., Aggression replacement training in Norway: Outcome evaluation of 11 Norwegian student projects, *Scandinavian Journal of Educational Research* 2006; 50(1):63–81.

Guyot, D., *Policing as Though People Matter*, Temple University Press, Philadelphia, PA, 1991.

Haapasalo, J. and Tremblay, R.E., Physically aggressive boys from ages 6 to 12: Family background, parenting behavior, and prediction of delinquency, *Journal of Consulting and Clinical Psychology* 1994; 62:1044–1052.

REFERENCES

Haeberle, S.H., Neighborhood identity and citizen participation, *Administration and Security* 1987; 19:178–196.

Hahn, A., Leavitt, T., and Aaron, P., Evaluation of the quantum opportunities program: Did the program work? A report on the post secondary outcomes and cost-effectiveness of the QOP program (1989–1993), Heller Graduate School, Center for Human Resources, Brandeis University, Waltham, MA, 1994.

Hale, L.F. and Canter, A., School dropout prevention: Information and strategies for educators, http://www.naspcenter.org/adol_sdpe.html (accessed November 19, 2013).

Hall, B.L., Participatory research, popular knowledge and power: A personal reflection, *Convergence* 1981; 14(3):6–17.

Hamilton, S.F., Hamilton, M.A., Hirsch, B.J., Hughes, J., King, J., and Maton, K., Community contexts for mentoring, *Journal of Community Psychology* 2006; 34(6):727–746.

Hartmann, D. and Depro, B., Rethinking sports-based community crime prevention. A preliminary analysis of the relationship between midnight basketball and urban crime rates, *Journal of Sport & Social Issues* 2006; 30(2):180–196.

Harvey, D., *The Urbanization of Capital: Studies in the History and Theory of Capitalist Urbanization*, John Hopkins University Press, Baltimore, MD, 1985.

Hastings, R. and Jamieson, W., Community mobilization and crime prevention: Report to the National Crime Prevention Centre, Department of Justice Canada, Ottawa, Ontario, Canada, 2002.

Hastings, R., Workshop report: Developing a strategic approach to criminal youth gangs, Institute for the Prevention of Crime, University of Ottawa, Ottawa, Ontario, Canada, 2010.

Hauber, A.R., Hofstra, L.J., Toornvliet, L.G., and Zanderbergen, J.G., *Stadswachten*, Department of Justice, The Hague, the Netherlands, 1994.

Hawkins, J.D. and Lam, T., Teacher practices, social development, and delinquency, in *Prevention of Delinquent Behavior*, Burchard, J.D. and Burchard, S.N., Eds., Sage, Newbury Park, CA, 1987.

Hawkins, J.D., Catalano, R.F., Morrison, D.M., O'Donnell, J., Abbott, R.D., and Day, L.E., The Seattle social development project: Effects of the first four years on protective factors and problem behaviors, in *Preventing Adolescent Antisocial Behavior: Interventions from Birth through Adolescence*, McCord, J. and Tremblay, R.E., Eds., Guilford Press, New York, 1992, pp. 139–161.

Hawkins, J.D., Doueck, H.J., and Lishner, D.M., Changing teaching practices in mainstream classrooms to improve bonding and behavior of low achievers, *American Educational Research Journal* 1988; 25:31–50.

Hawkins, J.D., Von Cleve, E., and Catalano, R.F., Reducing early childhood aggression: Results of a primary prevention program, *Journal of the American Academy of Child and Adolescent Psychiatry* 1991; 30:208–217.

Hayes, C.D., *Risking the Future: Adolescent Sexuality, Pregnancy, and Childbearing*, National Academies Press, Washington, DC, 1987.

Head Start Association, 2014, http://www.nhsa.org/ (accessed December, 2013).

Hedges, A., Blaber, A., and Mostyn, B., Community planning project: Cunningham road improvement scheme—Final report, Social and Community Planning and Research Agency, London, U.K., 1979.

Heilbrun, K., DeMatteo, D., Yasuhara, K., Brooks-Holliday, S., Shah, S., King, C., Bingham Dicarlo, A., Hamilton, D., and Laduke, C., Community-based alternatives for justice-involved individuals with severe mental illness: Review of the relevant research, *Criminal Justice and Behavior* 2012; 39(4):351–419.

Henggeler, S.W., Clingempeel, W.G., Brondino, M.J., and Pickrel, S.G., Four-year follow-up of multisystemic therapy with substance-abusing and substance dependent juvenile offenders, *Journal of the American Academy of Child and Adolescent Psychiatry* 2002; 41:868–874.

Henggeler, S.W., *Delinquency in Adolescence*, Sage, Newbury Park, CA, 1989.

Henggeler, S.W., Melton, G.B., Brondino, M.J., Scherer, D.G., and Hanley, J.H., Multisystemic therapy with violent and chronic juvenile offenders and their families: The role of treatment fidelity in successful dissemination, *Journal of Consulting and Clinical Psychology* 1997; 65:821–833.

REFERENCES

Henggeler, S.W., Rowland, M.D., Randall, J., Ward, D.M., Pickrel, S.G., Cunningham, P.B., Miller, S.L. et al., Home-based multisystemic therapy as an alternative to the hospitalization of youths in psychiatric crisis: Clinical outcomes, *Journal of the American Academy of Child and Adolescent Psychiatry* 1999; 38:1331–1339.

Henggeler, S.W., Schoenwald, S.K., Borduin, C.M., Rowland, M.D., and Cunningham, P.B., *Multisystemic Treatment of Antisocial Behaviour in Children and Adolescents*, Guilford Press, New York, 1998.

Henig, J.R., Citizens against crime: An assessment of the Neighborhood Watch Program in Washington, D.C., George Washington University, Center for Washington Area Studies, Washington, DC, 1984.

Herrenkohl, T.L. et al., School and community risk factors and interventions, in *Child Delinquents: Development, Intervention, and Service Needs*, Loeber, R. and Farrington, D.P. Eds., Sage Publications, Thousand Oaks, CA, 2009, pp. 211–246.

Hesseling, R., Thefts from cars: Reduced or displaced? *European Journal of Criminal Policy and Research* 1995; 3:79–92.

Heywood, P.R., Crane, P.R., Egginton, A., and Gleeson, J., *Out and About: In or Out? Better Outcomes from Young People's Use of Public & Community Space in the City of Brisbane*, Vol. 1: Introduction, Overview and Key Recommendations, Brisbane City Council, Brisbane, Queensland, Australia, 1998b.

Heywood, P.R., Crane, P.R., Egginton, A., and Gleeson, J., Young people in major centres: Needs, wants, constraints & recommended policies. A policy investigation and development project for Brisbane City Council, Brisbane City Council, Queensland, Brisbane, Australia, 1998a.

Hicks, D.C., Denat, F., and Arsenault, B., *Inspiring Police Practices: Crime Prevention Partnerships*, International Centre for the Prevention of Crime, Montreal, Quebec, Canada, 2000.

Hilborn, J., Dealing with crime and disorder in parks. Problem-Oriented Guides for Police, Response Guides Series, Number 9. US Department of Justice Office of Community Oriented Policing. Washington, DC, 2009. http://www.popcenter.org/responses/urban_parks (accessed March, 2013).

Hill, K.G. et al., Childhood risk factors for adolescent gang membership: Results from the Seattle Social Development Project, *Journal of Research in Crime and Delinquency* 1999; 36:300–322.

Hinkle, J.C. and Weisburd, D., The irony of broken windows policing: A micro-place study of the relationship between disorder, focused police crackdowns and fear of crime, *Journal of Criminal Justice* 2008; 36:503–512.

Hirschi, T., *Causes of Delinquency*, University of California Press, Berkeley, CA, 1969.

Hoeve, M., McReynolds, L.S., Wasserman, G.A., and McMillan, C., The influence of mental health disorders on severity of reoffending in juveniles, *Criminal Justice and Behavior* 2013; 40:289–301.

Hofferth, S.L., Programs for high risk adolescents: What works? *Evaluation and Program Planning* 1991; 14:3–16.

Homel, P., Delivering effective local crime prevention: Why understanding variations in municipal governance arrangements matters, in *International Report Crime Prevention and Community Safety: Trends and Perspectives*, International Centre for the Prevention of Crime, International Centre for the Prevention of Crime, Montreal, Quebec, Canada, 2010, pp. 118–120. http://www.crime-prevention-intl.org/fileadmin/user_upload/Publications/Crime_Prevention_and_Community_Safety_ANG.pdf (accessed July 21, 2014).

Homel, P., Nutley, S., Webb, B., and Tilly, N., Investing to deliver: Reviewing the implementation of the UK Crime Reduction Programme, Home Office Research, Development and Statistics Directorate, London, U.K., 2004.

Homel, R. and Homel, P., Implementing crime prevention: Good governance and a science of implementation, in *The Oxford Handbook of Crime Prevention*, Welsh, B.C. and Farrington, D.P., Eds., Oxford University Press, Oxford, U.K., 2012, pp. 423–445.

REFERENCES

Homel, R., Hauritz, M., Wortley, R., McIlwain, G., and Carvolth, R., Preventing alcohol-related crime through community action: The surfers paradise safety action project, in *Policing for Prevention: Reducing Crime, Public Intoxication and Injury*, Homel, R., Ed., Crime Prevention Studies, Vol. 7, Criminal Justice Press, Monsey, NY, 1997, pp. 35–90.

Home Office, *A New Approach to Fighting Crime*, Home Office, London, U.K., 2011.

Home Office, *Youth Crime Action Plan 2008*, Home Office, London, U.K., 2008.

Hope, T. and Foster, J., Conflicting forces: Changing the dynamics of crime and community on a 'problem' estate, *British Journal of Criminology* 1992; 32(4):488–504.

Hope, T., Building design and burglary, in *Coping with Burglary*, Clarke, R. and Hope, T., Eds., Kluwer-Nijhoff, Boston, MA, 1984, pp. 45–60.

Hope, T., Community crime prevention, in *Building a Safer Society: Strategic Approaches to Crime Prevention*, Tonry, M. and Farrington, D., Eds., University of Chicago Press, Chicago, IL, 1995, pp. 21–89.

Hope, T., Support for neighbourhood watch: A British crime survey analysis, in *Communities and Crime Reduction*, Hope, T. and Shaw, M., Eds., Her Majesty's Stationary Office, London, U.K., 1988, pp. 146–163.

Hough, M., Clarke, R., and Mayhew, P., Introduction, in *Designing Out Crime*, Clarke, R. and Mayhew, P., Eds., Her Majesty's Stationary Office, London, U.K., 1980.

House of Umoja, n.d. http://www.houseofumoja.org/ (accessed August 27, 2014).

Howell, J.C., Gang prevention: An overview of research and programs, *Juvenile Justice Bulletin*, Office of Juvenile Justice and Delinquency Prevention, December 2010, pp. 1–22, https://www.ncjrs.gov/pdffiles1/ojjdp/231116.pdf (accessed July, 2014).

Howell, J.C., Promising programs for youth gang violence prevention and intervention, in *Serious and Violent Offenders: Risk Factors and Successful Interventions*, Loeber, R. and Farrington, D., Eds., Sage, Thousand Oaks, CA, 1998, pp. 284–312.

Hudson, J. and Galaway, B., Introduction, in *Restorative Justice: International Perspectives*, Galaway, B. and Hudson, J., Eds., Criminal Justice Press, Monsey, NY, 1996, pp. 1–14.

Human Rights Watch, Ill-equipped: U.S. prisons and offenders with mental illness, Human Rights Watch, New York, 2003, http://www.hrw.org/reports/2003/usa1003/usa1003.pdf (accessed April, 2007).

Husain, S., Guidance on local safety audits: A compendium of international practice, Public Safety Canada, National Crime Prevention Centre, Ottawa, Ontario, Canada, 2007. http://efus.eu/files/fileadmin/efus/secutopics/EFUS_Safety_Audit_e_WEB.pdf (accessed July 21, 2014).

Husain, S., *Neighbourhood Watch and Crime: An Assessment of Impact*, Police Foundation, London, U.K., 1990.

Hutchings, J., Lane, E., Owen, R.E., and Gwyn, R., The Introduction of the Webster-Stratton Classroom Dinosaur School Programme in Gwynedd, North Wales: A pilot study, *Educational and Child Psychology* 2004; 21(4):4–15.

Immen, W., Team effort to cut crime transforms Jane-Finch, *Globe and Mail*, June 9, 2003, p. A10.

Institute for the Prevention of Crime Making cities safer: Action briefs for municipal stakeholders, Institute for the Prevention of Crime, University of Ottawa, Ottawa, Ontario, Canada, 2009. http://www.sciencessociales.uottawa.ca/ipc/eng/MCS_actionbriefs.asp (accessed March 20, 2013).

International Centre for the Prevention of Crime, International report crime prevention and community safety: Trends and perspectives, ICPC, Montreal, Quebec, Canada, 2008. http://www.crime-prevention-intl.org/fileadmin/user_upload/Publications/International_Report_on_Crime_Prevention_and_Community_Safety_ANG.pdf (accessed July 21, 2014).

International Centre for the Prevention of Crime, International report crime prevention and community safety: Trends and perspectives, ICPC, Montreal, Quebec, Canada, 2010. http://www.crime-prevention-intl.org/fileadmin/user_upload/Publications/Crime_Prevention_and_Community_Safety_ANG.pdf (accessed July 21, 2014).

International Centre for the Prevention of Crime, Police toolkit: The role of the police in crime prevention, ICPC, Montreal, Quebec, Canada, 2002, http://www.crime-prevention-intl.org/publications/pub_21_1.pdf (accessed February 27, 2003).

International Centre for the Prevention of Crime, The role of local government in community safety, Bureau of Justice Assistance, Department of Justice, 2001, Washington, DC, http://www.ncjrs.gov/pdffiles1/bja/184218.pdf (accessed July 21, 2014).

International Centre for the Prevention of Crime, Worldwide best practice in crime prevention: ICPC 100 best practices as of October 1997, n.d., http://www.crime-prevention-intl.org/publications/pub_107_1.pdf (accessed May, 2000).

Jacobs, J., *Death and Life of Great American Cities*, Random House, New York, 1961.

Jain, S. and Cohen, A.K., *The Power of Developmental Assets in Building Behavioral Adjustment among Youth Exposed to Community Violence: A Multidisciplinary Longitudinal Study of Resilience*, National Institute of Justice, Washington, DC, 2012.

James, D.J. and Glaze, L.E., Highlights: Mental health problems of prison and jail inmates, Bureau of Justice Statistics, Special Report, U.S. Department of Justice, Office of Justice Programs, September 2006, http://www.bjs.gov/content/pub/pdf/mhppji.pdf (accessed July 21, 2014).

Jamieson, W., Factors related to successful mobilization of communities for crime prevention, in *Towards More Comprehensive Approaches to Prevention and Safety. IPC Review*, Hastings, R. and Bania, M., Eds., Institute for the Prevention of Crime, University of Ottawa, Ottawa, Ontario, Canada, 2008, pp. 12–33.

John Howard Society of Alberta, Crime prevention through social development: A literature review, John Howard Society of Alberta, Edmonton, Alberta, Canada, 1995.

Johnson, C.A., Pentz, M.A., Weber, M.D., Dwyer, J.H., Baer, N., MacKinnon, D.P., Hansen, W.B., and Flay, B.R., Relative effectiveness of comprehensive community programming for drug abuse prevention with high-risk and low-risk adolescents, *Journal of Consulting & Clinical Psychology* 1990; 58:447–456.

Johnson, M.K., Crosnoe, R., and Elder, G.H., Student attachment and academic engagement: The role of ethnicity, *Sociology of Education* 2001; 74:318–340.

Johnson, S.D., Guerette, R., and Bowers, K., Crime displacement and diffusion of benefits, in *The Oxford Handbook of Crime Prevention*, Welsh, B.C. and Farrington, D.P., Eds., Oxford University Press, Oxford, U.K., 2012, pp. 337–353.

Jolliffe, D. and Farrington, D.P., Empathy and offending: A systematic review and metaanalysis, *Aggression and Violent Behaviour* 2004; 9:441–476.

Jones, M.B and Offord, D.R., Reduction of anti-social behavior in poor children by nonschool skill development, *Journal of Child Psychology and Psychiatry and Allied Disciplines* 1989; 30:737–750.

Jurich, S. and Estes, S., Raising academic achievement for America's youth: A study of 20 successful programs, American Youth Policy Forum, Washington, DC, 2000. http://www.aypf.org/publications/RAA/RAA.pdf (accessed July 21, 2014).

Kam, C.M., Greenberg, M., and Kusche, C., Sustained effects of the paths curriculum on the social and psychological adjustment of children in social and psychological adjustment of children in special education, *Journal of Emotional & Behavioral Disorders* 2004; 12(2):66–78.

Kappeler, V.E. and Gaines, L.K., *Community Policing: A Contemporary Perspective*, 6th edn., Anderson Publishing, Cincinnati, OH, 2012.

Kellan, K., Psycopaths have different brains: Study, *National Post*, May 7, 2012. http://news.nationalpost.com/2012/05/07/psychopaths-have-different-brains-study/ (accessed July, 2014).

Kelling, G.L. and Coles, C., *Broken Windows: Restoring Order and Reducing Crime in our Communities*, The Free Press, New York, 1996.

Kelling, G.L. and Moore, M., From political to reform to community: The evolving strategy of police, in *Community Policing: Rhetoric or Reality?*, Greene, J. and Mastrofski, S., Eds., Praeger, New York, 1988.

Kelling, G.L., Acquiring a taster for order: The community and police, *Crime and Delinquency* 1987; 33(1):90–102.

Kelling, G.L., Pate, A., Ferrara, A., Utne, M., and Brown, C.E., *Newark Foot Patrol Experiment*, The Police Foundation, Washington, DC, 1981.

REFERENCES

Kelly, B.T., Loeber, R., Keenan, K., and DeLamatre, M., Developmental pathways in boys' disruptive and delinquent behavior, Office of Juvenile Justice and Delinquency Prevention, Washington, DC, 1997.

Kelly, R., The nature of organized crime, in *Major Issues in Organized Crime Control*, Edelhertz, H., Ed., National Institute of Justice, Washington, DC, 1987.

Kendall, P.C., Cognitive-behavioral therapies with youth: Guiding theory, current status, and emerging developments, *Journal of Consulting and Clinical Psychology* 1993; 61(2):235–247.

Kennedy, D.M., Braga, A.A., and Piehl, A.M., *Reducing Gun Violence: The Boston Gun Project's Operation Ceasefire*, National Institute of Justice, Washington, DC, 2001. https://www.ncjrs. gov/pdffiles1/nij/188741.pdf (accessed July 21, 2014).

Kennedy, D.M., Piehl, A.M., and Braga, A.A., Youth violence in Boston: Gun markets, serious youth offenders, and a use-reduction strategy, *Law and Contemporary Problems* 1996; 59:147–196.

Kennedy, D.M., Pulling levers: Chronic offenders, high-crime settings, and a theory of prevention, *Valparaiso University Law Review* 1997; 31(2):449–484.

Kenney, D.J., Crime on the subways: Measuring the effectiveness of the guardian angels, *Justice Quarterly* 1986; 3:481–496.

Kim, C., Losen, D., and Hewitt, D., *The School-To-Prison Pipeline: Structuring Legal Reform*, NYU Press, New York, 2010.

Kines, L., Neighbours band together to save their community, *The Vancouver Sun*, February 6, 1992, p. A1.

King, M., How to make social crime prevention work: The French experience, NACRO Occasional Paper, London, U.K., 1988.

Kinscherff, R., A primer for mental health practitioners working with youth involved in the juvenile justice system, Technical Assistance Partnership for Child and Family Mental Health, Washington, DC, 2012. http://www.tapartnership.org/docs/jjResource_mentalHealthPrimer. pdf (accessed July 21, 2014).

Klein, M.W. and Maxson, C.L., *Street Gang Patterns and Policies*, Oxford University Press, New York, 2006.

Klein, M.W., *Street Gangs and Street Workers*, Prentice-Hall, Englewood Cliffs, NJ, 1971.

Klinteberg, B.A., Andersson, T., Magnusson, D., and Stattin, H., Hyperactive behaviour in childhood as related to subsequent alcohol problems and violent offending: A longitudinal study of male subjects, *Personality and Individual Differences* 1993; 15:381–388.

Knutsson, J., Restoring public order in a city park, in *Policing for Prevention: Reducing Crime, Public Intoxication and Injury*, Homel, R., Ed., Crime Prevention Studies, Vol. 7, Criminal Justice Press, Monsey, NY, 1997, pp. 133–151.

Kochel, T.R., Constructing hot spots policing: Unexamined consequences for disadvantaged populations and for police legitimacy, *Criminal Justice Policy Review* 2011; 22:350–374.

Konnerup, M. and Gill, C., The Campbell Collaboration and evidence-based crime prevention, *Translational Criminology* 2012; Fall:8–9. http://cebcp.org/wp-content/TCmagazine/TC3-Fall2012 (accessed July 21, 2014).

Koopman, I.C.H., Surveillance in public places by long-term unemployed, in *Setting the Stage for Community Safety: Report on Progress Towards World Change. Final Report of the First International Conference for Crime Prevention Practitioners*, Vancouver, British Columbia, Canada, March 31–April 3, 1996, Pearcey, P., Welsh, B., Waller, I., and French, S., Eds., Correctional Service Canada, Ottawa, Ontario, Canada, 1996.

Krug, E.G., Dahlberg, L.L., Mercy, J.A., Zwi, A.B., and Lozano, R., World report on violence and health, World Health Organization, Geneva, Switzerland, 2002. http://whqlibdoc.who.int/ hq/2002/9241545615.pdf (accessed July 21, 2014).

Lab, S. and Hope, T., Assessing the impact of area context on crime prevention behavior, paper presented at the *Environmental Criminology and Crime Analysis Conference*, Barcelona, Spain, 1998.

Lab, S., Citizen crime prevention: Domains and participation, *Justice Quarterly* 1990; 7:467–492.

Lab, S., *Crime Prevention: Approaches, Practices, and Evaluations*, 5th edn., Anderson Publishing (Lexis Nexis), New York, 2004.

Lab, S., Crime prevention: Where have we been and which way should we go?, in *Crime Prevention at a Crossroads*, Lab, S., Ed., Anderson Publishers, Cincinnati, OH, 1997, pp. 1–13.

Lahey, B.B., McBurnett, K., and Loeber, R., Are attention-deficit/hyperactivity disorder and oppositional defiant disorder developmental precursors to conduct disorder?, in *Handbook of Developmental Psychopathology*, 2nd edn., Sameroff, A., Lewis, M., and Miller, S.M., Eds., Plenum Press, New York, 2000, pp. 431–446.

Landenberger, N.A. and Lipsey, M.W., The positive effects of cognitive–behavioral programs for offenders: A meta-analysis of factors associated with effective treatment, *Journal of Experimental Criminology* 2005; 1:451–476.

Lasley, J., Designing out gang homicides and street assaults, National Institute of Justice, Research in Brief, November 1998. https://www.ncjrs.gov/txtfiles/173398.txt (accessed July, 2014).

Latanne, B. and Daley, J., *The Unresponsive Bystander: Why Doesn't He Help?* Appleton-Century-Crofts, New York, 1970.

Latessa, E.J. and Allen, H.F., Using citizens to prevent crime: An example of deterrence and community involvement, *Journal of Police Science and Administration* 1980; 8(1):69–74.

Latimer, J., Dowden, C., and Muise, D., The effectiveness of restorative justice practices: A meta-analysis, *The Prison Journal* 2005; 85:127–144.

Lattimore, P.K., Dryden-Witte, A., and Baker, J.R., Experimental assessment of the effect of vocational training on youthful property offenders, *Evaluation Review* 1990; 14(2):115–133.

La Vigne, N.G. and Lowry, S.S., Evaluation of camera use to prevent crime in commuter parking facilities: A randomized controlled trial. Report submitted to the National Institute of Justice, Washington, DC, Document No.: 236740, 2011. https://www.ncjrs.gov/pdffiles1/nij/grants/236740.pdf (accessed July 21, 2014).

Lavrakas, P.J. and Herz, L., Citizen participation in neighborhood crime prevention, *Criminology* 1982; 20:479–498.

Lavrakas, P.J. and Kushmuk, J.W., Evaluating crime prevention through environmental design: The Portland commercial demonstration project, in *Community Crime Prevention: Does it Work?*, Rosenbaum, D., Ed., Sage, Beverly Hills, CA, 1986, pp. 202–227.

Lavrakas, P.J., Citizen Self help and neighborhood crime prevention policy, in *American Violence and Public Policy*, Curtis, L.A., Ed., Yale University Press, New Haven, CT, 1985, pp. 87–115.

Laycock, G. and Austin, C., Crime prevention in parking facilities, *Security Journal* 1992; 3:154–160.

Laycock, G. and Webb, B., Designing out crime from the U.K. vehicle licensing system, in *Designing out Crime from Products and Systems,* Clarke, R.V. and Newman, G.R., Eds., Crime Prevention Studies, Vol. 18, Criminal Justice Press, Monsey, NY, 2005, pp. 203–230.

Laycock, G., Property marking: A deterrent to domestic burglary. Crime Prevention Unit Paper No. 3, Home Office, London, U.K., 1985.

LeBlanc, M. et al., The prediction of males' adolescent and adult offending from school experience, *Canadian Journal of Criminology* 1993; 35(4):459–478.

Lee, V.E. and Loeb, S., Where do head start attendees end up? One reason why preschool effects fade out, *Educational Evaluation and Policy Analysis* 1995; 17(1):62–82.

Leighton, B., The community concept in criminology: Toward a social network approach, *Journal of Research in Crime and Delinquency* 1988; 25(4):351–374.

Leighton, B., Visions of community policing: Rhetoric and reality in Canada, *Canadian Journal of Criminology* 1991; 33(3–4):485–522.

Leishman, F., Koban: Neighbourhood policing in contemporary Japan, *Policing: A Journal of Practice and Policy* 2007; 1(2):196–202.

Lenoir, E., Contractualization in the field of crime prevention in France, International report crime prevention and community safety: Trends and perspectives, International Centre for the Prevention of Crime, Montreal, Quebec, Canada, 2010, pp. 118–120. Nashville, Tennessee. http://www.crime-prevention-intl.org/fileadmin/user_upload/Publications/Crime_Prevention_and_Community_Safety_ANG.pdf (accessed July 21, 2014).

Lersch, K.M., *Space, Time, and Crime*, Carolina Academic Press, Durham, NC, 2007.

Leschied, A. and Cunningham, A., Seeking effective interventions for serious young offenders: Interim results of a four-year randomized study of multisystemic therapy in Ontario, Canada, London Family Court Clinic, London, Ontario, Canada, 2002.

Lewis, D.A. and Salem, G., Community crime prevention: An analysis of a developing perspective, *Crime and Delinquency* 1981; 27:405–421.

Lewis, D.A., Design problems in public policy development: The case of the community anti-crime program, *Criminology* 1979; 17:172–183.

Lewis, D.A., Grant, J.A., and Rosenbaum, D.P., *The Social Construction of Reform: Community Organizations and Crime Prevention*, Transaction Books, New Brunswick, NJ, 1988.

Lichterman, P., Beyond the seesaw model: Public commitment in a culture of self-fulfillment, *Sociological Theory* 1995; 13(3):275–300.

Liederbach, J., Fritsch, E.J., Carter, D.L., and Bannister, A., Exploring the limits of collaboration in community policing: A direct comparison of police and citizen views, *Policing: An International Journal of Police Strategies & Management* 2008; 31(2):271–291.

Lilly, J., Cullen, F., and Ball, R., *Criminological Theory: Context and Consequences*, Sage, Thousand Oaks, CA, 2007.

Limber, S.P. and Olweus, D., Evaluation research on the implementation of the Olweus Bullying Prevention Program in Pennsylvania Schools Summary of Findings, presented at the *Annual Meeting of the International Bullying Prevention Association*, 2013. https://www.clemson.edu/olweus/Summary%20of%20OBPP%20findings%20presented%20at%20IBPA.pdf (accessed July, 2014).

Linden, R., Building a safer community: A community-based crime prevention manual, Department of Justice, Ottawa, Ontario, Canada, 1996.

Linden, R., Crime prevention and urban safety in residential environments: Final report, Canadian Mortgage and Housing Corporation, Ottawa, Ontario, Canada, 1990.

Lindsay, B. and McGillis, D., Citywide community crime prevention: An assessment of the Seattle Program, in *Community Crime Prevention: Does it Work?*, Rosenbaum, D., Ed., Sage, Beverly Hills, CA, 1986, pp. 46–67.

Linquanti, R., Using community-wide collaboration to foster resilience in kids: A conceptual framework, *ERIC Digest*, Clearinghouse on Elementary and Early Childhood Education, Champaign, IL, 1992.

Lipsey, M.W. and Derzon, J.H., Predictors of violent or serious delinquency in adolescence and early adulthood: A synthesis of longitudinal research, in *Serious and Violent Juvenile Offenders: Risk Factors and Successful Interventions*, Loeber, R. and Farrington, D.P., Eds., Sage Publications, Thousand Oaks, CA, 1998, pp. 86–105.

Lipsey, M.W., Chapman, G.L., and Landenberger, N.A., Cognitive-behavioral programs for offenders, *The American Academy of Political and Social Science* 2001; 571(1):144–157.

Lipsey, M.W., The primary factors that characterize effective interventions with juvenile offenders: A meta-analytic overview of effective interventions, *Victims and Offenders: An International Journal of Evidence-Based Research, Policy, and Practice* 2009; 4(2):124–147.

Litschge, C.M., Vaughn, M.G., and McCrea, C., The empirical status of treatments for children and youth with conduct problems an overview of meta-analytic studies, *Research on Social Work Practice* 2010; 20(1):21–35.

Little, G.L., Meta-analysis of moral reconation therapy: Recidivism results from probation and parole implementations, *Cognitive-Behavioral Treatment Review* 2005; 14:14–16.

Little, G.L., Meta-analysis of MRT recidivism research on postincarceration adult felony offenders, *Cognitive-Behavioral Treatment Review* 2001; 10:4–6.

Lloyd, S., Farrell, G., and Pease, K., Preventing repeated domestic violence: A demonstration project on Merseyside, Home Office Crime Prevention Unit Paper 49, Home Office, London, U.K., 1994.

Lochman, J.E., Boxmeyer, C., Powell, N., Qu, L., Wells, K., and Windle, M., Dissemination of the coping power program: Importance of intensity of counselor training, *Journal of Consulting and Clinical Psychology* 2009; 77(3):397–409.

Lochman, J.E., Boxmeyer, C., Powell, N., Roth, D.L., and Windle, M., Masked intervention effects: Analytic methods for addressing low dosage of intervention, *New Directions for Evaluation* 2006; 110:19–32.

Lochman, J.E. and Wells, K.C., Contextual social–cognitive mediators and child outcome: A test of the theoretical model in the coping power program, *Development and Psychopathology* 2002; 14:945–967.

Lock, S. and Barrett, P.M., A longitudinal study of developmental differences in universal preventive intervention for child anxiety, *Behavior Change* 2003; 20:183–199.

Lockwood, S., Nally, J.M., Ho, T., and Knutson, K., The effect of correctional education on postrelease employment and recidivism: A 5-year follow-up study in the state of Indiana, *Crime & Delinquency* 2012; 58(3):380–396.

Loeber, R. and Hay, D.F., Developmental approaches to aggression and conduct problems, in *Development through Life: A Handbook for Clinicians*, Rutter, M.L. and Hay, D.H., Eds., Blackwell, Oxford, U.K., 1994, pp. 488–515.

Loeber, R. and Stouthamer-Loeber, M., Family factors as correlates and predictors of juvenile conduct problems and delinquency, in *Crime and Justice*, Tonry, M. and Morris, N., Eds., University of Chicago Press, Chicago, IL, 1986, pp. 29–149.

Lowman, J., Street prostitution control: Some Canadian reflections on the Finsbury Experience, *The British Journal of Criminology* 1992; 32(1):1–17.

Lowry-Webster, H., Barrett, P., and Lock, S., A universal prevention trial of anxiety symptomatology during childhood: Results at one-year follow-up, *Behaviour Change* 2003; 20(1):25–43.

Lurigio, A.J. and Rosenbaum, D.P., Evaluation research in community crime prevention: A critical look at the field, in *Community Crime Prevention: Does it Work?*, Rosenbaum, D.P., Ed., Sage Criminal Justice System Annuals, Vol. 22, Sage, Beverly Hills, CA, 1986, pp. 19–44.

Lurigio, A.J. and Rosenbaum, D.P., The impact of community policing on police personnel, in *The Challenge of Community Policing: Testing the Promises*, Rosenbaum, D.P., Ed., Sage, Thousand Oaks, CA, 1994, pp. 147–163.

Lynam, D.R., Pursuing the psychopath: Capturing the fledgling psychopath in a nomological net, *Journal of Abnormal Psychology* 1997; 106:425–438.

Lösel, F. and Beelmann, A., Effects of child social skills training in preventing antisocial behavior: A systematic review of randomized evaluations, *Annals of the American Academy of Political and Social Science* 2003; 587:84–109.

Lösel, F. and Bender, D., Child social skills training in the prevention of antisocial development and crime, in *The Oxford Handbook of Crime Prevention*, Welsh, B.C. and Farrington, D.P., Eds., Oxford University Press, Oxford, U.K., 2012, pp. 101–129.

Maccoby, E.E., Church, J.P., and Church, R.M., Community integration and the social control of juvenile delinquency, *Journal of Social Issues* 1958; 14:38–51.

Macdonald, J., The effectiveness of community policing in reducing urban violence, *Crime and Delinquency* 2002; 48(4):592–618.

MacDonald, L. and Frey, H.E., Families and schools together: Building relationships, *Juvenile Justice Bulletin*, Office of Juvenile Justice and Delinquency Prevention, November 1999. https://www.ncjrs.gov/html/ojjdp/9911_2/contents.html (accessed July 21, 2014).

MacKenzie, D.L., Preventing future criminal activities of delinquents and offenders, in *The Oxford Handbook of Crime Prevention*, Welsh, B.C. and Farrington, D.P., Eds., Oxford University Press, Oxford, U.K., 2012, pp. 466–486.

MacKenzie, D.L., *What Works in Corrections: Reducing the Criminal Activities of Offenders and Delinquents*, Cambridge University Press, New York, 2006.

REFERENCES

MacKenzie, D.L., Wilson, D.B., and Kider, S.B., Effects of correctional boot camps on offending, *Annals of the American Academy of Political and Social Science* 2001; 578:126–143.

Magnuson, K.A., Ruhm, C.J., and Waldfogel, J., Does Prekindergarten improve school preparation and performance? NBER working paper no. 10452, National Bureau of Economic Research, Cambridge, MA, 2004.

Maguin, E. and Loeber, R., Academic performance and delinquency, in *Crime and Justice: A Review of Research*, Vol. 20, Tonry, M., Ed., University of Chicago Press, Chicago, IL, 1996.

Maher, J., Youth gang crime, in *Handbook on Crime*, Brookman, F., Macguire, M., Pierpoint, H., and Bennett, T., Eds., Willan Publishing, New York, 2010.

Mair, J.S. and Mair, M., Violence prevention and control through environmental modifications, *Annual Review of Public Health* 2003; 24:209–225.

Mann, K., Punitive civil sanctions: The middleground between criminal and civil law, *Yale Law Journal* 1992; 101:1795–1873.

Manning, P. and Stoshine, M., Police technology, in *Encyclopedia of Crime and Punishment*, Vol. 3, Levinson, D., Ed., Sage, Thousand Oaks, CA, 2002, pp. 1194–1200.

Markie-Dadds, C. and Sanders, M.R., A controlled evaluation of an enhanced self-directed behavioural family intervention for parents of children with conduct problems in rural and remote areas, *Behaviour Change* 2006; 23(1):55–72.

Marshall, T.F., The evolution of restorative justice in Britain, *European Journal of Criminal Policy and Research* 1996; 4:21–42.

Martin, A.J., and Sanders, M.R., Balancing work and family: A controlled evaluation of the triple P-Positive Parenting Program as a work-site intervention, *Child and Adolescent Mental Health* 2003; 8(4):161–169.

Martinson, R., What works? Questions and answers about prison reform, *The Public Interest* 1974; 35(Spring):22–54.

Maruna, S., *Understanding Desistence from Crime*, United Kingdom, Ministry of Justice, Rehabilitation Services Group, National Offender Management Group, London, U.K., 2010.

Marx, G.T., Commentary: Some trends and issues in citizen involvement in the law enforcement process, *Crime and Delinquency* 1989; 35(3):500–519.

Mastrofski, S.D., Community policing as reform: A cautionary tale, in *Thinking about Policing*, Klockers, C.B. and Mastrofski, S.D., Eds., McGraw-Hill, New York, 1991.

Masuda, B., An alternative approach to the credit card fraud problem, *Security Journal* 1996; 7(1):15–21.

Mathews, D., *Politics for People: Finding a Responsible Public Voice*, University of Illinois Press, Chicago, IL, 1994.

Maxfield, M.G. and Widom, C.S., The cycle of violence: Revisited six years later, *Archives of Pediatrics & Adolescent Medicine* 1996; 150:390–395.

Maxfield, M.G., Lifestyle and routine activity theories of crime: Empirical studies of victimization, delinquency and offender decision-making, *Journal of Quantitative Criminology* 1987; 3(4):275–282.

Maxson, C.L., Egley Jr., A., Miller, J., and Klein, M.W., Section VIII introduction, in *The Modern Gang Reader*, Maxson, C.L., Egley Jr., A., Miller, J., and Klein, M.W., Eds., Oxford University Press, New York, 2014, pp. 441–442.

Maxson, C.L., Street gangs: How research can inform policy, in *Crime & Public Policy*, Wilson, J.Q. and Petersilia, J., Eds., Oxford University Press, New York, 2011.

Maxwell, C.D, Garner, J.H., and Skogan, W.G., Collective efficacy and criminal behavior in Chicago, 1995–2004, Final report submitted to the National Institute of Justice for Grant No. 2008-IJ-CX-0013, Washington, DC, 2000. https://www.ncjrs.gov/pdffiles1/nij/grants/235154.pdf (accessed July 21, 2014).

Mayhew, P., Crime in public view: Surveillance and crime prevention, in *Environmental Criminology*, Brantingham, P.J., and Brantingham, P.L., Eds., Sage, London, U.K., 1981, pp. 119–133.

Mayhew, P., Target-hardening—How much of an answer? in *Coping with Burglary*, Clark, R.V. and Hope, T., Eds., Kluwer-Nijhoff Publishing, Hingham, MA, 1984, pp. 29–44.

Mazerolle, L. and Ransley, J., *Third Party Policing*, Cambridge University Press, Cambridge, U.K., 2005.

Mazerolle, L., Soole, D., and Rombouts, S., Drug law enforcement: A review of the evaluation literature, *Police Quarterly* 2007; 10:115–153.

Mazerolle, L.G. and Roehl, J., Controlling drug and disorder problems: A focus on Oakland's Beat Health Program, *National Institute of Justice Research in Brief*, National Institute of Justice, Washington, DC, 1999, http://www.ncjrs.gov/pdffiles1/175051.pdf (accessed July 21, 2014).

Mazerolle, L.G. and Roehl, J., Eds., Civil remedies and crime prevention: An introduction, *Crime Prevention Studies* 1988; 9:1–20.

Mazerolle, L.G., Price, J., and Roehl, J., Civil remedies and drug control: A randomized field trial in Oakland, California, *Evaluation Review* 2000; 24(2):212–241.

McConville, M. and Shepherd, D., *Watching Police Watching Communities*, Routledge, London, U.K., 1992.

McDonald, L. and Frey, H.E., *Families and Schools Together: Building Relationships*. OJJDP Family Strengthening Series, November 1999, Office of Juvenile Justice and Delinquency Prevention, Washington, DC.

McGarrell, E., Cutting crime through police-citizen cooperation, Sagamore Institute for Policy Research, March 1, 1998, http://www.sagamoreinstitute.org/article/cutting-crime-through-police-citizen-cooperation/ (accessed July, 2014).

McGarrell, E.F., Bynum, T., Corsaro, N., and Cobbina, J., Attempting to reduce firearms violence through a comprehensive anti-gang initiative (CAGI): An evaluation of process and impact, *Journal of Criminal Justice* 2013b; 41:33–43.

McGarrell, E.F., Corsaro, N., Melde, C., Hipple, N., Cobbina, J., Bynum, T., and Perez, H., An assessment of the comprehensive anti-fang initiative: Final project report, National Institute of Justice, Washington, DC, 2013a.

McKeown, K. and Brosnan, M., Police and community: An evaluation of neighbourhood watch and community alert in Ireland. A report prepared for the Garda Síochána, Kieran McKeown Limited, Drumcondra, Dublin, 1998.

McNally, M.H. and Newman, G.R., Eds., *Perspectives on Identity Theft*, Crime Prevention Studies, Vol. 23, Criminal Justice Press, Monsey, NY, 2007.

McPherson, M. and Siloway, G., Planning to prevent crime, in *Reactions to Crime*, Lewis, D.A., Ed., Sage, Beverly Hills, CA, 1981, pp. 149–166.

Meek, S., assisted by K. Bowen-Willer, Eds., *Report of the International Conference for Crime Prevention Partnerships to Build Community Safety*, Johannesburg, South Africa, October 26–30, 1998, http://www.unhabitat.org/downloads/docs/1902_96378_Conference_on_crime.pdf (accessed August 23, 2000).

Merry, S.E., Defensible space undefended: Social factors in crime control through environmental design, *Urban Affairs Quarterly* 1981; 16(4):397–422.

Merton, R., Social structure and anomie, *American Sociological Review* 1938; 3:672–682.

Messner, S.F. and Zimmerman, G.M., Child social skills training in the prevention of antisocial development and crime, in *The Oxford Handbook of Crime Prevention*, Welsh, B.C. and Farrington, D.P., Eds., Oxford University Press, Oxford, U.K., 2012, pp. 155–172.

Metro Action Committee on Public Violence against Women and Children, *Moving Forward: Making Transit Safer for Women*, METRAC, Toronto, Ontario, Canada, 1989.

Milkman, H. and Wanberg, K., *Cognitive Behavioral Treatment: A Review and Discussion for Corrections Professionals*, National Institute of Justice, Washington, DC, 2007.

Miller, L.L., *The Politics of Community Crime Prevention: Implementing Operation Weed and Seed in Seattle*, Ashgate, Burlington, VT, 2001.

Millie, A. and Hough, M., Assessing the impact of the reducing burglary initiative in Southern England and Wales, 2nd edn., Home Office Online Report 42/04, Home Office, London, U.K., 2004.

Mitchell, O., Wilson, D.B., Eggers, A., and MacKenzie, D.L., Assessing the effectiveness of drug courts on recidivism: A meta-analytic review of traditional and nontraditional drug courts, *Journal of Criminal Justice* 2012; 40(1):60–71.

Moffitt, T.E., Adolescence-limited and life-course-persistent antisocial behavior: A developmental taxonomy, *Psychological Review* 1993; 100(4):674–701.

Moffitt, T.E., Juvenile delinquency and attention deficit disorder: Boy's developmental trajectories from age 13 to age 15, *Child Development* 1990; 61:893–910.

Morenoff, J.D., Sampson, R.J., and Raudenbush, S., Neighborhood inequality, collective efficacy, and the spatial dynamics of urban violence, *Criminology* 2001; 39:517–559.

Motiuk, L. and Frank, P., *An Examination of Sex Offender Case Histories in Federal Corrections*, Research and Statistics Branch, Correctional Service Canada, Ottawa, Ontario, Canada, 1993.

Moughtin, J.C. and Gardiner, A.R., Towards an improved and protected environment, *The Planner* 1990; 9–12.

Mugford, J. and Nelson, D., Violence prevention in practice: Australian Award-Winning Programs, Australian Institute of Criminology, Canberra, Australian Capital Territory, Australia, 1996, http://www.aic.gov.au/documents/7/1/2/%7B712FA7CD-66BE-4B81-B118-3D770464F827%7DRPP03.pdf (accessed July 21, 2014).

Mukherjee, S. and Wilson, P., Neighborhood watch: Issues and policy implications, in *Trends and Issues in Crime and Criminal Justice*, No. 8, Australian Institute of Criminology, Canberra, Australian Capital Territory, Australia, 1987.

Murray, T. and McKim, E., Introduction: The policy issues in policing and private security, in *Police and Private Security: What the Future Holds*, Richardson, J., Ed., Canadian Association of Chiefs of Police, Ottawa, Ontario, Canada, 2000, pp. 4–14.

Nagin, D.S., Imprisonment and crime control: Building evidence-based policy, in *Contemporary Issues in Criminological Theory and Research: The Role of Social Institutions (Papers from the American Society of Criminology 2010 Conference)*, Rosenfeld, R., Quinet, K., and Garcia, C., Eds., Wadsworth, Belmont, CA, 2010.

Natarajan, M. and Hough, M., Eds., *Illegal Drug Markets: From Research to Prevention Policy*, Crime Prevention Studies, Vol. 11, Criminal Justice Press, Monsey, NY, 2000.

National Association of Drug Court Professionals, *Adult Drug Court Best Practice Standards*, National Association of Drug Court Professionals, Vol. 1, Alexandria, VA, 2013.

National Center on Addiction and Substance Abuse, *National Survey of American Attitudes on Substance Abuse VIII: Teens and Parents*, National Center on Addiction and Substance Abuse, Columbia University, New York, 2003.

National Crime Council of Ireland, A crime prevention strategy for Ireland: Tackling the concerns of local communities, The Stationary Office, Dublin, Ireland, 2003, http://www.irlgov.ie/crimecouncil/downloads/CrimePrevention.pdf (accessed February 1, 2008).

National Crime Prevention Centre [Canada], Clear limits and real opportunities: The keys to preventing youth crimes, NCPC, Ottawa, Ontario, Canada, 1995.

National Crime Prevention Centre [Canada], *Focus on Children and Youth: Proceedings of the Workshop on Community Safety and Crime Prevention*, NCPC, Ottawa, Ontario, Canada, 1994.

National Crime Prevention Centre [Canada], Prevention of youth gang violence: Overview of strategies and approaches, National Crime Prevention Centre, Public Safety Canada, Ottawa, Ontario, Canada, 2012.

National Crime Prevention Centre [Canada], Promising and model crime prevention programs, National Crime Prevention Centre, Ottawa, Ontario, Canada, 2008.

National Crime Prevention Council, Crime prevention and community policing: A vital partnership, Bureau of Justice Statistics, U.S. Department of Justice, Washington, DC, 1997, http://www.ncjrs.gov/txtfiles/166819.txt (accessed July 21, 2014).

National Crime Prevention Institute, *Understanding Crime Prevention*, Vol. 1, National Crime Prevention Institute Press, Lexington, KY, 1978.

National Gang Center, *Best Practices to Address Community Gang Problems: OJJDP's Comprehensive Gang Model*, National Gang Center, Tallahassee, FL, 2010.

National Gang Center, National youth gang survey analysis: Measuring the extent of gang problems, n.d. https://www.nationalgangcenter.gov/Survey-Analysis/Measuring-the-Extent-of-Gang-Problems (accessed July 21, 2104).

National Institute of Justice, *Solving Crime Problems in Residential Neighborhoods: Comprehensive Changes in Design, Management, and Use*, National Institute of Justice, U.S. Department of Justice, Washington, DC, 1997.

National Institute on Drug Abuse, *Preventing Drug Abuse among Children and Adolescents. A Research Based Guide for Parents, Educators and Community Leaders*, U.S. Department of Health and Human Services, Washington, DC, 2003. http://www.drugabuse.gov/sites/default/files/preventingdruguse_2.pdf (accessed July 21, 2014).

National Youth Network, Planning a successful crime prevention project, Youth in action, Office of Juvenile Justice and Delinquency Prevention, Department of Justice, No. 1, Washington, DC, April 1998, https://www.ncjrs.gov/pdffiles/94266.pdf (accessed July 21, 2014).

Netherlands Ministry of Justice, Crime control in the Netherlands, investing in quality: Crime prevention in the Netherlands, Ministry of Justice, The Hague, the Netherlands, 2001.

Newburn, T. and Shiner, M., with Young, T., *Dealing with Disaffection: Young People, Mentoring and Social Inclusion*, Willan Publishing, Portland, OR, 2005.

Newburn, T., *Criminology*, Willan Publishing, Devon, U.K., 2007.

Newman, G.R. and Clarke, R.V., *Superhighway Robbery: Preventing E-commerce Crime*, Willan Publishing, Portland, OR, 2003.

Newman, O. and Franck, K.A., *Influencing Crime and Stability in Urban Housing Development*. National Institute of Justice, US Department of Justice, 1980.

Newman, O. and Franck, K.A., The effects of building size on personal crime and fear of crime, *Population and Environment* 1982; 5(4):203–220.

Newman, O., *Creating Defensible Space*, U.S. Department of Housing and Urban Development, Washington, DC, 1996. http://www.huduser.org/publications/pdf/def.pdf (accessed July 21, 2014).

Newman, O., *Defensible Space: People and Design in the Violent City*, MacMillan, New York, 1972.

Newman, O., *Design Guidelines for Creating Defensible Space*, National Institute of Law Enforcement and Criminal Justice, Washington, DC, 1995.

Newman, O., *Design Guidelines for Improving Defensible Space*. National Institute of Law Enforcement and Criminal Justice, US Government Printing Office, Washington, DC, 1976.

New South Wales Government, Department of Premier and Cabinet, NSW crime prevention framework, strengthening, focusing and coordinating crime prevention in NSW, Department of Premier and Cabinet, New South Wales Government, Sydney, New South Wales, Australia, 2008.

Nicholas, S., Povey, D., Walker, A., and Kershaw, C., *Crime in England and Wales, 2004/2005*, Home Office, London, U.K., 2005.

Nova Scotia Task Force on Bullying and Cyberbullying, Respectful and responsible relationships: There's no app for that. The report of the Nova Scotia Task Force on bullying and cyberbullying, Nova Scotia Task Force on Bullying and Cyberbullying, Halifax, Nova Scotia, Canada, 2012. http://www.nssba.ca/research-resources/doc_download/58-nova-scotia-task-force-on-bullying-and-cyber-bullying (accessed July 21, 2014).

Office of Community Oriented Policing Services, *COPS Innovations, Promising Strategies from the Field. Community Policing in Smaller Jurisdictions*, Office of Community-Oriented Policing Services, Department of Justice, Washington, DC, 2003, http://www.cops.usdoj.gov/html/cd_rom/inaction1/pubs/PromisingStratediesFieldPolicingSmallerJurisdictions.pdf (accessed July 21, 2014).

Office of Justice Programs, http://www.ojp.usdoj.gov/about/about.htm (accessed July 21, 2014).

Office of Juvenile Justice and Delinquency Center, *Best Practices to Address Community Gang Problems*, Office of Juvenile Justice and Delinquency Prevention, Washington, DC, 2007.

Office of Juvenile Justice and Delinquency Center, Comprehensive anti-gang initiative, n.d. http://www.ojjdp.gov/programs/antigang/ (accessed July 21, 2014).

Office of Juvenile Justice and Delinquency Center, Mission statement, http://ojjdp.ncjrs.org/about/missionstatement.html (accessed March 21, 2008).

Office of Juvenile Justice and Delinquency Center, Model programs guide, http://www.dsgonline.com/mpg2.5//mpg_index.htm (accessed July 21, 2014).

Office of Juvenile Justice and Delinquency Center, OJJDP model programs guide, cognitive behavioral treatment, http://www.dsgonline.com/mpg2.5/cognitive_behavioral_treatment_reentry.htm (accessed March 1, 2008).

Office of Juvenile Justice and Delinquency Center, OJJDP model programs guide, Early risers 'skills for success' program, http://demoatgetfit.net/mpg_program_detail.aspx?ID=320 (accessed March 21, 2007).

Office of Juvenile Justice and Delinquency Prevention, 1998 Report to congress, Title V incentive grants for local delinquency prevention programs, Office of Juvenile Justice and Delinquency Prevention, U.S. Department of Justice, Washington, DC, 1998b, http://ojjdp.ncjrs.org/pubs/98report/report_iii-5.html (accessed November 3, 2003).

Office of Juvenile Justice and Delinquency Prevention, A primer for OJJDP training and technical assistance, providers training, technical assistance, and evaluation protocols, Office of Juvenile Justice and Delinquency Prevention, U.S. Department of Justice, Washington, DC, 1998c.

Office of Juvenile Justice and Delinquency Prevention, Juvenile mentoring program, 1998 report to congress, Office of Juvenile Justice and Delinquency Prevention, U.S. Department of Justice, Washington, DC, 1998a, http://www.ncjrs.org/pdffiles1/952872.pdf (accessed November 1, 2003).

Office of Juvenile Justice and Delinquency Prevention, Juvenile offenders and victims: A national report, OJJDP, Washington, DC, 1996,

Office of Juvenile Justice and Delinquency Prevention, OJJDP annual report, 1998, Office of Juvenile Justice and Delinquency Prevention, U.S. Department of Justice, Washington, DC, 1999, http://www.ncjrs.org/html/ojjdp/annualreport99/ch1_d.html (accessed November 5, 2003).

Office of the Deputy Prime Minister, Social Exclusion Unit, *Bringing Britain Together: A National Strategy for Neighbourhood Renewal*, Home Office, London, U.K., 1998.

Office of the Deputy Prime Minister, *Tackling Social Exclusion: Taking Stock and Looking to the Future, Emerging Findings*, ODPM Publications, London, U.K., 2004.

Office of the Surgeon General, Youth violence: A report of the surgeon general, Office of the Surgeon General, Rockville, MD, 2001. http://www.ncbi.nlm.nih.gov/pubmed/20669522 (accessed July 21, 2014).

Olds, D. and Henderson, C.R., Does prenatal and infancy nurse home visitation have enduring effects on qualities of parental caregiving and child health at 25–50 months of life? *Pediatrics* 1994; 93:89–98.

Olds, D., Henderson, C.R., Cole, R., Eckenrode, J., Kitzman, H., Luckey, D., Pettitt, L., Sidora, K., Morris, P., and Powers, J., Long-term effects of nurse home visitation on children's criminal and antisocial behavior: 15-year follow-up of a randomized controlled trial, *Journal of the American Medical Association* 1998; 280(14):1238–1244.

Olds, D., Henderson, C.R., Tatelbaum, R., and Chamberlin, R., Improving the delivery of prenatal care and outcomes of pregnancy: A randomized trial of nurse home visitation, *Pediatrics* 1986; 77(1):16–28.

Olweus, D., *Bullying at School: What We Know and What We Can Do*, Blackwell, Cambridge, U.K., 1993.

Oregon Social Learning Center, http://www.oslc.org/about/overview.html (accessed July 21, 2014).

Ostroff, C., The relationship between satisfaction, attitudes, and performance: An organizational level analysis, *Journal of Applied Psychology* 1992; 77:963–974.

O'Donnell, J., Hawkins, J.D., Catalano, R.F., Abbott, R.D., and Day, L.E., Preventing school failure, drug use, and delinquency among low-income children: Long-term intervention in elementary schools, *American Journal of Orthopsychiatry* 1995; 65:87–100.

Palmer, E.J., Hollin, C.R., and Caulfield, L.S., Surveying fear: Crime, buses and new paint, *Crime Prevention and Community Safety: An International Journal* 2005; 7(4):47–58.

Palmiotto, M., *Community Policing: A Policing Strategy for the 21st Century*, Jones & Bartlett, Sudbury, MA, 2000.

Parada, M.M., Parental responsibility for youth crime: Comparative study of legislation in four countries, thesis submitted in partial fulfillment of the requirements of Masters of Arts, University of Manitoba, Winnipeg, Manitoba, Canada, 2010.

Parent, D., *Correctional Boot Camps: Lessons From a Decade of Research*, National Institute of Justice, Research for Practice Series, Washington, DC, 2003. https://www.ncjrs.gov/pdffiles1/nij/197018.pdf (accessed July 21, 2014).

Parliament of Canada, Standing Committee on Justice and the Solicitor General, Crime prevention in Canada: Toward a national strategy, Twelfth report of the Standing Committee on Justice and the Solicitor General, Parliament of Canada, Queen's Printer for Canada, Ottawa, Ontario, Canada, 1993.

Patrick, M., Proving the SARA model: A problem solving approach to street crime reduction in the London Borough of Lewisham, InfoTech Enterprises Europe, London, U.K., 2002.

Patterson, G.R., Crosby, L., and Vuchinich, S., Predicting risk for early police arrest, *Journal of Quantitative Criminology* 1992; 8:335–355.

Pavlich, G., Preventing crime: 'Social' versus 'Community' governance in Aotearoa/New Zealand, in *Governable Places: Readings on Governmentality and Crime Control*, Smandych, R., Ed., Ashgate, Brookfield, VT, 2002, pp. 103–131.

Paynich, R. and Hill, B., *Fundamentals of Crime Mapping: Principles and Practice*, Jones and Bartlett Learning, Burlington, MA, 2010.

Pearsall, B., Predictive policing: The future of law enforcement? *NIJ Journal* 2010; (266). http://www.nij.gov/journals/266/pages/predictive.aspx (accessed July, 2014).

Pearson, F.S., Lipton, D.S., Cleland, C.M., and Yee, D.S., The effects of behavioral/cognitive-behavioral programs on recidivism, *Crime and Delinquency* 2002; 48(3):476–496.

Pearson, S.S. and Voke, V.H., *Building an Effective Citizenry: Lessons Learned from Initiatives in Youth Engagement*, American Youth Policy, Forum, Washington, DC, 2003. http://www.aypf.org/publications/building-an-effective-citizenry.pdf (accessed July 21, 2014).

Pease, K., A review of street lighting evaluations: Crime reduction effects, in *Surveillance of Public Space, CCTV, Street Lighting and Crime Prevention*, Painter, K. and Tilly, N., Eds., Crime Prevention Studies, Vol. 10, Criminal Justice Press, Monsey, NY, 1999, pp. 47–76.

Pennell, S.C., Curtis, C., and Henderson, J., *Guardian Angels: An Assessment of Citizen Responses to Crime*, National Institute of Justice, Washington, DC, 1986.

Pepinsky, H.E. and Quinney, R., Eds., *Criminology as Peacemaking*, Indiana University Press, Bloomington, IN, 1991.

Pepinsky, H.E., Issues of citizen involvement in policing, *Crime and Delinquency* 1998; 35(3):458–470.

Perkins, D.D., Florin, P., Rich, R.C., Chavis, D.M., and Wandersman, A., Participation and the social and physical environment of residential blocks: Crime and community context, *American Journal of Community Psychology* 1990; 18(1):83–115.

Perkins, D.D., Wandersman, A., Rich, R.C., and Taylor, R.B., The physical environment of street crime: Defensible space, territoriality and incivilities, *Journal of Environmental Psychology* 1993; 13:29–49.

Perkins, D.F. and Noam, G.G., Characteristics of sports-based youth development programs, *New Directions for Youth Development* 2007; 115:75–84.

Perrault, S., Homicide in Canada, 2011, Statistics Canada, Ottawa, Ontario, Canada, 2012. http://www.statcan.gc.ca/pub/85-002-x/2012001/article/11738-eng.pdf (accessed July 21, 2014).

Perrault, S., Police-reported crime statistics in Canada, 2012, Statistics Canada, Ottawa, Ontario, Canada, 2013. http://www.statcan.gc.ca/pub/85-002-x/2013001/article/11854-eng.pdf (accessed July 21, 2014).

Petrosino, A., How can we respond effectively to juvenile crime? *Pediatrics* 2000; 105:635–637.

Petrosino, A., Turpin-Petrosino, C., and Buehler, J., "Scared Straight" and other juvenile awareness programs for preventing juvenile delinquency, Campbell Systematic Reviews, Oslo, Norway, 2004. http://www.campbellcollaboration.org/lib/download/13/Scared+Straight_R.pdf (accessed July 21, 2014).

Petrosino, A., Turpin-Petrosino, C., and Guckenburg, S., Formal system processing of juveniles: Effects on delinquency, Campbell Systematic Reviews, Philadelphia, PA, 2010. http://www.campbellcollaboration.org/lib/download/761/Review_System_Process_Effect_Juvenile_Delinquency_100129.pdf (accessed July 21, 2014).

487

REFERENCES

Piquero, A., Farrington, D., Welsh, B., Tremblay, R., and Jennings, W., *Effects of Early Family/Parent Training Programs on Antisocial Behavior & Delinquency*, U.S. Department of Justice, Washington, DC, 2008. https://www.ncjrs.gov/pdffiles1/nij/grants/224989.pdf (accessed July 21, 2014).

Piquero, A.R. and Jennings, W.G., Parent training and the prevention of crime, in *The Oxford Handbook of Crime Prevention*, Welsh, B.C. and Farrington, D.P., Eds., Oxford University Press, Oxford, U.K., 2012, pp. 89–101.

Pitts, J. and Hope, T., The local politics of inclusion: The state and community safety, *Social Policy and Administration* 1997; 31(5):37–58.

Pitts, J. and Smith, P., Preventing school bullying, Police Research Group, Paper 63, Home Office, London, U.K., 1995.

Pitts, J., Intervening in gang-affected neighbourhoods, in *Prevention and Youth Crime: Is Early Intervention Working?*, Blyth, M. and Solomon, E., Eds., The Policy Press, Bristol, U.K., 2009, pp. 21–40.

Plaster, S., Community CPTED, *The Journal of the International Crime Prevention through Environmental Design Association* 2002; 1(1):15–24.

Podolefsky, A. and Dubow, F., *Strategies for Community Crime Prevention: Collective Responses to Crime in Urban America*, Thomas, Springfield, IL, 1981.

Police Futures Group, Private policing. A policy discussion paper (draft), Police Futures Group, Ottawa, Ontario, Canada, n.d., pp. 14–15.

Poyner, B. and Webb, B., *Successful Crime Prevention: Case Studies*, Tavistock Institute of Human Relations, London, U.K., 1987.

Poyner, B., An evaluation of a walkway demolition on a British housing estate, in *Situational Crime Prevention: Successful Case Studies*, 2nd edn., Clarke, R.V., Ed., Harrow and Heston, Albany, NY, 1997, pp. 59–73.

Poyner, B., *Design against Crime: Beyond Defensible Space*, Butterworths, London, U.K., 1983.

Poyner, B., Lessons from Lisson Green: An evaluation of walkway demolition on a British housing estate, *Crime Prevention Studies* 1994; 3:127–150.

Pratkanis, A.R. and Turner, M.E., Persuasion and democracy: Strategies for increasing deliberative participation and enacting social change, *Journal of Social Issues* 1996; 52(1):187–205.

Pratt, T.C., Cullen, F.T., Blevins, K.R., Daigle, L., and Unnever, J.D., The relationship of attention deficit hyperactivity disorder to crime and delinquency: A meta-analysis, *International Journal of Police Science and Management* 2002; 4:344–360.

President's Commission on Law Enforcement and Administration of Justice, Task force on organized crime, Task force report: Organized crime, United States Government Printing Office, Washington, DC, 1967.

Presman, D., Chapman, R., and Rosen, L., Creative partnerships supporting youth, building communities: A closer look, Office of Community-Oriented Policing Services, U.S. Department of Justice, Washington, DC, 2002, http://www.cops.usdoj.gov/pdf/e03021471.pdf (accessed July 21, 2014).

Price, M., Personalizing crime: Mediation produces restorative justice for victims and offenders, *Dispute Resolution Magazine*, 2001, http://www.vorp.com/articles/justice.html (accessed July 21, 2014).

Prime, J., White, S., Liriano, S., and Patel, K., Criminal careers of those born between 1953 and 1978, UK Home Office Statistical Bulletin 4/01 2001.

Promising Practices Network on Children, Families and Communities, Nurse Family Partnership, n.d. http://www.promisingpractices.net/program.asp?programid=16 (accessed July 21, 2014).

Promising Practices Network on Children, Families, and Communities, n.d. http://www.promisingpractices.net/programs.asp (accessed July 21, 2014).

Promising Practices Network on Children, Families, and Communities, Quantum opportunity program, n.d. http://www.promisingpractices.net/program.asp?programid=27 (accessed July 21, 2014).

Public Safety Canada, A blueprint for effective crime prevention, Public Safety Canada, Ottawa, Ontario, Canada, 2007.

REFERENCES

Public Safety Canada, Crime prevention funding programs, 2013 (accessed January 29, 2014). Available at: http://www.publicsafety.gc.ca/cnt/cntrng-crm/crm-prvntn/fndng-prgrms/index-eng.aspx.

Public Safety Canada, National Crime Prevention Centre, n.d. Available at: http://www.publicsafety.gc.ca/cnt/cntrng-crm/crm-prvntn/ntnl-crm-prvntn-cntr-eng.aspx (accessed February 22, 2014).

Public Safety Canada, National Crime Prevention Centre, http://www.publicsafety.gc.ca/cnt/cntrng-crm/crm-prvntn/ntnl-crm-prvntn-cntr-eng.aspx (accessed July 21, 2014).

Puma, M., Cook, S., Bell, R., and Heid, C., Head start impact study final report, prepared for: Office of Planning, Research and Evaluation, Administration for Children and Families, U.S. Department of Health and Human Services, Washington, DC, 2010. http://www.acf.hhs.gov/sites/default/files/opre/hs_impact_study_final.pdf (accessed July 21, 2014).

Purdue, D., Neighbourhood governance: Leadership, trust and social capital, *Urban Studies* 2001; 38(12):2211–2224.

Putnam, R.D. with Leonardi, R., and Nanetti, R.Y., *Making Democracy Work: Civic Traditions in Modern Italy*, Princeton University Press, Princeton, NJ, 1993.

Putnam, R.D., Bowling alone: America's declining social capital, *Journal of Democracy* 1995; 6(1):65–78.

Raine, A., Liu, J., Venables, P., and Mednick, S.A., Preventing crime and schizophrenia using early environmental enrichment, in *Crime and Schizophrenia: Causes and Cures*, Raine, A., Ed., Nova Sciences Publishers, New York, 2003.

Raine, A., Mellingen, K., Liu, J., Venables, P., and Mednick, S.A., Effects of environmental enrichment at ages 3–5 years on schizotypal personality and antisocial behavior at ages 17 and 23 years, *The American Journal of Psychiatry* 2003; 160(9):1627–1635.

Ralph, A. and Sanders, M.R., Preliminary evaluation of the group Teen Triple P Program for parents of teenagers making the transition to high school, *Australian e-Journal for the Advancement of Mental Health* 2003; 2(3):1–9.

Ramsey, M. and Newton, R., The effect of better street lighting on crime and rear: A review, Crime Prevention Unit Paper 29, Crime Prevention Unit, Home Office, London, U.K., 1991.

RAND, *Proven Benefits of Early Childhood Interventions*, RAND Labor and Population Research Brief, Santa Monica, CA, 2005. http://www.rand.org/pubs/research_briefs/RB9145.html (accessed July 21, 2014).

Rapp-Paglicci, L. and Roberts, A.R., Mental illness and juvenile offending, in *Juvenile Justice Sourcebook: Past, Present, and Future*, Roberts, A.R., Ed., Oxford University Press, Oxford, U.K., 2004, pp. 289–307.

Rapp-Paglicci, L. et al., Addressing the hispanic delinquency and mental health relationship through cultural arts programming: A research note from the prodigy evaluation, *Journal of Contemporary Criminal Justice* 2011; 27(1):110–121.

Rapp-Paglicci, L., Stewart, C., and Rowe, W., Evaluating the effects of the prodigy cultural arts program on mental health symptoms in at-risk and adjudicated youth, *Best Practices in Mental Health* 2009; 5(1):65–73.

Rapp-Paglicci, L., Stewart, C., and Rowe, W., Improving outcomes for at-risk youth: Findings from the prodigy cultural arts program, *Journal of Evidence-Based Social Work* 2012; 9(5):512–513.

Rasmussen, M., Muggli, W., and Crabill, C.M., *Evaluation of the Minneapolis Community Crime Prevention Demonstration*, Crime Control Planning Board, St. Paul, MN, 1979.

Ratcliffe, J.H. and Guidetti, R., State police investigative structure and the adoption of intelligence-led policing, *Policing: An International Journal of Police Strategies and Management* 2008; 31(1):109–128.

Ratcliffe, J.H., Taniguchi, T., Groff, E.R., and Wood, J.D., The Philadelphia foot patrol experiment: A randomized controlled trial of police patrol effectiveness in violent crime hotspots, *Criminology* 2011; 49(3):795–831.

Read, T. and Tilley, N., Not rocket science? Problem-solving and crime reduction, Crime reduction research series paper 6, Police Research Group, Home Office, London, U.K., 2000.

REFERENCES

Reaves, B.A. and Goldberg, A.L., Law enforcement management and administrative statistics, 1997: Data for individual state and local agencies with 100 or more officers, U.S. Bureau of Justice Statistics, Washington, DC, 1999.

Reiss, A.J. and Roth, J., Eds., *Understanding and Preventing Violence*, National Academy of Sciences, Washington, DC, 1993.

Rempel, M., Green, M., and Kralstein, D., The impact of adult drug courts on crime and incarceration: Findings from a multi-site quasi-experimental design, *Journal of Experimental Criminology* 2012; 8:165–192.

Rena, L., Liqun, C., Lovrich, N., and Gaffney, M., Linking confidence in the police with the performance of the police: Community policing can make a difference, *Journal of Criminal Justice* 2005; 33:55–66.

Rennie Center for Education Research & Policy, *Forgotten Youth: Re-Engaging Students through Dropout Recovery*, Rennie Center for Education Research & Policy, Cambridge, MA, 2012.

Reppetto, T., *Residential Crime*, Ballinger, Cambridge, MA, 1974.

Republic of South Africa, Integrated social crime prevention strategy, Department of Social Development, Pretoria, Republic of South Africa, 2011.

Research Press Publishers, https://www.researchpress.com/books/599/impulse-control-game (accessed July 20, 2014).

Resilience Research Centre, Pathways to youth resilience: Community-based programs and services for youth in Labrador and Nova Scotia, Resilience Research Centre, Dalhousie University, Halifax, Nova Scotia, Canada, 2011. http://www.resilienceproject.org/research/resources/publications/25-reports (accessed July 21, 2014).

Reynald, D., Translating CPTED into crime prevention action: A critical examination of CPTED as a tool for active guardianship, *European Journal on Criminal Policy & Research* 2011; 17(1):69–81.

Rhodes, J.E., Grossman, J.B., and Resch, N.L., Agents of change: Pathways through which mentoring relationships influence adolescents' academic adjustment, *Child Development* 2000; 71(6):1662–1671.

Rhodes, J.E., *Stand By Me: The Risk and Rewards of Mentoring Today's Youth*, Harvard University Press, Boston, MA, 2002.

Ringwalt, C., Greene, J., Ennett, S., Lachan, R., Clayton, R.R., and Leukefeld, C.G., Past and future directions of the DARE program: An evaluation review: Draft final report, National Institute of Justice, Washington, DC, 1994.

Rink, E. and Tricker, R., Resilience-based research and adolescent health behaviors, *The Prevention Researcher* 2003; 10(1):13–14.

Ritter, N., CeaseFire: A public health approach to reduce shootings and killings, *National Institute of Justice Journal* 2009; (264):20–25. https://www.ncjrs.gov/pdffiles1/nij/228386.pdf (accessed July, 2014).

Rocque, M. and Paternoster, R., Understanding the antecedents of the 'School-to-Jail' link: The relationship between race and school discipline, *The Journal of Criminal Law & Criminology* 2011; 101(2):633–665.

Rocque, M., Welsh, B.C., and Raine, A., Biosocial criminology and modern crime prevention, *Journal of Criminal Justice* 2012; 40:306–312.

Roehl, J.A., Civil remedies for controlling crime: The role of community organizations, *Crime Prevention Studies* 1998; 9:241–259.

Roehl, J.A., Huitt, R., Wycoff, M.A., Pate, A., Rebovich, D., and Coyle, K., National process evaluation of operation weed and seed, *National Institute of Justice Research in Brief*, National Institute of Justice, Washington, DC, October 1996, www.ncjrs.gov/pdffiles/weedseed.pdf (accessed July 21, 2014).

Roethof, H., *Interimrapport van de Commisie Kleine Criminaliteit. Staatsuitgeverij*, Den Haag, 1984.

Rohe, W.M., Crime prevention through informal social control, *Social Science Newsletter* 1985; 70(3):162–165.

Rosen, H., What works in reentry clearinghouse update—New content on the effectiveness of employment and education programs, 2013. Available at: http://csgjusticecenter.org (accessed July 21, 2014).

Rosenbaum, D.P. and Schuck, A.M., Comprehensive community partnerships for preventing crime, in *The Oxford Handbook of Crime Prevention*, Welsh, B.C. and Farrington, D.P., Eds., Oxford University Press, Oxford, U.K., 2012, pp. 226–246.

Rosenbaum, D.P., Community crime prevention: A review and synthesis of the literature, *Justice Quarterly* 1988; 5:323–395.

Rosenbaum, D.P., Ed., *Community Crime Prevention: Does it Work?* Sage, Beverly Hills, CA, 1986.

Rosenbaum, D.P., Evaluating multi-agency anti-crime partnerships: Theory, design, and measurement issues, in *Crime Prevention Studies*, vol. 14, Willan Publishing, London, U.K., 2002, pp. 171–225.

Rosenbaum, D.P., Lewis, D., and Grant, J., *The Impact of Community Crime Prevention Programs in Chicago: Can Neighborhood Organizations Make a Difference*, Northwestern University, Center for Urban Affairs and Policy Research, Evanston, IL, 1985.

Rosenbaum, D.P., The theory and research behind neighborhood watch: Is it a sound fear and crime reduction strategy? *Crime and Delinquency* 1987; 33(1):103–134.

Ross, R.R. and Ross, R.D., Eds., *Thinking Straight: The Reasoning and Rehabilitation Programme for Delinquency Prevention and Offender Rehabilitation*, Air Training and Publications, Ottawa, Ontario, Canada, 1995.

Rossman, S., Roman, B., Zweig, J., Rempel, J.M.M., and Lindquist, C., *The Multi-Site Adult Drug Court Evaluation: Executive Summary*, Urban Institute, Washington, DC, 2011. http://www.urban.org/publications/412353.html (accessed July 21, 2014).

Royal Canadian Mounted Police, Community policing problem solving model, http://www.rcmp-grc.gc.ca/ccaps-spcca/capra-eng.htm (accessed July 21, 2014).

Royal Canadian Mounted Police, Reduction of opportunity for crime: Handbook for police officers, Royal Canadian Mounted Police, Ottawa, Ontario, Canada, 1985.

Rubin, H.J. and Rubin, I.S., *Community Organizing and Development*, Macmillan, New York, 1992.

Sadd, S. and Grinc, R., Innovative neighborhood oriented policing: An evaluation of community policing programs in eight cities, in *The Challenge of Community Policing: Testing the Promises*, Rosenbaum, D.P., Ed., Sage, Newbury Park, CA, 1994, pp. 27–52.

Safe in Tees Valley and the Home Office, Informing the effective use of publicity and media campaigns to reduce crime and the fear of crime, Safe in Tees Valley, Stockton on Tees, U.K., 2003, http://www.safeinteesvalley.org/ (accessed May 20, 2005).

Samaha, J., *Criminal Justice*, Thomson, Wadsworth, New York, 2006.

Sampson, R.J. and Laub, J., Desistance from crime over the life course, in *Handbook of the Life Course*, Mortimer, J. and Shanahan, M., Eds., Kluwer Academic/Plenum, New York, 2003.

Sampson, R.J. and Lauritsen, J.L., Violent victimization and offending: Individual-, situational-, and community-level risk factors. in *Understanding and Preventing Violence: Social Influence*, Vol. 3, Reiss, A.J. and Roth, J.A., Eds., National Academy Press, Washington, DC, 1994, pp. 1–115.

Sampson, R.J. and Scott, M.S., *Tackling Crime and Other Public-Safety Problems: Case Studies in Problem-Solving*, U.S. Department of Justice, Office of Community Oriented Policing Services, Washington, DC, 1999.

Sampson, R.J., Bullying in schools, Problem-Oriented Guides for Police Problem-Specific Guides Series No. 12, Office of Community Oriented Policing Services, U.S. Department of Justice, Washington, DC, 2002. http://www.cops.usdoj.gov/Publications/e07063414-guide.pdf (accessed July 21, 2014).

Sampson, R.J., Neighborhood and crime: The structural determinants of personal victimization, *Journal of Crime and Delinquency* 1985; 22:7–40.

Sampson, R.J., Raudenbush, S.W., and Earls, F., Neighborhoods and violent crime: A multilevel study of collective efficacy, *Science* 1997; 277:919–924.

Sampson, R.J., Transcending tradition: New directions in community research, Chicago style, *Criminology* 2002b; 40:213–230.

Sanders, M.R. et al., Stepping stones triple P: The theoretical basis and development of an evidence-based positive parenting program for families with a child who has a disability, *Journal of Intellectual & Developmental Disability* 2007; 29(3):265–283.

Sanders, M.R., Mazzucchelli, T.G., and Studman, L.J., Stepping Stones Triple P: The theoretical basis and development of an evidence-based positive parenting program for families with a child who has a disability, *Journal of Intellectual & Developmental Disability* 2004; 29(3):265–283.

Sansfaçon, D. and Welsh, B., *Crime Prevention Digest II: Summary*, International Centre for the Prevention of Crime, Montreal, Quebec, Canada, 1999.

Sansfaçon, D., Of prevention and security, Reflections on sustainable governance of community security, International Centre for the Prevention of Crime, Montreal, Quebec, Canada, 2004, http://www.crime-prevention-intl.org (accessed March 15, 2007).

Santa Cruz Police Department, Time Magazine names SCPD's predictive policing as one of top 50 inventions of 2011, http://santacruzpolice.blogspot.ca/2011/11/time-magazine-names-scpds-predictive.html (accessed July 21, 2014).

Sargeant, E., Wickes, R., and Mazerolle, L., Policing community problems: Exploring the role of formal social control in shaping collective efficacy, *Australian & New Zealand Journal of Criminology* 2013; 46(1):70–87.

Satterfield, J.H., Childhood diagnostic and neurophysiological predictors of teenage arrest rages: An eight-year prospective study, in *The Causes of Crime: New Biological Approaches*, Mednick, S.A., Moffitt, T.A., and Stack, S.A., Eds., Cambridge University Press, Cambridge, U.K., 1987.

Savignac, J., Families, youth and delinquency: The state of knowledge, and family-based juvenile delinquency prevention programs, National Crime Prevention Centre, Ottawa, Ontario, Canada, 2009. http://www.publicsafety.gc.ca/cnt/rsrcs/pblctns/fmls-yth-dlnqnc/fmls-yth-dlnqnc-eng.pdf (accessed July 21, 2014).

Saville, G. and Cleveland, G., Second generation CPTED: An antidote to the social Y2K virus of urban design, paper presented to *the Third International CPTED Association Conference*, Washington, DC, 1998.

Saville, G. and Cleveland, G., Second-generation CPTED: Rise and fall of opportunity theory, in *21st Century Security and CPTED: Designing for Critical Infrastructure and Crime Prevention*, 2nd edn., Atlas, R., Ed., CRC Press, Boca Raton, FL, 2013, pp. 91–106.

Saville, G. and Cleveland, G., Second-generation CPTED: Rise and fall of opportunity theory, in *21st Century Security and CPTED: Designing for Critical Infrastructure and Crime Prevention*, Atlas, R., Ed., CRC Press, Boca Raton, FL, 2010, pp. 79–90.

Savoie, J., *Neighbourhood Characteristics and the Distribution of Crime: Edmonton, Halifax and Thunder Bay*, Crime and Justice Research Paper Series, Canadian Centre for Justice Statistics, Statistics Canada, Ottawa, 2008.

Scales, P. and Leffert, N., *Developmental Assets*, Search Institute, Minneapolis, MN, 1999.

Scarborough Surface Transit, *Scarborough Moves Forward: Making Transit Stops Safer for Women*, Scarborough Surface Transit, Toronto, Ontario, Canada, 1991.

Schindler, H.S. and Yoshikawa, H., Preventing crime through intervention in the preschool years, in *The Oxford Handbook of Crime Prevention*, Welsh, B.C. and Farrington, D.P., Eds., Oxford University Press, Oxford, U.K., 2012, pp. 70–88.

Schinke, S.P. and Gilchrest, L.D., Primary prevention of tobacco smoking, *Journal of School Health* 1983; 53:416–419.

Schinke, S.P., Orlandi, M.A., and Cole, K.C., Boys & Girls Clubs in public housing developments: Prevention services for youth at risk, *Journal of Community Psychology* 1992; 28:118–128.

Schirm, A., and Rodriguez-Planas, N., *The Quantum Opportunities Program Demonstration: Initial Post-Intervention Impacts*, Mathematica Policy Research, Washington, DC, 2004. http://www.doleta.gov/reports/searcheta/occ/papers/June_04_QOP_report.pdf (accessed July 21, 2014).

Schmalleger, F., *Criminology Today: An Integrative Introduction*, Prentice Hall, Upper Saddle River, NJ, 2006.

Schneider, A.L. and Schneider, P.R., *Private and Public Minded Citizen Responses to a Neighborhood Based Crime Prevention Strategy*, Institute for Policy Analysis, Eugene, OR, 1978.

Schneider, A.L., Co-production of public and private safety: An analysis of bystander intervention, private neighboring and personal protection, *Western Political Science Quarterly* 1987; 40:611–630.

Schneider, R., Crime prevention through environmental design: Themes, theories, practice, and conflict, *Journal of Architectural & Planning Research* 2005; 22(4):271–357.

Schneider, S.R., Organizational obstacles to participation in community crime prevention programs: The case of Mount Pleasant (Vancouver, British Columbia, Canada), *International Criminal Justice Review* 2000; 10:32–53.

Schneider, S.R., *Refocusing Crime Prevention: Collective Action and the Quest for Community*, University of Toronto Press, Toronto, Ontario, Canada, 2007a.

Schneider, S.R., The theories, principles, and strategies underlying the PALS program, unpublished document, 2007b.

Schubert, C.A., Mulvey, E.P., and Glasheen, C., Influence of mental health and substance use problems and criminogenic risk on outcomes in serious juvenile offenders, *Journal of the American Academy of Child and Adolescent Psychiatry* 2011; 50:925–937.

Schweinhart, L.J., Barnes, H.V., and Weikart, D.P., Significant benefits: The high/scope preschool study through age 27, Monographs of the High/School Education Research Foundation, No. 10, HighScope Press, Ypsilanti, MI, 1993.

Schweinhart, L.J., Montie, J., Xiang, Z., Belfield, W.S., Barnett, C.R., and Nores, M., *Lifetime Effects: The HighScope Perry Preschool Study Through Age 40*, HighScope Press, Ypsilanti, MI, 2005.

Scott, M.S., *Problem-Oriented Policing: Reflections on the First 20 Years*, Office of Community-Oriented Policing Services, U.S. Department of Justice, Washington, DC, 2000. http://www.popcenter.org/library/reading/pdfs/reflectionsfull.pdf (accessed July 21, 2014).

Search Institute, Developmental assets for adolescents (ages 12–18), Search Institute, Minneapolis, MN, 2006. http://reachdevelopment.org/assets/40AssetsList.pdf (accessed January, 2014).

Secretary of State for the Home Department, *Criminal Justice: The Way Ahead*, The Stationery Office, London, U.K., 2001.

Sedlak, A., and McPherson, K., Conditions of confinement: Findings from the survey of youth in residential placement, *OJJDP Bulletin*, May 2010.

Sells, S.P., Winokur-Early, K., and Smith, T.E., Reducing adolescent oppositional and conduct disorders: An experimental design using parenting with love and limits, *Professional Issues in Criminal Justice* 2011; 6(3):9–30.

Sevigny, E.L., Fuleihan, B.K., and Ferdik, F.V., Do drug courts reduce the use of incarceration? A meta-analysis, *Journal of Criminal Justice* 2013; 41(6):416–425.

Shaffer, D.K., Looking inside the black box of drug courts: A meta-analytic review, *Justice Quarterly* 2011; 28:493–521.

Shaftoe, H., A chronology of British developments and key publications in urban security and crime prevention during the last two decades, University of West England, Bristol, U.K., 1997, http://www.uwe.ac.uk/fbe/commsafe/ukcron.htm (accessed March 1, 2005).

Shaftoe, H., *Southmead —Is it Getting Better? An Evaluation of Community Safety Initiatives*, Bristol City Council, Bristol, U.K., 2002.

Shaftoe, H., Southmead—Is it getting better? An evaluation of community safety initiatives, Bristol City Council, Bristol, U.K., 2002.

Shaftoe, H., Turksen, U., Lever, J., and Williams, S.-J., Dealing with terrorist threats through a crime prevention and community safety approach, *Crime Prevention and Community Safety: An International Journal* 2007; 9(4):291–307.

Shaw, C.T. and McKay, H.D., *Juvenile Delinquency and Urban Areas*, University of Chicago Press, Chicago, IL 1942.

Shaw, C.T. and McKay, H.D., Report on the causes of crime, Vol. 2, U.S. Government Printing Office, Washington, DC, 1931.

Shaw, M., Investing in youth: International approaches to preventing crime and victimization, International Centre for the Prevention of Crime, Montreal, Quebec, Canada, n.d., http://www.iau-idf.fr/fileadmin/Etudes/etude_548/Investing_In_Youth_M_Shaw_pdf.pdf (accessed July 21, 2014).

REFERENCES

Shaw, M., Youth and gun violence: The outstanding case for prevention, International Centre for the Prevention of Crime, Montreal, Quebec, Canada, 2005. http://www.crime-prevention-intl.org/fileadmin/user_upload/Publications/Youth_and_Gun_Violence._The_Outstanding_Case_for_Prevention_ANG.pdf (accessed July 21, 2014).

Shehayeb, D.K., Safety and security in public space, in *2008 International Report Crime Prevention and Community Safety: Trends and Perspectives*, International Centre for the Prevention of Crime, ICPC, Montreal, Quebec, Canada, 2008, pp. 107–111.

Shelde, R.G., Detention diversion advocacy: An evaluation, *Juvenile Justice Bulletin*, September 1999, pp. 1–16.

Sheridan, M., *Future of Netcrime Now: Part 2—Responses*, Research Development and Statistics Directorate, Home Office, London, U.K., 2004.

Sherman, L. and Strang, H., *Restorative Justice: The Evidence*, The Smith Institute, London, U.K., 2007.

Sherman, L.W. et al., *Preventing Crime: What Works, What Doesn't, What's Promising, National Institute of Justice Research in Brief*. US Department of Justice, Office of Justice Programs, Washington, DC, 1998.

Sherman, L.W. and Eck, J., Policing for crime prevention, in *Evidence-Based Crime Prevention*, Sherman, L.W., Farrington, D.P., Welsh, B.C., and MacKenzie, D.L., Eds., Routledge, London, U.K., 2006, pp. 295–329.

Sherman, L.W., Communities and crime prevention, in *Preventing Crime: What Works, What Doesn't, What's Promising. A Report to the United States Congress*, Sherman, L.W. et al., Eds., National Institute of Justice, Washington, DC, 1997c, Chap. 3. https://www.ncjrs.gov/works/ (accessed July 21, 2014).

Sherman, L.W., Family-based crime prevention, in *Preventing Crime: What Works, What Doesn't, What's Promising. A Report to the United States Congress*, Sherman, L.W. et al., Eds., National Institute of Justice, Washington, DC, 1997b, Chap. 4. https://www.ncjrs.gov/works/ (accessed July 21, 2014).

Sherman, L.W., Farrington, D.P., Welsh, B.C., and MacKenzie, D.L., Preventing crime, in *Evidence-Based Crime Prevention*, Sherman, L.W., Farrington, D.P., Welsh, B.C., and MacKenzie, D.L., Eds., Routledge, London, U.K., 2006, pp. 1–12.

Sherman, L.W., Gottfredson, D.C., MacKenzie, D.L., Eck, J., Reuter, P., and Bushway, S.D., Eds., *Preventing Crime: What Works, What Doesn't, What's Promising. A Report to the United States Congress*, National Institute of Justice, Washington, DC, 1997. https://www.ncjrs.gov/works/ (accessed July, 2014).

Sherman, L.W., Gun carrying and homicide prevention, *Journal of the American Medical Association* 2000; 283:1193–1195.

Sherman, L.W., Policing for crime prevention, in *Preventing Crime: What Works, What Doesn't, What's Promising. A Report to the United States Congress*, Sherman, L.W. et al., Eds., National Institute of Justice, Washington, DC, 1997d, Chap. 8. https://www.ncjrs.gov/works/ (accessed July 21, 2014).

Sherman, L.W., Shaw, J.W., and Rogan, D.P., *The Kansas City Gun Experiment: Research in Brief*, National Institute of Justice, Washington, DC, 1995.

Sherman, L.W., Thinking about crime prevention, in *Preventing Crime: What Works, What Doesn't, What's Promising. A Report to the United States Congress*, Sherman, L.W. et al., Eds., National Institute of Justice, Washington, DC, 1997a, Chap. 2. https://www.ncjrs.gov/works/ (accessed July 21, 2014).

Shonholtz, R., The citizens' role in justice: Building a primary justice and prevention system at the neighborhood level, *Annals of the American Academy of Political and Social Science* 1987; 494:43–53.

Shortt, A., Barrett, P., and Fox, T., Evaluating the friends program: A cognitive-behavioural group treatment of childhood anxiety disorders, *Journal of Clinical Child Psychology* 2001; 30(4):523–533.

Shropshire, S. and McFarquhar, M., Developing multi-agency strategies to address street gang culture and reduce gun violence, young people, gang culture and gun violence, Briefing No. 4, International Action Network on Small Arms, London, U.K., 2002.

Shufelt, J.S. and Cocozza, J.C., Youth with mental health disorders in the juvenile justice system: Results from a multistate, multi-system prevalence study, National Center for Mental Health and Juvenile Justice, Delmar, NY, 2006. http://www.unicef.org/tdad/usmentalhealthprevalence06(3).pdf (accessed July 21, 2014).

Shure, M.B. and Spivack, G., Interpersonal cognitive problem solving and primary prevention: Programming for preschool and kindergarten children, *Journal of Clinical Child Psychology*, 1979; 2(Summer):89–94.

Shure, M.B. and Spivack, G., Interpersonal problem solving in young children: A cognitive approach to prevention, *American Journal of Community Psychology* 1982; 10:341–356.

Shure, M.B., Interpersonal cognitive problem solving: Primary prevention of early high-risk behaviors in the preschool and primary years, in *Primary Prevention Works*, Albee, G.W. and Gullotta, T.P., Eds., Sage, Thousand Oaks, CA, 1997, pp. 167–188.

Shure, M.B., Interpersonal problem solving and prevention, a comprehensive report of research and training, Report #MH-40801, National Institute of Mental Health, Washington, DC, 1993.

Shure, M.B., Interpersonal problem solving in ten-year-olds, Final report #MH-27741, National Institute of Mental Health, Washington, DC, 1980.

Sickmund, M., Snyder, H.N., and Poe-Yamagata, E., Juvenile offenders and victims: 1997 update on violence, Office of Juvenile Justice and Delinquency Prevention, Washington, DC, 1997.

Siegel, L.J. and Welsh, B.C., *Juvenile Delinquency: The Core*, Cengage Learning, New York, 2011.

Silverman, E., Compstat's innovation, in *Police Innovation: Contrasting Perspectives*, Weisburd, D. and Braga, A., Eds., Cambridge University Press, Cambridge, U.K., 2006.

Sims, L., Neighbourhood watch: Findings from the 2000 British crime survey, Home Office Research Findings 150, Home Office, London, U.K., 2001.

Sinclair, A., Participation programs and techniques, in *The Community Participation Handbook*, Sarkissian, W. and Perlgut, D., Eds., Institute for Science and Technology, Murdoch University, Perth, Western Australia, Australia, 1994, pp. 17–35.

Skogan, W.G. and Maxfield, N.G., *Coping with Crime: Individual and Neighborhood Reactions*, Sage, Beverly Hills, CA, 1981.

Skogan, W.G. et al., Community policing in Chicago, years five-six: An interim report, Institute for Policy Research, Northwestern University, Chicago, IL, 1999, http://www.northwestern.edu/ipr/publications/policing_papers/caps99.pdf (accessed June 10, 2005).

Skogan, W.G., Community organizations and crime, in *Crime and Justice: A Review of Research*, Vol. 10, Tonry, M. and Morris, N., Eds., University of Chicago Press, Chicago, IL, 1988, pp. 39–78.

Skogan, W.G., *Disorder and Decline: Crime and the Spiral of Decay in American Neighborhoods*, Free Press, New York, 1990.

Skogan, W.G., *Evaluating Problem Solving Policing: The Chicago Experience*, Institute for Policy Research, Evanston, IL, 1996.

Skogan, W.G., Hartnett, S.M., Bump, N., and Dubois, J., *Evaluation of CeaseFire-Chicago*, Northwestern University, Chicago, IL, 2008.

Skogan, W.G., Representing the community in community policing, in *Community Policing: Can it Work?*, Skogan, W.G., Ed., National Institute of Justice, Washington, DC, 2004, pp. 57–75.

Skogan, W.G., The impact of community policing on neighborhood residents: A cross site analysis, in *Community Crime Prevention: Does It Work?*, Rosenbaum, D.P., Ed., Sage, Newbury Park, CA, 1994.

Skolnick, J.H. and Bayley, D.H., *Community Policing: Issues and Practices Around the World*, U.S. Government Printing Office, Washington, DC, 1988.

Sloan-Howitt, M. and Kelling, G.L., Subway graffiti in New York City: 'Gettin Up' vs. 'Meanin It and Cleanin it', in *Situational Crime Prevention: Successful Case Studies*, Clarke, R.V., Ed., Harrow and Heston, Albany, NY, 1992, pp. 242–249.

Smith, M. and Clarke, R., Situational crime prevention: Classifying techniques using 'Good Enough' theory, in *The Oxford Handbook of Crime Prevention*, Welsh, B.C. and Farrington, D.P., Eds., Oxford University Press, Oxford, U.K., 2012, pp. 291–315.

Smith, M.J., Exploring target attractiveness in vandalism: An experimental approach, in *Theory for Practice in Situational Crime Prevention*, Smith, M.J. and Cornish, D.B., Eds., Crime Prevention Studies, Vol. 16, Criminal Justice Press, Monsey, NY, 2003, pp. 97–236.

Smith, R.L., In the service of youth: A common denominator, *Juvenile Justice* 1993; 1(2):9–15.

Snyder, H.N. et al., *Juvenile Offenders and Victims: 1997 Update on Violence*. Office of Juvenile Justice and Delinquency Prevention, Washington, DC, 1997.

Social Finance, n.d. http://www.socialfinance.org.uk/ (accessed July 21, 2014).

Sorg, E.T., Haberman, C.P., Ratcliffe, J.H., and Groff, E.R., Foot patrol in violent crime hot spots: The longitudinal impact of deterrence and posttreatment effects of displacement, *Criminology* 2013; 51(1):65–101.

Spergel, I.A. and Curry, G.D., The National Youth Gang Survey: A research and development process, in *The Gang Intervention Handbook*, Goldstein, A. and Huff, C.R., Eds., Research Press, Champaign, IL, 1993, pp. 359–400.

Spergel, I.A. and Grossman, S.F., The Little Village Project: A community approach to the gang problem, *Social Work* 1997; 42:456–470.

Spergel, I.A., Grossman, S.F., Wa, K.M., Choi, S., and Jacob, A., Evaluation of the little village gang violence reduction project: The first three years, Illinois Criminal Justice Information Authority, Chicago, IL, 1999.

Spergel, I.A., *Reducing Youth Gang Violence: The Little Village Gang Project in Chicago*, AltaMira Press, Lanham, MD, 2007.

Spergel, I.A., *The Youth Gang Problem*, Oxford University Press, New York, 1995.

Spergel, I.A., Wa, K.M., and Sosa, R.V., The comprehensive, community-wide gang program model: Success and failure, in *The Modern Gang Reader*, Maxson, C.L., Egley Jr., A., Miller, J., and Klein, M.W., Eds., Oxford University Press, New York, 2014, pp. 451–466.

Spohn, C. and Holleran, D., The effect of imprisonment on recidivism rates of felony offenders: A focus on drug offenders, *Criminology* 2002; 40(2):329–358.

Stansfield, R.T., *Issues in Policing: A Canadian Perspective*, Thompson Educational Publishing Inc., Toronto, Ontario, Canada, 1996.

Statistics Canada, Literacy scores, human capital and growth 1960 to 1995, *The Daily*, Ottawa, Ontario, Canada, 2004. http://www.statcan.gc.ca/daily-quotidien/040622/dq040622d-eng.htm (accessed July, 2014).

Steadman, H.J., Redlich, A., Callahan, L., Robbins, P.C., and Vesselinov, R., Effect of mental health courts on arrest and jail days, *Archives of General Psychiatry* 2011; 68(2):167–172.

Steinberg, A. and Almeida, C., *The Dropout Crisis: Promising Approaches in Prevention and Recovery*, Jobs for the Future, Boston, MA, 2004.

Stevens, M., *A Brief Guide to Police History*, 2005. http://faculty.ncwc.edu/mstevens/205/205lect04.htm.

Stewart, E.A., Simons, R.L., and Conger, R., Assessing neighborhood and social psychological influences on childhood violence in an African-American Sample, *Criminology* 2002; 40:801–824.

Stone, C. and Travis, J., Toward a new professionalism in policing, New perspectives in policing, Harvard Kennedy School, Program in Criminal Justice Policy and Management National Institute of Justice, Washington, DC, 2011.

Sullivan, C.J. and Jolliffe, D., Peer influence, mentoring, and the prevention of crime, in *The Oxford Handbook of Crime Prevention*, Welsh, B.C. and Farrington, D.P., Eds., Oxford University Press, Oxford, U.K., 2012, pp. 207–225.

Sutherland, E., in *Edwin Sutherland: On Analyzing Crime*, Schuessler, K., Ed., University of Chicago Press, Chicago, IL, 1973.

Tagart, R., Quantum opportunity program, Opportunities Industrialization Centers of America, Philadelphia, PA, 1995.

Talen, E., Sense of community and neighborhood form: An assessment of the social doctrine, *Urban Studies* 1999; 36(8):1361–1379.

Taub, R.P., Taylor, D.G., and Dunham, J., *Patterns of Neighborhood Change: Race and Crime in Urban America*, University of Chicago Press, Chicago, IL, 1984.

REFERENCES

Taylor, K., assisted by Avellino, M., and Simpkins, M., *Crime Prevention for First Nations Communities. Self Evaluation Manual*, Solicitor General Canada, Ottawa, Ontario, Canada, 1998.

Taylor, M. and Quayle, E., Internet and abuse images of children: Search, pre-criminal situational and opportunity, in *Situational Prevention of Child Sexual Abuse*, Wortley, R. and Smallbone, S., Eds., Crime Prevention Studies, Vol. 19, Criminal Justice Press, Monsey, NY, 2006, pp. 169–195.

Taylor, R.B., Gotfredson, S.D., and Bower, S., Block crime and fear: Defensible space, local social ties and territorial functioning, *Journal of Research in Crime and Delinquency* 1984; 21(4):303–331.

Tell, R., Fighting crime: An architectural approach, *Journal of Housing* 1990; 47(4):207–212.

Teplin, L., Abram, K., McClelland, G., Mericle, A., Dulcan, M., and Washburn, J., Psychiatric disorders of youth in detention, *OJJDP Bulletin*, Washington, DC, 2006. https://www.ncjrs.gov/pdffiles1/ojjdp/210331.pdf (accessed July 21, 2014).

Terry, K.J. and Ackerman, A., Child sexual abuse in the catholic church: How situational crime prevention strategies can help create safe environments, *Criminal Justice and Behavior* 2008; 35(5):643–657.

Thigpen, M., Forward, in *Cognitive-Behavioral Treatment: A Review and Discussion for Corrections Professionals*, Milkman, H. and Wanberg, K., Eds., National Institute of Justice, Washington, DC, 2007, p. vii.

Thornberry, T., Huizinga, D., and Loeber, R., The causes and correlates studies: Findings and policy implications, *Juvenile Justice* 2004; 9(1):3–19.

Thornberry, T.P., Krohn, M.D., Lizotte, A.J., Smith, C.A., and Tobin, K., *Gangs and Delinquency in Developmental Perspective*, Cambridge University Press, New York, 2003.

Thurman, T., Parental responsibility laws/are they the answer to juvenile delinquency, *Journal of Law & Family Studies* 2003; 5(1):99–111.

Tien, J.M. and Rich, T.F., The Hartford's Compass Program: Experiences with a weed and seed-related program, in *The Challenge of Community Policing: Testing the Promises*, Rosenbaum, D.P., Ed., Sage, Thousand Oaks, CA, 1994, pp. 192–206.

Tierney, J.P. and Grossman, J.B., with Resch, N.L., *Making a Difference: An Impact Study of Big Brothers/Big Sisters*, Public/Private Ventures, Philadelphia, PA, 1995.

Tilley, N., Crime prevention and the safer cities story, *The Howard Journal of Criminal Justice* 1993; 32(1):40–57.

Tilley, N., Whither problem-oriented policing, *Criminology & Public Policy* 2010; 9(1):183–195.

Titus, R., Residential burglary and the community response, in *Coping with Burglary*, Clarke, R.V. and Hope, T., Eds., Kluwer-Nijhoff, Boston, MA, 1984, pp. 97–130.

Toch, H. and Grant, J.D., *Police as Problem Solvers*, Plenum, New York, 1991.

Todhunter, C., Undertaking action research: Negotiating the road ahead, UNIS social research update, Issue 34, University of Surrey, Surrey, U.K., 2001.

Tolan, P., Crime prevention: Focus on youth, in *Crime: Public Policies for Crime Control*, Wilson, J.Q. and Petersilia, J., Eds., ICS Press, Oakland, CA, 2002, pp. 109–127.

Tom, A., Yuen, S., Fong, G., Nemoto, M., Hisatake, T., and Choy, A., Raising resilient children during tough economic times, Center on the Family, University of Hawaii, Honolulu, HI, 2009.

Tonry, M.H. and Farrington, D.P., *Building a Safer Society: Strategic Approaches to Crime Prevention*, University of Chicago Press, Chicago, IL, 1995.

Toronto Transit Commission, Moving forward: Making transit safer for women, Toronto Transit Commission, Toronto, Ontario, Canada, 1989.

Toronto Transit Commission, Safety and security on the TTC, Toronto Transit Commission, Toronto, Ontario, Canada, 2014a.

Toronto Transit Commission, Special constable services, 2014b, https://www.ttc.ca/Riding_the_TTC/Safety_and_Security/Transit_Enforcement_Unit.jsp (accessed November 1, 2008).

Totten, M., *Promising practices for addressing youth involvement in gangs: A comprehensive and coordinated provincial action plan*, Research report prepared in support of the strategy, preventing youth gang violence in BC, 2008. http://www.pssg.gov.bc.ca/crimeprevention/shareddocs/pubs/totten-report.pdf (accessed July, 2014).

REFERENCES

Treasury Board of Canada Secretariat, RPP 2004–2005, Public Safety and Emergency Preparedness Canada, n.d. http://www.tbs-sct.gc.ca/est-pre/20042005/PSEPC-SPPCC/PSEPC-SPPCCr4501_e. asp (accessed July 21, 2014).

Tremblay, R. and Craig, W.M., Developmental crime prevention, in *Building a Safer Society. Crime and Justice*, Vol. 19, Tonry, M. and Farrington, D.P., Eds., University of Chicago Press, Chicago, IL, 1995.

Tremblay, R.E., Pihl, R.O., Vitaro, F., and Dobkin, P.L., Predicting early onset of male antisocial behavior from preschool behavior, *Archives of General Psychiatry* 1994; 51:732–739.

Trojanowicz, R., Kappeler, V.E., Gaines, L.K., and Bucqueroux, B., *Community Policing: A Contemporary Perspective*, Anderson Publishing, Cincinnati, OH, 1998.

Trojanowicz, R.C. and Bucqueroux, B., Eds., *Community Policing: How to Get Started*, 2nd edn., Anderson Publishing, Cincinnati, OH, 1988.

Ucida, C.D., Forst, B., and Annan, S., Modern policing and the control of illegal drugs: Testing new strategies in two American cities. Research report, National Institute of Justice, Washington, DC, 1992.

Umbreit, M.S., *Victim Meets Offender: The Impact of Restorative Justice and Mediation*, Willow Tree Press, Monsey, NY, 1994.

Underwood, G., *The Security of Buildings*, Architectural Press, London, U.K., 1984.

United Kingdom Ministry of Justice, National Offender Management Service, *Understanding Desistance from Crime*, Ministry of Justice, National Offender Management Service, London, U.K., 2010.

United Nations Habitat, Safer cities programme, n.d. http://www.unhabitat.org/programmes/safercities/approach.asp#3 (accessed February 4, 2008).

United Nations, Congress for the prevention of crime and the treatment of offenders, Urban policies and crime prevention, UN, Vienna, Austria, 1993.

United Nations, Office on drugs and crime, *Handbook on the Crime Prevention Guidelines: Making Them Work*, United Nations Office on Drugs and Crime, Vienna, Austria, 2010. http://www.unodc.org/pdf/criminal_justice/Handbook_on_Crime_Prevention_Guidelines_-_Making_them_work.pdf (accessed July 21, 2014).

United Nations, *Twelfth United Nations Congress on Crime Prevention and Criminal Justice*, Salvador, Brazil, April 12–19, 2010, Making the United Nations guidelines on crime prevention work, working paper prepared by the Secretariat, 2010 (accessed February 1, 2104). Available at: http://www.unodc.org/documents/crime-congress/12th-Crime-Congress/Documents/A_CONF.213_18/V1053828e.pdf.

United Nations, *United Nations Standards and Norms in Crime Prevention*, United Nations Office on Drugs and Crime, Vienna, Austria, 2002.

United States Conference on Mayors, Best practices, City of Salt Lake City, UT, Mayor Deedee Corradini, Community Action Teams (CATs), 1999, http://www.mayors.org (accessed May 5, 2008).

United States Department of Health and Human Services, Head start impact study final report, Executive Summary, U.S. Department of Health and Human Services, Administration for Children and Families, Office of Planning, Research and Education, Washington, DC, 2010. http://www.acf.hhs.gov/sites/default/files/opre/executive_summary_final.pdf (accessed July 21, 2104).

United States Department of Health and Human Services, Making a difference in the lives of infants and toddlers and their families: The impacts of early head start, Executive Summary, U.S. Department of Health and Human Services, Washington, DC, 2002.

United States Department of Health and Human Services, Strengthening families and communities. 2011 Resource guide, Department of Health and Human Services, Administration for Children and Families, Washington, DC, 2011. https://www.childwelfare.gov/pubs/guide2011/guide.pdf (accessed July 21, 2014).

United States Department of Justice, Community-oriented policing services program, http://www.cops.usdoj.gov/Default.asp?Item=36 (accessed July 21, 2014).

United States Department of Justice, Excellence in problem-oriented policing: The 1999 Herman Goldstein Award winners, National Institute of Justice, Washington, DC, 2000a, http://www.ncjrs.gov/pdffiles1/nij/182731.pdf (accessed July 2, 2007).

REFERENCES

United States Department of Justice, Excellence in problem-oriented policing: The 1999 Herman Goldstein Award winners, U.S. Department of Justice, National Institute of Justice, Washington, DC, 1999, http://www.ncjrs.org/pdffiles1/nij/182731.pdf (accessed July 2, 2007).

United States Department of Justice, Excellence in problem-oriented policing: The 2000 Herman Goldstein Award winners, U.S. Department of Justice, National Institute of Justice Washington, DC, 2000b, http://www.ncjrs.org/pdffiles1/nij/185279.pdf (accessed July 2, 2007).

United States Department of Justice, Guidelines manual: Guide to discretionary grant programs, Government Printing Office, Washington, DC, 1977.

United States Department of Labor, Job corps career development resource center, n.d. http://www.jccdrc.org/ (accessed May 1, 2008).

United States Department of Labor, Job corps, http://www.jobcorps.gov (accessed July 21, 2014).

United States Department of Labor, What's working (and what's not), Office of the Chief Economist, U.S. Department of Labor, Washington, DC, 1995.

United States National Advisory Council on Criminal Justice Standards and Goals, *A National Strategy to Reduce Crime*, U.S. Government Printing Office, Washington, DC, 1973.

University of Chicago Crime Lab, BAM—Sports edition, University of Chicago Crime Lab Research and Policy Brief, Chicago, IL, 2012. https://crimelab.uchicago.edu/page/becoming-man-bam-sports-edition-findings (accessed July 21, 2014).

University of Colorado at Boulder, Center for the Study and Prevention of Violence, Blueprints for Healthy Development, Promoting alternative THinking strategies (PATHS), Program summary, 2014, http://www.blueprintsprograms.com/factSheet.php?pid=b6692ea5df920cad691c20319a6fffd7a4a766b8 (accessed January 15, 2008).

University of Colorado at Boulder, Center for the Study and Prevention of Violence, Blueprints for Healthy Youth Development, http://www.blueprintsprograms.com/ (accessed July 21, 2014).

University of the West of England, International Learning & Information Network for Crime Prevention & Community Safety, A chronology of British developments and key publications in urban security and crime prevention during the last two decades, in Creating safer communities in Europe: A crime prevention sourcebook, 2004a, http://www.uwe.ac.uk/fbe/commsafe/ukcron.htm (accessed February 1, 2008).

University of the West of England, International Learning & Information Network for Crime Prevention & Community Safety, France, in Creating safer communities in Europe: A crime prevention sourcebook, 2004b, http://environment.uwe.ac.uk/commsafe/eufranc.asp (accessed February 3, 2008).

University of the West of England, International Learning & Information Network for Crime Prevention & Community Safety, Netherlands, in Creating safer communities in Europe: A crime prevention sourcebook, 2004c, http://environment.uwe.ac.uk/commsafe/euneth.asp (accessed February 4, 2008).

Vancouver Echo, Mount Pleasant residents protest prostitution, March 12, 1992, p. 1.

Vancouver Police Department and Vancouver Police Board, Improving community safety, Community deliberative dialogue session, Saturday, March 27, 2004, Morris J. Wosk, Centre for Dialogue. Session summary report, Vancouver, British Columbia, Canada, n.d., www.city.vancouver.bc.ca/police/What%27sNew/DeliberativeDialogue.pdf.

Vancouver Police Department, Community deliberative dialogue session, Vancouver Police Department 2004, www.city.vancouver.bc.ca/police/What%27sNew/DeliberativeDialogue.htm (accessed May 5, 2007).

Van de Bunt, H.G. and Van der Schoot, C., *Prevention of Organised Crime: A Situational Approach*, Boom Juridische Unitgevers (Royal Boom Publishers), Meppel, the Netherlands, 2003.

Vanderberg, S., Weekes, J., and Millson, W., Early substance use and its impact on adult offender alcohol and drug problems, *Forum on Corrections Research* 1995; 7(1): 14–16.

Van Dijk, J.J.M. and De Waard, J., A two dimensional typology of crime prevention projects; with a bibliography, *Criminal Justice Abstracts* 1991; 23(3):483–490.

Van Dijk, J.J.M., Towards effective public-private partnerships in crime control: Experiences in the Netherlands, in *Business and Crime Prevention*, Felson, M. and Clarke, R.V., Eds., Criminal Justice Press, Monsey, NY, 1997, pp. 97–124.

van Steden, R., van Caem, B., and Boutellier, H., The 'Hidden Strength' of active citizenship: The involvement of local residents in public safety projects, *Criminology and Criminal Justice* 2011; 11:433–450.

Veater, P., *Evaluation of Kingsdown Neighbourhood Watch Project Bristol*, Avon and Somerset Constabulary, Bristol, U.K., 1984.

Verbruggen, J., Blokland, A.A., and van der Geest, V.R., Effects of employment and unemployment on serious offending in a high-risk sample of men and women from ages 18 to 32 in the Netherlands, *British Journal of Criminology* 2012; 52:845–869.

Verma, A., Anatomy of riots: A situational crime prevention approach, *Crime Prevention and Community Safety* 2007; 9(3):201–221.

Vermeiren, R., Jespers, I., and Moffitt, T.E., Mental health problems in juvenile justice populations, *Child and Adolescent Psychiatric Clinics of North America* 2006; 15:333–351.

Verrfaillie, K. and Vander Beken, T., Proactive policing and the assessment of organised crime, *Policing: An International Journal of Police Strategies & Management* 2008; 31(4):534–552.

Violence Institute of New Jersey, University of Medicine and Dentistry of New Jersey, SourceBook of drug and violence prevention programs for children and adolescents, The Violence Institute of New Jersey, Piscataway, NJ, n.d., http://www.umdnj.edu/vinjweb/publications/sourcebook/about_sourcebook.html (accessed May 1, 2007).

Volk, R. and Schmalleger, F., *Canadian Criminology Today*, Pearson Prentice Hall, Toronto, Ontario, Canada, 2005.

Wald, J., and Losen, D.J., Defining and redirecting a school-to-prison pipeline, *New Directions for Youth Development* 2003; 99:9–15.

Walker, C.R. and Walker, S.G., The role of citizen volunteers, User report community policing series, 1993–2006, Solicitor General Canada, Ottawa, Ontario, Canada, 1993.

Walker, S.G., Walker, C.R., Johnson, C., and Savageau, J., You can do it: A practical tool kit to evaluating police and community crime prevention programs, National Crime Prevention Centre, Ottawa, Ontario, Canada, 2001.

Waller, I. and Sansfaçon, D., *Investing Wisely in Crime Prevention*, Bureau of Justice Assistance, U.S. Department of Justice, Washington, DC, 2000.

Walsh, A. and Beaver, K., Biosocial criminology, in *Handbook on Crime and Deviance*, Krohn, M.D. et al., Eds., Springer, New York, 2009, Chap. 5.

Walsh, M.L., *Building Citizen Involvement: Strategies for Local Government*, National League of Cities, International City/County Management Association, Washington, DC, 1997.

Wang, S.-Y., *Contingencies in the Long-Term Impact of Work on Crime Among Youth*, National Institute of Justice, Washington, DC, 2010.

Waples, S. et al., Does CCTV displace crime? *Criminology & Criminal Justice*, 2009; 9(2):207–224.

Wasserman, G.A. and Miller, L.S., The prevention of serious and violent juvenile offending, in *Serious and Violent Juvenile Offenders: Risk Factors and Successful Interventions*, Loeber, R. and Farrington, D.P., Eds., Sage, Thousand Oaks, CA, 1998, pp. 197–247.

Wasserman, G.A., Jensen, P.S., Ko, S.J., Cocozza, J., Trupin, E., Angold, A., and Grisso, T., Mental health assessments in juvenile justice: Report on the consensus conference, *Journal of the American Academy of Child and Adolescent Psychiatry* 2003b; 42:751–761.

Wasserman, G.A., Keenan, K., Tremblay, R.E., Coie, J.D., Herrenkohl, T.I., Loeber, R., and Petechuk, D., Risk and protective factors of child delinquency, *Child Delinquency Bulletin Series*, Office of Juvenile Justice and Delinquency Prevention, Washington, DC, April 2003, http://www.ncjrs.gov/pdffiles1/ojjdp/193409.pdf (accessed July 21, 2014).

Wasserman, G.A., Keenan, K., Tremblay, R.E., Coie, J.D., Herrenkohl, T.I., Loeber, R., and Petechuk, D., Risk and protective factors of child delinquency, *Child Delinquency Bulletin Series*, U.S. Department of Justice, Office of Juvenile Justice and Delinquency Prevention, Washington, DC, 2003a.

Wasserman, G.A., McReynolds, L.S., Schwalbe, C.S., Keating, J.M., and Jones, S.A., Psychiatric disorder, comorbidity, and suicidal behavior in juvenile justice youth, *Criminal Justice and Behavior* 2010; 37:1361–1376.

Waterloo Region Crime Prevention Council, *Governance Policy*, Waterloo Region Crime Prevention Council, Kitchener, Ontario, Canada, 2008.

Webb, B. and Laycock, G., *Reducing Crime on the London Underground: An Evaluation of Three Pilot Projects*, Home Office Crime Prevention Unit Paper 30, Home Office, London, U.K., 1992.

Websdale, N., *Policing the Poor: From Slave Plantation to Public Housing*, Northeastern University Press, Boston, MA, 2001.

Weiler, R., Community consultative committees, Ministry of the Solicitor General Canada, Ottawa, Ontario, Canada, 1993.

Weisburd, D., Hinkle, J.C., Famega, C., and Ready, J., Legitimacy, fear and collective efficacy in crime hot spots: Assessing the impacts of broken windows policing strategies on citizen attitudes, National Institute of Justice, Washington, DC, 2010. https://www.ncjrs.gov/pdffiles1/nij/grants/239971.pdf (accessed July 21, 2014).

Weisburd, D., Mastrofski, S., Willis, J., and Greenspan, R., Changing everything so that everything can remain the same: Compstat and American Policing, in *Police Innovation: Contrasting Perspectives*, Weisburd, D. and Braga, A., Eds., Cambridge University Press, Cambridge, U.K., 2006.

Weisburd, D., Telep, C.W., Hinkle, J.C., and Eck, J.E., Is problem-oriented policing effective in reducing crime and disorder? Findings from a Campbell systematic review, *Criminology & Public Policy* n.d.; 9(1):139–172.

Welsh, B.C. and Farrington, D.P., Effects of improved street lighting on crime, *Campbell Systematic Reviews* 2008:13, Accessed July 21, 2014.

Welsh, B.C. and Farrington, D.P., Public area CCTV and crime prevention: An updated systematic review and meta-analysis, *Justice Quarterly* 2009; 16(4):716–745.

Welsh, B.C. and Farrington, D.P., Toward an evidence-based approach to preventing crime, *Annals of the American Association of Political and Social Science* 2001; 578:158–173.

Welsh, B.C. and Farrington, D.P., Value for money? A review of the costs and benefits of situational crime prevention, *British Journal of Criminology* 1999; 39(3):345–368.

Welsh, B.C. and Hoshi, A., Communities and crime prevention, in *Evidence-Based Crime Prevention*, Sherman, L.W., Farrington, D.P., Welsh, B.C., and MacKenzie, D.L., Eds., Routledge, New York, 2006, pp. 165–197.

Welsh, B.C., Evidence-based crime prevention: Scientific basis, trends, results and implications for Canada, Research report: 2007–1, submitted to the National Crime Prevention Centre, Ottawa, Ontario, Canada, 2007. http://www.publicsafety.gc.ca/cnt/rsrcs/pblctns/vdnc-prvntn/vdnc-prvntn-eng.pdf (accessed July 21, 2014).

Welsh, B.C., Public health and the prevention of juvenile criminal violence, *Youth Violence and Juvenile Justice* 2005; 3:23–40.

Wermink, H., Blokland, A., Nieuwbeerta, P., Nagin, D., and Tollenaar, N., Comparing the effects of community service and short-term imprisonment on recidivism: A matched samples approach, *Journal of Experimental Criminology* 2010; 6:325–349.

Whitaker, C.J., Crime prevention measures. Bureau of Justice Statistics special report, U.S. Department of Justice, Washington, DC, 1986.

White, A., Substance use and the adolescent brain: An overview with the focus on alcohol, Duke University Medical Center, Durham, NC, 2004.

White, J.L., Moffitt, T.E., Earls, F., Robins, L., and Silva, P.A., How early can we tell? Predictors of childhood conduct disorder and delinquency, *Criminology* 1990; 28:507–533.

White, R., Social justice, community building, and restorative strategies, *Contemporary Justice Review* 2000; 3(1):55–72.

White House, Office of National Drug Control Policy, National drug control strategy, 2012, Office of National Drug Control Policy, White House, Washington, DC, 2012. http://www.whitehouse.gov/sites/default/files/ondcp/2012_ndcs.pdf (accessed July 21, 2014).

Whitzman, C., Shaw, M., Andres, C., and Travers, K., The effectiveness of women's safety audits, *Security Journal* 2009; 22:205–218.

REFERENCES

Whitzman, C., Toronto task force on community safety, Canada, in Report of the *International Conference for Crime Prevention Partnerships to Build Community Safety*, October 26–30, 1998, Johannesburg, South Africa, Meek, S., Assisted by Bowen-Willer, K., Eds.

Widom, C.S., Does violence beget violence? A critical examination of the literature, *Psychological Bulletin* 1989a; 106:3–28.

Widom, C.S., The cycle of violence, *Science* 1989b; 244:160–166.

Wikström, P.-O., Oberwittler, D., Treiber, K., and Hardie, B., *Breaking Rules: The Social and Situational Dynamics of Young People's Urban Crime*, Oxford University Press, Oxford, U.K., 2012.

Willemse, H.M., Developments in Dutch crime prevention, in *Crime Prevention Studies*, Vol. 2, Clarke, R.V., Ed., Criminal Justice Press, Monsey, NY, 1994, pp. 33–47.

Willis, J.J. and Mastrofski, S.D., COMPSTAT and the New Penology: A paradigm shift in policing? *British Journal of Criminology* 2012; 52:73–92.

Wilson, D.B., Bouffard, L.A., and MacKenzie, D.L., A quantitative review of structured, group-oriented, cognitive-behavioral programs for offenders, *Journal of Criminal Justice and Behavior* 2005; 32(2):172–204.

Wilson, D.B., MacKenzie, D.L., and Mitchell, F.N., Effects of correctional boot camps on offending, Campbell Collaboration Systematic Review, Oslo, Norway, 2008. http://www.campbell-collaboration.org/lib/download/3/ (accessed July 21, 2014).

Wilson, D.B., MacKenzie, D.L., and Mitchell, F.N., Effects of correctional boot camps on offending. A Campbell Collaboration systematic review, Campbell Systematic Reviews, Oslo, Norway, 2005. http://www.campbellcollaboration.org/lib/download/3/ (accessed July 21, 2014).

Wilson, J. and Kelling, G., Broken windows, *Atlantic Monthly*, March 31, 1982, pp. 29–38.

Wilson, J., *Thinking about Crime*, Academic Press, New York, 1975.

Wilson, J.J. and Howell, J.C., *The Comprehensive Strategy for Serious, Violent, and Chronic Juvenile Offenders*, Office of Juvenile Justice and Delinquency Prevention, Washington, DC, 1993.

Wilson, J.J. and Howell, J.C., The comprehensive strategy for serious, violent, and chronic juvenile offenders, Office of Juvenile Justice and Delinquency Prevention, Washington, DC, 1993.

Wilson, L.C. and Scarpa, A., Criminal behavior: The need for an integrative approach that incorporates biological influences, *Journal of Contemporary Criminal Justice* 2012; 28(3):366–381.

Wilson, P., *Public Housing for Australia*, University of Queensland Press, St. Lucia, Queensland, Australia, 1976.

Wilson, S., Vandalism and 'Defensible Space' on London housing estates, in *Tackling Vandalism*, Clarke, R.V., Ed., Her Majesty's Stationary Office, London, U.K., 1978.

Winslow, C.-E.A., The untilled fields of public health, *Science* 1920; 51(1306):23–33.

Wirth, L., Urbanism, migration and tolerance: A reassessment, *American Sociological Review* 1938; 56:117–123.

Wolfgang, M. and Ferracuti, F., *The Subculture of Violence: Toward an Integrated Theory of Criminology*, Routledge, New York, 1967.

Women's Action Centre against Violence (Ottawa-Carleton), *Safety Audit Tools and Housing: The State of the Art and Implications for CMHC*, Canada Mortgage and Housing Corporation, Ottawa, Ontario, Canada, 1995.

Woodson, R.L., *A Summons to Life: Mediating Structures and the Prevention of Youth Crime*, Ballinger, Cambridge, MA, 1981.

Woollaston, V., An adult at 18? Not any more: Adolescence now ends at 25 to prevent young people getting an inferiority complex, *Daily Mail*, September 24, 2013. http://www.dailymail.co.uk/health/article-2430573/An-adult-18-Not-Adolescence-ends-25-prevent-young-people-getting-inferiority-complex.html (accessed July, 2013).

World Health Organization, Violence prevention: The evidence, WHO, Geneva, Switzerland, 2010. http://apps.who.int/iris/bitstream/10665/77936/1/9789241500845_eng.pdf?ua=1 (accessed July 21, 2014).

Wortley, R. and Smallbone, S., Eds., *Situational Prevention of Child Sexual Abuse*, Crime Prevention Studies, Vol. 19, Criminal Justice Press, Monsey, NY, 2006.

REFERENCES

Wortley, S. and Tanner, J., Criminal organizations or social groups? An exploration of the myths and realities of youth gangs in Toronto, 2005, http://ceris.metropolis.net/Virtual%20Library/EResources/WortleyTanner2007.pdf (accessed July, 2014).

Wortley, S. and Tanner, J., Social groups or criminal organizations? The extent and nature of youth gang activity in Toronto, in *From Enforcement and Prevention to Civic Engagement: Research on Community Safety*, Kidd, B. and Phillips, J., Eds., Centre of Criminology, University of Toronto, Toronto, Ontario, Canada, 2004, pp. 59–80.

Wright, E.M. and Fagan, A.A., The cycle of violence in context: Exploring the moderating roles of neighborhood disadvantage and cultural norms, *Criminology* 2013; 51(2):217–249.

Wright, J.P. and Beaver, K.M., Do parents matter in creating self-control in their children? A genetically informed test of Gottfredson and Hirschi's theory of low self-control, *Criminology* 2005; 43:1169–1202.

Wright, V., Deterrence in criminal justice: Evaluating certainty vs. severity of punishment, The Sentencing Project, Washington, DC, 2010, http://www.asca.net/system/assets/attachments/1463/Deterrence_Briefing_.pdf?1290182850 (accessed April 30, 2011).

Wyrick, P.A. and Howell, J.C., Strategic risk-based responses to youth gangs, *Juvenile Justice* 2004; 10:20–29.

Yang, Y. and Raine, A., Prefrontal structural and functional brain imaging findings in antisocial, violent, and psychopathic individuals: A meta-analysis, *Psychiatry Research* 2009; 174(2):81–88.

Yankelovich, D., *Coming to Public Judgment: Making Democracy Work in a Complex World*, Syracuse University Press, Syracuse, NY, 1991.

Yin, R.K., Vogel, M.E., Chaiken, J.M., and Both, D.R., *Citizen Patrol Projects: National Evaluation Program, Phase I Summary Report*, National Institute of Justice, Washington, DC, 1977.

Young, J., Identity, community and social exclusion, in *Crime, Disorder, and Community Safety: A New Agenda?*, Roger, M. and Pitts, J., Eds., Routledge, London, U.K., 2001.

Zahm, D., *Using Crime Prevention Through Environmental Design in Problem-Solving, Problem-Oriented Guides for Police Problem-Solving Tools Series No. 8*, National Institute of Justice, Washington, DC, 2007. http://www.popcenter.org/tools/pdfs/cpted.pdf (accessed July 21, 2014).

Zajicek-Farber, M.L., Building practice evidence for parent mentoring: Home visiting in early childhood, *Research on Social Work Practice* 2010; 20(1):46–64.

Zamora, D., Levels of academic achievement and further delinquency among detained delinquency, *The Southwest Journal of Criminal Justice* 2005; 2(1):42–53.

Zehr, H., *Changing Lens*, Herald Press, Scottsdale, PA, 1990.

Zenaida, R.R., Rajulton, F., and Turcotte, P., Youth integration and social capital: An analysis of the Canadian general social surveys on time use, *Youth & Society* 2003; 35(2):158–182.

Zimbardo, P., A field experiment in auto shaping, in *Vandalism*, Ward, C., Ed., Architectural Press, London, U.K., 1973.

Zweig, J., Yahner, J., and Redcross, C., For whom does a transitional jobs program work? Examining the recidivism effects of the center for employment opportunities program on former prisoners at high, medium, and low risk of reoffending, *Criminology & Public Policy* 2011; 10(4):945–972.

INDEX

Index